THE HYMNAL
for Worship & Celebration

Containing Scriptures from the
New American Standard Bible
Revised Standard Version
The Holy Bible, New International Version
The New King James Version

This hymnal is available in two editions: one has Scripture readings from *The King James Version of the Holy Bible;* the second contains readings taken from a combination of four translations—*New American Standard Bible, Revised Standard Version, The Holy Bible, New International Version,* and *The New King James Version.*

All musical selections from *The Hymnal* have been fully orchestrated: part books and score are available for any size ensemble.

WORD MUSIC
NASHVILLE, TENNESSEE

Printed in the United States of America.

97989900 QPH 302928

FOREWORD

I love to sing! Of greater importance, I love to sing with others.

I can think of no more glorious sound than a body of people who love their Lord, singing and making melody in their hearts. Whether the voices are blending together in harmonious a cappella or accompanied by a grand pipe organ or even a full orchestra, there is no sound on earth more heavenly than the sound of singing saints. As my minister of music has often said, "If you don't love to sing, then why in the world would you ever want to go to heaven?"

Music has its own international language, breaking down cultural barriers, cutting across age differences, and erasing denominational lines. For long centuries its soothing strains have calmed anxious hearts, incited courage in the fainthearted, comforted the grieving, healed the wounded, rescued the perishing, and drawn wanderers home.

Throughout my Christian life I have treasured the historic hymns of the church, having committed many of them to memory. They have been my dearest companions in dark hours of loneliness and discouragement and my greatest encouragers in times of celebration and adoration. In ministry, both at home and abroad, I have never failed to find new strength from these strong, timeless statements of faith.

The church will continue to sing her stately hymns, but, in addition to these, each new generation will continue to compose fresh choruses of worship and new psalms of praise. These songs give the church a relevant expression of her message. No longer is the singing of these current melodies and lyrics limited to the young. All of God's people are now joining the song . . . and when such singing is enjoyed alongside great preaching, it is a contagious combination.

The old Wittenberg monk, Martin Luther, was right:

> *Next to the Word of God, music deserves the highest praise. The gift of language combined with the gift of song was given to man that he should proclaim the Word of God through music.*

I commend Word, Incorporated, for its commitment to the church for providing this new collection of psalms, hymns, and spiritual songs, *The Hymnal for Worship and Celebration.* This fine volume maintains the continuity of history by including the hymns God's people have sung for centuries. But there is also variety in that the more recent songs of praise have been included, giving us a balanced blend of music so needed among congregations en route to the twenty-first century. All of this has been accomplished without the loss of theological integrity.

But there is more, so much more. *The Hymnal for Worship and Celebration* offers pastors, worship leaders, and ministers of music many tools for worship, prompting creativity, unpredictable ideas, and stimulating suggestions that enhance spontaneity. The *Brief Services* are designed to intensify the congregation's praise. They cover an abundance of relevant themes and each crafted arrangement possesses a natural flow that is easily understood and expressed. Even the indexes have been compiled and designed to prompt creative ideas for arranging one's own sequences of readings and musical selections.

Of special interest to leaders of worship and ministers of music is the provision of materials which fuse choir with congregation. The two work together as one—which they are—and yet the distinct presence of each is not ignored. And for those who have become weary of frequent repetition, due to a limited selection, you will be encouraged to discover a greater quantity of hymns and songs than in most other hymnals available today. And best of all, each selection is meaningful and singable.

As a minister I love to preach. I would be at a loss in the pulpit without my Bible. Nothing could or should replace the Scriptures in the church of Jesus Christ. This hymnal does not attempt to do that. The Bible is essential for the sowing of the seed. But over the years I have come to realize that nothing can or will prepare the soil of the heart like the hymns and the songs of faith. True worship therefore calls for companion volumes: a Bible and a hymnal. The two are as inseparable as the sword of the Spirit and the shield of faith. Christians need both to stand firm in the strength of His might.

If you love preaching there is no substitute for the Bible. If you love singing there is no substitute for the hymnal . . . and I know of none better today than *The Hymnal for Worship and Celebration.*

Charles R. Swindoll
Pastor, Radio Bible Teacher, Author

ACKNOWLEDGEMENTS

SENIOR EDITOR
Tom Fettke

ASSOCIATE EDITOR
Ken Barker

EXECUTIVE COMMITTEE
Tom Fettke—Chairman, Ken Barker, James C. Gibson, Bruce Howe, Dan Johnson and Kurt Kaiser

SCRIPTURE EDITOR AND THEOLOGICAL CONSULTANT
Dr. Kenneth L. Barker

ADVISORY BOARD
Cliff Barrows, C. Harry Causey, Dr. D. George Dunbar, Wilbur C. Ellsworth, Dr. Don Finto, Don G. Fontana, Richard M. Freeman, Gary Hallberg, Jack W. Hayford, Jr., Stan Jantz, Peter Kobe, Joseph Linn, Roger G. McMurrin, Thad Roberts, Jr., Tom Russell, Marshall J. Sanders, Barry Swanson and Dr. Edwin M. Willmington

CONSULTANTS
Neal Doty, Sean Doty, Donald W. Felice, Camp Kirkland, Anthony V. Klucznik, Jacquelyn Murray, Ronald Murray, Dr. Terry C. Terry and David S. Winkler

LOGO DESIGN
Dennis Hill, Patrick Pollei and Roger Sanders

COPYRIGHT ADMINISTRATION
Waverly Conlan and Cathy L. Donaldson

PRODUCTION ASSISTANTS
Mildred Burkett, Jenna L. Caraway, Jan Fettke, Ronald E. Garman, Jean Norwood and Kristin E. Payne

MUSIC TYPOGRAPHY
Musictype, Inc., Omaha, Arkansas; Don Ellingson

WORD INCORPORATED
Jarrell McCracken, Founder; Roland Lundy, President; Tom Ramsey, Executive Vice-President: Word Record and Music Group; Don Cason, Vice-President: Word Music

The Publisher gratefully acknowledges permission received from other publishers, organizations and individuals to reprint texts, music, and arrangements contained in this book.

PREFACE

At the heart of Christian worship, our songs and hymns are a treasure house of wisdom and beauty. They express praise, wonder, and awe. They contemplate the majesty, the mystery and the mercy of God, and in a profound way they express the depth of our response to God.

The Hymnal for Worship and Celebration combines the dignity of our musical heritage with the need for a worship resource book that speaks to the hearts of the 'people'—we who daily proclaim Him as Savior and Lord.

The Hymnal for Worship and Celebration possesses a number of unique characteristics which will enable pastors, ministers of music and worship leaders to create, plan and implement more effective and meaningful times of worship and celebration. Included in *The Hymnal* are 23 *Brief Services*—worship sequences that consist of a reading by a worship leader and/or congregation and two or more hymns, all relating to a central theme. Appropriate stanzas are clearly marked, and transitional or modulatory material is provided in the book, thereby allowing an uninterrupted flow from stanza to stanza and from one hymn to another. Each hymn is presented in a traditional format and can be used apart from the context of the *Brief Service.* By using the transitional material, any two of the selections in the *Brief Services* may be combined to form a medley. *The Hymnal* also includes a number of two-selection medleys on various themes (modulatory material is provided).

The Hymnal for Worship and Celebration includes optional choral introductions and endings for over 40 hymns and songs. Others have descants, while some include tastefully-arranged, optional last stanza harmonizations. Also included are many canons and rounds, which integrate individual and corporate worship very effectively.

The Hymnal for Worship and Celebration is fully orchestrated. Every selection is arranged in an interesting, yet accessible manner. The arrangements may be used in two different applications: to accompany congregational singing or to stand alone as preludes, postludes or offertories. Suggested keyboard introductions are bracketed in *The Hymnal.* These introductions are coordinated with suggested introductions in the orchestrations.

The Hymnal for Worship and Celebration includes the most comprehensive set of indexes ever assembled in one hymnal volume. I would encourage you to explore these vast resources. They are designed to provide you with the tools and the information necessary to create worship experiences tailored to meet the needs of your congregation.

I am convinced that you will find this volume to be one of quality, quantity, utility, and integrity. May it enable us to *Worship* and *Celebrate* the greatness of our God with more excitement and enthusiasm than ever before!

***Soli Deo Gloria* - To God Alone Be the Glory**

Tom Fettke
Senior Editor

CONTENTS

Worship and Celebrate . . .
GOD OUR FATHER **1-71**
His Adoration and Praise 1-24
His Majesty and Power 25-40
His Guidance and Care 41-57
His Works in Creation 58-64
His Love and Mercy 65-71

Worship and Celebrate . . .
JESUS OUR SAVIOR **72-246**
His Adoration and Praise 72-117
His Advent 118-125
His Birth 126-162
His Epiphany 163-166
His Life and Ministry 167-172
His Triumphal Entry 173-174
His Suffering and Death 175-181
His Redemptive Works
His Cross 182-189
His Cleansing Blood 190-196
His Grace, Love and Mercy 197-212
His Resurrection 213-227
His Ascension and Reign 228-235
His Second Coming 236-246

Worship and Celebrate . . .
THE HOLY SPIRIT **247-261**

Worship and Celebrate . . .
THE HOLY TRINITY **262-268**

THE WORD OF GOD **269-275**

THE CHURCH **276-325**
Its Nature and Foundation 276-280
Fellowship of Believers 281-287
Renewal and Revival 288-295
Missions and Evangelism 296-316
Dedication of Children 317-318
Baptism 319-320
The Lord's Supper 321-325

LIFE IN CHRIST **326-537**
Salvation
Invitation and Acceptance 326-335
Repentance and Forgiveness 336-342
Assurance and Trust 343-357
Commitment and Consecration 358-379
Aspiration 380-401
Faith and Hope 402-411
Comfort and Encouragement 412-424
Prayer and Intercession 425-435
Holiness and Purity 436-443
Stewardship and Service 444-456
Provision and Leading 457-471
Spiritual Warfare 472-486
Inner Peace and Joy 487-503
Testimony and Praise 504-532
Family and Home 533-537

LIFE EVERLASTING **538-555**

SPECIAL TIMES and SEASONS	**556-577**
Thanksgiving	556-566
New Year	567-568
Patriotic	569-577
CHILDREN'S HYMNS	**578-583**
OPENING OF SERVICE	**584-599**
Hymns and Songs	584-592
Calls to Worship	593-598
Spoken Calls to Worship	599
CLOSING OF SERVICE	**600-613**
Hymns and Songs	600-606
Benedictions	607-612
Spoken Benedictions	613
SERVICE MUSIC	**614-628**
Prayer Responses	614-619
Offertories	620-621
Glorias	622-623
Doxologies	624-627
Amens	628
SCRIPTURE RESOURCES for Worship and Celebration	
Preface and Acknowledgments	———
Scriptures for Individual, Unison, Responsive or Antiphonal Readings	629-689
Psalms for Unison Reading or Personal Meditation	690-715
AFFIRMATIONS OF FAITH AND TE DEUM	**716-719**
	PAGES
INDEXES FOR SCRIPTURE RESOURCES	**665-673**
Table of Contents	665
Alphabetical Index of Scripture and Other Readings	666
Topical Index of Scripture and Other Readings	667-670
Scriptural Index of Scripture Readings	671-672
Index of Spoken Calls to Worship and Benedictions	673
Index of Non-Scriptural Readings	673
INDEXES FOR THE HYMNS	**674-720**
Table of Contents	674
Index of Scripture Appearing with Hymn Titles	675-676
Index of Scripture Texts and Adaptations in Hymns	677
Index of Brief Services and Medleys	678-679
Index of Descants, Last Stanza Harmonizations and Choral Endings	680
Index of Copyright Owners	681-682
Alphabetical Index of Tunes	683-686
Metrical Index of Tunes	687-691
Index of Keys	692-695
Index of Authors, Composers, Sources, Translators and Arrangers	696-701
Topical Index of Hymns	702-713
Alphabetical Index of Titles and First Lines of Hymns	714-720

BRIEF SERVICES

A more descriptive listing may be found at page 678.

PRAISE GOD IN HIS SANCTUARY 7
A Brief Service of Worship and Exaltation

HOW MAJESTIC IS YOUR NAME 28
A Brief Service in Recognition of God's Majesty and Power

LEAD US, O GOD 48
A Brief Service of Prayer and Petition

GIVE HIM GLORY 86
A Brief Service Exalting Our Lord, Jesus Christ

THE NAME OF JESUS 99
A Brief Service of Worship and Praise

THE ADVENT OF OUR LORD 122
A Brief Service of Joyful Expectation

GLORIA IN EXCELSIS DEO 130
A Brief Service of Proclamation and Praise

FOR UNTO US A CHILD IS BORN 142
A Brief Service in Celebration of Our Lord's Birth

GLORY IN THE CROSS 182
A Brief Service of Reflection and Praise

I KNOW A FOUNT 194
A Medley

GOD'S AMAZING GRACE 200
A Brief Service in Recognition of His Love and Provision

HE IS RISEN! ALLELUIA! 214
A Brief Service in Celebration of Our Lord's Resurrection

THE LIVING CHURCH 290
A Brief Service of Prayer and Challenge

MY GOD, I LOVE THEE 361
A Brief Service of Adoration and Commitment

IN HIS IMAGE 386
A Brief Service of Aspiration and Hope

A LIVING HOPE 403
A Brief Service of Affirmation and Renewal

THE LORD IS MY SHEPHERD 459
A Brief Service in Recognition of His Leadership

SOLDIERS OF CHRIST, ARISE 476
A Brief Service of Challenge and Victory

PERFECT PEACE 491
A Brief Service in Recognition of His Provision

MY LIFE, MY JOY, MY ALL 509
A Brief Service of Testimony and Praise

AN UPWARD LOOK 540
A Brief Service of Joyful Anticipation

WITH A SONG OF THANKSGIVING 558
A Brief Service of Praise to God, the Creator

ONE NATION, UNDER GOD 570
A Medley

Worship *the Lord*
in the beauty of holiness!
Celebrate *His abundant*
goodness and joyfully sing
of His righteousness.

Joyful, Joyful, We Adore Thee 1

Your works are wonderful, I know that full well. Ps. 139:14

1. Joy - ful, joy - ful, we a - dore Thee, God of glo - ry, Lord of love;
2. All Thy works with joy sur-round Thee, Earth and heaven re - flect Thy rays,
3. Thou art giv - ing and for - giv - ing, Ev - er bless - ing, ev - er blest,
4. Mor - tals, join the hap - py cho - rus Which the morn-ing stars be - gan;

Hearts un - fold like flowers be - fore Thee, Open-ing to the sun a - bove.
Stars and an - gels sing a - round Thee, Cen - ter of un - bro - ken praise.
Well - spring of the joy of liv - ing, O - cean depth of hap - py rest!
Fa - ther love is reign - ing o'er us, Broth-er love binds man to man.

Melt the clouds of sin and sad - ness, Drive the dark of doubt a - way;
Field and for - est, vale and moun-tain, Flow-ery mead - ow, flash - ing sea,
Thou our Fa - ther Christ, our Broth - er— All who live in love are Thine;
Ev - er sing - ing, march we on - ward, Vic - tors in the midst of strife,

Giv - er of im - mor - tal glad-ness, Fill us with the light of day.
Chant-ing bird and flow-ing foun-tain, Call us to re - joice in Thee.
Teach us how to love each oth - er, Lift us to the joy di-vine.
Joy - ful mu - sic leads us sun-ward In the tri-umph song of life. A - men.

TEXT: Henry van Dyke
MUSIC: Ludwig van Beethoven; melody from *Ninth Symphony*; adapted by Edward Hodges

HYMN TO JOY
8.7.8.7.D.

2 Come, Thou Fount of Every Blessing

The blessing of the Lord brings wealth. Prov. 10:22

1. Come, Thou Fount of ev - ery bless - ing, Tune my heart to sing Thy grace;
2. Hith - er - to Thy love has blest me; Thou hast bro't me to this place;
3. O to grace how great a debt - or Dai - ly I'm con-strained to be!
Streams of mer - cy, nev - er ceas - ing, Call for songs of loud - est praise.
And I know Thy hand will bring me Safe - ly home by Thy good grace.
Let Thy good-ness, like a fet - ter, Bind my wan-dering heart to Thee:
Teach me some me - lo - dious son - net, Sung by flam-ing tongues a - bove;
Je - sus sought me when a stran - ger, Wan-dering from the fold of God;
Prone to wan - der, Lord, I feel it, Prone to leave the God I love;
Praise His name—I'm fixed up-on it— Name of God's re-deem-ing love.
He, to res - cue me from dan-ger, Bought me with His precious blood.
Here's my heart, O take and seal it; Seal it for Thy courts a - bove. A - men.

TEXT: Robert Robinson; adapted by Margaret Clarkson
MUSIC: Traditional American melody; John Wyeth's *Repository of Sacred Music,* 1813

NETTLETON
8.7.8.7.D.

Praise, My Soul, the King of Heaven 3

Praise the Lord, O my soul . . . praise His holy name. Ps. 103:1

Unison

1. Praise, my soul, the King of heav - en, To His feet thy
2. Praise Him for His grace and fa - vor To our fa - thers
3. Frail as sum - mer's flow'r we flour - ish; Blows the wind and
4. An - gels in the height, a - dore Him; Ye be - hold Him

trib - ute bring; Ran - somed, healed, re - stored, for - giv - en,
in dis - tress; Praise Him, still the same as ev - er,
it is gone; But, while mor - tals rise and per - ish,
face to face; Saints tri - um - phant, bow be - fore Him;

Ev - er - more His prais - es sing; Al - le - lu - ia!
Slow to chide, and swift to bless; Al - le - lu - ia!
God en - dures un - chang - ing on: Al - le - lu - ia!
Gath - ered in from ev - ery race; Al - le - lu - ia!

Al - le - lu - ia! Praise the ev - er - last - ing King.
Al - le - lu - ia! Glo - rious in His faith - ful - ness.
Al - le - lu - ia! Praise the high E - ter - nal One.
Al - le - lu - ia! Praise with us the God of grace.

TEXT: Henry F. Lyte; based on Psalm 103
MUSIC: Mark Andrews
Alternate tune: REGENT SQUARE, No. 241

LAUDA ANIMA (Andrews)
8.7.8.7.8.7.

4 How Great Thou Art

Great is the Lord, and most worthy of praise. Ps. 48:1

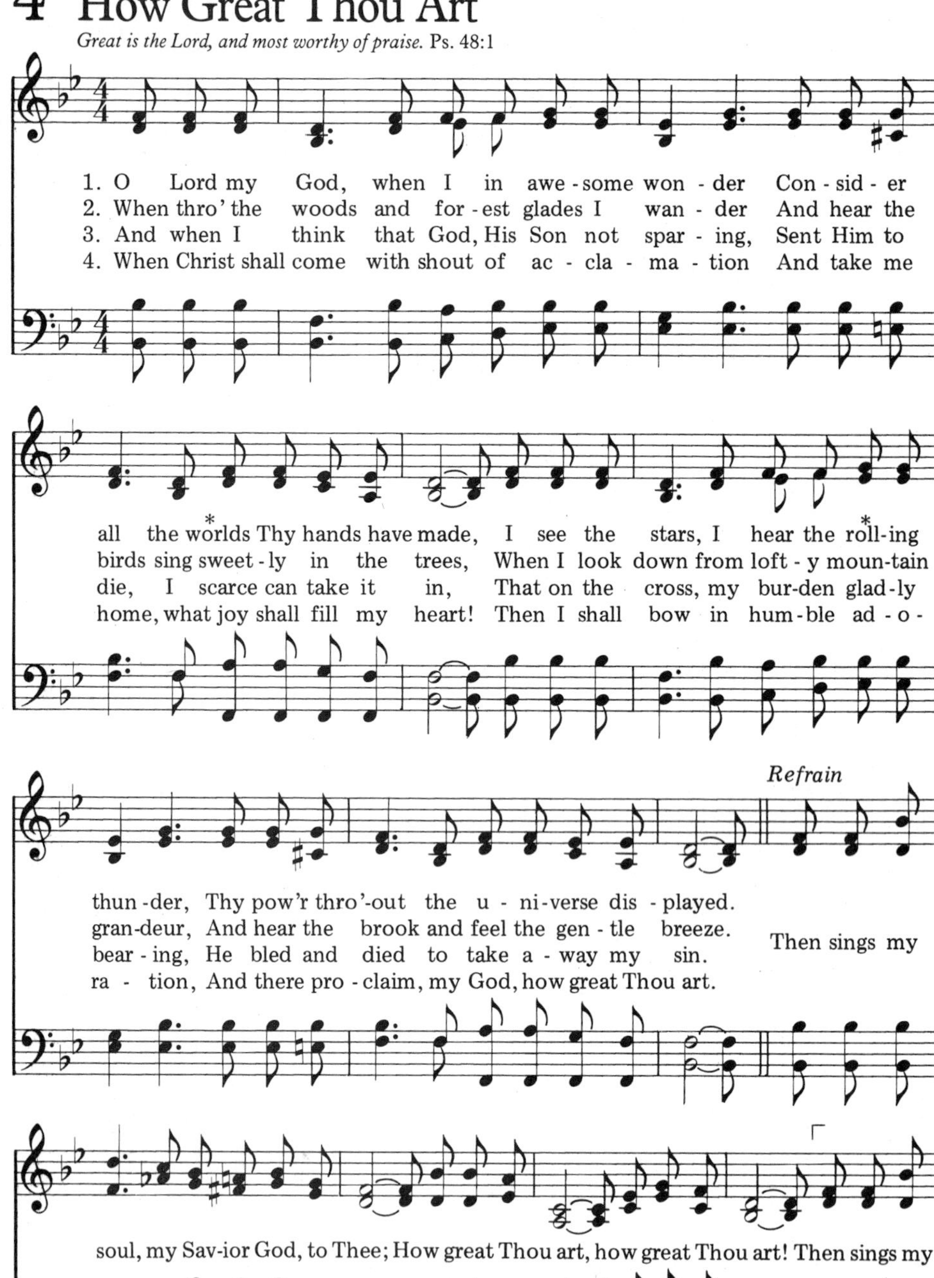
1. O Lord my God, when I in awe-some won-der Con-sid-er all the worlds* Thy hands have made, I see the stars, I hear the roll*-ing thun-der, Thy pow'r thro'-out the u-ni-verse dis-played.
2. When thro' the woods and for-est glades I wan-der And hear the birds sing sweet-ly in the trees, When I look down from loft-y moun-tain gran-deur, And hear the brook and feel the gen-tle breeze.
3. And when I think that God, His Son not spar-ing, Sent Him to die, I scarce can take it in, That on the cross, my bur-den glad-ly bear-ing, He bled and died to take a-way my sin.
4. When Christ shall come with shout of ac-cla-ma-tion And take me home, what joy shall fill my heart! Then I shall bow in hum-ble ad-o-ra-tion, And there pro-claim, my God, how great Thou art.
Refrain
Then sings my soul, my Sav-ior God, to Thee; How great Thou art, how great Thou art! Then sings my

*Translator's original words are "works" and "mighty."

TEXT and MUSIC: Stuart K. Hine;
Last stanza setting by Eugene Thomas

HOW GREAT THOU ART
11.10.11.10. with Refrain

soul, my Sav - ior God, to Thee: How great Thou art, how great Thou art!
Optional last stanza setting
Broader
art!
When Christ shall come with shout of ac - cla - ma - tion
8va
8va
8va
And take me home, what joy shall fill my heart! Then I shall bow in hum - ble ad - o -
Refrain
ra - tion, And there pro - claim, my God, how great Thou art! Then sings my
soul, my Sav - ior God, to Thee; How great Thou art, how great Thou art! Then sings my

continued on next page

soul, my Sav - ior God, to Thee: How great Thou art, how great Thou art!
Optional choral ending
rit.
How great Thou art, how great Thou art, how great Thou art!

5 Be Exalted, O God

Great is Your love . . . Be exalted, O God, above the heavens. Ps. 57:10-11

I will give thanks to Thee, O Lord, a - mong the peo - ple.

I will sing prais-es to Thee a - mong the na - tions.

For Thy stead - fast love is great, is great to the heav - ens;

TEXT and MUSIC: Brent Chambers; based on Psalm 57:9-11

BE EXALTED
Irregular meter

And Thy faith-ful-ness, Thy faith-ful-ness to the clouds.
Be ex - alt - ed, O God, a-bove the heav - ens;
Let Thy glo - ry be o - ver all the earth.
Be ex - alt - ed, O God, a-bove the heav - ens;
Let Thy glo - ry be o - ver all the earth.

6 Sing Praise to God Who Reigns Above

Oh, praise the greatness of our God! Deut. 32:3

1. Sing praise to God who reigns a-bove, The God of all cre-a-tion, The God of pow'r, the God of love, The God of our sal-va-tion. With heal-ing balm my soul He fills, And ev-'ry faith-less mur-mur stills: To God all praise and glo-ry!
2. What God's al-might-y pow'r hath made His gra-cious mer-cy keep-eth, By morn-ing glow or eve-ning shade His watch-ful eye ne'er sleep-eth. With-in the king-dom of His might, Lo! all is just and all is right: To God all praise and glo-ry!
3. The Lord is nev-er far a-way, But, thru all grief dis-tress-ing, An ev-er-pres-ent help and stay, Our peace and joy and bless-ing. As with a moth-er's ten-der hand He leads His own, His cho-sen band: To God all praise and glo-ry!
4. Thus all my toil-some way a-long I sing a-loud His prais-es, That men may hear the grate-ful song My voice un-wea-ried rais-es. Be joy-ful in the Lord, my heart! Both soul and bod-y bear your part: To God all praise and glo-ry! A-men.

TEXT: Johann J. Schütz; translated by Frances E. Cox
MUSIC: Bohemian Brethren's *Kirchengesänge,* Berlin, 1566

MIT FREUDEN ZART
8.7.8.7.8.8.7.

PRAISE GOD IN HIS SANCTUARY

A Brief Service of Worship and Exaltation

Suggested Hymn Stanzas

To facilitate an uninterrupted flow from stanza to stanza, the suggested stanzas have been marked with an arrow: ►

Praise to the Lord, the Almighty, stanzas 1, 4
Praise the Lord! Ye Heavens, Adore Him, stanzas 1, 3
O Worship the King, stanzas 1, 2, 4

WORSHIP LEADER:
Praise the Lord.

PEOPLE:
Praise the Lord.

WORSHIP LEADER:
Praise God in His sanctuary;
praise Him in His mighty heavens.
Praise Him for His acts of power;
praise Him for His surpassing greatness.
Praise Him with the sounding of the trumpet,
praise Him with the harp and lyre,
Praise Him with tambourine and dancing,
praise Him with the strings and flute,
Praise Him with the clash of cymbals,
praise Him with resounding cymbals.
Let everything that has breath praise the Lord.

ALL:
Praise the Lord.

Psalm 150. (NIV)

Optional introduction to "Praise to the Lord, the Almighty"
f

8 Praise to the Lord, the Almighty

Praise and exalt and glorify the King of heaven. Dan. 4:37

1. Praise to the Lord, the Al - might-y, the King of cre - a - tion!
2. Praise to the Lord, who o'er all things so won-drous-ly reign - eth,
3. Praise to the Lord, who doth pros - per thy work and de - fend thee;
4. Praise to the Lord! O let all that is in me a - dore Him!
O my soul, praise Him, for He is thy health and sal - va - tion!
Shel-ters thee un - der His wings, yes, so gen - tly sus - tain - eth!
Sure - ly His good - ness and mer - cy here dai - ly at - tend thee.
All that hath life and breath, come now with prais - es be - fore Him.
All ye who hear, Now to His tem - ple draw near; Join me in
Hast thou not seen How all thy long - ings have been Grant-ed in
Pon - der a - new What the Al - might - y can do, If with His
Let the A - men Sound from His peo - ple a - gain: Glad - ly for
glad ad - o - ra - tion!
what He or - dain - eth?
love He be - friend thee.
aye we a - dore Him. A - men. Him.
Optional transition to "Praise the Lord!"

TEXT: Joachim Neander; translated by Catherine Winkworth
MUSIC: *Stralsund Gesangbuch,* 1665

LOBE DEN HERREN
14.14.4.7.8.

Praise the Lord! Ye Heavens, Adore Him 9

Praise the Lord from the heavens . . . Praise the Lord from the earth. Ps. 148:1,7

1. Praise the Lord! ye heav'ns, a-dore Him; Praise Him an - gels in the height;
2. Praise the Lord! for He is glo - rious; Nev - er shall His prom-ise fail;
3. Wor-ship, hon - or, glo - ry, bless-ing, Lord, we of - fer un - to Thee;

Sun and moon, re - joice be - fore Him; Praise Him, all ye stars of light.
God hath made His saints vic - to - rious; Sin and death shall not pre - vail.
Young and old, Thy praise ex-press - ing, In glad hom-age bend the knee.

Praise the Lord! for He hath spo - ken; Worlds His might-y voice o-beyed;
Praise the God of our sal - va - tion! Hosts on high, His pow'r pro-claim;
All the saints in heav'n a-dore Thee; We would bow be - fore Thy throne:

Laws which nev-er shall be bro-ken For their guid-ance He hath made.
Heav'n and earth and all cre - a - tion, Laud and mag-ni - fy His name.
As Thine an - gels serve be-fore Thee, So on earth Thy will be done.* A - men.

*Optional segue to "O Worship the King" no transition is needed

TEXT: *Foundling Hospital Collection,* 1796; Edward Osler, stanza 3; based on Psalm 148
MUSIC: Franz Joseph Haydn
A higher setting may be found at No. 278; Alternate tune: HYFRYDOL, No. 89

AUSTRIAN HYMN
8.7.8.7.D.

10 O Worship the King

Praise the Lord . . . clothed with splendor and majesty. Ps. 104:1

1. O worship the King, all glorious above, And gratefully sing His wonderful love; Our Shield and Defender, the Ancient of Days, Pavilioned in splendor, and girded with praise.
2. O tell of His might, O sing of His grace, Whose robe is the light, whose canopy space! His chariots of wrath the deep thunder-clouds form, And dark is His path on the wings of the storm.
3. Thy bountiful care what tongue can recite? It breathes in the air, it shines in the light, It streams from the hills, it descends to the plain, And sweetly distills in the dew and the rain.
4. Frail children of dust, and feeble as frail, In Thee do we trust, nor find Thee to fail: Thy mercies how tender, how firm to the end, Our Maker, Defender, Redeemer, and Friend. Amen.
Optional last stanza harmonization
Descant
4. Frail children of dust, and
Broaden
Unison
storm.
4. Frail children of dust, and

TEXT: Robert Grant
MUSIC: William Gardiner's *Sacred Melodies,* 1815; arranged from Johann M. Haydn; Last stanza harmonization and descant by Herbert Colvin

LYONS
10.10.11.11.

fee - ble as frail, In Thee do we trust, nor find Thee to
fee - ble as frail, In Thee do we trust, nor find Thee to

fail: Thy mer - cies, firm to the end, Our
fail: Thy mer - cies how ten - der, how firm to the end, Our

Mak - er, De - fend - er, Re - deem - er, and Friend. A - men.
Mak - er, De - fend - er, Re - deem - er, and Friend. A - men.

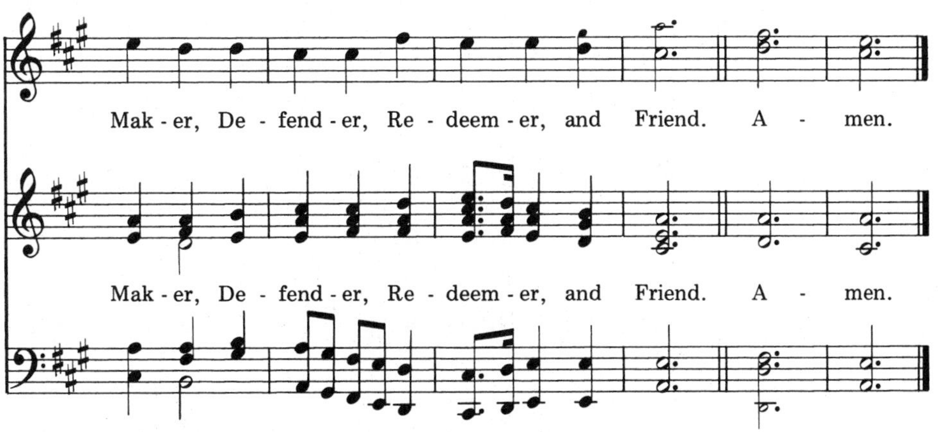

The end of "PRAISE GOD IN HIS SANCTUARY—A Brief Service of Worship and Exaltation"

11 My Tribute

Not to us, O Lord . . . but to Your name be the glory. Ps. 115:1

How can I say thanks for the things You have done for me— Things

so un - de - served, yet You give to prove Your love for me? The voic-es

of a mil - lion an - gels could not ex - press my grat - i - tude— All

that I am and ev-er hope to be, I owe it all to Thee. To

Refrain

God be the glo - ry, To God be the glo - ry; To

TEXT and MUSIC: Andraé Crouch

MY TRIBUTE
Irregular meter

God be the glo - ry for the things He has done. With His
blood He has saved me; With His pow'r He has raised me; To
God be the glo - ry For the things He has done.
Fine
*On introduction, hold 4 beats.
Just let me live my life; Let it be pleas-ing, Lord, to Thee. And
should I gain an - y praise, Let it go to Cal - va - ry. With His
D.S. al Fine

12 Holy God, We Praise Thy Name

I will praise Your name for ever and ever. Ps. 145:1

Descant, last stanza
3. Ho - ly Fa - ther, ho - ly Son, Ho - ly Spir - it:
three we name Thee, Though in es - sence on - ly one;
Un - di - vid - ed God we claim Thee, And a - dor - ing, bend the knee.
1. Ho - ly God, we praise Thy name; Lord of all, we
2. Hark, the glad ce - les - tial hymn An - gel choirs a -
3. Ho - ly Fa - ther, ho - ly Son, Ho - ly Spir - it:
bow be - fore Thee; All on earth Thy scep - ter claim,
bove are rais - ing; Cher - u - bim and ser - a - phim,
three we name Thee, Though in es - sence on - ly one;
All in heaven a - bove a - dore Thee: In - fi - nite Thy vast do -
In un - ceas - ing cho - rus prais-ing; Fill the heavens with sweet ac -
Un - di - vid - ed God we claim Thee, And a - dor - ing, bend the

TEXT: Attributed to Ignace Franz; translated by Clarence A. Walworth; based on *Te Deum*

MUSIC: Melody in *Katholisches Gesangbuch*, Vienna, c. 1774; Descant by Ken Barker

GROSSER GOTT
7.8.7.8.7.7.

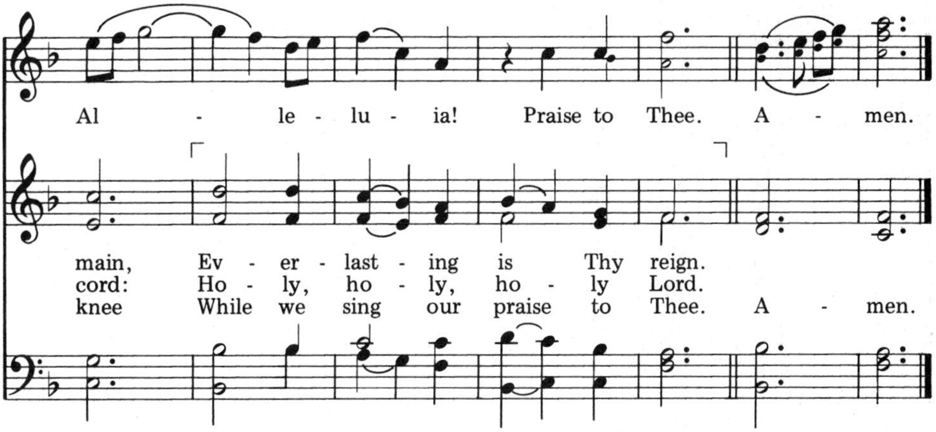

Al - le - lu - ia! Praise to Thee. A - men.

main, Ev - er - last - ing is Thy reign.
cord: Ho - ly, ho - ly, ho - ly Lord.
knee While we sing our praise to Thee. A - men.

Bless His Holy Name 13

Praise the Lord, O my soul. Ps. 103:22

Bless the Lord, O my soul, and all that is with - in me, Bless His

Fine

ho - ly Name. He has done great things, He has done great

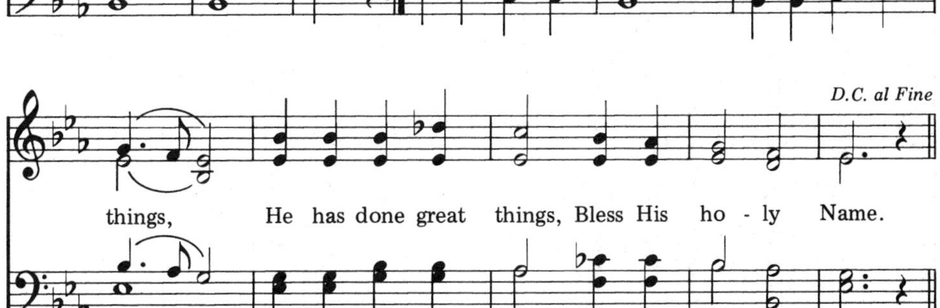
D.C. al Fine
things, He has done great things, Bless His ho - ly Name.

TEXT and MUSIC: Andraé Crouch; based on Psalm 103

BLESS HIS HOLY NAME
Irregular meter

14 Come, Let Us Worship and Bow Down

Come, let us bow down in worship. Ps. 95:6

Unison
Come, let us wor-ship and bow down, let us kneel be-fore the Lord, our God, our
accompaniment
1
D.C.
2
Mak - er. Mak - er. For He is our
God, and we are the peo-ple of His pas - ture, and the

TEXT: Psalm 95:6, 7; adapted by Dave Doherty
MUSIC: Dave Doherty

WORSHIP AND BOW DOWN
Irregular meter

sheep of His hand, just the sheep of His hand.

Abba Father 15

You received the Spirit of sonship. And by Him we cry, "Abba, Father." Rom. 8:15

1. "Ab - ba Fa - ther, Ab - ba Fa - ther," Deep with- in my soul I cry.
2. Fa - ther, Fa - ther, Je - ho - vah Sham - mah, You are the One who's stand-ing near.

Ab - ba Fa - ther, Ab - ba Fa - ther, I will nev - er cease to love You.

TEXT and MUSIC: Steven Fry; arranged by David Allen

ABBA FATHER
Irregular meter

16 We Praise Thee, O God, Our Redeemer

Great is the Lord and most worthy of praise. 1 Chr. 16:25

Descant, last stanza
3. With voic - es u - nit - ed our prais - es we of - fer To Thee, great Je -
1. We praise Thee, O God, our Re - deem - er, Cre - a - tor In grate - ful de -
2. We wor - ship Thee, God of our fa - thers, we bless Thee Thru life's storm and
3. With voic - es u - nit - ed our prais - es we of - fer To Thee, great Je -
ho - vah, glad an - thems we raise; Thy strong arm will guide us,
vo - tion our trib - ute we bring; We lay it be - fore Thee, we kneel
tem - pest our Guide hast Thou been; When per - ils o'er - take us, es - cape
ho - vah, glad an - thems we raise; Thy strong arm will guide us, our God
and our God is be - side us, great Re - deem - er, for - ev - er be praise!
and a - dore Thee, We bless Thy ho - ly Name, glad prais - es we sing.
Thou wilt make us, And with Thy help, O Lord, our bat - tles we win.
is be - side us, To Thee, our great Re - deem - er, for - ev - er be praise!

TEXT: Julia Cady Cory
MUSIC: Netherlands Folk song; arranged by Edward Kremser;
Descant and choral ending by Steve Holcomb
A lower setting may be found at No. 561

KREMSER
12.11.12.11.

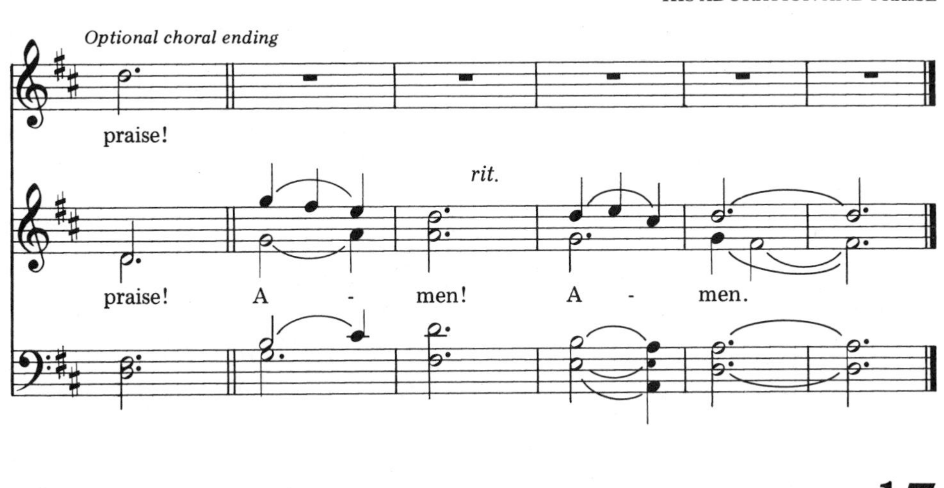
Optional choral ending
praise!
rit.
praise! A - men! A - men.

Ye Servants of God 17

Salvation belongs to our God, who sits on the throne, and to the Lamb. Rev. 7:10

1. Ye ser - vants of God, your Mas - ter pro - claim, And pub - lish a -
2. God rul - eth on high, al - might - y to save, And still He is
3. "Sal - va - tion to God, who sits on the throne!" Let all cry a -
4. Then let us a - dore, and give Him His right— All glo - ry and

broad His won - der - ful name; The name, all - vic - to - rious, of Je - sus
nigh, His pres - ence we have; The great con - gre - ga - tion His tri - umph
loud, and hon - or the Son; The prais - es of Je - sus the an - gels
pow'r, all wis - dom and might, All hon - or and bless - ing, with an - gels

ex - tol: His king - dom is glo - rious, He rules o - ver all.
shall sing, As - crib - ing sal - va - tion to Je - sus, our King.
pro - claim, Fall down on their fac - es and wor - ship the Lamb.
a - bove, And thanks nev - er - ceas - ing, and in - fi - nite love. A - men.

TEXT: Charles Wesley
MUSIC: William Croft

HANOVER
10.10.11.11.

18 Come, We That Love the Lord

Praise the Lord. Sing to the Lord a new song. Ps. 149:1

1. Come, we that love the Lord, And let our joys be known; Join in a song with sweet ac - cord, And thus sur - round the throne.
2. Let those re - fuse to sing Who nev - er knew our God; But chil - dren of the heav'n-ly King May speak their joys a - broad.
3. The men of grace have found Glo - ry be - gun be - low; Ce - les - tial fruit on earth - ly ground From faith and hope may grow.
4. The hill of Zi - on yields A thou - sand sa - cred sweets Be - fore we reach the heav'n-ly fields, Or walk the gold - en streets.
5. Then let our songs a - bound, And ev - ery tear be dry; We're march-ing thro' Em - man - uel's ground To fair - er worlds on high. A - men.

TEXT: Isaac Watts
MUSIC: Aaron Williams
A higher setting may be found at No. 21

ST. THOMAS
S.M.

19 We Worship and Adore You

They sang praises with gladness and bowed their heads and worshiped. 2 Chr. 29:30

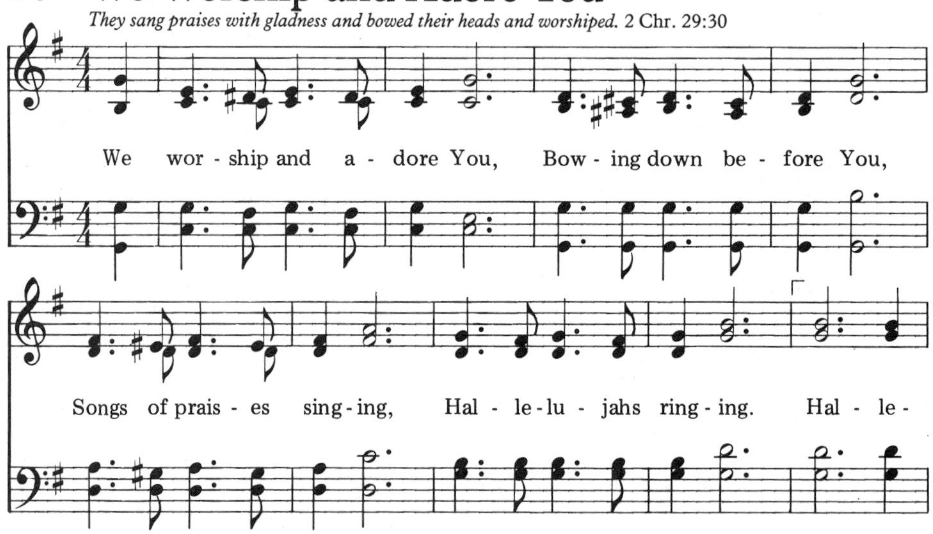
We wor - ship and a - dore You, Bow - ing down be - fore You,
Songs of prais - es sing - ing, Hal - le - lu - jahs ring - ing. Hal - le -

TEXT and MUSIC: Traditional

WORSHIP AND ADORE
7.6.6.6.8.6.

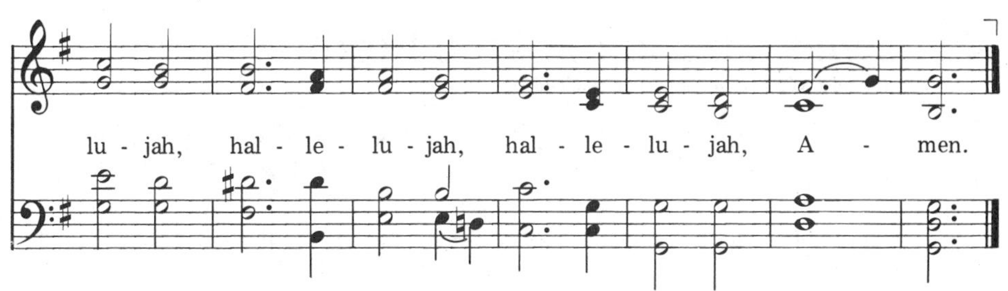
lu - jah, hal - le - lu - jah, hal - le - lu - jah, A - men.

All People That on Earth Do Dwell 20

Shout for joy to the Lord, all the earth. Ps. 100:1

1. All people that on earth do dwell, Sing to the Lord with cheerful voice; Him serve with fear, His praise forth tell, Come ye before Him and rejoice.

2. The Lord, ye know, is God indeed; Without our aid He did us make; We are His flock, He doth us feed, And for His sheep He doth us take.

3. O enter then His gates with praise, Approach with joy His courts unto; Praise, laud, and bless His name always, For it is seemly so to do.

4. For why? The Lord our God is good, His mercy is forever sure; His truth at all times firmly stood, And shall from age to age endure.

5. To Father, Son, and Holy Ghost, the God whom heaven and earth adore, From earth and from the angel host Be praise and glory evermore. Amen.

TEXT: William Kethe and *Scottish Psalter,* 1565; based on Psalm 100
MUSIC: *Genevan Psalter,* 1551; attributed to Louis Bourgeois

OLD HUNDREDTH
L.M.

21 Stand Up and Bless the Lord

Stand up and praise the Lord your God. Neh. 9:5

1. Stand up and bless the Lord, Ye people of His choice; Stand up and bless the Lord your God With heart and soul and voice.
2. Though high above all praise, Above all blessing high, Who would not fear His holy name, And laud and magnify?
3. O for the living flame, From His own altar brought, To touch our lips, our minds inspire, And wing to heav'n our thought.
4. God is our strength and song, And His salvation ours; Then be His love in Christ proclaim'd With all our ransomed pow'rs.
5. Stand up and bless the Lord, The Lord your God adore; Stand up and bless His glorious name Henceforth forevermore. Amen.

TEXT: James Montgomery
MUSIC: Aaron Williams
A lower setting may be found at No. 18

ST. THOMAS
S.M.

22 Isaiah 6:3

Holy, holy, holy is the Lord Almighty; the whole earth is full of His glory! Isa. 6:3

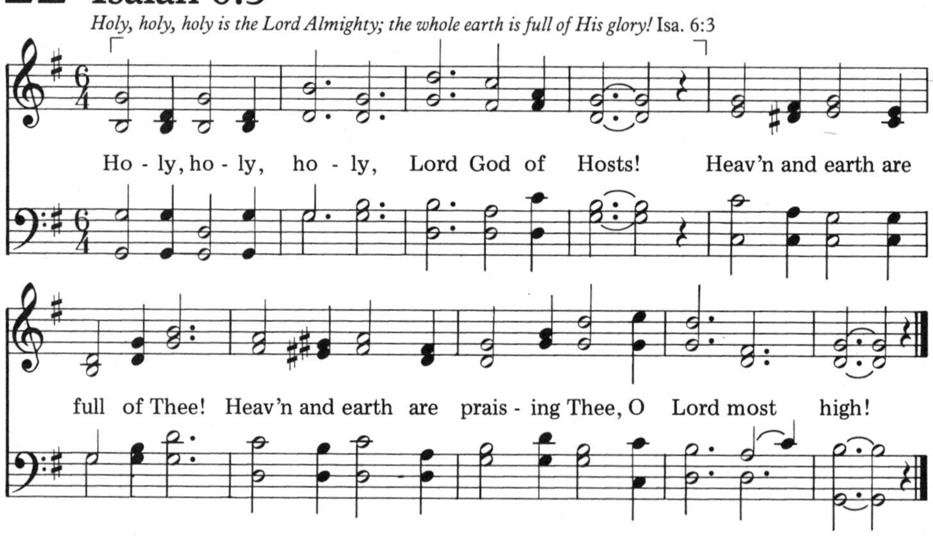
Ho - ly, ho - ly, ho - ly, Lord God of Hosts! Heav'n and earth are
full of Thee! Heav'n and earth are prais - ing Thee, O Lord most high!

TEXT: Mary A. Lathbury; from Isaiah 6:3
MUSIC: William F. Sherwin

CHAUTAUQUA (Refrain only)
Irregular meter

Make a Joyful Noise 23

Shout for joy to the Lord, all the earth. Ps. 98:4

4 Part Canon

Make a joyful noise unto the Lord, all the earth! Make a joyful noise unto the Lord!

Make a joyful noise unto the Lord, all the earth! Make a joyful noise unto the Lord! Make a

loud noise and re - joice! Sing prais-es! Make a joyful noise unto the Lord! Make a

loud noise and re - joice! Sing prais - es! Make a joy-ful noise un-to the Lord!

TEXT and MUSIC: Jimmy Owens; based on Psalm 98:4

JOYFUL NOISE
12.8.12.8.10.8.10.8.

Clap Your Hands 24

Clap your hands, all you nations: shout to God with cries of joy. Ps. 47:1

2 Part Canon

Clap your hands, all you peo-ple; Shout un-to God with a voice of tri-umph!

Clap your hands, all you peo-ple; Shout un-to God with a voice of praise! Ho-

san - na! Ho - san - na! Shout un-to God with a voice of tri-umph!

Praise Him! Praise Him! Shout un-to God with a voice of praise!

TEXT and MUSIC: Jimmy Owens; based on Psalm 47:1

CLAP YOUR HANDS
Irregular meter

25 Immortal, Invisible

Now to the King eternal, immortal, invisible, the only God, be honor. 1 Tim. 1:17

1. Im - mor - tal, in - vis - i - ble, God on - ly wise,
2. Un - rest - ing, un - hast - ing, and si - lent as light,
3. To all, life Thou giv - est— to both great and small,
4. Great Fa - ther of glo - ry, pure Fa - ther of light,

In light in - ac - ces - si - ble hid from our eyes,
Nor want - ing, nor wast - ing, Thou rul - est in might;
In all life Thou liv - est— the true life of all;
Thine an - gels a - dore Thee, all veil - ing their sight;

Most bless - ed, most glo - rious, the An - cient of Days,
Thy jus - tice, like moun - tains, high soar - ing a - bove
We blos - som and flour - ish as leaves on the tree,
All praise we would ren - der— O help us to see

Al - might-y, vic - to - rious—Thy great name we praise.
Thy clouds, which are foun-tains of good - ness and love.
And with - er and per - ish— but naught chang-eth Thee.
'Tis on - ly the splen-dor of light hid - eth Thee! A - men.

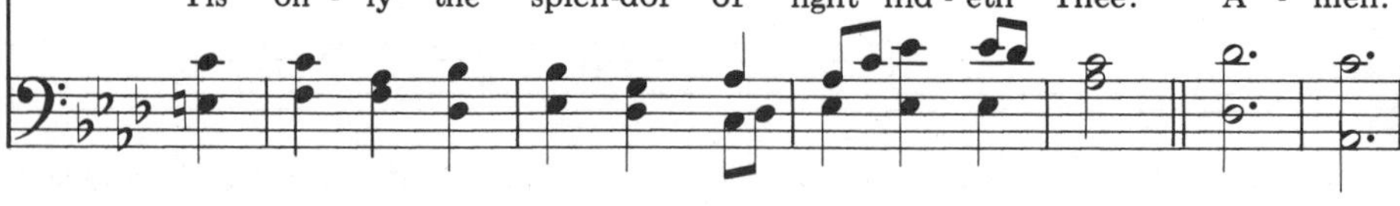

TEXT: Walter Chalmers Smith; based on 1 Timothy 1:17
MUSIC: Traditional Welsh Hymn melody
from John Roberts' *Canaidau y Cyssegr*, 1839

ST. DENIO
11.11.11.11.

A Mighty Fortress Is Our God 26

The Lord Almighty is with us; the God of Jacob is our fortress. Ps. 46:7

1. A might-y for-tress is our God, A bul-wark nev-er fail - ing;
2. Did we in our own strength con-fide, Our striv-ing would be los - ing,
3. And tho this world, with dev-ils filled, Should threat-en to un-do us,
4. That word a-bove all earth-ly pow'rs, No thanks to them, a-bid - eth;
Our help-er He a-mid the flood Of mor-tal ills pre-vail - ing.
Were not the right man on our side, The man of God's own choos - ing.
We will not fear, for God hath willed His truth to tri-umph thru us.
The Spir-it and the gifts are ours Thru Him who with us sid - eth.
For still our an-cient foe Doth seek to work us woe—His craft and pow'r are
Dost ask who that may be? Christ Je-sus, it is He— Lord Sab-a-oth His
The prince of dark-ness grim, We trem-ble not for him— His rage we can en-
Let goods and kin-dred go, This mor-tal life al-so— The bod-y they may
great, And, armed with cru-el hate, On earth is not his e - qual.
name, From age to age the same, And He must win the bat - tle.
dure, For lo, his doom is sure: One lit-tle word shall fell him.
kill; God's truth a-bid-eth still: His king-dom is for-ev - er. A-men.

TEXT: Martin Luther; translated by Frederick H. Hedge; based on Psalm 46
MUSIC: Martin Luther

EIN' FESTE BURG
8.7.8.7.6.6.6.6.7.

27 Tell Out, My Soul

The Mighty One has done great things for me. Luke 1:49

Unison

1. Tell out, my soul, the great - ness of the Lord! Un - num - bered bless - ings give my spir - it voice; Ten - der to me the prom - ise of His Word; In God my Sav - ior shall my heart re - joice.
2. Tell out, my soul, the great - ness of His Name! Make known His might, the deeds His arm has done; His mer - cy sure, from age to age the same; His ho - ly Name, the Lord, the Might - y One.
3. Tell out, my soul, the great - ness of His might! Pow'rs and do - min - ions lay their glo - ry by. Proud hearts and stub - born wills are put to flight, The hun - gry fed, the hum - ble lift - ed high.
4. Tell out, my soul, the glo - ries of His Word! Firm is His prom - ise, and His mer - cy sure. Tell out, my soul, the great - ness of the Lord To chil - dren's chil - dren and for - ev - er - more!

TEXT: Timothy Dudley-Smith; based on Luke 1:46-55
MUSIC: Walter Greatorex

WOODLANDS
10.10.10.10.

28

HOW MAJESTIC IS YOUR NAME

A Brief Service in Recognition of God's Majesty and Power

Suggested Hymn Stanzas

To facilitate an uninterrupted flow from stanza to stanza, the suggested stanzas have been marked with an arrow: ►

Glorify Thy Name, stanza 1
How Majestic Is Your Name, complete
Great Is the Lord, complete

WORSHIP LEADER and PEOPLE:

O Lord, our Lord,
how majestic is Your name in all the earth!

You have set Your glory
above the heavens.
From the lips of children and infants
You have ordained praise
because of Your enemies,
to silence the foe and the avenger.

When I consider Your heavens,
the work of Your fingers,
the moon and the stars,
which You have set in place,
what is man that You are mindful of him,
the son of man that You care for him?
You made him a little lower than the heavenly beings
and crowned him with glory and honor.

You made him ruler over the works of Your hands;
You put everything under his feet:
all flocks and herds,
and the beasts of the field,
the birds of the air, and the fish of the sea,
all that swim the paths of the seas.

O Lord, our Lord,
how majestic is Your name in all the earth!

Psalm 8. (NIV)

Optional introduction to "Glorify Thy Name"

"HOW MAJESTIC IS YOUR NAME—A Brief Service in Recognition of God's Majesty and Power"

29 Glorify Thy Name

Father, glorify Your name! John 12:28

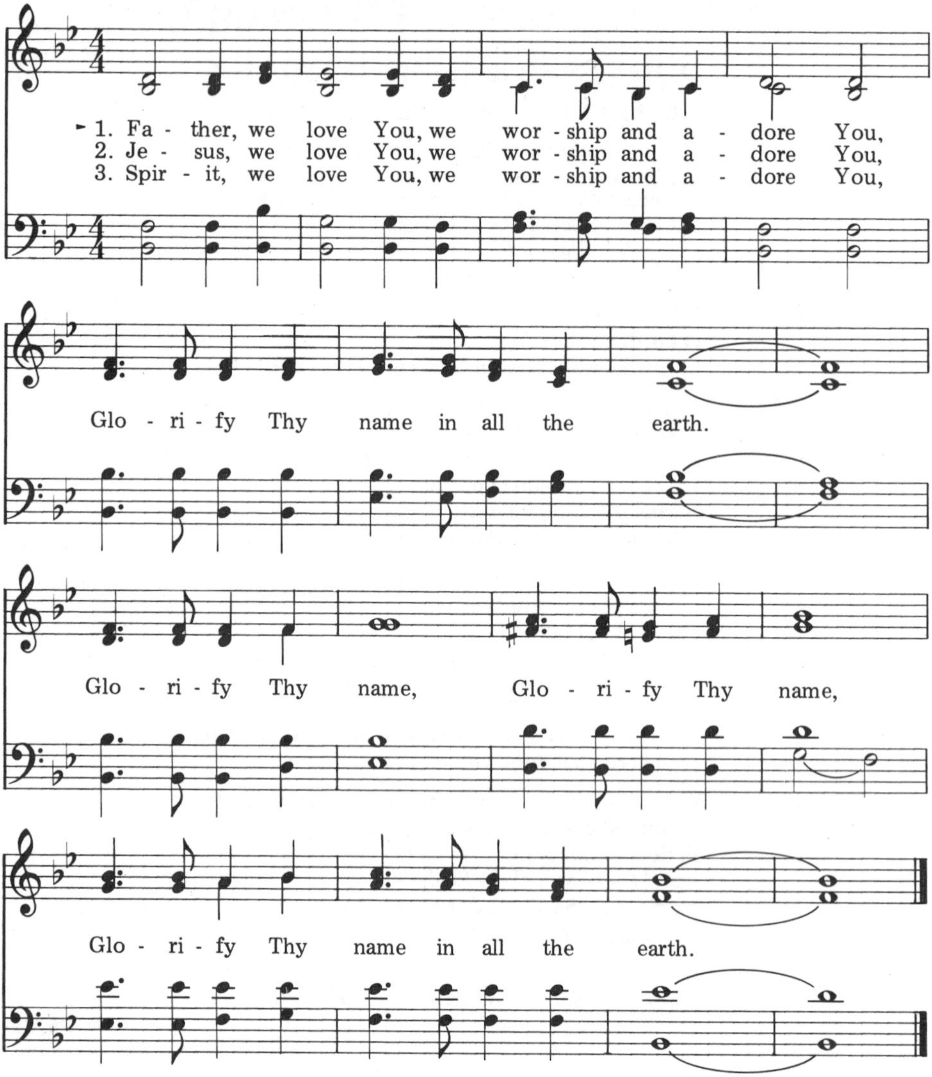
1. Fa - ther, we love You, we wor - ship and a - dore You,
2. Je - sus, we love You, we wor - ship and a - dore You,
3. Spir - it, we love You, we wor - ship and a - dore You,
Glo - ri - fy Thy name in all the earth.
Glo - ri - fy Thy name, Glo - ri - fy Thy name,
Glo - ri - fy Thy name in all the earth.

TEXT and MUSIC: Donna Adkins

GLORIFY THY NAME
Irregular meter

Optional transition to "How Majestic Is Your Name"

Bright and Energetic

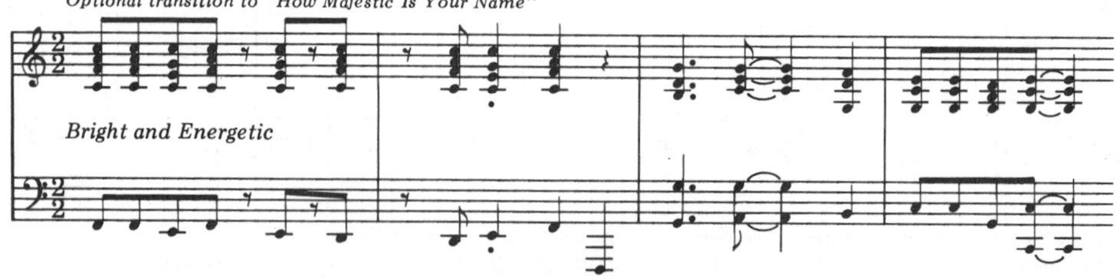

How Majestic Is Your Name 30

O Lord, our Lord, how majestic is Your name in all the earth! Ps. 8:1

1
2
D.S.
O Lord, our Lord, how ma - jes - tic is Your name in all the
earth. O earth. O Lord, we praise Your name. O
Lord, we mag - ni - fy Your name: Prince of Peace, might-y
God; O Lord God Al - might - y. O y.

TEXT and MUSIC: Michael W. Smith

HOW MAJESTIC
Irregular meter

Optional transition to "Great Is the Lord"

New tempo
♩. = ca. 63

31 Great Is the Lord

Great is the Lord and most worthy of praise. Ps. 145:3

Unison
Great is the Lord, He is ho-ly and just; By His pow-er we trust in His love.
Great is the Lord, He is faith-ful and true; By His mer-cy He proves He is love.
Parts optional
1, 2. Great is the Lord and wor-thy of glo-ry!
(D.S.) Great are You, Lord, and wor-thy of glo-ry!
Great is the Lord and wor-thy of praise. Great is the Lord; now
Great are You, Lord, and wor-thy of praise. Great are You, Lord; I
lift up your voice, Now lift up your voice: Great is the
lift up my voice, I lift up my voice: Great are You,

TEXT and MUSIC: Michael W. Smith and Deborah D. Smith

GREAT IS THE LORD
Irregular meter

3rd time to Coda 1 | 2 D.S. al Coda

Lord! Great is the Lord!
Lord! Great are You, Lord!

Coda

Optional choral ending

Lord! Great are You, Lord! Great are You, Lord!

*Observe fermatas if choral ending is not used.

Great are You, Lord!

8va 8va

The end of "HOW MAJESTIC IS YOUR NAME—A Brief Service in Recognition of God's Majesty and Power"

Holy Lord 32

The glory of the Lord fills the whole earth. Num. 14:21

3 Part canon
I
Ho-ly, ho-ly, Lord, God al-might-y; Your glo-ry fills the earth, Lord God of hosts.
II
Ho - ly, Lord, God al-might-y; Your glo-ry fills the earth, Lord God of hosts.
III
Ho - ly, Lord, God al-might-y; Your glo-ry fills the earth, Lord God of hosts.

TEXT: Gerald S. Henderson; based on Isaiah 6:3
MUSIC: Source unknown; adapted by Gerald S. Henderson

DONA NOBIS PACEM
Irregular meter

33 God the Omnipotent

He will proclaim peace to the nations. Zech. 9:10

1. God the Om - nip - o - tent! King, who or - dain - est
2. God the All - mer - ci - ful! Earth hath for - sak - en
3. God the All - right - eous One! Man hath de - fied Thee;
4. So shall Thy peo - ple, with thank - ful de - vo - tion,
Thun - der Thy clar - ion, the light - ning Thy sword;
Meek - ness and mer - cy, and slight - ed Thy Word;
Yet to e - ter - ni - ty stand - eth Thy Word;
Praise Him who saved them from per - il and sword,
Show forth Thy pit - y on high where Thou reign - est;
Let not Thy wrath in its ter - rors a - wak - en;
False - hood and wrong shall not tar - ry be - side Thee;
Sing - ing in cho - rus from o - cean to o - cean,
Give to us peace in our time, O Lord.
Give to us peace in our time, O Lord.
Give to us peace in our time, O Lord.
Peace to the na - tions, and praise to the Lord. A - men.

TEXT: Henry F. Chorley, stanzas 1, 2; John Ellerton, stanzas 3, 4
MUSIC: Alexis F. Lvov

RUSSIAN HYMN
11.10.11.9.

The God of Abraham Praise 34

[*Abraham*] *was strengthened in his faith and gave glory to God.* Rom. 4:20

1. The God of A - braham praise, Who reigns en - throned a - bove;
2. The God of A - braham praise, At whose su - preme com - mand
3. He by Him - self hath sworn, I on His oath de - pend,
4. The whole tri - um - phant host Give thanks to God on high;
An - cient of ev - er - last - ing days, And God of love.
From earth I rise, and seek the joys At His right hand.
I shall, on ea - gles wings up - borne, To heaven as - cend;
"Hail, Fa - ther, Son and Ho - ly Ghost!" They ev - er cry.
Je - ho - vah, great I AM, By earth and heaven con - fessed;
I all on earth for - sake, Its wis - dom, fame, and power;
I shall be - hold His face, I shall His power a - dore,
Hail, A - braham's God and mine! I join the heaven - ly lays;
I bow and bless the sa - cred name, For - ev - er blest.
And Him my on - ly por - tion make, My shield and tower.
And sing the won - ders of His grace For - ev - er - more.
All might and ma - jes - ty are Thine, And end - less praise. A - men.

TEXT: Thomas Olivers; based on Jewish *Doxology*
MUSIC: Traditional Hebrew melody; adapted by Meyer Lyon
A lower setting may be found at No. 472

LEONI
6.6.8.4.D.

35 The Majesty and Glory of Your Name

How majestic is Your name in all the earth! Ps. 8:9

mp
Al - le - lu - ia, Al - le - lu - ia!
cresc.
The maj - es - ty and glo - ry of Your name. Al - le - lu - ia,
Al - le - lu - ia!
cresc.
The maj - es - ty and glo - ry of Your
cresc.
name. Al - le - lu - ia, Al - le - lu - ia, Al - le -
ff
dim. and rit.
mp
lu - ia, Al - le - lu - ia! Al - le -

TEXT: Linda Lee Johnson; based on Psalm 8
MUSIC: Tom Fettke

SOLI DEO GLORIA
Irregular meter

dim.
lu - ia, Al - le - lu - ia, Al - le - lu - ia!

El Shaddai 36

I am God Almighty; walk before Me and be blameless. Gen. 17:1

Unison

*El Shad-dai, El Shad-dai, El El - yon na A - do-nai;

Age to age You're still the same By the pow-er of the name.

El Shad-dai, El Shad-dai, Er-kahm - ka na A - do-nai;

We will praise and lift You high, El Shad - dai.

*Translations of Hebrew terms:
El Shaddai: God Almighty — na Adonai: O Lord
El Elyon: The Most High God — Erkahmka: we will love You

TEXT and MUSIC: Michael Card and John Thompson

EL SHADDAI
Irregular meter

37 Hallelujah Chorus

Hallelujah! For our Lord God Almighty reigns. Rev. 19:6

Allegro
f
f
Hal-le - lu - jah! Hal - le-lu -jah! Hal-le - lu-jah! Hal-le-lu-jah! Hal - le - lu-jah!
Hal - le - lu-jah! Hal - le - lu - jah! Hal-le - lu-jah! Hal-le-lu-jah! Hal - le - lu - jah!
for the Lord God om-nip-o-tent reign-eth. Hal - le - lu -jah! Hal-le-lu-jah! Hal-le-
lu - jah! Hal-le -lu -jah! for the Lord God om-nip - o-tent reign - eth. Hal - le-

TEXT and MUSIC: George Frederick Handel

HALLELUJAH CHORUS
Irregular meter

This vocal score is complete and uniform with most editions.

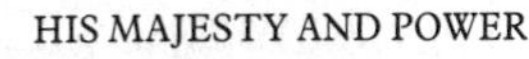

lu-jah! Hal-le-lu-jah! Hal-le - lu-jah! Hal-le-lu-jah! for the Lord
Hal-le-lu-jah! Hal-le-

God om-nip - o-tent reign - eth. Hal-le-lu-jah! Hallelujah! Hallelu-
Hal-le-lu-jah! Hal-le-lu-jah! Hal-le-lu-jah! Hal-le-lu-jah! Hal-le-lu-
lu-jah! Hal-le-lu-jah! Hal - le - lu - jah! Hal-le-lu-jah! for the Lord
Hal-le-lu-jah!

jah! Hal-le-lu-jah! Hal -le - lu - jah! Hal-le-lu-jah! Hal-le-lu-jah! Hal-le-lu -jah!
jah! Hal-le-lu-jah! Hal - le - lu - jah! Hal-le - lu-jah! Hal-le-lu-jah!
God om-nip - o-tent reign - eth. Hal-le-lu-jah! Hal-le - lu-jah! Hal-le - lu-jah!
Hal-le - lu-jah! Hal-le-lu-jah!

Hal-le-lu-jah! Hal-le-lu-jah! Hal-le-lu-jah! Hal-le-lu-jah! Hal - le-lu-jah! Hal -
for the Lord God om-nip - o - tent reign - eth. Hal-le-lu-jah!
for the Lord God om-nip - o - tent reign - eth. Hal -
Hal-le-lu-jah! Hal-le-lu-jah! Hal-le-lu-jah! Hal-le-lu-jah! Hallelujah! Hal-le-
le - lu - jah!
Hal-le - lu-jah!
le - lu-jah! The king-dom of this world is be -
is be -
lu-jah! Hallelujah!
is be -
come the king-dom of our Lord, and of His Christ, and of His Christ;
come
And He shall
alto
tenor
And He shall reign for ev - er and ev -
reign for ev - er and ev - er, for ev-er and ev - er, and He shall

f
And
And He shall reign for ev - er and ev - er, for ev - er
er, And He shall reign for ev - er and ev - er,
reign, and He shall reign for ev - er, for ev - er, for ev - er, for
He shall reign for ev - er and ev - er, King of kings,
and ev - er, for ev - er and ev - er, King of kings,
And He shall reign for ev - er and ev - er, for ev - er and
ev - er and ev - er, for ev - er, for ev - er and ev - er,
and Lord of lords,
ev - er, Hal - le - lu - jah! Hal - le - lu - jah! for ev - er and
King of kings,
ev - er, Hal - le - lu - jah! Hal - le - lu - jah! for ev - er and

and Lord of lords,
ev - er, Hal-le-lu-jah! Hal-le - lu-jah! for ev - er and
King of kings,
ev - er, Hal-le-lu - jah! Hal-le - lu-jah! for ev-er and
and Lord of lords, and Lord of
ff
ev-er, Hal-le-lu-jah! Hal-le - lu - jah! King of kings, and Lord of
lords, and He shall reign, and
f
lords, and He shall reign, and He shall
lords, and He shall reign, and He shall reign,
lords, and He shall reign for ev - er and ev - er,
He shall reign for ev - er and ev - er, for ev-er and
ff
reign for ev - er and ev - er, King of kings, for ev-er and
and He shall reign for ev - er and ev - er, King of kings,
and He shall reign for ev - er and ev-er, King of kings, for ev-er and

ev - er, Hal-le - lu - jah! Hal-le - lu - jah! And He shall
ev - er, and Lord of lords, Hal-le - lu - jah! Hal-le - lu - jah! And
and Lord of lords, And He shall
ev - er, and Lord of lords, Hal-le - lu - jah! Hal-le - lu - jah!
reign for ev - er, for ev - er and ev - er,
He shall reign for ev - er and ev - er, King of kings! and Lord of lords!
reign for ev - er, for ev - er and ev - er,
King of kings! and Lord of lords! And He shall reign for ev - er and ev -
And He shall reign for ev-er and ev - er, and ev -
er, King of kings! and Lord of lords! Hal-le - lu - jah!
er, for ev - er, and ev - er, for ev - er, and ev - er,
adagio
Hal-le - lu - jah! Hal-le - lu - jah! Hal-le - lu - jah! Hal - le - lu - jah!

38 I Will Call upon the Lord

I call to the Lord, who is worthy of praise. Ps. 18:3

Optional descant
I will call up-on the Lord
Unison
I will call up-on the Lord who is wor-thy to be
who is wor-thy to be praised. So shall I be
praised. So shall I be saved from my en - e - mies.
1
2
saved from my en - e-mies. I will call up-on the Lord. Lord. The
I will call up-on the Lord. Lord. The

TEXT and MUSIC: Michael O'Shields; based on Psalm 18:3; 2 Samuel 22:47

O'SHIELDS
Irregular meter

Lord liv - eth, and bless-ed be the Rock, And let the God of my sal-va-tion be ex-
alt - ed. The Lord liv-eth, and bless-ed be the Rock, and let the God of
my sal-va-tion be ex - alt - ed. The ed.
1
2
3 Part Canon
I
1. God, our Fa - ther, we a - dore You, mag - ni - fy You;
2. Heav'n and earth pro - claim Your pow - er, show Your glo - ry;
3. Al - le - lu - ia, al - le - lu - ia, al - le - lu - ia;
II
God, our Fa - ther, we a - dore You, mag - ni - fy You;
Heav'n and earth pro - claim Your pow - er, show Your glo - ry;
Al - le - lu - ia, al - le - lu - ia, al - le - lu - ia;
III
Great are You, O Lord!
Great are You, O Lord!
Great are You, O Lord!

Great Are You, O Lord 39

Great is our Lord and mighty in power. Ps. 147:5

TEXT: Gerald S. Henderson
MUSIC: Traditional English melody; adapted by Gerald S. Henderson

ENGLAND
Irregular meter

40 A Perfect Heart

I will give you a new heart and put a new spirit in you. Ezek. 36:26

Bless the Lord (bless the Lord) who reigns in beau-ty; Bless the Lord (bless the Lord)

who reigns in wis - dom and with pow'r. Bless the Lord (bless the Lord)

who fills my life with so much love, He can make a per-fect heart.

TEXT and MUSIC: Dony McGuire and Reba Rambo

A PERFECT HEART
Irregular meter

GOD OUR FATHER: HIS GUIDANCE AND CARE

41 God Is So Good

Give thanks to the Lord, for He is good. 1 Chr. 16:34

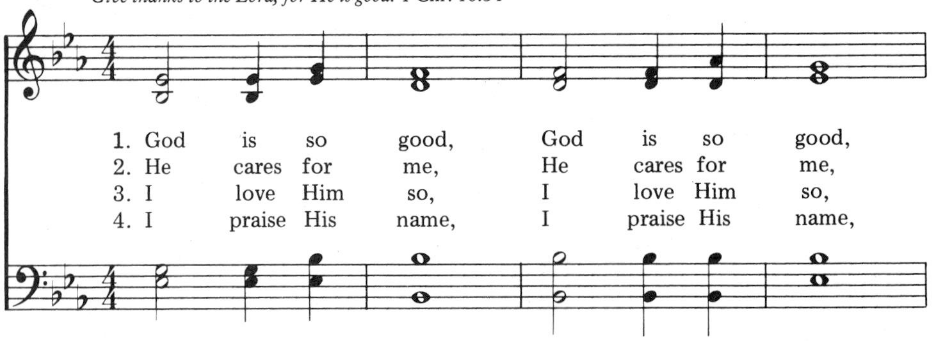
1. God is so good, God is so good,
2. He cares for me, He cares for me,
3. I love Him so, I love Him so,
4. I praise His name, I praise His name,

TEXT and MUSIC: Traditional

GOD IS SO GOOD
Irregular meter

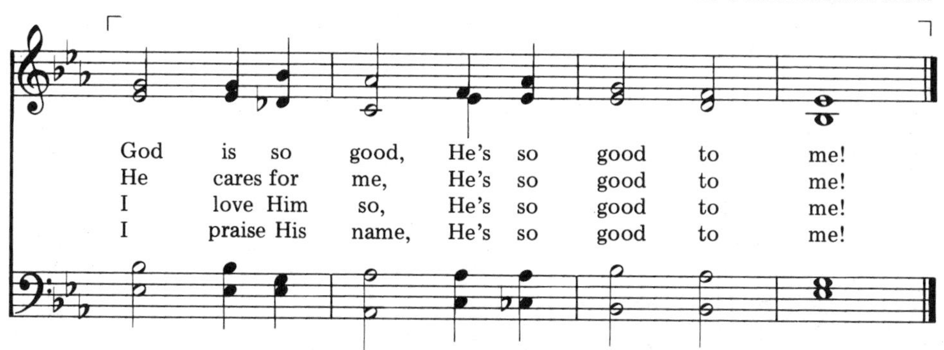
God is so good, He's so good to me!
He cares for me, He's so good to me!
I love Him so, He's so good to me!
I praise His name, He's so good to me!

Seek Ye First 42

Seek first His kingdom and His righteousness. Matt. 6:33

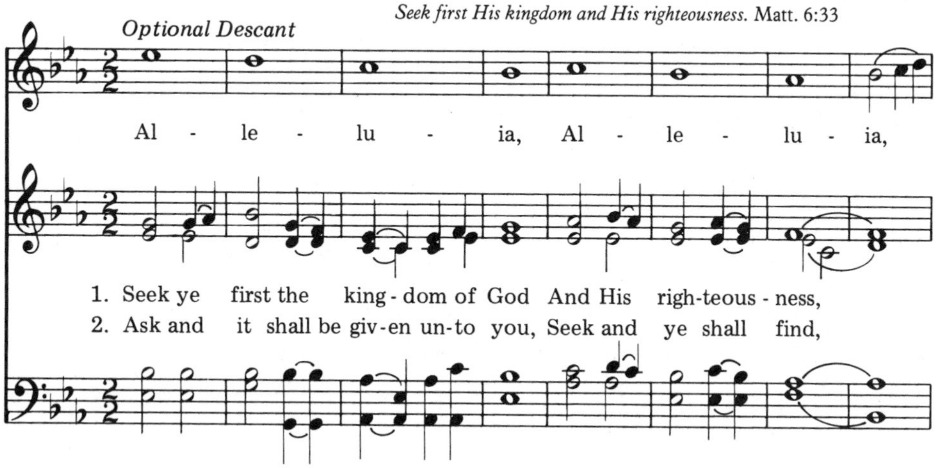

Optional Descant

Al - le - lu - ia, Al - le - lu - ia,

1. Seek ye first the king - dom of God And His righ-teous - ness,
2. Ask and it shall be giv-en un-to you, Seek and ye shall find,

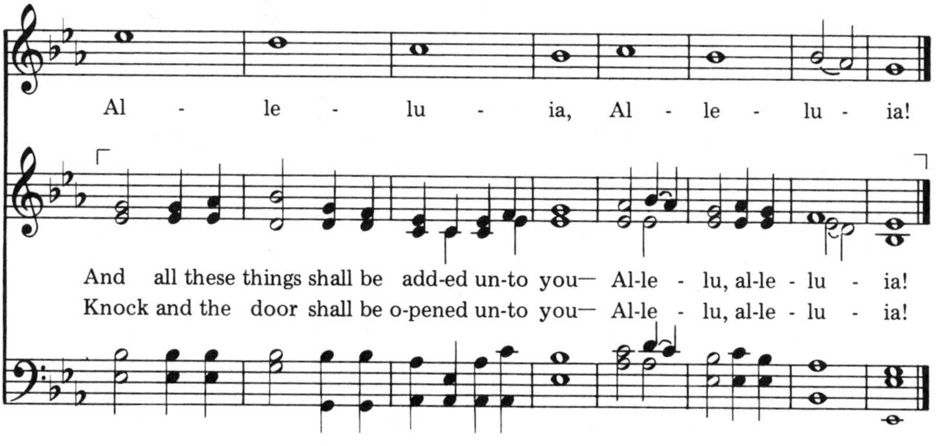

Al - le - lu - ia, Al - le - lu - ia!

And all these things shall be add-ed un-to you— Al-le - lu, al-le - lu - ia!
Knock and the door shall be o-pened un-to you— Al-le - lu, al-le - lu - ia!

TEXT and MUSIC: Karen Lafferty; based on Matthew 6:33; 7:7

LAFFERTY
Irregular meter

43 Great Is Thy Faithfulness

The Lord's . . . compassions . . . are new every morning; great is Your faithfulness. Lam. 3:22-23

1. Great is Thy faith - ful - ness, O God my Fa - ther, There is no
2. Sum - mer and win - ter, and spring-time and har - vest, Sun, moon and
3. Par - don for sin and a peace that en - dur - eth, Thy own dear
shad - ow of turn - ing with Thee; Thou chang-est not, Thy com-
stars in their cours - es a - bove Join with all na - ture in
pres - ence to cheer and to guide; Strength for to - day and bright
pas - sions they fail not; As Thou hast been Thou for - ev - er wilt be.
man - i - fold wit - ness To Thy great faith - ful - ness, mer - cy and love.
hope for to - mor - row, Bless - ings all mine, with ten thou-sand be - side!
Refrain
Great is Thy faith - ful - ness! Great is Thy faith - ful - ness! Morn - ing by
morn - ing new mer - cies I see; All I have need - ed Thy

TEXT: Thomas O. Chisholm
MUSIC: William M. Runyan

FAITHFULNESS
11.10.11.10 with Refrain

hand hath pro - vid - ed— Great is Thy faith - ful-ness, Lord, un - to me!
Optional choral ending
gradual cresc.
rit.
Slowly
ff
Great is Thy faith-ful-ness, Great is Thy faith-ful-ness, Lord, un-to me!

Children of the Heavenly Father 44

How great is the love the Father has lavished on us . . . children of God! 1 John 3:1

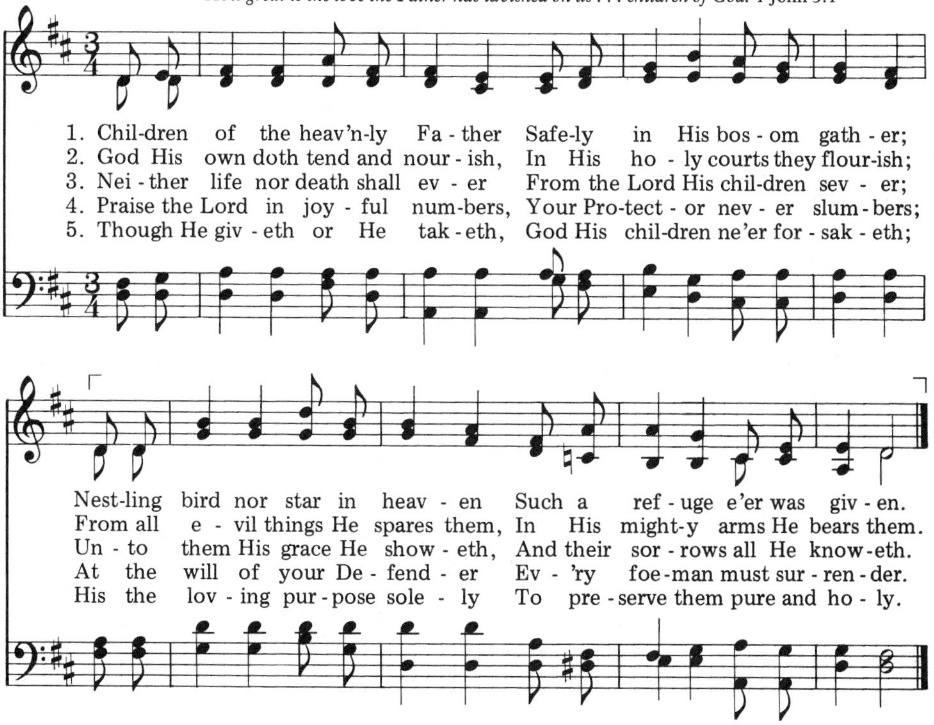

1. Chil-dren of the heav'n-ly Fa - ther Safe-ly in His bos - om gath - er;
Nest-ling bird nor star in heav - en Such a ref - uge e'er was giv - en.

2. God His own doth tend and nour - ish, In His ho - ly courts they flour-ish;
From all e - vil things He spares them, In His might-y arms He bears them.

3. Nei - ther life nor death shall ev - er From the Lord His chil-dren sev - er;
Un - to them His grace He show - eth, And their sor - rows all He know-eth.

4. Praise the Lord in joy - ful num-bers, Your Pro-tect - or nev - er slum - bers;
At the will of your De - fend - er Ev - 'ry foe-man must sur - ren - der.

5. Though He giv - eth or He tak - eth, God His chil-dren ne'er for - sak - eth;
His the lov - ing pur - pose sole - ly To pre - serve them pure and ho - ly.

TEXT: Carolina Sandell Berg; translated by Ernst W. Olson
MUSIC: Swedish Folk melody

TRYGGARE KAN INGEN VARA
L.M.

45 Surely Goodness and Mercy

Surely goodness and love will follow me all the days of my life. Ps. 23:6

1. A pil - grim was I, and a - wan-d'ring— In the cold night of sin I did roam When Je - sus the kind Shep-herd found me— And now I am on my way home.

2. He re - stor - eth my soul when I'm wea - ry, He giv - eth me strength day by day; He leads me be - side the still wa - ters, He guards me each step of the way.

3. When I walk thru the dark lone-some val - ley, My Sav - ior will walk with me there; And safe - ly His great hand will lead me To the man-sions He's gone to pre - pare.

Refrain

Sure - ly good - ness and mer - cy shall fol - low me All the days, all the days of my life; Sure - ly good - ness and mer - cy shall

TEXT and MUSIC: John W. Peterson and Alfred B. Smith; based on Psalm 23

SURELY GOODNESS AND MERCY
Irregular meter

(optional D.C.)
fol - low me All the days, all the days of my life.
May be omitted until final Refrain
And I shall dwell in the house of the Lord for - ev - er, And I shall
feast at the ta - ble spread for me; Sure - ly good - ness
and mer - cy shall fol - low me All the days, all the days of
my life, All the days, all the days of my life.

46 God Leads Us Along

When you pass through the waters, I will be with you. Isa. 43:2

1. In shad - y, green pas-tures, so rich and so sweet, God leads His dear
2. Some-times on the mount where the sun shines so bright, God leads His dear
3. Though sor-rows be - fall us and Sa - tan op - pose, God leads His dear
chil-dren a - long; Where the wa - ter's cool flow bathes the wea-ry one's feet,
chil-dren a - long; Some - times in the val - ley, in dark-est of night,
chil-dren a - long; Through grace we can con - quer, de - feat all our foes,
God leads His dear chil-dren a - long.
God leads His dear chil-dren a - long.
God leads His dear chil-dren a - long.
Refrain
Some thro' the wa-ters, some thro' the
flood, Some thro' the fire, but all thro' the blood; Some thro' great sorrow, but
God gives a song, In the night sea - son and all the day long.

TEXT and MUSIC: G. A. Young

GOD LEADS US
11.8.11.8. with Refrain

God Will Take Care of You 47

He cares for those who trust in Him. Nah. 1:7

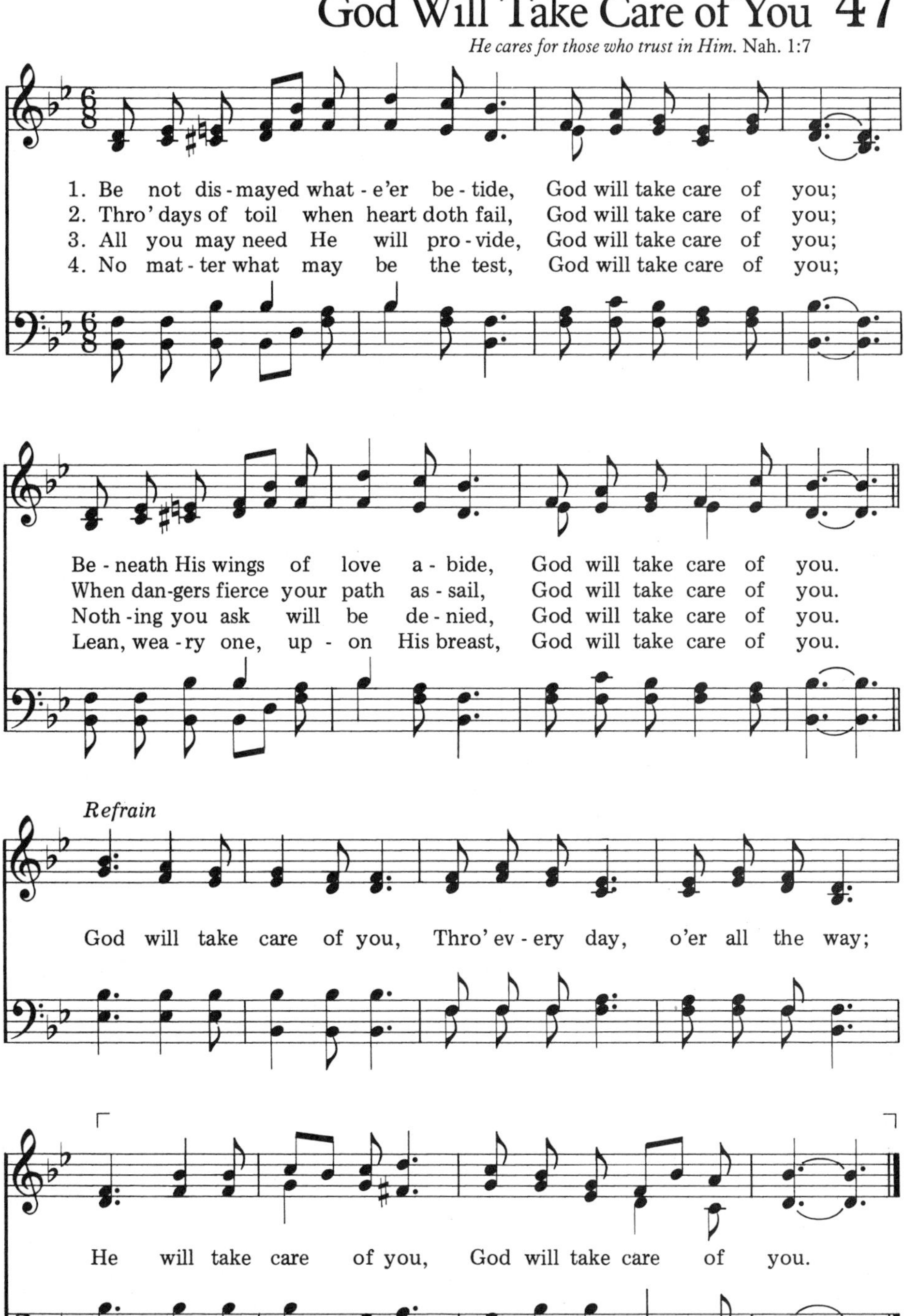
1. Be not dis-mayed what-e'er be-tide, God will take care of you;
2. Thro' days of toil when heart doth fail, God will take care of you;
3. All you may need He will pro-vide, God will take care of you;
4. No mat-ter what may be the test, God will take care of you;
Be-neath His wings of love a-bide, God will take care of you.
When dan-gers fierce your path as-sail, God will take care of you.
Noth-ing you ask will be de-nied, God will take care of you.
Lean, wea-ry one, up-on His breast, God will take care of you.
Refrain
God will take care of you, Thro' ev-ery day, o'er all the way;
He will take care of you, God will take care of you.

TEXT: Civilla D. Martin
MUSIC: W. Stillman Martin

GOD CARES
C.M. with Refrain

48

LEAD US, O GOD

A Brief Service of Prayer and Petition

Suggested Hymn Stanzas

To facilitate an uninterrupted flow from stanza to stanza, the suggested stanzas have been marked with an arrow: ►

Lead Me, Lord, complete
The Lord's My Shepherd, I'll Not Want, stanzas 1, 2, 3
Guide Me, O Thou Great Jehovah, stanzas 1, 2
O God, Our Help in Ages Past, stanzas 1, 2, 3, 6

WORSHIP LEADER and PEOPLE:

In You, O Lord, I put my trust; Let me never be ashamed; Deliver me in Your righteousness. Bow down Your ear to me, Deliver me speedily; Be my Rock of refuge, A fortress of defense to save me. For You are my rock and my fortress; Therefore for Your name's sake, Lead me and guide me.

Psalm 31:1-3. (NKJV)

49 Lead Me, Lord

Lead me, O Lord, in Your righteousness. Ps. 5:8

Choir or Congregation
Introduction
Lead me, Lord, lead me in Thy right-eous-ness;
make Thy way plain be - fore my face. For it is Thou, Lord,
Thou, Lord, on - ly, that mak - est me dwell in safe - ty.

TEXT: Based on Psalms 5:8 and 4:8
MUSIC: Samuel S. Wesley

LEAD ME, LORD
Irregular meter

"LEAD US, O GOD - A Brief Service of Prayer and Petition"

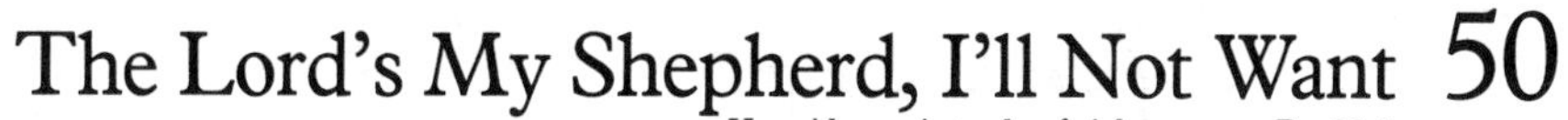

The Lord's My Shepherd, I'll Not Want 50

He guides me in paths of righteousness. Ps. 23:3

1. The Lord's my Shep-herd, I'll not want; He makes me down to lie
2. My soul He doth re - store a - gain; And me to walk doth make
3. Yea, though I walk through death's dark vale, Yet will I fear no ill;
4. My ta - ble Thou hast fur-nish - ed In pres-ence of my foes;
5. Good-ness and mer - cy all my life Shall sure - ly fol - low me;

In pas-tures green; He lead-eth me The qui - et wa-ters by.
With-in the paths of right-eous-ness, E'en for His own name's sake.
For Thou art with me, and Thy rod And staff me com-fort still.
My head Thou dost with oil a - noint, And my cup o - ver-flows.
And in God's house for - ev - er-more My dwell-ing place shall be. A-men.

TEXT: *Scottish Psalter,* 1650; William Whittingham and others; based on Psalm 23
MUSIC: Jessie S. Irvine; arranged by David Grant

CRIMOND
C.M.

51 Guide Me, O Thou Great Jehovah

The Lord will guide you always; He will satisfy your needs. Isa. 58:11

1. Guide me, O Thou great Je - ho - vah, Pil - grim through this bar - ren land; I am weak, but Thou art might - y; Hold me with Thy pow'r - ful hand; Bread of heav - en, Bread of heav - en, Feed me till I want no more, Feed me till I want no more.
2. O - pen now the crys - tal foun - tain, Whence the heal - ing stream doth flow; Let the fire and cloud - y pil - lar Lead me all my jour - ney through; Strong De - liv - erer, strong De - liv - erer, Be Thou still my strength and shield, Be Thou still my strength and shield.
3. When I tread the verge of Jor - dan, Bid my anx - ious fears sub - side; Bear me thro' the swell - ing cur - rent, Land me safe on Ca - naan's side; Songs of prais - es, songs of prais - es I will ev - er give to Thee, I will ev - er give to Thee. A - men.

TEXT: William Williams; translated by Peter Williams and William Williams
MUSIC: John Hughes

CWM RHONDDA
8.7.8.7.8.7.7.

Optional transition to "O God, Our Help in Ages Past"

mf

O God, Our Help in Ages Past 52

Lord, You have been our dwelling place throughout all generations. Ps. 90:1

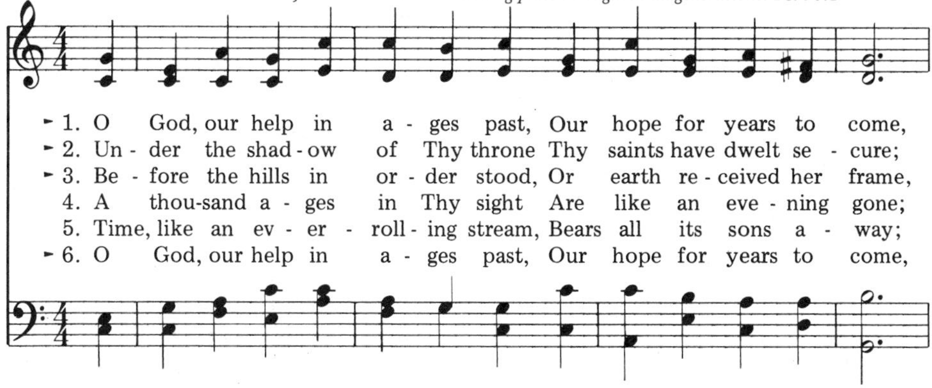

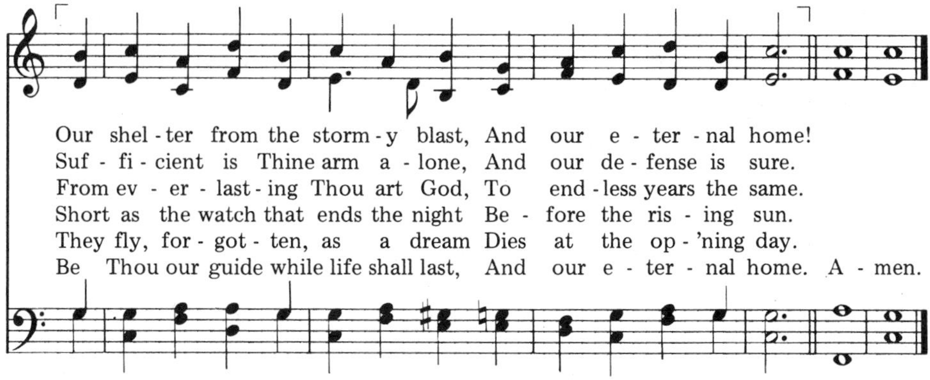

1. O God, our help in ages past, Our hope for years to come,
Our shelter from the stormy blast, And our eternal home!

2. Under the shadow of Thy throne Thy saints have dwelt secure;
Sufficient is Thine arm alone, And our defense is sure.

3. Before the hills in order stood, Or earth received her frame,
From everlasting Thou art God, To endless years the same.

4. A thousand ages in Thy sight Are like an evening gone;
Short as the watch that ends the night Before the rising sun.

5. Time, like an ever-rolling stream, Bears all its sons away;
They fly, forgotten, as a dream Dies at the op'ning day.

6. O God, our help in ages past, Our hope for years to come,
Be Thou our guide while life shall last, And our eternal home. Amen.

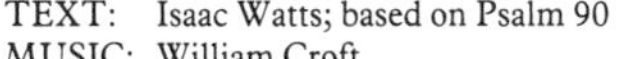

TEXT: Isaac Watts; based on Psalm 90
MUSIC: William Croft

ST. ANNE
C.M.

Optional choral ending

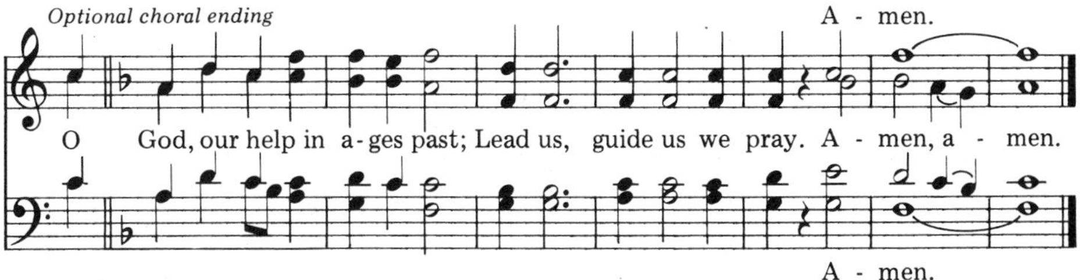
A - men.
O God, our help in a-ges past; Lead us, guide us we pray. A - men, a - men.
A - men.

The end of "LEAD US, O GOD—A Brief Service of Prayer and Petition"

53 The New 23rd

The Lord is my Shepherd, I shall not be in want. Ps. 23:1

Be - cause the Lord is my Shep-herd, I have ev - 'ry-thing that I need. He
lets me rest in mead-ows green And leads me be-side the qui-et stream; He
keeps on giv - ing life to me And helps me to do what hon-ors Him the most.
E-ven when walk-ing thru the dark val - ley of death, val-ley of death,
I will nev - er be a - fraid, For He is close be - side me,

TEXT and MUSIC: Ralph Carmichael; based on Psalm 23

THE NEW 23RD
Irregular meter

Guard-ing, guid-ing all the way; He spreads a feast be - fore me In the pres-ence
of my en-e-mies. He wel-comes me as His spe-cial guest. With bless-ing o-ver-
flow-ing, His good-ness and un-fail-ing kind - ness Shall be with me all of my
then
Shall
life And af-ter-ward I will live with Him for - ev-er, for - ev-er
my life
I
live with Him
in His home, for - ev - er in His home, for - ev - er in His home.
rit.

54 His Way

So are my ways higher than your ways. Isa. 55:9

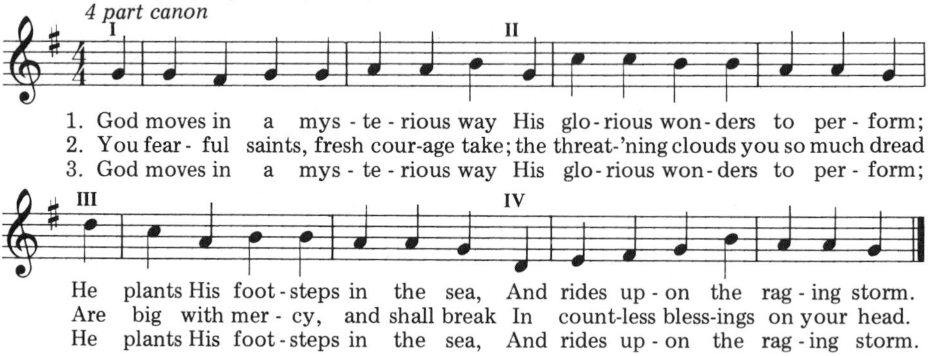

4 part canon
I
II
III
IV
1. God moves in a mys - te - rious way His glo - rious won - ders to per - form;
2. You fear - ful saints, fresh cour - age take; the threat-'ning clouds you so much dread
3. God moves in a mys - te - rious way His glo - rious won - ders to per - form;
He plants His foot - steps in the sea, And rides up - on the rag - ing storm.
Are big with mer - cy, and shall break In count-less bless-ings on your head.
He plants His foot - steps in the sea, And rides up - on the rag - ing storm.

TEXT: William Cowper; altered and adapted by Gerald S. Henderson — TALLIS' CANON
MUSIC: Thomas Tallis — L.M.

55 Day by Day—A Prayer

Love the Lord your God and keep His requirements . . . always. Deut. 11:1

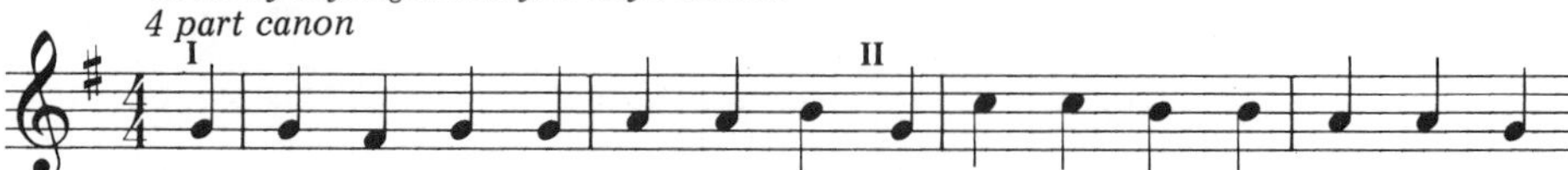

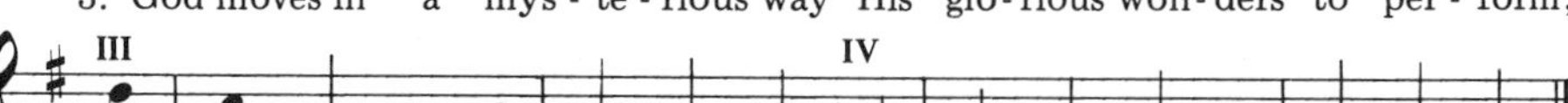

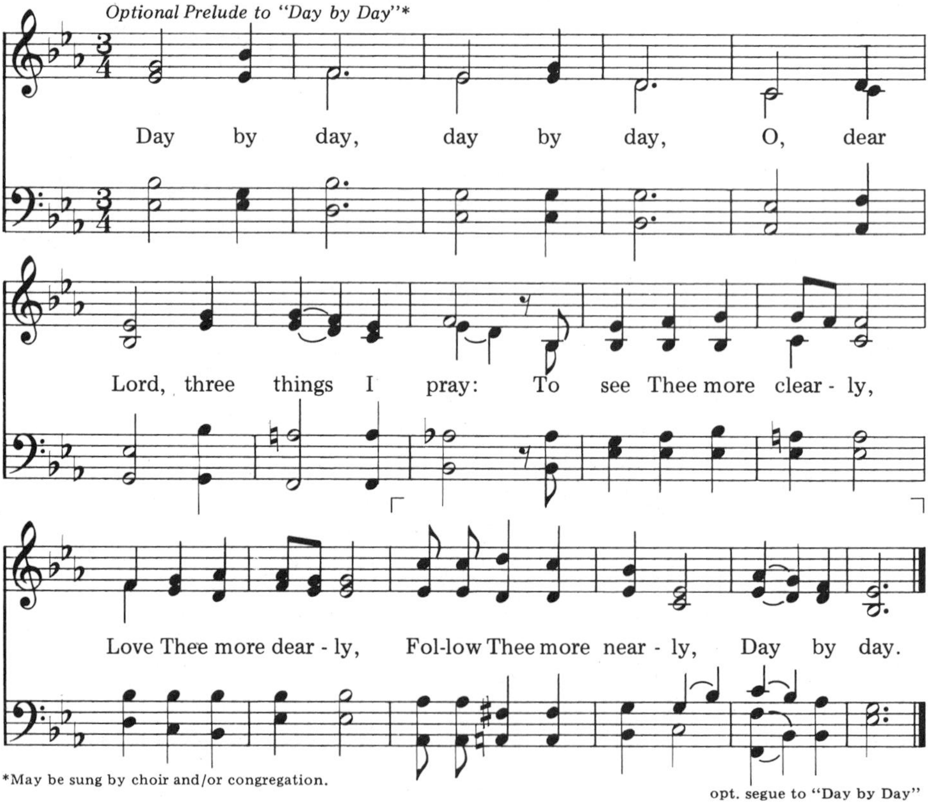

Optional Prelude to "Day by Day"*
Day by day, day by day, O, dear
Lord, three things I pray: To see Thee more clear - ly,
Love Thee more dear - ly, Fol - low Thee more near - ly, Day by day.
opt. segue to "Day by Day"

*May be sung by choir and/or congregation.

TEXT: St. Richard of Chichester — FAYE
MUSIC: Ken Barker — Irregular meter

Day by Day 56

My grace is sufficient for you, for My power is made perfect in weakness. 2 Cor. 12:9

1. Day by day and with each pass-ing mo-ment, Strength I find to meet my tri-als here; Trust-ing in my Fa-ther's wise be-stow-ment, I've no cause for wor-ry or for fear. He whose heart is kind be-yond all meas-ure Gives un-to each day what He deems best— Lov-ing-ly, its part of pain and pleas-ure, Min-gling toil with peace and rest.
2. Ev-'ry day the Lord Him-self is near me With a spe-cial mer-cy for each hour; All my cares He fain would bear, and cheer me, He whose name is Coun-sel-lor and Pow'r. The pro-tec-tion of His child and treas-ure Is a charge that on Him-self He laid; "As your days, your strength shall be in meas-ure," This the pledge to me He made.
3. Help me then in ev-'ry trib-u-la-tion So to trust Your prom-is-es, O Lord, That I lose not faith's sweet con-so-la-tion Of-fered me with-in Your ho-ly Word. Help me, Lord, when toil and trou-ble meet-ing, E'er to take, as from a fa-ther's hand, One by one, the days, the mo-ments fleet-ing, Till I reach the prom-ised land.

TEXT: Carolina Sandell Berg; translated by Andrew L. Skoog
MUSIC: Oscar Ahnfelt

BLOTT EN DAG
Irregular meter

57 He Careth for You

Cast your cares on the Lord and He will sustain you. Ps. 55:22

Unison
He car-eth for you, He car-eth for you.
When the wor-ries and cares of your life seem to block out the rays of His
light, nev-er for-get, nev-er lose sight for He
car-eth for you, for He car-eth for you.

TEXT and MUSIC: Kurt Kaiser

HE CARETH FOR YOU
Irregular meter

This Is My Father's World 58

The world is Mine, and all that is in it. Ps. 50:12

1. This is my Fa - ther's world, And to my lis - tening ears
2. This is my Fa - ther's world, The birds their car - ols raise,
3. This is my Fa - ther's world, O let me ne'er for - get
All na - ture sings, and round me rings The mu - sic of the spheres.
The morn - ing light, the lil - y white, De - clare their Mak-er's praise.
That though the wrong seems oft so strong, God is the Rul - er yet.
This is my Fa - ther's world: I rest me in the thought
This is my Fa - ther's world: He shines in all that's fair;
This is my Fa - ther's world: The bat - tle is not done;
Of rocks and trees, of skies and seas—His hand the won-ders wrought.
In the rus - tling grass I hear Him pass, He speaks to me ev-ery - where.
Je - sus who died shall be sat - is - fied, And earth and heav'n be one.

TEXT: Maltbie D. Babcock
MUSIC: Franklin L. Sheppard

TERRA BEATA
S.M.D.

59 I Sing the Mighty Power of God

The Lord made the heavens and the earth, the sea, and all that is in them. Ex. 20:11

1. I sing the might-y pow'r of God, That made the moun-tains rise;
2. I sing the good-ness of the Lord, That filled the earth with food;
3. There's not a plant or flow'r be - low, But makes Thy glo - ries known;

That spread the flow - ing seas a - broad, And built the loft - y skies.
He formed the crea - tures with His word, And then pro-nounced them good.
And clouds a - rise, and tem-pests blow, By or - der from Thy throne;

I sing the wis - dom that or-dained The sun to rule the day;
Lord, how Thy won - ders are dis-played, Wher - e'er I turn my eye:
While all that bor - rows life from Thee Is ev - er in Thy care,

The moon shines full at His com-mand, And all the stars o - bey.
If I sur - vey the ground I tread, Or gaze up - on the sky!
And ev - 'ry-where that man can be, Thou, God, art pres - ent there. A - men.

TEXT: Isaac Watts, altered
MUSIC: From *Gesangbuch der Herzogl,* Württemberg, 1784;
Last stanza harmonization and choral ending by Dick Bolks
A lower setting may be found at No. 174.

ELLACOMBE
C.M.D.

Optional last stanza harmonization
Broader - unison
rit.
3. There's not a plant or flow'r be - low, But makes Thy glo-ries known; And clouds a - rise, and tem-pests blow, By or - der from Thy throne; While all that bor-rows life from Thee Is ev - er in Thy care, And ev - 'ry - where that man can be, Thou, God, art pres - ent there.
8va
Optional choral ending
ff
Sing the pow - er, the might-y pow'r of God!

60 Morning Has Broken

I will awaken the dawn. I will praise You, O Lord. Ps. 57:8-9

Unison
1. Morn-ing has bro - ken Like the first morn - ing,
2. Sweet the rain's new fall Sun - lit from heav - en,
3. Mine is the sun - light! Mine is the morn - ing,
Black-bird has spo - ken Like the first bird.
Like the first dew - fall On the first grass.
Born of the one light E - den saw play!
Praise for the sing - ing! Praise for the morn - ing!
Praise for the sweet - ness Of the wet gar - den,
Praise with e - la - tion, Praise ev - 'ry morn - ing,
Praise for them spring - ing Fresh from the Word!
Sprung in com - plete - ness Where His feet pass.
God's re - cre - a - tion Of the new day!

TEXT: Eleanor Farjeon
MUSIC: Traditional Gaelic melody; arranged by Tom Fettke

BUNESSAN
5.5.5.4.D.

Lavish Love, Abundant Beauty 61

Great is His love for those who fear Him. Ps. 103:11

1. Lav-ish love, a - bun - dant beau - ty, Gra - cious gifts for heart and hand,
2. Who am I that You should love me, Meet my ev - 'ry need from birth?
3. I am Yours, E - ter - nal Fa - ther, All my bod - y, mind and heart.

Life that fills the soul and sen - ses— All burst forth at Your com-mand.
Why in - vest Your-self so ful - ly In a crea - ture made of earth?
Take and use me to Your glo - ry, Form Your-self in ev - 'ry part.

Lord, our Lord, E - ter - nal Fa - ther, Great Cre - a - tor, God and Friend,
In Your lov - ing heart You planned me, Fash-ioned me with great-est care;
Lord, Your love brings joy and glad - ness Flow - ing forth with - in my soul.

Bound - less pow'r gave full ex - pres - sion To Your love which knows no end.
Through my soul You breathed Your Spir - it, Plant-ed Your own im - age there.
May my ver - y breath and be - ing Rise to You, their source and goal.

TEXT: Peter Ellis
MUSIC: Rowland H. Prichard; arranged by Robert Harkness
Alternate tune: HYMN TO JOY, No. 1; Higher key, No. 124

HYFRYDOL
8.7.8.7.D.

62 The Spacious Firmament

The skies proclaim the work of His hands. Ps. 19:1

1. The spa - cious fir - ma - ment on high, With all the
2. Soon as the eve - ning shades pre - vail, The moon takes
3. What though in sol - emn si - lence all Move round the
blue e - the - real sky, And span - gled heav'ns, a
up the won - drous tale; And night - ly to the
dark ter - res - trial ball? What though no re - al
shin - ing frame, Their great O - rig - i - nal pro -
lis - tening earth Re - peats the sto - ry of her
voice nor sound A - mid their ra - diant orbs be
claim. Th'un - wear - ied sun, from day to day, Does
birth; While all the stars that round her burn, And
found? In rea - son's ear they all re - joice, And
his Cre - a - tor's pow'r dis - play; And pub - lish - es to
all the plan - ets in their turn, Con - firm the ti - dings
ut - ter forth a glo - rious voice, For - ev - er sing - ing

TEXT: Joseph Addison; based on Psalm 19
MUSIC: Franz Joseph Haydn

CREATION
L.M.D.

ev - ery land The work of an al - might - y hand.
as they roll, And spread the truth from pole to pole.
as they shine, "The hand that made us is di - vine." A - men.

Psalm 136 63

Give thanks to the Lord, for He is good. Ps. 136:1

Parts optional

Give thanks to the Lord for He is so good, His mer - cy en-

1,3,5
dures for - ev - er. (for - ev - er.) Give

2,4,6
dures for - ev - er. (for- ev - er.)

Last time fine

1. To Him a - lone who does might - y won - ders,
2. He made the sun to gov - ern the day - time,

Who by His un - der - stand - ing made the hea - vens.
The moon and stars to gov - ern o'er the night - time.

D.C.

TEXT: Brenda Barker; a paraphrase of Psalm 136
MUSIC: Ken Barker and Debi Parker Ladd

CATHERINE
Irregular meter

64 All Creatures of Our God and King

Let them praise the name of the Lord, for His name alone is exalted. Ps. 148:13

1. All crea-tures of our God and King, Lift up your voice and with us sing
2. Thou rush-ing wind that art so strong, Ye clouds that sail in heav'n a - long,
3. Thou flow-ing wa-ter, pure and clear, Make mu-sic for thy Lord to hear,
4. And all ye men of ten - der heart, For - giv - ing oth-ers, take your part,
5. Let all things their Cre - a - tor bless, And wor-ship Him in hum - ble - ness,
Al-le - lu - ia, Al-le - lu - ia! Thou burn - ing sun with gold-en beam,
O praise Him, Al-le - lu - ia! Thou ris - ing morn in praise re - joice,
Al-le - lu - ia, Al-le - lu - ia! Thou fire so mas - ter - ful and bright,
O sing ye, Al-le - lu - ia! Ye who long pain and sor - row bear,
O praise Him, Al-le - lu - ia! Praise, praise the Fa-ther, praise the Son,
Thou sil - ver moon with soft-er gleam, O praise Him, O praise Him,
Ye lights of eve - ning, find a voice, O praise Him, O praise Him,
That giv - est man both warmth and light, O praise Him, O praise Him,
Praise God and on Him cast your care, O praise Him, O praise Him,
And praise the Spir - it, Three in One, O praise Him, O praise Him,
Al - le - lu - ia, al - le - lu - ia, al - le - lu - ia! A - men.

TEXT: St. Francis of Assisi; translated by William H. Draper
MUSIC: *Geistliche Kirchengesänge,* Cologne, 1623, Arranged by Ralph Vaughan Williams
From the English Hymnal *by permission of Oxford University Press.*

LASST UNS ERFREUEN
L.M. with Alleluias

The Wonder of It All 65

What is man . . . that You care for him? Heb. 2:6

1. There's the won-der of sun-set at eve-ning, The won-der as sun-rise I see; But the won-der of won-ders that thrills my soul Is the won-der that God loves me.
2. There's the won-der of spring-time and har-vest, The sky, the stars, the sun; But the won-der of won-ders that thrills my soul Is a won-der that's on-ly be-gun.
Refrain
O, the won-der of it all! The won-der of it all! Just to think that God loves me. O, the won-der of it all! The won-der of it all! Just to think that God loves me.

TEXT and MUSIC: George Beverly Shea

WONDER OF IT ALL
Irregular meter

66 To God Be the Glory

The Lord has done great things for us, and we are filled with joy. Ps. 126:3

3/4
1. To God be the glo - ry—great things He hath done! So loved He the world that He gave us His Son, Who yield - ed His life an a - tone-ment for sin And o - pened the Life-gate that all may go in.
2. O per - fect re - demp - tion, the pur - chase of blood! To ev - 'ry be - liev - er the prom - ise of God; The vil - est of - fen - der who tru - ly be - lieves, That mo - ment from Je - sus a par - don re - ceives.
3. Great things He hath taught us, great things He hath done, And great our re - joic - ing thru Je - sus the Son; But pur - er and high - er and great - er will be Our won - der, our trans - port, when Je - sus we see.
Descant
Praise the Lord, hear His voice! Praise the
Refrain
Praise the Lord, Praise the Lord, Let the earth hear His voice! Praise the Lord,

TEXT: Fanny J. Crosby
MUSIC: William H. Doane;
Descant and choral ending by Doug Holck

TO GOD BE THE GLORY
11.11.11.11. with Refrain

Lord, Let the peo-ple re-joice! Come to the Fa-ther thru
Praise the Lord, Let the peo-ple re-joice! O come to the Fa-ther thru
Je-sus the Son, And give Him the glo-ry—great things He hath done!
Je-sus the Son, And give Him the glo-ry—great things He hath done!
Optional choral ending
mf
cresc. poco a poco
To God be the glo-ry, to God be the glo-ry; Oh, give Him the
rit.
glo-ry great things He hath done, great things He hath done! (He hath done!)

*sing cued notes if choral ending is not used.

67 The Love of God

I have loved you with an everlasting love. Jer. 31:3

1. The love of God is great-er far Than tongue or pen can ev - er
2. When years of time shall pass a - way And earth-ly thrones and king-doms
3. Could we with ink the o - cean fill And were the skies of parch-ment
tell, It goes be - yond the high-est star And reach-es to the low - est
fall, When men, who here re - fuse to pray, On rocks and hills and mountains
made, Were ev-'ry stalk on earth a quill And ev - 'ry man a scribe by
hell; The guilt-y pair, bowed down with care, God gave His Son to
call, God's love so sure shall still en - dure, All mea - sure - less and
trade, To write the love of God a - bove Would drain the o - cean
win: His err - ing child He rec - on - ciled And par - doned from his sin.
strong: Re-deem-ing grace to Ad-am's race— The saints' and an - gels' song.
dry, Nor could the scroll con-tain the whole Tho stretched from sky to sky.

TEXT and MUSIC: Frederick M. Lehman

LOVE OF GOD
Irregular meter

Refrain
O love of God, how rich and pure! How mea-sure - less and strong!
It shall for - ev - er-more en - dure— The saints' and an - gels' song.

There's a Wideness in God's Mercy 68

His mercy is very great. 1 Chr. 21:13

1. There's a wide-ness in God's mer-cy Like the wide-ness of the sea;
2. There is wel-come for the sin - ner And more grac - es for the good;
3. For the love of God is broad-er Than the meas-ure of man's mind;
4. If our love were but more sim-ple We should take Him at His word,
There's a kind-ness in His jus - tice Which is more than lib - er - ty.
There is mer - cy with the Sav-ior; There is heal - ing in His blood.
And the heart of the E - ter - nal Is most won - der - ful - ly kind.
And our lives would be all sun-shine In the sweet-ness of our Lord. A-men.

TEXT: Frederick W. Faber
MUSIC: Lizzie S. Tourjée

WELLESLEY
8.7.8.7.

69 Thy Loving Kindness

Because Your love is better than life, my lips will glorify You. Ps. 63:3

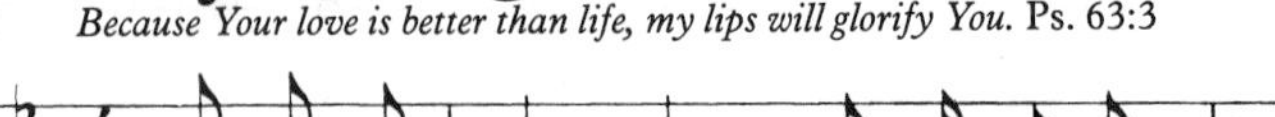

1. Thy lov - ing kind - ness is bet - ter than life. Thy lov-ing
2. I lift my hands, Lord, un - to Thy name. I lift my

kind - ness is bet-ter than life. My lips shall praise Thee, thus will I
hands, Lord, un - to Thy name. My lips shall praise Thee, thus will I

bless Thee: I will lift up my hands un - to Thy name.
bless Thee: I will lift up my hands un - to Thy name.

TEXT and MUSIC: Hugh Mitchell; based on Psalm 63:3, 4

THY LOVING KINDNESS
10.10.10.10.

70 Begin, My Tongue, Some Heavenly Theme

My tongue will tell of Your righteous acts all day long. Ps. 71:24

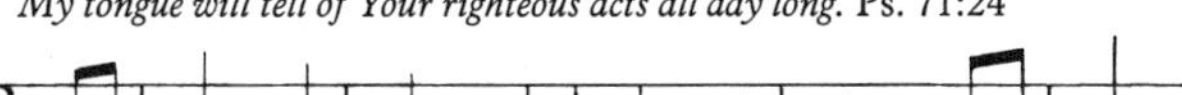

1. Be - gin, my tongue, some heav'n-ly theme And speak some bound-less thing:
2. Tell of His won - drous faith-ful - ness And sound His pow'r a - broad;
3. His ver - y word of grace is strong As that which built the skies;
4. O might I hear Thy heav'n-ly tongue But whis - per, "Thou art mine!"

TEXT: Isaac Watts
MUSIC: From Henry W. Greatorex's *Collection of Church Music,* 1851
A lower setting may be found at No. 321

MANOAH
C.M.

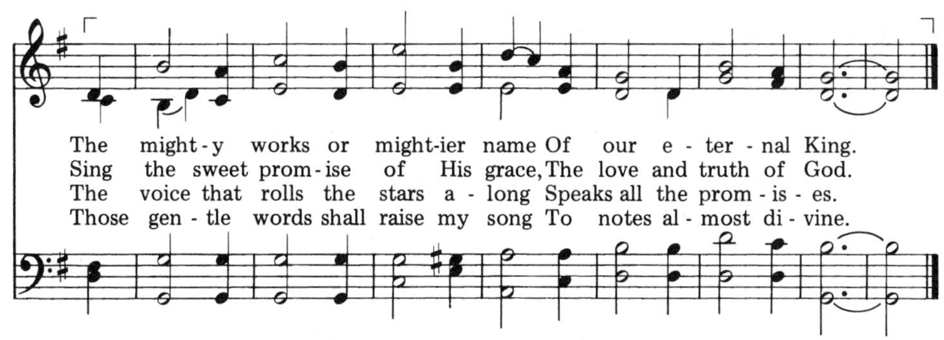
The mighty-y works or might-ier name Of our e - ter - nal King.
Sing the sweet prom - ise of His grace, The love and truth of God.
The voice that rolls the stars a - long Speaks all the prom - is - es.
Those gen - tle words shall raise my song To notes al - most di - vine.

71 Behold, What Manner of Love

How great is the love the Father has lavished on us. 1 John 3:1

May be sung as a 2 part canon

I

Be - hold, what man - ner of love the Fa - ther has giv - en un - to us, Be - hold what man - ner of love the Fa - ther has giv - en un - to us,

II

that we should be called the sons of God, that we should be called the sons of God.

TEXT and MUSIC: Patricia Van Tine; based on 1 John 3:1; arranged by Lee Herrington

MANNER OF LOVE
Irregular meter

72 We Will Glorify

To Him who sits on the throne and to the Lamb be praise and honor and glory. Rev. 5:13

1. We will glo-ri-fy the King of kings, we will glo-ri-fy the
2. Lord Je-ho-vah reigns in maj-es-ty, we will bow be-fore His
3. He is Lord of heav-en, Lord of earth, He is Lord of all who
4. Hal-le-lu-jah to the King of kings, hal-le-lu-jah to the

Lamb; We will glo-ri-fy the Lord of lords, who is the great I Am.
throne; We will wor-ship Him in right-eous-ness, we will wor-ship Him a-lone.
live; He is Lord a-bove the u-ni-verse, all praise to Him we give.
Lamb; Hal-le-lu-jah to the Lord of lords, who is the great I Am.

Optional last stanza setting

rit. *Broader*

give. 4. Hal-le-lu-jah to the King of kings, hal-le-lu-jah to the Lamb; Hal-le-lu-jah to the Lord of lords, who is the great I Am. Hal-le- [1] Am. [2] *mp*

TEXT and MUSIC: Twila Paris; arranged by David Allen

WE WILL GLORIFY
9.7.9.6.

Thou Art Worthy 73

You are worthy, our Lord and God . . . for You created all things. Rev. 4:11

Thou art wor-thy, Thou art wor-thy, Thou art wor-thy, O Lord,
To re-ceive glo - ry, glo - ry and hon - or, Glo - ry and
hon - or and pow'r. For Thou hast cre - at - ed, hast all things cre -
at - ed; Thou hast cre - at - ed all things. And for Thy
plea-sure they are cre - at - ed; For Thou art wor-thy, O Lord.

TEXT and MUSIC: Pauline M. Mills; based on Revelation 4:11; 5:9

WORTHY
Irregular meter

74 Majesty

We see Jesus . . . now crowned with glory and honor. Heb. 2:9

Maj - es - ty, wor-ship His maj - es - ty. Un - to
Je - sus be all glo - ry, hon - or, and praise. Maj - es - ty,
king-dom au - thor - i - ty flow from His throne un - to His own;
His an-them raise. So ex - alt, lift up on high the name of
Je - sus. Mag-ni - fy, come glo-ri - fy Christ Je-sus, the King.

TEXT and MUSIC: Jack Hayford; arranged by Eugene Thomas

MAJESTY
Irregular meter

Maj - es - ty, wor-ship His maj - es - ty;
Je - sus who died, now glo-ri - fied, King of all kings.

*cued notes optional for a few choir sopranos.

Praise the Savior 75

. . . that we . . . might be for the praise of His glory. Eph. 1:12

1. Praise the Sav - ior, ye who know Him! Who can tell how much we owe Him?
2. Je - sus is the name that charms us, He for con - flict fits and arms us;
3. Trust in Him, ye saints, for - ev - er— He is faith - ful, chang-ing nev - er;
4. Keep us, Lord, O keep us cleav - ing To Thy - self, and still be - liev - ing,
5. Then we shall be where we would be, Then we shall be what we should be;

Glad - ly let us ren - der to Him All we are and have.
Noth - ing moves and noth - ing harms us While we trust in Him.
Nei - ther force nor guile can sev - er Those He loves from Him.
Till the hour of our re - ceiv - ing Prom - ised joys with Thee.
Things that are not now, nor could be, Soon shall be our own.

TEXT: Thomas Kelly
MUSIC: Traditional German melody

ACCLAIM
8.8.8.5.

76 O for a Thousand Tongues

My tongue will speak . . . of Your praises all day long. Ps. 35:28

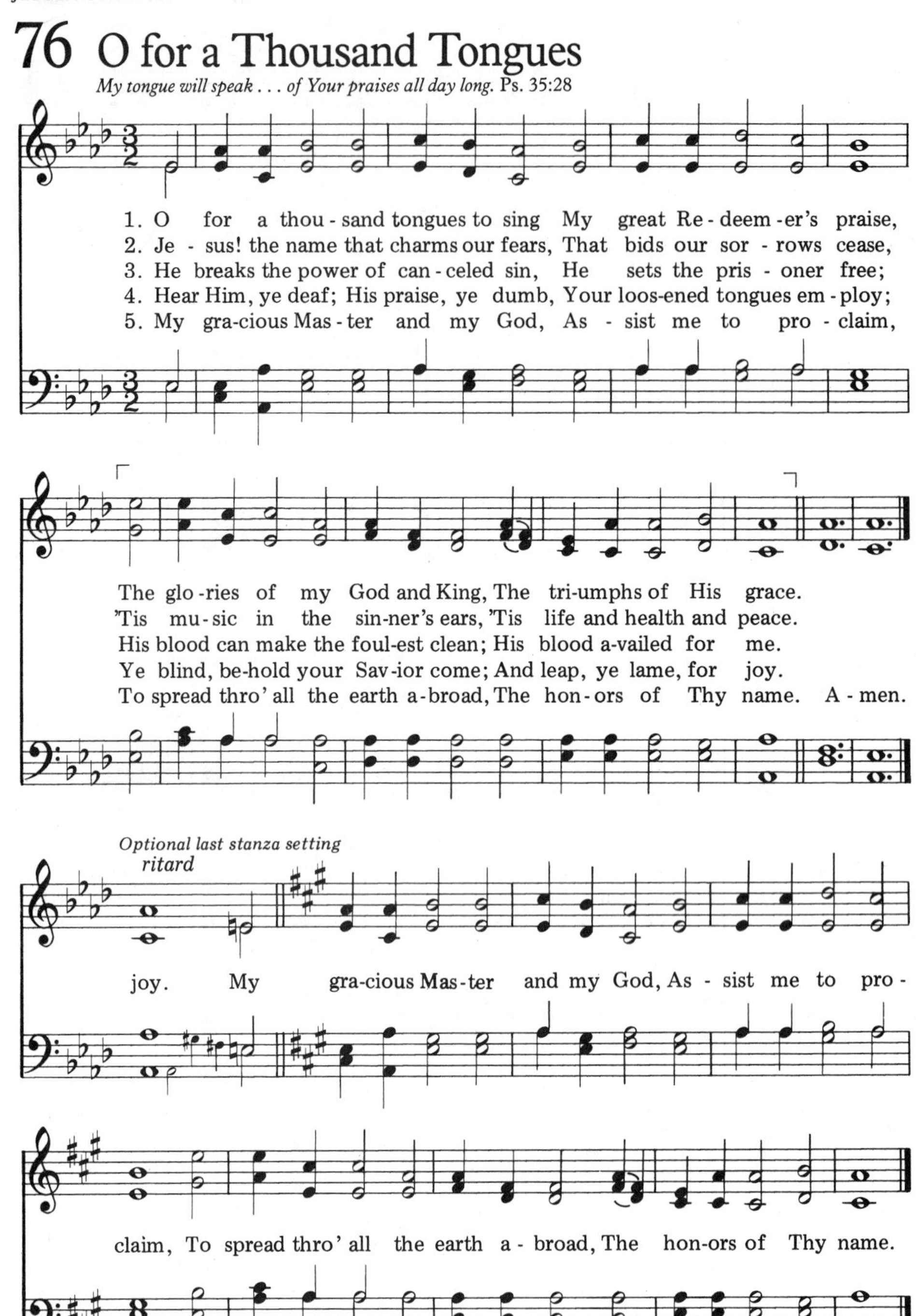
1. O for a thou - sand tongues to sing My great Re - deem - er's praise,
2. Je - sus! the name that charms our fears, That bids our sor - rows cease,
3. He breaks the power of can - celed sin, He sets the pris - oner free;
4. Hear Him, ye deaf; His praise, ye dumb, Your loos-ened tongues em - ploy;
5. My gra-cious Mas - ter and my God, As - sist me to pro - claim,
The glo - ries of my God and King, The tri-umphs of His grace.
'Tis mu - sic in the sin-ner's ears, 'Tis life and health and peace.
His blood can make the foul-est clean; His blood a-vailed for me.
Ye blind, be-hold your Sav-ior come; And leap, ye lame, for joy.
To spread thro' all the earth a-broad, The hon-ors of Thy name. A - men.
Optional last stanza setting
ritard
joy. My gra-cious Mas-ter and my God, As - sist me to pro -
claim, To spread thro' all the earth a - broad, The hon-ors of Thy name.

TEXT: Charles Wesley
MUSIC: Carl G. Gläzer; arranged by Lowell Mason;
Choral ending by Robert F. Douglas
A lower setting may be found at No. 440

AZMON
C.M.

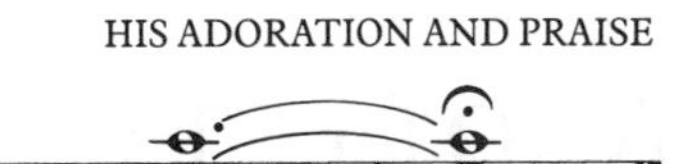

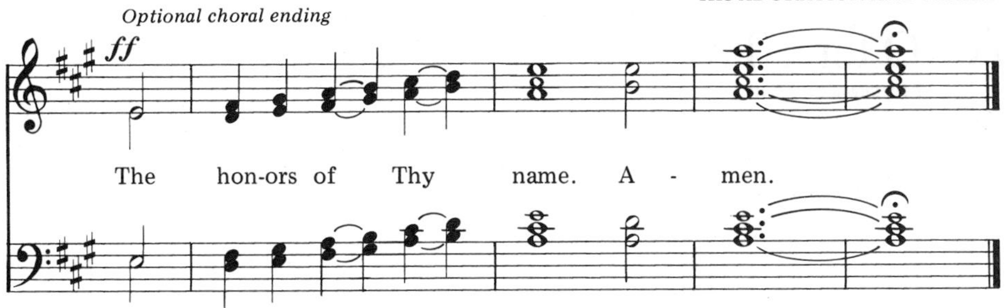
Optional choral ending
ff
The hon-ors of Thy name. A - men.

King of Kings 77

The King of kings and Lord of lords. 1 Tim. 6:15

2 Part Canon (optional)
I Unison or 2 part
King of kings and Lord of lords, glo - ry, hal - le - lu - jah!
II
Je - sus, Prince of Peace, glo - ry, hal - le - lu - jah!

TEXT: Sophie Conty and Naomi Batya
MUSIC: Ancient Hebrew Folk song

KING OF KINGS
Irregular meter

Blessing and Honor 78

To Him . . . be praise and honor and glory. Rev. 5:13

3 Part Canon
I
Bless - ing and hon - or and glo - ry be Thine;
II
Wor - thy are You, O Lord, to re - ceive end - less praise;
III
Bless - ing and hon - or and glo - ry be Thine.

TEXT: Gerald S. Henderson; based on Revelation 5:12, 13
MUSIC: German Folk song; adapted by Gerald S. Henderson

GERMAN FOLK
10.12.10.

79 Jesus, the Very Thought of Thee

Consider Him . . . so that you will not grow weary and lose heart. Heb. 12:3

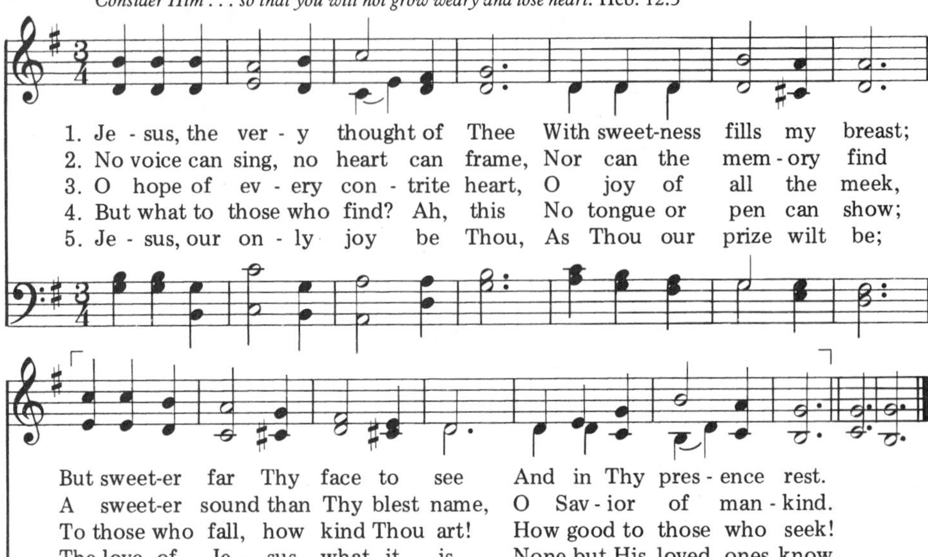
1. Je - sus, the ver - y thought of Thee With sweet-ness fills my breast;
2. No voice can sing, no heart can frame, Nor can the mem - ory find
3. O hope of ev - ery con - trite heart, O joy of all the meek,
4. But what to those who find? Ah, this No tongue or pen can show;
5. Je - sus, our on - ly joy be Thou, As Thou our prize wilt be;
But sweet-er far Thy face to see And in Thy pres - ence rest.
A sweet-er sound than Thy blest name, O Sav - ior of man - kind.
To those who fall, how kind Thou art! How good to those who seek!
The love of Je - sus, what it is None but His loved ones know.
Je - sus, be Thou our glo - ry now And thru e - ter - ni - ty. A-men.

TEXT: Attributed to Bernard of Clairvaux; translated by Edward Caswall
MUSIC: John B. Dykes
A lower setting may be found at No. 536

ST. AGNES
C.M.

80 I Love You, Lord

Love the Lord, all His saints! Ps. 31:23

I love You, Lord, and I lift my voice to wor - ship
You. O my soul, re - joice! Take joy, my King, in

TEXT and MUSIC: Laurie Klein; arranged by Eugene Thomas

I LOVE YOU LORD
Irregular meter

what You hear: may it be a sweet, sweet sound in Your ear.
What a Wonderful Savior! 81
We know that this Man really is the Savior of the world. John 4:42
1. Christ has for sin a - tone - ment made—What a won - der - ful Sav-ior!
2. I praise Him for the cleans - ing blood—What a won - der - ful Sav-ior!
3. He cleansed my heart from all its sin— What a won - der - ful Sav-ior!
4. He gives me o - ver - com - ing pow'r— What a won - der - ful Sav-ior!
We are re - deemed, the price is paid—What a won - der-ful Sav - ior!
That rec - on - ciled my soul to God—What a won - der-ful Sav - ior!
And now He reigns and rules there - in— What a won - der-ful Sav - ior!
And tri - umph in each try - ing hour—What a won - der-ful Sav - ior!
Refrain
What a won - der - ful Sav - ior is Je - sus, my Je - sus!
What a won - der - ful Sav - ior is Je - sus, my Lord!

TEXT and MUSIC: Elisha A. Hoffman

BENTON HARBOR
8.7.8.7. with Refrain

82 O Come, Let Us Adore Him

We . . . have come to worship Him. Matt. 2:2

1. O come, let us a - dore Him, O come, let us a - dore Him, O come, let us a - dore Him, Christ the Lord.
2. We'll praise His name for - ev - er, We'll praise His name for - ev - er, We'll praise His name for - ev - er, Christ the Lord.
3. We'll give Him all the glo - ry, We'll give Him all the glo - ry, We'll give Him all the glo - ry, Christ the Lord.
4. For He a - lone is wor - thy, For He a - lone is wor - thy, For He a - lone is wor - thy, Christ the Lord.

TEXT: Traditional
MUSIC: Wade's *Cantus Diversi,* 1751

ADESTE FIDELES (Refrain only)
7.7.10.

83 Lord, We Praise You

Praise be to the God and Father of our Lord Jesus Christ. 2 Cor. 1:3

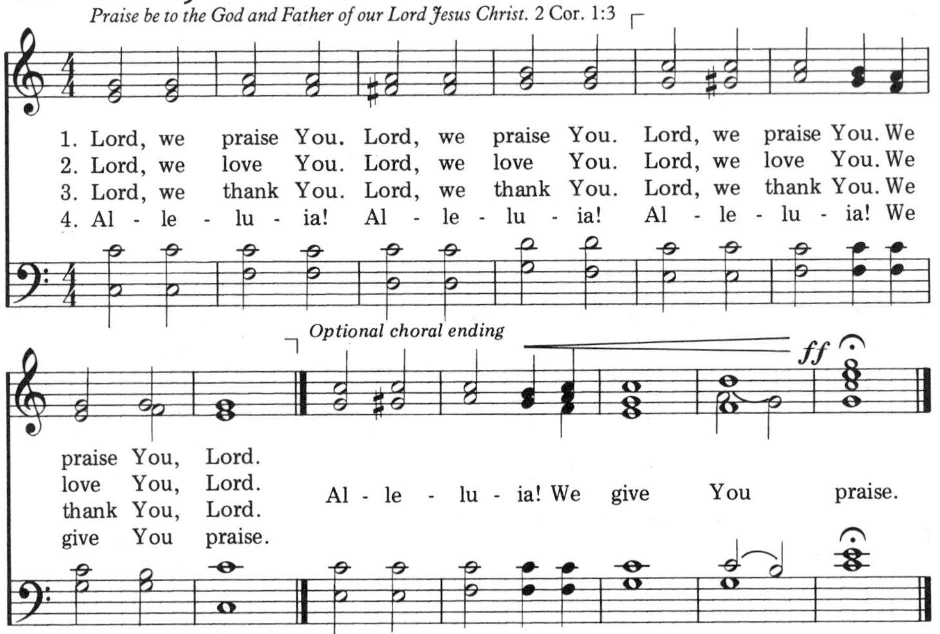
1. Lord, we praise You. Lord, we praise You. Lord, we praise You. We praise You, Lord.
2. Lord, we love You. Lord, we love You. Lord, we love You. We love You, Lord.
3. Lord, we thank You. Lord, we thank You. Lord, we thank You. We thank You, Lord.
4. Al - le - lu - ia! Al - le - lu - ia! Al - le - lu - ia! We give You praise.
Optional choral ending
ff
Al - le - lu - ia! We give You praise.

TEXT and MUSIC: Otis Skillings

LORD, WE PRAISE YOU
4.4.4.4.

Hallowed Be the Name 84

Give Him the name Jesus. He will be great . . . He will reign. Luke 1:31-33

Unison
1. Hal-low-ed be the name of Je - sus.
2. Wor - thy is the Lamb, Lord Je - sus.
Ho - ly is the name of Je - sus. Oth - er
Right-eous I can stand in Je - sus. We were
king - doms rise and fall, but He reign - eth o - ver all.
chained to death, but then You raised us up a - gain.
Hal-low-ed be the name of Je - sus.
Wor - thy is the Lamb, Lord Je - sus.

TEXT and MUSIC: Lilly Green; arranged by Robert F. Douglas

HALLOWED BE THE NAME
Irregular meter

85 Glorious Is Thy Name

Our God, we give You thanks, and praise Your glorious name. 1 Chr. 29:13

1. Bless-ed Sav - ior, we a - dore Thee, We Thy love and grace pro-claim;
2. Great Re-deem - er, Lord and Mas - ter, Light of all e - ter - nal days;
3. From the throne of heav-en's glo - ry To the cross of sin and shame,
4. Come, O come, im - mor - tal Sav - ior, Come and take Thy roy - al throne;

Thou art might-y, Thou art ho - ly, Glo - rious is Thy match-less name!
Let the saints of ev - 'ry na - tion Sing Thy just and end - less praise!
Thou didst come to die a ran - som, Guilt - y sin - ners to re - claim!
Come, and reign, and reign for - ev - er, Be the king-dom all Thine own!

Refrain

Glo - ri- ous, Glo - ri - ous,

Glo-rious is Thy name, O Lord! Glo-rious is Thy name, O Lord!

1. 2.

Glo-rious is Thy name, O Lord! name, O Lord! A - men.

TEXT and MUSIC: B. B. McKinney

GLORIOUS NAME
8.7.8.7. with Refrain

GIVE HIM GLORY

A Brief Service
Exalting Our Lord, Jesus Christ

Suggested Hymn Stanzas

To facilitate an uninterrupted flow from stanza to stanza,
the suggested stanzas have been marked with an arrow: ►
May Jesus Christ Be Praised, stanzas 1, 3, 4, 6
Fairest Lord Jesus, stanzas 1, 4
Our Great Savior, stanzas 1, 2, 4

WORSHIP LEADER:

Christ is the image of the invisible God, the firstborn over all creation. For by Him all things were created: things in heaven and on earth, visible and invisible, whether thrones or powers or rulers or authorities; all things were created by Him and for Him. He is before all things, and in Him all things hold together. And He is the head of the body, the church; He is the beginning and the firstborn from among the dead, so that in everything He might have the supremacy. For God was pleased to have all His fullness dwell in Him, and through Him to reconcile to Himself all things, whether things on earth or things in heaven, by making peace through His blood, shed on the cross. Let us fix our eyes on Jesus, the author and perfecter of our faith, who for the joy set before Him endured the cross, scorning its shame, and sat down at the right hand of the throne of God.

WORSHIP LEADER and PEOPLE:

Worthy is the Lamb, who was slain, to receive power and wealth and wisdom and strength and honor and glory and praise! To Him who sits on the throne and to the Lamb be praise and honor and glory and power, for ever and ever!

Col. 1:15-20; Heb. 12:2;
Rev. 5:12, 13. (NIV)

Optional introduction to "May Jesus Christ Be Praised"

"GIVE HIM GLORY—A Brief Service Exalting Our Lord, Jesus Christ"

87 May Jesus Christ Be Praised

Christ . . . is God over all, forever praised! Rom. 9:5

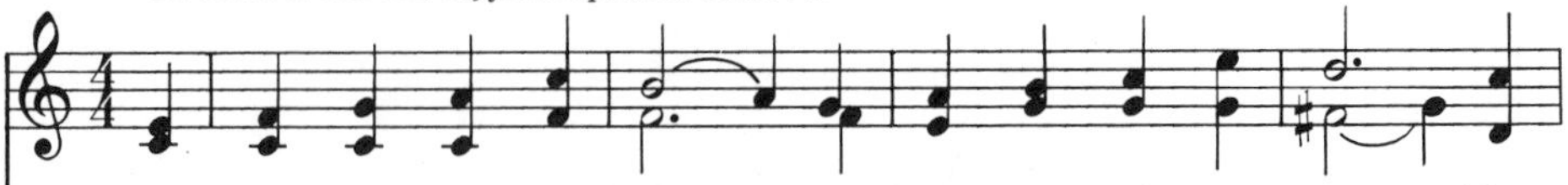

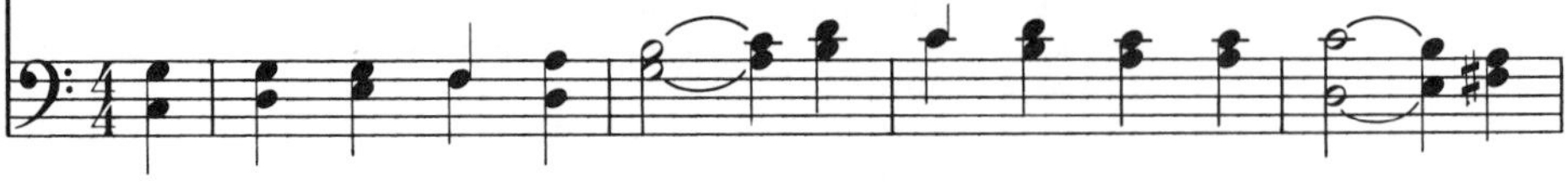

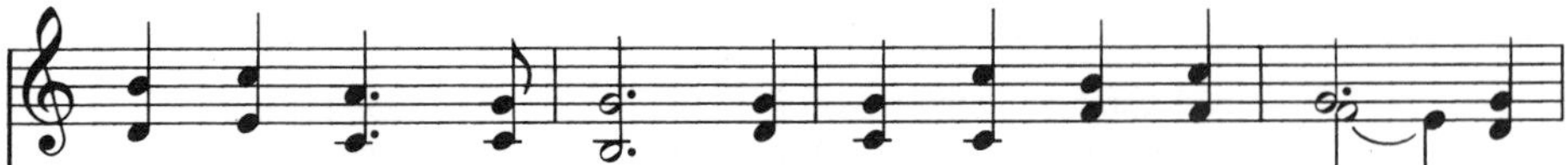

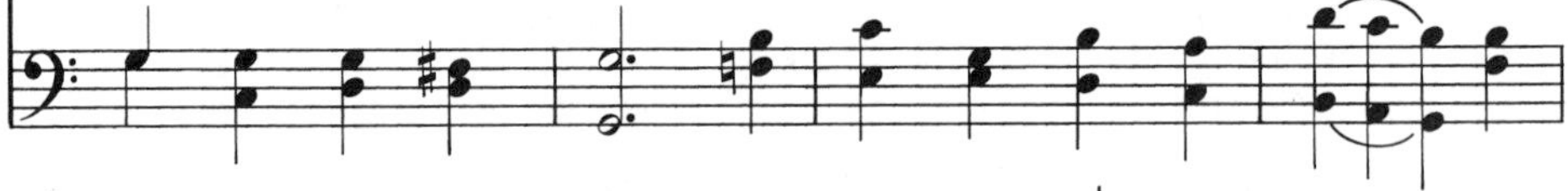

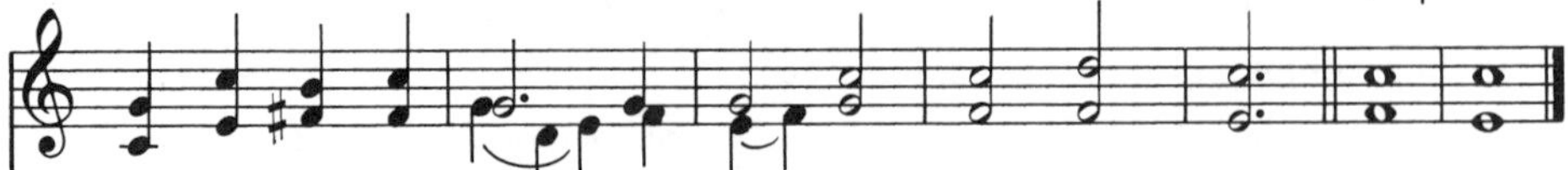

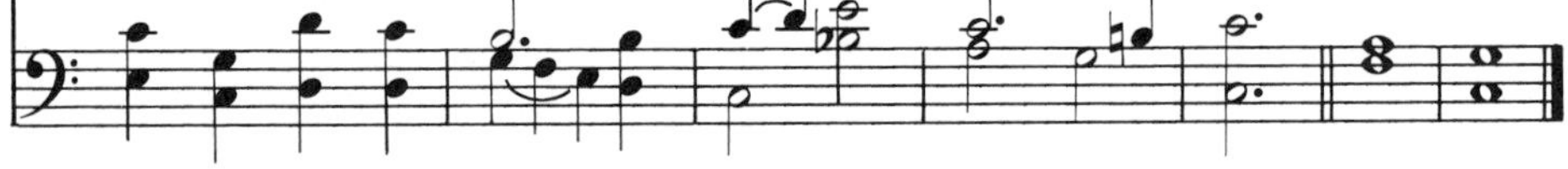

1. When morning gilds the skies,
My heart awaking cries,
May Jesus Christ be praised!
Alike at work and prayer
To Jesus I repair,
May Jesus Christ be praised!

2. Does sadness fill my mind?
A solace here I find,
May Jesus Christ be praised!
Or fades my earthly bliss?
My comfort still is this,
May Jesus Christ be praised!

3. The night becomes as day,
When from the heart we say,
May Jesus Christ be praised!
The pow'rs of darkness fear
When this sweet chant they hear,
May Jesus Christ be praised!

4. Ye nations of mankind,
In this your concord find,
May Jesus Christ be praised!
Let all the earth around
Ring joyous with the sound,
May Jesus Christ be praised!

5. Sing, suns and stars of space,
Sing, ye that see His face,
May Jesus Christ be praised!
God's whole creation o'er,
For aye and evermore
May Jesus Christ be praised!

6. Be this, while life is mine,
My canticle divine,
May Jesus Christ be praised!
Be this th'eternal song
Thro' all the ages long,
May Jesus Christ be praised! Amen.

TEXT: *Katholisches Gesangbuch,* Würzburg, 1828; translated by Edward Caswall
MUSIC: Joseph Barnby

LAUDES DOMINI
6.6.6.6.6.6.

Fairest Lord Jesus 88

Your eyes will see the King in His beauty. Isa. 33:17

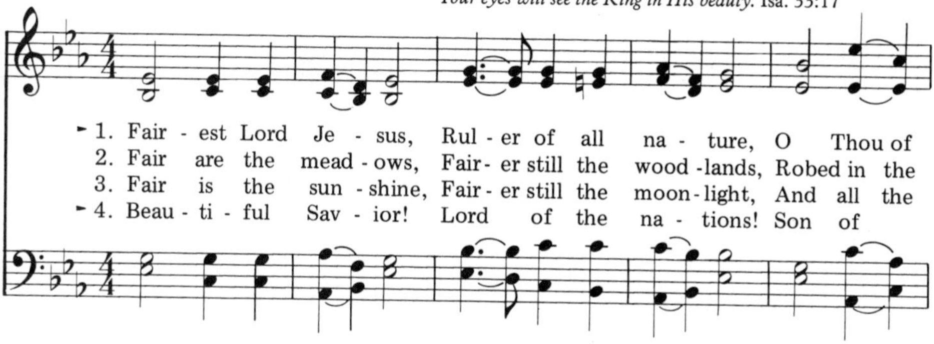

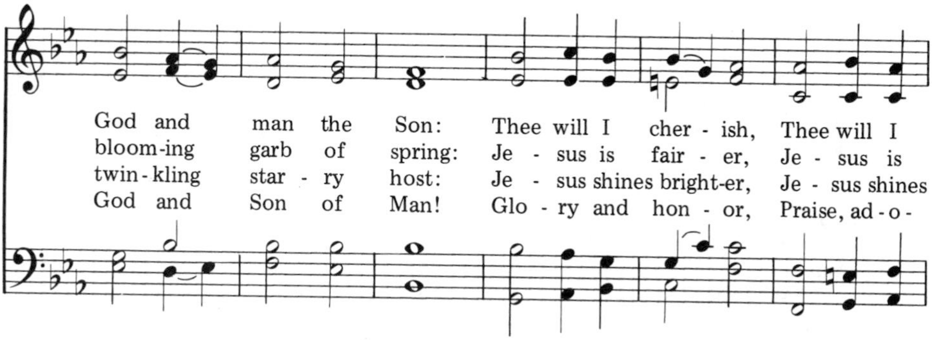

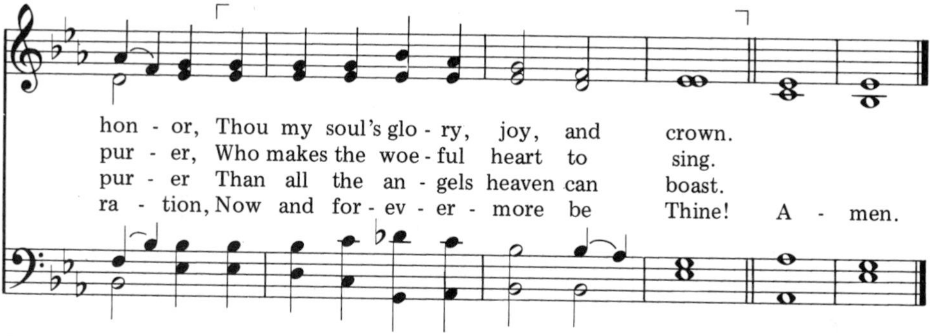

1. Fairest Lord Jesus, Ruler of all nature, O Thou of God and man the Son:
Thee will I cherish, Thee will I honor, Thou my soul's glory, joy, and crown.

2. Fair are the meadows, Fairer still the woodlands, Robed in the blooming garb of spring:
Jesus is fairer, Jesus is purer, Who makes the woeful heart to sing.

3. Fair is the sunshine, Fairer still the moonlight, And all the twinkling starry host:
Jesus shines brighter, Jesus shines purer Than all the angels heaven can boast.

4. Beautiful Savior! Lord of the nations! Son of God and Son of Man!
Glory and honor, Praise, adoration, Now and forevermore be Thine! Amen.

TEXT: Anonymous German Hymn, *Münster Gesangbuch,* 1677; translated, Source unknown, stanzas 1-3; Joseph A. Seiss, stanza 4

MUSIC: *Schlesische Volkslieder,* 1842; arranged by Richard S. Willis

CRUSADERS' HYMN
5.6.8.5.5.8.

89 Our Great Savior

Our great God and Savior, Jesus Christ, . . . gave Himself for us. Titus 2:13-14

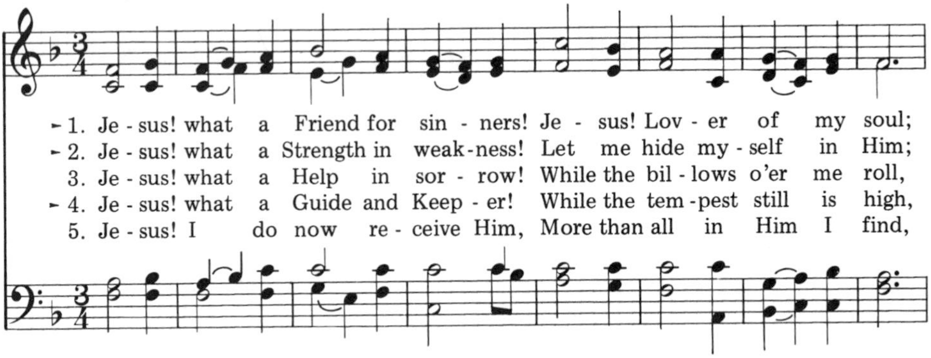

1. Je - sus! what a Friend for sin - ners! Je - sus! Lov - er of my soul;
2. Je - sus! what a Strength in weak-ness! Let me hide my - self in Him;
3. Je - sus! what a Help in sor - row! While the bil - lows o'er me roll,
4. Je - sus! what a Guide and Keep - er! While the tem - pest still is high,
5. Je - sus! I do now re - ceive Him, More than all in Him I find,

Friends may fail me, foes as - sail me, He, my Sav - ior, makes me whole.
Tempt - ed, tried, and some-times fail - ing, He, my Strength, my vic - t'ry wins.
E - ven when my heart is break - ing, He, my Com - fort, helps my soul.
Storms a - bout me, night o'er-takes me, He, my Pi - lot, hears my cry.
He hath grant - ed me for - give - ness, I am His, and He is mine.

Descant
Hal - le - lu - jah! what a Sav - ior! Hal - le -
Refrain
Hal - le - lu - jah! what a Sav - ior! Hal - le -

TEXT: J. Wilbur Chapman
MUSIC: Rowland H. Prichard; arranged by Robert Harkness;
Descant and choral ending by Tom Fettke
A higher setting may be found at No. 233

HYFRYDOL
8.7.8.7.D.

lu - jah! what a, what a Friend! Sav - ing, help - ing,
lu - jah! what a Friend! Sav - ing, help - ing,

keep-ing, lov - ing, He is with me to the end.
keep - ing, lov - ing, He is with me to the end.

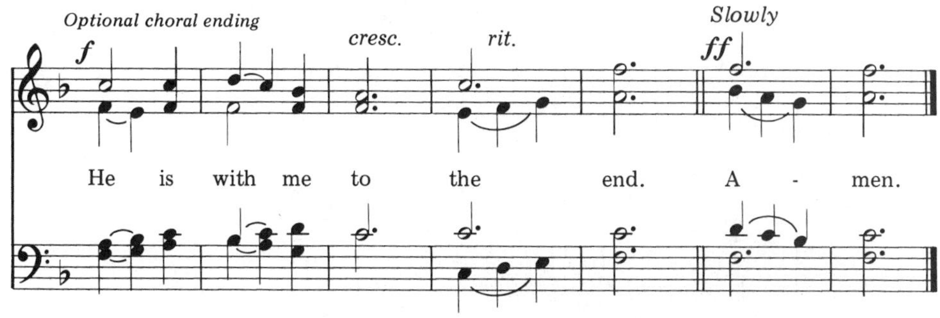
Optional choral ending
f
cresc.
rit.
Slowly
ff
He is with me to the end. A - men.

The end of "GIVE HIM GLORY—A Brief Service Exalting Our Lord, Jesus Christ"

90 In the Name of the Lord

I will do whatever you ask in My name. John 14:13

Unison
There is strength in the name of the Lord; There is pow'r in the name of the Lord;
There is hope in the name of the Lord! Bless-ed is He who comes in the
name of the Lord. There is
Parts optional
strength in the name of the Lord;
There is pow'r in the name of the Lord; There is hope in the
name of the Lord! Bless-ed is He who comes in the name of the Lord.
2nd time fine

TEXT and MUSIC: Phill McHugh, Gloria Gaither and Sandi Patti Helvering; arranged by Robert F. Douglas

NAME OF THE LORD
Irregular meter

Alleluia 91

Hallelujah! Salvation and glory and power belong to our God. Rev. 19:1

TEXT and MUSIC: Jerry Sinclair

ALLELUIA
L.M.

92 Love Divine, All Loves Excelling

God showed His love among us: He sent His one and only Son. 1 John 4:9

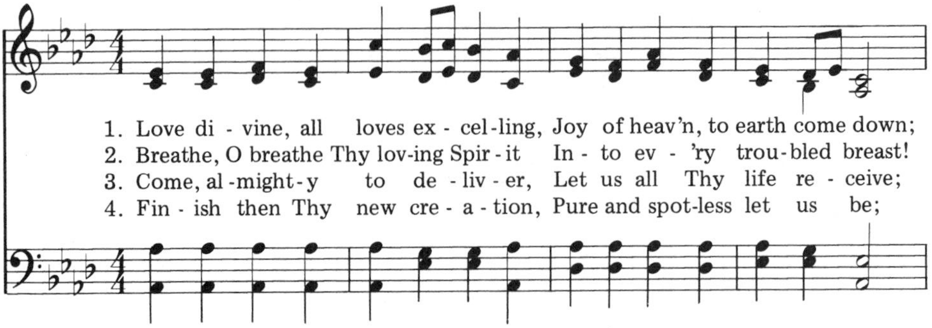

1. Love di - vine, all loves ex - cel-ling, Joy of heav'n, to earth come down;
2. Breathe, O breathe Thy lov-ing Spir - it In - to ev - 'ry trou-bled breast!
3. Come, al-might-y to de - liv - er, Let us all Thy life re - ceive;
4. Fin - ish then Thy new cre - a - tion, Pure and spot-less let us be;

Fix in us Thy hum - ble dwell-ing, All Thy faith-ful mer - cies crown.
Let us all in Thee in - her - it, Let us find that prom - ised rest.
Sud-den - ly re - turn, and nev - er, Nev - er - more Thy tem - ples leave.
Let us see Thy great sal - va - tion Per - fect - ly re - stored in Thee:

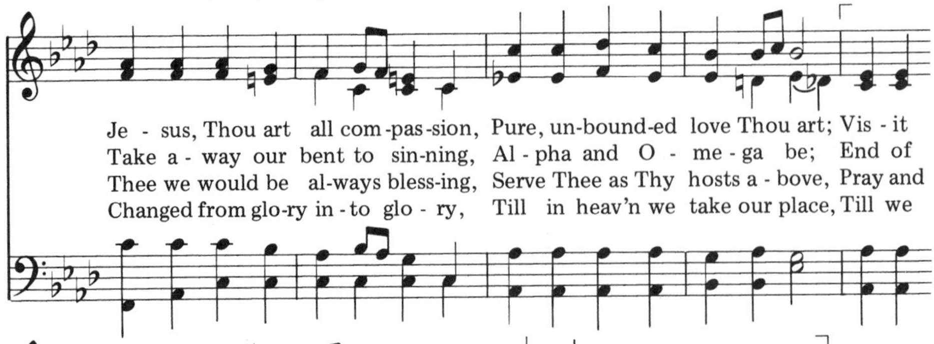

Je - sus, Thou art all com-pas-sion, Pure, un-bound-ed love Thou art; Vis - it
Take a - way our bent to sin-ning, Al - pha and O - me - ga be; End of
Thee we would be al-ways bless-ing, Serve Thee as Thy hosts a - bove, Pray and
Changed from glo-ry in - to glo - ry, Till in heav'n we take our place, Till we

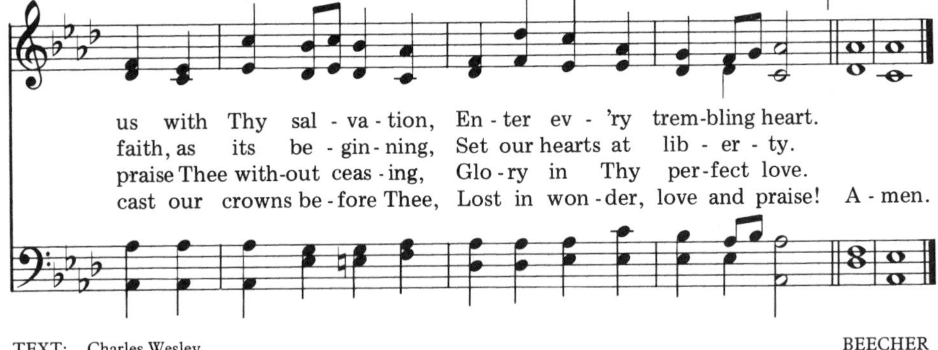

us with Thy sal - va - tion, En - ter ev - 'ry trem-bling heart.
faith, as its be - gin - ning, Set our hearts at lib - er - ty.
praise Thee with-out ceas - ing, Glo - ry in Thy per-fect love.
cast our crowns be - fore Thee, Lost in won - der, love and praise! A - men.

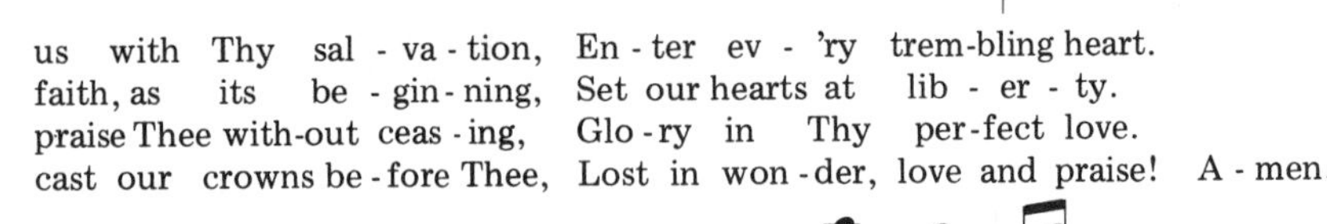

TEXT: Charles Wesley
MUSIC: John Zundel; Choral ending arranged by David Allen
A higher setting may be found at No. 268; Alternate tune: HYFRYDOL, No. 89

BEECHER
8.7.8.7.D.

Optional choral ending
f
Till we cast our crowns be - fore Thee, Lost in won - der,
love, and praise! A men.

Praise the Name of Jesus 93

The Lord is my Rock, my Fortress and my Deliverer. Ps. 18:2

Praise the name of Je - sus, Praise the name of Je - sus.

He's my Rock, He's my For - tress, He's my De - liv - er - er, in

Him will I trust. Praise the name of Je - sus.

TEXT and MUSIC: Roy Hicks, Jr.; based on Psalm 18:1

HICKS
Irregular meter

94 How Sweet the Name of Jesus Sounds

Call on the name of our Lord Jesus Christ. 1 Cor. 1:2

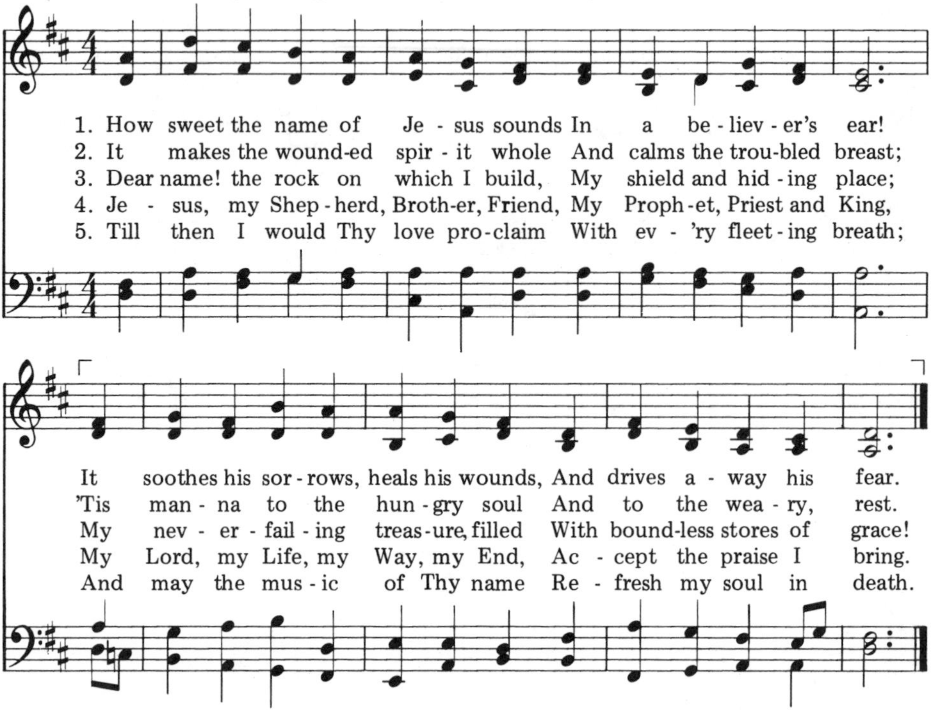

1. How sweet the name of Je - sus sounds In a be - liev - er's ear!
It soothes his sor - rows, heals his wounds, And drives a - way his fear.

2. It makes the wound-ed spir - it whole And calms the trou-bled breast;
'Tis man - na to the hun - gry soul And to the wea - ry, rest.

3. Dear name! the rock on which I build, My shield and hid - ing place;
My nev - er - fail - ing treas - ure, filled With bound-less stores of grace!

4. Je - sus, my Shep - herd, Broth-er, Friend, My Proph - et, Priest and King,
My Lord, my Life, my Way, my End, Ac - cept the praise I bring.

5. Till then I would Thy love pro-claim With ev - 'ry fleet - ing breath;
And may the mus - ic of Thy name Re - fresh my soul in death.

TEXT: John Newton
MUSIC: Alexander R. Reinagle

ST. PETER
C.M.

95 Jesus Is the Sweetest Name I Know

Jesus Christ is the same yesterday and today and forever. Heb. 13:8

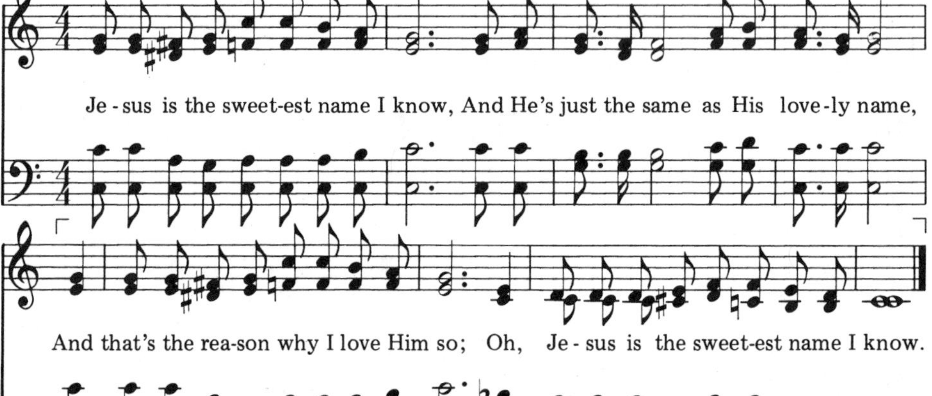
Je - sus is the sweet-est name I know, And He's just the same as His love-ly name,
And that's the rea-son why I love Him so; Oh, Je - sus is the sweet-est name I know.
8

TEXT and MUSIC: Lela Long

SWEETEST NAME
9.10.10.10.

All Hail the Power of Jesus' Name 96

God . . . gave Him the name that is above every name . . . Jesus Christ is Lord. Phil. 2:9-11

1. All hail the pow'r of Je - sus' name! Let an-gels pros-trate fall, Let an - gels pros-trate fall; Bring forth the roy - al di - a - dem,
2. Ye cho - sen seed of Is - rael's race, Ye ran-somed from the fall, Ye ran - somed from the fall; Hail Him who saves you by His grace, And crown Him, crown Him,
3. Let ev - ery kin - dred, ev - 'ry tribe, On this ter-res-trial ball, On this ter - res - trial ball; To Him all maj - es - ty as - cribe,
4. O that with yon - der sa - cred throng We at His feet may fall, We at His feet may fall! We'll join the ev - er - last - ing song, And crown Him, crown Him, crown Him, crown Him, crown Him,
crown
crown Him, crown Him, And crown Him Lord of all. A - men.
Him,

TEXT: Edward Perronet; adapted by John Rippon
MUSIC: James Ellor

DIADEM
C.M. with Refrain

97 All Hail the Power of Jesus' Name

God . . . gave Him the name that is above every name . . . Jesus Christ is Lord. Phil. 2:9-11

1. All hail the pow'r of Je - sus' name! Let an - gels pros - trate fall;
2. Ye cho - sen seed of Is - rael's race, Ye ran-somed from the fall,
3. Let ev - 'ry kin - dred, ev - 'ry tribe, On this ter - res - trial ball,
4. O that with yon - der sa - cred throng We at His feet may fall!

Bring forth the roy - al di - a - dem, And crown Him Lord of all;
Hail Him who saves you by His grace, And crown Him Lord of all;
To Him all maj - es - ty as - cribe, And crown Him Lord of all;
We'll join the ev - er - last - ing song, And crown Him Lord of all;

Bring forth the roy - al di - a - dem, And crown Him Lord of all!
Hail Him who saves you by His grace, And crown Him Lord of all!
To Him all maj - es - ty as - cribe, And crown Him Lord of all!
We'll join the ev - er - last - ing song, And crown Him Lord of all!

Optional choral ending

f

all! Crown Him, crown Him, al - le - lu - ia! Crown Him, crown Him,

Crown

Crown

TEXT: Edward Perronet; adapted by John Rippon
MUSIC: Oliver Holden; Choral ending by Tom Fettke

CORONATION
C.M. with Repeats

Him, cresc.
rit.
ff
crown Him, And crown Him Lord of all. A - men.
Him,

Jesus, We Just Want to Thank You 98

Thanks be to God for His indescribable gift! 2 Cor. 9:15

1. Je - sus, we just want to thank You,
Je - sus, we just want to thank You,
Je - sus, we just want to thank You,
Thank You for be - ing so good.

2. Je - sus, we just want to praise You,
Je - sus, we just want to praise You,
Je - sus, we just want to praise You,
Praise You for be - ing so good.

3. Je - sus, we just want to tell You,
Je - sus, we just want to tell You,
Je - sus, we just want to tell You,
We love You for be - ing so good.

4. Sav - ior, we just want to serve You,
Sav - ior, we just want to serve You,
Sav - ior, we just want to serve You,
Serve You for be - ing so good.

5. Je - sus, we know You are com - ing,
Je - sus, we know You are com - ing,
Je - sus, we know You are com - ing,
Take us to live in Your home.

TEXT: Gloria Gaither and William J. Gaither
MUSIC: William J. Gaither

THANK YOU
8.8.8.7.

99

THE NAME OF JESUS

A Brief Service of Worship and Praise

Suggested Hymn Stanzas

To facilitate an uninterrupted flow from stanza to stanza, the suggested stanzas have been marked with an arrow: ►

There Is No Name So Sweet on Earth, complete
His Name Is Wonderful, complete
There's Something About That Name, complete
Blessed Be the Name, complete

WORSHIP LEADER: **Therefore God has highly exalted Him and bestowed on Him the name which is above every name, that at the name of Jesus every knee should bow, in heaven and on earth and under the earth, and every tongue confess that Jesus Christ is Lord, to the glory of God the Father.**

Philippians 2:9-11. (RSV)

100 There Is No Name So Sweet on Earth

. . . *the good news that Jesus is the Christ.* Acts 5:42

Optional introduction
mf
*Choir or congregation
We love to sing of Christ our King, And hail Him, bless-ed Je - sus; For
there's no word ear ev - er heard So dear, so sweet as "Je - sus."
Optional transition to "His Name Is Wonderful"

*This song may be used as a choir introduction to the medley.

TEXT: George W. Bethune
MUSIC: William B. Bradbury

GOLDEN CHAIN (Refrain only)
8.7.8.7.

"THE NAME OF JESUS—A Brief Service of Worship and Praise"

His Name Is Wonderful 101

No one can say, "Jesus is Lord," except by the Holy Spirit. 1 Cor. 12:3

His name is Won-der-ful, His name is Won-der-ful, His name is Won-der-ful,
Je-sus, my Lord; He is the might-y King, Mas-ter of ev-ery-thing,
His name is Won-der-ful, Je-sus, my Lord. He's the great Shep-herd, the
Rock of all a-ges, Al-might-y God is He; Bow down be-
fore Him, Love and a-dore Him, His name is Won-der-ful, Je-sus, my Lord.

TEXT and MUSIC: Audrey Mieir

MIEIR
Irregular meter

Optional transition to
"There's Something About That Name"
L.H.
mf

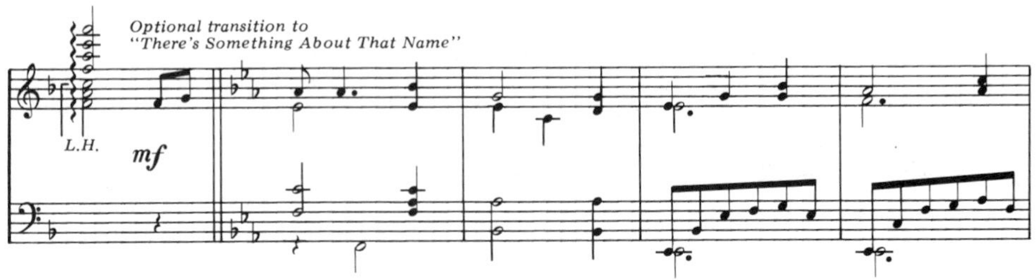

102 There's Something About That Name

There is no other name . . . by which we must be saved. Acts 4:12

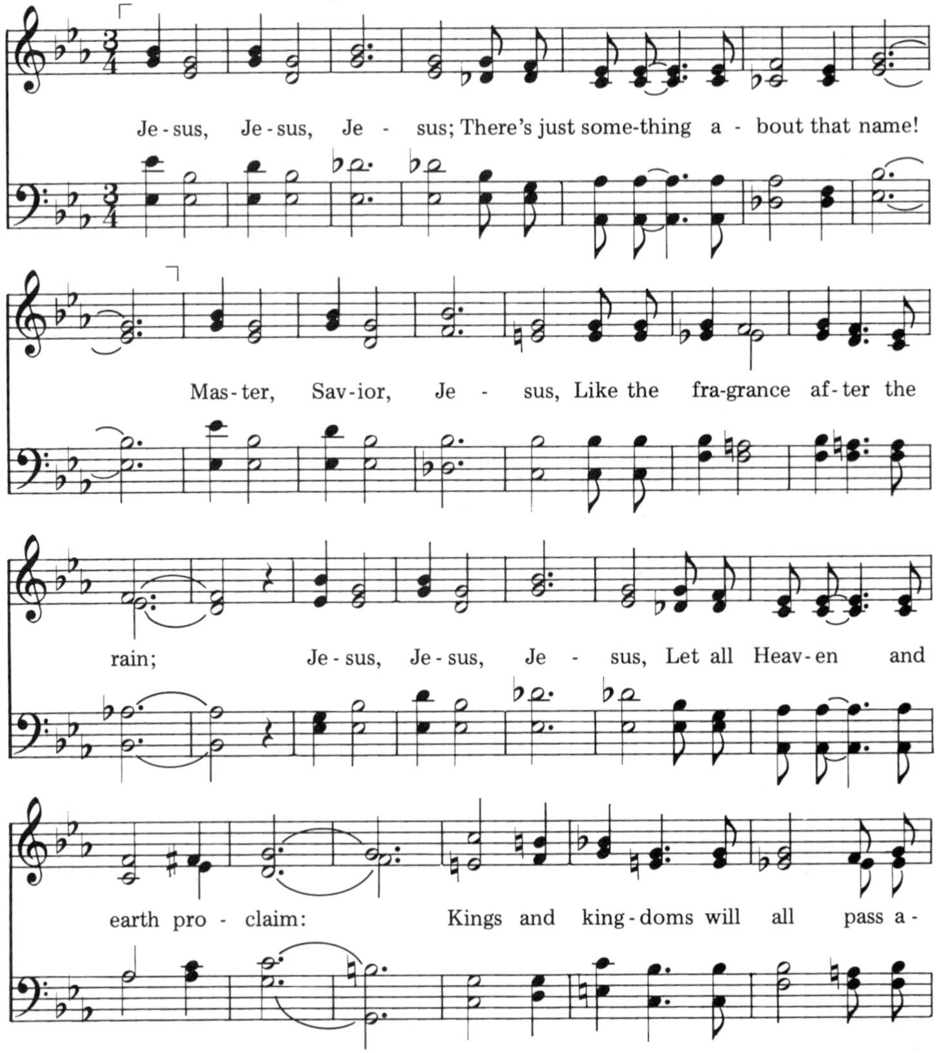
Je - sus, Je - sus, Je - sus; There's just some-thing a - bout that name!
Mas - ter, Sav - ior, Je - sus, Like the fra-grance af - ter the
rain; Je - sus, Je - sus, Je - sus, Let all Heav - en and
earth pro - claim: Kings and king - doms will all pass a -

TEXT: Gloria Gaither and William J. Gaither
MUSIC: William J. Gaither

THAT NAME
Irregular meter

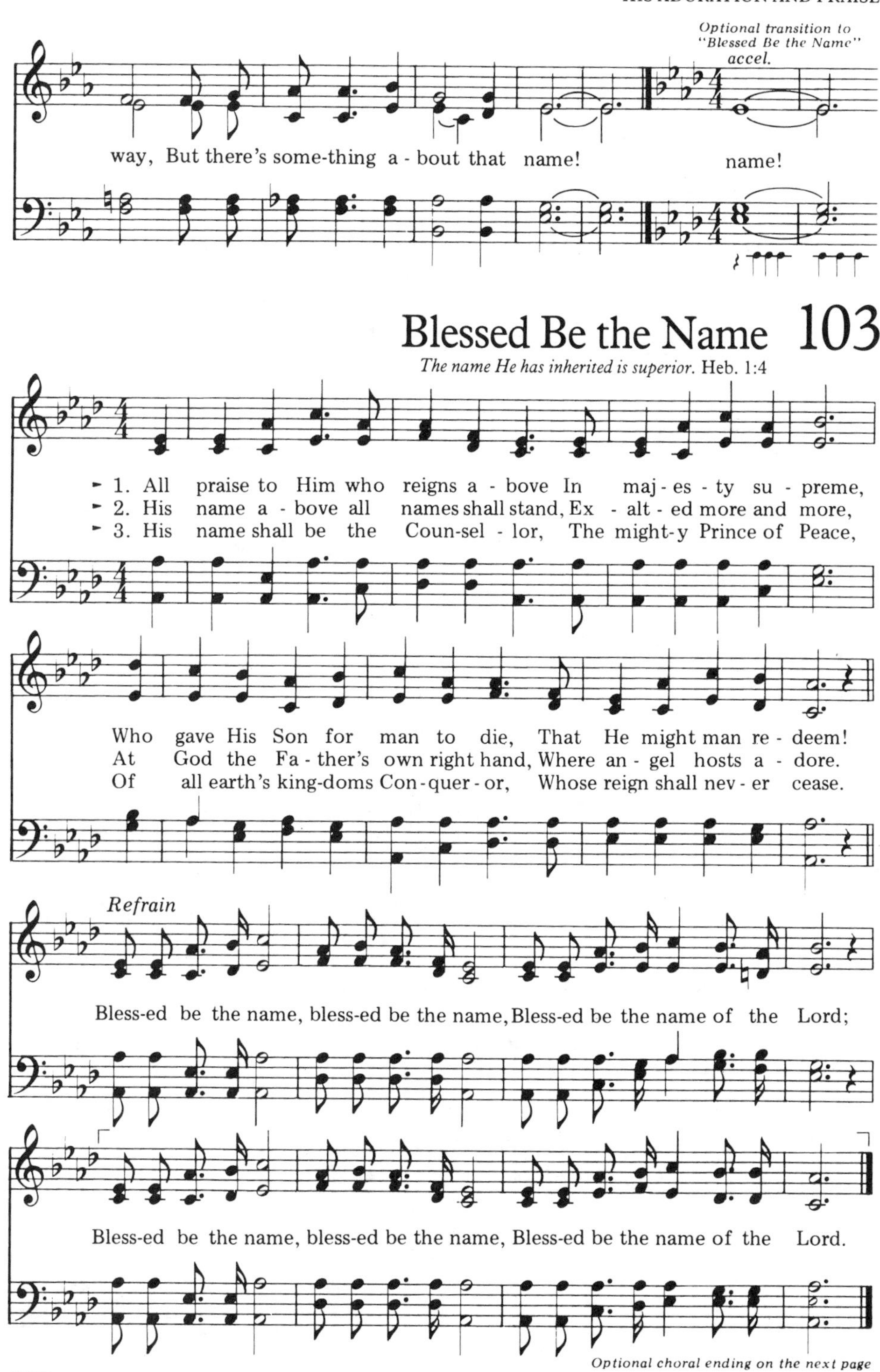
Optional transition to "Blessed Be the Name"
accel.
way, But there's some-thing a - bout that name! name!
Blessed Be the Name 103
The name He has inherited is superior. Heb. 1:4
1. All praise to Him who reigns a - bove In maj - es - ty su - preme,
2. His name a - bove all names shall stand, Ex - alt - ed more and more,
3. His name shall be the Coun-sel - lor, The might-y Prince of Peace,
Who gave His Son for man to die, That He might man re - deem!
At God the Fa - ther's own right hand, Where an - gel hosts a - dore.
Of all earth's king-doms Con-quer - or, Whose reign shall nev - er cease.
Refrain
Bless-ed be the name, bless-ed be the name, Bless-ed be the name of the Lord;
Bless-ed be the name, bless-ed be the name, Bless-ed be the name of the Lord.
Optional choral ending on the next page

TEXT: William H. Clark; Ralph E. Hudson, Refrain
MUSIC: Source unknown; arranged by Ralph E. Hudson and William J. Kirkpatrick

BLESSED BE THE NAME
C.M. with Refrain

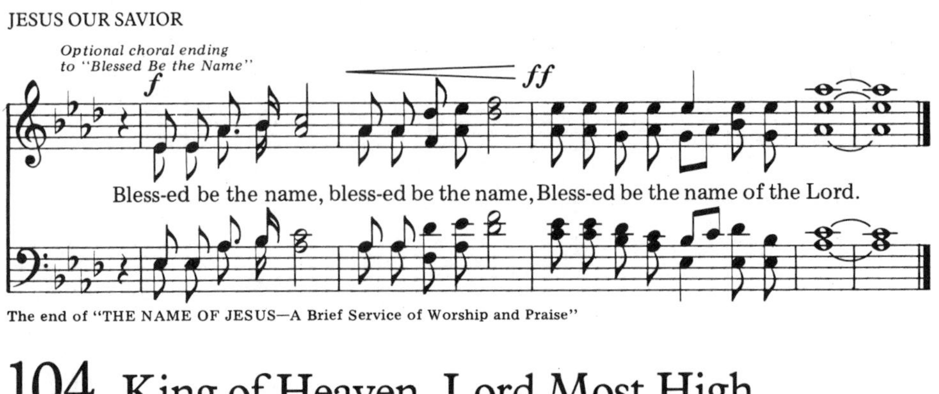
Optional choral ending
to "Blessed Be the Name"
f
ff
Bless-ed be the name, bless-ed be the name, Bless-ed be the name of the Lord.

The end of "THE NAME OF JESUS—A Brief Service of Worship and Praise"

104 King of Heaven, Lord Most High

God . . . is immortal . . . whom no one has seen or can see. 1 Tim. 6:15-16

1. Im - mor - tal, in - vis - i - ble King of Hea - ven, Lord Most High.
Hon - or now we give to You, Au - thor of e - ter - nal life. Power, wisdom,
strength and bless-ing; You are wor - thy to re-ceive our praise. Im - mor - tal, in -
vis - i - ble Lord, to You all prais - es be!

2. Im - mor - tal, in - vis - i - ble, Ev - er faith - ful, ev - er true.
O - ver-come with love and awe, Lord of Hosts we wor-ship You. Now in hum-ble
ad - o - ra - tion, Plac - ing all be - fore Your roy-al throne. Im - mor - tal, in -
vis - i - ble Sav - ior, we are Yours a - lone! A - men.

TEXT and MUSIC: Niles Borop and Dwight Liles

KING OF HEAVEN
Irregular meter

Confess with thy mouth the Lord Jesus, . . . believe . . . that God raised Him. Rom. 10:9

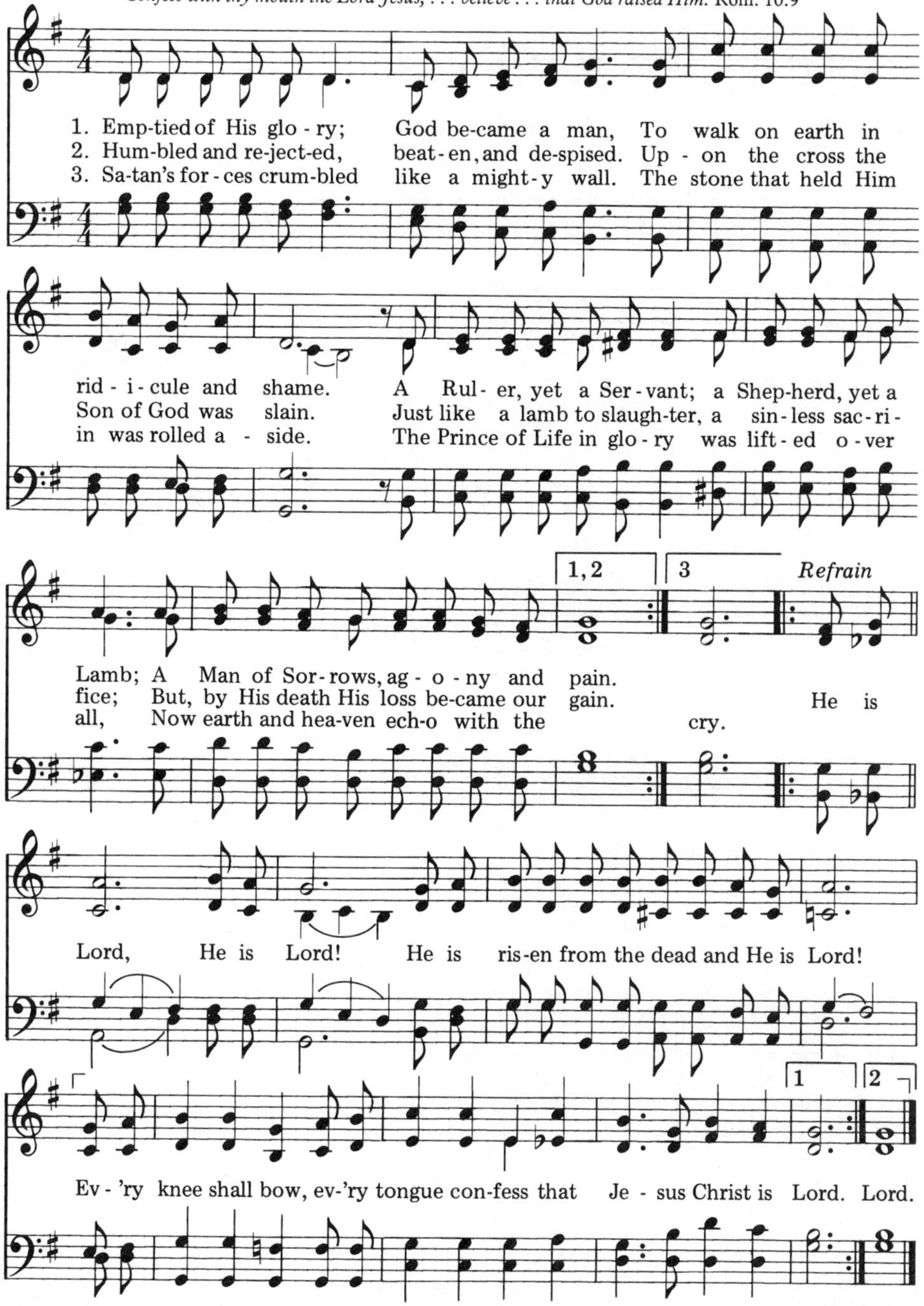

1. Emp-tied of His glo - ry; God be-came a man, To walk on earth in rid - i - cule and shame. A Rul - er, yet a Ser - vant; a Shep-herd, yet a Lamb; A Man of Sor-rows, ag - o - ny and pain.
2. Hum-bled and re-ject-ed, beat - en, and de-spised. Up - on the cross the Son of God was slain. Just like a lamb to slaugh-ter, a sin-less sac-ri - fice; But, by His death His loss be-came our gain.
3. Sa-tan's for - ces crum-bled like a might - y wall. The stone that held Him in was rolled a - side. The Prince of Life in glo - ry was lift - ed o - ver all, Now earth and hea-ven ech-o with the cry.

1, 2 | 3 | *Refrain*

He is Lord, He is Lord! He is ris-en from the dead and He is Lord! Ev - 'ry knee shall bow, ev-'ry tongue con-fess that Je - sus Christ is Lord. Lord.

TEXT: Linda Lee Johnson, Claire Cloninger and Tom Fettke, stanzas; Traditional, Refrain; based on Isaiah 53 and Philippians 2:6-11
MUSIC: Tom Fettke, stanzas and arrangement; Traditional, Refrain

HE IS LORD
11.10.12.10. with Refrain

106 Praise Him! Praise Him!

You are worthy . . . with Your blood You purchased men for God. Rev. 5:9

1. Praise Him! praise Him! Je - sus, our bless-ed Re - deem-er! Sing, O Earth, His won-der-ful love pro-claim! Hail Him! hail Him! high-est arch-an-gels in glo - ry; Strength and hon - or give to His ho - ly name! Like a shep-herd Je - sus will guard His chil - dren, In His arms He car-ries them all day long:
2. Praise Him! praise Him! Je - sus, our bless-ed Re - deem-er! For our sins He suf-fered, and bled and died; He our Rock, our hope of e - ter-nal sal - va-tion, Hail Him! hail Him! Je - sus the Cru - ci - fied. Sound His prais-es! Je - sus who bore our sor - rows; Love un-bound-ed, won-der-ful, deep and strong:
3. Praise Him! praise Him! Je - sus, our bless-ed Re - deem-er! Heav'n-ly por - tals loud with ho-san - nas ring! Je - sus, Sav - ior, reign-eth for-ev-er and ev - er; Crown Him! crown Him! Proph-et and Priest and King! Christ is com - ing! o - ver the world vic - to - rious, Pow'r and glo - ry un - to the Lord be - long:
Refrain
Praise Him! praise Him! tell of His ex - cel - lent great - ness;

TEXT: Fanny J. Crosby
MUSIC: Chester G. Allen

JOYFUL SONG
Irregular meter

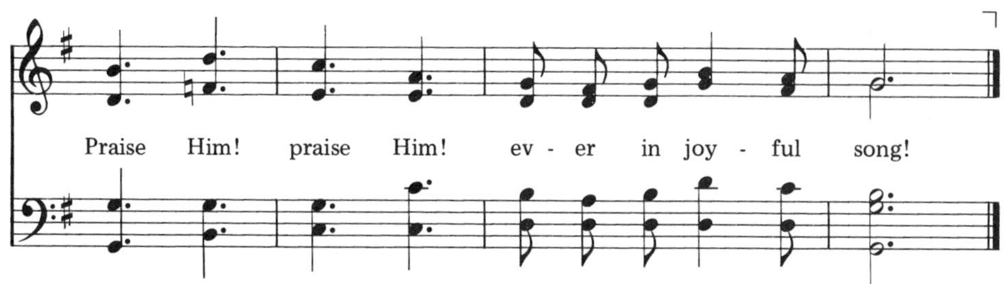
Praise Him! praise Him! ev - er in joy - ful song!

Let's Just Praise the Lord 107

Lift up your hands . . . and praise the Lord. Ps. 134:2

Let's just praise the Lord! Praise the Lord! Let's just lift our hearts* to heav - en and praise the Lord;

Let's just praise the Lord, Praise the Lord, Let's just lift our hearts* to heav - en and praise the Lord!

*Alternate words "voice," "hands."

TEXT: Gloria Gaither and William J. Gaither
MUSIC: William J. Gaither

LET'S JUST PRAISE THE LORD
Irregular meter

108 Come, Christians, Join to Sing

Sing and make music in your heart to the Lord, always giving thanks. Eph. 5:19-20

1. Come, Chris - tians, join to sing Al - le - lu - ia! A - men!
2. Come, lift your hearts on high, Al - le - lu - ia! A - men!
3. Praise yet our Christ a - gain, Al - le - lu - ia! A - men!
Loud praise to Christ our King; Al - le - lu - ia! A - men!
Let prais - es fill the sky; Al - le - lu - ia! A - men!
Life shall not end the strain; Al - le - lu - ia! A - men!
Let all, with heart and voice, Be - fore His throne re - joice;
He is our Guide and Friend; To us He'll con - de - scend;
On heav - en's bliss - ful shore His good - ness we'll a - dore,
Praise is His gra - cious choice: Al - le - lu - ia! A - men!
His love shall nev - er end: Al - le - lu - ia! A - men!
Sing - ing for - ev - er - more, "Al - le - lu - ia! A - men!"

TEXT: Christian H. Bateman
MUSIC: Traditional Spanish melody; arranged by David Evans;
Choral ending arranged by Eugene Thomas

MADRID
6.6.6.6.D.

Optional choral ending
mf cresc.
f rit.
ff
Al - le - lu - ia, al - le - lu - ia. Al - le - lu - ia! A - men!
Majestic Sweetness Sits Enthroned
109
All . . . were amazed at the gracious words that came from His lips. Luke 4:22
1. Ma - jes - tic sweet - ness sits en-throned Up - on the Sav - ior's
2. No mor - tal can with Him com-pare A - mong the sons of
3. He saw me plunged in deep dis - tress And flew to my re -
4. To Him I owe my life and breath And all the joys I
5. Since from His boun - ty I re - ceive Such proofs of love di -
brow; His head with ra - diant glo - ries crowned, His lips with
men; Fair - er is He than all the fair Who fill the
lief; For me He bore the shame - ful cross And car - ried
have; He makes me tri - umph o - ver death And saves me
vine, Had I a thou - sand hearts to give, Lord, they should
grace o'er - flow, His lips with grace o'er - flow.
heav'n - ly train, Who fill the heav'n - ly train.
all my grief, And car - ried all my grief.
from the grave, And saves me from the grave.
all be Thine, Lord, they should all be Thine. A - men.

TEXT: Samuel Stennett
MUSIC: Thomas Hastings

ORTONVILLE
C.M. with Repeats

110 O Could I Speak the Matchless Worth

We have seen His glory . . . full of grace and truth. John 1:14

1. O could I speak the matchless worth, O could I sound the glories forth Which in my Savior shine, I'd sing His glorious righteousness, And magnify the wondrous grace Which made salvation mine, Which made salvation mine.
2. I'd sing the characters He bears, And all the forms of love He wears, Exalted on His throne: In loftiest songs of sweetest praise, I would to everlasting days Make all His glories known, Make all His glories known.
3. Soon the delightful day will come When my dear Lord will bring me home, And I shall see His face; Then with my Savior, Brother, Friend, A blest eternity I'll spend, Triumphant in His grace, Triumphant in His grace.

TEXT: Samuel Medley
MUSIC: Source unknown; arranged by Lowell Mason

ARIEL
8.8.6.8.8.6.6.

Join All the Glorious Names 111

. . . *far above . . . every title that can be given.* Eph. 1:21

1. Join all the glo - rious names Of wis - dom, love, and pow'r,
2. Great Proph - et of my God, My tongue would bless Thy name:
3. Je - sus, my great High Priest, Of - fered His blood, and died;
4. Thou art my Coun - sel - lor, My Pat - tern, and my Guide,
5. My Sav - ior and my Lord, My Con - qu'ror and my King,
That ev - er mor - tals knew, That an - gels
By Thee the joy - ful news Of our sal -
My guilt - y con - science seeks No sac - ri -
And Thou my Shep - herd art; O, keep me
Thy scep - tre and Thy sword, Thy reign - ing
ev - er bore: All are too poor to speak His worth,
va - tion came, The joy - ful news of sins for - giv'n,
fice be - side: His pow'r - ful blood did once a - tone
near Thy side; Nor let my feet e'er turn a - stray
grace, I sing: Thine is the pow'r; be - hold I sit
Too poor to set my Sav - ior forth.
Of hell sub - dued and peace with heav'n.
And now it pleads be - fore the throne.
To wan - der in the crook - ed way.
In will - ing bonds be - neath Thy feet. A - men.

TEXT: Isaac Watts
MUSIC: John Darwall
A lower setting may be found at No. 117

DARWALL
6.6.6.6.8.8.

112 Jesus, Name Above All Names

We pray this so that the name of our Lord Jesus may be glorified in you. 2 Thess. 1:12

Unison

Je - sus, name a - bove all names, beau-ti - ful Sav - ior,
glo - ri - ous Lord. Em - man - u - el, God is
with us, bless-ed Re - deem - er, Liv - ing Word.

TEXT and MUSIC: Naida Hearn

HEARN
7.8.8.8.

113 I Just Came to Praise the Lord

I will sing praise to my God as long as I live. Ps. 146:2

1. I just came to praise the Lord, I just came to praise the Lord;
2. I just came to thank the Lord, I just came to thank the Lord;
3. I just came to love the Lord, I just came to love the Lord;

TEXT and MUSIC: Wayne Romero

ROMERO
7.7.9.7.

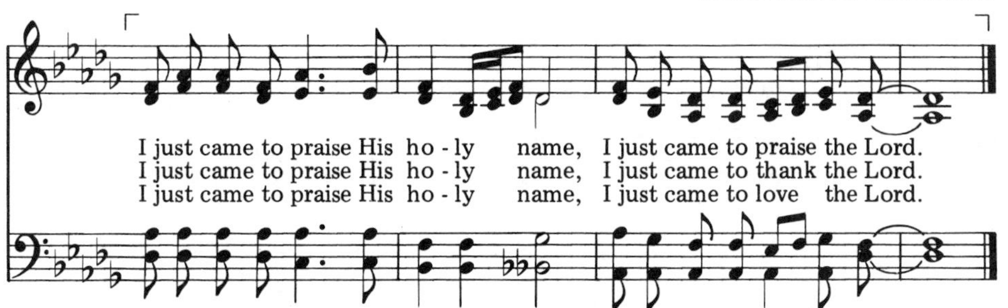
I just came to praise His ho - ly name, I just came to praise the Lord.
I just came to praise His ho - ly name, I just came to thank the Lord.
I just came to praise His ho - ly name, I just came to love the Lord.

His Name Is Life 114

I am . . . the Life. John 14:6

His name is Mas-ter, Sav-ior, Li - on of Ju - dah, Bless - ed Prince of Peace. Shep-herd, For-tress, Rock of Sal - va-tion, Lamb of God is He. Son of Dav-id, King of the Ag - es, E - ter - nal Life, Ho - ly Lord of Glo - ry, His name is Life.

TEXT and MUSIC: Carman, Gloria Gaither and William J. Gaither; arranged by Eugene Thomas

HIS NAME IS LIFE
Irregular meter

115 Sometimes "Alleluia"

Praise be to the God and Father of our Lord Jesus Christ! 1 Pet. 1:3

Some-times "Al - le - lu - ia," Some-times "Praise the Lord,"
Some-times gent - ly sing - ing; Our hearts in one ac - cord.
Last time: Fine
1. O let us lift our voic - es, Look toward the sky and start to sing;
2. O let our joy be un-con-fined; Let us sing with free-dom un - re - strained;
3. O let us feel His pres - ence, Let the sound of prais-es fill the air.
4. O let the Spir -it o - ver-flow As we are filled from head to toe.
O let us now re - turn His love, Just let our voic - es ring.
Let's take this feeling that we're feeling now Outside these walls and let it rain.
O let us sing the song of Je - sus' love To peo-ple ev - 'ry -where.
We love You, Father, Son, and Ho-ly Ghost; And we want this world to know.
D.C.

TEXT and MUSIC: Chuck Girard

SOMETIMES ALLELUIA
Irregular meter

Take the Name of Jesus with You 116

Whatever you do . . . do it all in the name of the Lord Jesus. Col. 3:17

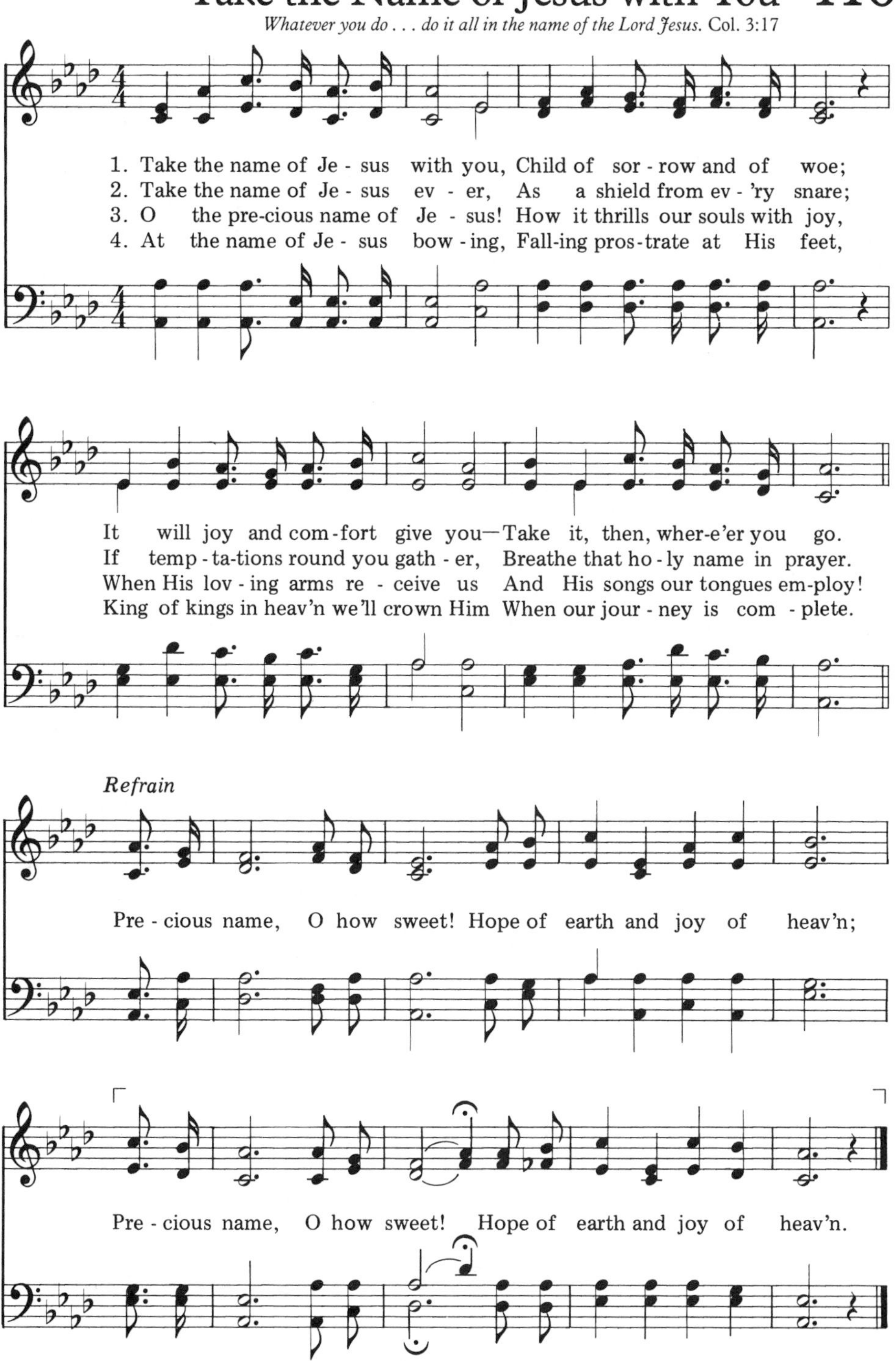
1. Take the name of Je - sus with you, Child of sor - row and of woe;
2. Take the name of Je - sus ev - er, As a shield from ev - 'ry snare;
3. O the pre-cious name of Je - sus! How it thrills our souls with joy,
4. At the name of Je - sus bow - ing, Fall-ing pros-trate at His feet,
It will joy and com-fort give you— Take it, then, wher-e'er you go.
If temp - ta-tions round you gath - er, Breathe that ho - ly name in prayer.
When His lov - ing arms re - ceive us And His songs our tongues em-ploy!
King of kings in heav'n we'll crown Him When our jour - ney is com - plete.
Refrain
Pre - cious name, O how sweet! Hope of earth and joy of heav'n;
Pre - cious name, O how sweet! Hope of earth and joy of heav'n.

TEXT: Lydia Baxter
MUSIC: William H. Doane

PRECIOUS NAME
8.7.8.7. with Refrain

117 We Come, O Christ, to You

Lord, to whom shall we go? You have the words of eternal life. John 6:68

1. We come, O Christ, to You, True Son of God and man, By Whom all things con - sist, In Whom all life be - gan: In You a - lone we live and move, And have our be - ing in Your love.
2. You are the Way to God, Your blood our ran - som paid; In You we face our Judge And Mak - er un - a - fraid. Be - fore the throne ab - solved we stand, Your love has met Your law's de - mand.
3. You are the liv - ing Truth! All wis - dom dwells in You, The Source of ev - ery skill, The One E - ter - nal True! O great I AM! In You we rest, Sure an - swer to our ev - ery quest.
4. You on - ly are true Life, To know You is to live The more a - bun - dant life That earth can nev - er give: O ris - en Lord! We live in You, in us each day Your life re - new!
5. We wor - ship You, Lord Christ, Our Sav - ior and our King, To You our youth and strength A - dor - ing - ly we bring: So fill our hearts, that all may view Your life in us, and turn to You! A - men.

TEXT: Margaret Clarkson
MUSIC: John Darwall
A higher setting may be found at No. 111

DARWALL
6.6.6.6.8.8.

Of the Father's Love Begotten 118

I am the Alpha and the Omega . . . the Beginning and the End. Rev. 22:13

Unison
1. Of the Fa - ther's love be - got - ten, Ere the worlds be - gan
2. O ye heights of heav'n a - dore Him; An - gel hosts, His prais -
3. Christ, to Thee with God the Fa - ther, And, O Ho - ly Ghost,
to be, He is Al - pha and O - me - ga, He the Source, the
es sing; Pow'rs, do-min - ions, bow be - fore Him, And ex - tol our
to Thee, Hymn and chant and high thanks-giv - ing And un - wea - ried
End - ing He, Of the things that are, that have been,
God and King; Let no tongue on earth be si - lent,
prais - es be: Hon - or, glo - ry, and do - min - ion,
And that fu-ture years shall see, Ev - er-more and ev - er-more!
Ev - 'ry voice in con - cert ring, Ev - er-more and ev - er-more!
And e - ter - nal vic - to - ry, Ev - er-more and ev - er-more! A - men.

TEXT: Aurelius C. Prudentius, 4th century; translated by John M. Neale and Henry W. Baker
MUSIC: Plainsong, 13th century; arranged by C. Winfred Douglas

DIVINUM MYSTERIUM
8.7.8.7.8.7.7.

119 O Thou Joyful, O Thou Wonderful

We also rejoice in God through our Lord Jesus Christ. Rom. 5:11

1. O thou joy - ful, O thou won-der-ful Grace-re - veal-ing
2. O thou joy - ful, O thou won-der-ful Love - re - veal-ing
3. O thou joy - ful, O thou won-der-ful Peace-re - veal-ing

Christ - mas - tide! Je - sus came to win us From all sin with-
Christ - mas - tide! Loud ho - san - nas sing - ing And all prais - es
Christ - mas - tide! Dark - ness dis - ap - pear - eth, God's own light now

in us; Glo - ri - fy the ho - ly Child!
bring - ing: May Thy love with us a - bide!
near - eth: Peace and joy to all be - tide!

TEXT: Johannes D. Falk, stanza 1; Source unknown, stanza 3; translated by Henry Katterjohn
MUSIC: Tattersall's *Psalmody*, 1794

O SANCTISSIMA
4.5.7.6.6.7.

120 The Advent of Our God

Be glad . . . for I am coming, and I will live among you. Zech. 2:10

1. The Ad - vent of our God With ea - ger hearts we greet; And
2. All glo - ry to the Son, Who comes to set us free; With

TEXT: Charles Coffin; translated by John Chandler, altered
MUSIC: Aaron Williams
A higher setting may be found at No. 21

ST. THOMAS
S.M.

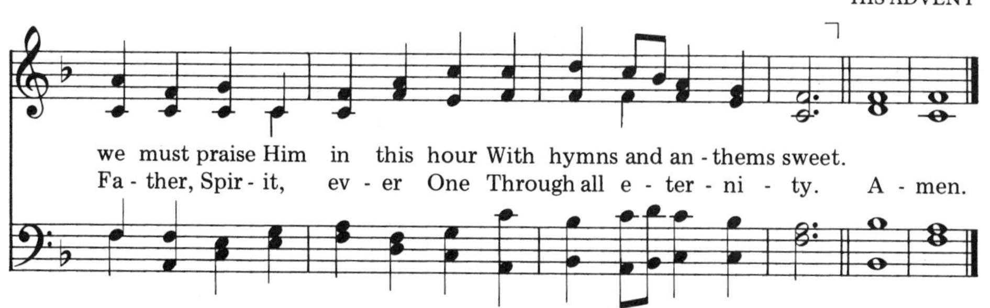
we must praise Him in this hour With hymns and an - thems sweet.
Fa - ther, Spir - it, ev - er One Through all e - ter - ni - ty. A - men.

The Word Made Flesh 121

From the fullness of His grace we have all received one blessing after another. John 1:16

1. The Word made flesh has dwelt a - mong us, full of grace and
2. The Word made flesh has dwelt a - mong us, from His full - ness

full of truth. We be - held His won-drous glo - ry of the on - ly
we re - ceived grace on grace and last - ing mer - cy, truth and wis - dom,

Son of God.
hope and peace.

Refrain

We have be - held His glo - ry, and we have seen the

light. A - noint - ed Prince of glo - ry, we mar - vel at Thy sight.

TEXT and MUSIC: John Purifoy; based on John 1:14-17;
arranged by Joseph Barlowe

VICKI
Irregular meter

122 THE ADVENT OF OUR LORD

A Brief Service of Joyful Expectation

Suggested Hymn Stanzas

To facilitate an uninterrupted flow from stanza to stanza, the suggested stanzas have been marked with an arrow: ►

O Come, O Come, Emmanuel, stanzas 1, 2
Come, Thou Long-Expected Jesus, complete
Joy to the World!, stanzas 1, 4

WORSHIP LEADER: **Who shall come in the fullness of time to gladden the hearts of men?**
Who shall bring new joy to the world and the poor and lonely defend?
Who shall come on a cold winter's night, when the world is hushed and still?
Only the silent stars keep watch as a promise is fulfilled.

Just as a Child newly born He shall come to a stable rough with sod.
'Tis gentle Jesus, Prince of Peace, the blessed Son of God!

WORSHIP LEADER and PEOPLE:

We await Him with reverent hearts,
O come Lord Jesus, come!

"Who Shall Come" by Mary E. Caldwell

123 O Come, O Come, Emmanuel

The virgin will . . . give birth to a Son, and will call Him Immanuel. Isa. 7:14

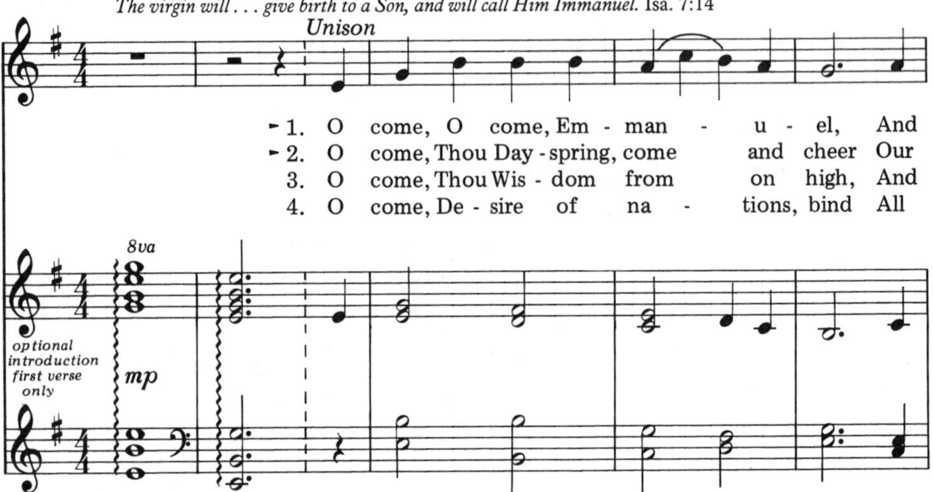
Unison
► 1. O come, O come, Em - man - u - el, And
► 2. O come, Thou Day - spring, come and cheer Our
3. O come, Thou Wis - dom from on high, And
4. O come, De - sire of na - tions, bind All
8va
optional introduction first verse only
mp

TEXT: Latin Hymn, *Psalteriolum Cantionum Catholicarum,* 1710; translated by John M. Neale, stanzas 1, 2, altered; Henry S. Coffin, stanzas 3, 4, altered
MUSIC: Adapted from Plainsong by Thomas Helmore; arranged by Tom Fettke

VENI EMMANUEL
L.M. with Refrain

ran - som cap - tive Is - ra - el, That mourns in lone - ly ex - ile
spir - its by Thine ad - vent here; Dis - perse the gloom-y clouds of
or - der all things, far and nigh; To us the path of knowl - edge
peo - ples in one heart and mind; Bid en - vy, strife and quar - rels
here, Un - til the Son of God ap - pear.
night, And death's dark shad - ows put to flight.
show, And cause us in her ways to go.
cease, Fill all the world with heav - en's peace.
Refrain
parts optional
Re - joice! Re -
joice! Em - man - u - el Shall come to thee, O Is - ra - el!
Optional transition to "Come, Thou Long-Expected Jesus"
accel. poco a poco
cresc.
no rit.

124 Come, Thou Long-Expected Jesus

He has sent me to bind up the brokenhearted, to proclaim freedom for the captives. Isa. 61:1

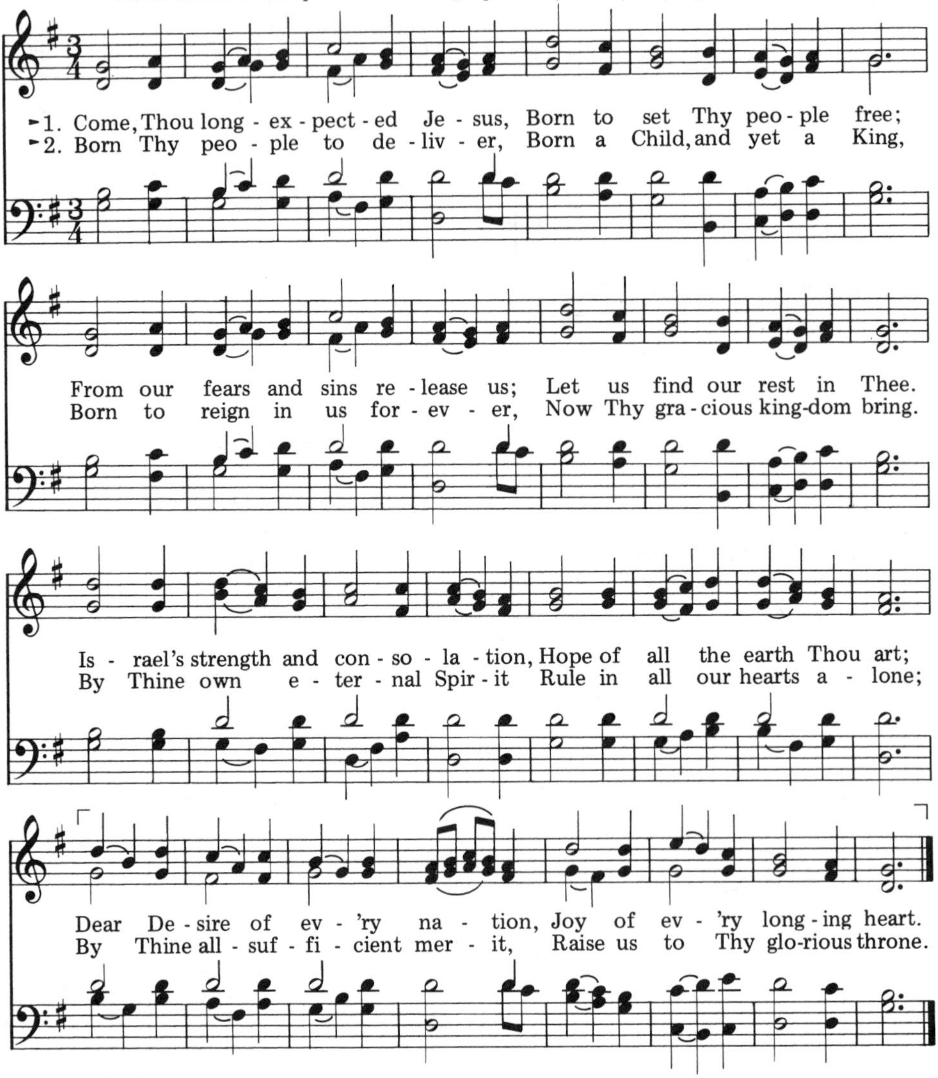

1. Come, Thou long-expected Jesus, Born to set Thy people free;
From our fears and sins release us; Let us find our rest in Thee.
Israel's strength and consolation, Hope of all the earth Thou art;
Dear Desire of every nation, Joy of every longing heart.

2. Born Thy people to deliver, Born a Child, and yet a King,
Born to reign in us forever, Now Thy gracious kingdom bring.
By Thine own eternal Spirit Rule in all our hearts alone;
By Thine all-sufficient merit, Raise us to Thy glorious throne.

TEXT: Charles Wesley
MUSIC: Rowland H. Prichard; arranged by Robert Harkness
A lower setting may be found at No. 89

HYFRYDOL
8.7.8.7.D.

Joy to the World! 125

Bethlehem . . . , out of you will come for Me One who will be ruler over Israel. Mic. 5:2

1. Joy to the world! the Lord is come; Let earth re-ceive her King;
2. Joy to the earth! the Sav-ior reigns; Let men their songs em-ploy;
3. No more let sins and sor-rows grow, Nor thorns in-fest the ground;
4. He rules the world with truth and grace, And makes the na-tions prove
Let ev-'ry heart pre-pare Him room,
While fields and floods, rocks, hills, and plains
He comes to make His bless-ings flow
The glo-ries of His righ-teous-ness,
And heav'n and na-ture sing, And heav'n and na-ture sing,
Re-peat the sound-ing joy, Re-peat the sound-ing joy,
Far as the curse is found, Far as the curse is found,
And won-ders of His love, And won-ders of His love,
1. And heav'n and na-ture sing,
1. And heav'n and na-ture sing, And heav'n and na-
And heav'n, and heav'n and na-ture sing.
Re-peat, re-peat the sound-ing joy.
Far as, far as the curse is found.
And won-ders, won-ders of His love.
ture sing,

Choral Ending on the following page.

TEXT: Isaac Watts
MUSIC: George Frederick Handel, arranged by Lowell Mason; Choral ending arranged by Tom Fettke

ANTIOCH
C.M.

Optional choral ending - "Joy to the World"
cresc.
A - men, a - men, a -
world! A - men!
rit.
men! Joy to the world! A - men!
world! A - men!

The end of "THE ADVENT OF OUR LORD—A Brief Service of Joyful Expectation"

126 A Nativity Prayer

Give Him the name Jesus, because He will save His people from their sins. Matt. 1:21

O ho - ly Child of Beth - le - hem! De - scend to us, we pray;

Cast out our sin, and en - ter in; Be born in us to - day. A - men.

TEXT: Phillips Brooks
MUSIC: William David Young

ELATA
C.M.

Thou Didst Leave Thy Throne 127

He came to that which was His own, but His own did not receive Him. John 1:11

1. Thou didst leave Thy throne and Thy king - ly crown When Thou cam - est to earth for me; But in Beth - le-hem's home was there found no room For Thy ho - ly na - tiv - i - ty.
2. Heav - en's arch - es rang when the an - gels sang, Pro - claim - ing Thy roy - al de - cree; But of low - ly birth didst Thou come to earth, And in great hu - mil - i - ty.
3. The fox - es found rest, and the birds their nest In the shade of the for - est tree; But Thy couch was the sod, O Thou Son of God, In the des - erts of Gal - i - lee.
4. Thou cam - est, O Lord, with the liv - ing word That should set Thy peo - ple free; But with mock - ing scorn and with crown of thorn They bore Thee to Cal - va - ry.
5. When the heav'ns shall ring and the an - gels sing At Thy com - ing to vic - to - ry, Let Thy voice call me home, say - ing, "Yet there is room— There is room at My side for thee."
Refrain
O come to my heart, Lord Je - sus—There is room in my heart for Thee!
O come to my heart, Lord Je - sus—There is room in my heart for Thee!
O come to my heart, Lord Je - sus—There is room in my heart for Thee!
O come to my heart, Lord Je - sus—There is room in my heart for Thee!
My heart shall re - joice, Lord Je - sus, When Thou com - est and call - est for me!

TEXT: Emily E. S. Elliott
MUSIC: Timothy R. Matthews

MARGARET
Irregular meter

128 It Came upon the Midnight Clear

An angel of the Lord appeared to them, and the glory of the Lord shone around them. Luke 2:9

1. It came up - on the mid-night clear, That glo - rious song of old,
2. Still thru the clo - ven skies they come With peace-ful wings un - furled,
3. And ye, be-neath life's crush-ing load, Whose forms are bend-ing low,
4. For lo, the days are has-t'ning on, By proph-ets seen of old,
From an - gels bend - ing near the earth To touch their harps of gold:
And still their heav'n - ly mu - sic floats O'er all the wea - ry world:
Who toil a - long the climb - ing way With pain - ful steps and slow,
When with the ev - er - cir - cling years Shall come the time fore - told,
"Peace on the earth, good - will to men, From heav'n's all-gra - cious King!"
A - bove its sad and low - ly plains They bend on hov - 'ring wing,
Look now! for glad and gold - en hours Come swift - ly on the wing:
When the new heav'n and earth shall own The Prince of Peace their King,
The world in sol - emn still - ness lay To hear the an - gels sing.
And ev - er o'er its Ba - bel sounds The bless - ed an - gels sing.
O rest be - side the wea - ry road And hear the an - gels sing.
And the whole world send back the song Which now the an - gels sing.

TEXT: Edmund H. Sears
MUSIC: Richard S. Willis

CAROL
C.M.D.

Break Forth, O Beauteous Heavenly Light 129

. . . a Light for revelation to the Gentiles and for glory to Your people. Luke 2:32

1. Break forth, O beau - teous heav'n - ly light, And ush - er in the
2. He comes, a Child, from realms on high, He comes the heav'ns a -
morn - ing; Ye shep - herds, shrink not with af - fright, But
dor - ing; He comes to earth to live and die, A
hear the an - gel's warn - ing. This Child, now weak in in - fan - cy,
bro - ken race re - stor - ing. Al - though the King of kings is He,
Our con - fi - dence and joy shall be. The pow'r of Sa - tan
He comes in deep hu - mil - i - ty; His peo - ple to de -
break - ing, Our peace e - ter - nal mak - ing.
liv - er, And reign in us for - ev - er.

TEXT: Johann Rist, stanza 1; translated by John Troutbeck; Joseph Barlowe, stanza 2
MUSIC: Johann Schop; harmonized by J. S. Bach

ERMUNTRE DICH
8.7.8.7.8.8.7.7.

130

GLORIA IN EXCELSIS DEO

A Brief Service of Proclamation and Praise

Suggested Hymn Stanzas

To facilitate an uninterrupted flow from stanza to stanza,
the suggested stanzas have been marked with an arrow: ►
Angels from the Realms of Glory, stanzas 1, 2
Angels We Have Heard on High, stanzas 1,3
Hark! the Herald Angels Sing, complete

WORSHIP LEADER:
Now there were in the same country shepherds living out in the fields, keeping watch over their flock by night. And behold, an angel of the Lord stood before them, and the glory of the Lord shone around them, and they were greatly afraid. Then the angel said to them, "Do not be afraid, for behold, I bring you good tidings of great joy which will be to all people. For there is born to you this day in the city of David a Savior, who is Christ the Lord. And this will be the sign to you: You will find a Babe wrapped in swaddling cloths, lying in a manger." And suddenly there was with the angel a multitude of the heavenly host praising God and saying:

WORSHIP LEADER and PEOPLE:
"Glory to God in the highest, and on earth peace, good will toward men!"

Luke 2:8-14. (NKJV)

Optional introduction to "Angels, from the Realms of Glory"

"GLORIA IN EXCELSIS DEO—A Brief Service of Proclamation and Praise"

Angels, from the Realms of Glory 131

Bethlehem, . . . out of you will come a Ruler who will be the Shepherd. Matt. 2:6

1. An - gels, from the realms of glo - ry, Wing your flight o'er all the earth;
2. Shep-herds, in the fields a - bid - ing, Watch-ing o'er your flocks by night,
3. Sag - es, leave your con - tem-pla - tions, Bright - er vi - sions beam a - far;
4. Saints be-fore the al - tar bend - ing, Watch-ing long in hope and fear,

Ye who sang cre - a - tion's sto - ry, Now pro-claim Mes - si - ah's birth:
God with man is now re - sid - ing, Yon - der shines the in - fant Light:
Seek the great De - sire of na - tions, Ye have seen His na - tal star:
Sud - den - ly the Lord, de - scend-ing, In His tem - ple shall ap - pear:

Come and wor-ship, come and wor-ship, Wor - ship Christ, the new - born King.

TEXT: James Montgomery
MUSIC: Henry T. Smart
A lower setting may be found at No. 241

REGENT SQUARE
8.7.8.7.8.7.

132 Angels We Have Heard on High

The heavenly host appeared with the angel, praising God. Luke 2:13

1. Angels we have heard on high, Sweetly singing o'er the plains,
2. Shepherds, why this jubilee? Why your joyous strains prolong?
3. Come to Bethlehem, and see Him whose birth the angels sing;
4. See within a manger laid Jesus, Lord of heav'n and earth!
And the mountains in reply Echo back their joyous strains.
Say what may the tidings be, Which inspire your heav'nly song?
Come, adore on bended knee Christ the Lord, the newborn King.
Mary, Joseph, lend your aid, With us sing our Savior's birth.
Refrain
Glo - - - ria in excelsis Deo,
Glo - - - ria in excelsis De - o.
Segue to "Hark! the Herald Angels Sing"

TEXT: Traditional French carol
MUSIC: Traditional French melody

GLORIA
7.7.7.7. with Refrain

Hark! the Herald Angels Sing 133

Glory to God in the highest, and on earth peace. Luke 2:14

1. Hark! the her - ald an - gels sing, "Glo - ry to the new - born King;
2. Christ, by high - est heav'n a - dored; Christ, the ev - er - last - ing Lord!
3. Hail the heav'n-born Prince of Peace! Hail the Sun of Right-eous-ness!
Peace on earth, and mer - cy mild, God and sin - ners rec - on-ciled!"
Late in time be - hold Him come, Off - spring of the Vir-gin's womb:
Light and life to all He brings, Ris'n with heal - ing in His wings.
Joy - ful, all ye na - tions, rise, Join the tri - umph of the skies;
Veiled in flesh the God - head see; Hail th'in - car - nate De - i - ty,
Mild He lays His glo - ry by, Born that man no more may die,
With th'an - gel - ic host pro - claim, "Christ is born in Beth - le - hem!"
Pleased as man with men to dwell, Je - sus, our Em - man - u - el.
Born to raise the sons of earth, Born to give them sec - ond birth.
Hark! the her - ald an - gels sing, "Glo - ry to the new - born King."

Optional choral ending on the next page

TEXT: Charles Wesley, altered
MUSIC: Felix Mendelssohn; arranged by William H. Cummings

MENDELSSOHN
7.7.7.7.D. with Refrain

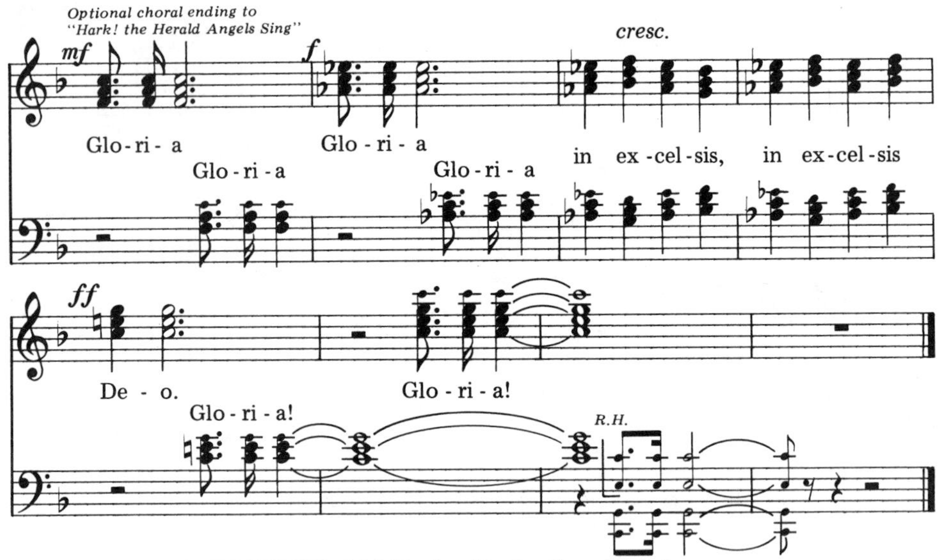
Optional choral ending to
"Hark! the Herald Angels Sing"
mf
f
cresc.
Glo-ri- a
Glo-ri- a
Glo-ri- a
Glo-ri- a
in ex-cel-sis, in ex-cel-sis
ff
De - o.
Glo-ri-a!
Glo-ri-a!
R.H.

The end of "GLORIA IN EXCELSIS DEO—A Brief Service of Proclamation and Praise"

134 Emmanuel

They will call Him Immanuel—which means, "God with us." Matt. 1:23

Unison

Em-man-u - el, Em - man-u - el,

His name is called Em-man-u - el;

God with us, re - vealed in us;

TEXT and MUSIC: Bob McGee

EMMANUEL
Irregular meter

His name is called Em - man - u - el.

While Shepherds Watched Their Flocks 135

Today in the town of David a Savior has been born to you. Luke 2:11

1. While shepherds watched their flocks by night,
All seated on the ground,
The angel of the Lord came down,
And glory shone around,
And glory shone around.

2. "Fear not!" said he; for mighty dread
Had seized their troubled mind,
"Glad tidings of great joy I bring
To you and all mankind,
To you and all mankind.

3. "To you, in David's town this day,
Is born of David's line,
The Savior who is Christ the Lord,
And this shall be the sign:
And this shall be the sign:

4. "The heav'nly Babe you there shall find
To human view displayed,
All meanly wrapped in swathing bands,
And in a manger laid;
And in a manger laid.

5. "All glory be to God on high,
And to the earth be peace:
Good will henceforth from heav'n to men,
Begin and never cease,
Begin and never cease."

TEXT: Nahum Tate
MUSIC: George Frederick Handel; from Weyman's, *Melodia Sacra,* 1815

CHRISTMAS
C.M. with Repeats

136 The First Noel

There were shepherds . . . in the fields . . . keeping watch over their flocks. Luke 2:8

1. The first No-el, the an-gel did say, Was to cer-tain poor shep-herds in fields as they lay; In fields where they lay keep-ing their sheep, On a cold win-ter's night that was so deep.
2. They look-ed up and saw a star Shin-ing in the east, be-yond them far, And to the earth it gave great light, And so it con-tin-ued both day and night.
3. And by the light of that same star Three wise men came from coun-try far; To seek for a king was their in-tent, And to fol-low the star wher-ev-er it went.
4. This star drew nigh to the north-west, O'er Beth-le-hem it took its rest, And there it did both stop and stay, Right o-ver the place where Je-sus lay.
5. Then en-tered in those wise men three, Full rev-'rent-ly up-on their knee, And of-fered there in His pres-ence Their gold, and myrrh, and frank-in-cense.
6. Then let us all with one ac-cord Sing prais-es to our heav'n-ly Lord, That hath made heav'n and earth of naught, And with His blood man-kind hath bought.
Refrain
No-el, No-el, No-el, No-el, Born is the King of Is-ra-el.

TEXT: Traditional English carol
MUSIC: W. Sandys' *Christmas Carols,* 1833; arranged by John Stainer

THE FIRST NOEL
Irregular meter

What Child Is This? 137

They spread the word concerning what had been told them about this Child. Luke 2:17

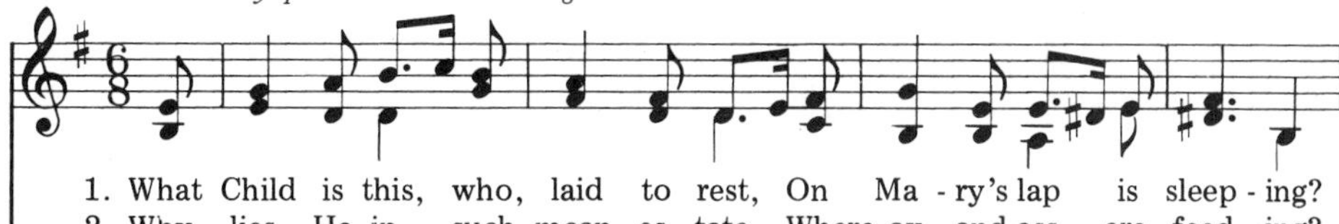

1. What Child is this, who, laid to rest, On Ma - ry's lap is sleep - ing?
2. Why lies He in such mean es - tate Where ox and ass are feed - ing?
3. So bring Him in - cense, gold and myrrh, Come, peas-ant, king, to own Him;

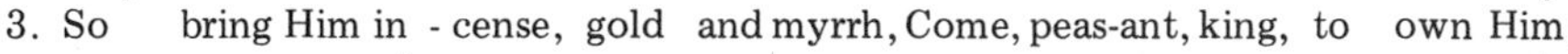

Whom an - gels greet with an - thems sweet, While shep-herds watch are keep-ing?
Good Chris-tian, fear; for sin - ners here The si - lent Word is plead-ing.
The King of kings sal - va - tion brings, Let lov - ing hearts en-throne Him.

Refrain

This, this is Christ the King, Whom shep - herds guard and an - gels sing:

Haste, haste to bring Him laud, The Babe, the Son of Ma - ry.

TEXT: William C. Dix
MUSIC: Traditional English melody, 16th century

GREENSLEEVES
8.7.8.7. with Refrain

138 Go, Tell It on the Mountain

Let them shout from the mountaintops. Let them give glory to the Lord. Isa. 42:11-12

Unison
Refrain: Go tell it on the moun - tain, O-ver the hills and ev - 'ry - where;
Go tell it on the moun - tain That Je - sus Christ is born.
Fine
1. While shep-herds kept their watch-ing O'er si - lent flocks by night, Be -
2. The shep-herds feared and trem-bled When, lo! a - bove the earth Rang
3. Down in a low - ly man - ger The hum-ble Christ was born And
hold, through-out the heav-ens There shone a ho - ly light.
out the an - gel cho - rus That hailed our Sav - ior's birth.
God sent us sal - va - tion That bless - ed Christ-mas morn.
D.C.

TEXT: Traditional Spiritual, stanzas written by John W. Work II
MUSIC: Traditional Spiritual; arranged by Bill Wolaver

GO TELL IT
Irregular meter

I Wonder as I Wander 139

All who heard it were amazed at what the shepherds said to them. Luke 2:18

Unison
1. I wonder as I wander, out under the sky, How
2. When Mary birthed Jesus, 'twas in a cow's stall, With
3. If Jesus had wanted for any wee thing, A
4. I wonder as I wander, out under the sky, How
Jesus the Savior did come for to die For
wise men and farmers and shepherds and all. But
star in the sky or a bird on the wing, Or
Jesus the Savior did come for to die For
poor, orn'ry people like you and like I; I
high from God's heaven a star's light did fall, The
all of God's angels in heav'n for to sing, He
poor, orn'ry people like you and like I; I
wonder as I wander, out under the sky.
promise of ages it then did recall.
surely could have it, 'cause He was the King.
wonder as I wander, out under the sky.
Optional Coda
Out under the sky.

TEXT: Appalachian carol; adapted by John Jacob Niles
MUSIC: John Jacob Niles; arranged by Donald P. Hustad

I WONDER AS I WANDER
Irregular meter

140 A Communion Hymn for Christmas

Proclaim the Lord's death until He comes. I Cor. 11:26

Unison
1. Gath-ered round Your ta - ble on this ho - ly eve,
2. Prince of Glo - ry, gra - cing Heav'n ere time be - gan,
3. Beth-lehem's In - car - na - tion, Cal - vary's bit - ter cross,
4. With pro-found - est won - der we Your bo - dy take—
5. Christ-mas Babe so ten - der, Lamb who bore our blame,
View - ing Beth - lehem's sta - ble we re - joice and grieve;
Now for us em - brac - ing death as Son of Man;
Wrought for us sal - va - tion by Your pain and loss;
Laid in man - ger yon - der, bro - ken for our sake;
How shall sin - ners ren - der prais - es due Your name?
Joy to see You ly - ing in Your man - ger bed,
By Your birth so low - ly, by Your love so true,
Now we fall be - fore You in this ho - ly place,
Hushed in ad - o - ra - tion we ap - proach the cup—
Do Your own good plea - sure in the lives we bring;
Weep to see You dy - ing in our sin - ful stead.
By Your cross most ho - ly, Lord, we wor-ship You!
Pros-trate we a - dore You, for Your gift of grace.
Beth-lehem's pure ob - la - tion free-ly of - fered up.
In Your ran - somed trea - sure reign for-ev - er King! A - men.

TEXT: Margaret Clarkson
MUSIC: Tom Fettke

GREENRIDGE
11.11.11.11.

O Little Town of Bethlehem 141

Bethlehem . . . , out of you will come for Me One who will be ruler over Israel. Mic. 5:2

1. O lit - tle town of Beth - le - hem, How still we see thee lie!
2. For Christ is born of Ma - ry, And gath-ered all a - bove,
3. How si - lent - ly, how si - lent - ly The won-drous gift is giv'n!
4. O ho - ly Child of Beth - le - hem! De - scend to us, we pray;
A - bove thy deep and dream-less sleep The si - lent stars go by.
While mor - tals sleep, the an - gels keep Their watch of won-d'ring love.
So God im - parts to hu - man hearts The bless - ings of His heav'n.
Cast out our sin, and en - ter in; Be born in us to - day.
Yet in thy dark streets shin - eth The ev - er - last - ing Light;
O morn - ing stars, to - geth - er Pro - claim the ho - ly birth!
No ear may hear His com - ing, But in this world of sin,
We hear the Christ - mas an - gels The great glad ti - dings tell;
The hopes and fears of all the years Are met in thee to - night.
And prais - es sing to God the King, And peace to men on earth.
Where meek souls will re - ceive Him still The dear Christ en - ters in.
O come to us, a - bide with us, Our Lord Em - man - u - el. A - men.

TEXT: Phillips Brooks
MUSIC: Lewis H. Redner

ST. LOUIS
8.6.8.6.7.6.8.6.

142

FOR UNTO US A CHILD IS BORN

A Brief Service in Celebration of Our Lord's Birth

Suggested Hymn Stanzas

To facilitate an uninterrupted flow from stanza to stanza, the suggested stanzas have been marked with an arrow: ►

Infant Holy, Infant Lowly, complete
How Great Our Joy!, stanzas 1, 2
O Come, All Ye Faithful, stanzas 1, 2
For Unto Us a Child Is Born, complete

WORSHIP LEADER:
Now the birth of Jesus Christ was as follows. When His mother Mary had been betrothed to Joseph, before they came together she was found to be with child by the Holy Spirit. And Joseph her husband, being a righteous man, and not wanting to disgrace her, desired to put her away secretly. But when he had considered this, behold, an angel of the Lord appeared to him in a dream, saying, "Joseph, son of David, do not be afraid to take Mary as your wife; for that which has been conceived in her is of the Holy Spirit. And she will bear a Son; and you shall call His name Jesus, for it is He who will save His people from their sins." Now all this took place that what was spoken by the Lord through the prophet might be fulfilled, saying, "Behold, the virgin shall be with child, and shall bear a Son, and they shall call His name Immanuel," which translated means,

WORSHIP LEADER and PEOPLE:
"God with us."

Matthew 1:18-23. (NASB)

"FOR UNTO US A CHILD IS BORN—A Brief Service in Celebration of Our Lord's Birth"

Infant Holy, Infant Lowly 143

He has this name written: KING OF KINGS AND LORD OF LORDS. Rev. 19:16

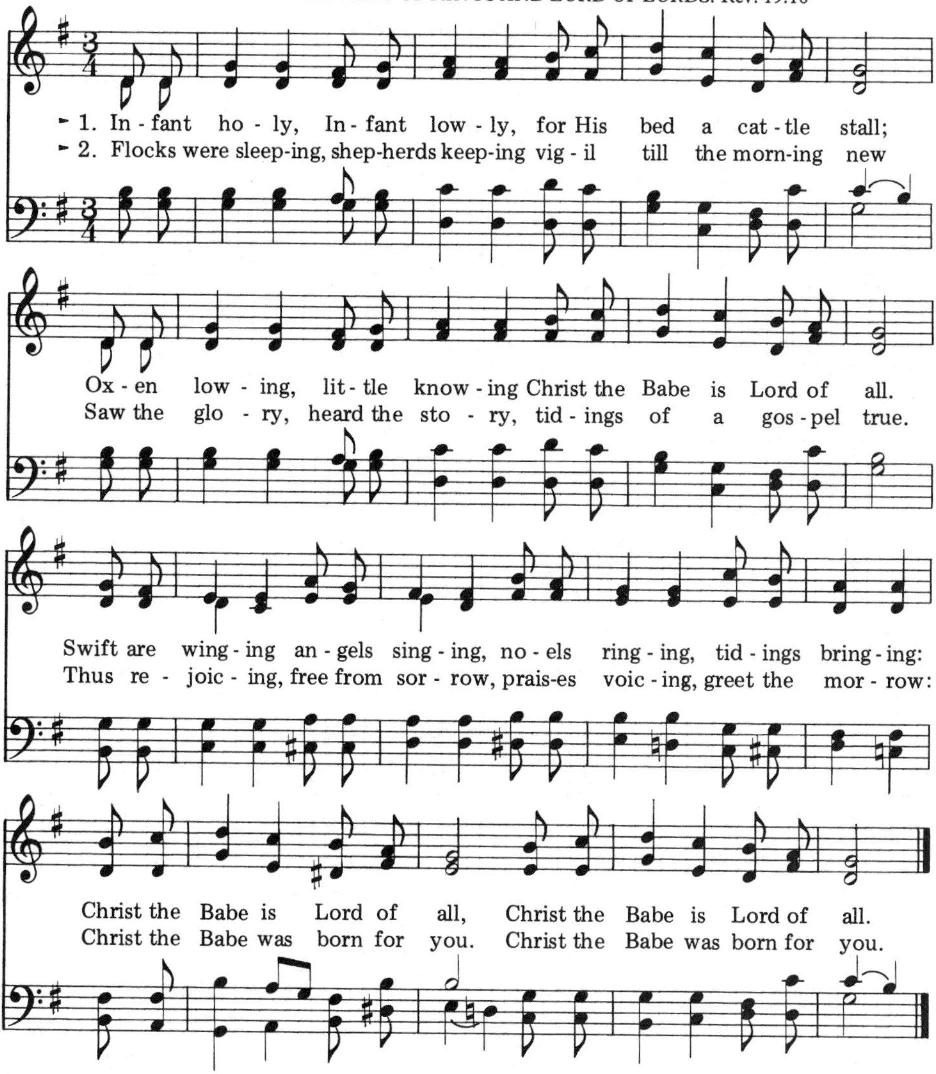

1. Infant holy, Infant lowly, for His bed a cattle stall;
Oxen lowing, little knowing Christ the Babe is Lord of all.
Swift are winging angels singing, noels ringing, tidings bringing:
Christ the Babe is Lord of all, Christ the Babe is Lord of all.

2. Flocks were sleeping, shepherds keeping vigil till the morning new
Saw the glory, heard the story, tidings of a gospel true.
Thus rejoicing, free from sorrow, praises voicing, greet the morrow:
Christ the Babe was born for you. Christ the Babe was born for you.

TEXT: Polish carol; paraphrase by Edith E. M. Reed
MUSIC: Traditional Polish carol; arranged by Joseph Barlowe

W ZLOBIE LEZY
8.7.8.7.8.8.7.7.

Optional transition to "How Great Our Joy"

144 How Great Our Joy!

I bring you good news of great joy. Luke 2:10

1. While by the sheep we watched at night, Glad tid-ings brought an an-gel bright.
2. There shall be born, so he did say, In Beth-le-hem a Child to-day.
3. There shall the Child lie in a stall, This Child who shall re-deem us all.
4. This gift of God we'll cher-ish well, That ev-er joy our hearts shall fill.

f How great our joy! *p echo* Great our joy!
f Joy, joy, joy, *p echo* Joy, joy, joy!
f Praise we the Lord in heav'n on high! *p echo* Praise we the Lord in heav'n on high!

TEXT: Traditional German carol
MUSIC: Traditional German melody; arranged by Hugo Jüngst

JÜNGST
Irregular meter

Optional transition to "O Come, All Ye Faithful"

O Come, All Ye Faithful 145

Let's go to Bethlehem and see this thing that has happened. Luke 2:15

1. O come, all ye faith - ful, joy - ful and tri - um - phant, O come ye, O come ye to Beth - le - hem! Come and be - hold Him, born the King of an - gels!
2. Sing choirs of an - gels, sing in ex - ul - ta - tion, O sing, all ye bright hosts of heav'n a - bove! Glo - ry to God, all glo - ry in the high - est!
3. Yea, Lord, we greet Thee, born this hap - py morn - ing, Je - sus, to Thee be all glo - ry giv'n; Word of the Fa - ther, now in flesh ap - pear - ing!
Refrain
O come, let us a - dore Him, O come, let us a - dore Him, O come, let us a - dore Him, Christ the Lord! Lord!
(slight rit. last time)
Optional transition to "For Unto Us"

TEXT: Latin Hymn; ascribed to John Francis Wade; translated by Frederick Oakeley
MUSIC: John Francis Wade

ADESTE FIDELES
Irregular meter

146 For Unto Us a Child Is Born

For to us a Child is born, to us a Son is given. Isa. 9:6

*Optional choral ending
f Unison
**For un-to us a Child is born, un-to us a Son is
Parts
S.A.
T.B.
giv-en, un-to us a Son is giv-en: and His
ff
name shall be call-ed Won-der-ful, Coun-se-lor,
The Might-y God, The Ev-er-last-ing Fa-ther, The Prince of Peace, The

*Congregation may join if desired.
**Harmonies and vocal parts conform to Handel's original score.

TEXT and MUSIC: George Frederick Handel; based on Isaiah 9:6, 7; arranged by Tom Fettke

FOR UNTO US
Irregular meter

Ev-er-last-ing Fa-ther, The Prince of Peace.

The end of "FOR UNTO US A CHILD IS BORN - A Brief Service in Celebration of Our Lord's Birth"

Silent Night! Holy Night! 147

They . . . found Mary and Joseph, and the Baby. Luke 2:16

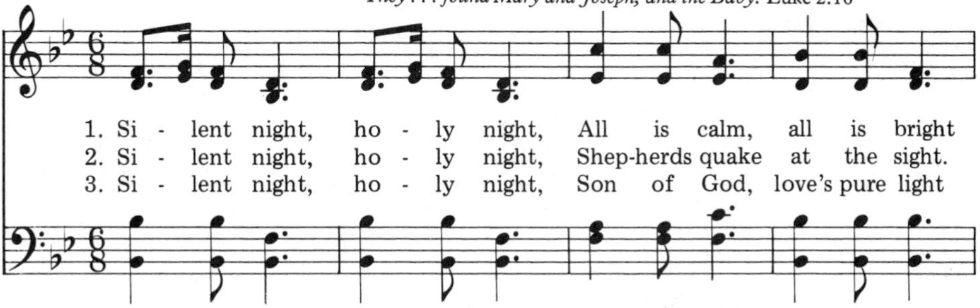

1. Si - lent night, ho - ly night, All is calm, all is bright
2. Si - lent night, ho - ly night, Shep-herds quake at the sight.
3. Si - lent night, ho - ly night, Son of God, love's pure light

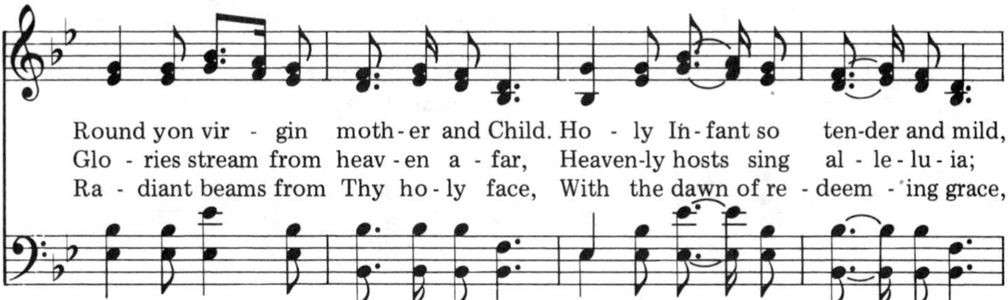

Round yon vir - gin moth-er and Child. Ho - ly In-fant so ten-der and mild,
Glo - ries stream from heav - en a - far, Heaven-ly hosts sing al - le - lu - ia;
Ra - diant beams from Thy ho - ly face, With the dawn of re - deem - ing grace,

Sleep in heav-en - ly peace, Sleep in heav - en - ly peace.
Christ the Sav - ior is born! Christ the Sav - ior is born!
Je - sus, Lord, at Thy birth, Je - sus, Lord, at Thy birth.

TEXT: Joseph Mohr; translated by John F. Young
MUSIC: Franz Grüber

STILLE NACHT
Irregular meter

148 O Holy Night!

The Holy One to be born will be called the Son of God. Luke 1:35

Introduction (use arpeggiated chords in a triplet feeling throughout)

1. O ho - ly night! the stars are bright-ly
2. Led by the light of faith se - rene - ly
3. Tru - ly He taught us to love one an -

use accompaniment figure from 1st 2 bars

shin - ing, It is the night of the dear Sav - ior's birth; Long lay the
beam-ing, With glow-ing hearts by His cra - dle we stand; So led by
oth - er; His law is love and His gos - pel is peace; Chains shall He

world in sin and er - ror pin - ing, Till He ap-peared and the soul felt its
light of a star sweet-ly gleam-ing, Here came the wise men from O - ri - ent
break, for the slave is our broth - er, And in His name all op-pres - sion shall

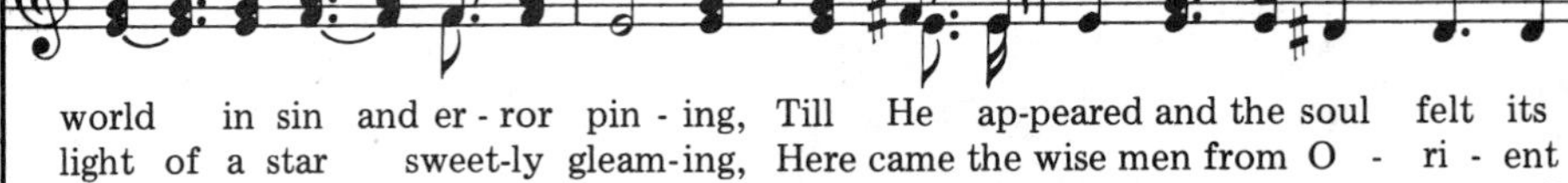

worth. A thrill of hope the wea - ry world re-joic - es, For yon-der breaks a
land. The King of kings lay thus in low - ly man - ger, In all our tri - als
cease. Sweet hymns of joy in grate-ful chor-us raise we, Let all with - in us

TEXT: John S. Dwight
MUSIC: Adolphe Adam

CANTIQUE DE NOËL
11.10.11.10.11.10.11.10.10.

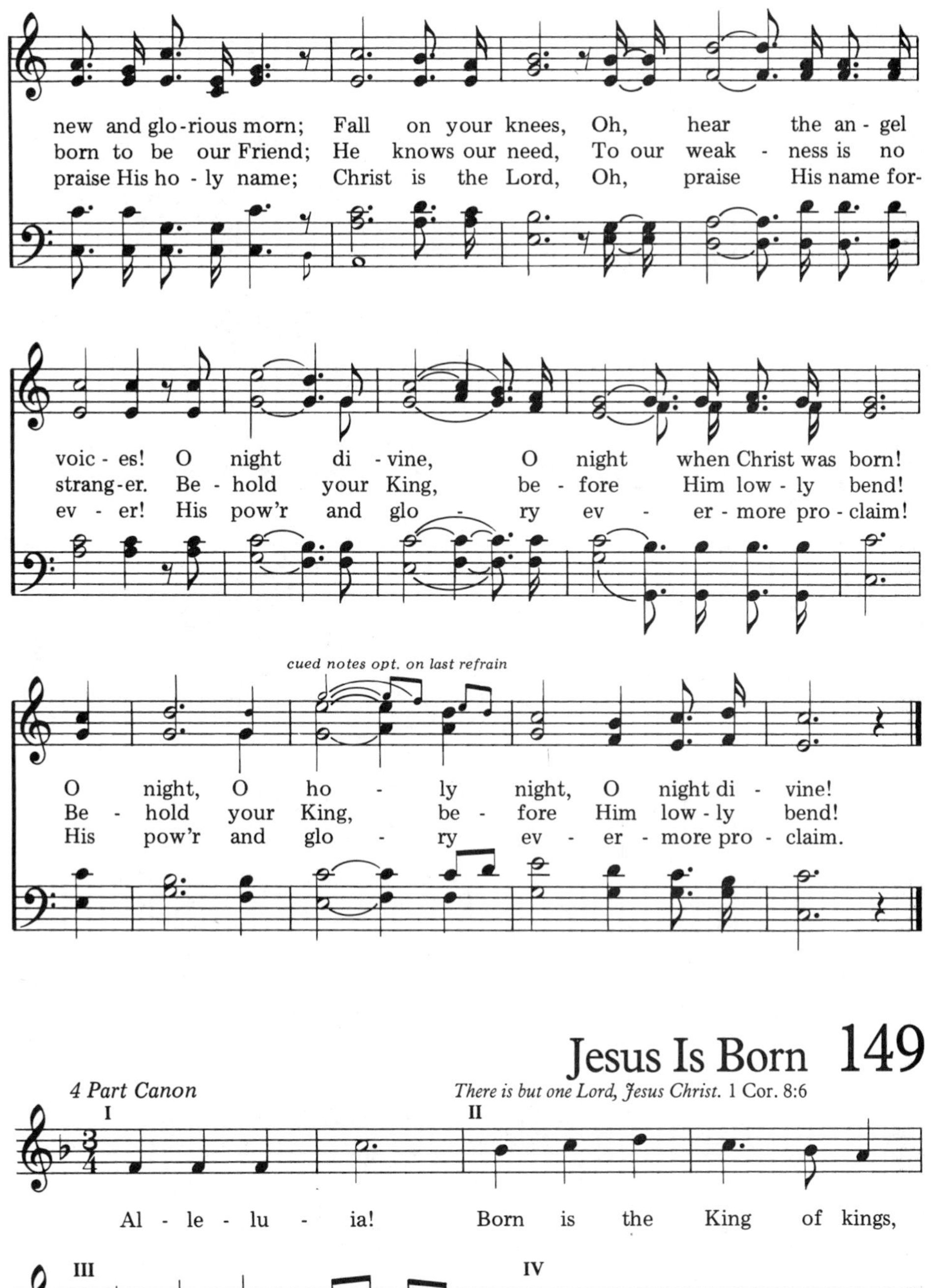
new and glo-rious morn; Fall on your knees, Oh, hear the an-gel
born to be our Friend; He knows our need, To our weak - ness is no
praise His ho - ly name; Christ is the Lord, Oh, praise His name for-
voic - es! O night di - vine, O night when Christ was born!
strang-er. Be - hold your King, be - fore Him low - ly bend!
ev - er! His pow'r and glo - ry ev - er - more pro - claim!
cued notes opt. on last refrain
O night, O ho - ly night, O night di - vine!
Be - hold your King, be - fore Him low - ly bend!
His pow'r and glo - ry ev - er - more pro - claim.
4 Part Canon
I
II
III
IV
Al - le - lu - ia! Born is the King of kings,
Born is the Lord of lords. Je - sus is born!

Jesus Is Born 149

There is but one Lord, Jesus Christ. 1 Cor. 8:6

TEXT and MUSIC: Gerald S. Henderson

NATIVITY CANON
4.6.6.4.

150 O Hearken Ye

My soul glorifies the Lord. Luke 1:46

1. O hearken ye who would believe, The gracious tidings
2. O hearken ye who long for peace, Your troubled searching
3. O hearken ye who long for love, And turn your hearts to
now receive: The
now may cease. Gloria, gloria, In excelsis Deo. For
God above. The
mighty Lord of heav'n and earth, Today is come to human birth.
at this cradle you shall find God's healing grace for all mankind.
angel's song the wonder tells: Now Love Incarnate with us dwells!
Gloria, gloria, In excelsis Deo.

TEXT: Wihla Hutson
MUSIC: Alfred Burt

O HEARKEN YE
8.8.6.6.D.

Good Christian Men, Rejoice 151

My spirit rejoices in God my Savior. Luke 1:47

1. Good Chris - tian men, re - joice With heart and soul and voice;
2. Good Chris - tian men, re - joice With heart and soul and voice;
3. Good Chris - tian men, re - joice With heart and soul and voice;
Give ye heed to what we say: News! news! Je - sus Christ is born to - day!
Now ye hear of end - less bliss: Joy! joy! Je - sus Christ was born for this!
Now ye need not fear the grave: Peace! peace! Je - sus Christ was born to save!
Ox and ass be - fore Him bow, And He is in the man - ger now:
He has o - pened heav - en's door, And man is bless - ed ev - er - more:
Calls you one and calls you all To gain His ev - er - last - ing hall:
Christ is born to - day! Christ is born to - day!
Christ was born for this! Christ was born for this!
Christ was born to save! Christ was born to save!

TEXT: Latin carol, 14th century; translated by John M. Neale
MUSIC: German melody, 14th century; harmonized by John Stainer

IN DULCI JUBILO
Irregular meter

152 I Heard the Bells on Christmas Day

He will be their peace. Mic. 5:5

1. I heard the bells on Christ - mas day Their old fa - mil - iar car - ols play, And wild and sweet the words re - peat Of peace on earth, good will to men.
2. I thought how, as the day had come, The bel - fries of all Chris - ten - dom Had rolled a - long th'un - bro - ken song Of peace on earth, good will to men.
3. And in de - spair I bowed my head: "There is no peace on earth," I said, "For hate is strong, and mocks the song Of peace on earth, good will to men."
4. Yet pealed the bells more loud and deep: "God is not dead, nor doth He sleep; The wrong shall fail, the right pre - vail, With peace on earth, good will to men."
5. Then ring - ing, sing - ing on its way, The world re-volved from night to day— A voice, a chime, a chant sub - lime Of peace on earth, good will to men! will to men!

Optional transition to "Come On, Ring Those Bells"

faster

TEXT: Henry W. Longfellow
MUSIC: Jean Baptiste Calkin

WALTHAM
L.M.

153 Come On, Ring Those Bells

Your King comes to you. Zech. 9:9

Unison
Come on, ring those bells, light the Christ-mas tree, Je- sus is the King

TEXT and MUSIC: Andrew Culverwell

RING THOSE BELLS
Irregular meter

born for you and me. Come on, ring those bells, ev - 'ry-bod - y
1
2
say, "Je-sus, we remember this Your birth - day." birth - day."

What Can I Give Him? 154

They gave themselves first to the Lord. 2 Cor. 8:5

What can I give Him, poor as I am? If I were a shep - herd I would bring a lamb; If I were a wise-man I would do my part; Yet what can I give Him? Give Him my heart.

TEXT: Christina Rossetti
MUSIC: Don Cason

CASTLE
9.11.11.10.

155 Once in Royal David's City

He will reign on David's throne. Isa. 9:7

1. Once in roy - al Da - vid's cit - y Stood a low - ly cat - tle
2. He came down to earth from heav - en Who is God and Lord of
3. Je - sus is our child-hood's pat - tern, Day by day like us He
4. And our eyes at last shall see Him Thro' His own re - deem - ing
shed, Where a moth - er laid her Ba - by In a
all, And His shel - ter was a sta - ble, And His
grew; He was lit - tle, weak, and help - less, Tears and
love; For that Child so dear and gen - tle Is our
man - ger for His bed: Ma - ry was that moth - er
cra - dle was a stall: With the poor, and mean, and
smiles like us He knew: And He feel - eth for our
Lord in heav'n a - bove, And He leads His chil - dren
mild, Je - sus Christ her lit - tle Child.
low - ly Lived on earth, our Sav - ior ho - ly.
sad - ness, And He shar - eth in our glad - ness.
on To the place where He is gone.

TEXT: Cecil F. Alexander
MUSIC: Henry J. Gauntlett

IRBY
8.7.8.7.7.7.

Child of Love 156

. . . the good news of peace through Jesus Christ, who is Lord of all. Acts 10:36

Descant - sing on repeat
Glo - - - - - ri - a in ex - cel - sis De - o!
King of ev - 'ry heart.
Unison
Je - sus, Je - sus, bless - ed Lord Thou art.
All men shall praise You, King of ev - 'ry heart.
King of ev - 'ry heart.
1
2

TEXT and MUSIC: Tina English
DESCANT: Traditional French melody

CHILD OF LOVE
Irregular meter

157 Away in a Manger

She gave birth to her firstborn, a Son . . . and placed Him in a manger. Luke 2:7

1. A - way in a man - ger, no crib for a bed, The lit - tle Lord
2. The cat - tle are low - ing, the Ba - by a - wakes, But lit - tle Lord
3. Be near me, Lord Je - sus, I ask Thee to stay Close by me for -

Je - sus laid down His sweet head; The stars in the sky looked
Je - sus no cry - ing He makes, I love Thee, Lord Je - sus, look
ev - er, and love me, I pray. Bless all the dear chil - dren in

down where He lay, The lit - tle Lord Je - sus, a - sleep on the hay.
down from the sky, And stay by my cra - dle till morn - ing is nigh.
Thy ten - der care, And fit us for heav - en, to live with Thee there.

TEXT: Source unknown, stanzas 1, 2; John Thomas McFarland, stanza 3
MUSIC: James R. Murray

AWAY IN A MANGER
11.11.11.11.

158 Away in a Manger

She gave birth to her firstborn, a Son . . . and placed Him in a manger. Luke 2:7

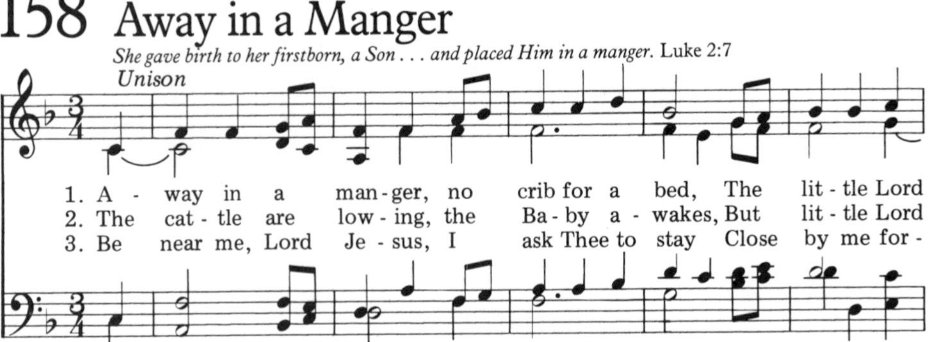
Unison
1. A - way in a man - ger, no crib for a bed, The lit - tle Lord
2. The cat - tle are low - ing, the Ba - by a - wakes, But lit - tle Lord
3. Be near me, Lord Je - sus, I ask Thee to stay Close by me for -

TEXT: Source unknown, stanzas 1, 2; John Thomas McFarland, stanza 3
MUSIC: William J. Kirkpatrick

CRADLE SONG
11.11.11.11.

Je - sus laid down His sweet head; The stars in the bright sky looked down where He lay, The lit - tle Lord Je - sus a - sleep on the hay.
Je - sus, no cry - ing He makes. I love Thee, Lord Je - sus, look down from the sky, And stay by my cra - dle till morn-ing is nigh.
ev - er, and love me, I pray. Bless all the dear chil - dren in Thy ten - der care, And fit us for heav - en, to live with Thee there.
A Thousand Candles 159
I have come into the world as a light. John 12:46
1. We light a thou - sand can - dles bright a - round the earth to - day, And all the beams will shine a - cross the heav-en's grand dis - play.
2. Yes o - ver land and sea to - night the joy - ful mes - sage brings The birth of Him, our Lord and Christ, our Sav - ior and our King.
3. Dear bright-est star o'er Beth - le - hem, O let your pre - cious light Shine in with hope and peace toward men in ev - 'ry home to - night.
4. In all our house so cold and dark please send your warmth sub - lime, The warmth that comes from Je - sus' love this bless-ed Christ-mas time.

TEXT: Swedish carol; translated by Evie Karlsson
MUSIC: Emmy Kohler; arranged by Eugene Thomas

THOUSAND CANDLES
8.7.8.6.

160 Lo! How a Rose E'er Blooming

A shoot will come up from the stump of Jesse. Isa. 11:1

1. Lo, how a Rose e'er bloom - ing From ten - der stem hath sprung!
2. I - sa - iah 'twas fore - told it, The Rose I have in mind;
3. This Flower, whose fra-grance ten - der With sweet-ness fills the air,
Of Jes - se's lin - eage com - ing As men of old have sung.
With Mar - y we be - hold it, The vir - gin moth - er kind.
Dis - pels with glo - rious splen - dor The dark-ness ev - ery - where.
It came, a Flow - er bright, A - mid the cold of
To show God's love a - right She bore to men a
True man, yet ver - y God, From sin and death He
win - ter, When half - gone was the night.
Sav - ior, When half - gone was the night.
saves us And light - ens ev - ery load.

TEXT: German carol, 16th century; translated by Theodore Baker, stanzas 1, 2 and Harriet Krauth Spaeth, stanza 3
MUSIC: *Geistliche Kirchengesäng,* Cologne, 1599; harmonized by Michael Praetorius

ES IST EIN' ROS'
7.6.7.6.6.7.6.

Our Day of Joy Is Here Again 161

The shepherds returned, glorifying and praising God. Luke 2:20

1. Our day of joy is here a-gain, With love and peace and song;
2. When dark-ness lay up-on this earth, A glo-rious light did shine;
3. Now to the man-ger let us go To wor-ship and a-dore
4. How won-der-ful that God's own Son Should so Him-self a-base!
Come, let us join th'an-gel-ic strain With voic-es clear and strong.
God sent a Gift of price-less worth And showed His love di-vine.
The ten-der Babe up-on the straw, Our Sav-ior ev-er-more.
He thrust the might-y from their throne, And gave the low-ly grace.
Refrain
Glo-ry to our God, we sing, Glo-ry to our Lord and King;
Peace, good-will with all a-bide This ho-ly Christ-mas tide.

TEXT and MUSIC: Andrew L. Skoog

NU GLÄDJENS TIMME
C.M. with Refrain

162 The Birthday of a King

I will raise up to David a righteous Branch, a King who will reign wisely. Jer. 23:5

Unison
1. In the lit - tle vil-lage of Beth - le-hem, there lay a Child one
2. 'Twas a hum-ble birth-place, but oh, how much God gave to us that
day, And the sky was bright with a ho - ly light o'er the
day, From the man - ger bed what a path has led, what a
place where Je - sus lay.
per - fect ho - ly way.
Refrain - Parts optional
Al - le - lu - ia! O how the
an - gels sang. Al - le - lu - ia! How it rang! And the
sky was bright with a ho - ly light, 'twas the birth-day of a King.

TEXT and MUSIC: William Harold Neidlinger; arranged by Robert F. Douglas

NEIDLINGER
10.6.10.7. with Refrain

As with Gladness Men of Old 163

When they saw the star, they were overjoyed . . . and they worshiped Him. Matt. 2:10-11

1. As with glad - ness men of old Did the guid - ing
2. As with joy - ful steps they sped To that low - ly
3. As they of - fered gifts most rare At that man - ger
4. Ho - ly Je - sus, ev - ery day Keep us in the
star be - hold; As with joy they hailed its light,
man - ger bed, There to bend the knee be - fore
rude and bare, So may we with ho - ly joy,
nar - row way; And when earth - ly things are past,
Lead - ing on - ward, beam - ing bright, So, most gra - cious
Him Whom heav'n and earth a - dore, So, may we with
Pure and free from sin's al - loy, All our cost - liest
Bring our ran - somed souls at last Where they need no
Lord, may we Ev - er - more be led to Thee.
will - ing feet Ev - er seek the mer - cy seat.
treas - ures bring, Christ, to Thee our heav'n-ly King.
star to guide, Where no clouds Thy glo - ry hide. A - men.

TEXT: William C. Dix
MUSIC: Conrad Kocher

DIX
7.7.7.7.7.7.

164 One Small Child

She gave birth to a Son, a male Child, who will rule all the nations. Rev. 12:5

Unison
1. One small Child in a land of a thou - sand, One small dream of a
2. One king bring - ing his gold and rich - es, One King rul - ing an
3. One small light from the flame of a can - dle, One small light from a
4. One small Child in a land of a thou - sand, One small dream in a
Sav - ior to - night, One small hand reach-ing out to the star - light,
ar - my of might, One king kneel - ing with in - cense and can-dle light,
cit - y of might, One small light from the stars in the end-less night,
peo - ple of might, One small hand reach-ing out to the star - light,
One small cit - y of life. Oh
One King bring - ing us life. Oh
One small light from a face. Oh
One small Sav - ior of life. Oh
1, 4
Fine
2, 3
2. See Him ly - ing, a cra-dle be-neath Him, See Him smil-ing in the
3. See the shep-herds kneel-ing be-fore Him, See the kings on bend - ed

TEXT and MUSIC: David Meece

ONE SMALL CHILD
Irregular meter

D.S. al Fine
stall. See His moth-er prais-ing His Fa-ther, See His tin - y eye - lids fall.
knee. See His moth-er prais-ing His Fa-ther, See the Bless-ed In - fant sleep.
Adoration 165
Worship the Lord in the splendor of His holiness. Ps. 96:9
1. Wor - ship the Lord in the beau - ty of ho - li - ness! Bow down be - fore Him, His glo - ry pro - claim; With gold of o - be - dience and in - cense of low - li - ness, kneel and a - dore Him: the Lord is His name!
2. Fear not to en - ter His pres - ence in pov - er - ty, Bear - ing no gifts to pre - sent as your own. Bring truth in its beau - ty and love in its pur - i - ty— these are the off - 'rings to lay at His throne. A - men.

TEXT: John S. B. Monsell, stanza 1; David Steele, stanza 2
MUSIC: Tom Fettke

JANICE
12.10.13.10.

166 We Three Kings

After Jesus was born in Bethlehem . . . Magi from the east came. Matt. 2:1

1. We three kings of O - ri - ent are: Bear - ing gifts we trav - erse a - far—
2. Born a King on Beth-le-hem's plain: Gold I bring to crown Him a-gain,
3. Frank-in - cense to of - fer have I: In - cense owns a De - i - ty nigh;
4. Myrrh is mine: its bit - ter per - fume Breathes a life of gath - er - ing gloom—
5. Glo - rious now be - hold Him a - rise: King and God and Sac - ri - fice;
Field and foun - tain, moor and moun-tain— Fol - low - ing yon - der star.
King for - ev - er, ceas - ing nev - er O - ver us all to reign.
Prayer and prais - ing, all men rais - ing, Wor-ship Him, God on high.
Sor - r'wing, sigh - ing, bleed - ing, dy - ing, Sealed in the stone-cold tomb.
Al - le - lu - ia, Al - le - lu - ia! Earth to heav'n re - plies.
Refrain
O star of won - der, star of night, Star with roy - al beau - ty bright,
West-ward lead - ing, still pro-ceed - ing, Guide us to thy per - fect light.

TEXT and MUSIC: John H. Hopkins, Jr.

KINGS OF ORIENT
8.8.4.4.6. with Refrain

O Sing a Song of Bethlehem 167

He appeared . . . was vindicated . . . was believed on . . . was taken up. 1 Tim. 3:16

1. O sing a song of Beth - le - hem, Of shep - herds watch-ing there,
2. O sing a song of Naz - a - reth, Of sun - ny days of joy,
3. O sing a song of Gal - i - lee, Of lake and woods and hill,
4. O sing a song of Cal - va - ry, Its glo - ry and dis - may;
And of the news that came to them From an - gels in the air:
O sing of fra - grant flow-ers' breath, And of the sin - less Boy:
Of Him who walked up - on the sea And bade the waves be still:
Of Him who hung up - on the tree, And took our sins a - way:
The light that shone on Beth - le - hem Fills all the world to - day;
For now the flowers on Naz - a - reth In ev - ery heart may grow;
For though like waves on Gal - i - lee, Dark seas of trou - ble roll,
For He who died on Cal - va - ry Is ris - en from the grave,
Of Je - sus' birth and peace on earth The an - gels sing al - way.
Now spreads the fame of His dear name On all the winds that blow.
When faith has heard the Mas - ter's word, Falls peace up - on the soul.
And Christ, our Lord, by heav'n a - dored, Is might - y now to save.

TEXT: Louis F. Benson
MUSIC: Melody collected by Lucy Broadwood; adapted & arranged by Ralph Vaughan Williams

KINGSFOLD
C.M.D.

168 Who Is He in Yonder Stall?

The Lamb . . . is Lord of lords and King of kings. Rev. 17:14

1. Who is He in yon-der stall, At whose feet the shep-herds fall?
2. Who is He the peo-ple bless For His words of gen-tle-ness?
3. Who is He that stands and weeps At the grave where Laz-arus sleeps?
4. Lo! at mid-night, who is He Prays in dark Geth-sem-a-ne?
5. Who is He that from the grave Comes to heal and help and save?
Who is He in deep dis-tress, Fast-ing in the wil-der-ness?
Who is He to whom they bring All the sick and sor-row-ing?
Who is He the gath-'ring throng Greet with loud tri-um-phant song?
Who is He on yon-der tree Dies in grief and ag-o-ny?
Who is He that from His throne Rules through all the world a-lone?
Refrain
'Tis the Lord! O won-drous sto-ry! 'Tis the Lord! the King of
glo-ry! At His feet we hum-bly fall, Crown Him! crown Him, Lord of all!

TEXT and MUSIC: Benjamin R. Hanby

LOWLINESS
7.7.7.7. with Refrain

The Unveiled Christ 169

. . . a new and living way opened for us through the curtain, that is, His body. Heb. 10:20

1. Once our bless-ed Christ of beau - ty Was veiled off from hu-man view;
2. Now He is with God the Fa - ther, In - ter - ced - ing there for you;
3. Ho - ly an-gels bow be - fore Him, Men of earth give prais-es due;
4. Thro'-out time and end-less a - ges, Heights and depths of love so true;
But thro' suf-f'ring, death and sor - row He has rent the veil in two.
For He is the might-y con-qu'ror Since He rent the veil in two.
For He is the well-be-lov - ed Since He rent the veil in two.
He a-lone can be the giv - er Since He rent the veil in two.
Refrain
O be-hold the Man of Sor - rows, O be-hold Him in plain view;
Lo! He is the might-y con-qu'ror, Since He rent the veil in two.
Lo! He is the might-y con-qu'ror, Since He rent the veil in two.

TEXT and MUSIC: N.B. Herrell

THE UNVEILED CHRIST
8.7.8.7. with Refrain

170 One Day

At just the right time, when we were still powerless, Christ died for the ungodly. Rom. 5:6

1. One day when heaven was filled with His praises, One day when sin was as black as could be, Jesus came forth to be born of a virgin, Dwelt among men— my example is He!
2. One day they led Him up Calvary's mountain, One day they nailed Him to die on the tree; Suffering anguish, despised and rejected, Bearing our sins, my Redeemer is He!
3. One day they left Him alone in the garden, One day He rested, from suffering free; Angels came down o'er His tomb to keep vigil— Hope of the hopeless, my Savior is He!
4. One day the grave could conceal Him no longer, One day the stone rolled away from the door; Then He arose, over death He had conquered, Now is ascended, my Lord evermore!
5. One day the trumpet will sound for His coming, One day the skies with His glory will shine; Wonderful day, my beloved ones bringing! Glorious Savior, this Jesus is mine!

Refrain

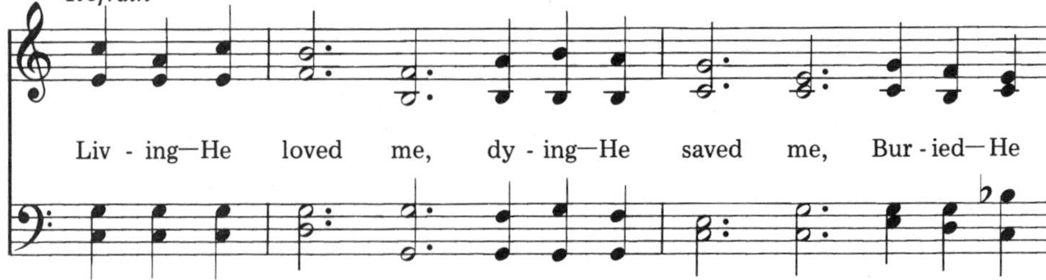
Liv - ing—He loved me, dy - ing—He saved me, Bur - ied—He

TEXT: J. Wilbur Chapman
MUSIC: Charles H. Marsh

ONE DAY
11.10.11.10. with Refrain

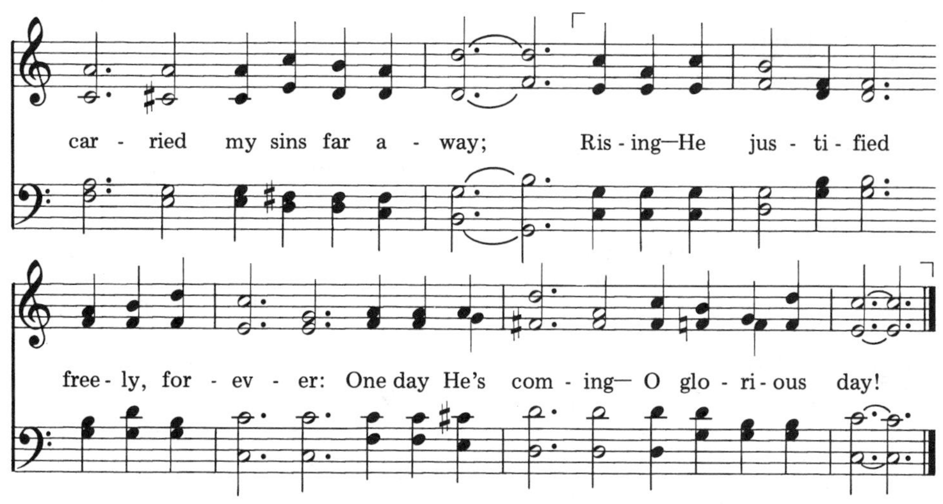
car - ried my sins far a - way; Ris - ing—He jus - ti - fied
free - ly, for - ev - er: One day He's com - ing— O glo - ri - ous day!

Come and Praise the Lord Our King 171

Continually offer to God a sacrifice of praise. Heb. 13:15

1. Come and praise the Lord our King, Al - le - lu, al - le - lu - ia!
2. Christ was born in Beth - le - hem, Al - le - lu, al - le - lu - ia!
3. He grew up an earth - ly child, Al - le - lu, al - le - lu - ia!
4. Je - sus died at Cal - va - ry, Al - le - lu, al - le - lu - ia!
5. He has con-quered death and sin, Al - le - lu, al - le - lu - ia!
6. Now He rules from heav'n a - bove, Al - le - lu, al - le - lu - ia!
7. We will live with Him some-day, Al - le - lu, al - le - lu - ia!

Lift your voice and with us sing, Al - le - lu, al - le - lu - ia!
Son of God and Son of Man, Al - le - lu, al - le - lu - ia!
In the world, but un - de - filed, Al - le - lu, al - le - lu - ia!
Rose a - gain tri - um - phant - ly, Al - le - lu, al - le - lu - ia!
Great His tri - umph— glo - rious win, Al - le - lu, al - le - lu - ia!
King of mer - cy, King of love, Al - le - lu, al - le - lu - ia!
And for - ev - er with Him stay, Al - le - lu, al - le - lu - ia!

TEXT: William David Young, stanzas 1b, 5, 6;
Traditional sources, stanzas 1a, 2, 3, 4, 7, altered
MUSIC: William David Young

CULL CANYON
7.7.7.7.

172 Tell Me the Story of Jesus

Philip began with that . . . Scripture and told him the good news about Jesus. Acts 8:35

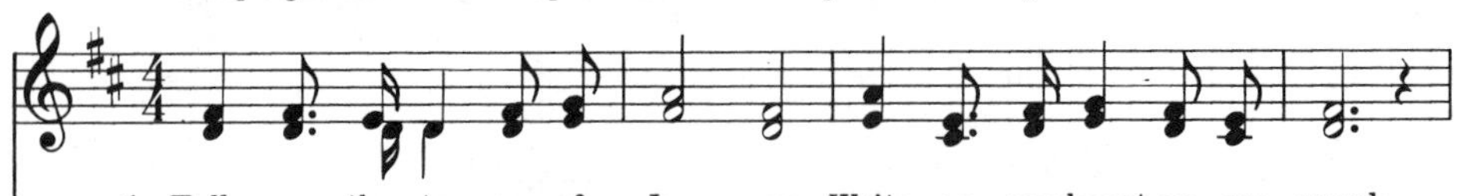

1. Tell me the sto - ry of Je - sus, Write on my heart ev - ery word;
2. Fast - ing a - lone in the des - ert, Tell of the days that are past,
3. Tell of the cross where they nailed Him, Writh-ing in an - guish and pain;

Refrain: Tell me the sto - ry of Je - sus, Write on my heart ev - ery word;

Tell me the sto - ry most pre - cious, Sweet-est that ev - er was heard.
How for our sins He was tempt - ed, Yet was tri - um-phant at last.
Tell of the grave where they laid Him, Tell how He liv - eth a - gain.
Tell me the sto - ry most pre - cious, Sweet-est that ev - er was heard.

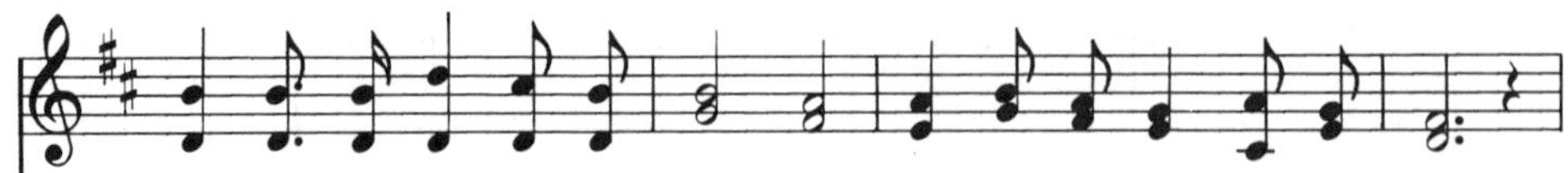

Tell how the an - gels in cho - rus Sang as they wel-comed His birth,
Tell of the years of His la - bor, Tell of the sor - row He bore,
Love in that sto - ry so ten - der, Clear - er than ev - er I see:

"Glo - ry to God in the high - est! Peace and good ti - dings to earth."
He was de-spised and af - flict - ed, Home-less, re - ject - ed and poor.
Stay, let me weep while you whis - per, Love paid the ran - som for me.

TEXT: Fanny J. Crosby
MUSIC: John R. Sweney

STORY OF JESUS
8.7.8.7.D. with Refrain

All Glory, Laud and Honor 173

Blessed is He who comes in the name of the Lord . . . the King of Israel! John 12:13

1. All glo - ry, laud and hon - or To Thee, Re - deem - er, King,
2. The com - pa - ny of an - gels Are prais - ing Thee on high,
3. To Thee, be - fore Thy pas - sion, They sang their hymns of praise;
To whom the lips of chil - dren Made sweet ho - san - nas ring: Thou
And mor - tal men and all things Cre - at - ed make re - ply: The
To Thee, now high ex - alt - ed, Our mel - o - dy we raise: Thou
art the King of Is - rael, Thou Da - vid's roy - al Son, Who
peo - ple of the He - brews With palms be - fore Thee went: Our
didst ac - cept their prais - es— Ac - cept the praise we bring, Who
in the Lord's name com - est, The King and bless - ed One!
praise and prayer and an - thems Be - fore Thee we pre - sent.
in all good de - light - est, Thou good and gra - cious King! A - men.

TEXT: Theodulph of Orleans; translated by John M. Neale
MUSIC: Melchior Teschner

ST. THEODULPH
7.6.7.6.D.

174 Hosanna, Loud Hosanna

Hosanna to the Son of David! . . . Hosanna in the highest! Matt. 21:9

1. Ho - san - na, loud ho - san - na The lit - tle chil - dren sang;
2. From Ol - i - vet they fol - lowed 'Mid an ex - ult - ant crowd,
3. "Ho - san - na in the high - est!" That an - cient song we sing,
Optional Children's Choir (1st and 3rd stanzas)
Ho - san - na, ho - san - na, ho - san - na to the King;
Through pil-lared court and tem - ple The love - ly an - them rang;
The vic - tor palm branch wav - ing, And chant-ing clear and loud;
For Christ is our Re - deem - er, The Lord of heav'n, our King;
Ho - san - na, praise ye the Lord, Sing in one ac - cord!
To Je - sus, who had blessed them Close fold - ed to His breast,
The Lord of men and an - gels Rode on in low - ly state,
O may we ev - er praise Him With heart and life and voice,

TEXT: Jenette Threlfall; based on Matthew 21:15, 16
MUSIC: *Gesangbuch der Herzogl,* Württemburg, 1784;
Descant, final ending and handbell parts by Bruce Greer
A higher setting may be found at No. 59

ELLACOMBE
7.6.7.6.D.

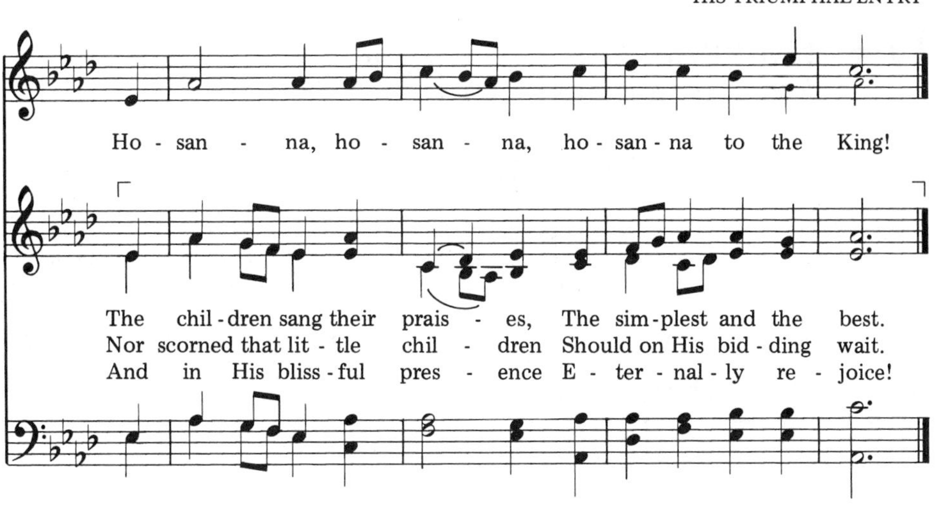
Ho - san - na, ho - san - na, ho - san - na to the King!
The chil - dren sang their prais - es, The sim - plest and the best.
Nor scorned that lit - tle chil - dren Should on His bid - ding wait.
And in His bliss - ful pres - ence E - ter - nal - ly re - joice!

Optional final ending
Children alone
ritard
King! Ho - san - na, ho - san - na, ho - san - na to the King!
joice! Keyboard only
ritard

Optional 2 Octave Handbells (2nd and 3rd stanzas)
tr

175 Hallelujah, What a Savior!

. . . a Man of Sorrows, and familiar with suffering. Isa. 53:3

1. "Man of Sor-rows!" what a name For the Son of God, who came Ru-ined sin-ners to re-claim! Hal-le-lu-jah, what a Sav-ior!
2. Bear-ing shame and scoff-ing rude, In my place con-demned He stood— Sealed my par-don with His blood: Hal-le-lu-jah, what a Sav-ior!
3. Guilt-y, vile and help-less we, Spot-less Lamb of God was He; Full a-tone-ment! can it be? Hal-le-lu-jah, what a Sav-ior!
4. Lift-ed up was He to die, "It is fin-ished!" was His cry; Now in heav'n ex-alt-ed high: Hal-le-lu-jah, what a Sav-ior!
5. When He comes, our glo-rious King, All His ran-somed home to bring, Then a-new this song we'll sing: Hal-le-lu-jah, what a Sav-ior!
Optional last stanza setting
Broader
rit.
5. When He comes, our glo-rious King, All His ran-somed home to bring, Then a-new this song we'll sing: Hal-le-lu-jah, what a Sav-ior!
rit.

TEXT and MUSIC: Philip P. Bliss

MAN OF SORROWS
7.7.7.8.

Lead Me to Calvary 176

I resolved to know nothing . . . except Jesus Christ and Him crucified. 1 Cor. 2:2

1. King of my life, I crown Thee now, Thine shall the glo - ry be;
Lest I for-get Thy thorn-crowned brow, Lead me to Cal - va - ry.

2. Show me the tomb where Thou wast laid, Ten - der-ly mourned and wept;
An - gels in robes of light ar - rayed Guard-ed Thee whilst Thou slept.

3. Let me like Ma - ry, through the gloom, Come with a gift to Thee;
Show to me now the emp - ty tomb, Lead me to Cal - va - ry.

4. May I be will - ing, Lord, to bear Dai - ly my cross for Thee;
E - ven Thy cup of grief to share, Thou hast borne all for me.

Refrain

Lest I for-get Geth - sem - a - ne; Lest I for-get Thine ag - o - ny;
Lest I for - get Thy love for me, Lead me to Cal - va - ry.

TEXT: Jennie Evelyn Hussey
MUSIC: William J. Kirkpatrick

DUNCANNON
C.M. with Refrain

177 What Wondrous Love Is This

Anyone who is hung on a tree is under God's curse. Deut. 21:23

Unison
1. What won-drous love is this, O my soul, O my soul! What
2. When I was sink - ing down, sink-ing down, sink - ing down, When
3. To God and to the Lamb I will sing, I will sing, To
4. And when from death I'm free, I'll sing on, I'll sing on, And
won - drous love is this, O my soul! What won-drous love is
I was sink - ing down, sink - ing down, When I was sink - ing
God and to the Lamb I will sing, To God and to the
when from death I'm free, I'll sing on, And when from death I'm
this That caused the Lord of bliss To bear the dread-ful curse
down Be - neath God's right - eous frown, Christ laid a - side His crown
Lamb Who is the great "I Am," While mil-lions join the theme,
free, I'll sing and joy - ful be, And thro' e - ter - ni - ty
for my soul, for my soul, To bear the dread-ful curse for my soul.
for my soul, for my soul, Christ laid a - side His crown for my soul.
I will sing, I will sing, While mil-lions join the theme, I will sing.
I'll sing on, I'll sing on, And thro' e - ter - ni - ty I'll sing on.

TEXT: American Folk Hymn
MUSIC: William Walker's *Southern Harmony*, 1835

WONDROUS LOVE
12.9.6.6.12.9.

O Sacred Head, Now Wounded 178

They . . . twisted together a crown of thorns and set it on Him. Mark 15:17

1. O sa - cred Head, now wound - ed, With grief and shame weighed down,
2. What Thou, my Lord, hast suf - fered Was all for sin - ners' gain;
3. What lan - guage shall I bor - row To thank Thee, dear-est Friend,
Now scorn-ful - ly sur - round - ed With thorns Thine on - ly crown:
Mine, mine was the trans - gres - sion, But Thine the dead - ly pain.
For this, Thy dy - ing sor - row, Thy pit - y with - out end?
How pale Thou art with an - guish, With sore a - buse and scorn, How
Lo, here I fall, my Sav - ior; 'Tis I de - serve Thy place; Look
O make me Thine for - ev - er, And should I faint - ing be, Lord,
does that vis - age lan - guish, Which once was bright as morn!
on me with Thy fa - vor, As - sist me with Thy grace.
let me nev - er, nev - er Out - live my love to Thee. A - men.

TEXT: Paul Gerhardt; based on Medieval Latin poem ascribed to Bernard of Clairvaux; translated from the German by James W. Alexander
MUSIC: Hans Leo Hassler; harmonized by J. S. Bach

PASSION CHORALE
7.6.7.6.D.

179 Behold the Lamb

. . . the Lamb that was slain from the creation of the world. Rev. 13:8

Be - hold the Lamb, be - hold the Lamb, slain from the foun-
da-tion of the world. For sin-ners cru-ci-fied, O ho - ly
Fine
sac - ri - fice, be-hold the Lamb of God, be-hold the Lamb.
play cued notes
first time only
More movement
Crown Him, crown Him, wor - thy is the Lamb.
D.S. al Fine
Praise Him, praise Him. Heav'n and earth re - sound. Be -

TEXT and MUSIC: Dottie Rambo; arranged by Lee Herrington

BEHOLD THE LAMB
Irregular meter

Worthy Is the Lamb 180

Worthy is the Lamb, who was slain. Rev. 5:12

Wor-thy is the Lamb that was slain, Wor-thy is the Lamb that was
slain, Wor-thy is the Lamb that was slain, to re - ceive:
Pow-er and rich-es and wis-dom and strength, Hon-or and glo-ry and
bless-ing! Wor-thy is the Lamb, Wor-thy is the Lamb, Wor-thy
is the Lamb that was slain, Wor - thy is the Lamb!

TEXT: Revelation 5:12; adapted by Don Wyrtzen
MUSIC: Don Wyrtzen

WORTHY IS THE LAMB
Irregular meter

181 Were You There?

It was the third hour when they crucified Him. Mark 15:25

1. Were you there when they cru - ci - fied my Lord? Were you
2. Were you there when they nailed Him to the tree? Were you
3. Were you there when they laid Him in the tomb? Were you
†opt. 4. Were you there when He rose up from the dead? Were you
there when they cru - ci - fied my Lord?
there when they nailed Him to the tree? O!
there when they laid Him in the tomb?
there when He rose up from the dead?
Some-times it caus - es me to trem-ble, trem-ble, trem-ble!
(4. Some-times I feel like shout-ing glo - ry, glo - ry, glo - ry!)
Were you there when they cru - ci - fied my Lord?
Were you there when they nailed Him to the tree?
Were you there when they laid Him in the tomb?
Were you there when He rose up from the dead?

†May be omitted, especially for Holy Week services.

TEXT and MUSIC: Traditional Spiritual

WERE YOU THERE?
Irregular meter

GLORY IN THE CROSS

A Brief Service of Reflection and Praise

Suggested Hymn Stanzas

To facilitate an uninterrupted flow from stanza to stanza,
the suggested stanzas have been marked with an arrow: ►
Beneath the Cross of Jesus, stanzas 1, 2
In the Cross of Christ I Glory, stanzas 1, 2
When I Survey the Wondrous Cross, complete

WORSHIP LEADER:

And Jesus answered them saying, "The hour has come for the Son of Man to be glorified. Father, glorify Thy name." There came therefore a voice out of heaven: "I have both glorified it, and will glorify it again." The multitude therefore, who stood by and heard it, were saying that it had thundered; others were saying, "An angel has spoken to Him." Jesus answered and said, "This voice has not come for My sake, but for your sakes. Now judgment is upon this world; now the ruler of this world shall be cast out. And I, if I be lifted up from the earth, will draw all men to Myself." But He was saying this to indicate the kind of death by which He was to die.

PEOPLE:

And being found in appearance as a man, He humbled Himself by becoming obedient to the point of death, even death on a cross. Therefore also God highly exalted Him, and bestowed on Him the name which is above every name, . . .

WORSHIP LEADER:

. . . fixing our eyes on Jesus, the author and perfecter of faith, who for the joy set before Him endured the cross, despising the shame, and sat down at the right hand of the throne of God.

ALL:

But may it never be that I should boast, except in the cross of our Lord Jesus Christ, through which the world has been crucified to me, and I to the world.

**John 12:23,28-33; Phil. 2:8-9;
Heb. 12:2; Gal. 6:14. (NASB)**

"GLORY IN THE CROSS—A Brief Service of Reflection and Praise"

183 Beneath the Cross of Jesus

Near the cross of Jesus stood His mother . . . John 19:25

1. Be - neath the cross of Je - sus I fain would take my stand—
2. Up - on that cross of Je - sus Mine eye at times can see
3. I take, O cross, thy shad - ow For my a - bid - ing place;
The shad - ow of a might - y Rock With - in a wea - ry land;
The ver - y dy - ing form of One Who suf-fered there for me;
I ask no oth - er sun - shine than The sun-shine of His face;
A home with - in the wil - der - ness, A rest up - on the way,
And from my smit - ten heart with tears Two won-ders I con - fess—
Con - tent to let the world go by, To know no gain nor loss,
From the burn - ing of the noon - tide heat, And the bur - den of the day.
The won-ders of re - deem - ing love And my un-wor - thi - ness.
My sin - ful self my on - ly shame, My glo - ry all the cross.

TEXT: Elizabeth C. Clephane
MUSIC: Frederick C. Maker

ST. CHRISTOPHER
7.6.8.6.8.6.8.6.

Optional transition to "In the Cross of Christ I Glory"

In the Cross of Christ I Glory 184

Jesus . . . for the joy set before Him endured the cross, scorning its shame. Heb. 12:2

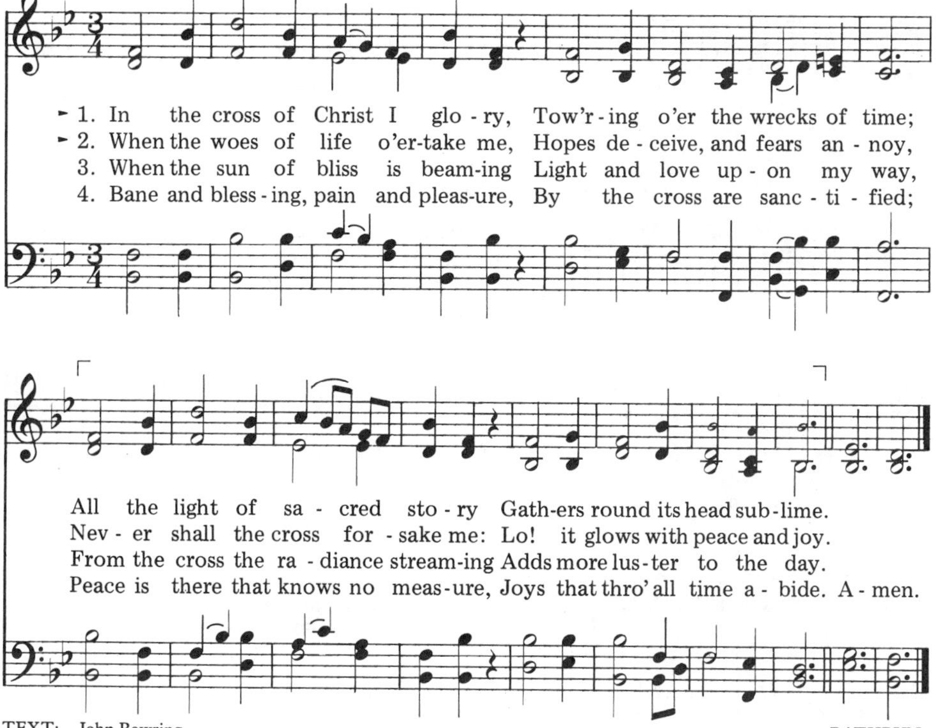

1. In the cross of Christ I glo - ry, Tow'r - ing o'er the wrecks of time; All the light of sa - cred sto - ry Gath-ers round its head sub-lime.
2. When the woes of life o'er-take me, Hopes de - ceive, and fears an - noy, Nev - er shall the cross for - sake me: Lo! it glows with peace and joy.
3. When the sun of bliss is beam-ing Light and love up - on my way, From the cross the ra - diance stream-ing Adds more lus-ter to the day.
4. Bane and bless - ing, pain and pleas-ure, By the cross are sanc - ti - fied; Peace is there that knows no meas-ure, Joys that thro' all time a - bide. A - men.

TEXT: John Bowring
MUSIC: Ithamar Conkey

RATHBUN
8.7.8.7.

Optional transition to "When I Survey the Wondrous Cross"

185 When I Survey the Wondrous Cross

They will look on the One they have pierced. John 19:37

1. When I survey the wondrous cross On which the Prince of glory died, My richest gain I count but loss, And pour contempt on all my pride.
2. Forbid it, Lord, that I should boast, Save in the death of Christ, my God; All the vain things that charm me most— I sacrifice them to His blood.
3. See, from His head, His hands, His feet, Sorrow and love flow mingled down; Did e'er such love and sorrow meet, Or thorns compose so rich a crown?
4. Were the whole realm of nature mine, That were a present far too small: Love so amazing, so divine, Demands my soul, my life, my all.
Optional last stanza harmonization
crown?
rit.
Broader
Unison
4. Were the whole realm of na - ture

TEXT: Isaac Watts
MUSIC: Based on a Gregorian chant; arranged by Lowell Mason;
Last stanza harmonization by Robert F. Douglas; Alternate tune: APPALACHIA at No. 401

HAMBURG
L.M.

mine, That were a pres - ent far too small:
Love so a - maz - ing, so di - vine,
Play cued notes if opt. choral ending is used
De - mands my soul, my life, my all.
Optional choral ending
Great rit.
8va
De - mands my soul, my life, my all.
8va

The end of "GLORY IN THE CROSS—A Brief Service of Reflection and Praise"

186 The Old Rugged Cross

He humbled Himself and became obedient to death . . . on a cross! Phil. 2:8

1. On a hill far a - way stood an old rug-ged cross, The em - blem of suf-f'ring and shame; And I love that old cross where the dear - est and best For a world of lost sin - ners was slain.
2. O that old rug-ged cross, so de - spised by the world, Has a won-drous at - trac - tion for me; For the dear Lamb of God left His glo - ry a - bove To bear it to dark Cal - va - ry.
3. In the old rug-ged cross, stained with blood so di - vine, A won - drous beau - ty I see; For 'twas on that old cross Je - sus suf - fered and died To par - don and sanc - ti - fy me.
4. To the old rug-ged cross I will ev - er be true, Its shame and re - proach glad - ly bear; Then He'll call me some day to my home far a - way, Where His glo - ry for - ev - er I'll share.
Refrain
So I'll cher - ish the old rug - ged cross, Till my
cross, the old rug - ged cross,

TEXT and MUSIC: George Bennard

OLD RUGGED CROSS
Irregular meter

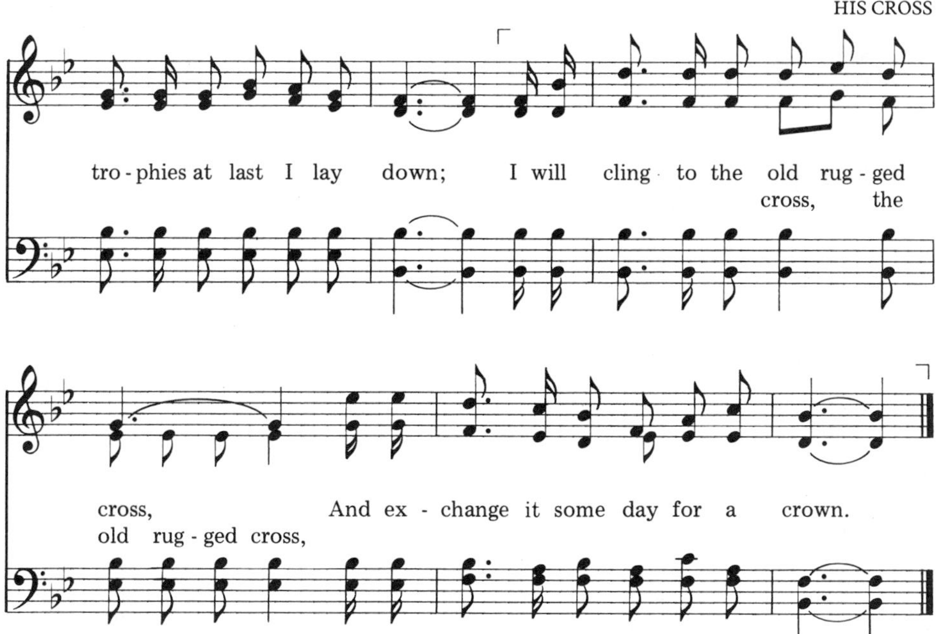
tro - phies at last I lay down; I will cling to the old rug - ged
cross, the
cross, And ex - change it some day for a crown.
old rug - ged cross,

In His Cross I Glory 187

. . . justified freely by His grace through the redemption that came by Christ. Rom. 3:24

I
2 part Canon
II
1. In the cross of Christ I glo - ry, There for all was
2. In the cross of Christ I glo - ry, Not in pow - er,

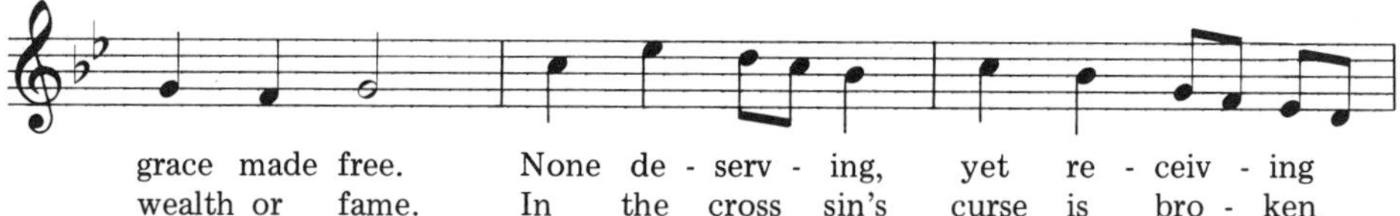
grace made free. None de - serv - ing, yet re - ceiv - ing
wealth or fame. In the cross sin's curse is bro - ken

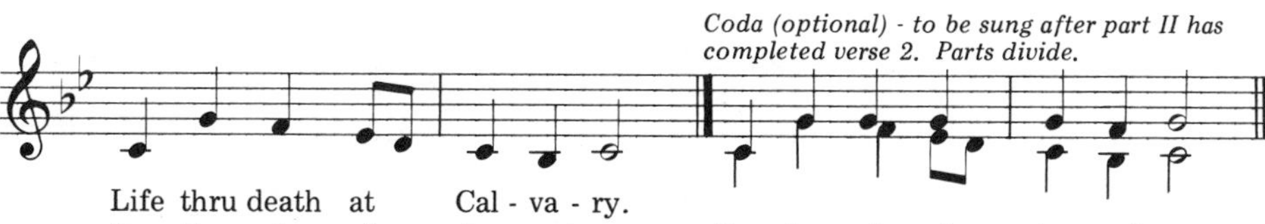
Coda (optional) - to be sung after part II has completed verse 2. Parts divide.
Life thru death at Cal - va - ry.
For the sake of Je - sus' name. For the sake of Je - sus' name.

TEXT and MUSIC: Tricia Walker

WALKER
8.7.8.7.

188 At the Cross

The message of the cross . . . is the power of God. 1 Cor. 1:18

1. A - las! and did my Sav - ior bleed? And did my Sov - 'reign die?
2. Was it for crimes that I have done He groaned up - on the tree?
3. Well might the sun in dark-ness hide And shut His glo - ries in,
4. But drops of grief can ne'er re - pay The debt of love I owe:
Would He de - vote that sa - cred head For sin - ners such as I!
A - maz - ing pit - y! grace un-known! And love be - yond de - gree!
When Christ, the might - y Mak - er, died For man the crea - ture's sin.
Here, Lord, I give my - self a - way— 'Tis all that I can do!
Refrain
At the cross, at the cross where I first saw the light And the
bur - den of my heart rolled a - way— It was there by faith
I re - ceived my sight, And now I am hap - py all the day!

TEXT: Isaac Watts; Ralph E. Hudson, Refrain
MUSIC: Ralph E. Hudson

HUDSON
C.M. with Refrain

Calvary Covers It All 189

He forgave us all our sins. Col. 2:13

1. Far dear - er than all that the world can im - part Was the mes - sage that came to my heart; How that Je - sus a - lone for my sin did a - tone, And Cal - va - ry cov - ers it all.
2. The stripes that He bore and the thorns that He wore Told His mer - cy and love ev - er - more; And my heart bowed in shame as I called on His name,
3. How match-less the grace, when I looked on the face Of this Je - sus, my cru - ci - fied Lord; My re - demp-tion com-plete I then found at His feet,
4. How bless - ed the thought, that my soul by Him bought, Shall be His in the glo - ry on high; Where with glad - ness and song I'll be one of the throng,
Refrain
Cal - va - ry cov - ers it all, My past with its sin and stain; My guilt and de - spair Je - sus took on Him there, And Cal - va - ry cov - ers it all.

TEXT and MUSIC: Mrs. Walter G. Taylor

CALVARY COVERS IT
Irregular meter

190 Are You Washed in the Blood?

They have washed their robes and made them white in the blood of the Lamb. Rev. 7:14

1. Have you been to Je - sus for the cleans-ing power? Are you washed in the blood of the Lamb? Are you ful - ly trust-ing in His grace this hour? Are you washed in the blood of the Lamb?
2. Are you walk - ing dai - ly by the Sav - ior's side? Are you washed in the blood of the Lamb? Do you rest each mo-ment in the Cru - ci - fied? Are you washed in the blood of the Lamb?
3. When the Bride-groom com-eth will your robes be white? Are you washed in the blood of the Lamb? Will your soul be read - y for the man-sions bright, And be washed in the blood of the Lamb?
4. Lay a - side the gar-ments that are stained with sin, And be washed in the blood of the Lamb? There's a foun-tain flow-ing for the soul un - clean, O be washed in the blood of the Lamb?
Refrain
Are you washed in the blood,
Are you washed in the blood,
In the soul - cleans-ing blood of the Lamb?
of the Lamb?
Are your gar - ments spot-less? Are they white as snow? Are you washed in the blood of the Lamb?

TEXT and MUSIC: Elisha A. Hoffmann

WASHED IN THE BLOOD
11.9.11.9. with Refrain

There Is Power in the Blood 191

They overcame Him by the blood of the Lamb. Rev. 12:11

1. Would you be free from the bur - den of sin? There's pow'r in the blood, pow'r in the blood; Would you o'er e - vil a vic - to - ry win? There's won - der - ful pow'r in the blood.
2. Would you be free from your pas - sion and pride? There's pow'r in the blood, pow'r in the blood; Come for a cleans - ing to Cal - va - ry's tide? There's won - der - ful pow'r in the blood.
3. Would you be whit - er, much whit - er than snow? There's pow'r in the blood, pow'r in the blood; Sin - stains are lost in its life - giv - ing flow; There's won - der - ful pow'r in the blood.
4. Would you do serv - ice for Je - sus your King? There's pow'r in the blood, pow'r in the blood; Would you live dai - ly His prais - es to sing? There's won - der - ful pow'r in the blood.

Refrain

There is pow'r, pow'r, won - der - work - ing pow'r (there is) In the blood (In the blood) of the Lamb; (of the Lamb;) There is pow'r, pow'r, (there is) won - der - work - ing pow'r In the pre - cious blood of the Lamb.

TEXT and MUSIC: Lewis E. Jones

POWER IN THE BLOOD
10.9.10.8. with Refrain

192 The Blood Will Never Lose Its Power

. . . the blood of the eternal covenant. Heb. 13:20

1. The blood that Je - sus shed for me, 'Way back on Cal - va - ry; The blood that gives me strength from day to day, It will nev - er lose its power.
2. It soothes my doubts and calms my fears, And it dries all my tears; The blood that gives me strength from day to day, It will nev - er lose its power.
Refrain
It reach - es to the high - est moun - tain. It flows to the low - est val - ley. The blood that gives me strength from

TEXT and MUSIC: Andraé Crouch

THE BLOOD
Irregular meter

day to day, It will nev - er lose its power.

Jesus, Thy Blood and Righteousness 193

God presented Him as a sacrifice of atonement, through faith in His blood. Rom. 3:25

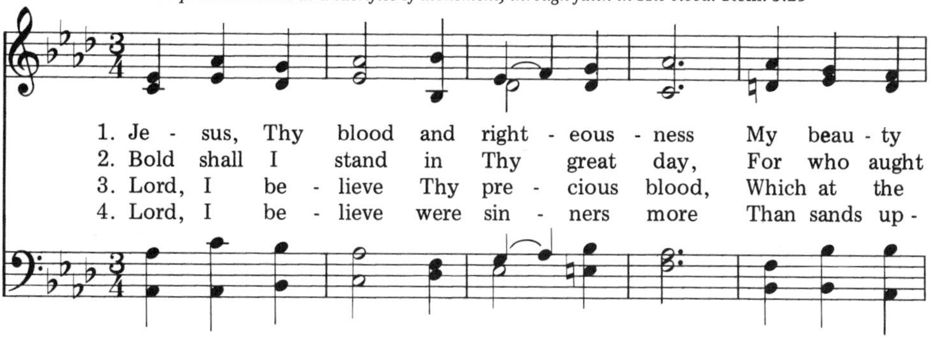

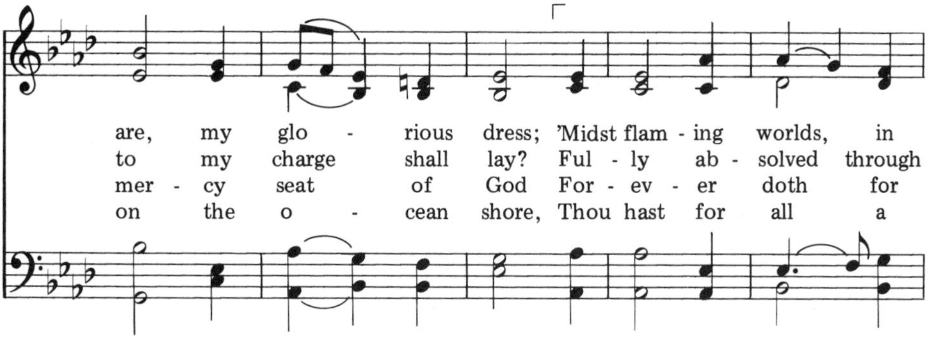

1. Jesus, Thy blood and righteousness
My beauty are, my glorious dress;
'Midst flaming worlds, in these arrayed,
With joy shall I lift up my head.

2. Bold shall I stand in Thy great day,
For who aught to my charge shall lay?
Fully absolved through these I am,
From sin and fear, from guilt and shame.

3. Lord, I believe Thy precious blood,
Which at the mercy seat of God
Forever doth for sinners plead,
For me, e'en for my soul, was shed.

4. Lord, I believe were sinners more
Than sands upon the ocean shore,
Thou hast for all a ransom paid,
For all a full atonement made.

TEXT: Nicolaus L. von Zinzendorf; translated by John Wesley
MUSIC: William Gardiner's *Sacred Melodies,* 1815

GERMANY
L.M.

194 I KNOW A FOUNT
A Medley

WORSHIP LEADER:
You know that you were ransomed from the futile ways inherited from your fathers, not with perishable things, such as silver or gold, but with the precious blood of Christ, like that of a lamb without spot or blemish. Through Him you have confidence in God who raised Him from the dead and gave Him glory, so that your faith and hope are in God.

1 Pet. 1:18-19, 21. (RSV)

I know a fount where sins are washed a - way,
I know a place where night is turned to day;
Bur - dens are lift - ed, blind eyes made to see; There's a
won - der work - ing pow'r in the blood of Cal - va - ry.
Cued notes for transition to "Nothing But the Blood"

TEXT and MUSIC: Oliver Cooke

I KNOW A FOUNT
10.10.10.15.

Nothing But the Blood 195

The blood of Jesus, His Son, purifies us from all sin. 1 John 1:7

1. What can wash a - way my sin? Noth-ing but the blood of Je - sus;
2. For my par - don this I see, Noth-ing but the blood of Je - sus;
3. Noth - ing can for sin a - tone, Noth-ing but the blood of Je - sus;
4. This is all my hope and peace, Noth-ing but the blood of Je - sus;
What can make me whole a - gain? Noth-ing but the blood of Je - sus.
For my cleans-ing, this my plea, Noth-ing but the blood of Je - sus.
Naught of good that I have done, Noth-ing but the blood of Je - sus.
This is all my right-eous - ness, Noth-ing but the blood of Je - sus.
Refrain
Oh! pre - cious is the flow That makes me white as snow;
No oth - er fount I know, Noth-ing but the blood of Je - sus.

The end of "I KNOW A FOUNT - a medley"

TEXT and MUSIC: Robert Lowry

PLAINFIELD
7.8.7.8. with Refrain

196 There Is a Fountain

A fountain will be opened . . . to cleanse them from sin. Zech. 13:1

1. There is a foun-tain filled with blood Drawn from Im-man-uel's veins,
2. The dy - ing thief re - joiced to see That foun-tain in his day,
3. Dear dy - ing Lamb, Thy pre-cious blood Shall nev - er lose its pow'r,
4. E'er since by faith I saw the stream Thy flow - ing wounds sup - ply,
5. When this poor lisp-ing, stam-m'ring tongue Lies si - lent in the grave,
And sin - ners plunged be-neath that flood Lose all their guilt - y stains:
And there may I, though vile as he, Wash all my sins a - way:
Till all the ran-somed Church of God Be saved to sin no more:
Re - deem - ing love has been my theme And shall be till I die:
Then in a no - bler, sweet-er song I'll sing Thy pow'r to save:
Lose all their guilt - y stains, Lose all their guilt - y stains;
Wash all my sins a - way, Wash all my sins a - way;
Be saved to sin no more, Be saved to sin no more;
And shall be till I die, And shall be till I die;
I'll sing Thy pow'r to save, I'll sing Thy pow'r to save;
And sin - ners plunged be-neath that flood Lose all their guilt - y stains.
And there may I, though vile as he, Wash all my sins a - way.
Till all the ran-somed Church of God Be saved to sin no more.
Re - deem - ing love has been my theme And shall be till I die.
Then in a no - bler, sweet-er song I'll sing Thy pow'r to save.

TEXT: William Cowper
MUSIC: Traditional American melody; arranged by Lowell Mason

CLEANSING FOUNTAIN
C.M.D.

Lamb of Glory 197

Look, the Lamb of God, who takes away the sin of the world! John 1:29

1. Hear the sto - ry from God's Word That kings and priests and pro - phets heard; There would be a sac - ri - fice And blood would flow to pay sin's price.
2. On the cross God loved the world While all the pow'rs of hell were hurled; No one there could un - der - stand The One they saw was Christ the Lamb.
rit.
Refrain
a tempo
Pre - cious Lamb of glo - ry, Love's most won - drous sto - ry. Heart of God's re - demp-tion of man; Wor-ship the Lamb of glo - ry.

TEXT and MUSIC: Greg Nelson and Phill McHugh; arranged by Eugene Thomas

LAMB OF GLORY
7.8.7.8. with Refrain

198 Wonderful Grace of Jesus

You know the grace of our Lord Jesus Christ. 2 Cor. 8:9

1. Won - der - ful grace of Je - sus, Great - er than all my sin;
2. Won - der - ful grace of Je - sus, Reach - ing to all the lost,
3. Won - der - ful grace of Je - sus, Reach - ing the most de - filed,
How shall my tongue de - scribe it, Where shall its praise be - gin?
By it I have been par - doned, Saved to the ut - ter - most;
By its trans-form - ing pow - er Mak - ing him God's dear child,
Tak - ing a - way my bur - den, Set - ting my spir - it free,
Chains have been torn a - sun - der, Giv - ing me lib - er - ty,
Pur - chas - ing peace and heav - en For all e - ter - ni - ty;
For the won - der - ful grace of Je - sus reach - es me.
For the won - der - ful grace of Je - sus reach - es me.
For the won - der - ful grace of Je - sus reach - es me.
Refrain
the match-less grace of Je - sus,
Won-der-ful the match-less grace of Je - sus, Deep - er

TEXT and MUSIC: Haldor Lillenas

WONDERFUL GRACE
Irregular meter

the roll - ing sea;
Won -
than the might - y roll - ing sea;
High - er than the
der - ful grace, all - suf - fi - cient for
moun-tain, spar-kling like a foun - tain, All - suf - fi - cient grace for e - ven
me, for e - ven me;
Broad - er than the scope of my trans-
me;
trans-
gres - sions, Great - er far than all my sin and shame;
gres-sions, sing it!
my sin and shame;
O mag - ni - fy the pre - cious name of Je - sus, Praise His name!

199 Arise, My Soul, Arise

He always lives to intercede for them. Heb. 7:25

1. A - rise, my soul, a - rise. Shake off thy guilt - y fears.
2. He ev - er lives a - bove For me to in - ter - cede,
3. Five bleed - ing wounds He bears, Re - ceived on Cal - va - ry.
4. The Fa - ther hears Him pray, His dear A - noint - ed One;
5. My God is rec - on - ciled; His par - d'ning voice I hear.
The bleed - ing Sac - ri - fice In my be - half ap - pears.
His all - re - deem - ing love, His pre - cious blood to plead.
They pour ef - fec - tual prayers; They strong - ly plead for me.
He can - not turn a - way The pres - ence of His Son.
He owns me for His child; I can no lon - ger fear.
Be - fore the throne my Sure - ty stands, Be - fore the throne my
His blood a - toned for all our race, His blood a - toned for
"For - give him, oh, for - give," they cry, "For - give him, oh, for -
His Spir - it an - swers to the blood, His Spir - it an - swers
With con - fi - dence I now draw nigh, With con - fi - dence I
Sure - ty stands; My name is writ - ten on His hands.
all our race, And sprin - kles now the throne of grace.
give," they cry, "Nor let that ran - somed sin - ner die."
to the blood, And tells me I am born of God.
now draw nigh, And, "Fa - ther, Ab - ba, Fa - ther," cry. A - men.

TEXT: Charles Wesley
MUSIC: Lewis Edson

LENOX
6.6.6.6.8.8. with Repeat

200

GOD'S AMAZING GRACE

A Brief Service in Recognition of His Love and Provision

Suggested Hymn Stanzas

To facilitate an uninterrupted flow from stanza to stanza,
the suggested stanzas have been marked with an arrow: ►
Grace Greater Than Our Sin, stanzas 1, 4
Amazing Grace, stanzas 1, 2, 4
And Can It Be?, stanzas 1, 2, 4

PEOPLE:

From the fullness of His grace we have all received one blessing after another. For the law was given through Moses; grace and truth came through Jesus Christ.

WORSHIP LEADER:

Having loved His own who were in the world, He now showed them the full extent of His love.

PEOPLE:

God demonstrates His own love for us in this: While we were still sinners, Christ died for us.

WORSHIP LEADER:

You know the grace of our Lord Jesus Christ, that though He was rich, yet for your sakes He became poor, so that you through His poverty might become rich.

PEOPLE:

Because of His great love for us, God, who is rich in mercy, made us alive with Christ even when we were dead in transgressions—it is by grace you have been saved.

WORSHIP LEADER:

This is how God showed His love among us: He sent His one and only Son into the world that we might live through Him. This is love: not that we loved God, but that He loved us and sent His Son as an atoning sacrifice for our sins.

John 1:16-17; 13:1; Rom. 5:8;
2 Cor. 8:9; Eph. 2:4-5; 1 John 4:9-10. (NIV)

Optional introduction to "Grace Greater Than Our Sin"

201 Grace Greater Than Our Sin

Where sin increased, grace increased all the more. Rom. 5:20

1. Mar - vel - ous grace of our lov - ing Lord, Grace that ex - ceeds our
2. Sin and de - spair, like the sea - waves cold, Threat-en the soul with
3. Dark is the stain that we can - not hide— What can a - vail to
4. Mar - vel - ous, in - fi - nite, match - less grace, Free - ly be - stowed on
sin and our guilt! Yon - der on Cal - va - ry's mount out - poured—
in - fi - nite loss; Grace that is great - er—yes, grace un - told—
wash it a - way? Look! there is flow - ing a crim - son tide—
all who be - lieve! You that are long - ing to see His face,
There where the blood of the Lamb was spilt.
Points to the ref - uge, the might - y cross.
Whit - er than snow you may be to - day.
Will you this mo - ment His grace re - ceive?
Refrain
Grace, grace,
Mar - vel - ous grace,
God's grace, Grace that will par-don and cleanse with - in, Grace,
in - fi - nite grace,
Mar-vel-ous

TEXT: Julia H. Johnston
MUSIC: Daniel B. Towner

MOODY
9.9.9.9. with Refrain

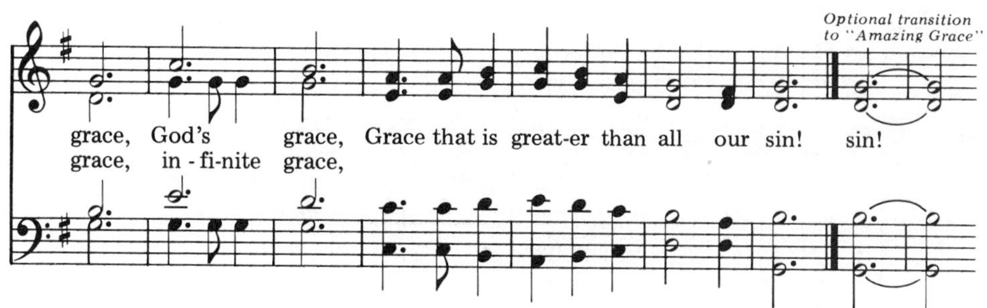
Optional transition to "Amazing Grace"
grace, God's grace, Grace that is great-er than all our sin! sin!
grace, in-fi-nite grace,

Amazing Grace 202

One thing I do know. I was blind but now I see! John 9:25

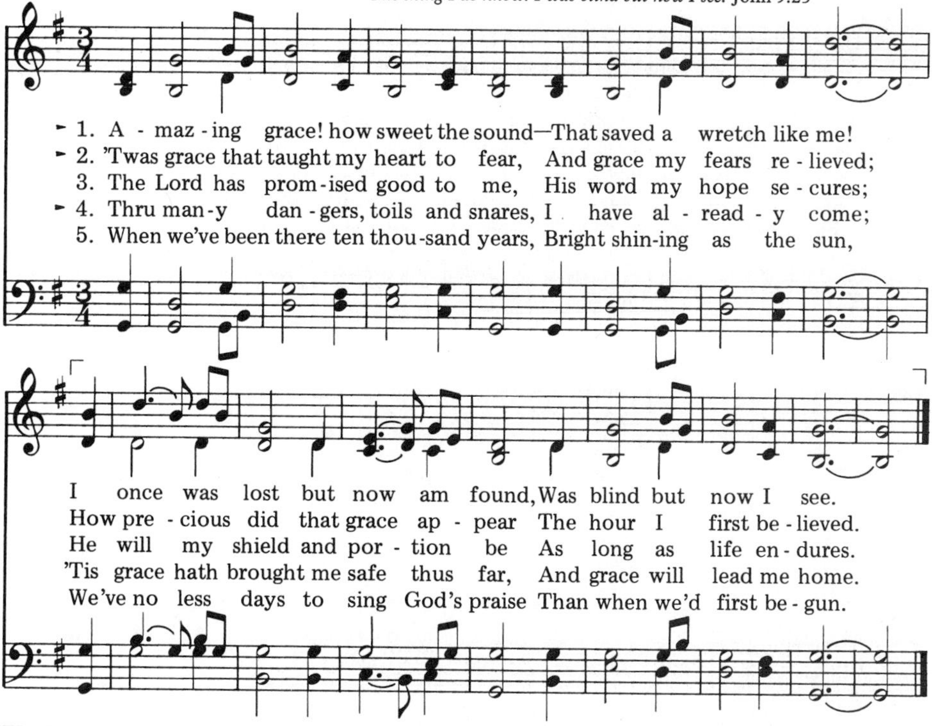

1. A - maz - ing grace! how sweet the sound—That saved a wretch like me!
I once was lost but now am found, Was blind but now I see.

2. 'Twas grace that taught my heart to fear, And grace my fears re - lieved;
How pre - cious did that grace ap - pear The hour I first be - lieved.

3. The Lord has prom - ised good to me, His word my hope se - cures;
He will my shield and por - tion be As long as life en - dures.

4. Thru man - y dan - gers, toils and snares, I have al - read - y come;
'Tis grace hath brought me safe thus far, And grace will lead me home.

5. When we've been there ten thou - sand years, Bright shin - ing as the sun,
We've no less days to sing God's praise Than when we'd first be - gun.

TEXT: John Newton; John P. Rees, stanza 5
MUSIC: Traditional American melody from Carrell and Clayton's *Virginia Harmony,* 1831; arranged by Edwin O. Excell

AMAZING GRACE
C.M.

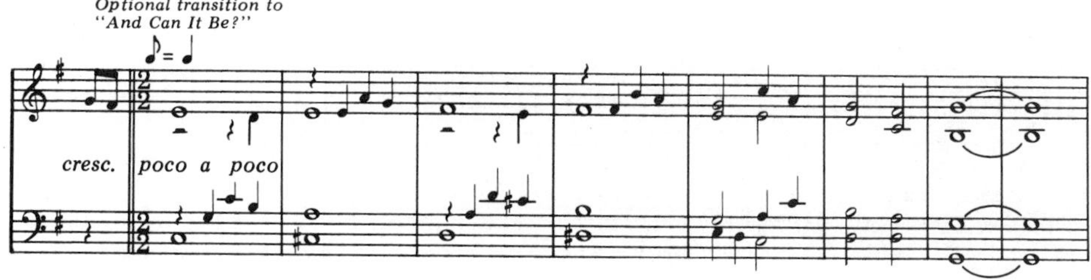
Optional transition to "And Can It Be?"
cresc.
poco a poco

203 And Can It Be?

. . . the incomparable riches of His grace . . . His kindness to us in Christ. Eph. 2:7
1. And can it be that I should gain An in - t'rest in
2. He left His Fa - ther's throne a - bove, So free, so in -
3. Long my im - pris - oned spir - it lay Fast bound in sin
4. No con - dem - na - tion now I dread: Je - sus, and all
the Sav - ior's blood? Died He for me, who caused His pain?
fi - nite His grace! Emp - tied Him - self of all but love,
and na - ture's night. Thine eye dif - fused a quick - 'ning ray:
in Him, is mine! A - live in Him, my liv - ing Head,
For me, who Him to death pur - sued? A - maz-ing love!
And bled for Ad - am's help - less race! 'Tis mer-cy all,
I woke— the dun - geon flamed with light! My chains fell off,
And clothed in right - eous - ness di - vine, Bold I ap - proach
how can it be That Thou, my God shouldst
im - mense and free, For, O my God, it
my heart was free, I rose, went forth, and
th'e - ter - nal throne, And claim the crown, thru

TEXT: Charles Wesley
MUSIC: Thomas Campbell; Choral ending by Joseph Linn

SAGINA
8.8.8.8.8.8. with Refrain

Refrain
die for me?
found out me.
fol - lowed Thee.
Christ my own.
A - maz - ing love! how can it
A -maz-ing love! how
be That Thou, my God, shouldst die for me!
can it be
Optional choral ending
sop. A - men, a - men,
A - men, a -
me! A - men, a -
A - men, a -
a - men,
men, a - men.
men, a - men.
A - men.
men, a - men.

The End of "GOD'S AMAZING GRACE—A Brief Service in Recognition of His Love and Provision"

204 Rock of Ages

They drank from the spiritual Rock that accompanied them, and that Rock was Christ. 1 Cor. 10:4

1. Rock of A - ges, cleft for me, Let me hide my - self in Thee;
2. Not the la - bors of my hands Can ful - fill Thy law's de - mands;
3. Noth-ing in my hand I bring, Sim - ply to Thy cross I cling;
4. While I draw this fleet - ing breath, When my eyes shall close in death,

Let the wa - ter and the blood, From Thy riv - en side which flowed,
Could my zeal no res - pite know, Could my tears for - ev - er flow,
Na - ked, come to Thee for dress, Help - less, look to Thee for grace;
When I soar to worlds un - known, See Thee on Thy judg-ment throne,

Be of sin the dou - ble cure, Cleanse me from its guilt and pow'r.
All for sin could not a - tone; Thou must save and Thou a - lone.
Foul, I to the foun-tain fly, Wash me, Sav - ior, or I die!
Rock of A - ges, cleft for me, Let me hide my-self in Thee. A-men.

TEXT: Augustus M. Toplady
MUSIC: Thomas Hastings

TOPLADY
7.7.7.7.7.7.

205 For God So Loved

. . . that everyone who believes in Him may have eternal life. John 3:15

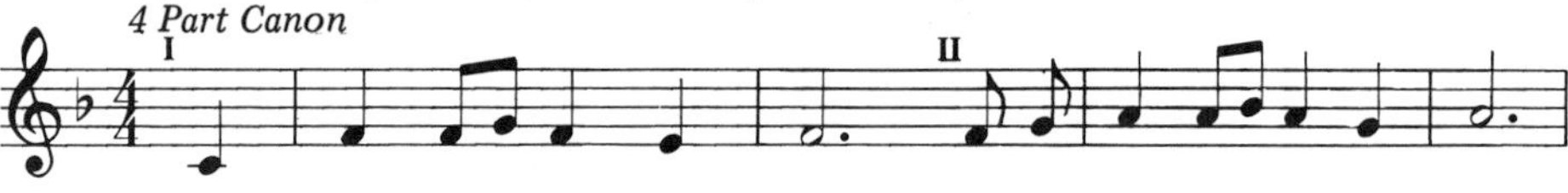

For God so loved the world That He gave His Son to die;

TEXT: John 3:16; adapted by Gerald S. Henderson
MUSIC: Gerald S. Henderson; based on an English Folk song

GIFT OF LIFE
6.7.8.6.

III
IV
And who - so - ev - er be - lieves in Him shall have ev - er-last-ing life.

There Is a Redeemer 206

Christ Jesus . . . is made unto us . . . righteousness, and sanctification, and redemption. 1 Cor. 1:30

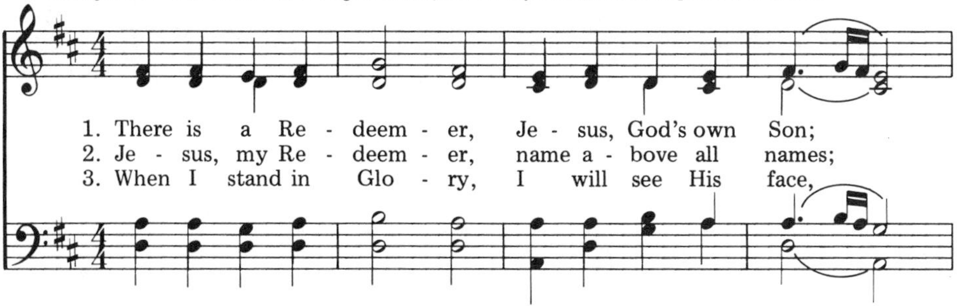

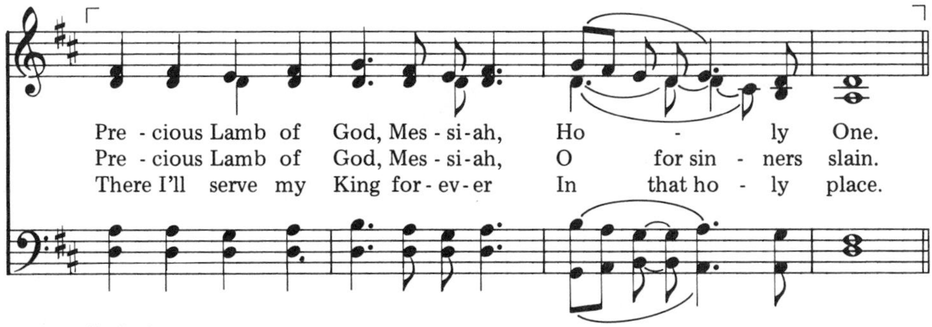

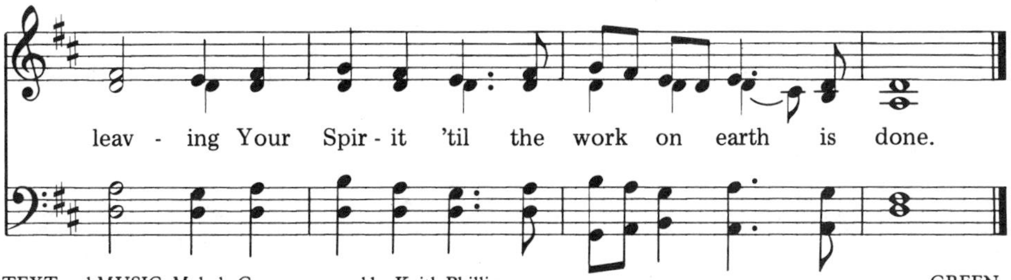

1. There is a Re - deem - er, Je - sus, God's own Son;
Pre - cious Lamb of God, Mes - si - ah, Ho - ly One.

2. Je - sus, my Re - deem - er, name a - bove all names;
Pre - cious Lamb of God, Mes - si - ah, O for sin - ners slain.

3. When I stand in Glo - ry, I will see His face,
There I'll serve my King for - ev - er In that ho - ly place.

Refrain

Thank You, oh, my Fa - ther, for giv - ing us Your Son, and
leav - ing Your Spir - it 'til the work on earth is done.

TEXT and MUSIC: Melody Green; arranged by Keith Phillips

GREEN
Irregular meter

207 God So Loved the World

For God so loved the world that He gave His one and only Son. John 3:16

p
cresc.
God so loved the world, God so loved the world,

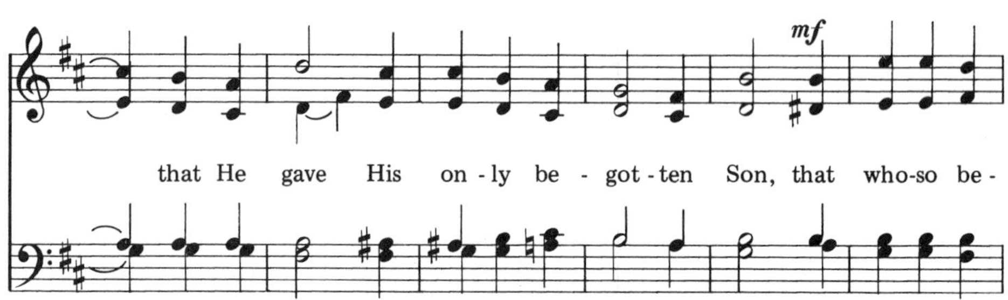
mf
that He gave His on - ly be - got - ten Son, that who-so be -

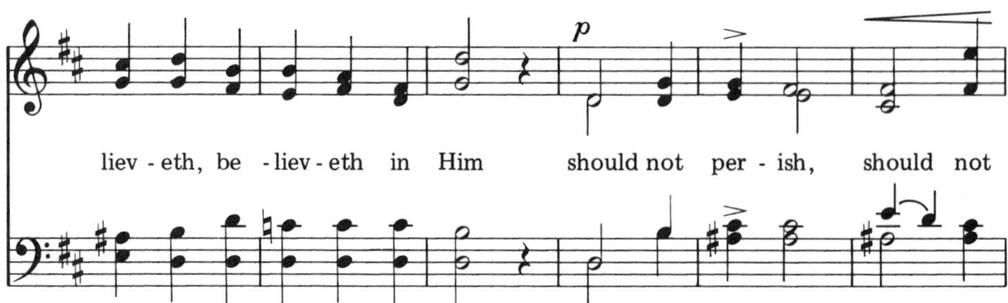
p
liev - eth, be - liev - eth in Him should not per - ish, should not

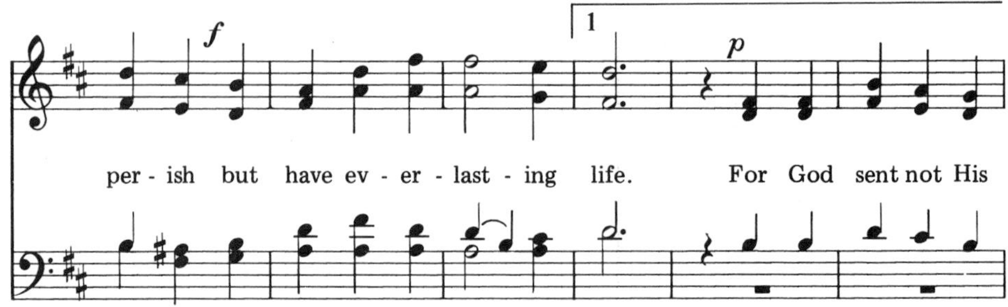
f
1
p
per - ish but have ev - er - last - ing life. For God sent not His

TEXT: John 3:16, 17
MUSIC: John Stainer

STAINER
Irregular meter

mf
Son in - to the world to con - demn the world, God sent not His Son in-to the
p
world to con - demn the world; But that the world through Him might be
D.C.
2
sav - ed. life, ev - er - last - ing life, ev - er - last - ing, ev - er -
dim. e rall.
pp
last - ing life. God so loved the world,
ppp
rall.
God so loved the world, God so loved the world.

208 Alas! and Did My Savior Bleed?

The message of the cross . . . is the power of God. 1 Cor. 1:18

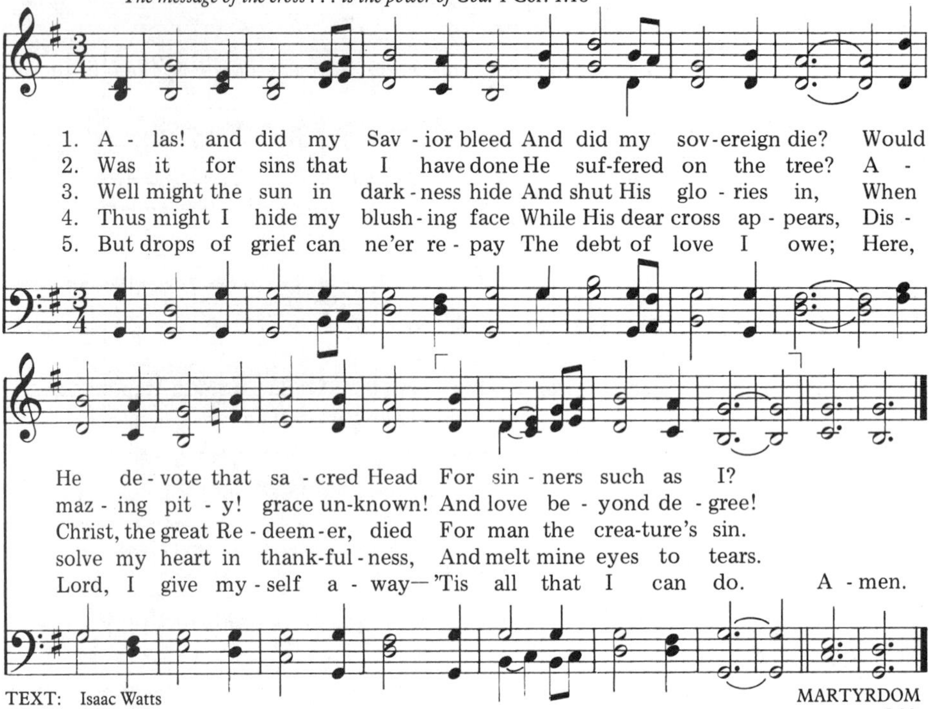

1. A - las! and did my Sav - ior bleed And did my sov - ereign die? Would
He de - vote that sa - cred Head For sin - ners such as I?
2. Was it for sins that I have done He suf - fered on the tree? A -
maz - ing pit - y! grace un - known! And love be - yond de - gree!
3. Well might the sun in dark - ness hide And shut His glo - ries in, When
Christ, the great Re - deem - er, died For man the crea - ture's sin.
4. Thus might I hide my blush - ing face While His dear cross ap - pears, Dis -
solve my heart in thank - ful - ness, And melt mine eyes to tears.
5. But drops of grief can ne'er re - pay The debt of love I owe; Here,
Lord, I give my - self a - way—'Tis all that I can do. A - men.

TEXT: Isaac Watts
MUSIC: Hugh Wilson
Alternate tune with Refrain: HUDSON, No. 188

MARTYRDOM
C.M.

209 We Are the Reason

While we were still sinners, Christ died for us. Rom. 5:8

Unison
We are the rea - son that He gave His life,
We are the rea - son that He suf - fered and died.
To a world that was lost He gave all He could give,

TEXT and MUSIC: David Meece

MEECE
Irregular meter

Jesus Paid It All 210

You are not your own; you were bought at a price. Therefore honor God. 1 Cor. 6:19-20

1
D.C.
2
to show us the rea - son to live. live.
1. I hear the Sav - ior say, "Thy strength in - deed is small!
2. Lord, now in - deed I find Thy pow'r, and Thine a - lone,
3. For noth - ing good have I Where - by Thy grace to claim—
4. And when be - fore the throne I stand in Him com - plete,
Child of weak - ness, watch and pray, Find in Me thine all in all."
Can change the lep - er's spots And melt the heart of stone.
I'll wash my gar - ments white In the blood of Cal - v'ry's Lamb.
"Je - sus died my soul to save," My lips shall still re - peat.
Refrain
Je - sus paid it all, All to Him I owe;
Sin had left a crim - son stain— He washed it white as snow.

TEXT: Elvina M. Hall
MUSIC: John T. Grape

ALL TO CHRIST
6.6.7.7. with Refrain

211 O the Deep, Deep Love of Jesus

... to grasp how ... deep is the love of Christ. Eph. 3:18

1. O the deep, deep love of Je - sus, Vast, un - meas - ured, bound - less, free!
2. O the deep, deep love of Je - sus, Spread His praise from shore to shore!
3. O the deep, deep love of Je - sus, Love of ev - ery love the best;
Roll - ing as a might - y o - cean In its full - ness o - ver me,
How He lov - eth, ev - er lov - eth, Chang - eth nev - er, nev - er - more;
'Tis an o - cean vast of bless - ing, 'Tis a ha - ven sweet of rest,
Un - der - neath me, all a - round me, Is the cur - rent of Thy love;
How He watch - es o'er His loved ones, Died to call them all His own;
O the deep, deep love of Je - sus, 'Tis a heav'n of heav'ns to me;
Lead - ing on - ward, lead - ing home - ward To my glo - rious rest a - bove.
How for them He in - ter - ced - eth, Watch - eth o'er them from the throne.
And it lifts me up to glo - ry, For it lifts me up to Thee. A - men.

TEXT: Samuel Trevor Francis
MUSIC: Thomas J. Williams
A higher setting may be found at No. 475

EBENEZER
8.7.8.7.D.

O the Deep, Deep Love of Jesus 212

. . . to grasp how . . . deep is the love of Christ. Eph. 3:18

Unison
1. O the deep, deep love of Je - sus,
2. Un - der-neath me, all a - round me
3. O the deep, deep love of Je - sus,
4. O the deep, deep love of Je - sus,
5. O the deep, deep love of Je - sus,
Vast, un - mea - sured, bound - less free!
Is the cur - rent of His love;
Love of ev - 'ry love the best;
'Tis a heav'n of heav'ns to me;
Spread His praise from shore to shore;
Roll - ing as a might - y o - cean
Lead - ing on - ward, lead - ing home - ward
'Tis an o - cean vast of bless - ing,
And it lifts me up to glo - ry,
Sing of His great - ness, sing of His good - ness,
In its full - ness o - ver me.
To my glo - rious rest a - bove.
'Tis the source of peace and rest.
For it lifts me up to Thee.
Sing of His love for - ev - er - more.

TEXT: Samuel Trevor Francis, altered; adapted by Tom Fettke
MUSIC: Traditional Gaelic melody; arranged by Tom Fettke

BUNESSAN
5.5.5.4.D.

213 Because He Lives

Because I live, you also will live. John 14:19

1. God sent His Son, they called Him Je - sus, He came to love, heal, and for - give; He lived and died to buy my par - don, An emp - ty grave is there to prove my Sav - ior lives.
2. How sweet to hold a new-born ba - by, And feel the pride, and joy he gives; But great - er still the calm as - sur - ance, This child can face un - cer - tain days be-cause He lives.
3. And then one day I'll cross the riv - er, I'll fight life's fi - nal war with pain; And then as death gives way to vic - tory, I'll see the lights of glo - ry and I'll know He lives.
Refrain
Be - cause He lives I can face to - mor - row, Be-cause He lives all fear is gone; Be - cause I know

TEXT: Gloria Gaither and William J. Gaither
MUSIC: William J. Gaither

RESURRECTION
Irregular meter

He holds the fu - ture. And life is worth the liv-ing just be-cause He
1,2
D.C.
3
Optional repeat of last Refrain
lives. lives. Be - cause He lives
I can face to - mor - row; Be - cause He lives all fear is
gone; Be - cause I know He holds the fu - ture.
rit.
And life is worth the liv - ing just be-cause He lives.

214

HE IS RISEN! ALLELUIA!

A Brief Service in Celebration of Our Lord's Resurrection

Suggested Hymn Stanzas

To facilitate an uninterrupted flow from stanza to stanza,
the suggested stanzas have been marked with an arrow: ►
Alleluia! Alleluia!, complete
Christ Arose, stanzas 1, 2
Christ the Lord Is Risen Today, complete

WORSHIP LEADER:
After the Sabbath, at dawn on the first day of the week, Mary Magdalene and the other Mary went to look at the tomb.

PEOPLE:
There was a violent earthquake, for an angel of the Lord came down from heaven and, going to the tomb, rolled back the stone and sat on it.

WORSHIP LEADER:
His appearance was like lightning, and his clothes were white as snow. The guards were so afraid of him that they shook and became like dead men.

PEOPLE:
The angel said to the women, "Do not be afraid, for I know that you are looking for Jesus, who was crucified.

WORSHIP LEADER:
He is not here; He is risen, just as He said."

PEOPLE:
He is not here; He is risen! Alleluia!

Matthew 28:1-6. (NIV)

Alleluia! Alleluia! 215

After His suffering, He . . . gave many convincing proofs that He was alive. Acts 1:3

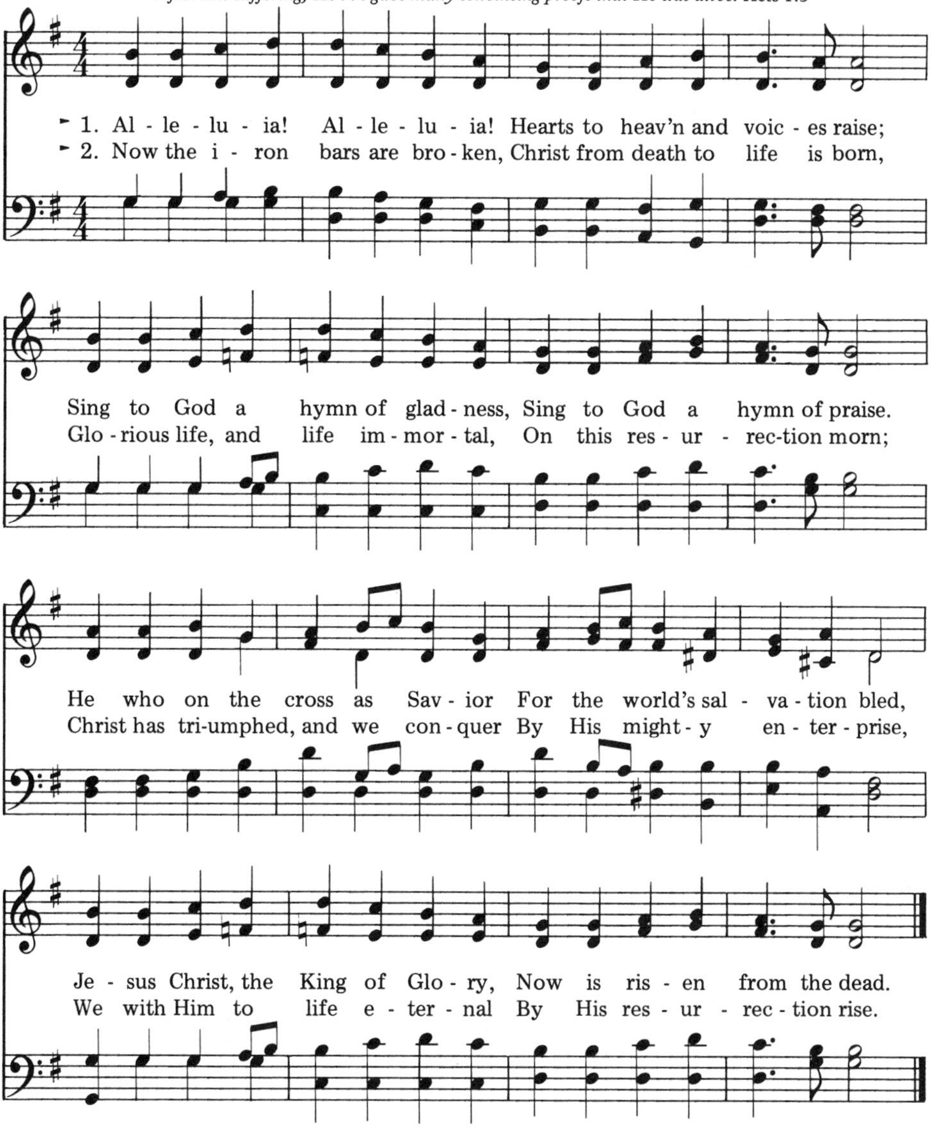
1. Al - le - lu - ia! Al - le - lu - ia! Hearts to heav'n and voic - es raise;
2. Now the i - ron bars are bro - ken, Christ from death to life is born,
Sing to God a hymn of glad - ness, Sing to God a hymn of praise.
Glo - rious life, and life im - mor - tal, On this res - ur - rec-tion morn;
He who on the cross as Sav - ior For the world's sal - va - tion bled,
Christ has tri-umphed, and we con - quer By His might - y en - ter - prise,
Je - sus Christ, the King of Glo - ry, Now is ris - en from the dead.
We with Him to life e - ter - nal By His res - ur - rec - tion rise.

TEXT: Christopher Wordsworth, altered
MUSIC: Ludwig van Beethoven; adapted by Edward Hodges

HYMN TO JOY
8.7.8.7.D.

Optional transition to "Christ Arose"
decresc.
mp

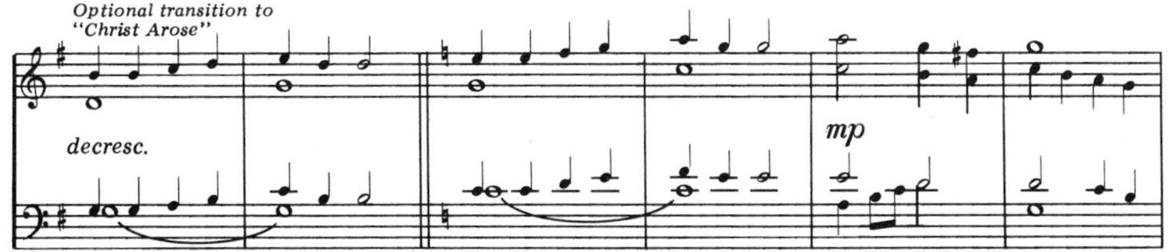

216 Christ Arose

It was impossible for death to keep its hold on Him. Acts 2:24

1. Low in the grave He lay, Je - sus my Sav - ior! Wait - ing the com - ing day,
2. Vain - ly they watch His bed, Je - sus my Sav - ior! Vain - ly they seal the dead,
3. Death can-not keep his prey, Je - sus my Sav - ior! He tore the bars a - way,
Je - sus my Lord!
Refrain
Up from the grave He a - rose, He a-rose, With a mighty - y tri-umph o'er His foes; He a-rose! He a - rose a Vic-tor from the dark do - main, And He lives for - ev - er with His saints to reign, He a - rose! He a-rose! He a - rose! He a-rose! Hal - le - lu - jah! Christ a - rose!

Segue to "Christ the Lord Is Risen Today"

TEXT and MUSIC: Robert Lowry

CHRIST AROSE
6.5.6.4. with Refrain

Christ the Lord Is Risen Today 217

Where, O death, is your victory? Where, O death, is your sting? 1 Cor. 15:55

1. Christ the Lord is ris'n to - day, Al - le - lu - ia!
2. Lives a - gain our glo - rious King, Al - le - lu - ia!
3. Love's re - deem - ing work is done, Al - le - lu - ia!
4. Soar we now where Christ has led, Al - le - lu - ia!
Sons of men and an - gels say: Al - le - lu - ia!
Where, O death, is now thy sting? Al - le - lu - ia!
Fought the fight, the bat - tle won, Al - le - lu - ia!
Fol - l'wing our ex - alt - ed Head, Al - le - lu - ia!
Raise your joys and tri - umphs high, Al - le - lu - ia!
Dy - ing once He all doth save, Al - le - lu - ia!
Death in vain for - bids Him rise, Al - le - lu - ia!
Made like Him, like Him we rise, Al - le - lu - ia!
Sing, ye heav'ns, and earth re - ply: Al - le - lu - ia!
Where thy vic - to - ry, O grave? Al - le - lu - ia!
Christ has o - pened Par - a - dise, Al - le - lu - ia!
Ours the cross, the grave, the skies, Al - le - lu - ia!

Optional choral ending on the next page

TEXT: Charles Wesley
MUSIC: from *Lyra Davidica,* London, 1708

EASTER HYMN
7.7.7.7. with Alleluias

Optional choral ending to "Christ the Lord Is Risen Today"
ff
Je - sus Christ, the King of Glo - ry, Now is ris - en from the
dead. Al - le - lu - ia!
tenor
bass
keyboard
8va
The End of "HE IS RISEN! ALLELUIA!—A Brief Service in Celebration of Our Lord's Resurrection"

218 I Know That My Redeemer Liveth

I am the Resurrection and the Life. John 11:25

Optional introduction

I know, I know that Je - sus liv - eth, And on the earth a - gain shall stand. I know, I know that life He giv - eth, That grace and pow'r are in His hand. hand.

1 2

TEXT: Jessie B. Pounds
MUSIC: James H. Fillmore and George Frederick Handel (introduction); arranged by Keith Phillips

HANNAH (Refrain only)
9.8.9.8.

He Rose Triumphantly 219

Jesus died and rose again. 1 Thess. 4:14

Slowly
1. Our bless - ed Lord was slain, (was slain), The Christ who came to
2. They sor-rowed when He died, (He died), Nor sought their tears to
3. The stone was rolled a - way, (a - way), For Christ was raised that
accel.
reign, And in a grave He lay, To wait the com - ing
hide; But soon their bit - ter pain Was turned to joy a -
day; And now He lives a - bove To man - i - fest His
Refrain
Brightly
day. gain. love.
He rose tri - um-phant-ly, In pow'r and maj - es - ty,
The Sav-ior rose no more to die; O let us now pro-claim
The glo - ry of His name, And tell to all, He lives to - day.

TEXT: Oswald J. Smith
MUSIC: Bentley D. Ackley

HE ROSE TRIUMPHANTLY
6.6.6.6. with Refrain

220 He Lives

I am the Living One. I was dead, and behold I am alive for ever and ever! Rev. 1:18

1. I serve a ris - en Sav - ior, He's in the world to - day;
2. In all the world a - round me I see His lov - ing care,
3. Re - joice, re - joice, O Chris - tian, lift up your voice and sing
I know that He is liv - ing, what - ev - er men may say;
And tho' my heart grows wea - ry, I nev - er will de - spair;
E - ter - nal hal - le - lu - jahs to Je - sus Christ the King!
I see His hand of mer - cy, I hear His voice of cheer,
I know that He is lead - ing thro' all the storm - y blast,
The Hope of all who seek Him, the Help of all who find,
And just the time I need Him He's al - ways near.
The day of His ap - pear - ing will come at last.
None oth - er is so lov - ing, so good and kind.
Refrain
He lives, He lives, Christ Je - sus lives to - day! He walks with me and
He lives, He lives,

TEXT and MUSIC: Alfred H. Ackley

ACKLEY
Irregular meter

talks with me a - long life's nar - row way. He lives, He lives, sal-
He lives, He lives,

va - tion to im - part! You ask me how I know He lives? He lives with - in my heart.

Resurrection Canon 221

3 Part Canon

He is not here; He has risen, just as He said. Matt. 28:6

I *not too fast*
Al - le - lu - ia! Christ is ris - en from the dead.
II
Al - le - lu - ia! He is ris - en as He said.

III
Al - le - lu - ia! Christ is ris - en from the dead.

Optional choral ending - to be sung after part 3 completes canon.

Al - le - lu - ia! He is ris - en!

TEXT: Gerald S. Henderson; based on Matthew 28:6, 7
MUSIC: German Folk song; arranged by Gerald S. Henderson

RESURRECTION CANON
11.11.11.

222 Easter Song

He has risen! He is not here . . . go, tell His disciples. Mark 16:6-7

1. Hear the bells ring - ing, they're sing - ing that we can be born a - gain!
2. Hear the bells ring - ing, they're sing - ing "Christ is ris - en from the dead!"
1
2
The an - gel up - on the tomb - stone said, "He is ris - en just as He said. Quick - ly now, go tell His dis - ci - ples that Je - sus Christ is no long - er

TEXT and MUSIC: Anne Herring

EASTER SONG
Irregular meter

dead!" Joy to the world, He is
ris - en, al - le - lu - ia! He's ris - en, al-
le - lu - ia! He's ris - en, al - le - lu - ia,
al - le - lu - ia!

Be Joyful 223

2 Part Canon *They worshiped Him and returned to Jerusalem with great joy.* Luke 24:52

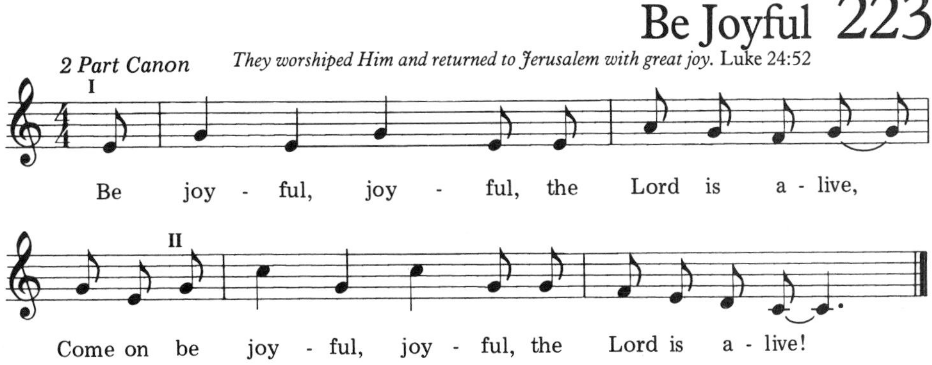
I
Be joy - ful, joy - ful, the Lord is a - live,
II
Come on be joy - ful, joy - ful, the Lord is a - live!

TEXT and MUSIC: Kurt Kaiser

BE JOYFUL
Irregular meter

224 Jesus Lives, and So Shall I

Christ has indeed been raised . . . the first fruits of those who have fallen asleep. 1 Cor. 15:20

1. Je - sus lives, and so shall I: Death, thy sting is gone for - ev - er! He for me hath deigned to die, Lives the bands of death to sev - er. He shall raise me from the dust: Je - sus is my hope and trust.
2. Je - sus lives and reigns su - preme: And, His king - dom still re - main - ing, I shall al - so be with Him, Ev - er liv - ing, ev - er reign - ing. God has prom - ised— be it must: Je - sus is my hope and trust.
3. Je - sus lives—and by His grace, Vic - t'ry o'er my pas - sions giv - ing, I will change my heart and ways, Ev - er to His glo - ry liv - ing. Me He rais - es from the dust: Je - sus is my hope and trust.
4. Je - sus lives— I know full well Naught from Him my heart can sev - er, Life nor death nor pow'rs of hell, Joy nor grief, hence - forth for - ev - er. None of all His saints is lost: Je - sus is my hope and trust.
5. Je - sus lives—and death is now But my en - trance in - to glo - ry; Cour - age, then, my soul, for thou Hast a crown of life be - fore thee. Thou shalt find thy hopes were just: Je - sus is my hope and trust. A - men.

TEXT: Christian F. Gellert; translated by Philip Schaff
MUSIC: Johann Crüger

ZUVERSICHT
7.8.7.8.7.7.

Worship Christ the Risen King 225

My Lord and my God! John 20:28

1. Rise, O Church, and lift your voi - ces, Christ has con - quered
2. See the tomb where death had laid Him, Emp - ty now, its
3. Hear the earth pro - test and trem - ble, See the stone re -
4. Doubt may lift its head to mur - mur, Scof - fers mock and
5. We ac - claim Your life, O Je - sus, Now we sing Your
death and hell. Sing as all the earth re - joi - ces;
mouth de - clares; "Death and I could not con - tain Him,
moved with pow'r; All hell's min - ions may as - sem - ble
sin - ners jeer; But the truth pro - claims a won - der
vic - to - ry; Sin or hell may seek to seize us
Re - sur - rec - tion an - thems swell. Come and wor - ship,
For the Throne of Life He shares." Come and wor - ship,
But can - not with - stand His hour. He has con - quered,
Thought-ful hearts re - ceive with cheer. He is ris - en,
But Your con - quest keeps us free. Stand in tri - umph,
come and wor - ship, Wor - ship Christ, the Ris - en King!
come and wor - ship, Wor - ship Christ, the Ris - en King!
He has con - quered, Christ the Lord, the Ris - en King!
He is ris - en, Now re - ceive the Ris - en King!
Stand in tri - umph, Wor - ship Christ, the Ris - en King! A - men.

TEXT: Jack W. Hayford
MUSIC: Henry T. Smart
A lower setting may be found at No. 241

REGENT SQUARE
8.7.8.7.8.7.

226 The Day of Resurrection

Suddenly Jesus met them. "Greetings," He said. Matt. 28:9

1. The day of res - ur - rec - tion! Earth, tell it out a - broad;
2. Our hearts be pure from e - vil, That we may see a - right
3. Now let the heav'ns be joy - ful! Let earth her song be - gin!

The Pass - o - ver of glad - ness, The Pass - o - ver of God.
The Lord in rays e - ter - nal Of res - ur - rec - tion light;
The world re - sound in tri - umph, And all that is there - in;

From death to life e - ter - nal, From earth un - to the sky,
And, lis - t'ning to His ac - cents, May hear, so calm and plain,
Let all things seen and un - seen Their notes of glad - ness blend;

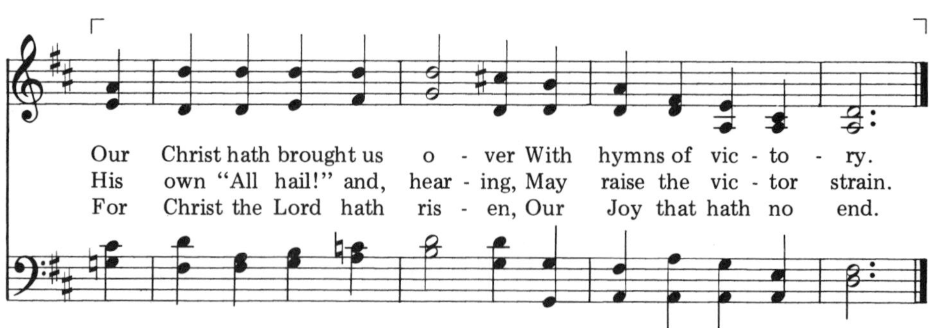
Our Christ hath brought us o - ver With hymns of vic - to - ry.
His own "All hail!" and, hear - ing, May raise the vic - tor strain.
For Christ the Lord hath ris - en, Our Joy that hath no end.

TEXT: John of Damascus, 8th century; translated by John M. Neale
MUSIC: Henry T. Smart
A lower setting may be found at No. 483

LANCASHIRE
7.6.7.6.D.

Thine Is the Glory 227

Death has been swallowed up in victory. 1 Cor. 15:54

1. Thine is the glo - ry, Ris - en, con - qu'ring Son; End - less is the
2. Lo! Je - sus meets us, Ris - en, from the tomb; Lov - ing - ly He
3. No more we doubt Thee, Glo - rious Prince of Life! Life is naught with-
vic - t'ry Thou o'er death hast won. An - gels in bright rai - ment
greets us, Scat - ters fear and gloom; Let His church with glad - ness
out Thee; Aid us in our strife; Make us more than con - qu'rors,
Rolled the stone a - way, Kept the fold - ed grave-clothes Where Thy
Hymns of tri - umph sing, For her Lord now liv - eth; Death hath
Through Thy death-less love; Bring us safe through Jor - dan With Thy
bod - y lay.
lost its sting.
power and love.
Refrain
Thine is the glo - ry, Ris - en, con - qu'ring Son;
End - less is the vic - t'ry Thou o'er death hast won. A - men.

TEXT: Edmund L. Budry; translated by Richard B. Hoyle
MUSIC: George Frederick Handel

MACCABEUS
10.11.11.11. with Refrain

228 Rejoice, the Lord Is King

Rejoice in the Lord always. I will say it again: Rejoice! Phil. 4:4

Descant - last stanza
4. Re-joice, our Lord shall come a-gain.
And take His ser - vants to their e - ter - nal home:
Lift up your heart, Re -
1. Re - joice, the Lord is King! Your Lord and King a - dore!
2. The Lord, our Sav - ior, reigns, The God of truth and love;
3. His king - dom can - not fail, He rules o'er earth and heav'n;
4. Re - joice in glo - rious hope! Our Lord the Judge shall come
Re - joice, give thanks, and sing, And tri - umph ev - er - more:
When He had purged our stains, He took His seat a - bove:
The keys of death and hell Are to our Je - sus giv'n:
And take His ser - vants up To their e - ter - nal home:
Lift up your heart, lift up your voice! Re -

TEXT: Charles Wesley; based on Philippians 4:4
MUSIC: John Darwall;
Descant and choral ending by Camp Kirkland
A higher setting may be found at No. 111

DARWALL
6.6.6.6.8.8.

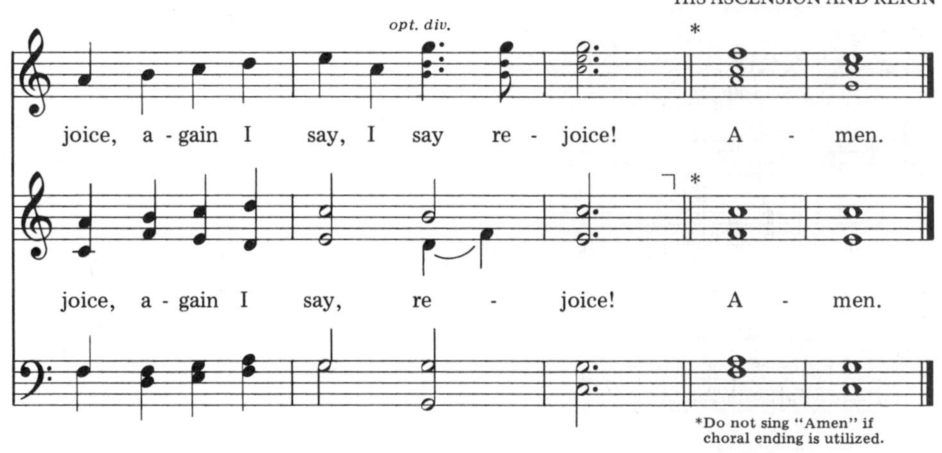
opt. div.
joice, a - gain I say, I say re - joice! A - men.
joice, a - gain I say, re - joice! A - men.
*Do not sing "Amen" if choral ending is utilized.

Optional choral ending
Unison
ff
div.

Lift up your voice! Re - joice, a - gain I say, re -

ff
Keyboard

joice, re - joice! A - men.

8va

8va

229 Our God Reigns

How beautiful . . . are the feet of those who bring good news . . . "Your God reigns!" Isa. 52:7

1. How love - ly on the moun-tains are the feet of him who brings good news, good news An - nounc-ing peace, pro - claim - ing news of hap - pi - ness. Our God reigns, Our God reigns!
2. He had no state - ly form, He had no maj - es - ty, That we should be drawn to Him. He was de - spised and we took no ac - count of Him, Yet now He reigns with the Most High.
3. Out from the tomb He came with grace and maj - es - ty, He is a - live, He is a - live. God loves us so, see here His hands, His feet, His side. Yes, we know, He is a - live.
Refrain
Our God reigns!

TEXT and MUSIC: Leonard E. Smith, Jr.; arranged by Eugene Thomas

OUR GOD REIGNS
Irregular meter

Our God reigns! Our God reigns! Our God reigns!

OPTIONAL STANZAS: *To be sung after verse 2. Verse 3 is to be sung last.*

It was our sin and guilt that bruised and wounded Him.
It was our sin that brought Him down.
When we like sheep had gone astray, our Shepherd came
And on His shoulders bore our shame.

Refrain

Meek as a lamb that's led out to the slaughterhouse,
Dumb as a sheep before its shearer,
His life ran down upon the ground like pouring rain,
That we might be born again.

Refrain

Jesus Is King 230

3 Part Canon

I am a King. In fact, for this reason I was born. John 18:37

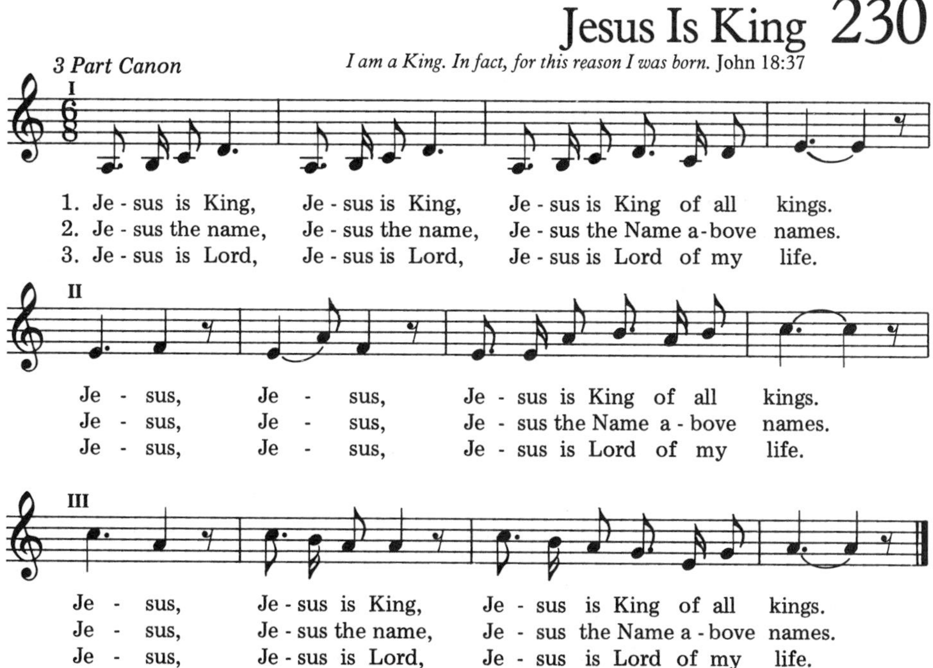
I
1. Je - sus is King, Je - sus is King, Je - sus is King of all kings.
2. Je - sus the name, Je - sus the name, Je - sus the Name a - bove names.
3. Je - sus is Lord, Je - sus is Lord, Je - sus is Lord of my life.
II
Je - sus, Je - sus, Je - sus is King of all kings.
Je - sus, Je - sus, Je - sus the Name a - bove names.
Je - sus, Je - sus, Je - sus is Lord of my life.
III
Je - sus, Je - sus is King, Je - sus is King of all kings.
Je - sus, Je - sus the name, Je - sus the Name a - bove names.
Je - sus, Je - sus is Lord, Je - sus is Lord of my life.

TEXT: Gerald S. Henderson
MUSIC: Traditional Appalachian melody; adapted by Gerald S. Henderson

JESUS IS KING
Irregular meter

231 Jesus Shall Reign

He will rule from sea to sea and from the River to the ends of the earth. Ps. 72:8

1. Je - sus shall reign wher - e'er the sun Does His suc - ces-sive jour-neys run;
2. To Him shall end - less prayer be made, And end-less prais-es crown His head;
3. Peo-ple and realms of ev - 'ry tongue Dwell on His love with sweet-est song;
4. Let ev - 'ry crea - ture rise and bring His grate-ful hon-ors to our King;
His king-dom spread from shore to shore, Till moons shall wax and wane no more.
His name like sweet per - fume shall rise With ev - 'ry morn - ing sac - ri - fice.
And in - fant voic - es shall pro - claim Their ear - ly bless - ings on His name.
An - gels de - scend with songs a - gain, And earth re - peat the loud "A-men!"

Optional last stanza harmonization

Descant

4. Let ev - 'ry crea - ture

Broader

Unison

Broaden

4. Let ev - 'ry crea - ture rise and

TEXT: Isaac Watts, altered; based on Psalm 72
MUSIC: John Hatton; Descant and last stanza harmonization by Ken Barker

DUKE STREET
L.M.

rise and bring His grate-ful hon - ors to our
bring His grate-ful hon - ors to our King;

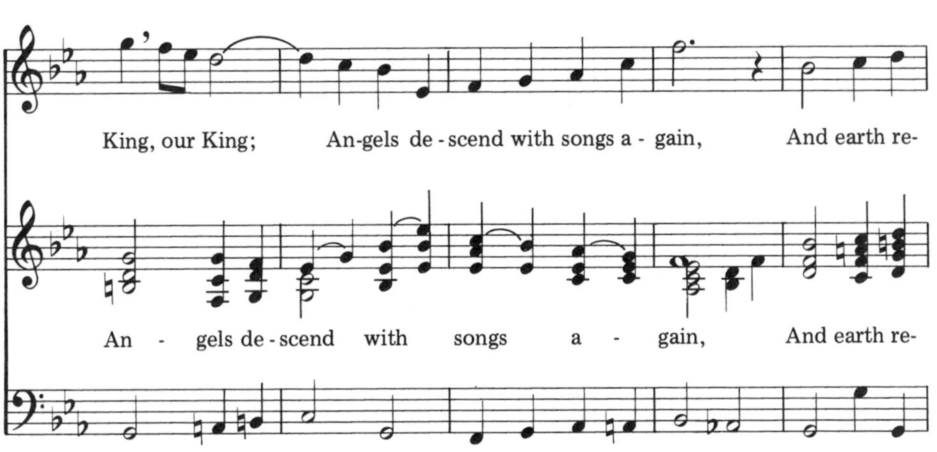
King, our King; An-gels de - scend with songs a - gain, And earth re-
An - gels de - scend with songs a - gain, And earth re-

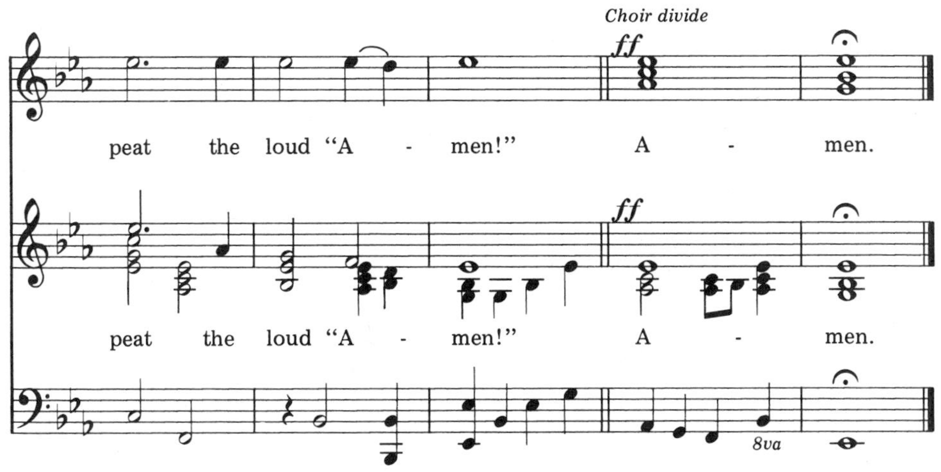
Choir divide
ff
peat the loud "A - men!" A - men.
ff
peat the loud "A - men!" A - men.
8va

232 Hail the Day That Sees Him Rise

When He ascended on high, He led captives in His train. Eph. 4:8

1. Hail the day that sees Him rise, Al - le - lu - ia!
2. There for Him high tri - umph waits; Al - le - lu - ia!
3. See, He lifts His hands a - bove! Al - le - lu - ia!
4. Lord, be - yond our mor - tal sight, Al - le - lu - ia!
To His throne a - bove the skies; Al - le - lu - ia!
Lift your heads, e - ter - nal gates, Al - le - lu - ia!
See, He shows the prints of love! Al - le - lu - ia!
Raise our hearts to reach Thy height, Al - le - lu - ia!
Christ, the Lamb for sin - ners giv'n, Al - le - lu - ia!
He hath con - quered death and sin, Al - le - lu - ia!
Hark! His gra - cious lips be - stow, Al - le - lu - ia!
There Thy face un - cloud - ed see, Al - le - lu - ia!
En - ters now the high - est heav'n. Al - le - lu - ia!
Take the King of glo - ry in! Al - le - lu - ia!
Bless-ings on His church be - low. Al - le - lu - ia!
Find our heav'n of heav'ns in Thee! Al - le - lu - ia! A - men.

TEXT: Charles Wesley
MUSIC: Welsh Hymn melody; arranged by John Roberts

LLANFAIR
7.7.7.7. with Alleluias

Alleluia! Sing to Jesus 233

There . . . was a great multitude . . . from every nation . . . standing . . . in front of the Lamb. Rev. 7:9

1. Al - le - lu - ia! sing to Je - sus! His the scep - tre, His the throne;
2. Al - le - lu - ia! not as or - phans Are we left in sor - row now;
3. Al - le - lu - ia! Bread of Heav - en, You on earth our food, and stay!
Al - le - lu - ia! His the tri - umph, His the vic - to - ry a - lone;
Al - le - lu - ia! He is near us, Faith be - lieves, nor ques - tions how:
Al - le - lu - ia! here the sin - ful Flee to You from day to day;
Hark! the songs of peace - ful Zi - on Thun - der like a might - y flood;
Though the clouds from sight re - ceived Him When the for - ty days were o'er,
In - ter - ces - sor, Friend of sin - ners, Earth's Re - deem - er, plead for me,
"Je - sus, out of ev - 'ry na - tion Has re-deemed us by His blood."
Shall our hearts for-get His prom - ise, "I am with you ev - er - more"?
Where the songs of all the sin - less Sweep a-cross the crys-tal sea. A - men.

TEXT: William C. Dix
MUSIC: Rowland H. Prichard; arranged by Robert Harkness
A lower setting may be found at No. 89

HYFRYDOL
8.7.8.7.D.

234 Crown Him with Many Crowns

On His head are many crowns. Rev. 19:12

1. Crown Him with man - y crowns, The Lamb up - on His throne:
2. Crown Him the Lord of love: Be - hold His hands and side—
3. Crown Him the Lord of life: Who tri - umphed o'er the grave,
4. Crown Him the Lord of heav'n: One with the Fa - ther known,
Hark! how the heav'n-ly an - them drowns All mu - sic but its own!
Rich wounds, yet vis - i - ble a - bove, In beau - ty glo - ri - fied.
Who rose vic - to - rious to the strife For those He came to save.
One with the Spir - it thru Him giv'n From yon-der glo - rious throne.
A - wake, my soul, and sing Of Him who died for thee, And
No an - gel in the sky Can ful - ly bear that sight, But
His glo - ries now we sing, Who died and rose on high, Who
To Thee be end - less praise, For Thou for us hast died; Be
hail Him as thy match-less King Thru all e - ter - ni - ty.
down-ward bends his won-d'ring eye At mys - ter - ies so bright.
died e - ter - nal life to bring And lives that death may die.
Thou, O Lord, thru end - less days A - dored and mag - ni - fied. A - men.

TEXT: Matthew Bridges, stanzas 1, 2, 4; Godfrey Thring, stanza 3
MUSIC: George J. Elvey; Last stanza harmonization by Mark Hayes
A higher setting may be found at No. 478

DIADEMATA
S.M.D.

Optional last stanza harmonization
Unison
die. Broaden 4. Crown Him the Lord of heav'n: One
with the Fa - ther known, One with the Spir - it thru Him giv'n
From yon-der glo - rious throne. To Thee be end - less praise,
For Thou for us hast died; Be Thou, O Lord, thru
end - less days A - dored and mag - ni - fied. A - men.
ff
Optional choir divisi– sing cued notes

235 At the Name of Jesus

Whoever acknowledges Me before men, I will also acknowledge him before My Father. Matt. 10:32

1. At the name of Je - sus Ev - 'ry knee shall bow,
2. At His voice cre - a - tion Sprang at once to sight,
3. Hum-bled for a sea - son, To re - ceive a name
4. In your hearts en - throne Him; There let Him sub - due
5. Broth-ers, this Lord Je - sus Shall re - turn a - gain,
Ev - 'ry tongue con - fess Him King of glo - ry now;
All the an - gel fac - es, All the hosts of light,
From the lips of sin - ners, Un - to whom He came,
All that is not ho - ly, All that is not true:
With the Fa - ther's glo - ry O'er the earth to reign;
'Tis the Fa - ther's pleas - ure We should call Him Lord,
Thrones and dom - i - na - tions, Stars up - on their way,
Faith - ful - ly He bore it Spot - less to the last,
Crown Him as your Cap - tain In temp - ta - tion's hour;
For all wreaths of em - pire Meet up - on His brow,
Who from the be - gin - ning Was the might - y Word.
All the heav'n-ly or - ders In their great ar - ray.
Brought it back vic - to - rious, When from death He passed.
Let His will en - fold you In its light and power.
All our hearts con - fess Him King of glo - ry now. A - men.

TEXT: Caroline M. Noel; based on Philippians 2:5-11
MUSIC: Ronn Huff

ASHLYNE
6.5.6.5.D.

Is It the Crowning Day? 236

He will appear a second time . . . to bring salvation to those who are waiting for Him. Heb. 9:28

1. Je - sus may come to - day, Glad day! Glad day! And I would see my Friend; Dan - gers and trou - bles would end If Je - sus should come to - day.
2. I may go home to - day, Glad day! Glad day! Seem - eth I hear their song; Hail to the ra - di - ant throng! If I should go home to - day.
3. Why should I anx - ious be? Glad day! Glad day! Lights ap - pear on the shore, Storms will af - fright nev - er - more, For He is "at hand" to - day.
4. Faith-ful I'll be to - day, Glad day! Glad day! And I will free - ly tell Why I should love Him so well, For He is my all to - day.
Refrain
Glad day! Glad day! Is it the crown - ing day? I'll live for to - day, nor anx - ious be, Je - sus my Lord I soon shall see; Glad day! Glad day! Is it the crown - ing day?

TEXT: George Walker Whitcomb
MUSIC: Charles H. Marsh

CROWNING DAY
Irregular meter

237 We Shall Behold Him

We shall be like Him, for we shall see Him as He is. 1 John 3:2

1. The sky shall un - fold, pre - par - ing His en-trance; The stars shall ap-plaud Him with thun-ders of praise. The sweet light in His eyes shall en-hance those a - wait - ing; And we shall be - hold Him then face to face.
2. The an - gel shall sound the shout of His com-ing; The sleeping shall rise from their slum-ber-ing place. And those who re - main shall be changed in a mo - ment; And we shall be - hold Him then face to face.
Refrain
And we shall be - hold Him, We shall be - hold Him Face to face in all of His glo - ry. O we shall be - hold Him, We shall be-

TEXT and MUSIC: Dottie Rambo; arranged by Tom Fettke

WE SHALL BEHOLD HIM
Irregular meter

hold Him Face to face, our Sav-ior and Lord.
Optional choral ending
f Broaden
rit.
And we shall be - hold Him, our Sav - ior and Lord.

The King Is Coming 238

The Lord is coming with thousands . . . of His holy ones. Jude 14

O the King is com-ing, the King is com-ing! I just heard the trum-pets sound-ing, And now His face I see; O the King is com-ing, the King is com-ing! Praise God, He's com-ing for me!

TEXT: Gloria Gaither, William J. Gaither and Charles Millhuff
MUSIC: William J. Gaither

KING IS COMING
Irregular meter

239 Jesus Is Coming Again

I will come back and take you to be with Me. John 14:3

1. Mar-vel-ous mes-sage we bring, Glo-ri-ous car-ol we sing,
2. For-est and flow-er ex-claim, Moun-tain and mead-ow the same,
3. Stand-ing be-fore Him at last, Tri-al and trou-ble all past,
Won-der-ful word of the King— Je-sus is com-ing a-gain! (a-gain!)
All earth and heav-en pro-claim— Je-sus is com-ing a-gain! (a-gain!)
Crowns at His feet we will cast— Je-sus is com-ing a-gain! (a-gain!)
Refrain—Unison
Com-ing a-gain, Com-ing a-gain;
May-be morn-ing, may-be noon, May-be eve-ning and may-be soon!
Com-ing a-gain, Com-ing a-gain;

TEXT and MUSIC: John W. Peterson

COMING AGAIN
7.7.7.7. with Refrain

Parts
O what a won-der-ful day it will be— Je-sus is com-ing a - gain!
When He Shall Come 240
They will walk with Me, dressed in white, for they are worthy. Rev. 3:4
1. When He shall come, re - splen-dent in His glo - ry, To take His own from out this vale of night, O may I know the joy at His ap - pear - ing— On - ly at morn to walk with Him in white!
2. When I shall stand with - in the court of heav - en Where white-robed pil - grims pass be - fore my sight— Earth's mar-tyred saints and blood-washed o-ver - com - ers— These then are they who walk with Him in white!
3. When He shall call, from earth's re-mot-est cor - ners, All who have stood tri - um-phant in His might, O to be wor - thy then to stand be - side them, And in that morn to walk with Him in white!

TEXT and MUSIC: Almeda J. Pearce; based on Rev. 3:4 and 7:9

PEARCE
11.10.11.10.

241 Lo, He Comes with Clouds Descending

They will see the Son of Man coming on the clouds of the sky. Matt. 24:30

1. Lo, He comes with clouds de-scend-ing, Once for fa - vored sin - ners slain;
2. Ev - ery eye shall now be-hold Him, Robed in dread-ful maj - es - ty;
3. Now re-demp-tion, long ex-pect-ed, See in sol - emn pomp ap-pear:
4. Yea, A - men! let all a-dore Thee, High on Thine e - ter - nal throne;

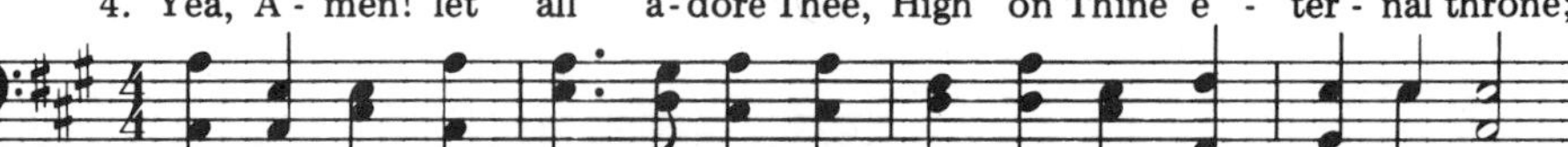

Thou-sand thou-sand saints at-tend-ing, Swell the tri - umph of His train:
Those who set at naught and sold Him, Pierced and nailed Him to the tree,
All His saints, by men re - ject-ed, Now shall meet Him in the air:
Sav - ior, take the pow'r and glo - ry, Claim the king - dom for Thine own:

Al - le - lu - ia! al - le - lu - ia! God ap-pears on earth to reign.
Deep-ly wail - ing, deep - ly wail - ing, Shall the true Mes - si - ah see.
Al - le - lu - ia! al - le - lu - ia! See the day of God ap-pear.
O, come quick-ly, O, come quick-ly! Ev - er - last - ing God, come down. A-men.

TEXT: Charles Wesley and Martin Madan; based on John Cennick — REGENT SQUARE
MUSIC: Henry T. Smart — 8.7.8.7.8.7.
A higher setting may be found at No. 225

242 While We Are Waiting, Come

Behold, I am coming soon! My reward is with Me. Rev. 22:12

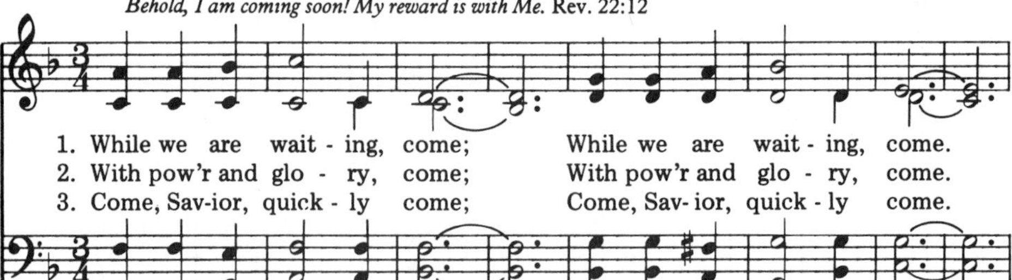

1. While we are wait - ing, come; While we are wait - ing, come.
2. With pow'r and glo - ry, come; With pow'r and glo - ry, come.
3. Come, Sav-ior, quick - ly come; Come, Sav- ior, quick - ly come.

TEXT: Claire Cloninger — WAITING
MUSIC: Don Cason — S.M.

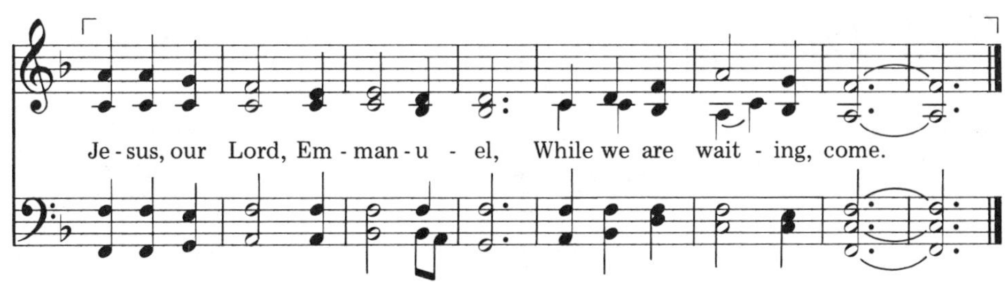
Je - sus, our Lord, Em - man - u - el, While we are wait - ing, come.

O Come, Messiah, Come Again 243

He waits for His enemies to be made His footstool. Heb. 10:13

8va

Unison

O come, Mes - si - ah, come a - gain, And rid the world of death and sin. Re - turn, Thou ris - en Sav - ior and King. That heav'n and earth at last may sing

Refrain—parts optional

Re - joice, re - joice, Em - man - u - el has come to thee, O Is - ra - el!

TEXT: Vann Trapp
MUSIC: Adapted from Plainsong by Thomas Helmore; arranged by Tom Fettke

VENI EMMANUEL
L.M. with Refrain

244 The Trees of the Field

You will go out in joy . . . and all the trees of the field will clap. Isa. 55:12

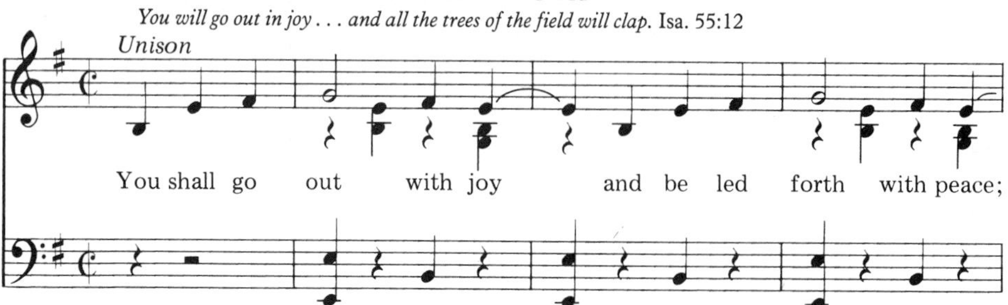
Unison
You shall go out with joy and be led forth with peace;

The moun-tains and the hills will break forth be -

fore you. There'll be shouts of joy, and all the trees of the

field Will clap, will clap their hands.

TEXT: Steffi Geiser Rubin; based on Isaiah 55:12
MUSIC: Stuart Dauermann

THE TREES OF THE FIELD
Irregular meter

And all the trees of the field will
claps
clap their hands, The trees of the
field will clap their hands, The trees of the
field will clap their hands While
you go out with joy.

245 What If It Were Today?

Lift up your heads, because your redemption is drawing near. Luke 21:28

1. Je - sus is com-ing to earth a-gain— What if it were to - day?
2. Sa-tan's do-min-ion will then be o'er— O that it were to - day!
3. Faith-ful and true would He find us here If He should come to - day?

Com - ing in pow - er and love to reign— What if it were to - day?
Sor - row and sigh-ing shall be no more— O that it were to - day!
Watch-ing in glad -ness and not in fear, If He should come to - day?

Com - ing to claim His cho - sen Bride, All the re - deemed and pu - ri - fied,
Then shall the dead in Christ a - rise, Caught up to meet Him in the skies;
Signs of His com - ing mul - ti - ply, Morn-ing light breaks in east-ern sky;

rit. *a tempo*

O - ver this whole earth scat - tered wide— What if it were to - day?
When shall these glo - ries meet our eyes? What if it were to - day?
Watch, for the time is draw - ing nigh— What if it were to - day?

Refrain

Glo - ry, glo - ry! Joy to my heart 'twill bring; Glo - ry, glo - ry!

TEXT and MUSIC: Lelia N. Morris

SECOND COMING
Irregular meter

When we shall crown Him King; Glo - ry! glo - ry! Haste to pre -
pare the way; Glo - ry, glo - ry! Je - sus will come some-day.

He Is Coming 246

He is coming with the clouds, and every eye will see Him. Rev. 1:7

3 Part Canon
I
1. Oh, Je - sus my Sav - ior, He is com - ing a - gain.
2. In clouds of great glo - ry, He is com - ing a - gain.
3. And we shall be like Him, He is com - ing a - gain.
II
Oh, Je - sus my Sav - ior, He is com - ing a - gain.
In clouds of great glo - ry, He is com - ing a - gain.
And we shall be like Him, He is com - ing a - gain.
III
Com - ing, com - ing, com - ing a - gain.

TEXT: Gerald S. Henderson; based on 1 Thessalonians 4:16-17; 1 John 3:2; Revelation 1:7
MUSIC: From *The Diapason,* 1860; adapted by Gerald S. Henderson

DIAPASON
Irregular meter

247 Spirit of the Living God

Live by the Spirit, and you will not gratify the desires of the sinful nature. Gal. 5:16

Spir - it of the Liv - ing God, fall fresh on me. Spir - it of the Liv - ing God, fall fresh on me. Melt me, mold me, fill me, use me. Spir - it of the Liv - ing God, fall fresh on me.

TEXT and MUSIC: Daniel Iverson

IVERSON
Irregular meter

248 Holy Ghost, with Light Divine

"Not by might nor by power, but by My Spirit," says the Lord Almighty. Zech. 4:6

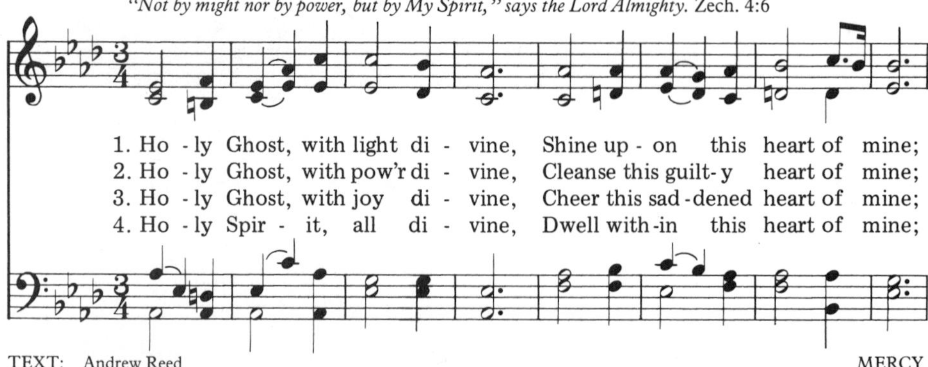
1. Ho - ly Ghost, with light di - vine, Shine up - on this heart of mine;
2. Ho - ly Ghost, with pow'r di - vine, Cleanse this guilt - y heart of mine;
3. Ho - ly Ghost, with joy di - vine, Cheer this sad - dened heart of mine;
4. Ho - ly Spir - it, all di - vine, Dwell with - in this heart of mine;

TEXT: Andrew Reed
MUSIC: Louis M. Gottschalk; adapted by Edwin P. Parker

MERCY
7.7.7.7.

Chase the shades of night a - way, Turn my dark-ness in - to day.
Long hath sin with-out con - trol Held do - min - ion o'er my soul.
Bid my man - y woes de - part, Heal my wound-ed, bleed-ing heart.
Cast down ev - 'ry i - dol - throne, Reign su-preme and reign a - lone. A-men.
Spirit of God, Descend upon My Heart 249
Since we live by the Spirit, let us keep in step with the Spirit. Gal. 5:25
1. Spir - it of God, de - scend up - on my heart: Wean it from earth, thro' all its puls - es move. Stoop to my weak - ness, might-y as Thou art, And make me love Thee as I ought to love.
2. Hast Thou not bid us love Thee, God and King? All, all Thine own— soul, heart and strength and mind. I see Thy cross— there teach my heart to cling; O let me seek Thee, and O let me find.
3. Teach me to feel that Thou art al - ways nigh; Teach me the strug-gles of the soul to bear— To check the ris - ing doubt, the reb - el sigh; Teach me the pa - tience of un - an - swered prayer.
4. Teach me to love Thee as Thine an - gels love, One ho - ly pas - sion fill - ing all my frame: The bap - tism of the heav'n-de-scend-ed Dove— My heart an al - tar and Thy love the flame. A - men.

TEXT: George Croly
MUSIC: Frederick C. Atkinson

MORECAMBE
10.10.10.10.

250 Come, Holy Spirit

The law of the Spirit of life set me free from the law of sin and death. Rom. 8:2

1. Come as a wis - dom to chil-dren, Come as new sight to the
2. Come as a rest to the wea -ry, Come as a balm for the
3. Come like a spring in the des - ert, Come to the with-ered of
blind, Come, Lord, as strength to my weak - ness,
sore, Come as a dew to my dry - ness:
soul; O let Your sweet heal - ing pow - er
Take me: soul, bod - y and mind.
Fill me with joy ev - er - more.
Touch me and make me whole.
Refrain
Come, Ho - ly Spir - it, I
need You, Come, sweet Spir - it, I pray; Come in Your
strength and Your pow - er, Come in Your own gen - tle way.

TEXT: Gloria Gaither and William J. Gaither
MUSIC: William J. Gaither

COME, HOLY SPIRIT
8.7.8.7.D.

Breathe on Me 251

He breathed on them and said, "Receive the Holy Spirit." John 20:22

1. Ho - ly Spir - it, breathe on me, Un - til my heart is clean;
2. Ho - ly Spir - it, breathe on me, My stub-born will sub - due;
3. Ho - ly Spir - it, breathe on me, Fill me with pow'r di - vine;
4. Ho - ly Spir - it, breathe on me, Till I am all Thine own,
Let sun-shine fill its in - most part, With not a cloud be - tween.
Teach me in words of liv - ing flame What Christ would have me do.
Kin - dle a flame of love and zeal With - in this heart of mine.
Un - til my will is lost in Thine, To live for Thee a - lone.
Refrain
Breathe on me, breathe on me, Ho - ly Spir - it, breathe on me;
Take Thou my heart, cleanse ev - 'ry part, Ho - ly Spir - it, breathe on me.

TEXT: Edwin Hatch; adapted by B. B. McKinney; based on John 20:22
MUSIC: B. B. McKinney

TRUETT
7.6.8.6. with Refrain

252 Sweet, Sweet Spirit

The fruit of the Spirit is love, joy, peace. Gal. 5:22

There's a sweet, sweet Spir - it in this place, And I
sweet ex - pres-sions on each face, And I
know that it's the Spir - it of the Lord; There are
know that it's the pres - ence of the
1
2
Lord.
Refrain
Sweet Ho - ly Spir - it, Sweet heav-en-ly Dove,
Stay right here with us, Fill - ing us with Your love; And for these
bless - ings We lift our hearts in praise: With - out a doubt we'll know

TEXT and MUSIC: Doris Akers

MANNA
Irregular meter

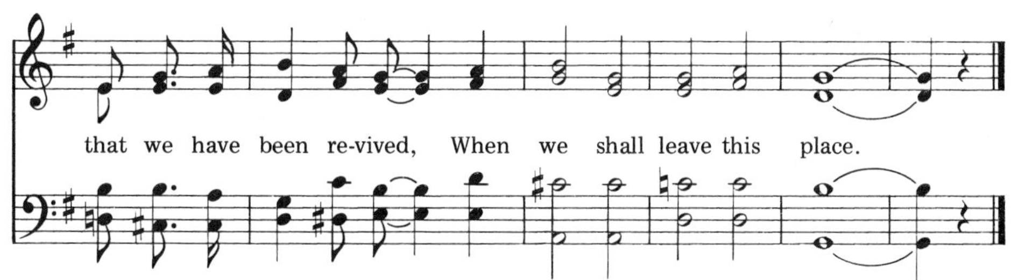
that we have been re-vived, When we shall leave this place.

Where the Spirit of the Lord Is 253

Where the Spirit of the Lord is, there is freedom. 2 Cor. 3:17

Where the Spir - it of the Lord is, there is peace; Where the Spir-it of the Lord is, there is love. There is com-fort in life's dark - est hour, there is light and life; There is help and pow-er in the Spir - it, in the Spir - it of the Lord.

TEXT and MUSIC: Stephen R. Adams; based on 2 Corinthians 3:17

ADAMS
Irregular meter

254 Heavenly Spirit, Gentle Spirit

The Spirit will take from what is Mine and make it known to you. John 16:15

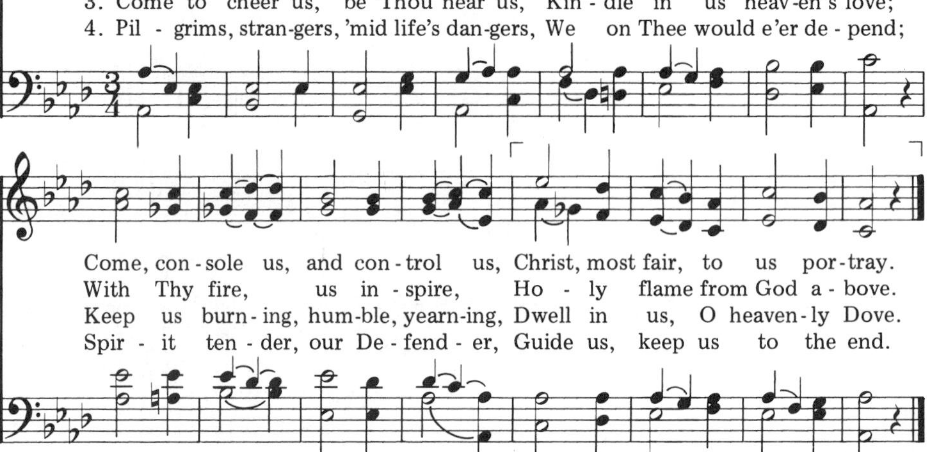
1. Heaven-ly Spir - it, gen - tle Spir - it, O de - scend on us, we pray;
2. Hear us plead-ing, in - ter - ced - ing, Thou in - ter - pre - ter of love;
3. Come to cheer us, be Thou near us, Kin - dle in us heav - en's love;
4. Pil - grims, stran-gers, 'mid life's dan-gers, We on Thee would e'er de - pend;
Come, con - sole us, and con - trol us, Christ, most fair, to us por - tray.
With Thy fire, us in - spire, Ho - ly flame from God a - bove.
Keep us burn - ing, hum-ble, yearn-ing, Dwell in us, O heaven - ly Dove.
Spir - it ten - der, our De - fend - er, Guide us, keep us to the end.

TEXT: Joel Blomquist; translated by Gerhard W. Palmgren
MUSIC: Joel Blomquist

HIMLADUVA
8.7.8.7.

255 Greater Is He That Is in Me

The One who is in you is greater than the one who is in the world. 1 John 4:4

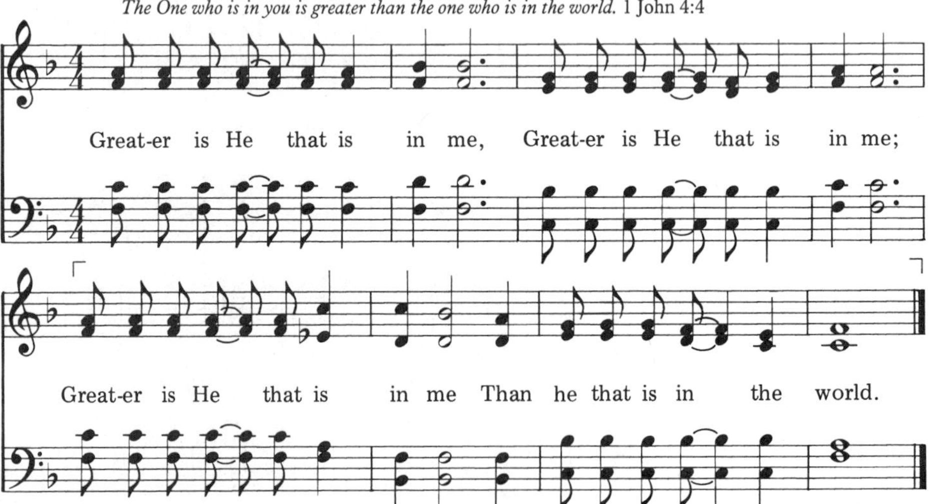
Great-er is He that is in me, Great-er is He that is in me;
Great-er is He that is in me Than he that is in the world.

TEXT and MUSIC: Lanny Wolfe; based on 1 John 4:4

GREATER IS HE
8.8.8.7.

He Is Here, He Is Here 256

Where two or three come together in My name, there am I with them. Matt. 18:20

Unison
1. He is here, He is here, He is mov - ing a - mong us. He is
2. He is Lord, He is Lord, let us wor - ship be - fore Him. He is
here, He is here, as we gath - er in His name! He is
Lord, He is Lord, as we gath - er in His name! He is
here, He is here and He wants to work a won-der. He is here as we
Lord, He is Lord, let us
1
gath - er in His name.
D.C.
2
praise and a - dore Him—yes-ter-
day and to - day and for - ev - er-more the same.

TEXT and MUSIC: Jimmy Owens; arranged by Lee Herrington

HE IS HERE
Irregular meter

257 The Comforter Has Come

I will ask the Father, and He will give you another Counselor to be with you. John 14:16

1. O spread the ti - dings 'round wher - ev - er man is found, Wher - ev - er hu-man hearts and hu - man woes a - bound; Let ev-'ry Christian tongue pro - claim the joy-ful sound: The Com-fort - er has come!
2. Lo, the great King of kings, with heal - ing in His wings, To ev - 'ry cap-tive soul a full de - liv-'rance brings; And thru the vacant cells the song of tri-umph rings: The Com-fort - er has come!
3. O bound - less love di - vine! how shall this tongue of mine To won-d'ring mor-tals tell the match-less grace di - vine— That I, a child of hell, should in His im - age shine! The Com-fort - er has come!
Refrain
The Com - fort - er has come, the Com - fort - er has come! The Ho - ly Ghost from heav'n—the Fa - ther's prom-ise giv'n; O spread the ti-dings

TEXT: Frank Bottome
MUSIC: William J. Kirkpatrick

COMFORTER
12.12.12.6. with Refrain

'round wher - ev - er man is found—The Com - fort - er has come!

We Are Gathered for Thy Blessing 258

My message and my preaching were . . . with a demonstration of the Spirit's power. 1 Cor. 2:4

1. We are gath - ered for Thy bless - ing, We will wait up - on our God;
We will trust in Him who loved us, And who bought us with His blood.

2. We will glo - ry in Thy pow - er, We will sing of won - drous grace;
In our midst as Thou hast prom - ised, Come, O come and take Thy place.

3. Bring us low in prayer be - fore Thee, And with faith our souls in - spire,
Till we claim by faith the prom - ise Of the Ho - ly Ghost and fire.

Refrain

Spir - it, now melt and move All of our hearts with love,
Breathe on us from a - bove With old - time pow'r. A - men.

TEXT and MUSIC: Paul Rader

TABERNACLE
8.7.8.7. with Refrain

259 Breathe on Me, Breath of God

He breathed on them and said, "Receive the Holy Spirit." John 20:22

1. Breathe on me, Breath of God, Fill me with life a - new, That I may love what Thou dost love, And do what Thou wouldst do.
2. Breathe on me, Breath of God, Un - til my heart is pure, Un - til my will is one with Thine, To do and to en - dure.
3. Breathe on me, Breath of God, Till I am whol - ly Thine, Un - til this earth - ly part of me Glows with Thy fire di - vine.
4. Breathe on me, Breath of God, So shall I nev - er die, But live with Thee the per - fect life Of Thine e - ter - ni - ty. A - men.

TEXT: Edwin Hatch
MUSIC: Robert Jackson

TRENTHAM
S.M.

260 Welcome, Welcome

You . . . are God's temple and . . . God's Spirit lives in you. 1 Cor. 3:16

Wel - come, wel-come, wel-come, wel-come! Ho - ly Ghost we wel-come Thee.
Come in power and fill this tem-ple; Ho - ly Ghost we wel-come Thee.

TEXT: Lelia N. Morris
MUSIC: Daniel Read; arranged by Kurt Kaiser

WELCOME
8.7.8.7.

Fill Me Now 261

Be filled with the Spirit. Eph. 5:18

1. Hov - er o'er me, Ho - ly Spir - it, Bathe my trem-bling heart and brow;
Fill me with Thy hal-low'd pres - ence, Come, O come and fill me now.

2. Thou canst fill me, gra-cious Spir - it, Tho I can - not tell Thee how;
But I need Thee, great - ly need Thee, Come, O come and fill me now.

3. I am weak-ness, full of weak-ness, At Thy sa - cred feet I bow;
Blest, di-vine, e - ter - nal Spir - it, Fill with pow'r, and fill me now.

4. Cleanse and com-fort, bless and save me, Bathe, O bathe my heart and brow;
Thou art com - fort - ing and sav - ing, Thou art sweet - ly fill - ing now.

Refrain

Fill me now, fill me now, Je - sus, come and fill me now;
Fill me with Thy hal-lowed pres - ence—Come, O come and fill me now.

TEXT: Elwood H. Stokes
MUSIC: John R. Sweney

FILL ME NOW
8.7.8.7. with Refrain

262 Holy, Holy, Holy

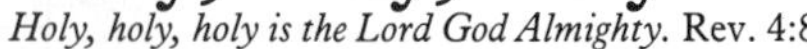

Holy, holy, holy is the Lord God Almighty. Rev. 4:8

Descant - last stanza

4. Ho - ly, ho - ly, ho - ly, ho - ly! Lord God Al - might - y!

1. Ho - ly, ho - ly, ho - ly! Lord God Al - might - y!
2. Ho - ly, ho - ly, ho - ly! all the saints a - dore Thee,
3. Ho - ly, ho - ly, ho - ly! though the dark - ness hide Thee,
4. Ho - ly, ho - ly, ho - ly! Lord God Al - might - y!

All Thy works shall praise Thy name in earth and sky;

Ear - ly in the morn - ing our song shall rise to
Cast - ing down their gold - en crowns a - round the glass - y
Though the eye of sin - ful man Thy glo - ry may not
All Thy works shall praise Thy name in earth and sky and

We praise Thy name, O Lord, most Ho - ly, ho - ly, ho - ly, ho - ly!

Thee; Ho - ly, ho - ly, ho - ly!
sea; Cher - u - bim and ser - a - phim
see; On - ly Thou art ho - ly—
sea; Ho - ly, ho - ly, ho - ly!

TEXT: Reginald Heber
MUSIC: John B. Dykes; Descant by Gary Rhodes

NICAEA
11.12.12.10.

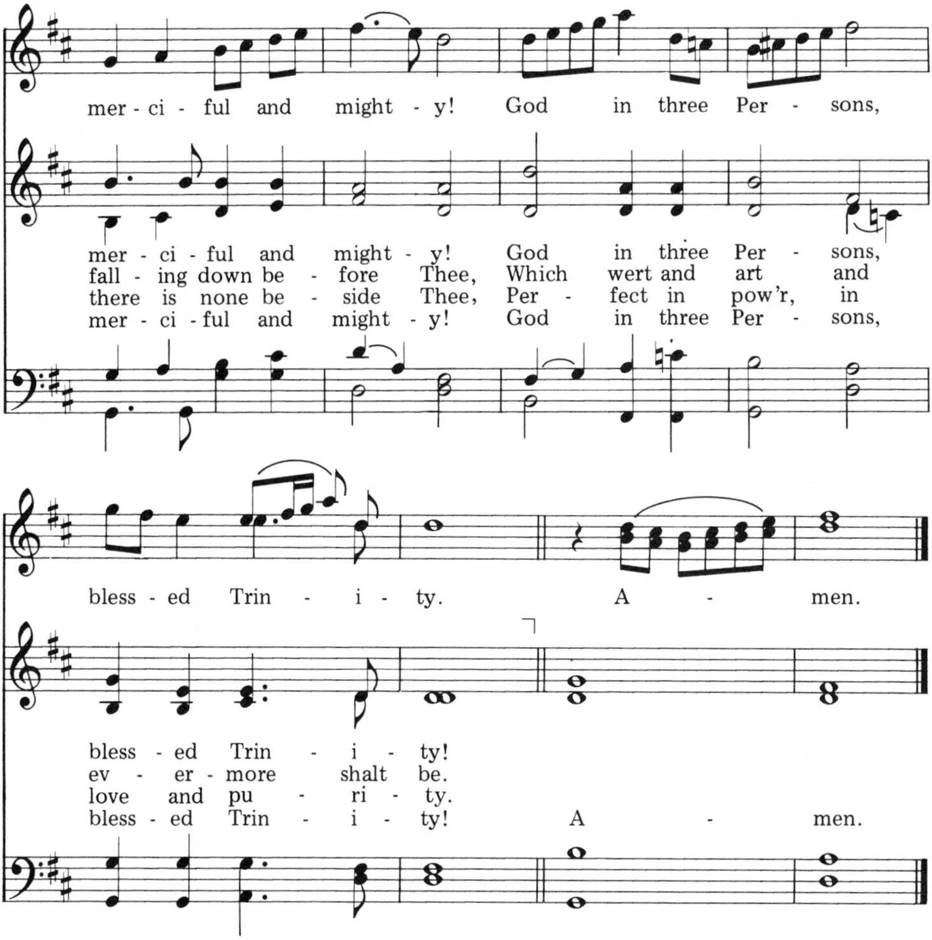

mer - ci - ful and might - y! God in three Per - sons,
mer - ci - ful and might - y! God in three Per - sons,
fall - ing down be - fore Thee, Which wert and art and
there is none be - side Thee, Per - fect in pow'r, in
mer - ci - ful and might - y! God in three Per - sons,
bless - ed Trin - i - ty. A - men.
bless - ed Trin - i - ty!
ev - er - more shalt be.
love and pu - ri - ty.
bless - ed Trin - i - ty! A - men.

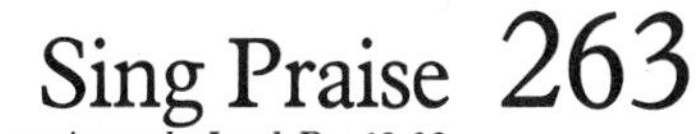

Sing Praise 263

Sing praise to the Lord. Ps. 68:32

3 Part Canon

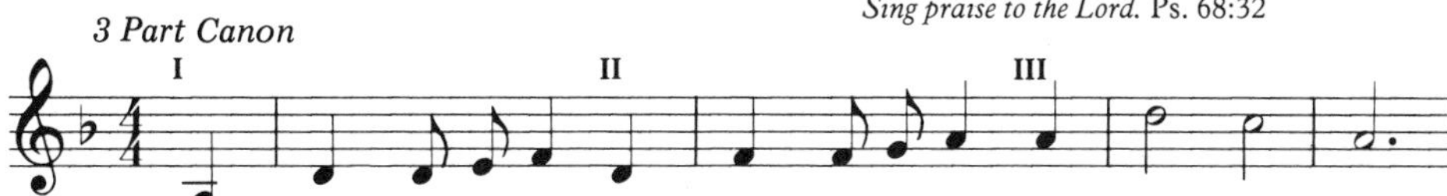

I
II
III
Sing praise to the Fa - ther, praise to the Son; Sing praise, sing praise.
Sing praise to the Spir - it, Three in One; Sing praise, sing praise.

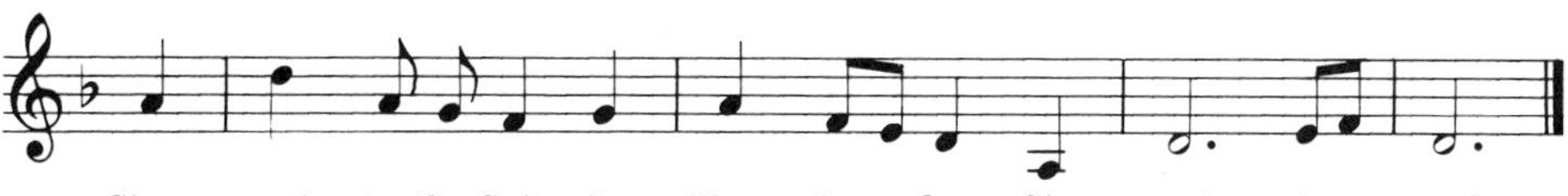

TEXT: Gerald S. Henderson
MUSIC: Israeli Folk song; adapted by Gerald S. Henderson

SING PRAISE
Irregular meter

264 Praise Ye the Triune God

I will . . . praise Your name for Your love and Your faithfulness. Ps. 138:2

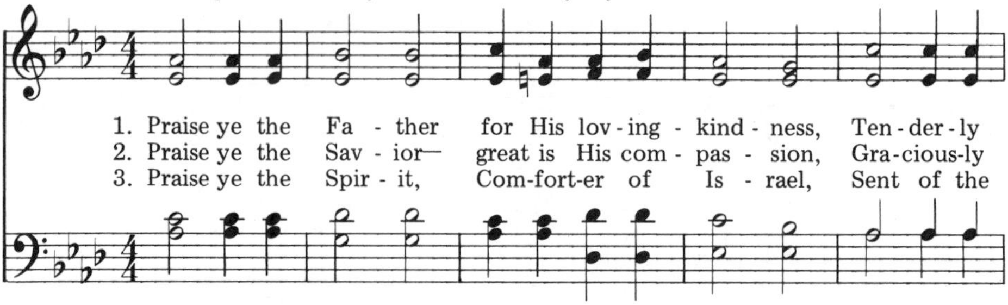

1. Praise ye the Fa - ther for His lov - ing - kind - ness, Ten - der - ly
2. Praise ye the Sav - ior— great is His com - pas - sion, Gra - cious - ly
3. Praise ye the Spir - it, Com - fort - er of Is - rael, Sent of the

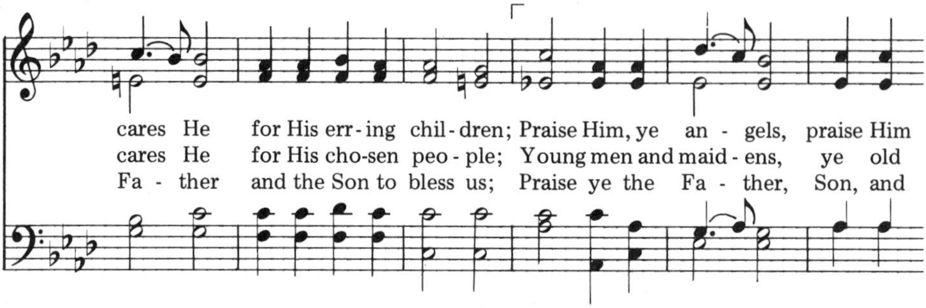

cares He for His err - ing chil - dren; Praise Him, ye an - gels, praise Him
cares He for His cho - sen peo - ple; Young men and maid - ens, ye old
Fa - ther and the Son to bless us; Praise ye the Fa - ther, Son, and

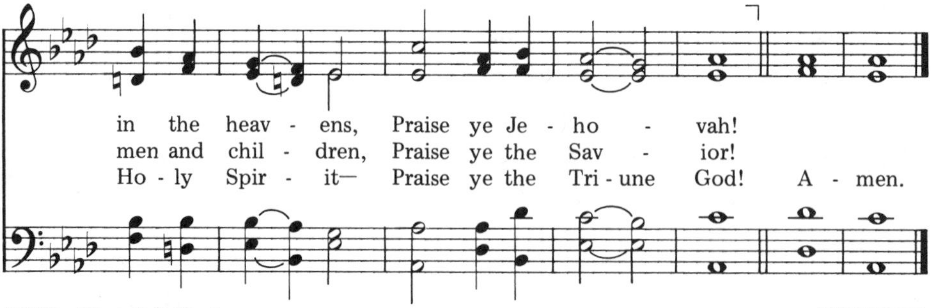

in the heav - ens, Praise ye Je - ho - vah!
men and chil - dren, Praise ye the Sav - ior!
Ho - ly Spir - it— Praise ye the Tri - une God! A - men.

TEXT: Elizabeth R. Charles
MUSIC: Friedrich F. Flemming

FLEMMING
11.11.11.6.

265 Father, I Adore You

True worshipers will worship the Father in spirit and truth. John 4:23

3 Part Round

1. Fa - ther, I a - dore You, Lay my life be - fore You, How I love You.
2. Je - sus, I a - dore You, Lay my life be - fore You, How I love You.
3. Spir - it, I a - dore You, Lay my life be - fore You, How I love You.

TEXT and MUSIC: Terrye Coelho

MARANATHA
Irregular meter

Holy, Holy 266

You alone are holy. All nations will . . . worship before You. Rev. 15:4

1. Ho-ly, ho-ly, ho-ly, ho-ly, Ho-ly, ho-ly, Lord God Al-might-y; And we lift our hearts be-fore You as a tok-en of our love, Ho-ly, ho-ly, ho-ly, ho-ly.
2. Gra-cious Fa-ther, gra-cious Fa-ther, We're so blest to be Your child-ren, gra-cious Fa-ther; And we lift our heads be-fore You as a tok-en of our love, Gra-cious Fa-ther, gra-cious Fa-ther.
3. Pre-cious Je-sus, pre-cious Je-sus, We're so glad that You've re-deemed us, pre-cious Je-sus; And we lift our hands be-fore You as a tok-en of our love, Pre-cious Je-sus, pre-cious Je-sus.
4. Ho-ly Spir-it, Ho-ly Spir-it, Come and fill our hearts a-new, Ho-ly Spir-it; And we lift our voice be-fore You as a tok-en of our love, Ho-ly Spir-it, Ho-ly Spir-it.
5. Ho-ly, ho-ly, ho-ly, ho-ly, Ho-ly, ho-ly, Lord God Al-might-y; And we lift our hearts be-fore You as a tok-en of our love, Ho-ly, ho-ly, ho-ly, ho-ly.
6. Hal-le-lu-jah, hal-le-lu-jah, Hal-le-lu-jah, hal-le-lu-jah; And we lift our hearts be-fore You as a tok-en of our love, Hal-le-lu-jah, hal-le-lu-jah.

TEXT and MUSIC: Jimmy Owens

HOLY, HOLY
Irregular meter

267 Come, Thou Almighty King

The Lord is the great God, the great King. Ps. 95:3

1. Come, Thou Al - might - y King, Help us Thy name to sing, Help us to praise: Fa - ther! all - glo - ri - ous, O'er all vic - to - ri - ous, Come, and reign o - ver us, An - cient of Days.
2. Come, Thou In - car - nate Word, Gird on Thy might - y sword, Our prayer at - tend! Come, and Thy peo - ple bless, And give Thy word suc-cess: Spir - it of ho - li - ness, On us de - scend.
3. Come, Ho - ly Com - fort - er, Thy sa - cred wit - ness bear In this glad hour! Thou, who al - might - y art, Now rule in ev - 'ry heart And ne'er from us de - part, Spir - it of pow'r.
4. To Thee, great One in Three, E - ter - nal prais - es be, Hence ev - er - more; Thy sov - 'reign maj - es - ty May we in glo - ry see, And to e - ter - ni - ty Love and a - dore. A - men.

TEXT: Source unknown
MUSIC: Felice de Giardini;
Last stanza harmonization by O. D. Hall, Jr.

ITALIAN HYMN
6.6.4.6.6.6.4.

Optional last stanza harmonization
Broader
Unison
rall.
4. To Thee, great One in Three,
E - ter - nal prais - es be,
Hence ev - er - more;
Thy sov-'reign maj - es - ty
May we in glo - ry see,
And to e - ter - ni - ty
Love and a - dore.
rit.
a tempo
Optional choral ending
cresc.
play cued notes if opt. choral ending is used.
A - men.
div.
A - men.
tenor: Come, Thou Al - might - y King.
A - men.

268 God, Our Father, We Adore Thee

Our Father in heaven, hallowed be Your name. Matt. 6:9

1. God, our Fa - ther, we a - dore Thee! We, Thy chil - dren, bless Thy name!
2. Son E - ter - nal, we a - dore Thee! Lamb up - on the throne on high!
3. Ho - ly Spir - it, we a - dore Thee! Par - a - clete and heav'n - ly guest!
4. Fa - ther, Son, and Ho - ly Spir - it— Three in One! we give Thee praise!
Cho - sen in the Christ be - fore Thee, We are "ho - ly with - out blame."
Lamb of God, we bow be - fore Thee, Thou hast brought Thy peo - ple nigh!
Sent from God and from the Sav - ior, Thou hast led us in - to rest.
For the rich - es we in - her - it, Heart and voice to Thee we raise!
We a - dore Thee! we a - dore Thee! Ab - ba's prais - es we pro - claim!
We a - dore Thee! we a - dore Thee! Son of God, who came to die!
We a - dore Thee! we a - dore Thee! By Thy grace for - ev - er blest:
We a - dore Thee! we a - dore Thee! Thee we bless, thro' end - less days!
We a - dore Thee! we a - dore Thee! Ab - ba's prais - es we pro - claim!
We a - dore Thee! we a - dore Thee! Son of God, who came to die!
We a - dore Thee! we a - dore Thee! By Thy grace for - ev - er blest!
We a - dore Thee! we a - dore Thee! Thee we bless, thro' end - less days! A - men.

TEXT: George W. Frazier; Alfred S. Loizeaux, stanza 3
MUSIC: John Zundel
A lower setting may be found at No. 92; Alternate tune: HYFRYDOL, No. 89

BEECHER
8.7.8.7.D.

O Word of God Incarnate 269

The unfolding of Your words gives light. Ps. 119:130

1. O Word of God in - car - nate, O Wis - dom from on high,
2. The Church from her dear Mas - ter Re - ceived the gift di - vine,
3. It float - eth like a ban - ner Be - fore God's host un - furled;
4. O make Thy Church, dear Sav - ior, A lamp of pur - est gold,
O Truth un-changed, un - chang - ing, O Light of our dark sky;
And still that light she lift - eth O'er all the earth to shine.
It shin - eth like a bea - con A - bove the dark - ling world.
To bear be - fore the na - tions Thy true light as of old.
We praise Thee for the ra - diance That from the hal - lowed page,
It is the gold - en cas - ket Where gems of truth are stored;
It is the chart and com - pass That o'er life's surg - ing sea,
O teach Thy wan-d'ring pil - grims By this their path to trace,
A lan - tern to our foot - steps, Shines on from age to age.
It is the heav'n-drawn pic - ture Of Christ, the liv - ing Word.
'Mid mists and rocks and quick-sands, Still guides, O Christ, to Thee.
Till, clouds and dark - ness end - ed, They see Thee face to face. A-men.

TEXT: William W. How
MUSIC: *Neuvermehrtes Gesangbuch,* Meiningen, 1693; arranged by Felix Mendelssohn

MUNICH
7.6.7.6.D.

270 Wonderful Words of Life

The words I have spoken to you are spirit and they are life. John 6:63

1. Sing them o-ver a-gain to me, Won-der-ful words of Life;
Let me more of their beau-ty see, Won-der-ful words of Life.
Words of life and beau-ty, Teach me faith and du-ty;

2. Christ, the bless-ed One, gives to all Won-der-ful words of Life;
Sin-ner, list to the lov-ing call, Won-der-ful words of Life.
All so free-ly giv-en, Woo-ing us to Heav-en:

3. Sweet-ly ech-o the gos-pel call, Won-der-ful words of Life;
Of-fer par-don and peace to all, Won-der-ful words of Life.
Je-sus, on-ly Sav-ior, Sanc-ti-fy for-ev-er:

Refrain

Beau-ti-ful words, won-der-ful words, Won-der-ful words of Life.
Beau-ti-ful words, won-der-ful words, Won-der-ful words of Life.

TEXT and MUSIC: Philip P. Bliss

WORDS OF LIFE
8.6.8.6.6.6. with Refrain

Standing on the Promises 271

He has given us His very great and precious promises. 2 Pet. 1:4

1. Stand-ing on the prom - is - es of Christ my King, Thro' e - ter - nal a - ges let His prais - es ring; Glo - ry in the high - est, I will shout and sing, Stand-ing on the prom-is-es of God.
2. Stand-ing on the prom - is - es that can - not fail, When the howl-ing storms of doubt and fear as - sail, By the liv - ing Word of God I shall pre - vail,
3. Stand-ing on the prom - is - es of Christ the Lord, Bound to Him e - ter - nal-ly by love's strong cord, O - ver-com - ing dai - ly with the Spir - it's sword,
4. Stand-ing on the prom - is - es I can - not fall, Lis-t'ning ev - ery mo-ment to the Spir - it's call, Rest-ing in my Sav - ior as my all in all,
Refrain
Stand-ing, stand - ing, stand-ing on the prom-is-es,
Stand - ing on the prom - is - es of God my Sav - ior; Stand - ing, stand - ing, stand-ing on the prom-is-es,
I'm stand-ing on the prom-is - es of God.

TEXT and MUSIC: R. Kelso Carter

PROMISES
11.11.11.9. with Refrain

272 Thy Word

Your Word is a lamp to my feet and a light for my path. Ps. 119:105

Unison

Thy Word is a lamp un-to my feet and a light un-to my path.

Thy Word is a lamp un-to my feet and a light un-to my path.

2nd time rit. *2nd time Fine*

Thy Word is a lamp un-to my feet and a light un-to my path.

TEXT: Amy Grant; based on Psalm 119:105
MUSIC: Michael W. Smith; arranged by Keith Phillips

THY WORD
Irregular meter

273 Holy Bible, Book Divine

All Scripture is God-breathed and is useful. 2 Tim. 3:16

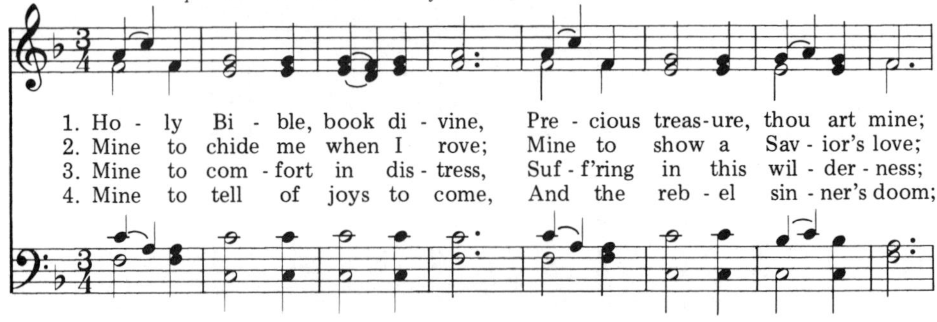
1. Ho - ly Bi - ble, book di - vine, Pre - cious treas-ure, thou art mine;
2. Mine to chide me when I rove; Mine to show a Sav - ior's love;
3. Mine to com - fort in dis - tress, Suf - f'ring in this wil - der - ness;
4. Mine to tell of joys to come, And the reb - el sin - ner's doom;

TEXT: John Burton
MUSIC: William B. Bradbury

ALETTA
7.7.7.7.

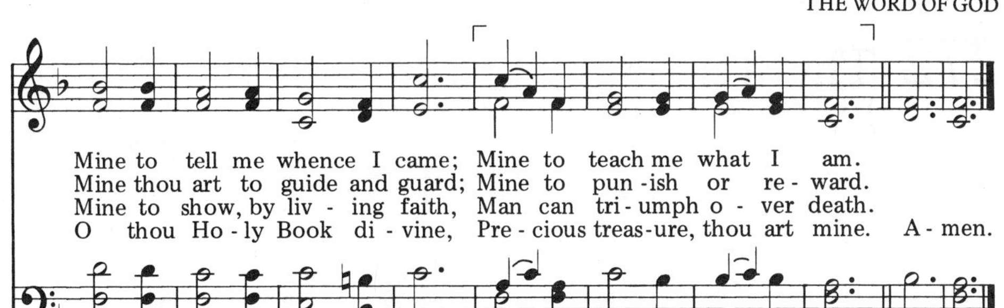
Mine to tell me whence I came; Mine to teach me what I am.
Mine thou art to guide and guard; Mine to pun-ish or re-ward.
Mine to show, by liv-ing faith, Man can tri-umph o-ver death.
O thou Ho-ly Book di-vine, Pre-cious treas-ure, thou art mine. A-men.

Break Thou the Bread of Life 274

Looking up to heaven, He gave thanks and broke the loaves. Mark 6:41

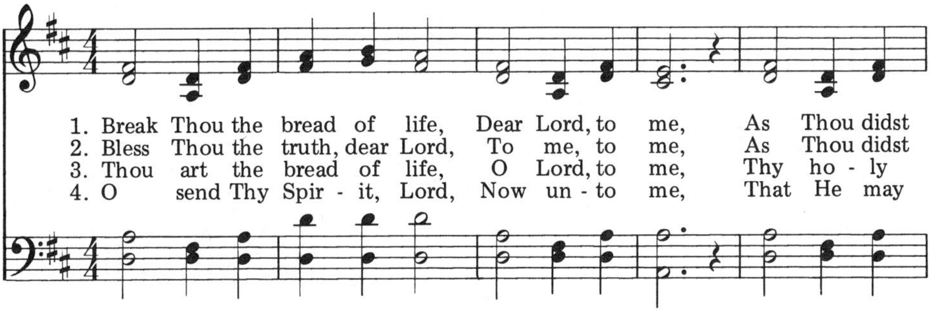

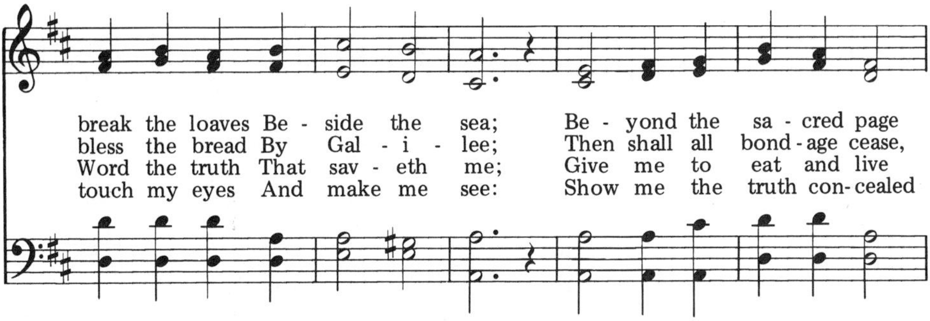

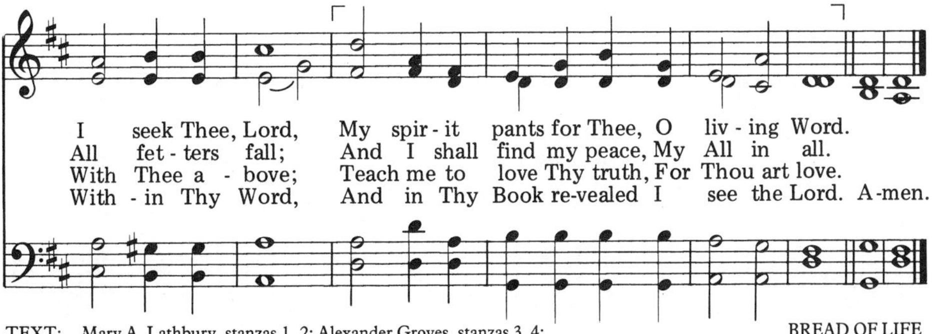

1. Break Thou the bread of life, Dear Lord, to me, As Thou didst break the loaves Be-side the sea; Be-yond the sa-cred page I seek Thee, Lord, My spir-it pants for Thee, O liv-ing Word.
2. Bless Thou the truth, dear Lord, To me, to me, As Thou didst bless the bread By Gal-i-lee; Then shall all bond-age cease, All fet-ters fall; And I shall find my peace, My All in all.
3. Thou art the bread of life, O Lord, to me, Thy ho-ly Word the truth That sav-eth me; Give me to eat and live With Thee a-bove; Teach me to love Thy truth, For Thou art love.
4. O send Thy Spir-it, Lord, Now un-to me, That He may touch my eyes And make me see: Show me the truth con-cealed With-in Thy Word, And in Thy Book re-vealed I see the Lord. A-men.

TEXT: Mary A. Lathbury, stanzas 1, 2; Alexander Groves, stanzas 3, 4; based on Matthew 14:19
MUSIC: William F. Sherwin

BREAD OF LIFE
6.4.6.4.D.

275 How Firm a Foundation

God's solid foundation stands firm . . . The Lord knows those who are His. 2 Tim. 2:19

1. How firm a foun - da - tion, ye saints of the Lord,
2. "Fear not, I am with thee; O be not dis - mayed,
3. "When through fier - y tri - als thy path - way shall lie,
4. "The soul that on Je - sus hath leaned for re - pose
Is laid for your faith in His ex - cel - lent Word!
For I am thy God, and will still give thee aid;
My grace, all suf - fi - cient, shall be thy sup - ply:
I will not, I will not de - sert to its foes;
What more can He say than to you He hath said,
I'll strength-en thee, help thee, and cause thee to stand,
The flame shall not hurt thee; I on - ly de - sign
That soul, though all hell should en - deav - or to shake,
To you who for ref - uge to Je - sus have fled?
Up - held by My right - eous, om - nip - o - tent hand.
Thy dross to con - sume and thy gold to re - fine.
I'll nev - er, no, nev - er, no, nev - er for - sake!"

TEXT: Rippon's *Selection of Hymns,* 1787
MUSIC: Traditional American melody; Caldwell's *Union Harmony,* 1837

FOUNDATION
11.11.11.11.

Christ Is Made the Sure Foundation 276

No one can lay any foundation other than . . . Jesus Christ. 1 Cor. 3:11

1. Christ is made the sure foun - da - tion, Christ the head and
2. To this tem - ple, where we call Thee, Come, O Lord of
3. Here vouch - safe to all Thy serv - ants What they ask of
4. Laud and hon - or to the Fa - ther, Laud and hon - or
cor - ner - stone, Chos - en of the Lord and pre - cious,
hosts, to - day; With ac - cus - tomed lov - ing - kind - ness
Thee to gain, What they gain from Thee for - ev - er
to the Son, Laud and hon - or to the Spir - it,
Bind - ing all the Church in one, Ho - ly Zi - on's
Hear Thy peo - ple as they pray, And Thy full - est
With the bless - ed to re - tain, And here - aft - er
Ev - er Three and ev - er One, One in might and
help for - ev - er, And her con - fi - dence a - lone.
ben - e - dic - tion Shed with - in its walls al - way.
in Thy glo - ry Ev - er - more with Thee to reign.
One in glo - ry While un - end - ing a - ges run. A - men.

TEXT: Latin Hymn, 7th century; translated by John M. Neale
MUSIC: Henry T. Smart
A lower setting may be found at No. 241

REGENT SQUARE
8.7.8.7.8.7.

277 The Church's One Foundation

I lay . . . a precious cornerstone for a sure foundation. Isa. 28:16

1. The Church-'s one foun - da - tion Is Je - sus Christ her Lord;
2. E - lect from ev - 'ry na - tion, Yet one o'er all the earth,
3. 'Mid toil and trib - u - la - tion And tu - mult of her war,
4. Yet she on earth hath un - ion With God the Three in One,
She is His new cre - a - tion By wa - ter and the Word:
Her char - ter of sal - va - tion One Lord, one faith, one birth;
She waits the con - sum - ma - tion Of peace for - ev - er - more;
And mys - tic sweet com - mun - ion With those whose rest is won:
From heav'n He came and sought her To be His ho - ly bride; With
One ho - ly name she bless - es, Par - takes one ho - ly food, And
Till with the vi - sion glo - rious Her long - ing eyes are blest, And
O hap - py ones and ho - ly! Lord, give us grace that we, Like
His own blood He bought her, And for her life He died.
to one hope she press - es, With ev - 'ry grace en - dued.
the great Church vic - to - rious Shall be the Church at rest.
them, the meek and low - ly, On high may dwell with Thee. A - men.

TEXT: Samuel J. Stone
MUSIC: Samuel S. Wesley
A lower setting may be found at No. 567

AURELIA
7.6.7.6.D.

Glorious Things of Thee Are Spoken 278

Glorious things are said of you, O city of God. Ps. 87:3

1. Glo - rious things of thee are spo - ken, Zi - on, cit - y of our God;
2. See, the streams of liv - ing wa - ters, Spring-ing from e - ter - nal Love,
3. Round each hab - i - ta - tion hov-ering, See the cloud and fire ap - pear
He whose word can - not be bro - ken Formed thee for His own a - bode.
Well sup-ply thy sons and daugh-ters, And all fear of want re - move.
For a glo - ry and a cov-ering, Show - ing that the Lord is near!
On the Rock of A - ges found-ed, What can shake thy sure re-pose?
Who can faint while such a riv - er Ev - er flows their thirst to assuage?
Thus de - riv - ing from their ban-ner Light by night and shade by day,
With sal-va- tion's walls sur-round-ed, Thou mayst smile at all thy foes.
Grace which, like the Lord, the Giv-er, Nev - er fails from age to age!
Safe they feed up - on the man-na Which He gives them when they pray. A - men.

TEXT: John Newton; based on Psalm 87:3 and Isaiah 33:20, 21
MUSIC: Franz Joseph Haydn
A lower setting may be found at No. 9

AUSTRIAN HYMN
8.7.8.7.D.

279 Faith of Our Fathers

Contend for the faith that was once for all entrusted to the saints. Jude 3

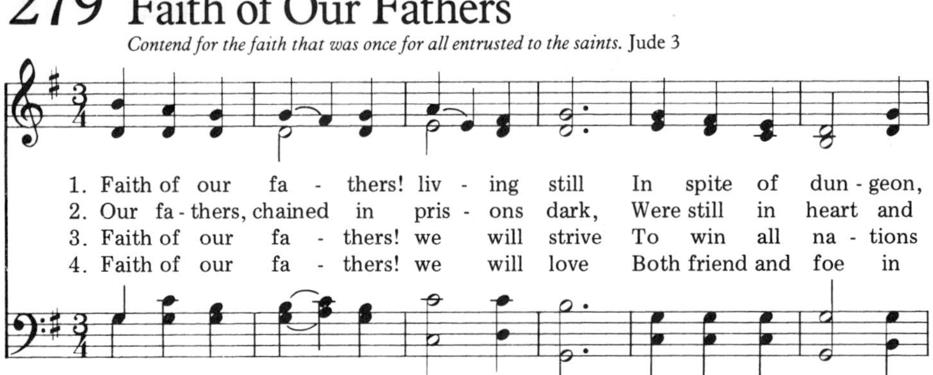
1. Faith of our fa - thers! liv - ing still In spite of dun - geon,
2. Our fa - thers, chained in pris - ons dark, Were still in heart and
3. Faith of our fa - thers! we will strive To win all na - tions
4. Faith of our fa - thers! we will love Both friend and foe in

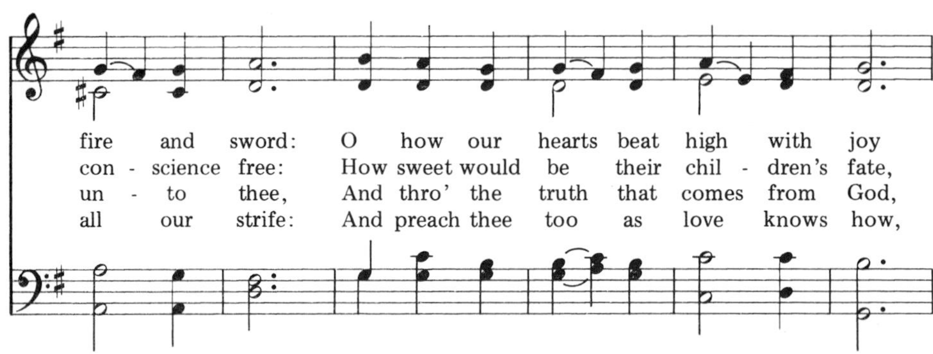
fire and sword: O how our hearts beat high with joy
con - science free: How sweet would be their chil - dren's fate,
un - to thee, And thro' the truth that comes from God,
all our strife: And preach thee too as love knows how,

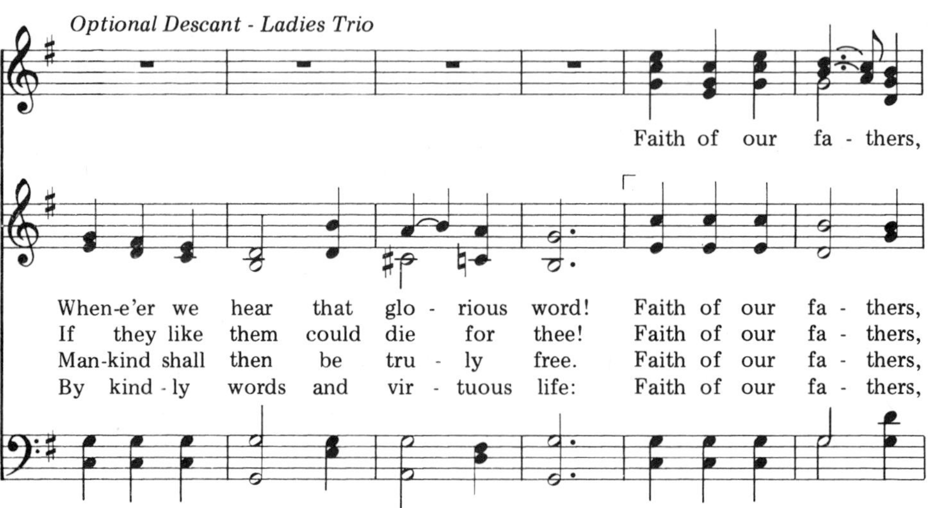
Optional Descant - Ladies Trio
Faith of our fa - thers,
When-e'er we hear that glo - rious word! Faith of our fa - thers,
If they like them could die for thee! Faith of our fa - thers,
Man-kind shall then be tru - ly free. Faith of our fa - thers,
By kind - ly words and vir - tuous life: Faith of our fa - thers,

TEXT: Frederick W. Faber
MUSIC: Henry F. Hemy; arranged by James G. Walton
Descant and choral ending by Ken Barker

ST. CATHERINE
8.8.8.8.8.8.

ho - ly faith! We will be true to thee till death!
ho - ly faith! We will be true to thee till death!
ho - ly faith! We will be true to thee till death!
ho - ly faith! We will be true to thee till death!
ho - ly faith! We will be true to thee till death!

Optional choral ending
mf
cresc.
We will be true, We will be true,

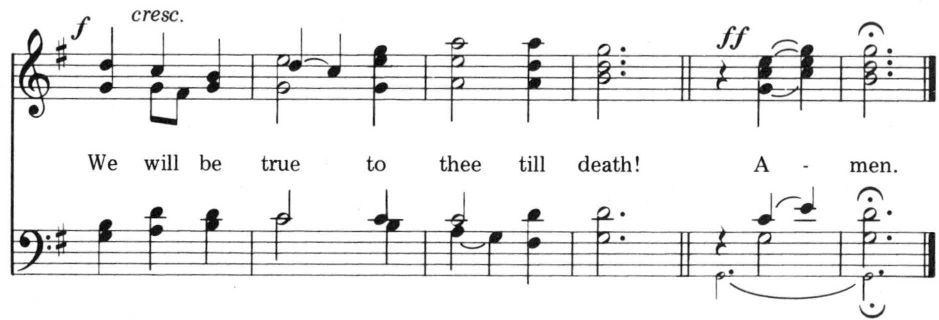
f
cresc.
ff
We will be true to thee till death! A - men.

280 I Love Thy Kingdom, Lord

I love the house where You live, O Lord. Ps. 26:8

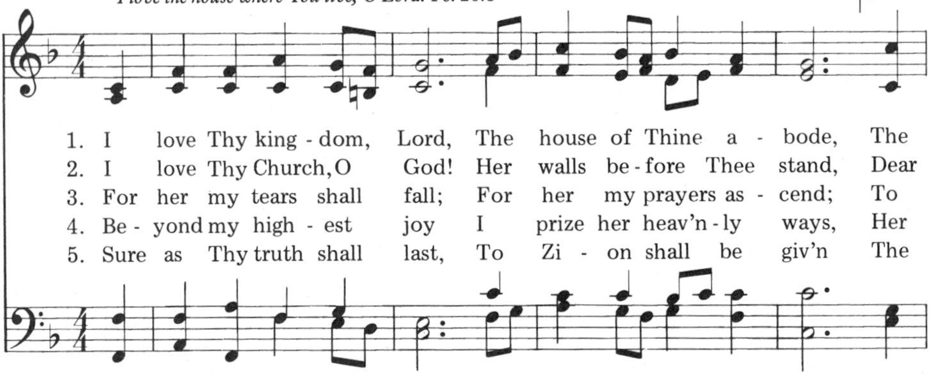

1. I love Thy king - dom, Lord, The house of Thine a - bode, The
2. I love Thy Church, O God! Her walls be - fore Thee stand, Dear
3. For her my tears shall fall; For her my prayers as - cend; To
4. Be - yond my high - est joy I prize her heav'n - ly ways, Her
5. Sure as Thy truth shall last, To Zi - on shall be giv'n The

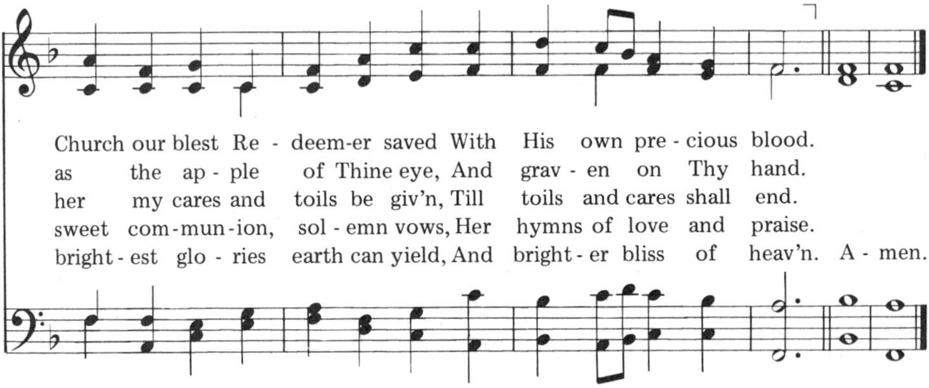

Church our blest Re - deem-er saved With His own pre - cious blood.
as the ap - ple of Thine eye, And grav - en on Thy hand.
her my cares and toils be giv'n, Till toils and cares shall end.
sweet com-mun-ion, sol - emn vows, Her hymns of love and praise.
bright - est glo - ries earth can yield, And bright - er bliss of heav'n. A - men.

TEXT: Timothy Dwight
MUSIC: Aaron Williams
A higher setting may be found at No. 21

ST. THOMAS
S.M.

281 The Bond of Love

We know that we have passed from death to life, because we love our brothers. 1 John 3:14

1. We are one in the bond of love; We are one in the
2. Let us sing now, ev - ery - one; Let us feel His

TEXT and MUSIC: Otis Skillings

BOND OF LOVE
Irregular meter

FELLOWSHIP OF BELIEVERS

bond of love. We have joined our spir - it with the
love be - gun. Let us join our hands that the
Spir - it of God; We are one in the bond of love.
world will know We are one in the bond of love.

The Family of God 282

. . . His whole family in heaven and on earth. Eph. 3:15

I'm so glad I'm a part of the fam-ily of God— I've been washed in the foun-tain, cleansed by His blood! Joint heirs with Je-sus as we trav-el this sod, For I'm part of the fam-ily, the fam-ily of God.

TEXT: Gloria Gaither and William J. Gaither
MUSIC: William J. Gaither

FAMILY OF GOD
Irregular meter

283 We Are God's People

You are a chosen people . . . a people belonging to God. 1 Pet. 2:9

Unison
1. We are God's peo-ple, the cho-sen of the Lord,
2. We are God's loved ones, the Bride of Christ our Lord,
3. We are the Bod-y of which the Lord is Head,
4. We are a Tem-ple, the Spir-it's dwell-ing place,
Born of His Spir-it, es-tab-lished by His Word; Our
For we have known it, the love of God out-poured; Now
Called to o-bey Him, now ris-en from the dead; He
Formed in great weak-ness, a cup to hold God's grace; We
cor-ner-stone is Christ a-lone, And strong in Him we stand: O let us
let us learn how to re-turn The gift of love once given: O let us
wills us be a fam-i-ly Di-verse yet tru-ly one: O let us
die a-lone, for on its own Each em-ber los-es fire: Yet joined in
live trans-par-ent-ly, And walk heart to heart and hand in hand.
share each joy and care, And live with a zeal that pleas-es Heaven.
give our gifts to God, And so shall His work on earth be done.
one the flame burns on To give warmth and light, and to in-spire.

SYMPHONY
11.11.13.8.9.

TEXT: Bryan Jeffery Leech
MUSIC: Johannes Brahms; arranged by Fred Bock

They'll Know We Are Christians by Our Love 284

By this all men will know that you are My disciples, if you love one another. John 13:35

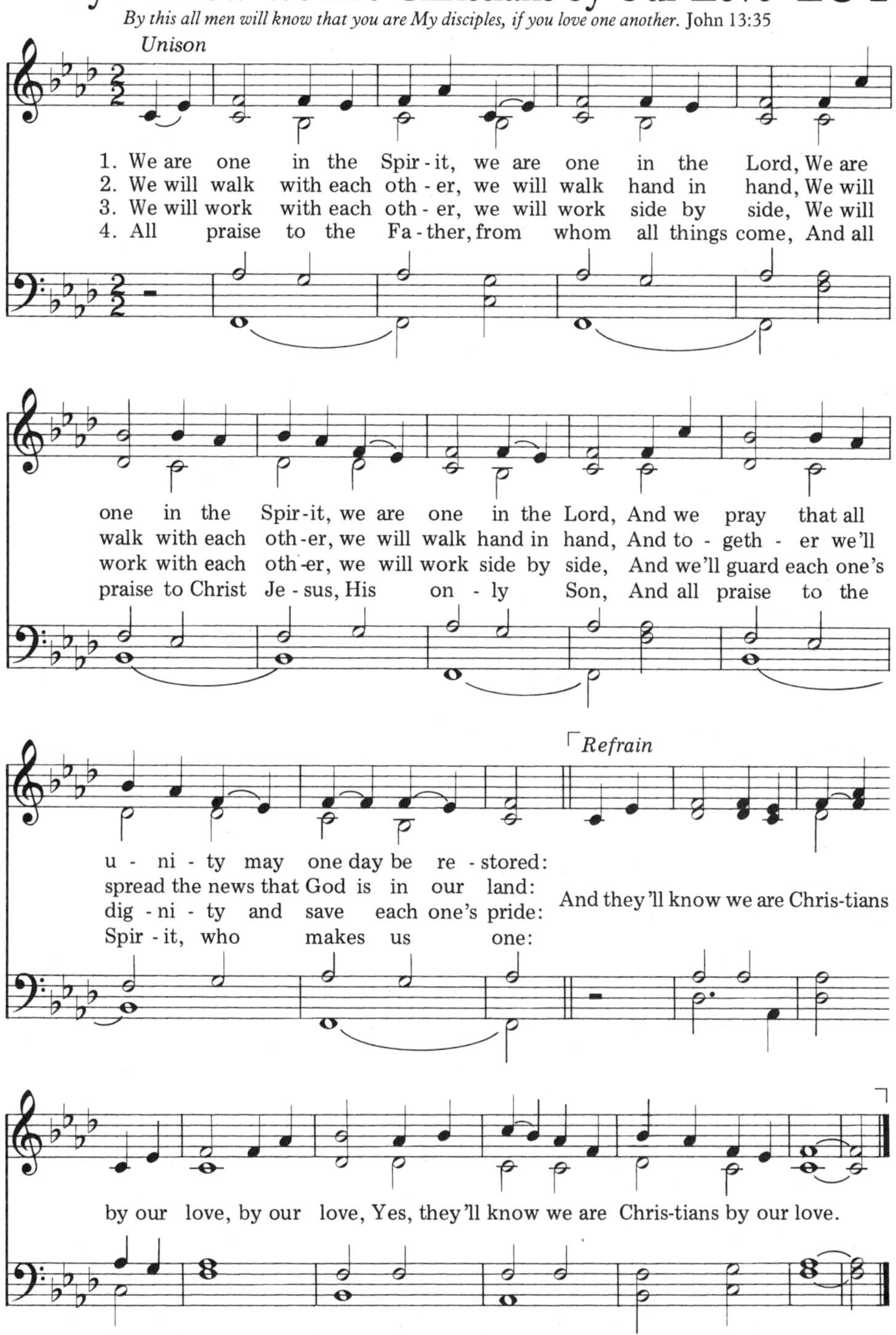
Unison
1. We are one in the Spir-it, we are one in the Lord, We are
2. We will walk with each oth-er, we will walk hand in hand, We will
3. We will work with each oth-er, we will work side by side, We will
4. All praise to the Fa-ther, from whom all things come, And all
one in the Spir-it, we are one in the Lord, And we pray that all
walk with each oth-er, we will walk hand in hand, And to-geth-er we'll
work with each oth-er, we will work side by side, And we'll guard each one's
praise to Christ Je-sus, His on-ly Son, And all praise to the
u-ni-ty may one day be re-stored:
spread the news that God is in our land:
dig-ni-ty and save each one's pride:
Spir-it, who makes us one:
Refrain
And they'll know we are Chris-tians
by our love, by our love, Yes, they'll know we are Chris-tians by our love.

TEXT and MUSIC: Peter Scholtes; based on John 13:35

ST. BRENDAN'S
Irregular meter

285 In Christ There Is No East or West

God does not show favoritism but accepts men from every nation. Acts 10:34-35

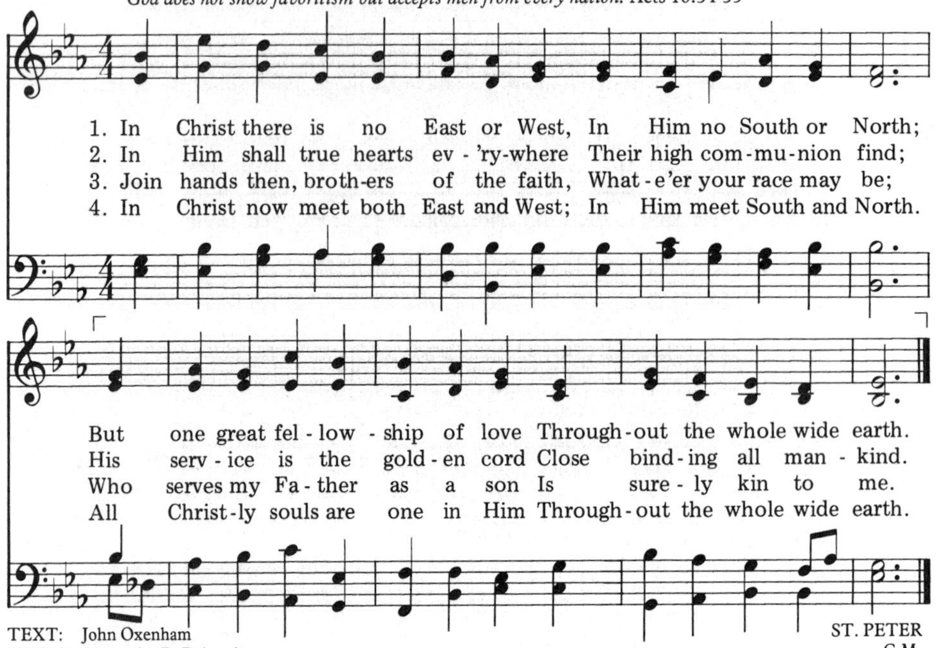
1. In Christ there is no East or West, In Him no South or North;
2. In Him shall true hearts ev - 'ry-where Their high com-mu-nion find;
3. Join hands then, broth-ers of the faith, What - e'er your race may be;
4. In Christ now meet both East and West; In Him meet South and North.
But one great fel - low - ship of love Through-out the whole wide earth.
His serv - ice is the gold - en cord Close bind - ing all man - kind.
Who serves my Fa - ther as a son Is sure - ly kin to me.
All Christ-ly souls are one in Him Through - out the whole wide earth.

TEXT: John Oxenham
MUSIC: Alexander R. Reinagle
A lower setting may be found at No. 94; Alternate setting: McKEE, No. 547

ST. PETER
C.M.

286 Blest Be the Tie That Binds

You are all one in Christ Jesus. Gal. 3:28

1. Blest be the tie that binds Our hearts in Chris - tian love;
2. Be - fore our Fa - ther's throne We pour our ar - dent prayers;
3. When we a - sun - der part, It gives us in - ward pain;
The fel - low - ship of kin - dred minds Is like to that a - bove.
Our fears, our hopes, our aims are one, Our com-forts and our cares.
But we shall still be joined in heart, And hope to meet a - gain. A-men.

TEXT: John Fawcett
MUSIC: Johann G. Naegeli; arranged by Lowell Mason

DENNIS
S.M.

Our God Has Made Us One 287

Keep the unity of the Spirit through the bond of peace. Eph. 4:3

1. Our God has made us one— In Him our hearts u - nite. When we His chil - dren share His love, Our joy is His de - light.
2. Our God has made us one— His glo - ry is dis - played. For as we build each oth - er up Our love be-comes His praise.
3. Our God has made us one— In sor - row and in joy; We share the cross of Christ, our Lord, In Him we now re - joice.
4. Our God has made us one— One Church to bear His name; One bod - y and one Bride of Christ, And with Him we shall reign. A - men.

TEXT: Niles Borop
MUSIC: Jim Weber

WEBER
S.M.

Faithful Men 288

Ask the Lord of the harvest . . . to send out workers into His harvest field. Matt. 9:38

1. Come and join the reap - ers; All the King - dom seek - ers; Lay - ing down your life to find it in the end.
2. Come and share the har - vest; Help to light the dark - ness, For the Lord is call - ing faith - ful men.
1
2

TEXT and MUSIC: Twila Paris

FAITHFUL MEN
6.6.11.6.6.9.

289 There Shall Be Showers of Blessing

There will be showers of blessing. Ezek. 34:26

1. "There shall be show-ers of bless - ing"— This is the prom-ise of love;
2. "There shall be show-ers of bless - ing"— Pre - cious re - viv - ing a - gain;
3. "There shall be show-ers of bless - ing"— Send them up - on us, O Lord;
4. "There shall be show-ers of bless - ing"— O that to - day they might fall,
There shall be sea - sons re - fresh - ing, Sent from the Sav - ior a - bove.
O - ver the hills and the val - leys, Sound of a - bun-dance of rain.
Grant to us now a re - fresh - ing, Come and now hon - or Your Word.
Now as to God we're con - fess - ing, Now as on Je - sus we call!
Refrain
Show - ers of bless - ing, Show-ers of bless-ing we need;
Show - ers, show-ers of bless - ing,
Mer - cy-drops round us are fall - ing, But for the show-ers we plead.

TEXT: Daniel W. Whittle; based on Ezekiel 34:26
MUSIC: James McGranahan

SHOWERS OF BLESSING
8.7.8.7. with Refrain

THE LIVING CHURCH

A Brief Service of Prayer and Challenge

Suggested Hymn Stanzas

To facilitate an uninterrupted flow from stanza to stanza, the suggested stanzas have been marked with an arrow: ►

O Breath of Life, stanzas 1, 2, 3
God of Grace and God of Glory, stanza 1
Rise Up, O Church of God, complete

WORSHIP LEADER:
God of the living church empow'r,
Thine ancient might reveal;
Give wisdom for this crucial hour,
And in Thy mercy, heal.

PEOPLE:
God of the living church forgive,
Renew, perfect, translate,
In Thee to be, and move, and live,
Immanuel, we wait.

WORSHIP LEADER:
God of the living church renew,
Fresh vision now impart,
And as we strive to live for You
Sustain each faithful heart.

ALL:
God of the living church, we plead,
Bestow Thy mighty pow'r,
Thy loving presence, Lord, we need,
To guide us in this hour.

"God of the Living Church"
by Alfred H. Ackley

Optional Introduction to "O Breath of Life"

mf

"God of the Living Church" by Alfred H. Ackley, altered

"THE LIVING CHURCH—A Brief Service of Prayer and Challenge"

291 O Breath of Life

I stand in awe of Your deeds, O Lord. Renew them in our day. Hab. 3:2

1. O Breath of Life, come sweeping thru us,
Revive Thy Church with life and pow'r;
O Breath of Life, come, cleanse, renew us,
And fit Thy Church to meet this hour.

2. O Wind of God, come bend us, break us,
Till humbly we confess our need;
Then in Thy tenderness remake us,
Revive, restore, for this we plead.

3. O Breath of Love, come breathe within us,
Renewing thought and will and heart;
Come, Love of Christ, afresh to win us,
Revive Thy Church in ev'ry part.

4. O Heart of Christ, once broken for us,
'Tis there we find our strength and rest;
Our broken, contrite hearts now solace,
And let Thy waiting Church be blest.

5. Revive us, Lord! Is zeal abating,
While harvest fields are vast and white?
Revive us, Lord, the world is waiting,
Equip Thy Church to spread the light.
Amen.

TEXT: Bessie Porter Head
MUSIC: Joel Blomquist

DET AR ETT FAST ORD
9.8.9.8.

God of Grace and God of Glory 292

Do not be discouraged, for the Lord your God will be with you. Josh. 1:9

1. God of grace and God of glo - ry, On Thy peo - ple
2. Lo! the hosts of e - vil round us Scorn Thy Christ, as -
3. Cure Thy chil - dren's war - ring mad - ness; Bend our pride to
4. Set our feet on loft - y plac - es, Gird our lives that
pour Thy power; Crown Thine an - cient Church's sto - ry, Bring her bud to
sail His ways! From the fears that long have bound us, Free our hearts to
Thy con - trol; Shame our wan - ton, self - ish glad - ness, Rich in things and
they may be Ar - mored with all Christ - like grac - es In the fight to
glo - rious flower. Grant us wis - dom, Grant us cour - age, For the
faith and praise. Grant us wis - dom, Grant us cour - age, For the
poor in soul. Grant us wis - dom, Grant us cour - age, Lest we
set men free. Grant us wis - dom, Grant us cour - age, That we
fac - ing of this hour, For the fac - ing of this hour.
liv - ing of these days, For the liv - ing of these days.
miss Thy king-dom's goal, Lest we miss Thy king-dom's goal.
fail not man nor Thee, That we fail not man nor Thee. A - men.

TEXT: Harry Emerson Fosdick
MUSIC: John Hughes

CWM RHONDDA
8.7.8.7.8.7.7.

Optional transition to "Rise Up, O Church of God"

293 Rise Up, O Church of God

Wake up! Strengthen what remains and is about to die. Rev. 3:2

1. Rise up, O Church of God! Have done with lesser things; Give heart and mind and soul and strength To serve the King of kings.
2. Rise up, O Church of God! His kingdom tarries long; Bring in the day of brotherhood And end the night of wrong.
3. Rise up, O sons of God! The Church for you doth wait, Her strength unequal to her task, Rise up, and make her great!
4. Lift high the cross of Christ! Tread where His feet have trod; As fol-l'wers of the Son of Man, Rise up, O Church of God!

Optional last stanza setting

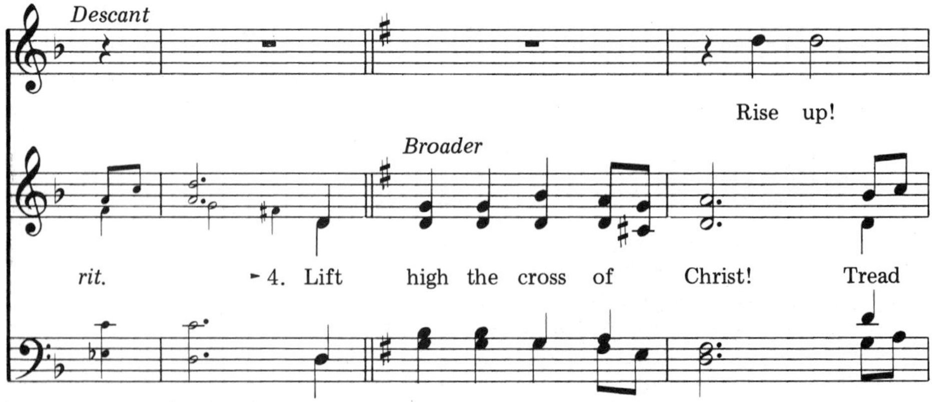

Descant

Rise up!

rit. *Broader*

4. Lift high the cross of Christ! Tread

TEXT: William P. Merrill, altered
MUSIC: Aaron Williams; Last stanza setting by Eugene Thomas

ST. THOMAS
S.M.

Rise up! As fol - l'wers of the Son of Man, Rise
where His feet have trod; As fol - l'wers of the Son of Man, Rise

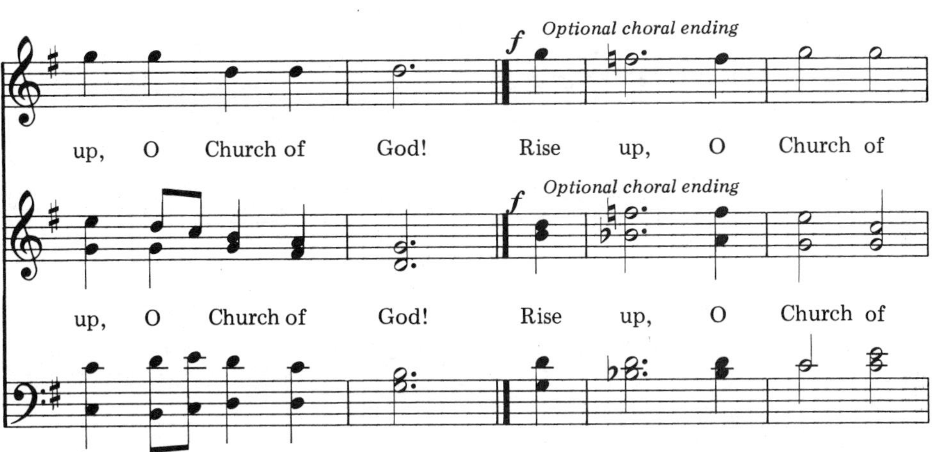
f
Optional choral ending
up, O Church of God! Rise up, O Church of
f
Optional choral ending
up, O Church of God! Rise up, O Church of

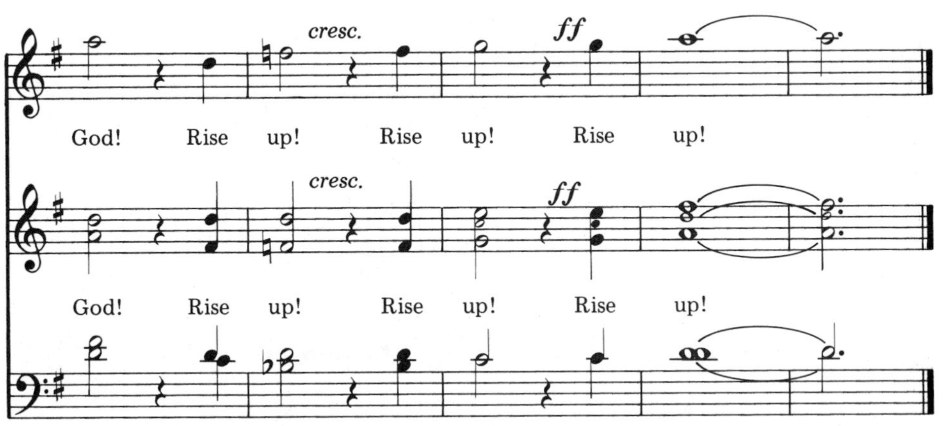
cresc.
ff
God! Rise up! Rise up! Rise up!
cresc.
ff
God! Rise up! Rise up! Rise up!

The end of "THE LIVING CHURCH—A Brief Service of Prayer and Challenge"

294 Set My Soul Afire

His Word is in my heart like a fire . . . I am weary of holding it in; indeed, I cannot. Jer. 20:9

1. Set my soul a - fire, Lord, for Thy ho - ly Word, Burn it deep with -
2. Set my soul a - fire, Lord, for the lost in sin, Give to me a
3. Set my soul a - fire, Lord, in my dai - ly life, Far too long I've
in me, let Thy voice be heard; Mil - lions grope in dark - ness
pas - sion as I seek to win; Help me not to fal - ter,
wan - dered in this day of strife; Noth - ing else will mat - ter
in this day and hour, I will be a wit - ness, fill me with Thy pow'r.
nev - er let me fail, Fill me with Thy Spir - it, let Thy will pre - vail.
but to live for Thee, I will be a wit - ness, for Christ lives in me.
Refrain
Set my soul a - fire, Lord, set my soul a - fire, Make my life a
wit - ness of Thy sav - ing pow'r. Mil - lions grope in dark - ness,

TEXT and MUSIC: Gene Bartlett

SCALES
11.11.11.11. with Refrain

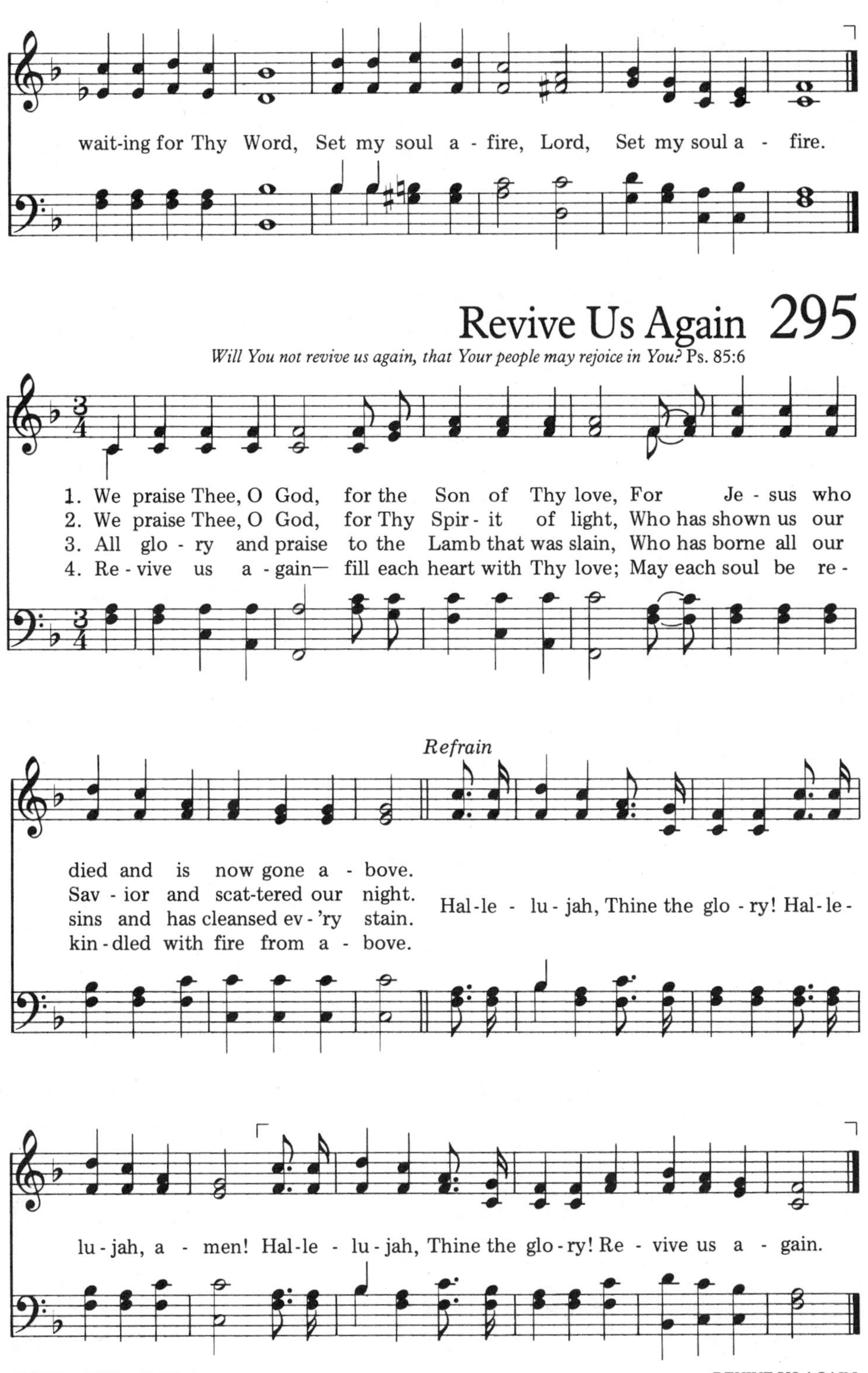
wait-ing for Thy Word, Set my soul a - fire, Lord, Set my soul a - fire.
Revive Us Again 295
Will You not revive us again, that Your people may rejoice in You? Ps. 85:6
1. We praise Thee, O God, for the Son of Thy love, For Je - sus who died and is now gone a - bove.
2. We praise Thee, O God, for Thy Spir - it of light, Who has shown us our Sav - ior and scat-tered our night.
3. All glo - ry and praise to the Lamb that was slain, Who has borne all our sins and has cleansed ev - 'ry stain.
4. Re - vive us a - gain— fill each heart with Thy love; May each soul be re - kin - dled with fire from a - bove.
Refrain
Hal-le - lu - jah, Thine the glo - ry! Hal-le - lu - jah, a - men! Hal-le - lu - jah, Thine the glo - ry! Re - vive us a - gain.

TEXT: William P. Mackay
MUSIC: John J. Husband

REVIVE US AGAIN
11.11. with Refrain

296 We've a Story to Tell to the Nations

Go and make disciples of all nations. Matt. 28:19

1. We've a sto - ry to tell to the na - tions That shall turn their hearts to the right, A sto - ry of truth and mer - cy, A sto - ry of peace and light, A sto - ry of peace and light.
2. We've a song to be sung to the na - tions That shall lift their hearts to the Lord, A song that shall con - quer e - vil And shat - ter the spear and sword, And shat - ter the spear and sword.
3. We've a mes - sage to give to the na - tions That the Lord who reign - eth a - bove Hath sent us His Son to save us, And show us that God is love, And show us that God is love.
4. We've a Sav - ior to show to the na - tions Who the path of sor - row hath trod, That all of the world's great peo - ples Might come to the truth of God, Might come to the truth of God.
Refrain
For the dark-ness shall turn to dawn-ing, And the dawn-ing to noon-day bright,
And Christ's great king-dom shall come to earth, The king-dom of love and light.

TEXT and MUSIC: H. Ernest Nichol

MESSAGE
10.8.8.7.7. with Refrain

I Love to Tell the Story 297

Those who had been scattered preached the Word wherever they went. Acts 8:4

1. I love to tell the sto - ry of un - seen things a - bove, Of Je - sus
2. I love to tell the sto - ry—'tis pleas-ant to re - peat What seems, each
3. I love to tell the sto - ry, for those who know it best Seem hun - ger-
and His glo - ry, of Je - sus and His love; I love to tell the
time I tell it, more won - der - ful - ly sweet; I love to tell the
ing and thirst-ing to hear it like the rest; And when in scenes of
sto - ry be - cause I know 'tis true, It sat - is - fies my long-ings
sto - ry, for some have nev - er heard The mes - sage of sal - va - tion
glo - ry I sing the new, new song, 'Twill be the old, old sto - ry
as noth-ing else can do.
from God's own ho - ly Word.
that I have loved so long.
Refrain
I love to tell the sto - ry! 'Twill be my
theme in glo - ry— To tell the old, old sto - ry Of Je - sus and His love.

TEXT: A. Catherine Hankey
MUSIC: William G. Fischer

HANKEY
7.6.7.6.D. with Refrain

298 O Zion, Haste

O Zion, bringer of good tidings . . . lift up your voice. Isa. 40:9

1. O *Zi - on, haste, thy mis - sion high ful - fill - ing, To tell to all the
2. Be - hold how man - y thou-sands still are ly - ing, Bound in the dark-some
3. Pro-claim to ev - ery peo - ple, tongue and na - tion That God, in whom they
4. Give of thy sons to bear the mes - sage glo - rious; Give of thy wealth to

world that God is Light; That He who made all na - tions is not will - ing
pris - on-house of sin, With none to tell them of the Sav - ior's dy - ing,
live and move, is love: Tell how He stooped to save His lost cre - a - tion,
speed them on their way; Pour out thy soul for them in prayer vic - to - rious;

One soul should per - ish, lost in shades of night.
Or of the life He died for them to win.
And died on earth that man might live a - bove.
And all thy spend-ing Je - sus will re - pay.

Refrain

Pub - lish glad ti - dings,

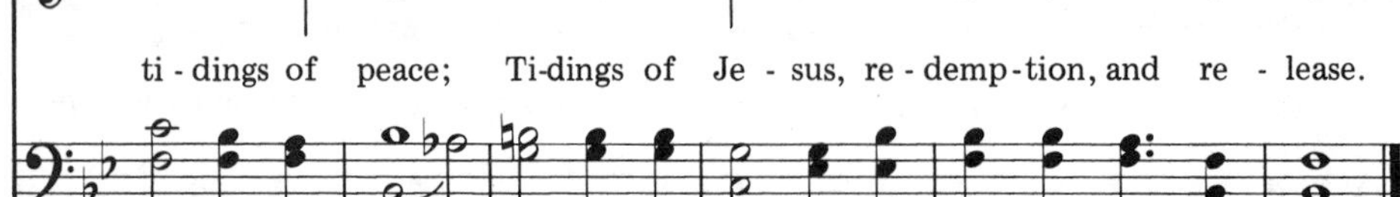
ti - dings of peace; Ti-dings of Je - sus, re - demp-tion, and re - lease.

TEXT: Mary A. Thomson
MUSIC: James Walch

TIDINGS
11.10.11.10. with Refrain

**Isaiah 40:9. By extension the word refers to the People of God.*

Rescue the Perishing 299

Snatch others from the fire and save them. Jude 23

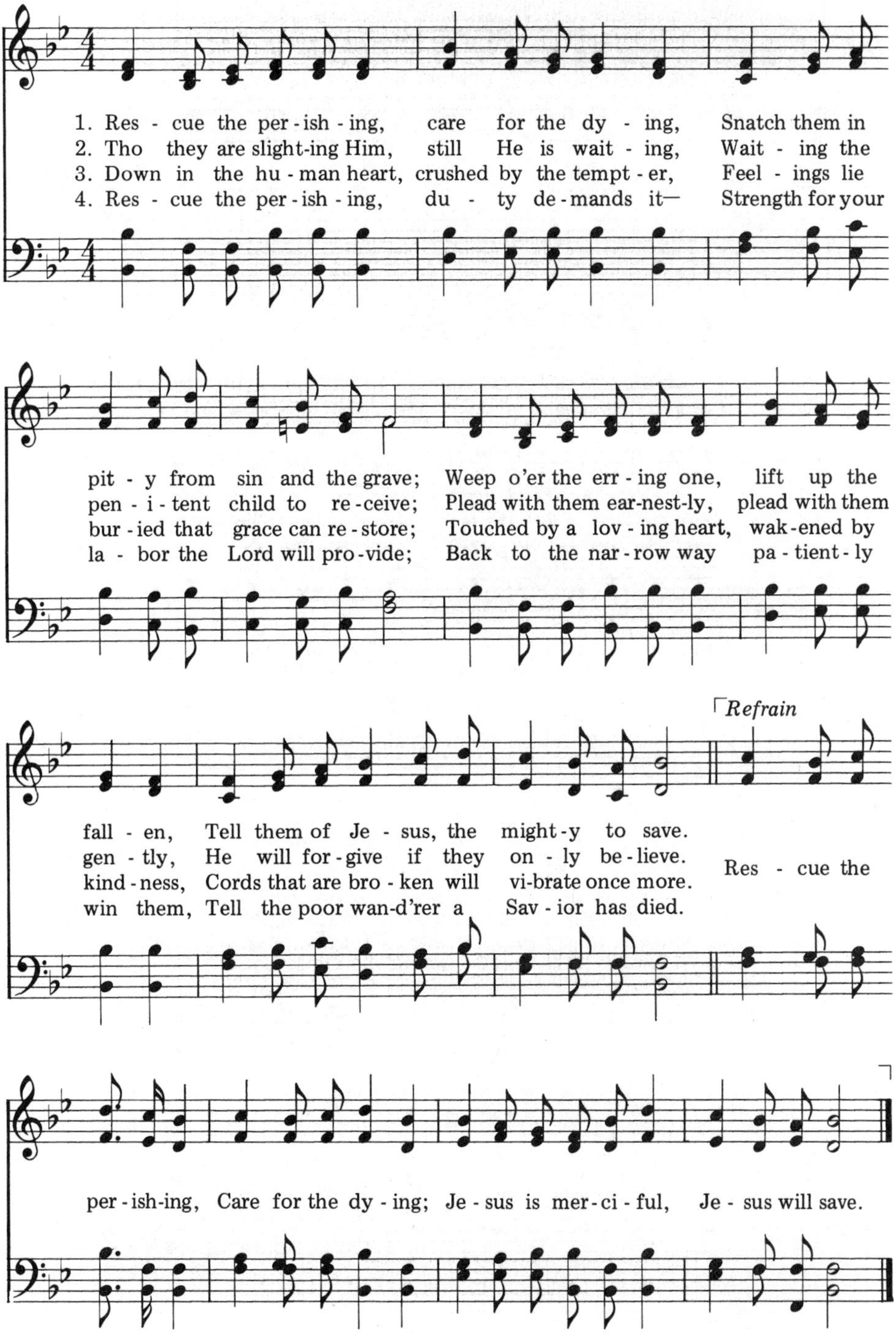

1. Res - cue the per - ish - ing, care for the dy - ing, Snatch them in
2. Tho they are slight-ing Him, still He is wait - ing, Wait - ing the
3. Down in the hu - man heart, crushed by the tempt - er, Feel - ings lie
4. Res - cue the per - ish - ing, du - ty de - mands it— Strength for your

pit - y from sin and the grave; Weep o'er the err - ing one, lift up the
pen - i - tent child to re - ceive; Plead with them ear-nest-ly, plead with them
bur - ied that grace can re - store; Touched by a lov - ing heart, wak-ened by
la - bor the Lord will pro - vide; Back to the nar - row way pa - tient - ly

fall - en, Tell them of Je - sus, the might - y to save.
gen - tly, He will for - give if they on - ly be - lieve.
kind - ness, Cords that are bro - ken will vi-brate once more.
win them, Tell the poor wan-d'rer a Sav - ior has died.

Refrain

Res - cue the per - ish-ing, Care for the dy - ing; Je - sus is mer - ci - ful, Je - sus will save.

TEXT: Fanny J. Crosby
MUSIC: William H. Doane

RESCUE
11.10.11.10. with Refrain

300 I'll Tell the World That I'm a Christian

I am not ashamed of the gospel. Rom. 1:16

1. I'll tell the world that I'm a Christian— I'm not a - shamed His name to bear; I'll tell the world that I'm a Christian— I'll take Him with me an - y - where. I'll tell the world how Je - sus saved me, And how He gave me a life brand - new; And I know that if you trust Him That all He gave me He'll give to you. I'll tell the world
2. I'll tell the world that He is com - ing— It may be near or far a - way; But we must live as if His com - ing Would be to - mor-row or to - day. For when He comes and life is o - ver, For those who love Him there's more to be; Eyes have nev - er seen the won-ders That He's pre - par - ing for you and me. O tell the world

TEXT and MUSIC: Baynard L. Fox

TUCKER
Irregular meter

that He's my Sav-ior, No oth-er one could love me so; My life, my
that you're a Chris-tian, Be not a-shamed His name to bear; O tell the

all is His for-ev-er, And where He leads me I will go.
world that you're a Chris-tian, And take Him with you ev-ery-where.

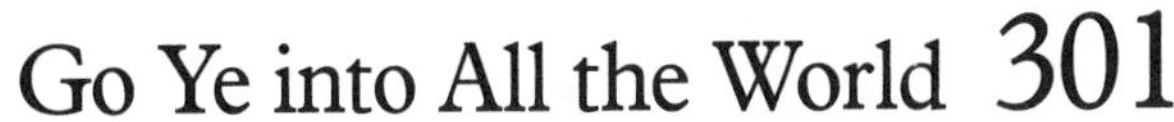
Go Ye into All the World 301

All authority in heaven and on earth has been given to Me. Matt. 28:18

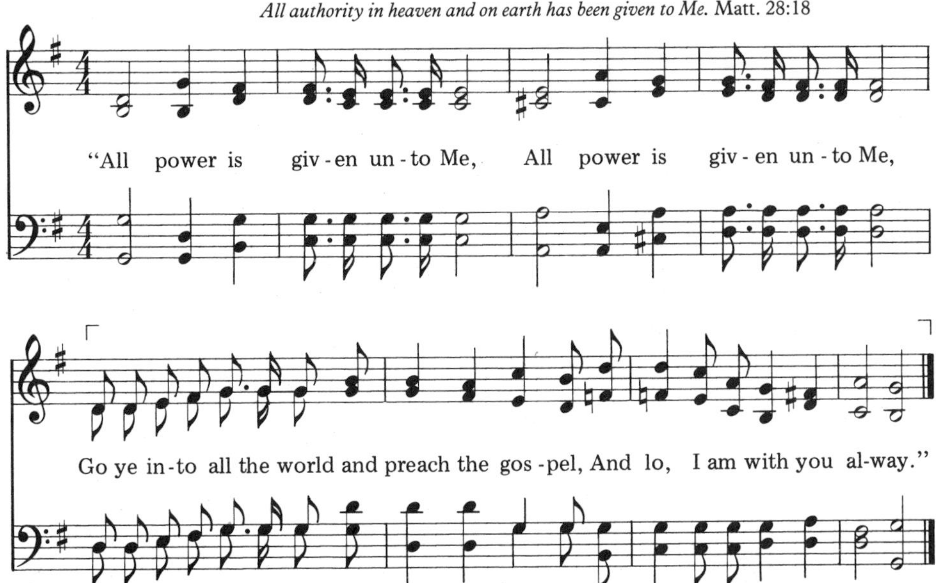
"All power is giv-en un-to Me, All power is giv-en un-to Me,
Go ye in-to all the world and preach the gos-pel, And lo, I am with you al-way."

TEXT and MUSIC: James McGranahan; based on Matthew 28:18-20

GO YE
8.8.12.8.

302 Share His Love

He . . . did not spare His own Son, but gave Him up for us all. Rom. 8:32

Unison
1. The love of God is broad - er than earth's vast ex - panse,
2. All those who have trust - ed in God's on - ly Son,
3. We show the love of God each day we live,
'Tis deep - er and wid - er than the sea.
And hold this pre - cious trea - sure in their hearts,
Re - veal Christ's pres - ence in our lives;
Love reach - es out to all to bring a - bun - dant life,
Seek ways to make it known to all who need to know
And how the Ho - ly Spir - it guides us day by day,
For God so loved the world His on - ly Son He gave.
That God so loved the world His on - ly Son He gave.
For God so loved the world His on - ly Son He gave.
Refrain
Share His love by tell - ing what the Lord has done for you,

TEXT and MUSIC: William J. Reynolds

SULLIVAN
Irregular meter

Share His love by shar - ing of your faith, and show the world that
Je - sus Christ is real to you ev - 'ry mo - ment, ev - 'ry day.
People Need the Lord 303
I am poor and needy . . . You are my help and my deliverer. Ps. 40:17
Unison
1. Peo-ple need the Lord, peo-ple need the Lord;
2. Peo-ple need the Lord, peo-ple need the Lord;
At the end of bro - ken dreams,
When will we re - al - ize
1
He's the o - pen door.
2
peo-ple need the Lord.

TEXT and MUSIC: Greg Nelson and Phill McHugh; arranged by David Allen

PEOPLE NEED THE LORD
Irregular meter

304 Lift High the Cross

I, when I am lifted up from the earth, will draw all men to Myself. John 12:32

Refrain - Unison
Lift high the Cross, the love of Christ pro - claim, Till
all the world a - dore His sa - cred name.
Fine
Parts Optional
1. Come, Chris - tians, fol - low where our Sav - ior trod,
2. Led on their way by this tri - um - phant sign,
3. O Lord, once lift - ed on this glo - rious Tree,
4. Set up Thy throne, that earth's de - spair may cease
5. For Thy blest Cross which doth for all a - tone,
Our King vic - to - rious, Christ, the Son of God.
The hosts of God in con - qu'ring ranks com - bine.
As Thou hast prom - ised, draw men un - to Thee.
Be - neath the shad - ow of its heal - ing peace.
Cre - a - tion's prais - es rise be - fore Thy throne.
Return to Refrain

TEXT: George W. Kitchin and Michael R. Newbolt
MUSIC: Sydney H. Nicholson

CRUCIFER
10.10.10.10.

Lord, Thy Church on Earth Is Seeking 305

Open your eyes and look at the fields! They are ripe for harvest. John 4:35

1. Lord, Thy church on earth is seek - ing Thy re - new - al
from a - bove;
Teach us all the art of speak - ing With the ac - cent of Thy love.
We would heed Thy great com - mis - sion:
"Go ye in - to ev - 'ry place;
Preach, bap - tize, ful - fill My mis - sion, Serve with love and share My grace."

2. Free - dom, give to those in bond - age, Lift the bur - dens caused by sin;
Give new hope, new strength and cour - age, Grant re - lease from fears with - in.
Light for dark - ness, joy for sor - row;
Love for ha - tred, peace for strife.
These and count - less bless - ings fol - low As the Spir - it gives new life.

3. In the streets of ev - 'ry cit - y Where the bruised and lone - ly dwell,
We shall show the Sav - ior's pit - y, We shall of His mer - cy tell.
In all lands and with all rac - es,
We shall serve and seek to bring
All the world to ren - der prais - es, Christ, to Thee, Re - deem - er, King.
A - men.

TEXT: Hugh Sherlock
MUSIC: William David Young

KINGSTON
8.7.8.7.D.

306 Jesus Saves!

Christ Jesus came into the world to save sinners. 1 Tim. 1:15

1. We have heard the joy - ful sound— Je - sus saves! Je - sus saves!
2. Waft it on the roll - ing tide— Je - sus saves! Je - sus saves!
3. Sing a - bove the bat - tle strife— Je - sus saves! Je - sus saves!
4. Give the winds a might - y voice— Je - sus saves! Je - sus saves!
Spread the ti - dings all a - round— Je - sus saves! Je - sus saves!
Tell to sin - ners far and wide— Je - sus saves! Je - sus saves!
By His death and end - less life— Je - sus saves! Je - sus saves!
Let the na - tions now re - joice— Je - sus saves! Je - sus saves!
Bear the news to ev - 'ry land, Climb the steeps and cross the waves;
Sing, ye is - lands of the sea! Ech - o back, ye o - cean caves!
Sing it soft - ly thru the gloom, When the heart for mer - cy craves;
Shout sal - va - tion full and free, High - est hills and deep - est caves;
On - ward! 'tis our Lord's com - mand— Je - sus saves! Je - sus saves!
Earth shall keep her ju - bi - lee— Je - sus saves! Je - sus saves!
Sing in tri - umph o'er the tomb— Je - sus saves! Je - sus saves!
This our song of vic - to - ry— Je - sus saves! Je - sus saves!

TEXT: Priscilla J. Owens
MUSIC: William J. Kirkpatrick

JESUS SAVES
7.6.7.6.7.7.7.6.

. . . the light of the gospel of the glory of Christ. 2 Cor. 4:4

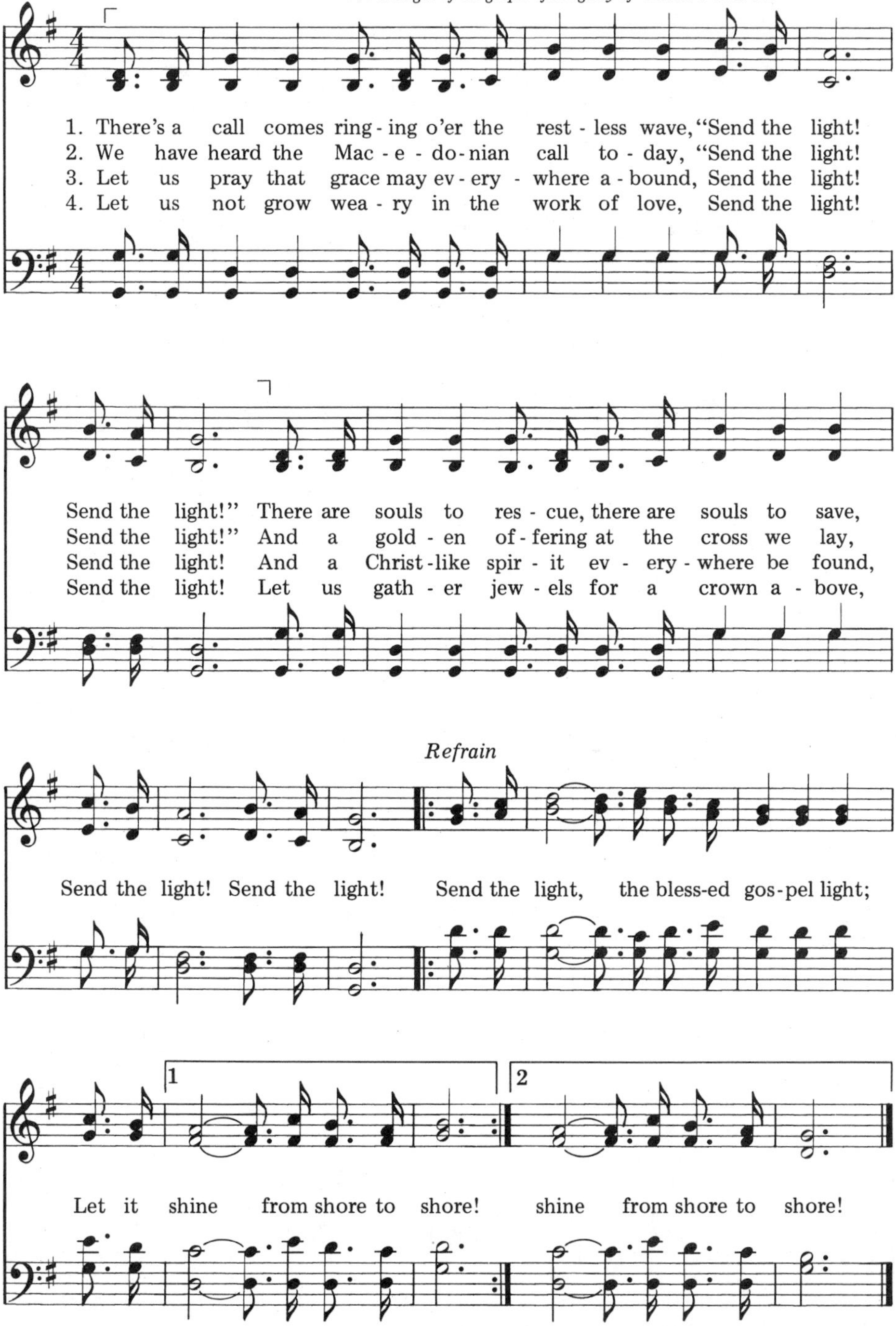

1. There's a call comes ring - ing o'er the rest - less wave, "Send the light! Send the light!" There are souls to res - cue, there are souls to save,
2. We have heard the Mac - e - do - nian call to - day, "Send the light! Send the light!" And a gold - en of - fering at the cross we lay,
3. Let us pray that grace may ev - ery - where a - bound, Send the light! Send the light! And a Christ - like spir - it ev - ery - where be found,
4. Let us not grow wea - ry in the work of love, Send the light! Send the light! Let us gath - er jew - els for a crown a - bove,

Send the light! Send the light!

Refrain

Send the light, the bless-ed gos-pel light; Let it shine from shore to shore! shine from shore to shore!

TEXT and MUSIC: Charles H. Gabriel

McCABE
11.6.11.6. with Refrain

308 Go

Surely I am with you always, to the very end of the age. Matt. 28:20

Parts optional
1. Go ye there-fore and teach all na - tions, go, go, go.
2. If you love Me, real - ly love Me, feed My sheep.
3. Go ye there-fore and teach all na - tions, go, go, go.
Go ye there-fore and teach all na - tions, go, go,
If you love Me, real - ly love Me, feed My
Go ye there-fore and teach all na - tions, go, go,
go. Bap-tiz - ing them in the name of the Fa - ther and Son, and
sheep. Lo, I'll be with you for - ev - er and ev - er, un - til the
go. Bap-tiz - ing them in the name of the Fa - ther and Son, and
Ho - ly Ghost. Go, go, go.
end of the world. Go, go, go.
Ho - ly Ghost. Go, go, go.

TEXT and MUSIC: Leon Patillo; arranged by Eugene Thomas

GO
Irregular meter

Pass It On 309

Since God so loved us, we also ought to love one another. 1 John 4:11

1. It only takes a spark to get a fire going,
2. What a wondrous time is spring—when all the trees are budding,
3. I wish for you, my friend, this happiness that I've found—
pass it on!
And soon all those around can warm up in its glowing;
The birds begin to sing, the flowers start their blooming;
You can depend on Him, it matters not where you're bound;
pass it on!
That's how it is with God's love, once you've experienced it: You
That's how it is with God's love, once you've experienced it: You
I'll shout it from the mountain top, I want my world to know: The
spread His love to ev-'ry-one, you want to pass it on.
want to sing, it's fresh like spring, you want to pass it on.
Lord of love has come to me, I want to pass it on.

TEXT and MUSIC: Kurt Kaiser

PASS IT ON
Irregular meter

310 So Send I You

As the Father has sent Me, I am sending you. John 20:21

1. So send I you— to labor unrewarded,
To serve unpaid, unloved, unsought, unknown,
To bear rebuke, to suffer scorn and scoffing—
So send I you, to toil for Me alone.

2. So send I you— to bind the bruised and broken,
O'er wand'ring souls to work, to weep, to wake,
To bear the burdens of a world aweary—
So send I you, to suffer for My sake.

3. So send I you— to loneliness and longing,
With heart ahung'ring for the loved and known,
Forsaking home and kindred, friend and dear one—
So send I you, to know My love alone.

4. So send I you— to leave your life's ambition,
To die to dear desire, self-will resign,
To labor long, and love where men revile you—
So send I you, to lose your life in Mine.

5. So send I you— to hearts made hard by hatred,
To eyes made blind because they will not see,
To spend, tho it be blood, to spend and spare not—
So send I you, to taste of Calvary.

1-4 D.C. 5

Coda

"As the Father hath sent Me, So send I you."

TEXT: Margaret Clarkson; based on John 20:21
MUSIC: John W. Peterson
Alternate tune: adaptable, without Coda, to FINLANDIA, No. 347

TORONTO
11.10.11.10. with Coda

So Send I You - by Grace Made Strong 311

As the Father has sent Me, I am sending you. John 20:21

1. So send I you— by grace made strong to tri - umph O'er hosts of hell,
2. So send I you— to take to souls in bond - age The Word of Truth
3. So send I you— My strength to know in weak - ness, My joy in grief,
4. So send I you— to bear My cross with pat - ience, And then one day
o'er dark - ness, death and sin, My name to bear and in that name to
that sets the cap - tive free, To break the bonds of sin, to loose death's
My per - fect peace in pain, To prove My pow'r, My grace, My prom-ised
with joy to lay it down, To hear My voice, "Well done, My faith-ful
con - quer— So send I you, My vic - to - ry to win.
fet - ters— So send I you, to bring the lost to Me.
pres - ence— So send I you, e - ter - nal fruit to gain.
ser - vant— Come share My throne, My king - dom and My crown!"
1-3
D.C.
4
Coda
"As the Fa - ther hath sent Me, so send I you."

TEXT: Margaret Clarkson; based on John 20:21
MUSIC: Kurt Kaiser
Alternate tunes: adaptable, without Coda to FINLANDIA, No. 347; TORONTO, No. 310

BY GRACE MADE STRONG
11.10.11.10. with Coda

312 To Be God's People

You shine like stars in the universe as you hold out the Word of life. Phil. 2:15-16

Unison

1. Al - might-y Fa - ther give us a vis - ion of a dy - ing world that needs Your love and care. We see the need, the yearn-ing for a Sav - ior, In Je - sus' name, grant this our prayer.

2. And when we fal - ter be Thou our com - fort; guide us as Your chil - dren that our lives may be A bea - con in this dark - ness that sur - rounds us, A light that oth - ers then may see.

Refrain

To be God's peo - ple in this place, live His

TEXT and MUSIC: Charles F. Brown

GOD'S PEOPLE
10.11.11.8. with Refrain

good - ness, share His grace, Pro - claim God's
mer - cy through His Son, be His
love to ev - 'ry - one.
Lord lay some soul up - on my heart, And love that soul through me;
And may I no - bly do my part To win that soul for Thee.

Lord, Lay Some Soul upon My Heart 313

I make myself a slave to everyone, to win as many as possible. 1 Cor. 9:19

TEXT: Dr. Leon Tucker
MUSIC: Ira D. Sankey

IRA
C.M.

314 Reach Out and Touch

Let us not love with words . . . but with actions and in truth. 1 John 3:18

Unison
1. Reach out and touch a soul that is hun-gry; Reach out and touch a spir-it in de-spair; Reach out and touch a life torn and dirt-y, A man who is lone-ly— If you care! Reach out and touch that neigh-bor who hates you; Reach out and touch that stran-ger who meets you; Reach out and touch the broth-er who needs you; Reach out and let the smile of
2. Reach out and touch a friend who is wea-ry; Reach out and touch a seek-er un-a-ware; Reach out and touch tho' touch-ing means los-ing A part of your own self— If you dare! Reach out and give your love to the love-less; Reach out and make a home for the home-less; Reach out and shed God's light in the dark-ness; Reach out and let the smile of

TEXT and MUSIC: Charles F. Brown

REACH OUT
Irregular meter

God touch thro' you.
you.

Let Your Heart Be Broken 315

When He saw the crowds, He had compassion on them. Matt. 9:36

1. Let your heart be broken For a world in need— Feed the mouths that hunger, Soothe the wounds that bleed, Give the cup of water And the loaf of bread— Be the hands of Jesus, Serving in His stead.

2. Here on earth applying Principles of love— Visible expression God still rules above, Living illustration Of the Living Word To the minds of all who've Never seen and heard.

3. Blest to be a blessing, Privileged to care, Challenged by the need Apparent ev'rywhere, Where mankind is wanting Fill the vacant place, Be the means thru which the Lord reveals His grace.

4. Add to your believing Deeds that prove it true— Knowing Christ as Savior, Make Him Master too: Follow in His footsteps, Go where He has trod, In the world's great trouble Risk yourself for God.

5. Let your heart be tender And your vision clear— See mankind as God sees, Serve Him far and near; Let your heart be broken By a brother's pain, Share your rich resources— Give and give again.

TEXT: Bryan Jeffery Leech
MUSIC: James Mountain

WYE VALLEY (abridged)
6.5.6.5.D.

316 Macedonia

Come over to Macedonia and help us. Acts 16:9

1. The vi - sion of a dy - ing world Is vast be - fore our eyes; We
2. The sav - age hugs his god of stone And fears de - scent of night; The
3. To - day, as un - der - stand - ing's bounds Are stretch'd on ev - ery hand, O
4. The warn - ing bell of judg - ment tolls, A - bove us looms the cross; A -
feel the heart - beat of its need, We hear its fee - ble cries: Lord
cit - y dwell - er cring - es lone A - mid the gar - ish light: Lord
clothe Thy Word in bright, new sounds, And speed it o'er the land; Lord
round are ev - er - dy - ing souls—How great, how great the loss! O
Je - sus Christ, re - vive Thy church In this, her cru - cial hour! Lord
Je - sus Christ, a - rouse Thy church To see their mute dis - tress! Lord
Je - sus Christ, em - pow - er us To preach by ev - ery means! Lord
Lord, con - strain and move Thy church The glad news to im - part! And
Je - sus Christ, a - wake Thy church With Spir - it - giv - en pow'r.
Je - sus Christ, e - quip Thy church With love and ten - der - ness.
Je - sus Christ, em - bold - en us In near and dis - tant scenes.
Lord, as Thou dost stir Thy church, Be - gin with - in my heart. A - men.

TEXT: Anne Ortlund
MUSIC: Henry S. Cutler

ALL SAINTS, NEW
C.M.D.

This Child We Dedicate to Thee 317

Bring them up in the training and instruction of the Lord. Eph. 6:4

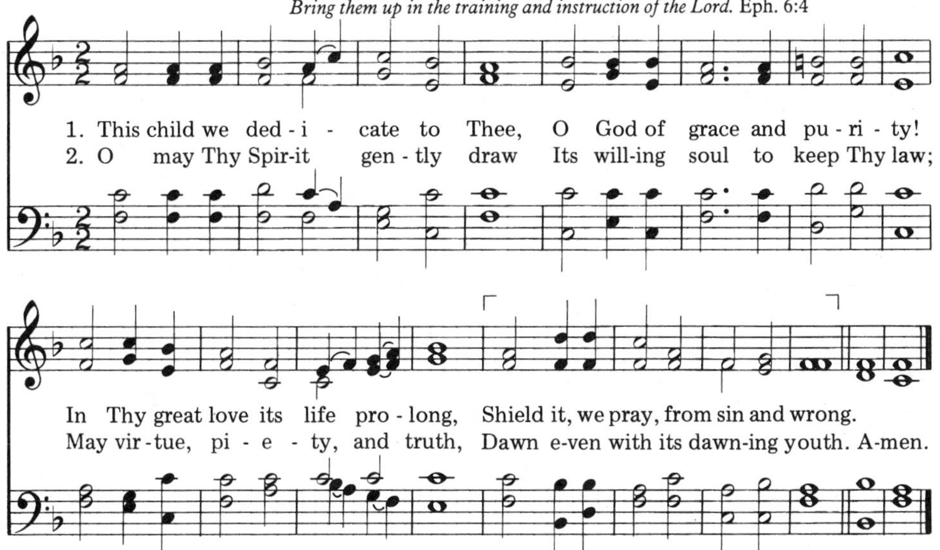
1. This child we ded - i - cate to Thee, O God of grace and pu - ri - ty!
2. O may Thy Spir-it gen - tly draw Its will-ing soul to keep Thy law;
In Thy great love its life pro - long, Shield it, we pray, from sin and wrong.
May vir - tue, pi - e - ty, and truth, Dawn e-ven with its dawn-ing youth. A-men.

TEXT: From the German; translated by Samuel Gilman
MUSIC: Henry K. Oliver

FEDERAL STREET
L.M.

Good Shepherd, Take This Little Child 318

He took the children in His arms, put His hands on them and blessed them. Mark 10:16

Unison
1. Good Shep - herd, take this lit - tle child in - to Your lov - ing
2. Good Shep - herd, we com - mit our - selves in ev - 'ry - thing we
3. Good Shep - herd, now we place this child in - to Your gen - tle
hands; And in the days that lie a - head pro - tect this lit - tle lamb.
do To be Your fam-'ly here on earth and love this child for You.
trust; This pre-cious gift we give to You is one You've giv - en us.

TEXT: Claire Cloninger
MUSIC: Ken Barker

AMY
C.M.

319 We Bless the Name of Christ, the Lord

It is proper for us to do this to fulfill all righteousness. Matt. 3:15

Unison

1. We bless the name of Christ the Lord, We bless Him for His ho - ly Word, Who loved to do His Fa - ther's will, And all His righ - teous - ness ful - fill.
2. We fol - low Him with pure de - light To sanc - ti - fy His sa - cred rite, And thus our faith with wa - ter seal To prove o - be - dience that we feel.
3. Bap - tized in God the Fa - ther, Son And Ho - ly Spir - it, Three in One, With con - science free we rest in God, In love and peace, thro' Je - sus' blood.
4. By grace we "Ab - ba, Fa - ther," cry; By grace the Com - fort - er comes nigh; And for Thy grace our love shall be For - ev - er, on - ly, Lord, for Thee.

TEXT: Samuel F. Coffman
MUSIC: Thomas Hastings
An alternate setting of this tune may be found at No. 432

RETREAT
L.M.

320 Come Holy Spirit, Dove Divine

We were therefore buried with Him through baptism into death. Rom. 6:4

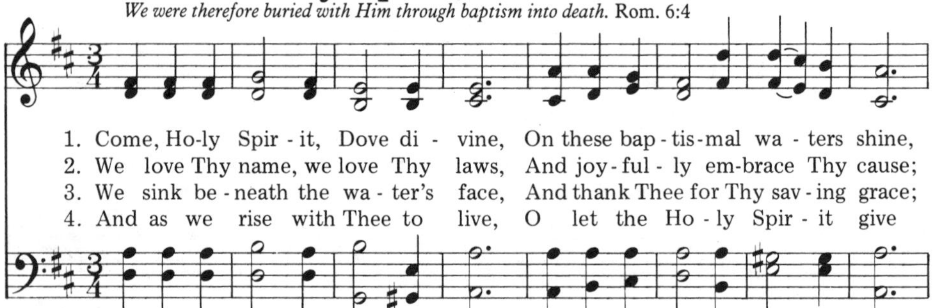
1. Come, Ho-ly Spir - it, Dove di - vine, On these bap - tis-mal wa - ters shine,
2. We love Thy name, we love Thy laws, And joy - ful - ly em-brace Thy cause;
3. We sink be - neath the wa - ter's face, And thank Thee for Thy sav - ing grace;
4. And as we rise with Thee to live, O let the Ho - ly Spir - it give

TEXT: Adoniram Judson
MUSIC: H. Percy Smith
A higher setting may be found at No. 451

MARYTON
L.M.

And teach our hearts, in high - est strain, To praise the Lamb for sin - ners slain.
We love Thy cross, the shame, the pain, O Lamb of God for sin - ners slain.
We die to sin and seek a grave With Thee, be-neath the yield-ing wave.
The seal - ing unc- tion from a - bove, The joy of life, the fire of love. A-men.

According to Thy Gracious Word 321

This is My body, which is for you; do this in remembrance of Me. 1 Cor. 11:24

1. Ac - cord - ing to Thy gra-cious word, In meek hu - mil - i - ty,
2. Thy bod - y, bro-ken for my sake, My bread from heav'n shall be;
3. When to the cross I turn mine eyes And rest on Cal - va - ry,
4. Re - mem - ber Thee and all Thy pains And all Thy love to me;
5. And when these fail - ing lips grow dumb And mind and mem - 'ry flee,

This will I do, my dy - ing Lord: I will re - mem - ber Thee.
Thy tes - ta - men - tal cup I take, And thus re - mem - ber Thee.
O Lamb of God, my sac - ri - fice, I must re - mem - ber Thee.
Yea, while a breath, a pulse re - mains, Will I re - mem - ber Thee.
When Thou shalt in Thy king - dom come, Je - sus, re - mem - ber me!

TEXT: James Montgomery
MUSIC: From Henry W. Greatorex's *Collection of Church Music,* 1851
A higher setting may be found at No. 70

MANOAH
C.M.

322 In Remembrance

This is My body given for you; do this in remembrance of Me. Luke 22:19

Introduction

In re - mem-brance of Me,
(In re -) mem-brance of Me,

eat this bread. In re - mem-brance of Me, drink this wine. In re-
heal the sick. In re - mem-brance of Me, feed the poor. In re-

mem-brance of Me, pray for the time when God's own will is
mem-brance of Me, o - pen the door and let your broth - er

1 done. In re-
2 in, Let him in.

Take, eat, and be com - fort - ed; drink and re - mem - ber

TEXT: Ragan Courtney
MUSIC: Buryl Red; arranged by Robert F. Douglas

RED
Irregular meter

too, That this is My bod - y and pre - cious blood shed for
you, shed for you. In re - mem-brance of Me
search for truth. In re-mem-brance of Me al-ways love. In re-
mem-brance of Me, don't look a - bove, but in your heart
Optional ending
Choir or Congregation
rit.
look for God. Do this in re - mem-brance of Me.

323 Let Us Break Bread Together

They devoted themselves . . . to the breaking of bread. Acts 2:42

1. Let us break bread to - geth - er on our knees; (on our knees;)
2. Let us drink the cup to - geth - er on our knees; (on our knees;)
3. Let us praise God to - geth - er on our knees; (on our knees;)
Let us break bread to - geth - er on our knees; (on our knees;)
Let us drink the cup to - geth - er on our knees; (on our knees;)
Let us praise God to - geth - er on our knees; (on our knees;)
Refrain
When I fall on my knees with my face to the ris - ing sun,
O Lord, have mer - cy on me. (on me.)

TEXT: Traditional Spiritual
MUSIC: Traditional Spiritual; arranged by Keith Phillips

LET US BREAK BREAD
Irregular meter

Come Celebrate Jesus 324

Do this . . . in remembrance of Me. 1 Cor. 11:25

Come cel - e - brate Je - sus, come cel - e - brate Je - sus,
The bread and the wine, the mo-ment in time. Come cel - e - brate
Je - sus, the Spir - it that frees us, His ta - ble
has been laid, come now and cel - e - brate Him.
1
D.C.
2
cel - e - brate Him. (cel - e - brate Him.)

TEXT: Claire Cloninger
MUSIC: John Rosasco; arranged by David Allen

CELEBRATE JESUS
Irregular meter

325 Here, O My Lord, I See Thee Face to Face

Your face, Lord, I will seek. Ps. 27:8

1. Here, O my Lord, I see Thee face to face,
2. Here would I feed up - on the bread of God,
3. I have no help but Thine, nor do I need
4. Mine is the sin, but Thine the right - eous - ness,
Here would I touch and han - dle things un - seen;
Here drink with Thee the roy - al wine of heaven;
An - oth - er arm save Thine to lean up - on;
Mine is the guilt, but Thine the cleans - ing blood;
Here grasp with firm - er hand e - ter - nal grace,
Here would I lay a - side each earth - ly load,
It is e - nough, my Lord, e - nough in - deed—
Here is my robe, my ref - uge, and my peace—
And all my wea - ri - ness up - on Thee lean.
Here taste a - fresh the calm of sin for - giv'n.
My strength is in Thy might, Thy might a - lone.
Thy blood, Thy right - eous - ness, O Lord, my God. A - men.

TEXT: Horatius Bonar
MUSIC: Edward Dearle

PENITENTIA
10.10.10.10.

Softly and Tenderly 326

Come to Me, all you who are weary and burdened, and I will give you rest. Matt. 11:28

1. Soft - ly and ten - der - ly Je - sus is call - ing, Call - ing for
2. Why should we tar - ry when Je - sus is plead - ing, Plead - ing for
3. Time is now fleet - ing, the mo - ments are pass - ing, Pass - ing from
4. O for the won - der - ful love He has prom - ised, Prom - ised for
you and for me; See, on the por - tals He's wait - ing and watch - ing,
you and for me? Why should we lin - ger and heed not His mer - cies,
you and from me; Shad - ows are gath - er - ing, death's night is com - ing,
you and for me! Though we have sinned, He has mer - cy and par - don,
Watch - ing for you and for me.
Mer - cies for you and for me?
Com - ing for you and for me.
Par - don for you and for me.
Refrain
Come home, come home,
Come home, come home,
Ye who are wea - ry, come home;
Ear - nest - ly, ten - der - ly,
Je - sus is call - ing, Call - ing, O sin - ner, come home!

TEXT and MUSIC: Will L. Thompson

THOMPSON
11.7.11.7. with Refrain

327 Jesus Is Calling

Today, if you hear His voice, do not harden your hearts. Heb. 4:7

1. Jesus is tenderly calling you home,
Calling today, calling today,
Why from the sunshine of love will you roam
Farther and farther away?

2. Jesus is calling the weary to rest,
Calling today, calling today,
Bring Him your burden and you shall be blest;
He will not turn you away.

3. Jesus is waiting, O come to Him now,
Waiting today, waiting today,
Come with your sins, at His feet lowly bow;
Come, and no longer delay.

4. Jesus is pleading, O list to His voice:
Hear Him today, hear Him today,
They who believe on His name shall rejoice;
Quickly arise and away.

Refrain

Calling today, (Calling, calling today, today,)
Calling today, (Calling, calling today, today,)
Jesus is calling, (Jesus is tenderly calling today,)
Is tenderly calling today.

TEXT: Fanny J. Crosby
MUSIC: George C. Stebbins

CALLING TODAY
10.8.10.7. with Refrain

Have You Any Room for Jesus? 328

Now is the time of God's favor, now is the day of salvation. 2 Cor. 6:2

1. Have you an - y room for Je - sus, He who bore your load of sin?
2. Room for pleas-ure, room for busi - ness— But, for Christ the Cru - ci - fied,
3. Have you an - y room for Je - sus, As in grace He calls a - gain?
4. Room and time now give to Je - sus, Soon will pass God's day of grace;
As He knocks and asks ad - mis - sion, Sin - ner, will you let Him in?
Not a place that He can en - ter In the heart for which He died?
O to - day is time ac - cept - ed, Lat - er you may call in vain.
Soon your heart left cold and si - lent, And your Sav-ior's plead-ing cease.
Refrain
Room for Je - sus, King of glo - ry! Has - ten now, His Word o - bey;
Swing the heart's door wide-ly o - pen, Bid Him en - ter while you may.

TEXT: Source unknown; adapted by Daniel W. Whittle
MUSIC: C. C. Williams

ANY ROOM
8.7.8.7. with Refrain

329 The Savior Is Waiting

Today, if you hear His voice, do not harden your hearts. Heb. 3:15

1. The Savior is waiting to enter your heart—Why don't you let Him come in? There's nothing in this world to keep you apart—What is your answer to Him?

2. If you'll take one step toward the Savior, my friend, You'll find His arms open wide; Receive Him and all of your darkness will end, Within your heart He'll abide.

Refrain

Time after time He has waited before, And now He is waiting again To see if you're willing to open the door—O how He wants to come in.

TEXT and MUSIC: Ralph Carmichael; arranged by Michael James

CARMICHAEL
11.7.11.7. with Refrain

Only Trust Him 330

Believe in the Lord Jesus Christ, and you shall be saved. Acts 16:31

Optional choral ending
Slowly
Oh, how He wants to come in.
wants to come in.
in.
1. Come, ev - 'ry soul by sin op-pressed—There's mer - cy with the Lord,
2. For Je - sus shed His pre-cious blood, Rich bless - ings to be - stow;
3. Yes, Je - sus is the Truth, the Way, That leads you in - to rest:
And He will sure - ly give you rest By trust - ing in His Word.
Plunge now in - to the crim - son flood That wash - es white as snow.
Be - lieve in Him with - out de - lay And you are ful - ly blest.
Refrain
On - ly trust Him, on - ly trust Him, On - ly trust Him now;
He will save you, He will save you, He will save you now.

TEXT and MUSIC: John H. Stockton

MINERVA
C.M. with Refrain

331 Room at the Cross for You

There is still room. Luke 14:22

1. The cross up - on which Je - sus died Is a shel - ter in
2. Tho mil - lions have found Him a friend And have turned from the
3. The hand of my Sav - ior is strong, And the love of my
which we can hide; And its grace so free is suf -
sins they have sinned, The Sav - ior still waits to
Sav - ior is long; Through sun - shine or rain, through
fi - cient for me, And deep is its foun - tain—as wide as the sea.
o - pen the gates And wel - comes a sin - ner be - fore it's too late.
loss or in gain, The blood flows from Cal - v'ry to cleanse ev - 'ry stain.
Refrain
There's room at the cross for you, There's room at the cross for you; Tho
mil-lions have come, There's still room for one—Yes, there's room at the cross for you.

TEXT and MUSIC: Ira F. Stanphill

ROOM AT THE CROSS
Irregular meter

Without Him 332

Apart from Me you can do nothing. John 15:5

1. With - out Him I could do noth - ing, With - out Him I'd sure - ly fail; With - out Him I would be drift - ing Like a ship with - out a sail.
2. With - out Him I would be dy - ing, With - out Him I'd be en - slaved; With - out Him life would be hope - less, But with Je - sus, thank God, I'm saved.
Refrain
Je - sus, O Je - sus! Do you know Him to - day? Do not turn Him a - way. O Je - sus, O Je - sus, With - out Him, how lost I would be.

TEXT and MUSIC: Mylon R. LeFevre

WITHOUT HIM
8.7.8.7. with Refrain

333 His Way with Thee

As for God, His way is perfect; . . . God . . . makes my way perfect. Ps. 18:30,32

1. Would you live for Je - sus and be al-ways pure and good? Would you walk with
2. Would you have Him make you free and fol-low at His call? Would you know the
3. Would you in His king-dom find a place of con-stant rest? Would you prove Him
Him with - in the nar - row road? Would you have Him bear your bur - den,
peace that comes by giv - ing all? Would you have Him save you, so that
true in prov - i - den - tial test? Would you in His serv - ice la - bor
car - ry all your load? Let Him have His way with thee.
you need nev-er fall? Let Him have His way with thee.
al-ways at your best? Let Him have His way with thee.
Refrain
His pow'r can make you what you ought to be; His blood can cleanse your heart and make you free; His love can fill your soul, and you will see 'Twas best for Him to have His way with thee.

TEXT and MUSIC: Cyrus S. Nusbaum

NUSBAUM
Irregular meter

Come, Ye Sinners, Poor and Needy 334

Come . . . take the free gift of the water of life. Rev. 22:17

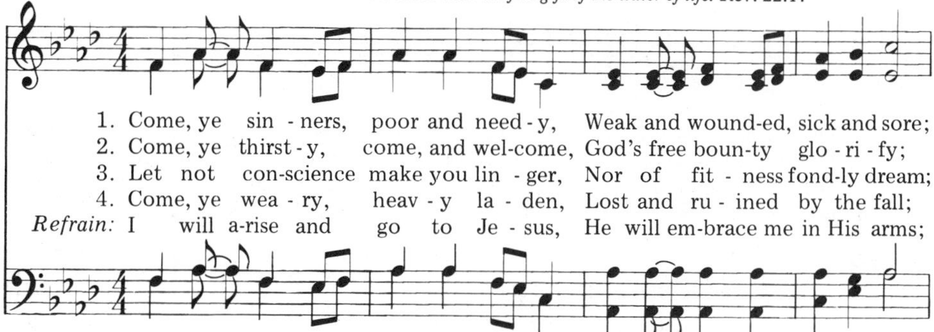

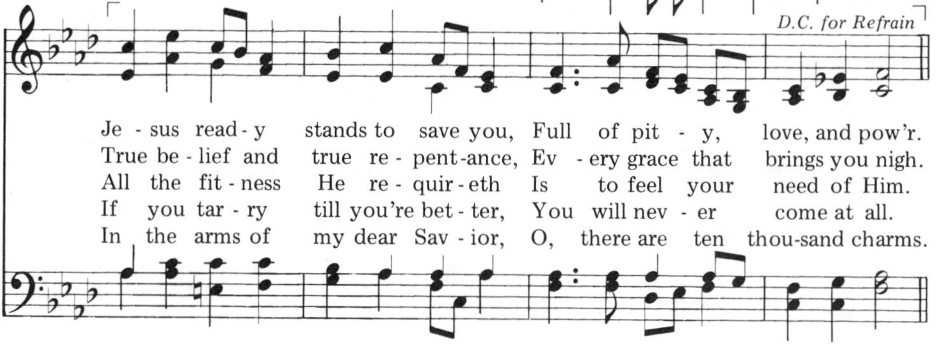

1. Come, ye sin-ners, poor and need-y, Weak and wound-ed, sick and sore;
Je-sus read-y stands to save you, Full of pit-y, love, and pow'r.

2. Come, ye thirst-y, come, and wel-come, God's free boun-ty glo-ri-fy;
True be-lief and true re-pent-ance, Ev-ery grace that brings you nigh.

3. Let not con-science make you lin-ger, Nor of fit-ness fond-ly dream;
All the fit-ness He re-quir-eth Is to feel your need of Him.

4. Come, ye wea-ry, heav-y la-den, Lost and ru-ined by the fall;
If you tar-ry till you're bet-ter, You will nev-er come at all.

Refrain: I will a-rise and go to Je-sus, He will em-brace me in His arms;
In the arms of my dear Sav-ior, O, there are ten thou-sand charms.

D.C. for Refrain

TEXT: Joseph Hart; Refrain, source unknown
MUSIC: Traditional American melody; Walker's *Southern Harmony,* 1835

ARISE
8.7.8.7. with Refrain

Turn Your Eyes upon Jesus 335

We . . . reflect the Lord's glory, . . . being transformed into His likeness. 2 Cor. 3:18

Turn your eyes up-on Je-sus, Look full in His won-der-ful face,
won-der-ful face,
And the things of earth will grow strange-ly dim In the light of His glo-ry and grace.

TEXT and MUSIC: Helen H. Lemmel

LEMMEL (Refrain only)
Irregular meter

336 Jesus, I Come

He has sent Me . . . to proclaim freedom for the captives. Isa. 61:1

1. Out of my bond-age, sor-row and night, Je-sus, I come, Je-sus, I come;
Out of my bond-age, sor-row and night,
In-to Thy free-dom, glad-ness and light, Je-sus, I come to Thee.
Out of my sick-ness in-to Thy health, Out of my want and in-to Thy wealth,
Out of my sin and in-to Thy-self, Je-sus, I come to Thee.

2. Out of my shame-ful fail-ure and loss, Je-sus, I come, Je-sus, I come;
In-to the glo-rious gain of Thy cross, Je-sus, I come to Thee.
Out of earth's sor-rows in-to Thy balm, Out of life's storms and in-to Thy calm,
Out of dis-tress to ju-bi-lant psalm, Je-sus, I come to Thee.

3. Out of un-rest and ar-ro-gant pride, Je-sus, I come, Je-sus, I come;
In-to Thy bless-ed will to a-bide, Je-sus, I come to Thee.
Out of my-self to dwell in Thy love, Out of de-spair in-to rap-tures a-bove,
Up-ward for aye on wings like a dove, Je-sus, I come to Thee.

4. Out of the fear and dread of the tomb, Je-sus, I come, Je-sus, I come;
In-to the joy and light of Thy home, Je-sus, I come to Thee.
Out of the depths of ru-in un-told, In-to the peace of Thy shel-ter-ing fold,
Ev-er Thy glo-rious face to be-hold, Je-sus, I come to Thee.

TEXT: William T. Sleeper
MUSIC: George C. Stebbins

JESUS, I COME
Irregular meter

Pass Me Not 337

The Lord is not slow in keeping His promise . . . not wanting anyone to perish. 2 Pet. 3:9

1. Pass me not, O gen - tle Sav - ior— Hear my hum - ble cry!
2. Let me at a throne of mer - cy Find a sweet re - lief;
3. Trust - ing on - ly in Thy mer - it, Would I seek Thy face;
4. Thou the spring of all my com - fort, More than life to me!
While on oth - ers Thou art call - ing, Do not pass me by.
Kneel - ing there in deep con - tri - tion— Help my un - be - lief.
Heal my wound-ed, bro-ken spir - it, Save me by Thy grace.
Whom have I on earth be - side Thee? Whom in heav'n but Thee?
Refrain
Sav - ior, Sav - ior, Hear my hum - ble cry!
While on oth - ers Thou art call - ing, Do not pass me by.

TEXT: Fanny J. Crosby
MUSIC: William H. Doane

PASS ME NOT
8.5.8.5. with Refrain

338 At Calvary

When they came to the place called the Skull, there they crucified Him. Luke 23:33

1. Years I spent in van - i - ty and pride, Car - ing not my Lord was cru - ci - fied, Know - ing not it was for me He died On Cal - va - ry.
2. By God's Word at last my sin I learned— Then I trem-bled at the law I'd spurned, Till my guilt - y soul im - plor - ing turned To Cal - va - ry.
3. Now I've giv'n to Je - sus ev - 'ry - thing, Now I glad - ly own Him as my King, Now my rap-tured soul can on - ly sing Of Cal - va - ry.
4. O the love that drew sal - va - tion's plan! O the grace that bro't it down to man! O the might - y gulf that God did span At Cal - va - ry.

Refrain

Mer - cy there was great and grace was free, Par - don there was mul - ti - plied to me, There my bur-dened soul found lib - er - ty—At Cal - va - ry.

TEXT: William R. Newell
MUSIC: Daniel B. Towner

CALVARY
9.9.9.4. with Refrain

Since I Have Been Redeemed 339

Christ redeemed us from the curse of the law. Gal. 3:13

1. I have a song I love to sing, Since I have been re - deemed,
2. I have a Christ who sat - is - fies, Since I have been re - deemed,
3. I have a wit - ness bright and clear, Since I have been re - deemed,
4. I have a home pre - pared for me, Since I have been re - deemed,
Of my Re - deem - er, Sav - ior, King, Since I have been re - deemed.
To do His will my high - est prize, Since I have been re - deemed.
Dis - pel - ling ev - ery doubt and fear, Since I have been re - deemed.
Where I shall dwell e - ter - nal - ly, Since I have been re - deemed.
Refrain
Since I have been re-deemed, Since I have been re-
Since I have been re-deemed, Since I have been re-deemed,
deemed, I will glo - ry in His name; Since I have been re-
Since I have been re - deemed, Since
deemed, I will glo - ry in my Sav - ior's name.
I have been re-deemed,

TEXT and MUSIC: Edwin O. Excell

OTHELLO
C.M. with Refrain

340 I Lay My Sins on Jesus

The Lord has laid on Him the iniquity of us all. Isa. 53:6

1. I lay my sins on Je - sus, The spot - less Lamb of God;
2. I lay my wants on Je - sus— All full - ness dwells in Him;
3. I long to be like Je - sus— Meek, lov - ing, low - ly, mild;
He bears them all, and frees us From the ac - curs - ed load.
He heals all my dis - eas - es, He doth my soul re - deem.
I long to be like Je - sus—The Fa - ther's ho - ly Child.
I bring my guilt to Je - sus, To wash my crim - son stains
I lay my griefs on Je - sus, My bur - dens and my cares;
I long to be with Je - sus, A - mid the heav'n-ly throng,
White in His blood most pre - cious, Till not a spot re - mains.
He from them all re - leas - es, He all my sor - rows shares.
To sing with saints His prais - es, To learn the an - gels' song.

TEXT: Horatius Bonar
MUSIC: Traditional Greek melody

CRUCIFIX
7.6.7.6.D.

Lord, I'm Coming Home 341

I will set out and go back to my father. Luke 15:18

1. I've wan-dered far a-way from God— Now I'm com-ing home;
The paths of sin too long I've trod— Lord, I'm com-ing home.

2. I've wast-ed man-y pre-cious years— Now I'm com-ing home;
I now re-pent with bit-ter tears— Lord, I'm com-ing home.

3. I've tired of sin and stray-ing, Lord— Now I'm com-ing home;
I'll trust Thy love, be-lieve Thy word— Lord, I'm com-ing home.

4. My soul is sick, my heart is sore— Now I'm com-ing home;
My strength re-new, my hope re-store— Lord, I'm com-ing home.

Refrain

Com-ing home, com-ing home, Nev-er-more to roam;
O-pen now Thine arms of love— Lord, I'm com-ing home.

TEXT and MUSIC: William J. Kirkpatrick

COMING HOME
8.5.8.5. with Refrain

342 Just As I Am

Whoever comes to Me I will never drive away. John 6:37

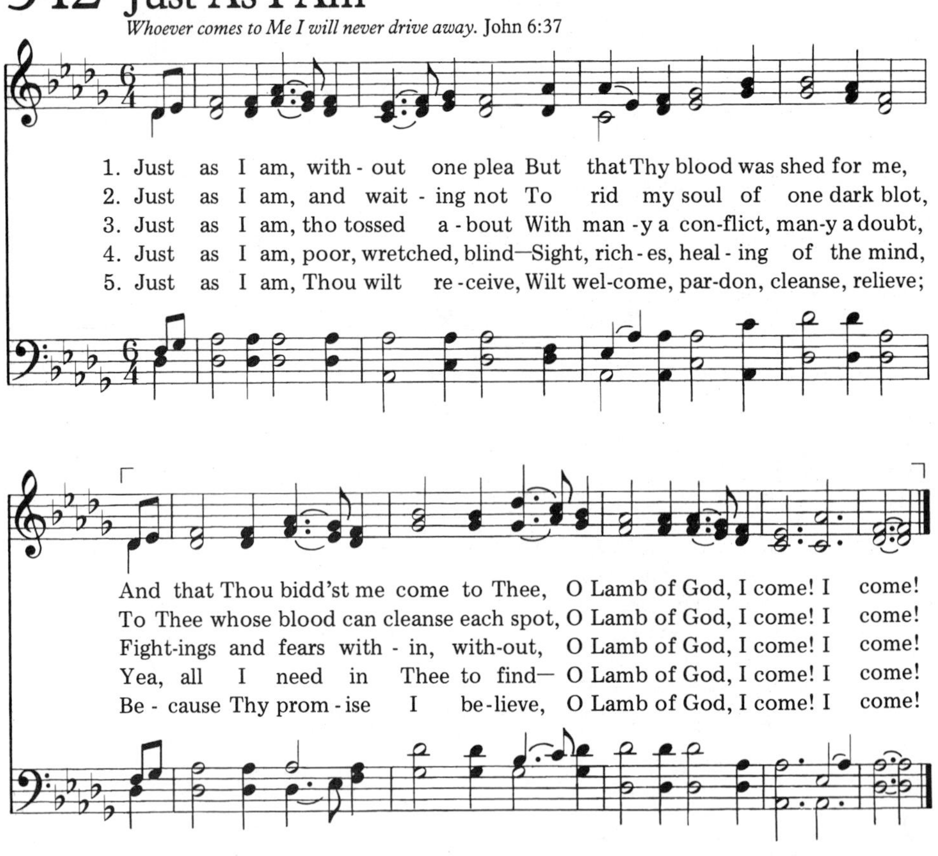
1. Just as I am, with - out one plea But that Thy blood was shed for me,
2. Just as I am, and wait - ing not To rid my soul of one dark blot,
3. Just as I am, tho tossed a - bout With man -y a con-flict, man-y a doubt,
4. Just as I am, poor, wretched, blind—Sight, rich - es, heal - ing of the mind,
5. Just as I am, Thou wilt re -ceive, Wilt wel-come, par-don, cleanse, relieve;
And that Thou bidd'st me come to Thee, O Lamb of God, I come! I come!
To Thee whose blood can cleanse each spot, O Lamb of God, I come! I come!
Fight-ings and fears with - in, with-out, O Lamb of God, I come! I come!
Yea, all I need in Thee to find— O Lamb of God, I come! I come!
Be - cause Thy prom - ise I be-lieve, O Lamb of God, I come! I come!

TEXT: Charlotte Elliott
MUSIC: William B. Bradbury

WOODWORTH
L.M.

343 Be Still and Know

I am the Lord, who heals you. Ex. 15:26

1. Be still and know that I am God. Be still and know that
2. I am the Lord that heal - eth thee. I am the Lord that

TEXT and MUSIC: Anonymous; based on Psalm 46:10, Exodus 15:26; arranged by Lee Herrington

BE STILL AND KNOW
8.8.8.

He's Got the Whole World in His Hands 344

In His hand is the life of every creature. Job 12:10

Unison

1. He's got the whole world in His hands, He's got the whole world in His hands, He's got the whole world in His hands, He's got the whole world in His hands.
2. He's got the wind and the rain in His hands, He's got the wind and the rain in His hands, He's got the wind and the rain in His hands, He's got the whole world in His hands.
3. He's got the ti - ny lit - tle ba - by in His hands, He's got the ti - ny lit - tle ba - by in His hands, He's got the ti - ny lit - tle ba - by in His hands, He's got the whole world in His hands.
4. He's got you and me, broth-er, in His hands, He's got you and me, sis - ter, in His hands, He's got you and me, broth - er, in His hands, He's got the whole world in His hands.

TEXT and MUSIC: Traditional Spiritual; arranged by Eugene Thomas

WHOLE WORLD
Irregular meter

345 Blessed Assurance

Is anyone happy? Let him sing songs of praise. James 5:13

1. Bless-ed as - sur - ance, Je - sus is mine! O what a fore - taste of glo - ry di - vine! Heir of sal - va - tion, pur-chase of God, Born of His Spir - it, washed in His blood.
2. Per - fect sub - mis - sion, per - fect de - light! Vi-sions of rap - ture now burst on my sight; An - gels de - scend - ing bring from a - bove Ech - oes of mer - cy, whis - pers of love.
3. Per - fect sub - mis - sion—all is at rest, I in my Sav - ior am hap - py and blest; Watch-ing and wait - ing, look - ing a - bove, Filled with His good - ness, lost in His love.
Descant
This is my sto - ry, this is my song, Prais-ing my Sav - ior all the day long; This is my
Refrain
This is my sto - ry, this is my song, Prais-ing my Sav - ior all the day long; This is my

TEXT: Fanny J. Crosby
MUSIC: Phoebe P. Knapp; Descant by James C. Gibson

ASSURANCE
9.10.9.9. with Refrain

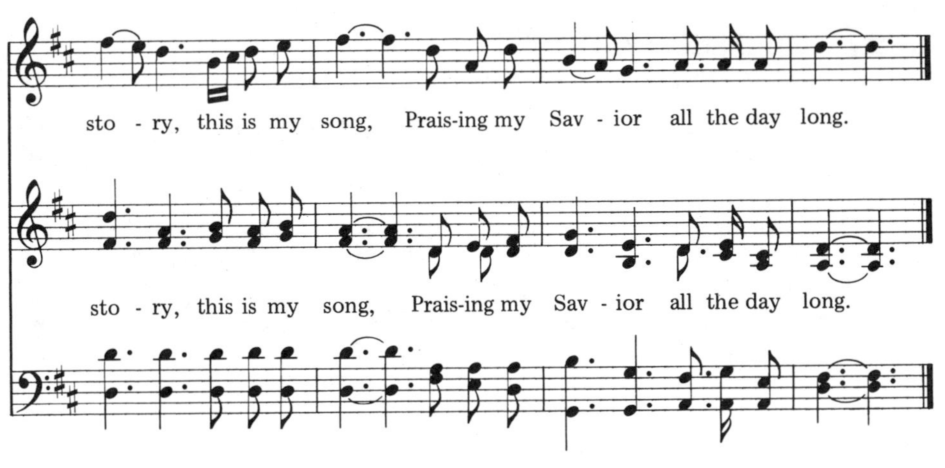
sto - ry, this is my song, Prais-ing my Sav - ior all the day long.
sto - ry, this is my song, Prais-ing my Sav - ior all the day long.

I Am Trusting Thee, Lord Jesus 346

. . . the Lord, in whom they had put their trust. Acts 14:23

1. I am trust - ing Thee, Lord Je - sus—Trust - ing on - ly Thee;
2. I am trust - ing Thee to guide me—Thou a - lone shalt lead,
3. I am trust - ing Thee for pow - er—Thine can nev - er fail;
4. I am trust - ing Thee, Lord Je - sus—Nev - er let me fall;

Trust - ing Thee for full sal - va - tion, Great and free.
Ev - 'ry day and hour sup - ply - ing All my need.
Words which Thou Thy - self shalt give me Must pre - vail.
I am trust - ing Thee for - ev - er, And for all. A - men.

TEXT: Frances Ridley Havergal
MUSIC: Ethelbert W. Bullinger

BULLINGER
8.5.8.3.

347 Be Still, My Soul

Be still, and know that I am God. Ps. 46:10

1. Be still, my soul! the Lord is on thy side; Bear pa - tient - ly the
2. Be still, my soul! thy God doth un - der - take To guide the fu - ture
3. Be still, my soul! the hour is has - tening on When we shall be for -
cross of grief or pain; Leave to thy God to or - der and pro - vide;
as He has the past. Thy hope, thy con - fi - dence let noth - ing shake;
ev - er with the Lord, When dis - ap - point - ment, grief, and fear are gone,
In ev - ery change He faith - ful will re - main. Be still, my soul! thy
All now mys - te - rious shall be bright at last. Be still, my soul! the
Sor - row for - got, love's pur - est joys re - stored. Be still, my soul! when
best, thy heaven - ly Friend Thro' thorn - y ways leads to a joy - ful end.
waves and winds still know His voice who ruled them while He dwelt be - low.
change and tears are past, All safe and bless - ed we shall meet at last.

TEXT: Katharina von Schlegel; translated by Jane L. Borthwick
MUSIC: Jean Sibelius
A lower setting may be found at No. 535

FINLANDIA
10.10.10.10.10.10.

Hiding in Thee 348

Lead me to the Rock that is higher than I. Ps. 61:2

1. O safe to the Rock that is high - er than I, My
2. In the calm of the noon - tide, in sor - row's lone hour, In
3. How oft in the con-flict, when pressed by the foe, I have
soul in its con - flicts and sor - rows would fly; So sin - ful, so
times when temp - ta - tion casts o'er me its power; In the tem - pests of
fled to my Ref - uge and breathed out my woe; How of - ten, when
wea - ry, Thine, Thine would I be; Thou blest Rock of A - ges, I'm
life, on its wide, heav - ing sea, Thou blest Rock of A - ges, I'm
tri - als like sea bil - lows roll, Have I hid - den in Thee, O Thou
Refrain
hid - ing in Thee.
hid - ing in Thee. Hid - ing in Thee, Hid - ing in
Rock of my soul.
Thee, Thou blest Rock of A - ges, I'm hid - ing in Thee.

TEXT: William O. Cushing
MUSIC: Ira D. Sankey

HIDING IN THEE
11.11.11.11. with Refrain

349 Trust and Obey

. . . that all nations might believe and obey Him. Rom. 16:26

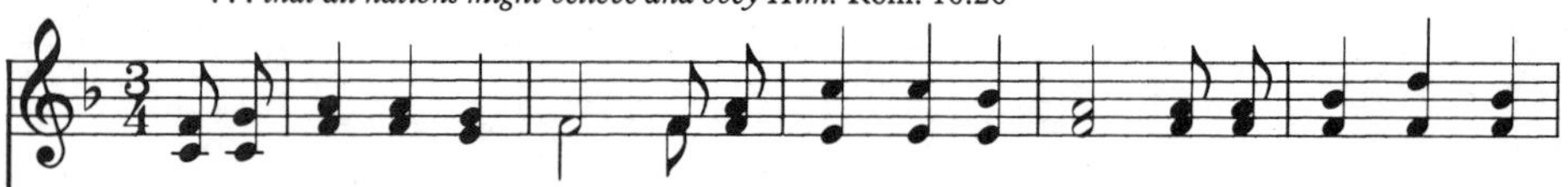

1. When we walk with the Lord in the light of His Word, What a glo - ry He
2. Not a shad-ow can rise, not a cloud in the skies, But His smile quick-ly
3. Not a bur-den we bear, not a sor - row we share, But our toil He doth
4. But we nev - er can prove the de - lights of His love Un - til all on the
5. Then in fel - low-ship sweet we will sit at His feet, Or we'll walk by His

sheds on our way! While we do His good will He a - bides with us still,
drives it a - way; Not a doubt nor a fear, not a sigh nor a tear,
rich - ly re - pay; Not a grief nor a loss, not a frown nor a cross,
al - tar we lay; For the fa - vor He shows and the joy He be - stows
side in the way; What He says we will do, where He sends we will go—

Refrain

And with all who will trust and o - bey.
Can a - bide while we trust and o - bey.
But is blest if we trust and o - bey. Trust and o - bey, for there's
Are for them who will trust and o - bey.
Nev - er fear, on - ly trust and o - bey.

no oth - er way To be hap - py in Je - sus, But to trust and o - bey.

TEXT: John H. Sammis
MUSIC: Daniel B. Towner

TRUST AND OBEY
6.6.9.D. with Refrain

'Tis So Sweet to Trust in Jesus 350

Trust in God; trust also in Me. John 14:1

1. 'Tis so sweet to trust in Je - sus, Just to take Him at His word,
2. O how sweet to trust in Je - sus, Just to trust His cleans - ing blood,
3. Yes, 'tis sweet to trust in Je - sus, Just from sin and self to cease,
4. I'm so glad I learned to trust Him, Pre - cious Je - sus, Sav - ior, Friend;
Just to rest up - on His prom-ise, Just to know "Thus saith the Lord."
Just in sim - ple faith to plunge me 'Neath the heal - ing, cleans - ing flood!
Just from Je - sus sim - ply tak - ing Life and rest and joy and peace.
And I know that He is with me, Will be with me to the end.
Refrain
Je - sus, Je - sus, how I trust Him! How I've proved Him o'er and o'er!
Je - sus, Je - sus, pre - cious Je - sus! O for grace to trust Him more!

TEXT: Louisa M. R. Stead
MUSIC: William J. Kirkpatrick

TRUST IN JESUS
8.7.8.7. with Refrain

351 Moment by Moment

Having loved His own . . . He now showed them the full extent of His love. John 13:1

1. Dy-ing with Je-sus, by death reck-oned mine; Liv-ing with Je-sus a new life di-vine; Look-ing to Je-sus till glo-ry doth shine, Mo-ment by mo-ment, O Lord, I am Thine.
2. Nev-er a tri-al that He is not there, Nev-er a bur-den that He doth not bear, Nev-er a sor-row that He doth not share, Mo-ment by mo-ment, I'm un-der His care.
3. Nev-er a weak-ness that He doth not feel, Nev-er a sick-ness that He can-not heal; Mo-ment by mo-ment, in woe or in weal, Je-sus my Sav-ior a-bides with me still.
Refrain
Mo-ment by mo-ment I'm kept in His love; Mo-ment by mo-ment I've life from a-bove; Look-ing to Je-sus till glo-ry doth shine; Mo-ment by mo-ment, O Lord, I am Thine.

TEXT: Daniel W. Whittle
MUSIC: May Whittle Moody

WHITTLE
10.10.10.10. with Refrain

A Child of the King 352

If we are children, then we are . . . heirs of God and co-heirs with Christ. Rom. 8:17

1. My Fa - ther is rich in hous - es and lands, He hold - eth the
2. My Fa - ther's own Son, the Sav - ior of men, Once wan-dered on
3. I once was an out - cast stran - ger on earth, A sin - ner by
4. A tent or a cot - tage, why should I care? They're build-ing a
wealth of the world in His hands! Of ru - bies and dia-monds, of
earth as the poor - est of them; But now He is reign-ing for -
choice, and an al - ien by birth; But I've been a - dopt - ed, my
pal - ace for me o - ver there; Though ex - iled from home, yet
sil - ver and gold, His cof - fers are full, He has rich - es un - told.
ev - er on high, And will give me a home in heav'n by and by.
name's writ-ten down, An heir to a man - sion, a robe, and a crown.
still I may sing; All glo - ry to God, I'm a child of the King.
Refrain
I'm a child of the King, A child of the King:
With Je - sus my Sav - ior, I'm a child of the King.

TEXT: Harriet E. Buell
MUSIC: John B. Sumner

BINGHAMTON
10.11.11.11. with Refrain

353 A Shelter in the Time of Storm

He is my mighty Rock, my Refuge. Ps. 62:7

1. The Lord's our Rock, in Him we hide, A shel - ter in the time of storm;
2. A shade by day, de - fense by night, A shel - ter in the time of storm;
3. The rag - ing storms may round us beat, A shel - ter in the time of storm;
4. O Rock di - vine, O Ref - uge dear, A shel - ter in the time of storm;
Se - cure what - ev - er ill be - tide, A shel - ter in the time of storm.
No fears a - larm, no foes af - fright, A shel - ter in the time of storm.
We'll nev - er leave our safe re - treat, A shel - ter in the time of storm.
Be Thou our help - er ev - er near, A shel - ter in the time of storm.
Refrain
O, Je - sus is a Rock in a wea - ry land, A wea - ry land, a wea - ry land;
O, Je - sus is a Rock in a wea - ry land, A shel-ter in the time of storm.

TEXT: Vernon J. Charlesworth; adapted by Ira D. Sankey
MUSIC: Ira D. Sankey

SHELTER
L.M. with Refrain

Leaning on the Everlasting Arms 354

The eternal God is your Refuge, and underneath are the everlasting arms. Deut. 33:27

1. What a fel - low-ship, what a joy di - vine, Lean - ing on the ev-er-
2. O how sweet to walk in this pil - grim way, Lean - ing on the ev-er-
3. What have I to dread, what have I to fear, Lean - ing on the ev-er-
last - ing arms; What a bless - ed-ness, what a peace is mine,
last - ing arms; O, how bright the path grows from day to day,
last - ing arms? I have bless - ed peace with my Lord so near,
Refrain
Lean - ing on the ev - er - last - ing arms. Lean - ing,
Lean - ing on the ev - er - last - ing arms. Lean - ing on Je - sus,
Lean - ing on the ev - er - last - ing arms.
lean - ing, Safe and se - cure from all a - larms; Lean -
lean - ing on Je - sus, Lean - ing on
ing, lean - ing, Lean - ing on the ev - er - last - ing arms.
Je - sus, lean - ing on Je - sus,

TEXT: Elisha A. Hoffman
MUSIC: Anthony J. Showalter

SHOWALTER
10.9.10.9. with Refrain

355 Trusting Jesus

I . . . delight to see . . . how firm your faith in Christ is. Col. 2:5

1. Sim - ply trust - ing ev - ery day, Trust - ing through a storm - y way;
2. Bright-ly doth His Spir - it shine In - to this poor heart of mine.
3. Sing - ing if my way is clear, Pray - ing if the path be drear;
4. Trust-ing Him while life shall last, Trust - ing Him till earth be past;
E - ven when my faith is small, Trust - ing Je - sus— that is all.
While He leads I can - not fall, Trust - ing Je - sus— that is all.
If in dan - ger, for Him call, Trust - ing Je - sus— that is all.
Till with - in the jas - per wall, Trust - ing Je - sus— that is all.
Refrain
Trust - ing as the mo - ments fly, Trust - ing as the days go by;
Trust - ing Him what - e'er be - fall, Trust - ing Je - sus— that is all.

TEXT: Edgar P. Stites
MUSIC: Ira D. Sankey

TRUSTING JESUS
7.7.7.7. with Refrain

Under His Wings 356

Under His wings you will find refuge. Ps. 91:4

1. Un - der His wings I am safe - ly a - bid - ing, Tho the night deep - ens and tem - pests are wild; Still I can trust Him, I know He will keep me, He has re-deemed me and I am His child.
2. Un - der His wings, what a ref - uge in sor - row! How the heart yearn - ing - ly turns to His rest! Of - ten when earth has no balm for my heal - ing, There I find com - fort and there I am blest.
3. Un - der His wings, O what pre - cious en - joy - ment! There will I hide till life's tri - als are o'er; Shel - tered, pro - tect - ed, no e - vil can harm me, Rest - ing in Je - sus I'm safe ev - er - more.
Refrain
Un-der His wings, un - der His wings, Who from His love can sev - er?
Un-der His wings my soul shall a - bide, Safe-ly a - bide for - ev - er.

TEXT: William O. Cushing
MUSIC: Ira D. Sankey

HINGHAM
11.10.11.10. with Refrain

357 Jesus Loves Even Me

Christ loved the church and gave Himself up for her. Eph. 5:25

1. I am so glad that our Fa - ther in heav'n Tells of His
2. Tho I for - get Him and wan - der a - way, Still He doth
3. O if there's on - ly one song I can sing When in His
love in the Book He has giv'n; Won - der - ful things in the
love me wher - ev - er I stray; Back to His dear lov - ing
beau - ty I see the great King, This shall my song in e -
Bi - ble I see— This is the dear - est, that Je - sus loves me.
arms would I flee When I re - mem - ber that Je - sus loves me.
ter - ni - ty be: "O what a won - der, that Je - sus loves me!"
Refrain
I am so glad that Je - sus loves me, Je - sus loves me, Je - sus loves me;
I am so glad that Je - sus loves me, Je - sus loves e - ven me.

TEXT and MUSIC: Philip P. Bliss

GLADNESS
10.10.10.10. with Refrain

I Am Thine, O Lord 358

Let us draw near to God with a sincere heart in full assurance of faith. Heb. 10:22

1. I am Thine, O Lord, I have heard Thy voice, And it told Thy love to me; But I long to rise in the arms of faith, And be clos - er drawn to Thee.
2. Con - se - crate me now to Thy serv - ice, Lord, By the pow'r of grace di - vine; Let my soul look up with a stead-fast hope, And my will be lost in Thine.
3. O, the pure de - light of a sin - gle hour That be - fore Thy throne I spend, When I kneel in prayer, and with Thee, my God, I com - mune as friend with friend!
4. There are depths of love that I can - not know Till I cross the nar - row sea; There are heights of joy that I may not reach Till I rest in peace with Thee.
Refrain
Draw me near - er,

near - er, bless - ed Lord, To the cross where Thou hast died; Draw me near - er, near - er, near-er, bless-ed Lord, To Thy pre - cious, bleed-ing side.

TEXT: Fanny J. Crosby
MUSIC: William H. Doane

I AM THINE
10.7.10.7. with Refrain

359 Jesus Is Lord of All

No one can serve two masters. . . . You cannot serve both God and money. Matt. 6:24

1. All my to - mor - rows, all my past, Je - sus is Lord of all. I've quit my strug - gles, con - tent - ment at last, Je - sus is Lord of all.
2. All of my con - flicts, all my thoughts, Je - sus is Lord of all. His love wins the bat - tles I could not have fought, Je - sus is Lord of all.
3. All of my long - ings, all my dreams, Je - sus is Lord of all. All of my fail - ures His pow - er re - deems, Je - sus is Lord of all.
Refrain
King of kings, Lord of lords, Je - sus is Lord of all; All my pos - sess - ions and all my life, Je - sus is Lord of all.

TEXT: Gloria Gaither and William J. Gaither
MUSIC: William J. Gaither

LORD OF ALL
Irregular meter

Jesus Is Lord of All 360

God has made this Jesus, whom you crucified, both Lord and Christ. Acts 2:36

1. Je - sus is Sav - ior and Lord of my life,
2. Bless - ed Re - deem - er, all glo - ri - ous King,
3. Will you sur - ren - der your all to Him now?
My hope, my glo - ry, my all; Won - der - ful Mas - ter in
Wor - thy of rev - 'rence I pay; Trib - ute and prais - es I
Fol - low His will and o - bey, Crown Him as Sov-'reign, be-
joy and in strife, On Him you too may call.
joy - ful - ly bring To Him, the Life, the Way.
fore His throne bow; Give Him your heart to - day.
Refrain
Je - sus is Lord of all, Je - sus is Lord of all, Lord of my
thoughts and my serv - ice each day, Je - sus is Lord of all.

TEXT and MUSIC: LeRoy McClard

LORDSHIP OF CHRIST
10.7.10.6. with Refrain

361

MY GOD, I LOVE THEE

A Brief Service of Adoration and Commitment

Suggested Hymn Stanzas

To facilitate an uninterrupted flow from stanza to stanza, the suggested stanzas have been marked with an arrow: ►

I Love Thee, stanzas 1, 2
More Love to Thee, stanza 1
My Jesus, I Love Thee, stanzas 1, 2, 4

ALL:
My God, I love Thee;
Not because I hope for heaven thereby,
Nor yet because who love Thee not
Must die eternally.

WORSHIP LEADER:
Thou, O my Jesus, Thou didst me
Upon the cross embrace,
For me didst bear the nails and spear,
And manifold disgrace.

PEOPLE:
Then why, O blessed Jesus Christ,
Should I not love Thee well?
Not for the hope of winning heaven,
Or of escaping hell.

ALL:
E'en so I love Thee, and will love
And in Thy praise will sing,
Solely because Thou art my God,
And my eternal King!

"My Eternal King" by Francis Xavier;
translated by Edward Caswall.

"MY GOD, I LOVE THEE—A Brief Service of Adoration and Commitment"

I Love Thee 362

I love You, O Lord, my strength. Ps. 18:1

1. I love Thee, I love Thee, I love Thee, my Lord; I love Thee, my Savior, I love Thee, my God; I love Thee, I love Thee, and that Thou dost know; But how much I love Thee my actions will show.
2. O Jesus, my Savior, with Thee I am blest, My life and salvation, my joy and my rest; Thy name be my theme, and Thy love be my song; Thy grace shall inspire both my heart and my tongue. tongue.
3. O, who's like my Savior? He's Salem's bright King; He smiles and He loves me and helps me to sing; I'll praise Him, I'll praise Him with notes loud and clear, While rivers of pleasure my spirit shall cheer.
Optional transition to "More Love to Thee"

TEXT: Source unknown
MUSIC: Ingalls' *Christian Harmony,* 1805

I LOVE THEE
11.11.11.11.

363 More Love to Thee

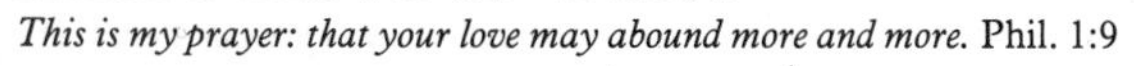

This is my prayer: that your love may abound more and more. Phil. 1:9

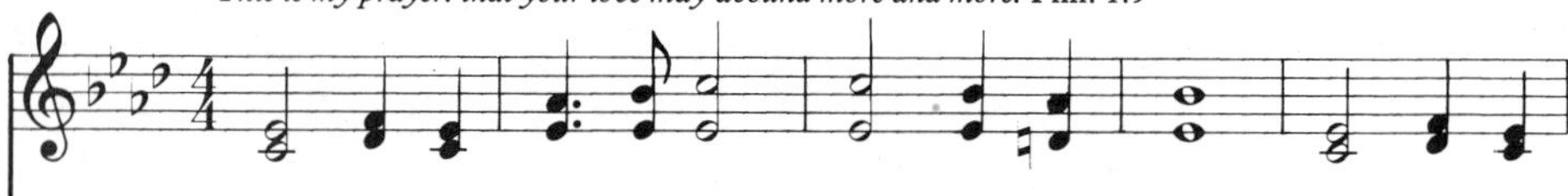

1. More love to Thee, O Christ, More love to Thee! Hear Thou the
2. Once earth-ly joy I craved, Sought peace and rest; Now Thee a-
3. Then shall my lat-est breath Whis-per Thy praise; This be the

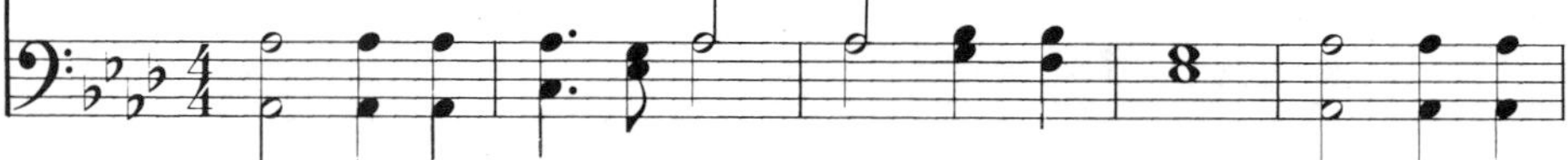

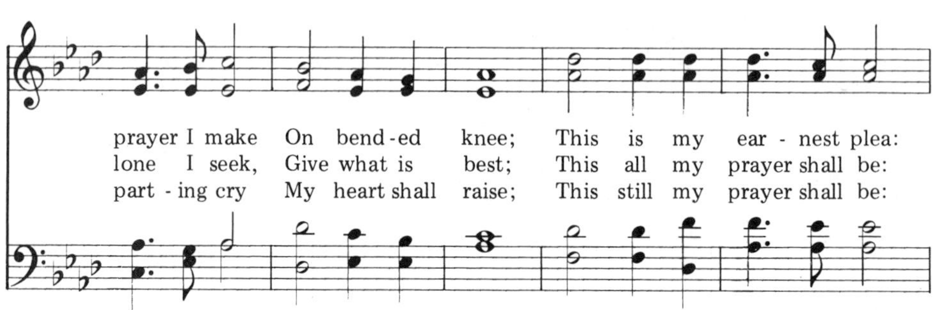
prayer I make On bend-ed knee; This is my ear-nest plea:
lone I seek, Give what is best; This all my prayer shall be:
part-ing cry My heart shall raise; This still my prayer shall be:

More love, O Christ to Thee, More love to Thee, More love to Thee!

TEXT: Elizabeth P. Prentiss
MUSIC: William H. Doane

MORE LOVE TO THEE
6.4.6.4.6.6.4.

Optional transition to "My Jesus, I Love Thee"

My Jesus, I Love Thee 364

I love the Lord, for He heard my voice. Ps. 116:1

1. My Je - sus, I love Thee, I know Thou art mine—For Thee all the fol - lies of sin I re - sign; My gra - cious Re - deem - er, my Sav - ior art Thou: If ev - er I loved Thee, my Je - sus, 'tis now.
2. I love Thee be - cause Thou hast first lov - ed me And pur-chased my par - don on Cal - va - ry's tree; I love Thee for wear - ing the thorns on Thy brow: If ev - er I loved Thee, my Je - sus, 'tis now.
3. I'll love Thee in life, I will love Thee in death, And praise Thee as long as Thou lend - est me breath; And say when the death-dew lies cold on my brow, "If ev - er I loved Thee, my Je - sus, 'tis now."
4. In man-sions of glo - ry and end - less de - light, I'll ev - er a - dore Thee in heav - en so bright; I'll sing with the glit - ter - ing crown on my brow, "If ev - er I loved Thee, my Je - sus, 'tis now."
TEXT: William R. Featherston
MUSIC: Adoniram J. Gordon
GORDON
11.11.11.11.
Optional choral ending
mp
decresc.
I love Thee, I love Thee, I love Thee, my Lord.
The end of "MY GOD, I LOVE THEE - A Brief Service of Adoration and Commitment."

365 Close to Thee

Come near to God and He will come near to you. James 4:8

1. Thou my ev - er-last-ing por-tion, More than friend or life to me;
2. Not for ease or world-ly pleas-ure, Nor for fame my prayer shall be;
3. Lead me through the vale of shad-ows, Bear me o'er life's fit - ful sea;
All a - long my pil-grim jour-ney, Sav-ior, let me walk with Thee.
Glad-ly will I toil and suf - fer, On - ly let me walk with Thee.
Then the gate of life e - ter - nal May I en - ter, Lord, with Thee.
Close to Thee, close to Thee, Close to Thee, close to Thee; All a -
Close to Thee, close to Thee, Close to Thee, close to Thee; Glad-ly
Close to Thee, close to Thee, Close to Thee, close to Thee; Then the
long my pil-grim jour - ney, Sav-ior, let me walk with Thee.
will I toil and suf - fer, On - ly let me walk with Thee.
gate of life e - ter - nal May I en - ter, Lord, with Thee.

TEXT: Fanny J. Crosby
MUSIC: Silas J. Vail

CLOSE TO THEE
8.7.8.7.6.6.8.7.

I Surrender All 366

Offer yourselves to God. Rom. 6:13

1. All to Je - sus I sur-ren - der, All to Him I free - ly give;
2. All to Je - sus I sur-ren - der, Hum-bly at His feet I bow,
3. All to Je - sus I sur-ren - der, Make me, Sav - ior, whol - ly Thine;
4. All to Je - sus I sur-ren - der, Lord, I give my - self to Thee;
I will ev - er love and trust Him, In His pres - ence dai - ly live.
World - ly pleas-ures all for - sak - en, Take me, Je - sus, take me now.
May Thy Ho - ly Spir - it fill me, May I know Thy pow'r di - vine.
Fill me with Thy love and pow - er, Let Thy bless - ing fall on me.
Refrain
I sur-ren - der all, I sur - ren - der all.
I sur-ren-der all, I sur-ren-der all.
All to Thee, my bless - ed Sav - ior, I sur - ren - der all.

TEXT: Judson W. VanDeVenter
MUSIC: Winfield S. Weeden

SURRENDER
8.7.8.7. with Refrain

367 Wherever He Leads I'll Go

If anyone would come after Me, he must . . . take up his cross and follow Me. Matt. 16:24

1. "Take up thy cross and fol - low Me," I heard my Mas - ter say;
2. He drew me clos - er to His side, I sought His will to know,
3. It may be thro' the shad-ows dim, Or o'er the storm - y sea,
4. My heart, my life, my all I bring To Christ who loves me so;
"I gave My life to ran - som thee, Sur - ren-der your all to - day."
And in that will I now a - bide, Wher - ev - er He leads I'll go.
I take the cross and fol - low Him, Wher - ev - er He lead - eth me.
He is my Mas - ter, Lord, and King, Wher - ev - er He leads I'll go.
Refrain
Wher - ev - er He leads I'll go, Wher - ev - er He leads I'll go,
I'll fol-low my Christ who loves me so, Wher - ev - er He leads I'll go.

TEXT and MUSIC: B. B. McKinney

FALLS CREEK
8.6.8.7. with Refrain

All for Jesus 368

Offer your bodies as living sacrifices . . . to God—this is your spiritual . . . worship. Rom. 12:1

1. All for Je - sus, all for Je - sus! All my be -ing's ran-somed pow'rs:
2. Let my hands per-form His bid - ding, Let my feet run in His ways;
3. Since my eyes were fixed on Je - sus, I've lost sight of all be - side;
4. Oh, what won-der! how a - maz - ing! Je - sus,-glo-rious King of kings,
All my tho'ts and words and do - ings, All my days and all my hours.
Let my eyes see Je - sus on - ly, Let my lips speak forth His praise.
So en-chained my spir - it's vi - sion, Look-ing at the Cru - ci - fied.
Deigns to call me His be - lov - ed, Lets me rest be-neath His wings.
Refrain
All for Je - sus! all for Je - sus! All my days and all my hours;
All for Je - sus! all for Je - sus! Let my lips speak forth His praise;
All for Je - sus! all for Je - sus! Look-ing at the Cru - ci - fied;
All for Je - sus! all for Je - sus! Rest - ing now be-neath His wings;
All for Je - sus! all for Je - sus! All my days and all my hours.
All for Je - sus! all for Je - sus! Let my lips speak forth His praise.
All for Je - sus! all for Je - sus! Look-ing at the Cru - ci - fied.
All for Je - sus! all for Je - sus! Rest - ing now be - neath His wings.

TEXT: Mary D. James
MUSIC: Source unknown

CONSTANCY
8.7.8.7. with Refrain

369 O Jesus, I Have Promised

Show . . . diligence to the very end, in order to make your hope sure. Heb. 6:11

1. O Je - sus, I have prom-ised To serve Thee to the end; Be Thou for-ev - er
2. O let me feel Thee near me, The world is ev - er near; I see the sights that
3. O Je - sus, Thou hast prom-ised To all who fol-low Thee, That where Thou art in

near me, My Mas - ter and my Friend: I shall not fear the bat-tle If Thou art
daz - zle, The tempt-ing sounds I hear: My foes are ev - er near me, A-round me
glo - ry, There shall Thy serv-ant be; And, Je-sus, I have prom-ised To serve Thee

by my side, Nor wan-der from the path-way If Thou wilt be my guide.
and with - in; But, Je - sus, draw Thou near-er, And shield my soul from sin.
to the end; O give me grace to fol - low, My Mas - ter and my Friend.

TEXT: John E. Bode
MUSIC: Arthur H. Mann

ANGEL'S STORY
7.6.7.6.D.

370 I'll Live for Him

Live self-controlled, upright and godly lives in this present age. Titus 2:12

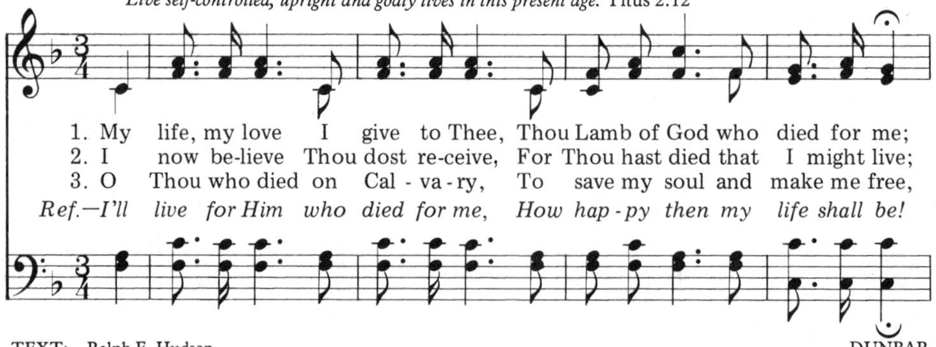
1. My life, my love I give to Thee, Thou Lamb of God who died for me;
2. I now be-lieve Thou dost re-ceive, For Thou hast died that I might live;
3. O Thou who died on Cal - va - ry, To save my soul and make me free,
Ref.—I'll live for Him who died for me, How hap - py then my life shall be!

TEXT: Ralph E. Hudson
MUSIC: C. R. Dunbar

DUNBAR
8.8.8.6. with Refrain

D.C. for Refrain
O may I ev - er faith - ful be, My Sav - ior and my God!
And now hence-forth I'll trust in Thee, My Sav - ior and my God!
I'll con - se - crate my life to Thee, My Sav - ior and my God!
I'll live for Him who died for me, My Sav - ior and my God!

Have Thine Own Way, Lord 371

We are the clay, You are the potter. Isa. 64:8

1. Have Thine own way, Lord! Have Thine own way! Thou art the Pot - ter, I am the clay. Mold me and make me af - ter Thy will, While I am wait - ing, yield - ed and still.
2. Have Thine own way, Lord! Have Thine own way! Search me and try me, Mas - ter, to - day! Whit - er than snow, Lord, wash me just now, As in Thy pres - ence hum - bly I bow.
3. Have Thine own way, Lord! Have Thine own way! Wound - ed and wea - ry, help me, I pray! Pow - er— all pow - er— sure - ly is Thine! Touch me and heal me, Sav - ior di - vine!
4. Have Thine own way, Lord! Have Thine own way! Hold o'er my be - ing ab - so - lute sway! Fill with Thy Spir - it till all shall see Christ on - ly, al - ways, liv - ing in me! A - men.

TEXT: Adelaide A. Pollard
MUSIC: George C. Stebbins

ADELAIDE
5.4.5.4.D.

372 Living for Jesus

Those who live should no longer live for themselves but for Him who died for them. 2 Cor. 5:15

1. Living for Jesus a life that is true, Striving to please Him in all that I do; Yielding allegiance, glad-hearted and free, This is the pathway of blessing for me.

2. Living for Jesus who died in my place, Bearing on Cal-v'ry my sin and disgrace; Such love constrains me to answer His call, Follow His leading and give Him my all.

3. Living for Jesus wherever I am, Doing each duty in His holy name; Willing to suffer affliction and loss, Deeming each trial a part of my cross.

4. Living for Jesus through earth's little while, My dearest treasure, the light of His smile; Seeking the lost ones He died to redeem, Bringing the weary to find rest in Him.

Refrain

O Jesus, Lord and Savior, I give myself to Thee; For Thou, in Thy atonement, Didst give Thyself for me. I own no other Master, My heart shall be Thy

TEXT: Thomas O. Chisholm
MUSIC: C. Harold Lowden

LIVING
10.10.10.10. with Refrain

throne. My life I give, hence-forth to live, O Christ, for Thee a - lone.

Where He Leads Me 373

My sheep listen to My voice; I know them, and they follow Me. John 10:27

1. I can hear my Sav - ior call - ing, I can
2. I'll go with Him thru the judg - ment, I'll go
3. He will give me grace and glo - ry, He will
Refrain: Where He leads me I will fol - low, where He

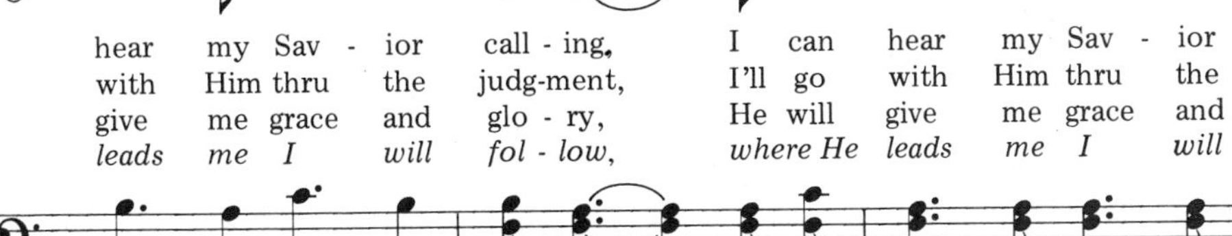
hear my Sav - ior call - ing, I can hear my Sav - ior
with Him thru the judg-ment, I'll go with Him thru the
give me grace and glo - ry, He will give me grace and
leads me I will fol - low, where He leads me I will

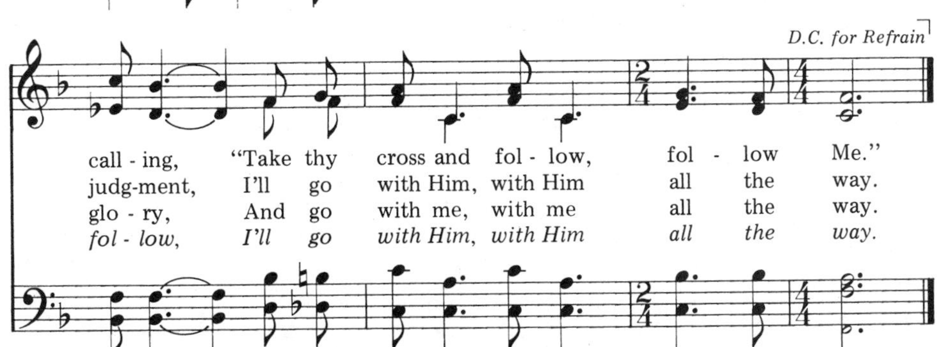
D.C. for Refrain
call - ing, "Take thy cross and fol - low, fol - low Me."
judg-ment, I'll go with Him, with Him all the way.
glo - ry, And go with me, with me all the way.
fol - low, I'll go with Him, with Him all the way.

TEXT: E. W. Blandy
MUSIC: John S. Norris

NORRIS
8.8.8.9. with Refrain

374 O Love That Will Not Let Me Go

. . . nor anything else . . . will be able to separate us from the love of God. Rom. 8:39

1. O Love that will not let me go, I rest my wea - ry soul in
2. O Light that fol-l'west all my way, I yield my flick-'ring torch to
3. O Joy that seek - est me thru pain, I can - not close my heart to
4. O Cross that lift - est up my head, I dare not ask to fly from

Thee; I give Thee back the life I owe, That in Thine
Thee; My heart re - stores its bor - rowed ray, That in Thy
Thee; I trace the rain - bow thru the rain, And feel the
Thee; I lay in dust life's glo - ry dead, And from the

o - cean depths its flow May rich - er, full - er be.
sun-shine's blaze its day May bright-er, fair - er be.
prom - ise is not vain That morn shall tear - less be.
ground there blos-soms red Life that shall end - less be. A - men.

TEXT: George Matheson
MUSIC: Albert L. Peace

ST. MARGARET
8.8.8.8.6.

375 Jesus Calls Us

"Come, follow Me," Jesus said. Matt. 4:19

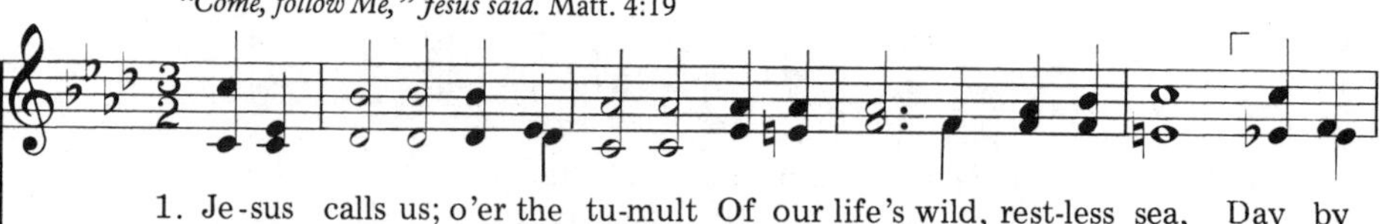

1. Je-sus calls us; o'er the tu-mult Of our life's wild, rest-less sea, Day by
2. Je-sus calls us from the wor-ship Of the vain world's gold-en store, From each
3. In our joys and in our sor-rows, Days of toil and hours of ease, Still He
4. Je-sus calls us: by Thy mer-cies, Sav-ior, may we hear Thy call, Give our

TEXT: Cecil F. Alexander
MUSIC: William H. Jude

GALILEE
8.7.8.7.

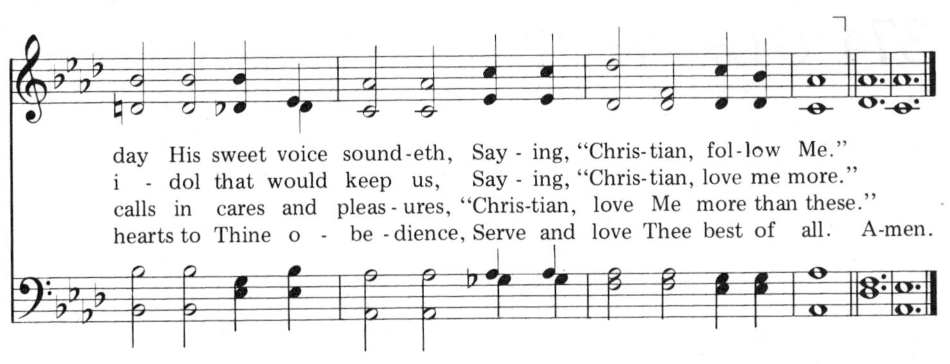

day His sweet voice sound-eth, Say - ing, "Chris-tian, fol-low Me."
i - dol that would keep us, Say - ing, "Chris-tian, love me more."
calls in cares and pleas - ures, "Chris-tian, love Me more than these."
hearts to Thine o - be - dience, Serve and love Thee best of all. A-men.

I Have Decided to Follow Jesus 376

Whoever serves Me must follow Me. John 12:26

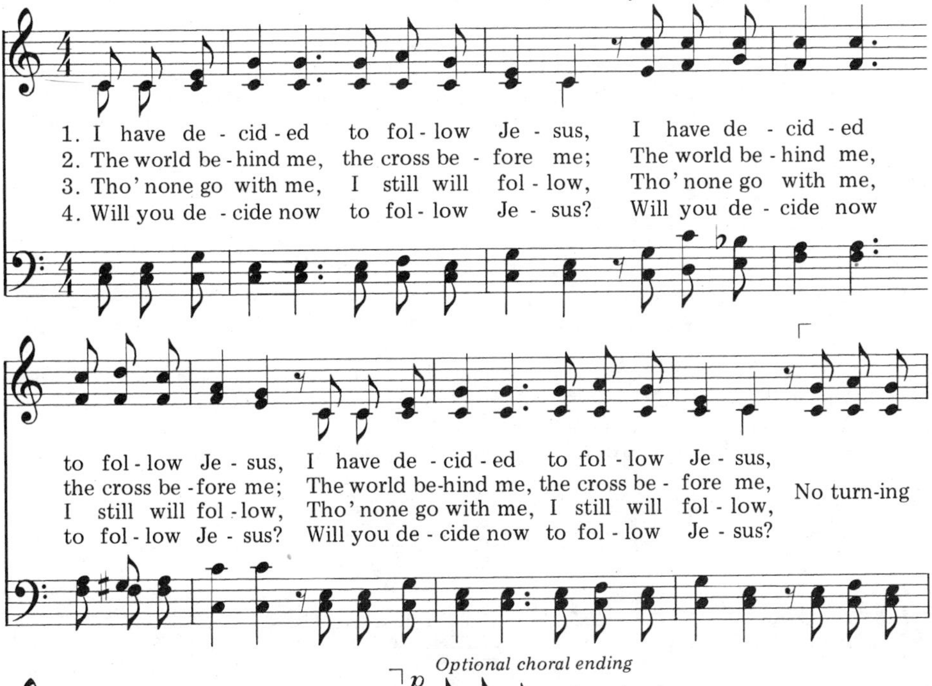

1. I have de - cid - ed to fol - low Je - sus, I have de - cid - ed to fol - low Je - sus, I have de - cid - ed to fol - low Je - sus,
2. The world be - hind me, the cross be - fore me; The world be - hind me, the cross be - fore me; The world be-hind me, the cross be - fore me,
3. Tho' none go with me, I still will fol - low, Tho' none go with me, I still will fol - low, Tho' none go with me, I still will fol - low,
4. Will you de - cide now to fol - low Je - sus? Will you de - cide now to fol - low Je - sus? Will you de - cide now to fol - low Je - sus?

No turn-ing back, no turn-ing back.

Optional choral ending

p I have de - cid - ed to fol - low Him.

TEXT: Source unknown
MUSIC: Folk melody from India; arranged by Eugene Thomas

ASSAM
Irregular meter

377 Jesus, I My Cross Have Taken

If anyone would come after Me, he must . . . take up his cross daily. Luke 9:23

1. Je - sus, I my cross have tak - en, All to leave and fol - low Thee;
2. Let the world de - spise and leave me, They have left my Sav - ior too;
3. Man may trou-ble and dis-tress me, 'Twill but drive me to Thy breast;
4. Has - ten on from grace to glo - ry, Armed by faith and winged by prayer;
Des - ti - tute, de - spised, for-sak - en, Thou from hence my all shalt be:
Hu - man hearts and looks de - ceive me; Thou art not, like man, un - true;
Life with tri - als hard may press me, Heav'n will bring me sweet - er rest.
Heav'n's e-ter - nal days be - fore me, God's own hand shall guide me there.
Per - ish ev - ery fond am - bi - tion, All I've sought, and hoped and known;
And, while Thou shalt smile up - on me, God of wis - dom, love, and might,
O 'tis not in grief to harm me, While Thy love is left to me;
Soon shall close my earth - ly mis - sion, Swift shall pass my pil - grim days,
Yet how rich is my con-di - tion, God and heav'n are still my own!
Foes may hate and friends may shun me; Show Thy face, and all is bright.
O 'twere not in joy to charm me, Were that joy un - mixed with Thee.
Hope shall change to glad fru - i - tion, Faith to sight, and prayer to praise. A - men.

TEXT: Henry F. Lyte
MUSIC: Leavitt's *The Christian Lyre*, 1831; attributed to Wolfgang A. Mozart; arranged by Hubert P. Main
A higher setting may be found at No. 584

ELLESDIE
8.7.8.7.D.

Only One Life 378

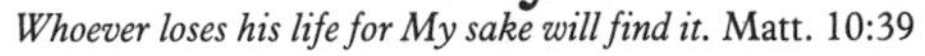
Whoever loses his life for My sake will find it. Matt. 10:39

1. Only one life to offer— Jesus, my Lord and King;
Only one tongue to praise Thee And of Thy mercy sing (forever);
Only one heart's devotion— Savior, O may it be
Consecrated alone to Thy matchless glory, Yielded fully to Thee.

2. Only this hour is mine, Lord— May it be used for Thee;
May ev'ry passing moment Count for eternity (my Savior);
Souls all about are dying, Dying in sin and shame;
Help me bring them the message of Calv'ry's redemption In Thy glorious name.

3. Only one life to offer— Take it, dear Lord, I pray;
Nothing from Thee withholding, Thy will I now obey (my Jesus);
Thou who hast freely given Thine all in all for me,
Claim this life for Thine own to be used, my Savior, Ev'ry moment for Thee.

TEXT: Avis B. Christiansen
MUSIC: Merrill Dunlop

ONLY ONE LIFE
7.6.7.6.7.6.12.6.

379 Take My Life and Let It Be

Consecrate yourselves and be holy, because I am holy. Lev. 11:44

1. Take my life and let it be Con-se-cra-ted,
2. Take my hands and let them move At the im-pulse
3. Take my voice and let me sing Al-ways, on-ly,
4. Take my sil-ver and my gold— Not a mite would
5. Take my will and make it Thine— It shall be no
6. Take my love— my Lord, I pour At Thy feet its
Lord, to Thee; Take my mo-ments and my days— Let them
of Thy love; Take my feet and let them be Swift and
for my King; Take my lips and let them be Filled with
I with-hold; Take my in-tel-lect and use Ev-'ry
long-er mine; Take my heart— it is Thine own, It shall
treas-ure store; Take my-self— and I will be Ev-er,
flow in cease-less praise, Let them flow in cease-less praise.
beau-ti-ful for Thee, Swift and beau-ti-ful for Thee.
mes-sag-es from Thee, Filled with mes-sag-es from Thee.
pow'r as Thou shalt choose, Ev-'ry pow'r as Thou shalt choose.
be Thy roy-al throne, It shall be Thy roy-al throne.
on-ly, all for Thee, Ev-er, on-ly, all for Thee.
Optional last stanza harmonization
Unison
6. Take my love—my Lord, I pour At Thy feet its treas-ure store;

TEXT: Frances Ridley Havergal
MUSIC: Henry A. César Malan; Last verse harmonization by David Allen

HENDON
7.7.7.7. with Repeat

Take my-self— and I will be Ev - er, on - ly, all for Thee,

Ev - er, on - ly, all for Thee. A - men.

ASPIRATION

Just a Closer Walk with Thee 380

I can do everything through Him who gives me strength. Phil. 4:13

1. I am weak but Thou art strong; Je - sus, keep me from all wrong;
2. Thro' this world of toil and snares, If I fal - ter, Lord, who cares?
3. When my fee - ble life is o'er, Time for me will be no more;
Refrain: Just a clos - er walk with Thee, Grant it, Je - sus, is my plea,
D.C. for Refrain
I'll be sat - is - fied as long As I walk, let me walk close to Thee.
Who with me my bur-den shares? None but Thee, dear Lord, none but Thee.
Guide me gent-ly, safe - ly o'er To Thy king-dom shore, to Thy shore.
Dai - ly, walk-ing close to Thee, Let it be, dear Lord, let it be.

TEXT and MUSIC: Traditional Folk song

CLOSER WALK
Irregular meter

381 Open My Eyes, That I May See

Open my eyes that I may see wonderful things in Your law. Ps. 119:18

1. O-pen my eyes, that I may see Glimp-ses of truth Thou hast for me;
2. O-pen my ears, that I may hear Voic-es of truth Thou send-est clear;
3. O-pen my mouth, and let it bear Glad-ly the warm truth ev-'ry-where;
Place in my hands the won-der-ful key, That shall un-clasp and set me free.
And while the wave-notes fall on my ear, Ev-'ry-thing false will dis-ap-pear.
O-pen my heart, and let me pre-pare Love with Thy chil-dren thus to share.
Si-lent-ly now I wait for Thee, Read-y, my God, Thy will to see;
O-pen my eyes, il-lu-mine me, Spir-it di-vine!
O-pen my ears, il-lu-mine me, Spir-it di-vine!
O-pen my heart, il-lu-mine me, Spir-it di-vine! A-men.

TEXT and MUSIC: Clara H. Scott

SCOTT
Irregular meter

Be Thou My Vision 382

Whatever was to my profit I now consider loss for the sake of Christ. Phil. 3:7

Unison
1. Be Thou my Vi - sion, O Lord of my heart;
2. Be Thou my Wis - dom, and Thou my true Word;
3. Rich - es I heed not, nor man's emp - ty praise,
4. High King of heav - en, my vic - to - ry won,
Naught be all else to me, save that Thou art—
I ev - er with Thee and Thou with me, Lord;
Thou mine in - her - i - tance, now and al - ways;
May I reach heav - en's joys, O bright heav'n's Sun!
Thou my best thought, by day or by night,
Thou my great Fa - ther, I Thy true son,
Thou and Thou on - ly, first in my heart,
Heart of my own heart, what - ev - er be - fall,
Wak - ing or sleep - ing, Thy pres - ence my light.
Thou in me dwell - ing, and I with Thee one.
High King of heav - en, my Treas - ure Thou art.
Still be my Vi - sion, O Rul - er of all. A - men.

TEXT: Ancient Irish hymn, translated by Mary E. Byrne; versified by Eleanor H. Hull
MUSIC: Irish Folk melody; arranged by David Allen

SLANE
10.10.10.10.

383 Open Our Eyes, Lord

Blessed are the pure in heart, for they will see God. Matt. 5:8

1. O - pen our eyes, Lord, we want to see Je - sus,
2. O - pen our ears, Lord, and help us to lis - ten,

to reach out and touch Him, and say that we love Him.

O - pen our eyes, Lord, we want to see Je - sus.

TEXT and MUSIC: Robert Cull;
arranged by David Allen

OPEN OUR EYES
11.12.11.11.

384 To Be Like Jesus

Follow my example, as I follow the example of Christ. 1 Cor. 11:1

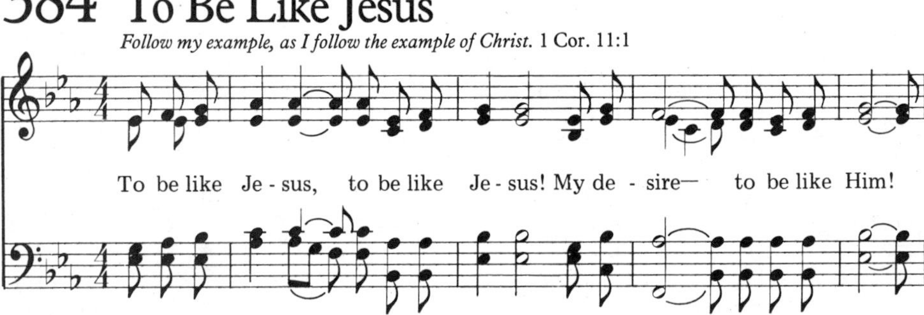
To be like Je - sus, to be like Je - sus! My de - sire— to be like Him!

TEXT and MUSIC: Traditional

TO BE LIKE JESUS
10.7.10.7.

All thru life's jour-ney from earth to glo - ry, My de - sire— to be like Him.

Near the Cross 385

May I never boast except in the cross of our Lord Jesus Christ. Gal. 6:14

1. Je - sus, keep me near the cross— There a pre - cious foun - tain,
Free to all, a heal - ing stream, Flows from Cal - v'ry's moun - tain.

2. Near the cross, a trem-bling soul, Love and mer - cy found me;
There the Bright and Morn-ing Star Sheds its beams a - round me.

3. Near the cross! O Lamb of God, Bring its scenes be - fore me;
Help my walk from day to day With its shad - ows o'er me.

4. Near the cross I'll watch and wait, Hop - ing, trust - ing ev - er,
Till I reach the gold - en strand Just be - yond the riv - er.

Refrain

In the cross, in the cross Be my glo - ry ev - er,
Till my rap - tured soul shall find Rest, be-yond the riv - er.

TEXT: Fanny J. Crosby
MUSIC: William H. Doane

NEAR THE CROSS
7.6.7.6. with Refrain

386

IN HIS IMAGE

A Brief Service of Aspiration and Hope

Suggested Hymn Stanzas

To facilitate an uninterrupted flow from stanza to stanza, the suggested stanzas have been marked with an arrow: ►

O to Be Like Thee!, stanzas 1, 2
I Would Be Like Jesus, stanzas 1, 3
More About Jesus, stanzas 1, 2, 4

WORSHIP LEADER:

For those God foreknew He also predestined to be conformed to the likeness of His Son, that He might be the firstborn among many brothers. For I resolved to know nothing while I was with you except Jesus Christ and Him crucified.

PEOPLE:

And we, who with unveiled faces all reflect the Lord's glory, are being transformed into His likeness with ever-increasing glory, which comes from the Lord, who is the Spirit.

WORSHIP LEADER:

My dear children, for whom I am again in the pains of childbirth until Christ is formed in you. . . . Your attitude should be the same as that of Christ Jesus.

PEOPLE:

What is more, I consider everything a loss compared to the surpassing greatness of knowing Christ Jesus my Lord, for whose sake I have lost all things. I consider them rubbish, that I may gain Christ. I want to know Christ and the power of His resurrection and the fellowship of sharing in His sufferings, becoming like Him in His death.

WORSHIP LEADER:

To this you were called, because Christ suffered for you, leaving you an example, that you should follow in His steps. Whoever claims to live in Him must walk as Jesus did.

Rom. 8:29; 1 Cor. 2:2; 2 Cor. 3:18; Gal. 4:19; Phil. 2:5; 3:8, 10; 1 Pet. 2:21; 1 John 2:6. (NIV)

Optional introduction to
"O to Be Like Thee"
mp

"IN HIS IMAGE—A Brief Service of Aspiration and Hope"

O to Be Like Thee! 387

I am . . . in the pains of childbirth until Christ is formed in you. Gal. 4:19

1. O to be like Thee! bless-ed Re - deem - er, This is my con - stant long - ing and prayer; Glad-ly I'll for - feit all of earth's treas - ures, Je - sus, Thy per - fect like-ness to wear.
2. O to be like Thee! full of com - pas - sion, Lov - ing, for - giv - ing, ten - der and kind; Help-ing the help - less, cheer-ing the faint - ing, Seek-ing the wan-d'ring sin - ner to find.
3. O to be like Thee! while I am plead - ing, Pour out Thy Spir - it, fill with Thy love; Make me a tem - ple meet for Thy dwell - ing, Fit me for life and heav-en a - bove.
Refrain
O to be like Thee! O to be like Thee, Bless-ed Re - deem-er, pure as Thou art! Come in Thy sweet-ness, come in Thy full-ness—Stamp Thine own im - age deep on my heart.

TEXT: Thomas O. Chisholm
MUSIC: William J. Kirkpatrick

RONDINELLA
10.9.10.9. with Refrain

388 I Would Be Like Jesus

Those God foreknew, He also predestined to be conformed to the likeness of His Son. Rom. 8:29

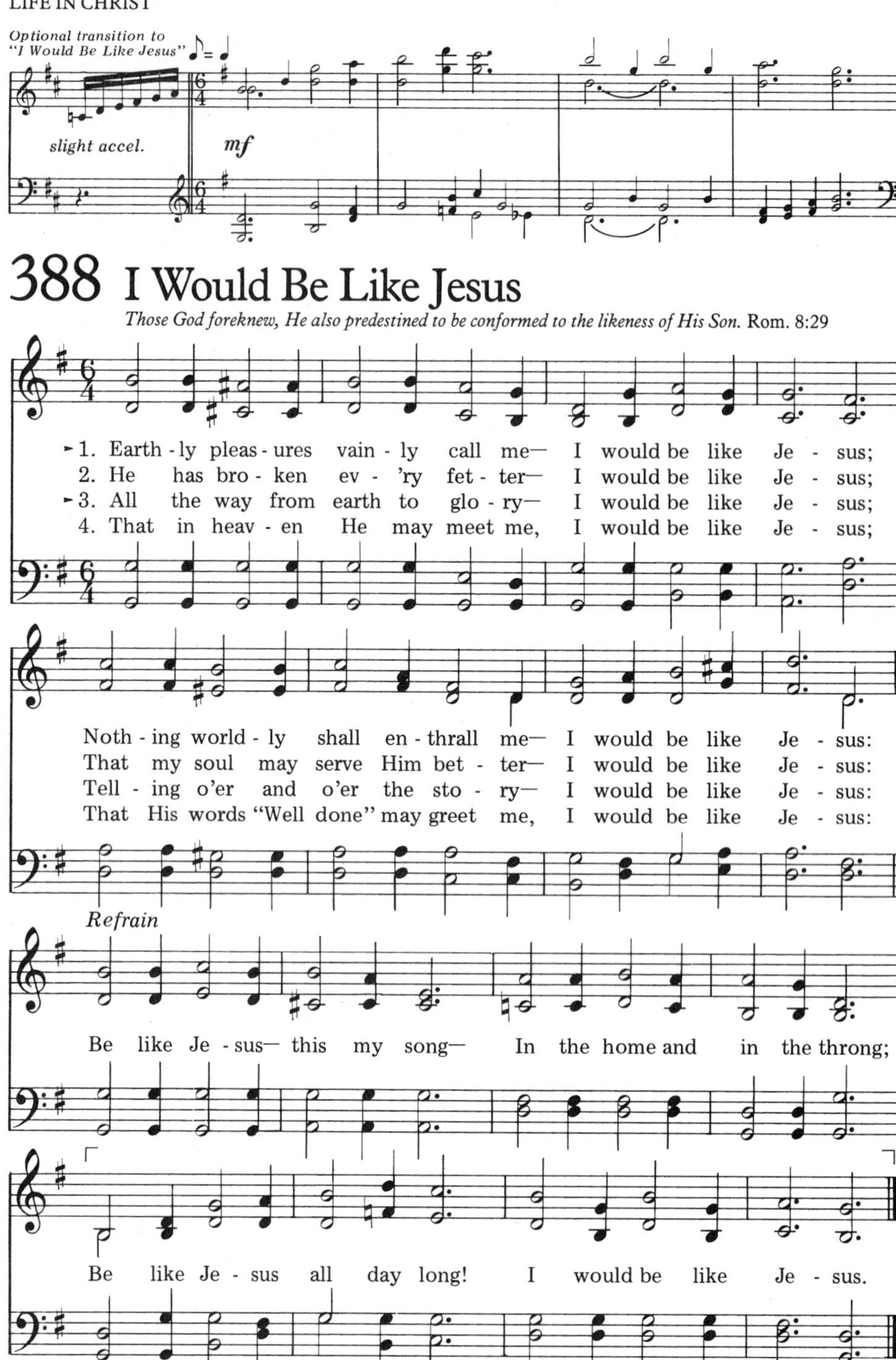
Optional transition to "I Would Be Like Jesus"
slight accel.
mf
1. Earth-ly pleas-ures vain-ly call me— I would be like Je-sus;
2. He has bro-ken ev-'ry fet-ter— I would be like Je-sus;
3. All the way from earth to glo-ry— I would be like Je-sus;
4. That in heav-en He may meet me, I would be like Je-sus;
Noth-ing world-ly shall en-thrall me— I would be like Je-sus:
That my soul may serve Him bet-ter— I would be like Je-sus:
Tell-ing o'er and o'er the sto-ry— I would be like Je-sus:
That His words "Well done" may greet me, I would be like Je-sus:
Refrain
Be like Je-sus— this my song— In the home and in the throng;
Be like Je-sus all day long! I would be like Je-sus.
Opt. segue to "More About Jesus"
Same tempo

TEXT: James Rowe
MUSIC: Bentley D. Ackley

SPRING HILL
C.M. with Refrain

More About Jesus 389
Grow in the grace and knowledge of our Lord and Savior Jesus Christ. 2 Pet. 3:18
1. More a - bout Je - sus would I know, More of His grace to oth - ers show,
2. More a - bout Je - sus let me learn, More of His ho - ly will dis - cern;
3. More a - bout Je - sus; in His Word, Hold - ing com - mun - ion with my Lord,
4. More a - bout Je - sus on His throne, Rich - es in glo - ry all His own,
More of His sav - ing full - ness see, More of His love who died for me.
Spir - it of God, my teach - er be, Show - ing the things of Christ to me.
Hear - ing His voice in ev - 'ry line, Mak - ing each faith - ful say - ing mine.
More of His king - dom's sure in - crease, More of His com - ing—Prince of Peace.
Refrain
More, more a - bout Je - sus, More, more a - bout Je - sus;
More of His sav - ing full - ness see, More of His love who died for me!
TEXT: Eliza E. Hewitt
MUSIC: John R. Sweney
SWENEY
L.M. with Refrain
Optional choral ending
decresc. rit.
O to be like Thee, Bless-ed Re-deem-er, I want to be like Je-sus, my Lord.

The end of "IN HIS IMAGE—A Brief Service of Aspiration and Hope"

390 May the Mind of Christ, My Savior

Your attitude should be the same as that of Christ Jesus. Phil. 2:5

1. May the mind of Christ my Sav-ior Live in me from day to day,
By His love and pow'r con-trol-ling All I do and say.

2. May the Word of God dwell rich-ly In my heart from hour to hour,
So that all may see I tri-umph On-ly thru His pow'r.

3. May the peace of God my Fa-ther Rule my life in ev-'ry-thing,
That I may be calm to com-fort Sick and sor-row-ing.

4. May the love of Je-sus fill me As the wa-ters fill the sea;
Him ex-alt-ing, self a-bas-ing— This is vic-to-ry.

5. May I run the race be-fore me, Strong and brave to face the foe,
Look-ing on-ly un-to Je-sus As I on-ward go.

6. May His beau-ty rest up-on me As I seek the lost to win,
And may they for-get the chan-nel, See-ing on-ly Him.

TEXT: Kate B. Wilkinson
MUSIC: A. Cyril Barham-Gould

ST. LEONARDS
8.7.8.5.

391 Aspiration Canon

If you love Me, you will obey what I command. John 14:15

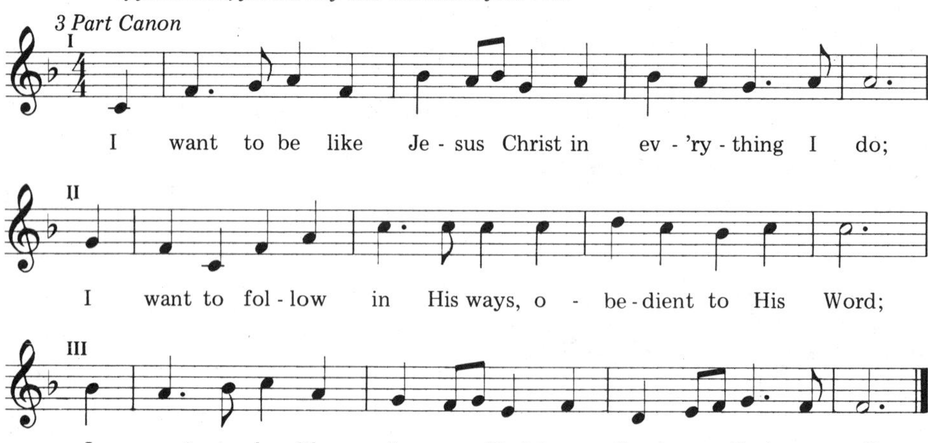
3 Part Canon
I
I want to be like Je-sus Christ in ev-'ry-thing I do;
II
I want to fol-low in His ways, o-be-dient to His Word;
III
I want to be like Je-sus Christ, my Lord, my God, my all.

TEXT and MUSIC: Bruce Greer

ASPIRATION CANON
8.6.8.6.8.6.

Nearer, Still Nearer 392

A better hope is introduced, by which we draw near to God. Heb. 7:19

1. Near - er, still near - er, close to Thy heart, Draw me, my Sav - ior, so pre - cious Thou art; Fold me, O fold me close to Thy breast, Shel - ter me safe in that "Ha - ven of Rest," Shel - ter me safe in that "Ha - ven of Rest."
2. Near - er, still near - er, noth - ing I bring, Naught as an of - fering to Je - sus my King; On - ly my sin - ful, now con-trite heart, Grant me the cleans - ing Thy blood doth im- part, Grant me the cleans - ing Thy blood doth im - part.
3. Near - er, still near - er, while life shall last, 'Til safe in glo - ry my an - chor is cast; Through end-less a - ges, ev - er to be, Near - er, my Sav - ior, still near - er to Thee, Near - er, my Sav - ior, still near - er to Thee. A - men.

TEXT and MUSIC: Lelia N. Morris

MORRIS
9.10.9.10.

393 Nearer, My God, to Thee

You are near, O Lord, and all Your commands are true. Ps. 119:151

1. Near - er, my God, to Thee, Near - er to Thee! E'en though it
2. Though like the wan - der - er, The sun gone down, Dark - ness be
3. *There let the way ap - pear Steps un - to heav'n; All that Thou
4. Then, with my wak - ing thoughts Bright with Thy praise, Out of my
5. Or if on joy - ful wing, Cleav - ing the sky, Sun, moon, and

be a cross That rais - eth me; Still all my song shall be, Near - er, my
o - ver me, My rest a stone; Yet in my dreams I'd be Near - er, my
send - est me In mer - cy giv'n; An - gels to beck - on me Near - er, my
ston - y griefs, **Beth - el I'll raise; So by my woes to be Near - er, my
stars for - got, Up - ward I fly, Still all my song shall be Near - er, my

God, to Thee, Near - er, my God, to Thee, Near - er to Thee. A - men.

*Genesis 28:12 **Genesis 35:15

TEXT: Sarah F. Adams; based on Genesis 28:10-22
MUSIC: Lowell Mason

BETHANY
6.4.6.4.6.6.6.4.

394 In My Life Lord, Be Glorified

Christ will be exalted in my body, whether by life or by death. Phil. 1:20

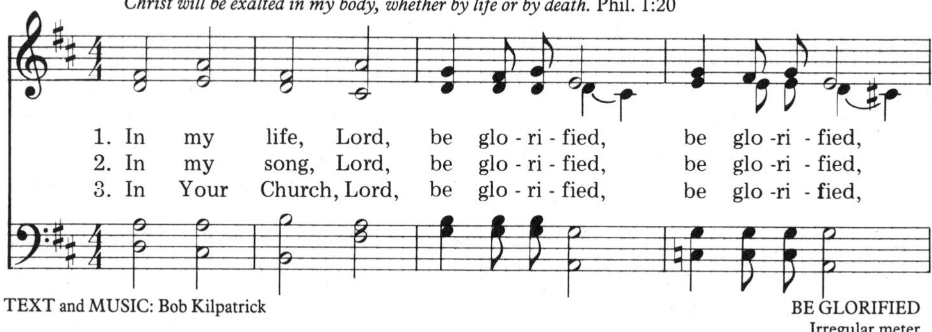
1. In my life, Lord, be glo - ri - fied, be glo - ri - fied,
2. In my song, Lord, be glo - ri - fied, be glo - ri - fied,
3. In Your Church, Lord, be glo - ri - fied, be glo - ri - fied,

TEXT and MUSIC: Bob Kilpatrick

BE GLORIFIED
Irregular meter

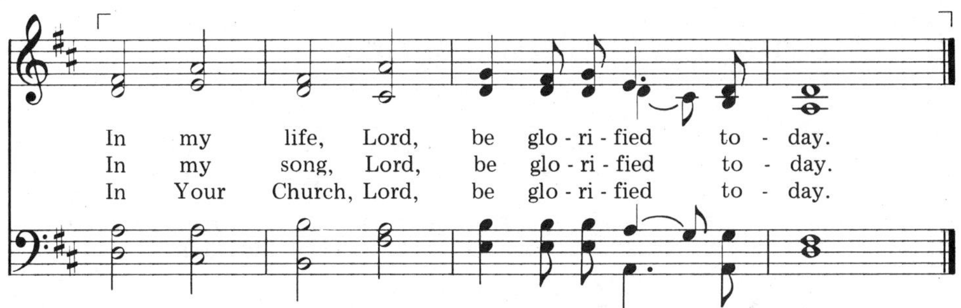
In my life, Lord, be glo-ri-fied to-day.
In my song, Lord, be glo-ri-fied to-day.
In Your Church, Lord, be glo-ri-fied to-day.

Teach Me Thy Way, O Lord 395

Teach me Your way, O Lord. Ps. 27:11

1. Teach me Thy way, O Lord, Teach me Thy way! Thy guid-ing grace af-ford— Teach me Thy way! Help me to walk a-right, More by faith, less by sight; Lead me with heav'n-ly light, Teach me Thy way!
2. When I am sad at heart, Teach me Thy way! When earth-ly joys de-part, Teach me Thy way! In hours of lone-li-ness, In times of dire dis-tress, In fail-ure or suc-cess, Teach me Thy way!
3. When doubts and fears a-rise, Teach me Thy way! When storms o'erspread the skies, Teach me Thy way! Shine thro' the cloud and rain, Thro' sor-row, toil and pain; Make Thou my path-way plain, Teach me Thy way!
4. Long as my life shall last, Teach me Thy way! Wher-e'er my lot be cast, Teach me Thy way! Un-til the race is run, Un-til the jour-ney's done, Un-til the crown is won, Teach me Thy way! A-men.

TEXT and MUSIC: B. Mansell Ramsey

CAMACHA
6.4.6.4.6.6.6.4.

396 Bring Back the Springtime

The winter is past. . . . flowers appear on the earth. Song. 2:11-12

1. When in the spring the flow'rs are bloom-ing bright and fair Aft - er the
2. Lord, make me like that stream that flows so cool and clear Down from the
gray of win - ter's gone,
mountains high a - bove;
Once a - gain the lark be - gins its
I will tell the world that won-drous
tun - ing
sto - ry
Back in the mead-ows of my home.
Of the streams that flowed from Cal - va - ry.
Refrain
Lord, to my heart bring back the spring - time,
Take a - way the
cold and dark of sin;
O re - turn to me, sweet Ho - ly

TEXT and MUSIC: Kurt Kaiser

SPRINGTIME
Irregular meter

Spir - it, May I warm and ten - der be a - gain.

Draw Nigh to God 397

Come near to God and He will come near to you. James 4:8

Draw nigh to God, and He will draw nigh to you.
Draw nigh to God, and He will draw nigh to you. Ac -
quaint thy-self with the Lord, ac - quaint thy-self with the Lord,
Draw nigh to God, and He will draw nigh to you.

TEXT and MUSIC: Colbert and Joyce Croft; based on James 4:8;
arranged by Robert F. Douglas

CROFT
11.11.7.7.11.

398 Fill My Cup, Lord

Whoever drinks the water I give him will never thirst. John 4:14

1. Like the woman at the well I was seeking For things that could not satisfy; And then I heard my Savior speaking: "Draw from My well that never shall run dry."
2. There are millions in this world who are craving The pleasures earthly things afford; But none can match the wondrous treasure That I find in Jesus Christ, my Lord.
3. So, my brother, if the things this world gave you Leave hungers that won't pass away, My blessed Lord will come and save you, If you kneel to Him and humbly pray:

Refrain

Fill my cup, Lord— I lift it up, Lord! Come and quench this thirsting of my soul; Bread of heaven, feed me till I want no more—Fill my cup, fill it up and make me whole!

TEXT and MUSIC: Richard Blanchard

FILL MY CUP
Irregular meter

Higher Ground 399

I press on toward the goal to win the prize. Phil. 3:14

1. I'm press-ing on the up - ward way, New heights I'm gain - ing ev - 'ry day—
2. My heart has no de - sire to stay Where doubts a-rise and fears dis-may;
3. I want to live a - bove the world, Tho Sa - tan's darts at me are hurled;
4. I want to scale the ut - most height And catch a gleam of glo - ry bright;

Still pray-ing as I'm on-ward bound, "Lord, plant my feet on high - er ground."
Tho some may dwell where these a - bound, My pray'r, my aim, is high - er ground.
For faith has caught the joy - ful sound, The song of saints on high - er ground.
But still I'll pray till heav'n I've found, "Lord, lead me on to high - er ground."

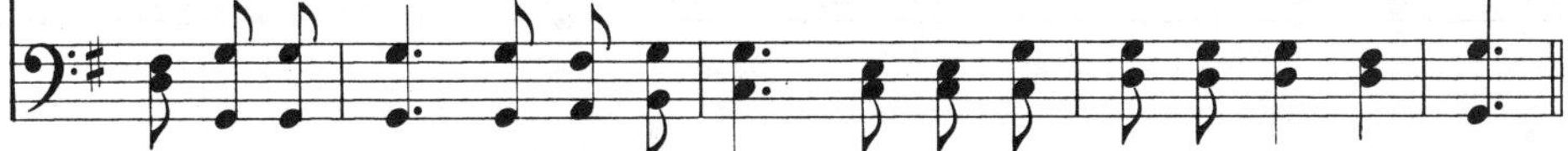

Refrain

Lord, lift me up and let me stand By faith on heav - en's ta - ble - land;

A high-er plane than I have found—Lord, plant my feet on high - er ground.

TEXT: Johnson Oatman, Jr.
MUSIC: Charles H. Gabriel

HIGHER GROUND
L.M. with Refrain

400 I Want to Be Like Jesus

You became imitators of us and of the Lord. 1 Thess. 1:6

1. I have one deep, su - preme de - sire, That I may be like Je - sus.
2. He spent His life in do - ing good; I want to be like Je - sus.
3. A ho - ly, harm - less life He led; I want to be like Je - sus.
4. Oh, per - fect life of Christ, my Lord! I want to be like Je - sus.
To this I fer - vent - ly as - pire, That I may be like Je - sus.
In low - ly paths of ser - vice trod; I want to be like Je - sus.
The Fa - ther's will, His drink and bread; I want to be like Je - sus.
My rec - om - pense and my re - ward, That I may be like Je - sus.
I want my heart His throne to be, So that a watch - ing world may
He sym - pa - thized with hearts dis - tressed; He spoke the words that cheered and
And when at last He comes to die, "For - give them, Fa - ther," hear Him
His Spir - it fill my hun - g'ring soul, His pow - er all my life con -
see His like - ness shin - ing forth in me. I want to be like Je - sus.
blessed; He wel - comed sin - ners to His breast. I want to be like Je - sus.
cry For those who taunt and cru - ci - fy. I want to be like Je - sus.
trol; My deep - est pray'r, my high - est goal, That I may be like Je - sus.

TEXT: Thomas O. Chisholm
MUSIC: David Livingstone Ives

IVES
8.7.8.7.8.8.8.7.

Psalm 42 401

Put your hope in God, for I will yet praise Him, my Savior and my God. Ps. 42:11

Unison
1. As the hart longs for flow-ing streams,
2. My tears have fed me day and night,
3. Why do I mourn and toil with - in,
So longs my soul for You, O God.
While men have said, "Where is your God?"
When it is mine to hope in God?
My soul does thirst for the liv - ing God.
But I re - call as my soul pours dry
I shall a - gain sing praise to Him,
Ritard last stanza
When shall I come to see Your face?
The days of praise with - in Your house.
He is my help, He is my God.

TEXT: Danna Harkin; based on Psalm 42
MUSIC: Appalachian Folk melody; arranged by Michael James

APPALACHIA
8.8.9.8.

402 The Solid Rock

A wise man . . . built his house on the rock. Matt. 7:24

1. My hope is built on nothing - ing less Than Je - sus' blood and
2. When dark - ness veils His love - ly face, I rest on His un -
3. His oath, His cov - e - nant, His blood, Sup - port me in the
4. When He shall come with trum - pet sound, O may I then in
right - eous - ness; I dare not trust the sweet - est frame, But
chang - ing grace; In ev - 'ry high and storm - y gale, My
whelm - ing flood; When all a - round my soul gives way, He
Him be found: Dressed in His right - eous - ness a - lone, Fault-
whol - ly lean on Je - sus' name. On Christ, the sol - id
an - chor holds with - in the veil. On Christ, the sol - id
then is all my hope and stay. On Christ, the sol - id
less to stand be - fore the throne. On Christ, the sol - id
Rock, I stand: All oth - er ground is sink - ing sand.
Rock, I stand: All oth - er ground is sink - ing sand.
Rock, I stand: All oth - er ground is sink - ing sand.
Rock, I stand: All oth - er ground is sink - ing sand. A - men.

TEXT: Edward Mote
MUSIC: John B. Dykes
Alternate tune: SOLID ROCK at No. 404

MELITA
8.8.8.8.8.8.

A LIVING HOPE

A Brief Service of Affirmation and Renewal

Suggested Hymn Stanzas

To facilitate an uninterrupted flow from stanza to stanza,
the suggested stanzas have been marked with an arrow: ►
The Solid Rock, stanzas 1, 3, 4
My Faith Has Found a Resting Place, stanzas 1, 2
My Hope Is in the Lord, stanzas 1, 3, 4

WORSHIP LEADER:

Therefore having been justified by faith, we have peace with God through our Lord Jesus Christ, through whom also we have obtained our introduction by faith into this grace in which we stand; and we exult in hope of the glory of God. And hope does not disappoint, because the love of God has been poured out within our hearts through the Holy Spirit who was given to us.

PEOPLE:

For while we were still helpless, at the right time Christ died for the ungodly. Much more then, having now been justified by His blood, we shall be saved from the wrath of God through Him. For if while we were enemies, we were reconciled to God through the death of His Son, much more, having been reconciled, we shall be saved by His life.

WORSHIP LEADER:

In the same way God, desiring even more to show to the heirs of the promise the unchangeableness of His purpose, interposed with an oath, in order that by two unchangeable things, in which it is impossible for God to lie, we may have strong encouragement, we who have fled for refuge in laying hold of the hope set before us.

ALL:

This hope we have as an anchor of the soul, a hope both sure and steadfast and one which enters within the veil, where Jesus has entered as a forerunner for us, having become a high priest forever.
Rom. 5:1-2, 5-6, 9-10; Heb. 6:17-20. (NASB)

404 The Solid Rock

A wise man . . . built his house on the rock. Matt. 7:24

1. My hope is built on nothing less Than Jesus' blood and righteousness;
I dare not trust the sweetest frame, But wholly lean on Jesus' name.
2. When darkness veils His lovely face, I rest on His unchanging grace;
In every high and stormy gale My anchor holds within the veil.
3. His oath, His covenant, His blood Support me in the whelming flood;
When all around my soul gives way, He then is all my hope and stay.
4. When He shall come with trumpet sound, O may I then in Him be found,
Dressed in His righteousness alone, Faultless to stand before the throne.
Refrain
On Christ, the solid Rock, I stand— All other ground is sinking sand, All other ground is sinking sand.
Optional transition to "My Faith Has Found a Resting Place"
mf
Same tempo

TEXT: Edward Mote
MUSIC: William B. Bradbury
Alternate tune: MELITA at No. 402

SOLID ROCK
L.M. with Refrain

My Faith Has Found a Resting Place 405

We who have believed enter that rest. Heb. 4:3

1. My faith has found a rest - ing place—Not in de - vice or creed:
2. E - nough for me that Je - sus saves—This ends my fear and doubt;
3. My heart is lean - ing on the Word—The writ-ten Word of God:
4. My great Phy - si - cian heals the sick— The lost He came to save;

I trust the Ev - er - liv - ing One— His wounds for me shall plead.
A sin - ful soul I come to Him— He'll nev - er cast me out.
Sal - va - tion by my Sav-ior's name— Sal - va - tion thru His blood.
For me His pre - cious blood He shed— For me His life He gave.

Refrain

I need no oth - er ar - gu - ment, I need no oth - er plea; It is e - nough that Je - sus died, And that He died for me.

TEXT: Lidie H. Edmunds
MUSIC: André Grétry; arranged by William J. Kirkpatrick

LANDAS
C.M. with Refrain

406 My Hope Is in the Lord

... Christ in you, the hope of glory. Col. 1:27

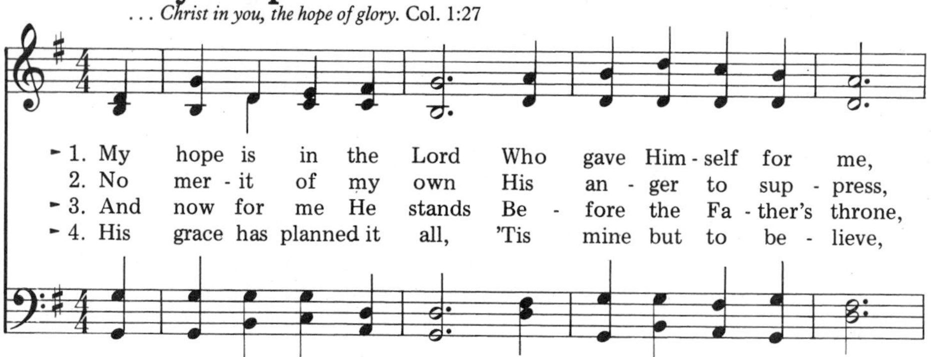
1. My hope is in the Lord Who gave Him-self for me,
2. No mer-it of my own His an-ger to sup-press,
3. And now for me He stands Be-fore the Fa-ther's throne,
4. His grace has planned it all, 'Tis mine but to be-lieve,

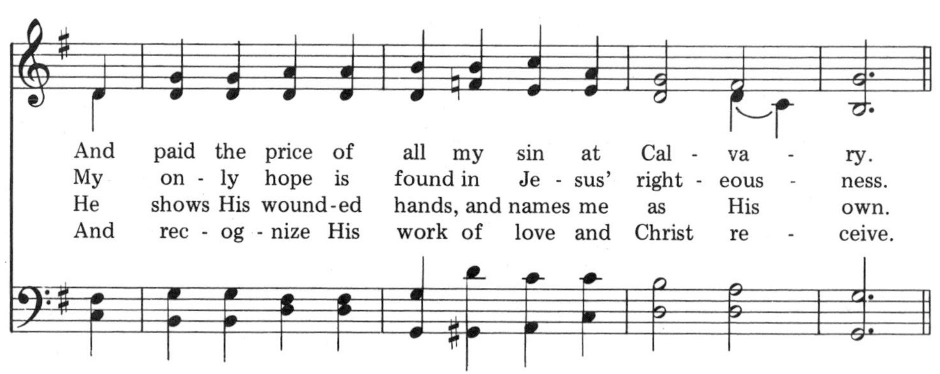
And paid the price of all my sin at Cal-va-ry.
My on-ly hope is found in Je-sus' right-eous-ness.
He shows His wound-ed hands, and names me as His own.
And rec-og-nize His work of love and Christ re-ceive.

Descant
For me He died, For me He lives,
Refrain
For me He died, For me He lives,
For me He died, For me He lives,

TEXT and MUSIC: Norman J. Clayton
Descant and choral ending by Michael James

WAKEFIELD
6.6.12. with Refrain

And ev - er - last - ing life and light He free - ly gives.
And ev - er - last - ing life and light He free - ly gives.
Optional choral ending
For me He died, For me He lives, And
For me He died, He died, For me He lives,
For me He died, For me He lives,
And
For me He died, He died, For me He lives, And
ev - er - last - ing life and light He free - ly gives.
Keyboard

The end of "A LIVING HOPE—A Brief Service of Affirmation and Renewal"

407 Hear Now the Name

Confess your sins to each other and pray for each other so that you may be healed. James 5:16

1. Hear now the Name I'm sing - ing, Here in this Name re - veal - ing All of God's love and heal - ing Comes to you this hour. O - pen your heart re - ceiv - ing, Speak now this Name be - liev - ing; No - thing be -
2. Pain and af - flic - tion bear - ing, Frail is the flesh we're wear - ing, Man - kind this weak - ness shar - ing— Cry - ing to be whole. Christ wore the stripes in sor - row, Paid all that we might bor - row Health for a
3. Heart - ache and men - tal an - guish Rip at the soul, men lan - guish. Hell - ish the sword now brand - ished, Pierc - ing hu - man minds. Comes now the Lord of heal - ing, Touched with our deep - est feel - ing; Truth from His
4. Thy King - dom come this ho - ur; Thy King - dom come with pow - er. Pour forth Your love, a show - er, Drench our thirst - y souls. Rule o - ver sin and sick - ness, Strength - en our ev - ery weak - ness. Son, rise, dis -

TEXT and MUSIC: Jack W. Hayford

ANNAMARIE
7.7.7.5.D. with Refrain

Refrain
yond con - ceiv - ing Lies be - yond His power.
bright to - mor - row, Bod - y, mind and soul.
lips is peal - ing, Free - ing hu - man - kind.
pel all bleak - ness, Come and make us whole.
Je - sus, the
Name a - bove all names. Je - sus, the Lord and King of
Kings. His Name is Life, His Name is health For bod - y, mind and
soul. Je - sus the Name we're sing - ing, In Je - sus'
Name we're bring-ing All of God's love and heal-ing Here to make you whole.

408 Have Faith in God

Have faith in God. Mark 11:22

1. Have faith in God when your path - way is lone - ly, He sees and
2. Have faith in God when your pray'rs are un - an - swered, Your ear - nest
3. Have faith in God in your pain and your sor - row, His heart is
4. Have faith in God tho all else fail a - bout you; Have faith in
knows all the way you have trod; Nev - er a - lone are the
plea He will nev - er for - get; Wait on the Lord, trust His
touched with your grief and de - spair; Cast all your cares and your
God, He pro - vides for His own; He can - not fail tho all
least of His chil - dren; Have faith in God, have faith in God.
Word and be pa - tient, Have faith in God, He'll an - swer yet.
bur - dens up - on Him, And leave them there, oh, leave them there.
king - doms shall per - ish, He rules, He reigns up - on His throne.
Refrain
Have faith in God, He's on His throne; Have faith in God, He watch-es o'er His own;
He can - not fail, He must pre - vail; Have faith in God, have faith in God.

TEXT and MUSIC: B. B. McKinney

MUSKOGEE
11.10.11.8. with Refrain

I Know Whom I Have Believed 409

I know whom I have believed. 2 Tim. 1:12

1. I know not why God's won-drous grace To me He hath made known,
2. I know not how this sav - ing faith To me He did im - part,
3. I know not how the Spir - it moves, Con - vinc - ing men of sin,
4. I know not when my Lord may come, At night or noon-day fair,

Nor why, un-wor-thy, Christ in love Re - deemed me for His own.
Nor how be-liev - ing in His Word Wrought peace with-in my heart.
Re - veal - ing Je - sus through the Word, Cre - at - ing faith in Him.
Nor if I'll walk the vale with Him, Or "meet Him in the air."

Refrain

But "I know whom I have be - liev - ed, And am per - suad - ed that He is

a - ble To keep that which I've com-mit-ted Un-to Him a-gainst that day."

TEXT: Daniel W. Whittle; based on 2 Timothy 1:12b
MUSIC: James McGranahan

EL NATHAN
C.M. with Refrain

410 My Faith Looks Up to Thee

Through faith in Him we may approach God with freedom and confidence. Eph. 3:12

1. My faith looks up to Thee, Thou Lamb of Cal - va - ry,
Sav - ior di - vine! Now hear me while I pray, Take all my
guilt a - way, O let me from this day Be whol - ly Thine!

2. May Thy rich grace im - part Strength to my faint - ing heart,
My zeal in - spire; As Thou hast died for me, O may my
love to Thee Pure, warm, and change-less be, A liv - ing fire!

3. While life's dark maze I tread And griefs a - round me spread,
Be Thou my guide; Bid dark - ness turn to day, Wipe sor - row's
tears a - way, Nor let me ev - er stray From Thee a - side.

4. When ends life's pass - ing dream, When death's cold, threat - ening stream
Shall o'er me roll, Blest Sav - ior, then, in love, Fear and dis -
trust re-move; O lift me safe a - bove, A ran-somed soul! A - men.

TEXT: Ray Palmer
MUSIC: Lowell Mason

OLIVET
6.6.4.6.6.6.4.

411 The Joy of the Lord

The joy of the Lord is your strength. Neh. 8:10

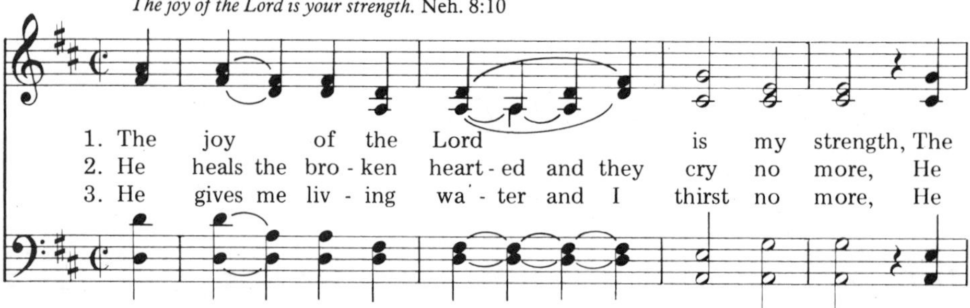
1. The joy of the Lord is my strength, The
2. He heals the bro - ken heart - ed and they cry no more, He
3. He gives me liv - ing wa - ter and I thirst no more, He

TEXT and MUSIC: Alliene G. Vale; based on Nehemiah 8:10

THE JOY OF THE LORD
8.8.7.7.8.

joy of the Lord is my strength, The joy of the
heals the bro - ken heart-ed and they cry no more, He heals the bro - ken
gives me liv - ing wa - ter and I thirst no more, He gives me liv - ing
Lord is my strength, The joy of the Lord is my strength.
heart-ed and they cry no more, The joy of the Lord is my strength.
wa - ter and I thirst no more, The joy of the Lord is my strength.

Sun of My Soul 412

The Lord God is a Sun and Shield. Ps. 84:11

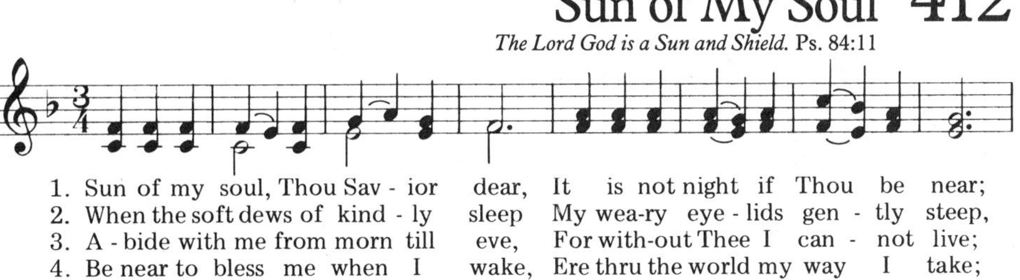
1. Sun of my soul, Thou Sav - ior dear, It is not night if Thou be near;
2. When the soft dews of kind - ly sleep My wea-ry eye - lids gen - tly steep,
3. A - bide with me from morn till eve, For with-out Thee I can - not live;
4. Be near to bless me when I wake, Ere thru the world my way I take;

O may no earth - born cloud a - rise To hide Thee from Thy ser-vant's eyes!
Be my last thought, how sweet to rest For-ev - er on my Sav - ior's breast!
A - bide with me when night is nigh, For with-out Thee I dare not die.
A - bide with me till in Thy love I lose my - self in heav'n a - bove.

TEXT: John Keble
MUSIC: *Katholisches Gesangbuch,* Vienna, c. 1774

HURSLEY
L.M.

413 Jesus, Priceless Treasure

Now to you who believe, this stone is precious. 1 Pet. 2:7

1. Je - sus, price - less treas - ure, Source of pur - est pleas - ure,
2. In Thy strength I rest me; Foes who would mo - lest me
3. Ban - ished is our sad - ness! For the Lord of glad - ness,
Tru - est friend to me: Long my heart hath pant - ed, 'Til it well - nigh
Can - not reach me here. Though the earth be shak - ing, Ev - ery heart be
Je - sus, en - ters in. Those who love the Fa - ther, Tho' the storms may
faint - ed, Thirst - ing aft - er Thee. Thine I am, O spot - less Lamb,
quak - ing, God dis - pels our fear. Sin and hell in con - flict fell
gath - er, Still have peace with - in. Yea, what - e'er we here must bear,
I will suf - fer nought to hide Thee, Ask for naught be - side Thee.
With their heav - iest storms as - sail us: Je - sus will not fail us.
Still in Thee lies pur - est pleas - ure, Je - sus, price - less treas - ure! A - men.

TEXT: Johann Franck; translated by Catherine Winkworth
MUSIC: Traditional German melody; adapted by Johann Crüger

JESU, MEINE FREUDE
6.6.5.6.6.5.7.8.6.

I Heard the Voice of Jesus Say 414

Take My yoke upon you . . . and you will find rest for your souls. Matt. 11:29

1. I heard the voice of Je - sus say, "Come un - to Me and rest;
2. I heard the voice of Je - sus say, "Be - hold, I free - ly give
3. I heard the voice of Je - sus say, "I am this dark world's Light;
Lay down, thou wea - ry one, lay down Thy head up - on My breast."
The liv - ing wa - ter; thirst - y one, Stoop down, and drink, and live."
Look un - to Me, thy morn shall rise, And all the day be bright."
I came to Je - sus as I was, Wea - ry, and worn, and sad;
I came to Je - sus, and I drank Of that life - giv - ing stream;
I looked to Je - sus, and I found In Him my Star, my Sun;
I found in Him a rest - ing place, And He has made me glad.
My thirst was quenched, my soul re - vived, And now I live in Him.
And in that Light of life I'll walk, Till trav - 'ling days are done.

TEXT: Horatius Bonar
MUSIC: John B. Dykes

VOX DILECTI
C.M.D.

415 He Giveth More Grace

He gives us more grace. James 4:6

1. He giv - eth more grace when the bur-den grows great-er; He send-eth more strength when the la - bors in - crease. To add - ed af - flic - tion He add - eth His mer - cy; To mul - ti-plied tri - als, His mul - ti - plied peace.
2. When we have ex - haust - ed our store of en - dur-ance, When our strength has failed ere the day is half done, When we reach the end of our hoard-ed re - sourc-es, Our Fa - ther's full giv - ing is on - ly be - gun.
Refrain
His love has no lim - it; His grace has no meas-ure; His pow'r has no bound - a - ry known un - to men. For out of His in - fi - nite

TEXT: Annie Johnson Flint
MUSIC: Hubert Mitchell

HE GIVETH MORE GRACE
Irregular meter

rich - es in Je - sus, He giv - eth, and giv - eth, and giv - eth a - gain!

Come, Ye Disconsolate 416

Let us then approach the throne of grace with confidence. Heb. 4:16

1. Come, ye dis - con - so - late, wher - e'er ye lan - guish; Come to the
2. Joy of the des - o - late, Light of the stray - ing, Hope of the
3. Here see the Bread of Life; see wa - ters flow - ing, Forth from the

mer - cy-seat, fer - vent - ly kneel; Here bring your wound-ed hearts, here tell your
pen - i - tent, fade - less and pure, Here speaks the Com - fort-er, ten - der - ly
throne of God, pure from a - bove; Come to the feast of love; come, ev - er

an - guish; Earth has no sor-row that heav'n can - not heal.
say - ing, "Earth has no sor-row that heav'n can - not cure."
know - ing Earth has no sor-row but heav'n can re - move. A - men.

TEXT: Thomas Moore, stanzas 1 and 2;
Thomas Hastings, stanza 3
MUSIC: Samuel Webbe

CONSOLATOR
11.10.11.10.

417 No One Understands Like Jesus

We do not have a High Priest who is unable to sympathize with our weaknesses. Heb. 4:15

1. No one un-der-stands like Je - sus, He's a friend be-yond com-pare;
2. No one un-der-stands like Je - sus, Ev - ery woe He sees and feels;
3. No one un-der-stands like Je - sus, When the foes of life as - sail;
4. No one un-der-stands like Je - sus, When you falt-er on the way;
Meet Him at the throne of mer - cy, He is wait-ing for you there.
Ten-der-ly He whis - pers com-fort, And the bro-ken heart He heals.
You should nev-er be dis - cour-aged, Je - sus cares and will not fail.
Tho' you fail Him, sad - ly fail Him, He will par-don you to - day.
Refrain
No one un-der-stands like Je - sus, When the days are dark and grim;
No one is so near, so dear as Je - sus, Cast your ev-ery care on Him.

TEXT and MUSIC: John W. Peterson

NO ONE UNDERSTANDS
8.7.8.7. with Refrain

All Your Anxiety 418

Cast all your anxiety on Him because He cares for you. 1 Pet. 5:7

1. Is there a heart o'er-bound by sor-row? Is there a life weighed
2. No oth-er friend so keen to help you, No oth-er friend so
3. Come then at once— de - lay no long-er! Heed His en - treat - y
down by care? Come to the cross—each bur - den bear-ing,
quick to hear; No oth-er place to leave your bur-den,
kind and sweet; You need not fear a dis - ap - point-ment—
All your anx - i - e - ty— leave it there.
No oth-er one to hear your prayer.
You shall find peace at the mer - cy seat.
Refrain
All your anx - i - e-ty,
all your care, Bring to the mer-cy seat— leave it there; Nev-er a
bur-den He can - not bear, Nev-er a friend like Je - sus!

TEXT and MUSIC: Edward Henry Joy

ALL YOUR ANXIETY
Irregular meter

419 Abide with Me

The Lord your God goes with you; He will never leave you nor forsake you. Deut. 31:6

1. A - bide with me! Fast falls the e - ven - tide. The dark - ness
deep - ens; Lord, with me a - bide! When oth - er help - ers fail and
com - forts flee, Help of the help - less, oh, a - bide with me!

2. Swift to its close ebbs out life's lit - tle day. Earth's joys grow
dim; its glo - ries pass a - way. Change and de - cay in all a -
round I see; O Thou who chang - est not, a - bide with me!

3. I need Thy pres - ence ev - 'ry pass - ing hour. What but Thy
grace can foil the tempt - er's pow'r? Who, like Thy - self, my guide and
stay can be? Thro' clouds and sun - shine, oh, a - bide with me!

4. I fear no foe, with Thee at hand to bless; Ills have no
weight, and tears no bit - ter - ness. Where is death's sting? Where, grave, thy
vic - to - ry? I tri - umph still if Thou a - bide with me!

5. Hold Thou Thy cross be - fore my clos - ing eyes; Shine thro' the
gloom, and point me to the skies. Heav'n's morn - ing breaks, and earth's vain
shad - ows flee! In life, in death, O Lord, a - bide with me! A - men.

TEXT: Henry F. Lyte
MUSIC: William H. Monk

EVENTIDE
10.10.10.10.

420 Only Believe

Everything is possible for him who believes. Mark 9:23

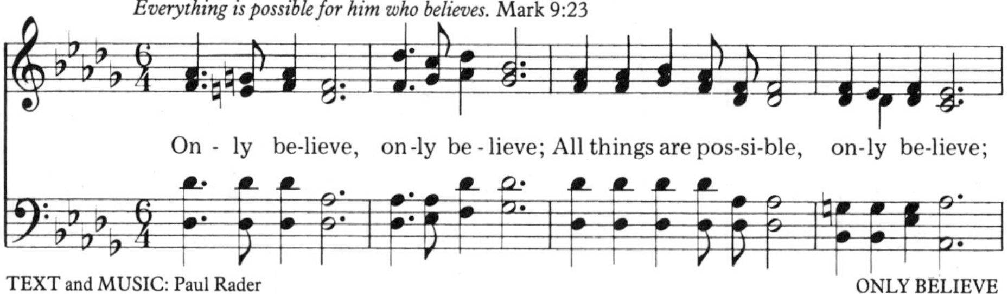
On - ly be-lieve, on-ly be - lieve; All things are pos-si-ble, on-ly be-lieve;

TEXT and MUSIC: Paul Rader

ONLY BELIEVE
8.10.8.10.

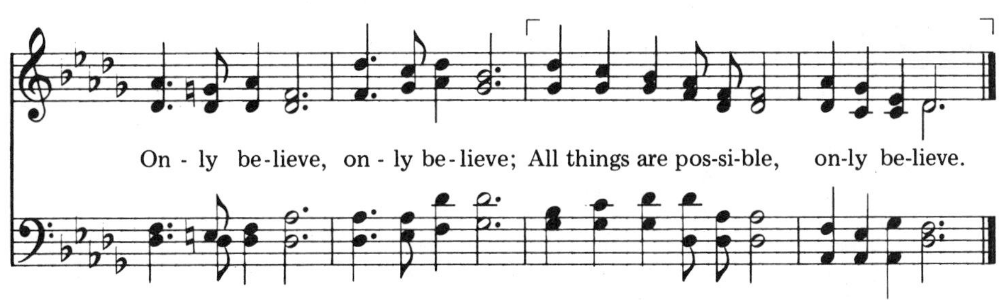
On - ly be-lieve, on - ly be-lieve; All things are pos-si-ble, on-ly be-lieve.

Be Calm My Soul 421

Be careful, keep calm and don't be afraid. Do not lose heart. Isa. 7:4

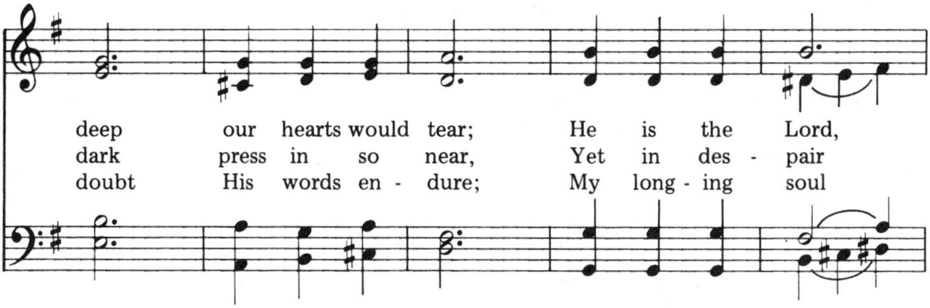

1. Be calm my soul, faint not with care Though bur - dens deep our hearts would tear; He is the Lord, all He com - mands, He hold - eth me Safe in His hands.
2. Be calm my soul, melt not in fear, Though shad-ows dark press in so near, Yet in des - pair I see His light; Lead me, O Lord, with won- d'rous sight.
3. Be calm my soul, rest in Him sure. No wave of doubt His words en - dure; My long - ing soul is sat - is - fied, He now leads forth, my Strength and Guide.

TEXT and MUSIC: Gloria Roe

BE CALM MY SOUL
L.M.

422 No, Not One!

I have called you friends. John 15:15

1. There's not a friend like the low - ly Je - sus— No, not one! no, not one!
2. No friend like Him is so high and ho - ly— No, not one! no, not one!
3. There's not an hour that He is not near us— No, not one! no, not one!
4. Did ev - er saint find this friend for-sake Him? No, not one! no, not one!
5. Was e'er a gift like the Sav - ior giv - en? No, not one! no, not one!
None else could heal all our soul's dis - eas - es— No, not one! no, not one!
And yet no friend is so meek and low - ly— No, not one! no, not one!
No night so dark but His love can cheer us— No, not one! no, not one!
Or sin - ner find that He would not take Him? No, not one! no, not one!
Will He re - fuse us a home in heav - en? No, not one! no, not one!
Refrain
Je - sus knows all a - bout our strug-gles, He will guide till the day is done;
There's not a friend like the low - ly Je - sus— no, not one! no, not one!

TEXT: Johnson Oatman, Jr.
MUSIC: George C. Hugg

NO NOT ONE
10.6.10.6. with Refrain

There Is a Balm in Gilead 423

Is there no balm in Gilead? Is there no physician there? Jer. 8:22

There is a balm in Gil - e - ad to make the wound-ed whole;
Fine
There is a balm in Gil - e - ad to heal the sin - sick soul.
1. Some - times I feel dis - cour - aged, And think my work's in vain,
2. If you can - not preach like Pe - ter, If you can - not pray like Paul,
D.C. al Fine
But then the Ho - ly Spir - it Re - vives my soul a - gain.
You can tell the love of Je - sus, And say, "He died for all."

TEXT and MUSIC: Traditional Spiritual

BALM IN GILEAD
Irregular meter

424 Tell Me the Old, Old Story

We love because He first loved us. 1 John 4:19

1. Tell me the old, old sto - ry Of un-seen things a - bove, Of Je - sus and His glo - ry, Of Je - sus and His love. Tell me the sto - ry sim - ply, As to a lit - tle child, For I am weak and wea - ry, And help - less and de - filed.
2. Tell me the sto - ry slow - ly, That I may take it in– That won - der - ful re - demp - tion, God's rem - e - dy for sin. Tell me the sto - ry oft - en, For I for - get so soon; The ear - ly dew of morn - ing Has passed a - way at noon.
3. Tell me the same old sto - ry When you have cause to fear That this world's emp - ty glo - ry Is cost - ing me too dear. Tell me the sto - ry al - ways, If you would real - ly be, In an - y time of trou - ble, A com - fort - er to me.
Refrain
Tell me the old, old sto - ry, Tell me the old, old sto - ry, Tell me the old, old sto - ry Of Je - sus and His love.

TEXT: A. Catherine Hankey
MUSIC: William H. Doane

EVANGEL
7.6.7.6.D. with Refrain

In the Garden 425

The disciples were overjoyed when they saw the Lord. John 20:20

1. I come to the gar - den a - lone, While the dew is still on the ros - es; And the voice I hear, fall-ing on my ear, The Son of God dis - clos - es.
2. He speaks, and the sound of His voice Is so sweet the birds hush their sing - ing; And the mel - o - dy that He gave to me With - in my heart is ring - ing.
3. I'd stay in the gar - den with Him Tho the night a - round me be fall - ing; But He bids me go— thru the voice of woe, His voice to me is call - ing.

Refrain

And He walks with me, and He talks with me, And He tells me I am His own; And the joy we share as we tar - ry there None oth - er has ev - er known.

TEXT and MUSIC: C. Austin Miles

GARDEN
Irregular meter

426 The Lord's Prayer

This, then, is how you should pray. Matt. 6:9

Unison
Our Fa - ther, which art in heav - en, Hal-low-ed
be Thy name. Thy king-dom come,
Thy will be done on earth as it is in heav -
en. Give us this day our dai - ly bread, And for - give us our

TEXT: Matthew 6:9-13
MUSIC: Albert Hay Malotte; arranged by Donald P. Hustad

MALOTTE
Irregular meter

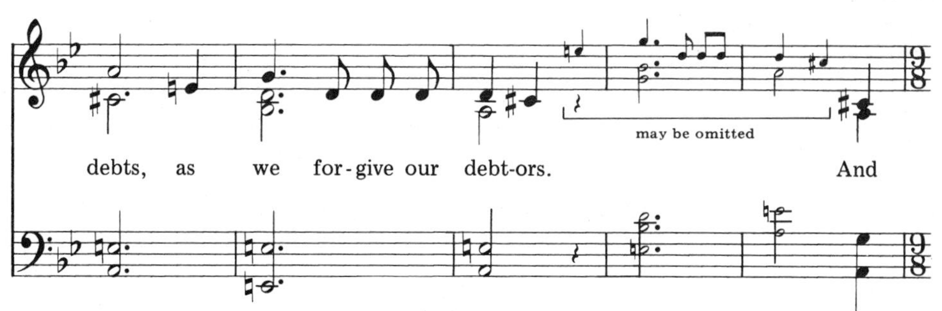
may be omitted
debts, as we for-give our debt-ors. And

lead us not in-to temp - ta - tion but de - liv - er us from e - vil; For

Thine is the king-dom, and the pow - er, and the glo - ry, For-

ev - er, A - men. A - men.

427 Dear Lord and Father of Mankind

Father, . . . forgive us our sins. Luke 11:2,4

1. Dear Lord and Fa - ther of man - kind, For - give our fool - ish ways! Re - clothe us in our right - ful mind; In pur - er lives Thy serv - ice find, In deep - er rev - 'rence, praise.
2. In sim - ple trust like theirs who heard, Be - side the Syr - ian Sea, The gra - cious call - ing of the Lord, Let us, like them, with - out a word, Rise up and fol - low Thee.
3. Drop Thy still dews of qui - et - ness, Till all our striv - ings cease; Take from our souls the strain and stress, And let our or - dered lives con - fess The beau - ty of Thy peace.
4. Breathe through the heats of our de - sire Thy cool - ness and Thy balm; Let sense be dumb, let flesh re - tire; Speak through the earth - quake, wind, and fire, O still small voice of calm! A - men.

TEXT: John G. Whittier
MUSIC: Frederick C. Maker

REST
8.6.8.8.6.

428 I Need Thee Every Hour

Hear, O Lord, and answer me, for I am poor and needy. Ps. 86:1

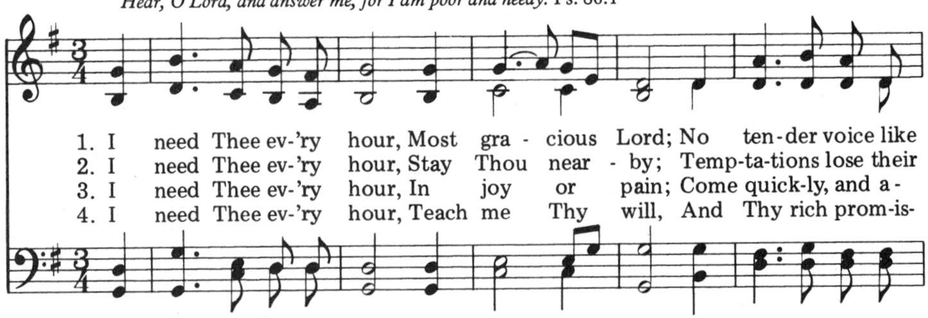
1. I need Thee ev-'ry hour, Most gra - cious Lord; No ten-der voice like
2. I need Thee ev-'ry hour, Stay Thou near - by; Temp-ta-tions lose their
3. I need Thee ev-'ry hour, In joy or pain; Come quick-ly, and a -
4. I need Thee ev-'ry hour, Teach me Thy will, And Thy rich prom-is-

TEXT: Annie S. Hawks; Robert Lowry, Refrain
MUSIC: Robert Lowry

NEED
6.4.6.4. with Refrain

Refrain
Thine Can peace af - ford.
pow'r When Thou art nigh.
bide, Or life is vain.
es In me ful - fill.
I need Thee, O I need Thee; Ev - 'ry
hour I need Thee! O bless me now, my Sav-ior, I come to Thee. A - men.
Lord, lis-ten to your chil-dren pray - ing, Lord, send Your Spir-it
in this place; Lord, lis-ten to Your chil-dren pray - ing,
Send us love, send us pow'r, send us grace.
1 (optional) D.C.
Final
grace!

Lord, Listen to Your Children Praying 429

If we ask anything according to His will, He hears us. 1 John 5:14

TEXT and MUSIC: Ken Medema

CHILDREN PRAYING
Irregular meter

430 I Must Tell Jesus

Because He Himself suffered . . . He is able to help those who are being tempted. Heb. 2:18

1. I must tell Je - sus all of my tri - als, I can-not bear these
2. I must tell Je - sus all of my trou - bles, He is a kind, com-
3. O how the world to e - vil al - lures me! O how my heart is

bur - dens a - lone; In my dis - tress He kind - ly will help me,
pas - sion-ate friend; If I but ask Him, He will de - liv - er,
tempt-ed to sin! I must tell Je - sus, and He will help me

He ev - er loves and cares for His own.
Make of my trou - bles quick - ly an end.
O - ver the world the vic - t'ry to win.

Refrain

I must tell Je - sus! I must tell Je - sus! I can-not bear my bur-dens a - lone; I must tell Je - sus! I must tell Je - sus! Je-sus can help me, Je - sus a - lone.

TEXT and MUSIC: Elisha A. Hoffman

ORWIGSBURG
10.9.10.9. with Refrain

I Am Praying for You 431

God our Savior . . . wants all men to be saved. 1 Tim. 2:3-4

1. I have a Sav - ior, He's plead - ing in glo - ry, A dear, lov - ing Sav - ior tho' earth - friends be few; And now He is watch - ing in ten - der - ness o'er me, But oh, that my Sav - ior were your Sav - ior, too!
2. I have a Fa - ther; to me He has giv - en A hope for e - ter - ni - ty, bless - ed and true; And soon He will call me to meet Him in heav - en, But oh, that He'd let me bring you with me too!
3. I have a robe; 'tis re - splen - dent in white - ness, A - wait - ing in glo - ry my won - der - ing view; Oh, when I re - ceive it all shin - ing in bright - ness, Dear friend, could I see you re - ceiv - ing one too!
4. When He has found you, tell oth - ers the sto - ry, That my lov - ing Sav - ior is your Sav - ior, too; Then pray that your Sav - ior may bring them to glo - ry, And prayer will be an - swered, 'twas an - swered for you!
Refrain
For you I am pray - ing, For you I am pray - ing, For you I am pray - ing, I'm pray - ing for you.

TEXT: Samuel Cluff
MUSIC: Ira D. Sankey

PRAYING FOR YOU
9.9.11.11. with Refrain

432 From Every Stormy Wind That Blows

We have confidence to enter the Most Holy Place by the blood of Jesus. Heb. 10:19

1. From ev - 'ry storm - y wind that blows, From ev - 'ry swell - ing
tide of woes, There is a calm, a sure re - treat:
'Tis found be - neath the mer - cy seat.

2. There is a scene where spir - its blend, Where friend holds fel - low-
ship with friend; Though sun - dered far, by faith they meet
A - round one com - mon mer - cy seat.

3. Ah! whith - er could we flee for aid, When tempt - ed, des - o-
late, dis - mayed: Or how the hosts of hell de - feat,
Had suf - f'ring saints no mer - cy seat.

4. Ah! there on ea - gle wings we soar, And sin and sense mo-
lest no more: And heav'n comes down our souls to greet,
While glo - ry crowns the mer - cy seat. A - men.

TEXT: Hugh Stowell
MUSIC: Thomas Hastings
Another key and alternate setting may be found at No. 319

RETREAT
L.M.

433 Sweet Hour of Prayer

Peter and John were going up to the temple at the time of prayer. Acts 3:1

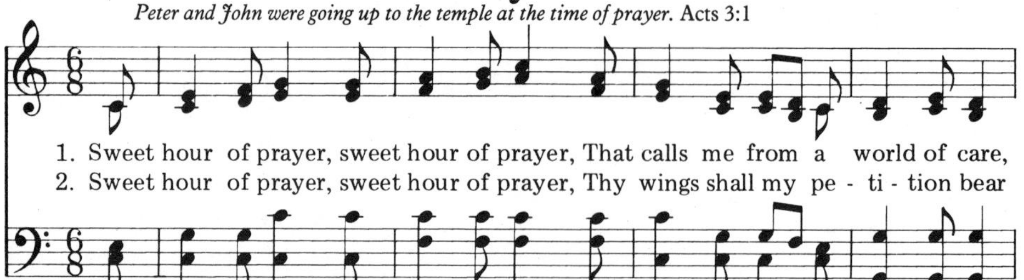
1. Sweet hour of prayer, sweet hour of prayer, That calls me from a world of care,
2. Sweet hour of prayer, sweet hour of prayer, Thy wings shall my pe - ti - tion bear

TEXT: William W. Walford
MUSIC: William B. Bradbury

SWEET HOUR
L.M.D.

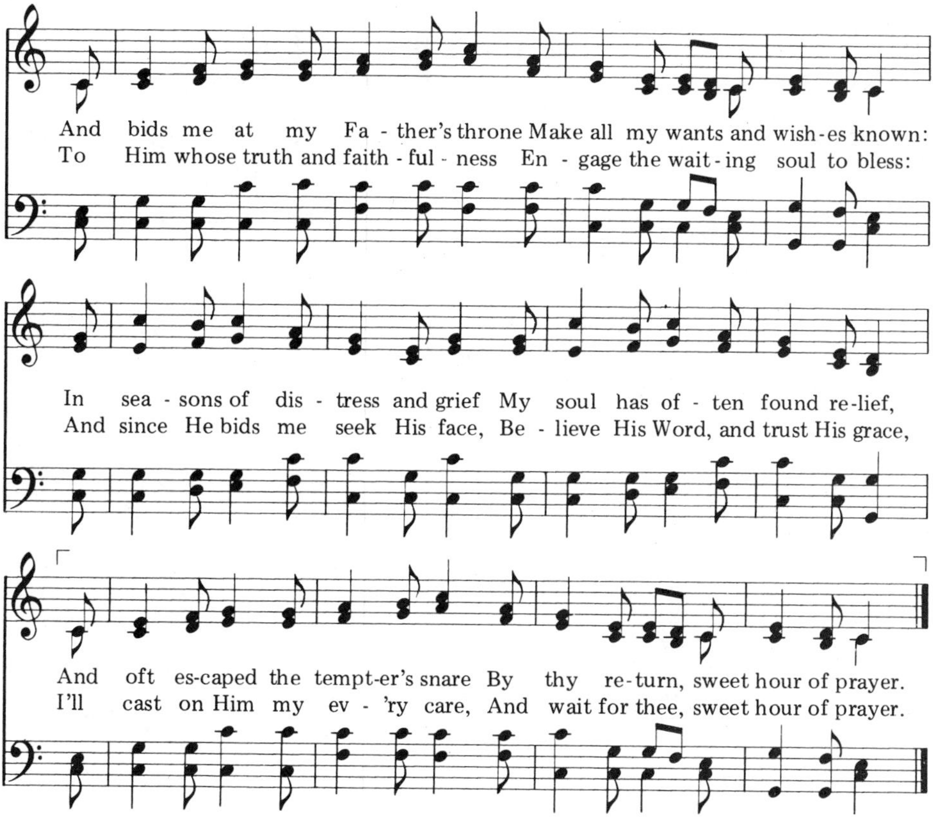

And bids me at my Fa - ther's throne Make all my wants and wish - es known:
To Him whose truth and faith - ful - ness En - gage the wait - ing soul to bless:

In sea - sons of dis - tress and grief My soul has of - ten found re - lief,
And since He bids me seek His face, Be - lieve His Word, and trust His grace,

And oft es-caped the tempt - er's snare By thy re - turn, sweet hour of prayer.
I'll cast on Him my ev - 'ry care, And wait for thee, sweet hour of prayer.

Search Me 434

Search me, O God, and know my heart. Ps. 139:23

4 Part Canon
I
II
III
IV
Search me, O God, and know my heart to - day! Try me, O
Fa - ther and know my thoughts I pray. See if there be some
wick - ed way in me; Lead me, O Lord, in Your ev - er - last - ing way!

TEXT and MUSIC: Ken Barker; based on Psalm 139:23, 24

DAVID
10.11.10.10.

435 What a Friend We Have in Jesus

In everything, by prayer and petition, . . . present your requests to God. Phil. 4:6

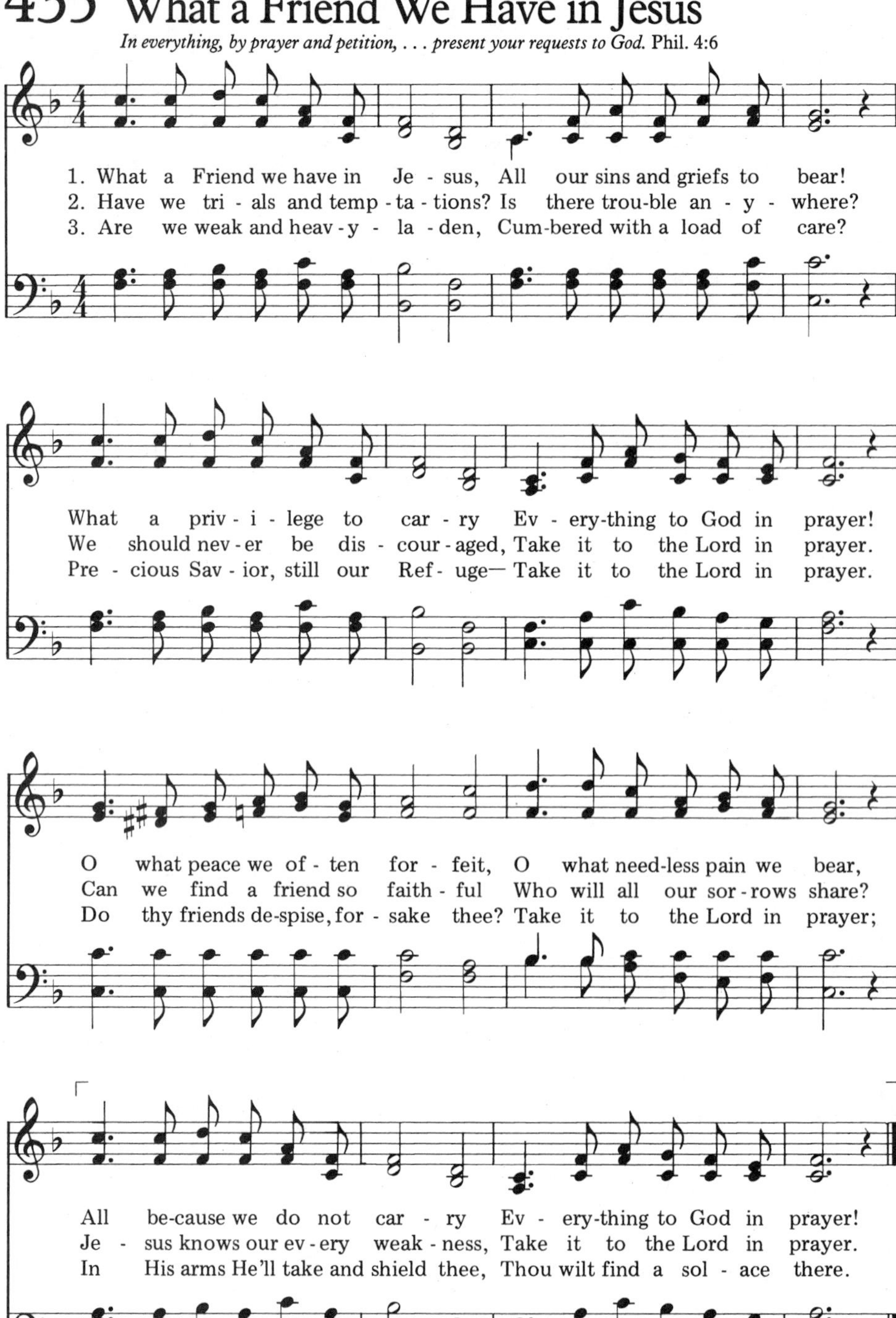
1. What a Friend we have in Je - sus, All our sins and griefs to bear!
2. Have we tri - als and temp - ta - tions? Is there trou-ble an - y - where?
3. Are we weak and heav - y - la - den, Cum-bered with a load of care?
What a priv - i - lege to car - ry Ev - ery-thing to God in prayer!
We should nev - er be dis - cour - aged, Take it to the Lord in prayer.
Pre - cious Sav - ior, still our Ref - uge— Take it to the Lord in prayer.
O what peace we of - ten for - feit, O what need-less pain we bear,
Can we find a friend so faith - ful Who will all our sor - rows share?
Do thy friends de-spise, for - sake thee? Take it to the Lord in prayer;
All be-cause we do not car - ry Ev - ery-thing to God in prayer!
Je - sus knows our ev - ery weak - ness, Take it to the Lord in prayer.
In His arms He'll take and shield thee, Thou wilt find a sol - ace there.

TEXT: Joseph M. Scriven
MUSIC: Charles C. Converse

CONVERSE
8.7.8.7.D.

Whiter Than Snow 436

Wash me, and I will be whiter than snow. Ps. 51:7

1. Lord Je - sus, I long to be per - fect - ly whole; I
2. Lord Je - sus, look down from Your throne in the skies And
3. Lord Je - sus, for this I most hum - bly en - treat; I
4. Lord Je - sus, be - fore You I pa - tient - ly wait; Come
want Thee for - ev - er to live in my soul. Break down ev - ery
help me to make a com - plete sac - ri - fice. I give up my-
wait, bless - ed Lord, at Thy cru - ci - fied feet. By faith, for my
now and with- in me a new heart cre - ate. To those who have
i - dol, cast out ev - ery foe— Now wash me and I shall be
self and what - ev - er I know— Now wash me and I shall be
cleans-ing I see Your blood flow— Now wash me and I shall be
sought You, You nev - er said, "No"— Now wash me and I shall be
whit - er than snow.
Refrain
Whit - er than snow, yes, whit - er than
snow— Now wash me and I shall be whit - er than snow.

TEXT: James Nicholson
MUSIC: William G. Fischer

FISCHER
11.11.11.11. with Refrain

437 Pure and Holy

Be holy because I, the Lord your God, am holy. Lev. 19:2

1. Pure and ho - ly I would be, wor - thy of Your love for me. Teach me while Your light is clear, change me while my heart is near.
2. You are great and I am small, You are King and God of all. You are wise in all You do, Lord I put my trust in You.
Optional descant
Ho - ly, ho - ly ho - ly Lord. ho - ly Lord.
Refrain
Ho - ly, ho - ly, ho - ly Lord. ho - ly Lord.
1
2

TEXT and MUSIC: Mike Hudson and Bob Farnsworth; arranged by David Allen

PURE and HOLY
7.7.7.7. with Refrain

Cleanse Me 438

Search me, O God, and know my heart. Ps. 139:23

Unison
1. Search me, O God, and know my heart to - day;
2. I praise Thee, Lord, for cleans-ing me from sin;
3. Lord, take my life, and make it whol - ly Thine;
4. O Ho - ly Ghost, re - viv - al comes from Thee;
Try me, O Sav - ior, know my thoughts, I pray.
Ful - fill Thy Word, and make me pure with - in.
Fill my poor heart with Thy great love di - vine.
Send a re - viv - al, start the work in me.
See if there be some wick - ed way in me;
Fill me with fire, where once I burned with shame;
Take all my will, my pas - sion, self and pride;
Thy Word de - clares Thou wilt sup - ply our need;
Cleanse me from ev - ery sin, and set me free.
Grant my de - sire to mag - ni - fy Thy name.
I now sur - ren - der, Lord—in me a - bide.
For bless - ings now, O Lord, I hum - bly plead.

TEXT: J. Edwin Orr; based on Psalm 139:23
MUSIC: Maori melody; arranged by Robert F. Douglas
Alternate tune: ELLERS at No. 439

MAORI
10.10.10.10.

439 Cleanse Me

Search me, O God, and know my heart. Ps. 139:23

1. Search me, O God, and know my heart to - day; Try me, O
2. I praise Thee, Lord, for cleans - ing me from sin; Ful - fill Thy
3. Lord, take my life and make it whol - ly Thine; Fill my poor
4. O Ho - ly Ghost, re - viv - al comes from Thee; Send a re -

Sav - ior, know my thoughts, I pray. See if there be some wick-ed
Word and make me pure with - in. Fill me with fire where once I
heart with Thy great love di - vine. Take all my will, my pas-sion,
viv - al, start the work in me. Thy Word de - clares Thou wilt sup-

way in me; Cleanse me from ev - 'ry sin and set me free.
burned with shame; Grant my de - sire to mag-ni - fy Thy name.
self, and pride; I now sur - ren - der; Lord, in me a - bide.
ply our need; For bless-ings now, O Lord, I hum-bly plead. A - men.

TEXT: J. Edwin Orr; based on Psalm 139:23
MUSIC: Edward J. Hopkins; arranged by Joseph Barlowe
Alternate tune: MAORI at No. 438

ELLERS
10.10.10.10.

440 O for a Heart to Praise My God

Create in me a pure heart, O God. Ps. 51:10

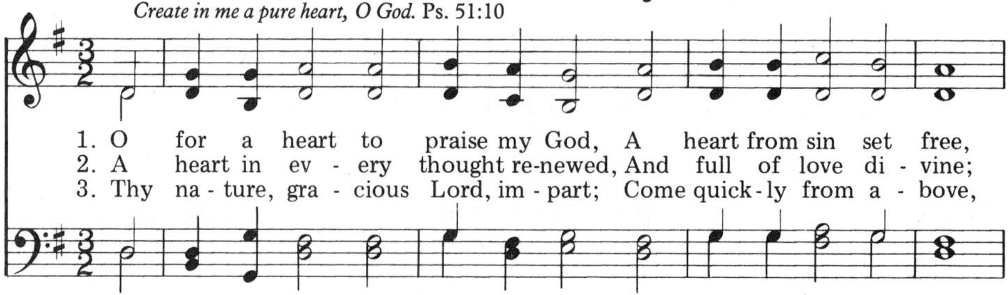
1. O for a heart to praise my God, A heart from sin set free,
2. A heart in ev - ery thought re-newed, And full of love di - vine;
3. Thy na - ture, gra - cious Lord, im - part; Come quick - ly from a - bove,

TEXT: Charles Wesley
MUSIC: Carl G. Gläser; arranged by Lowell Mason
A higher setting may be found at No. 76

AZMON
C.M.

A heart that al - ways feels Thy blood So free-ly shed for me!
Per - fect and right and pure and good, A cop -y, Lord, of Thine!
Write Thy new name up - on my heart, Thy new, best name of Love. A - men.

Take Time to Be Holy 441

Without holiness no one will see the Lord. Heb. 12:14

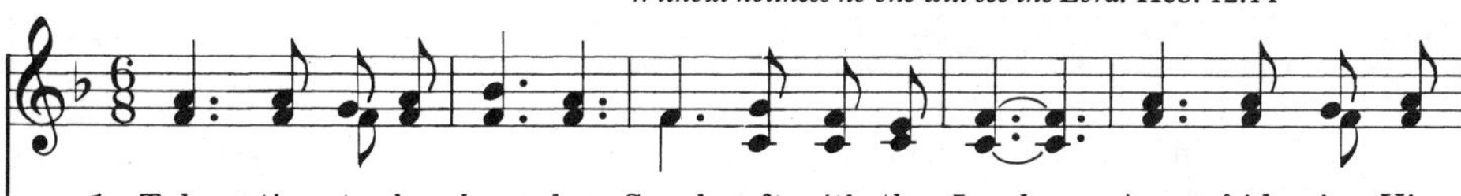
1. Take time to be ho - ly, Speak oft with thy Lord; A - bide in Him
2. Take time to be ho - ly, The world rush-es on; Much time spend in
3. Take time to be ho - ly, Let Him be thy guide, And run not be -
4. Take time to be ho - ly, Be calm in thy soul; Each thought and each

al - ways, And feed on His Word. Make friends of God's chil - dren; Help
se - cret With Je - sus a - lone; By look - ing to Je - sus, Like
fore Him What - ev - er be - tide; In joy or in sor - row Still
mo - tive Be - neath His con - trol; Thus led by His Spir - it To

those who are weak; For - get - ting in noth-ing His bless-ing to seek.
Him thou shalt be; Thy friends in thy con-duct His like-ness shall see.
fol - low thy Lord, And, look - ing to Je - sus, Still trust in His Word.
foun-tains of love, Thou soon shalt be fit - ted For ser - vice a - bove.

TEXT: William D. Longstaff
MUSIC: George C. Stebbins
Alternate tune: SLANE (altered) at No. 442

HOLINESS
6.5.6.5.D.

442 Take Time to Be Holy

Without holiness no one will see the Lord. Heb. 12:14

Unison
1. Take time to be holy, Speak often with God; Find rest in Him always And feed on His Word. Make friends of God's children; Help those who are weak, Forgetting in nothing His blessing to seek.
2. Take time to be holy, The world rushes on; Much time spend in secret With Jesus alone. By looking to Jesus, Like Him thou shalt be; Thy friends in thy conduct His likeness shall see.
3. Take time to be holy, Let Him be thy guide, And run not before Him, Whatever betide. In joy or in sorrow, Still follow thy Lord, And, looking to Jesus, Still trust in His Word.
A - men.

TEXT: William D. Longstaff
MUSIC: Irish Folk melody; adapted by Ronn Huff; arranged by David Allen
Alternate tune: HOLINESS at No. 441

SLANE (altered)
6.5.6.5.D.

Give Me Jesus 443

What good is it for a man to gain the whole world, yet forfeit his soul? Mark 8:36

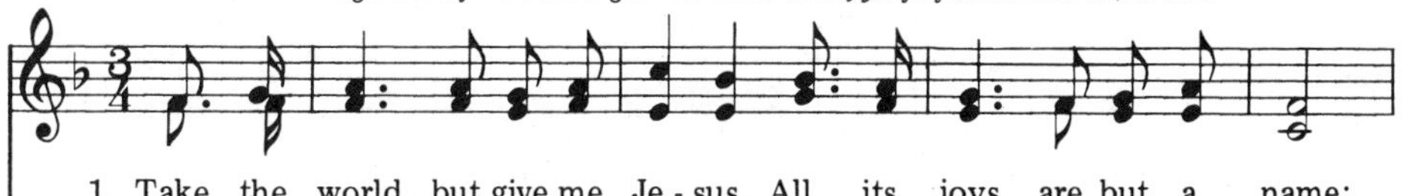

1. Take the world, but give me Je - sus, All its joys are but a name;
2. Take the world, but give me Je - sus, Sweet-est com - fort of my soul;
3. Take the world, but give me Je - sus, Let me view His con-stant smile;
4. Take the world, but give me Je - sus, In His cross my trust shall be;

But His love a - bid - eth ev - er, Thru e - ter - nal years the same.
With my Sav - ior watch-ing o'er me, I can sing tho bil-lows roll.
Then thru - out my pil - grim jour - ney Light will cheer me all the while.
Till, with clear - er, bright-er vi - sion, Face to face my Lord I see.

Refrain

O the height and depth of mer - cy! O the length and breadth of love!

O the full - ness of re - demp-tion, Pledge of end - less life a - bove!

TEXT: Fanny J. Crosby
MUSIC: John R. Sweney

GIVE ME JESUS
8.7.8.7. with Refrain

444 I'll Go Where You Want Me to Go

Go to everyone I send you to and say whatever I command you. Jer. 1:7

1. It may not be on the mountain's height Or o - ver the storm - y sea,
2. Per - haps to - day there are lov - ing words Which Je - sus would have me speak,
3. There's sure - ly somewhere a low - ly place In earth's har - vest fields so wide,
It may not be at the bat - tle's front My Lord will have need of me;
There may be now, in the paths of sin, Some wand'rer whom I should seek;
Where I may la - bor thru life's short day For Je - sus the Cru - ci - fied;
But if by a still, small voice He calls To paths I do not know,
O Sav - ior, if Thou wilt be my Guide, Tho dark and rug - ged the way,
So, trust - ing my all un - to Thy care— I know Thou lov - est me—
I'll an - swer, dear Lord, with my hand in Thine, I'll go where You want me to go.
My voice shall ech - o the mes - sage sweet, I'll say what You want me to say.
I'll do Thy will with a heart sin - cere, I'll be what You want me to be.
Refrain
I'll go where You want me to go, dear Lord, O'er mountain or plain or sea;

TEXT: Mary Brown, stanza 1; Charles E. Prior, stanzas 2, 3
MUSIC: Carrie E. Rounsefell

I'LL GO
9.7.9.7.9.8. with Refrain

I'll say what you want me to say, dear Lord, I'll be what You want me to be.

Something for Thee 445

Do your best to present yourself to God as one approved. 2 Tim. 2:15

1. Sav - ior, Thy dy - ing love Thou gav - est me,
Nor should I aught with-hold, Dear Lord, from Thee:
In love my soul would bow, My heart ful-fill its vow,
Some of - f'ring bring Thee now, Some - thing for Thee.

2. At the blest mer - cy seat, Plead - ing for me,
My fee - ble faith looks up, Je - sus, to Thee:
Help me the cross to bear, Thy won-drous love de-clare,
Some song to raise, or pray'r, Some - thing for Thee.

3. Give me a faith - ful heart, Like - ness to Thee,
That each de - part - ing day Hence-forth may see
Some work of love be - gun, Some deed of kind-ness done,
Some wan-d'rer sought and won, Some - thing for Thee.

4. All that I am and have, Thy gifts so free,
In joy, in grief, thro' life, Dear Lord, for Thee!
And when Thy face I see, My ran-som'd soul shall be,
Thro' all e - ter - ni - ty, Some - thing for Thee. A - men.

TEXT: Sylvanus D. Phelps
MUSIC: Robert Lowry

SOMETHING FOR JESUS
6.4.6.4.6.6.6.4.

446 I Will Serve Thee

It is the Lord Christ you are serving. Col. 3:24

I will serve Thee be-cause I love Thee, You have giv - en
life to me; I was noth-ing be-fore You found me,
You have giv - en life to me. Heart-aches, bro-ken
piec-es, Ru-ined lives are why You died on Cal-vary; Your touch
was what I longed for, You have giv - en life to me.

TEXT: Gloria Gaither and William J. Gaither
MUSIC: William J. Gaither

SERVING
Irregular meter

Freely, Freely 447

Freely you have received, freely give. Matt. 10:8

1. God for - gave my sin in Je - sus' name, I've been born a - gain in Je - sus' name; And in Je - sus' name I come to you To share His love as He told me to:
2. All pow'r is giv'n in Je - sus' name, In earth and heav'n in Je - sus' name; And in Je - sus' name I come to you To share His pow'r as He told me to:
Refrain
He said, "Free - ly, free - ly you have re - ceived—Free - ly, free - ly give; Go in My name and, be-cause you be - lieve, Oth-ers will know that I live."

TEXT and MUSIC: Carol Owens; based on Matthew 10:8; 28:18

FREELY, FREELY
9.9.9.9. with Refrain

448 A Charge to Keep I Have
Those who have been given a trust must prove faithful. 1 Cor. 4:2
1. A charge to keep I have, A God to glo - ri - fy, A nev - er - dy - ing soul to save, And fit it for the sky.
2. To serve the pres - ent age, My call - ing to ful - fill; O may it all my pow'rs en - gage To do my Mas - ter's will!
3. Arm me with watch - ful care As in Thy sight to live, And now Thy serv - ant, Lord, pre - pare A strict ac - count to give!
4. Help me to watch and pray, And still on Thee re - ly, O let me not my trust be - tray, But press to realms on high. A - men.
TEXT: Charles Wesley
MUSIC: Lowell Mason
BOYLSTON
S.M.
449 Must Jesus Bear the Cross Alone?
If anyone would come after Me, he must . . . take up his cross. Mark 8:34
1. Must Je - sus bear the cross a - lone And all the world go free? No, there's a cross for ev - 'ry - one, And there's a cross for me.
2. The con - se - crat - ed cross I'll bear Till death shall set me free, And then go home my crown to wear, For there's a crown for me.
3. Up - on the crys - tal pave - ment, down At Je - sus' pierc - ed feet, Joy - ful I'll cast my gold - en crown And His dear name re - peat.
4. O pre - cious cross! O glo - rious crown! O res - ur - rec - tion day! Ye an - gels, from the stars come down And bear my soul a - way.
TEXT: Thomas Shepherd and others
MUSIC: George N. Allen
MAITLAND
C.M.

Lord, Speak to Me 450

The things you have heard me say . . . entrust to reliable men. 2 Tim. 2:2

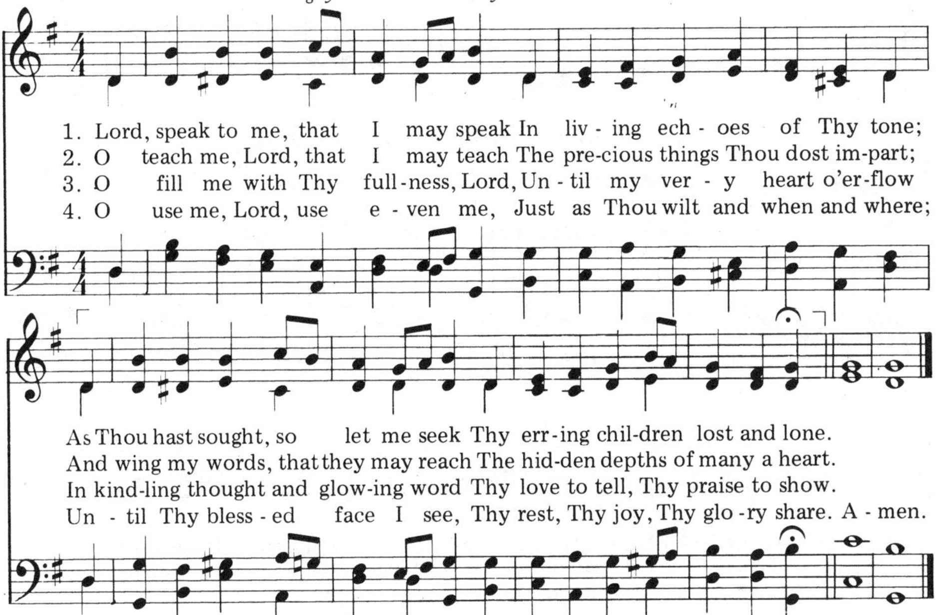

1. Lord, speak to me, that I may speak In liv - ing ech - oes of Thy tone;
As Thou hast sought, so let me seek Thy err-ing chil-dren lost and lone.

2. O teach me, Lord, that I may teach The pre-cious things Thou dost im-part;
And wing my words, that they may reach The hid-den depths of many a heart.

3. O fill me with Thy full-ness, Lord, Un - til my ver - y heart o'er-flow
In kind-ling thought and glow-ing word Thy love to tell, Thy praise to show.

4. O use me, Lord, use e - ven me, Just as Thou wilt and when and where;
Un - til Thy bless - ed face I see, Thy rest, Thy joy, Thy glo - ry share. A - men.

TEXT: Frances Ridley Havergal
MUSIC: Robert Schumann

CANONBURY
L.M.

O Master, Let Me Walk with Thee 451

Whoever claims to live in Him must walk as Jesus did. 1 John 2:6

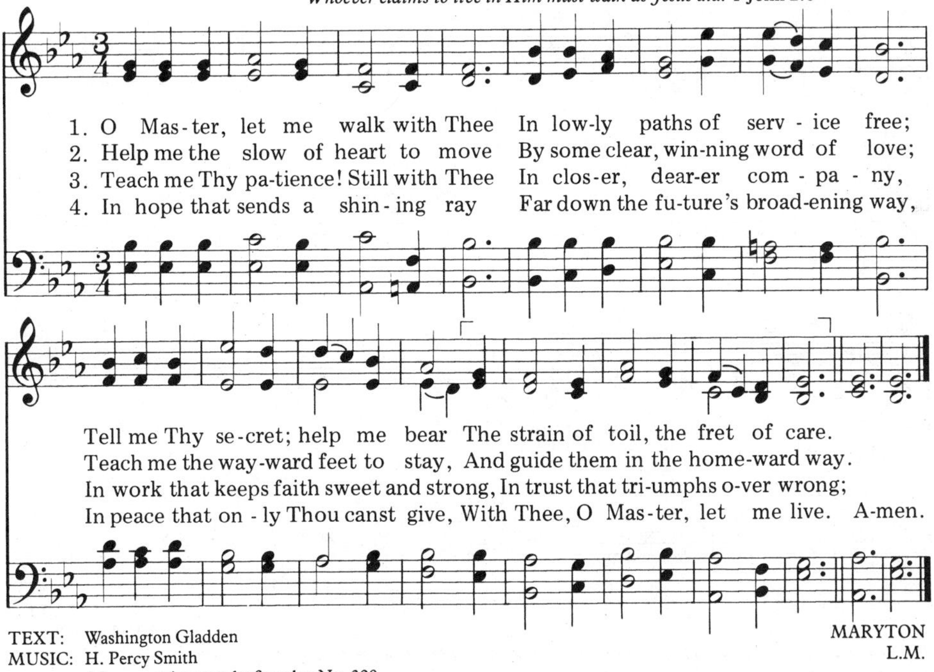

1. O Mas - ter, let me walk with Thee In low-ly paths of serv - ice free;
Tell me Thy se-cret; help me bear The strain of toil, the fret of care.

2. Help me the slow of heart to move By some clear, win-ning word of love;
Teach me the way-ward feet to stay, And guide them in the home-ward way.

3. Teach me Thy pa-tience! Still with Thee In clos-er, dear-er com - pa - ny,
In work that keeps faith sweet and strong, In trust that tri-umphs o-ver wrong;

4. In hope that sends a shin - ing ray Far down the fu-ture's broad-ening way,
In peace that on - ly Thou canst give, With Thee, O Mas-ter, let me live. A-men.

TEXT: Washington Gladden
MUSIC: H. Percy Smith
A lower setting may be found at No. 320

MARYTON
L.M.

452 Make Me a Blessing

Through the blessing of the upright a city is exalted. Prov. 11:11

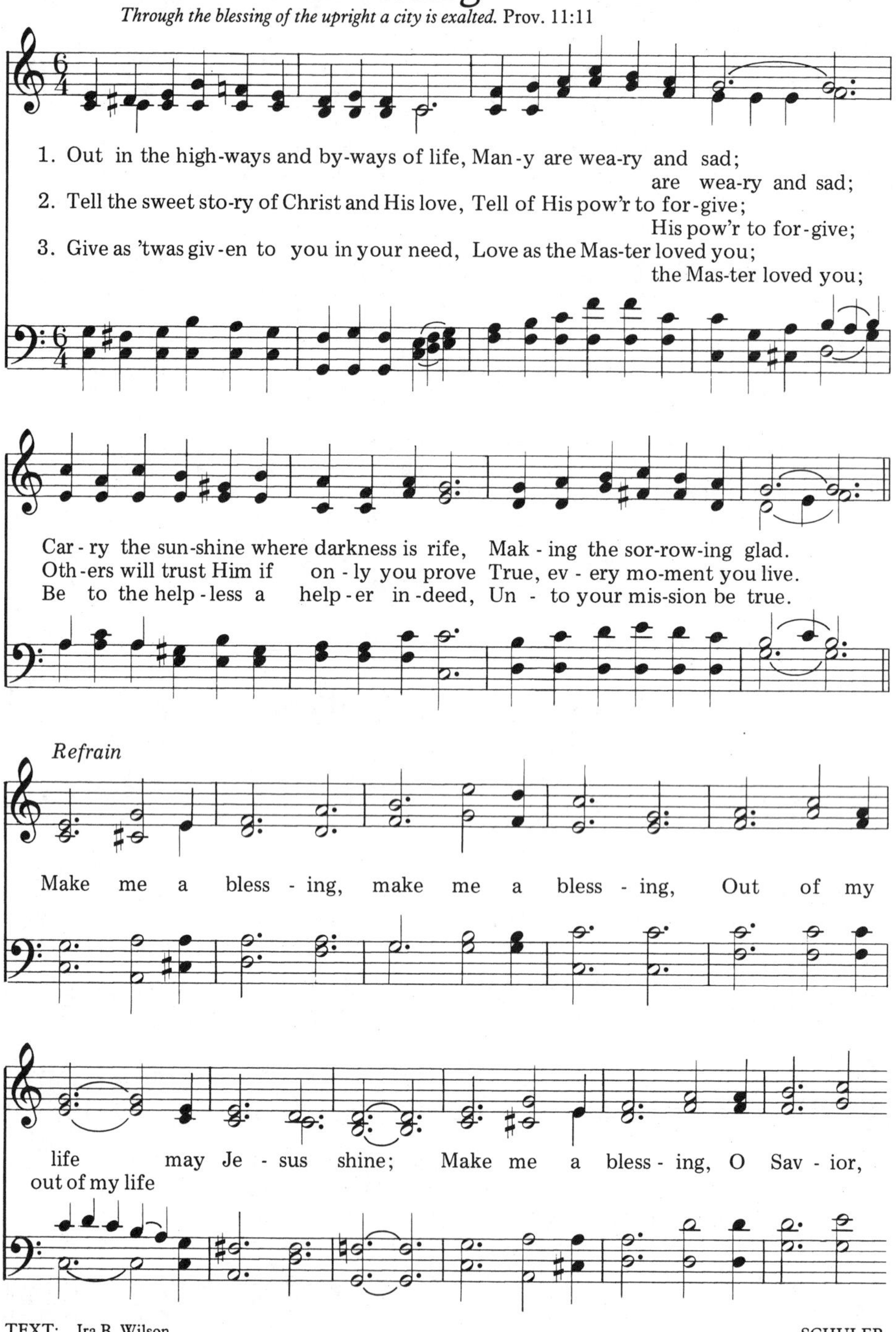
1. Out in the high-ways and by-ways of life, Man-y are wea-ry and sad;
are wea-ry and sad;
2. Tell the sweet sto-ry of Christ and His love, Tell of His pow'r to for-give;
His pow'r to for-give;
3. Give as 'twas giv-en to you in your need, Love as the Mas-ter loved you;
the Mas-ter loved you;
Car-ry the sun-shine where darkness is rife, Mak-ing the sor-row-ing glad.
Oth-ers will trust Him if on-ly you prove True, ev-ery mo-ment you live.
Be to the help-less a help-er in-deed, Un-to your mis-sion be true.
Refrain
Make me a bless-ing, make me a bless-ing, Out of my
life may Je-sus shine; Make me a bless-ing, O Sav-ior,
out of my life

TEXT: Ira B. Wilson
MUSIC: George S. Schuler

SCHULER
10.7.10.7. with Refrain

I pray,
I pray Thee, my Sav-ior, Make me a bless - ing to some - one to - day.

I Gave My Life for Thee 453

Greater love has no one than this, that he lay down his life for his friends. John 15:13

1. I gave My life for thee, My pre-cious blood I shed,
That thou might'st ran-somed be, And quick-ened from the dead;
I gave, I gave My life for thee, What hast thou given for Me?

2. My Fa-ther's house of light, My glo - ry - cir - cled throne,
I left, for earth - ly night, For wan-d'rings sad and lone;
I left, I left it all for thee, Hast thou left aught for Me?

3. I suf-fered much for thee, More than the tongue can tell,
Of bit - t'rest ag - o - ny, To res - cue thee from hell;
I've borne, I've borne it all for thee, What hast thou borne for Me?

4. And I have brought to thee, Down from My home a - bove,
Sal - va - tion full and free, My par - don and My love;
I bring, I bring rich gifts to thee, What hast thou brought to Me?

TEXT: Frances Ridley Havergal
MUSIC: Philip P. Bliss

KENOSIS
6.6.6.6.8.8.

454 Glorious Is Thy Name Most Holy

Do not forget to do good and to share with others. Heb. 13:16

1. Glorious is Thy name, Most Holy,
God and Father of us all;
We Thy servants bow before Thee,
Strive to answer ev'ry call.
Thou with life's great good hast blest us,
Cared for us from earliest years;
Unto Thee our thanks we render;
Thy deep love o'ercomes all fears.

2. For our world of need and anguish
We would lift to Thee our prayer.
Faithful stewards of Thy bounty,
May we with our brothers share.
In the name of Christ our Savior,
Who redeems and sets us free,
Gifts we bring of heart and treasure,
That our lives may worthier be.

3. In the midst of time we journey,
From Thy hand comes each new day;
We would use it in Thy service,
Humbly, wisely, while we may.
So to Thee, Lord and Creator,
Praise and honor we accord,
Thine the earth and Thine the heavens,
Thro' all the Eternal Word.

TEXT: Ruth Elliott
MUSIC: William Moore

HOLY MANNA
8.7.8.7.D.

Come, All Christians, Be Committed 455

Keep your spiritual fervor, serving the Lord. Rom. 12:11

1. Come, all Chris - tians, be com - mit - ted To the ser - vice of the
2. Of your time and tal - ents give ye, They are gifts from God a -
3. God's com - mand to love each oth - er Is re - quired of ev - ery
4. Come in praise and ad - o - ra - tion, All who on Christ's name be-
Lord. Make your lives for Him more fit - ted, Tune your hearts with one ac -
bove, To be used by Chris-tians free - ly To pro - claim His won-drous
man. Show-ing mer - cy to a broth - er Mir - rors His re - demp-tive
lieve. Wor - ship Him with con - se - cra - tion, Grace and love will you re -
cord. Come in - to His courts with glad - ness, Each his sa - cred vows re -
love. Come a - gain to serve the Sav - ior, Tithes and off - 'rings with you
plan. In com - pas - sion He has giv - en Of His love that is di -
ceive. For His grace give Him the glo - ry, For the Spir - it and the
new, Turn a - way from sin and sad - ness, Be trans-formed with life a - new.
bring. In your work with Him find fa - vor, And with joy His prais-es sing.
vine; On the cross sins were for - giv - en; Joy and peace are ful - ly thine.
Word, And re - peat the gos - pel sto - ry Till all men His name have heard.

TEXT: Eva B. Lloyd
MUSIC: Traditional American melody; *The Sacred Harp,* 1844; harmonized by James H. Wood

BEACH SPRING
8.7.8.7.D.

456 Reaching for Excellence

. . . that you may be able to discern what is best and may be . . . blameless. Phil. 1:10

1. Reach for the glor - ious prize, the prize of God's "Well done."
2. So fol - low Je - sus Christ who lived a life un - flawed.
3. Give to the Lord your best, the best that you can do.

Learn to fix your eyes on the long - ings of the Son. Sur -
Think of who it is you now rev - er - ence as Lord. Be -
As you hon - or Him, He will sure - ly hon - or you. So

ren - der all you are, let all be sac - ri - ficed.
cause He gave His all, a crown is His re - ward.
learn to run the race un - til the race is done.

Reach - ing for ex - cel - lence by giv - ing all to Christ,
Reach - ing for ex - cel - lence, our world He will re - store,
Reach - ing for ex - cel - lence un - til the prize is won,

Reach - ing for ex - cel-lence by giv - ing all to Christ.
Reach - ing for ex - cel-lence, our world He will re - store.
Reach - ing for ex - cel-lence un - til the prize is won. A - men.

TEXT: Bryan Jeffery Leech
MUSIC: Kurt Kaiser

EXCELLENCE
Irregular meter

I Will Sing of the Mercies 457

I will sing of the Lord's great love forever. Ps. 89:1

Unison
I will sing of the mer-cies of the Lord for - ev - er, I will
1
sing, I will sing, I will
2
sing of the mer-cies of the
Fine
Lord. With my mouth will I make known Thy
faith - ful-ness, Thy faith - ful-ness, With my mouth will I make
D.C. al Fine
known Thy faith-ful-ness to all gen-er - a - tions. I will

TEXT: Psalm 89:1
MUSIC: James H. Fillmore; arranged by Lee Herrington

FILLMORE
Irregular meter

458 Gentle Shepherd

He tends His flock like a shepherd . . . He gently leads. Isa. 40:11

Gen - tle Shep-herd, come and lead us, For we need You to help us find our way. Gen-tle Shep-herd, come and feed us, For we need Your strength from day to day. There's no oth - er we can turn to Who can help us face an-oth - er day; Gen-tle Shep-herd, come and lead us, For we need You to help us find our way.

TEXT: Gloria Gaither and William J. Gaither
MUSIC: William J. Gaither

GENTLE SHEPHERD
Irregular meter

THE LORD IS MY SHEPHERD

A Brief Service in Recognition of His Leadership

Suggested Hymn Stanzas

To facilitate an uninterrupted flow from stanza to stanza, the suggested stanzas have been marked with an arrow: ►

All the Way My Savior Leads Me, stanza 1
He Leadeth Me, stanza 1
Savior, Like a Shepherd Lead Us, stanzas 1, 2, 4

WORSHIP LEADER:
"I am the good Shepherd. The good Shepherd lays down His life for the sheep."

PEOPLE:
The Lord is my Shepherd, I shall not be in want. For this God is our God for ever and ever; He will be our guide even to the end. He tends His flock like a shepherd: He gathers the lambs in His arms and carries them close to His heart; He gently leads those that have young.

WORSHIP LEADER:
I Myself will tend My sheep and have them lie down, declares the Sovereign Lord. I will search for the lost and bring back the strays. I will bind up the injured and strengthen the weak, but the sleek and the strong I will destroy. I will shepherd the flock with justice. May the God of peace, who through the blood of the eternal covenant brought back from the dead our Lord Jesus, that great Shepherd of the sheep, equip you with everything good for doing His will, and may He work in us what is pleasing to Him, through Jesus Christ, to whom be glory for ever and ever. And when the Chief Shepherd appears, you will receive the crown of glory that will never fade away.

ALL:
For the Lamb at the center of the throne will be their Shepherd; He will lead them to springs of living water. And God will wipe away every tear from their eyes.

John 10:11; Ps. 23:1; 48:14; Isa. 40:11;
Ezek. 34:15-16; Heb. 13:20-21; 1 Pet. 5:4; Rev. 7:17. (NIV)

Optional introduction to "All the Way My Savior Leads Me"

460 All the Way My Savior Leads Me

He will be our guide even to the end. Ps. 48:14

1. All the way my Sav-ior leads me; What have I to ask be - side? Can I
2. All the way my Sav-ior leads me; Cheers each wind-ing path I tread, Gives me
3. All the way my Sav-ior leads me; Oh, the full-ness of His love! Per-fect

doubt His ten-der mer-cy, Who thru life has been my guide? Heav'n-ly
grace for ev - 'ry tri - al, Feeds me with the liv - ing bread: Tho my
rest to me is prom-ised In my Fa - ther's house a - bove: When my

peace, di - vin - est com - fort, Here by faith in Him to dwell! For I
wea - ry steps may fal - ter, And my soul a - thirst may be, Gush-ing
spir - it, cloth'd im - mor - tal, Wings its flight to realms of day, This my

1
2
know what-e'er be - fall me, Je - sus do - eth all things well; well.
from the Rock be - fore me, Lo! a spring of joy I see; see.
song thru end-less a - ges: Je - sus led me all the way; way.

opt. segue to "He Leadeth Me"

TEXT: Fanny J. Crosby
MUSIC: Robert Lowry

ALL THE WAY
8.7.8.7.D.

He Leadeth Me 461

In Your unfailing love You will lead the people You have redeemed. Ex. 15:13

1. He lead - eth me! O bless-ed thought! O words with heav'n-ly comfort fraught!
2. Lord, I would clasp Thy hand in mine, Nor ev - er mur - mur nor re - pine,
3. And when my task on earth is done, When, by Thy grace, the vic-t'ry's won,

What - e'er I do, wher-e'er I be, Still 'tis God's hand that lead - eth me!
Con - tent, what-ev - er lot I see, Since 'tis Thy hand that lead - eth me!
E'en death's cold wave I will not flee, Since God thru Jor - dan lead - eth me!

Refrain

He lead - eth me, He lead - eth me, By His own hand He lead - eth me:
His faith-ful fol - l'wer I would be, For by His hand He lead - eth me.

TEXT: Joseph Gilmore
MUSIC: William B. Bradbury

HE LEADETH ME
L.M. with Refrain

Optional transition to
"Savior, Like a Shepherd Lead Us"

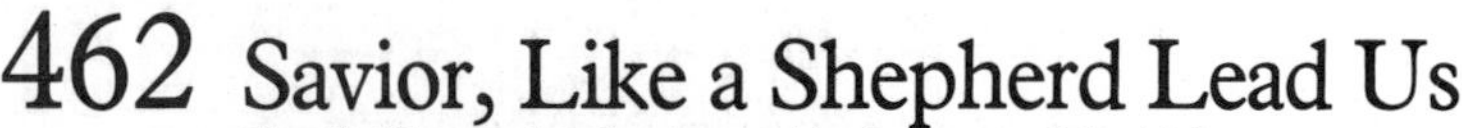

462 Savior, Like a Shepherd Lead Us

He calls His own sheep by name and leads them out. John 10:3

1. Sav - ior, like a shep-herd lead us, Much we need Thy ten-der care;
2. We are Thine; do Thou be-friend us, Be the Guard-ian of our way;
3. Thou hast prom-ised to re - ceive us, Poor and sin - ful though we be;
4. Ear - ly let us seek Thy fa - vor; Ear - ly let us do Thy will;

In Thy pleas-ant pas-tures feed us, For our use Thy folds pre-pare:
Keep Thy flock, from sin de - fend us, Seek us when we go a - stray:
Thou hast mer-cy to re - lieve us, Grace to cleanse, and pow'r to free:
Bless-ed Lord and on - ly Sav - ior, With Thy love our bos-oms fill:

Bless-ed Je - sus, bless-ed Je - sus, Thou hast bought us, Thine we are;
Bless-ed Je - sus, bless-ed Je - sus, Hear, O hear us when we pray;
Bless-ed Je - sus, bless-ed Je - sus, Ear - ly let us turn to Thee;
Bless-ed Je - sus, bless-ed Je - sus, Thou hast loved us, love us still;

Bless-ed Je-sus, bless-ed Je - sus, Thou hast bought us, Thine we are.
Bless-ed Je-sus, bless-ed Je - sus, Hear, O hear us when we pray.
Bless-ed Je-sus, bless-ed Je - sus, Ear - ly let us turn to Thee.
Bless-ed Je-sus, bless-ed Je - sus, Thou hast loved us, love us still.

TEXT: *Hymns for the Young,* 1836; attributed to Dorothy A. Thrupp
MUSIC: William B. Bradbury

BRADBURY
8.7.8.7.D.

Optional choral ending
mp
still. Bless-ed Je - sus, bless-ed Je - sus, Thou hast loved
us, love us still.
Sop. or ten. solo: Sav-ior, like a shep-herd lead us.
3
4
1. Pre-cious Lord, take my hand, Lead me on, help me stand— I am
2. When my way grows drear, Pre-cious Lord, lin - ger near— When my
tired, I am weak, I am worn; Thro' the storm, thro' the night, Lead me
life is al - most gone; Hear my cry, hear my call, Hold my

The end of "THE LORD IS MY SHEPHERD—A Brief Service in Recognition of His Leadership"

Precious Lord, Take My Hand 463

I am the Lord . . . who takes hold of your right hand. Isa. 41:13

on to the light— Take my hand, pre-cious Lord, lead me home.
hand lest I fall— Take my hand, pre-cious Lord, lead me home.

TEXT: Thomas A. Dorsey
MUSIC: George N. Allen; adapted by Thomas A. Dorsey

PRECIOUS LORD
6.6.9.6.6.9.

464 Shepherd of Love

Does he not . . . go after the lost sheep until he finds it? Luke 15:4

1. Shep-herd of love, You knew I had lost my way;
2. Shep-herd of love, Con-tent-ment at last is mine;
Shep-herd of love, You cared that I'd gone a - stray.
Deep in my heart There's peace and a joy di - vine.
You sought and found me, placed a - round me Strong arms that car-ried me home;
The fu - ture's bright-er, bur - den's light - er, My cup runs o - ver each day;
No foe can harm me or a - larm me— Nev - er a - gain will I roam!
Your grace sup- plied me now pro-vides me All that I need for the way.
Shep - herd of love, Sav - ior and Lord and Guide,
Shep - herd of love, Sav - ior and Lord and Guide,

TEXT and MUSIC: John W. Peterson

SHEPHERD OF LOVE
Irregular meter

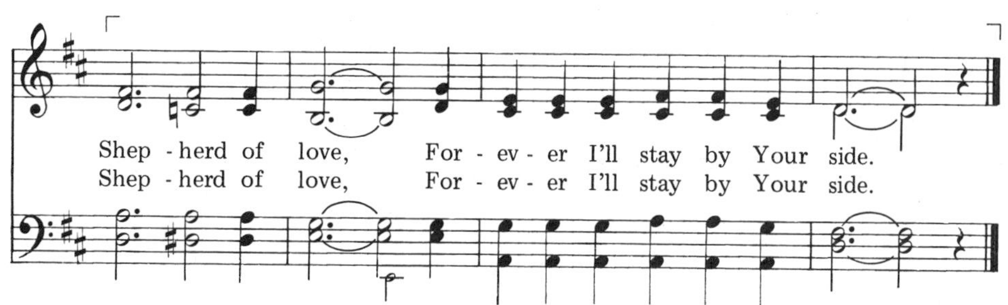
Shep - herd of love, For - ev - er I'll stay by Your side.
Shep - herd of love, For - ev - er I'll stay by Your side.

In His Time 465

He has made everything beautiful in its time. Eccl. 3:11

1. In His time (in His time), in His time (in His time);
He makes all things beau - ti - ful in His time (in His time).
Lord, please show me ev - 'ry day As You're teach-ing me Your way,
That You do just what You say in Your time (in Your time).

2. In Your time (in Your time), in Your time (in Your time);
You make all things beau - ti - ful in Your time (in Your time).
Lord, my life to You I bring; May each song I have to sing
Be to You a love - ly thing in Your time (in Your time).

TEXT and MUSIC: Diane Ball

IN HIS TIME
Irregular meter

466 Jesus, Lover of My Soul

You have been . . . a shelter from the storm. Isa. 25:4

1. Je - sus, Lov - er of my soul, Let me to Thy bos - om fly,
2. Oth - er ref - uge have I none; Hangs my help - less soul on Thee;
3. Thou, O Christ, art all I want; More than all in Thee I find;
4. Plen-teous grace with Thee is found, Grace to cov - er all my sin;
While the near - er wa - ters roll, While the tem - pest still is high;
Leave, ah! leave me not a - lone, Still sup - port and com - fort me.
Raise the fall - en, cheer the faint, Heal the sick and lead the blind.
Let the heal - ing streams a - bound; Make and keep me pure with - in.
Hide me, O my Sav - ior, hide, Till the storm of life is past;
All my trust on Thee is stayed, All my help from Thee I bring;
Just and ho - ly is Thy name, I am all un - right-eous - ness;
Thou of life the foun - tain art, Free - ly let me take of Thee;
Safe in - to the ha - ven guide; O re - ceive my soul at last!
Cov - er my de - fense-less head With the shad - ow of Thy wing.
False and full of sin I am, Thou art full of truth and grace.
Spring Thou up with - in my heart, Rise to all e - ter - ni - ty. A - men.

TEXT: Charles Wesley
MUSIC: Joseph Parry

ABERYSTWYTH
7.7.7.7.D.

Anywhere with Jesus 467

Never will I leave you; never will I forsake you. Heb. 13:5

1. An - y - where with Je - sus I can safe - ly go; An - y - where He leads me in this world be - low; An - y - where with - out Him dear-est joys would fade; An - y - where with Je - sus I am not a - fraid.
2. An - y - where with Je - sus I am not a - lone, Oth - er friends may fail me, He is still my own; Though His hand may lead me o - ver drear - y ways, An - y - where with Je - sus is a house of praise.
3. An - y - where with Je - sus o - ver land and sea, Tell - ing souls in dark - ness of sal - va - tion free; Read - y as He sum-mons me to go or stay, An - y - where with Je - sus when He points the way.
Refrain
An - y - where! an - y - where! Fear I can - not know;
An - y - where with Je - sus I can safe - ly go.

TEXT: Jessie Pounds, stanzas 1, 2; Helen C. Dixon, stanza 3
MUSIC: Kurt Kaiser

I CAN SAFELY GO
11.11.11.11. with Refrain

468 The King of Love My Shepherd Is

I am the Good Shepherd . . . I lay down My life for the sheep. John 10:14-15

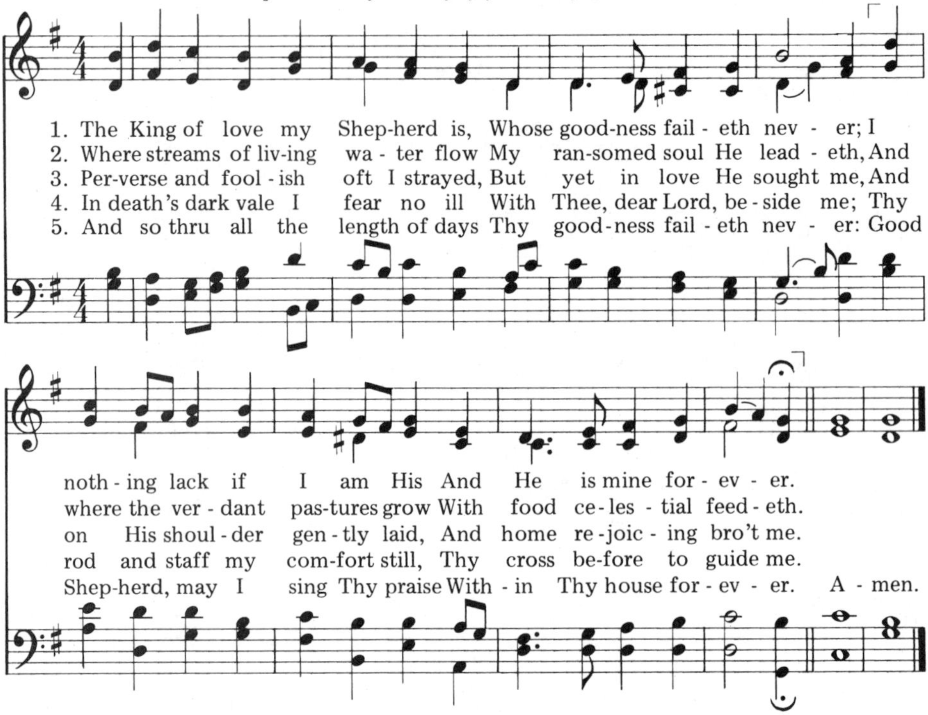

1. The King of love my Shepherd is, Whose good-ness fail - eth nev - er; I noth - ing lack if I am His And He is mine for - ev - er.
2. Where streams of liv-ing wa - ter flow My ran-somed soul He lead - eth, And where the ver - dant pas-tures grow With food ce - les - tial feed - eth.
3. Per-verse and fool - ish oft I strayed, But yet in love He sought me, And on His shoul - der gen - tly laid, And home re - joic - ing bro't me.
4. In death's dark vale I fear no ill With Thee, dear Lord, be - side me; Thy rod and staff my com-fort still, Thy cross be-fore to guide me.
5. And so thru all the length of days Thy good-ness fail - eth nev - er: Good Shep-herd, may I sing Thy praise With - in Thy house for - ev - er. A - men.

TEXT: Henry W. Baker
MUSIC: John B. Dykes

DOMINUS REGIT ME
8.7.8.7.

469 Cover Me

Clothe yourselves with the Lord Jesus Christ. Rom. 13:14

Cov-er me, Lord, with Your pres - ence, Cov-er me, Lord, with Your right-eous-ness,
Cov-er me, Lord, with Your ho - li - ness, Lord Je - sus, cov - er me.

TEXT and MUSIC: Andrew Culverwell

COVER ME
Irregular meter

Footsteps of Jesus 470

They . . . left everything and followed Him. Luke 5:11

1. Sweet-ly, Lord, have we heard Thee call - ing, "Come, fol - low Me!"
2. Tho they lead o'er the cold, dark moun-tains, Seek - ing His sheep,
3. If they lead thro' the tem - ple ho - ly, Preach-ing the Word,
4. Then at last, when on high He sees us, Our jour - ney done,
And we see where Thy foot-prints fall - ing, Lead us to Thee.
Or a - long by *Si - lo - am's foun - tains, Help - ing the weak.
Or in homes of the poor and low - ly, Serv - ing the Lord.
We will rest where the steps of Je - sus End at His throne.
Refrain
Foot - prints of Je - sus that make the path - way glow;
We will fol - low the steps of Je - sus wher - e'er they go.

*John 9:1-11

TEXT: Mary B. C. Slade
MUSIC: Asa B. Everett

FOOTSTEPS
9.4.9.4. with Refrain

471 The Way of the Cross Leads Home

There is . . . one Mediator between God and men, the Man Christ Jesus. 1 Tim. 2:5

1. I must needs go home by the way of the cross,
There's no other way but this;
I shall ne'er get sight of the gates of light,
If the way of the cross I miss.

2. I must needs go on in the blood-sprinkled way,
The path that the Savior trod,
If I ever climb to the heights sublime,
Where the soul is at home with God.

3. Then I bid farewell to the way of the world,
To walk in it nevermore;
For my Lord says, "Come," and I seek my home,
Where He waits at the open door.

Refrain

The way of the cross leads home, leads home,
The way of the cross leads home; leads home;
It is sweet to know as I onward go,
The way of the cross leads home.

TEXT: Jessie B. Pounds
MUSIC: Charles H. Gabriel

WAY OF THE CROSS
Irregular meter

The Battle Is the Lord's 472

The battle is the Lord's. 1 Sam. 17:47

1. The bat - tle is the Lord's! The har - vest fields are white:
2. The bat - tle is the Lord's! Not ours in strength or skill,
3. The bat - tle is the Lord's! The Vic - tor cru - ci - fied
4. The bat - tle is the Lord's! Stand still, my soul, and view
How few the reap - ing hands ap - pear, Their strength how slight!
But His a - lone, in sov - ereign grace, To work His will.
Must with the tra - vail of His soul Be sat - is - fied.
The great sal - va - tion God has wrought Re - vealed for you.
Yet vic - to - ry is sure— We face a van - quished foe;
Ours, count - ing not the cost, Un - flinch - ing, to o - bey;
The pow'rs of hell shall fail, And all God's will be done,
Then, rest - ing in His might, Lift high His tri - umph song,
Then for - ward with the ris - en Christ To bat - tle go!
And in His time His ho - ly arm Shall win the day.
Till ev - ery soul whom He has giv'n To Christ be won.
For pow'r, do - min - ion, king-dom, strength To Christ be - long! A - men.

TEXT: Margaret Clarkson
MUSIC: Traditional Hebrew melody; adapted by Meyer Lyon
A higher setting may be found at No. 34

LEONI
6.6.8.4.D.

473 Victory in Jesus

He gives us the victory through our Lord Jesus Christ. 1 Cor. 15:57

1. I heard an old, old sto - ry, how a Sav - ior came from glo - ry,
2. I heard a-bout His heal - ing, of His cleans-ing pow'r re - veal - ing,
3. I heard a-bout a man-sion He has built for me in glo - ry,

How He gave His life on Cal - va - ry to save a wretch like me:
How He made the lame to walk a - gain and caused the blind to see;
And I heard a - bout the streets of gold be - yond the crys - tal sea;

I heard a - bout His groan-ing, of His pre-cious blood's a - ton - ing,
And then I cried, "Dear Je - sus, come and heal my bro - ken spir - it,"
A - bout the an - gels sing - ing, and the old re - demp - tion sto - ry,

Then I re - pent - ed of my sins and won the vic - to - ry.
And some-how Je - sus came and bro't to me the vic - to - ry.
And some sweet day I'll sing up there the song of vic - to - ry.

Refrain

O vic - to - ry in Je - sus, my Sav - ior, for - ev - er, He sought me and

TEXT and MUSIC: Eugene M. Bartlett, Sr.

HARTFORD
Irregular meter

We Will Stand 474

Stand firm then. Eph. 6:14

bo't me with His re-deem-ing blood; He loved me ere I knew Him, and all my
love is due Him, He plunged me to vic-to-ry be-neath the cleans-ing flood.
Unison
You're my broth-er, you're my sis - ter, so take me by the hand. To-geth-er
we will work un-til He comes. There's no foe that can de-feat us when we're
walk-ing side by side; As long as there is love, we will stand.

TEXT: Russ Taff and Tori Taff
MUSIC: James Hollihan

WE WILL STAND
Irregular meter

475 Once to Every Man and Nation

If the Lord is God, follow Him. 1 Kings 18:21

1. Once to every man and nation Comes the moment to decide,
In the strife of truth with falsehood, For the good or evil side;
Some great cause, some great decision, Off'ring each the bloom or blight,
And the choice goes by forever 'Twixt that darkness and that light.
2. Then to side with truth is noble, When we share her wretched crust,
Ere her cause bring fame and profit, And 'tis prosp'rous to be just;
Then it is the brave man chooses While the coward stands aside,
Till the multitude make virtue Of the faith they had denied.
3. Though the cause of evil prosper, Yet the truth alone is strong;
Though her portion be the scaffold, And upon the throne be wrong,
Yet that scaffold sways the future, And, behind the dim unknown,
Standeth God within the shadow, Keeping watch above His own. Amen.

TEXT: James Russel Lowell
MUSIC: Thomas J. Williams
A lower setting may be found at No. 211

EBENEZER
8.7.8.7.D.

SOLDIERS OF CHRIST, ARISE

A Brief Service of Challenge and Victory

Suggested Hymn Stanzas

To facilitate an uninterrupted flow from stanza to stanza,
the suggested stanzas have been marked with an arrow: ►
Stand Up, Stand Up for Jesus, stanzas 1, 2
Soldiers of Christ, Arise, stanzas 1, 3
Onward, Christian Soldiers, stanzas 1, 4

WORSHIP LEADER:

Be strong in the Lord and in His mighty power. Put on the full armor of God so that you can take your stand against the devil's schemes. For our struggle is not against flesh and blood, but against the rulers, against the authorities, against the powers of this dark world and against the spiritual forces of evil in the heavenly realms. Therefore put on the full armor of God, so that when the day of evil comes, you may be able to stand your ground, and after you have done everything, to stand. Stand firm then, with the belt of truth buckled around your waist, with the breastplate of righteousness in place, and with your feet fitted with the readiness that comes from the gospel of peace. In addition to all this, take up the shield of faith, with which you can extinguish all the flaming arrows of the evil one. Take the helmet of salvation and the sword of the Spirit, which is the word of God.

Ephesians 6:10-17. (NIV)

Optional introduction to "Stand Up, Stand Up for Jesus"
f

"SOLDIERS OF CHRIST, ARISE—A Brief Service of Challenge and Victory"

477 Stand Up, Stand Up for Jesus

Stand firm in the faith; be men of courage; be strong. 1 Cor. 16:13

1. Stand up, stand up for Je - sus, Ye sol - diers of the cross, Lift high His roy-al
2. Stand up, stand up for Je - sus, The trum - pet call o - bey; Forth to the might-y
3. Stand up, stand up for Je - sus, Stand in His strength a-lone; The arm of flesh will
4. Stand up, stand up for Je - sus, The strife will not be long; This day the noise of

ban - ner, It must not suf - fer loss; From vic-tory un - to vic - tory His ar - my
con-flict In this His glo - rious day, Ye that are men, now serve Him A-gainst un-
fail you—Ye dare not trust your own; Put on the gos-pel ar-mor, Each piece put
bat - tle, The next, the vic-tor's song; To him who o - ver - com -eth A crown of

shall He lead, Till ev - ery foe is van-quished And Christ is Lord in - deed.
num-bered foes; Let cour-age rise with dan - ger, And strength to strength oppose.
on with prayer; Where du - ty calls, or dan - ger, Be nev - er want-ing there.
life shall be; He with the King of glo - ry Shall reign e - ter - nal - ly.

TEXT: George Duffield, Jr.
MUSIC: George J. Webb
Alternate tune: GEIBEL at No. 481

WEBB
7.6.7.6.D.

Optional transition to "Soldiers of Christ, Arise"

Soldiers of Christ, Arise 478

Be strong in the Lord. . . . Put on the full armor of God. Eph. 6:10-11

1. Sol - diers of Christ, a - rise And put your ar - mor on, Strong in the strength which God sup-plies Through His e - ter - nal Son; Strong in the Lord of hosts, And in His might - y pow'r, Who in the strength of Je - sus trusts Is more than con - quer - or.
2. Stand then in His great might, With all His strength en - dued, And take, to arm you for the fight, The *pan - o - ply of God; From strength to strength go on, Wres - tle and fight and pray; Tread all the pow'rs of dark - ness down, And win the well-fought day.
3. Leave no un-guard - ed place, No weak-ness of the soul; Take ev - ery vir - tue, ev - 'ry grace, And for - ti - fy the whole. That hav - ing all things done, And all your con - flicts past, Ye may o'er-come through Christ a-lone, And stand com-plete at last. A - men.

*"panoply"—anything protecting completely or forming a magnificent covering; esp. a full suit of armor; see Eph. 6:10-18.

TEXT: Charles Wesley
MUSIC: George J. Elvey
A lower setting may be found at No. 234.

DIADEMATA
S.M.D.

Optional introduction (or transition from "Soldiers of Christ, Arise")

479 Onward, Christian Soldiers

God . . . always leads us in triumphal procession in Christ. 2 Cor. 2:14

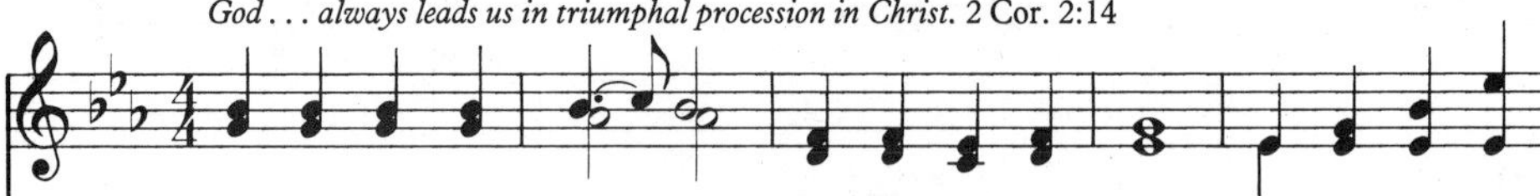

1. On-ward, Chris-tian sol - diers, March-ing as to war, With the cross of
2. At the sign of tri - umph Sa - tan's host doth flee; On, then, Chris-tian
3. Like a might-y ar - my Moves the Church of God; Broth-ers, we are
4. On-ward, then, ye peo - ple, Join our hap-py throng; Blend with ours your

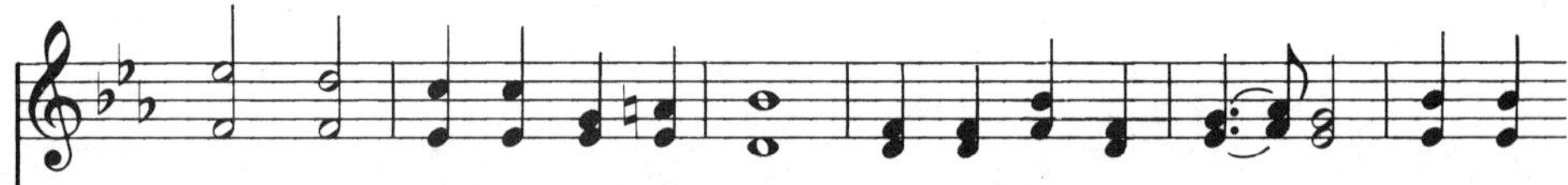

Je - sus Go - ing on be - fore! Christ, the roy-al Mas - ter, Leads a -
sol - diers, On to vic - to - ry! Hell's foun-da-tions quiv - er At the
tread - ing Where the saints have trod. We are not di - vid - ed, All one
voic - es In the tri - umph song. Glo - ry, laud and hon - or Un - to

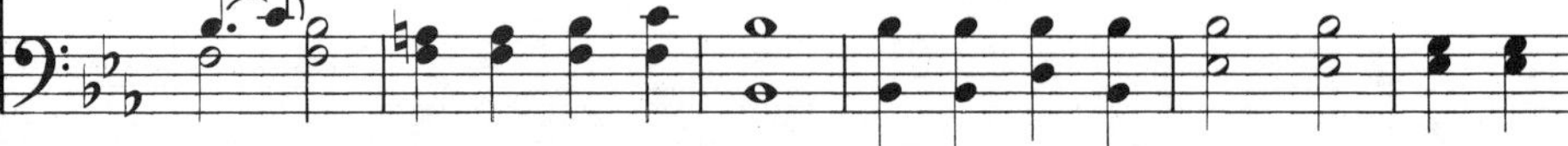

gainst the foe; For - ward in - to bat - tle See His ban-ners go!
shout of praise; Broth-ers, lift your voic - es, Loud your an-thems raise!
bod - y we— One in hope and doc - trine, One in char - i - ty.
Christ the King— This thru count-less a - ges Men and an - gels sing.

TEXT: Sabine Baring-Gould
MUSIC: Arthur S. Sullivan; Descant by David Allen

ST. GERTRUDE
6.5.6.5.D. with Refrain

Optional descant - final refrain

On - ward, ye sol - diers, march-ing as to war, With the

Refrain

On - ward, Chris-tian sol - diers, march-ing as to war, With the

cross of Je - sus go - ing on be - fore. A - men.

cross of Je - sus go - ing on be - fore. A - men.

The end of "SOLDIERS OF CHRIST, ARISE—A Brief Service of Challenge and Victory"

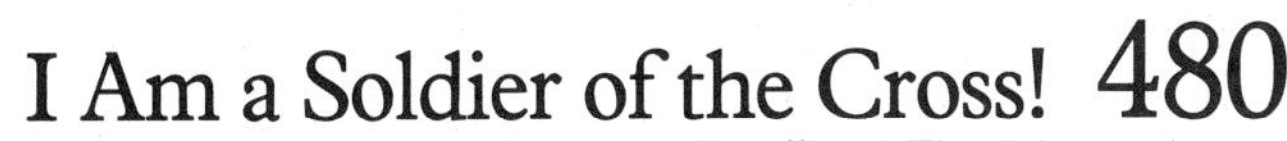

I Am a Soldier of the Cross! 480

A soldier . . . wants to please his commanding officer. 2 Tim. 2:4

4 Part Canon

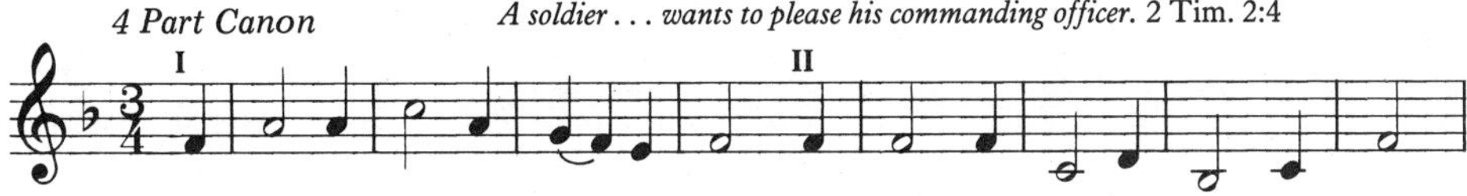
I
II
I am a sol-dier of the cross! A fol - l'wer of the pre - cious Lamb.

III
IV
I will not fear to own His cause Or blush to speak His glo - rious name.

TEXT: Isaac Watts and Gerald S. Henderson
MUSIC: William Billings; adapted by Gerald S. Henderson

AFFIRMATIVE
L.M.

481 Stand Up, Stand Up for Jesus

Stand firm in the faith; be men of courage; be strong. 1 Cor. 16:13

Unison
1. Stand up, stand up for Je - sus, Ye sol - diers of the cross;
2. Stand up, stand up for Je - sus, The trum - pet call o - bey;
3. Stand up, stand up for Je - sus, Stand in His strength a - lone;
4. Stand up, stand up for Je - sus, The strife will not be long.
Lift high His roy - al ban - ner, It must not suf - fer loss:
Forth to the might - y con - flict In this His glo - rious day:
The arm of flesh will fail you; Ye dare not trust your own.
This day the noise of bat - tle; The next, the vic - tor's song.
From vic - t'ry un - to vic - t'ry His ar - my shall He lead,
Ye that are men, now serve Him A - gainst un - num - bered foes;
Put on the gos - pel ar - mor; Each piece put on with prayer.
To him that o - ver - com - eth, A crown of life shall be;
Till ev - ery foe is van - quished And Christ is Lord in - deed.
Let cour - age rise with dan - ger, And strength to strength op - pose.
Where du - ty calls, or dan - ger, Be nev - er want - ing there.
He with the King of Glo - ry Shall reign e - ter - nal - ly.

TEXT: George Duffield, Jr.
MUSIC: Adam Geibel
Alternate tune: WEBB at No. 477

GEIBEL
7.6.7.6.D. with Refrain

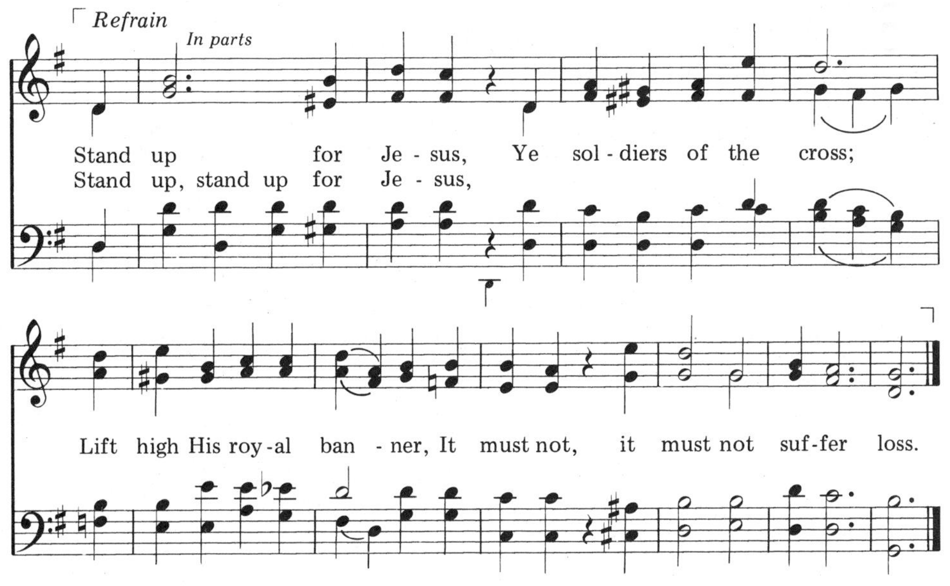
Refrain
In parts
Stand up for Je - sus, Ye sol - diers of the cross;
Stand up, stand up for Je - sus,
Lift high His roy - al ban - ner, It must not, it must not suf - fer loss.

Am I a Soldier of the Cross? 482

Endure hardship . . . like a good soldier of Christ Jesus. 2 Tim. 2:3

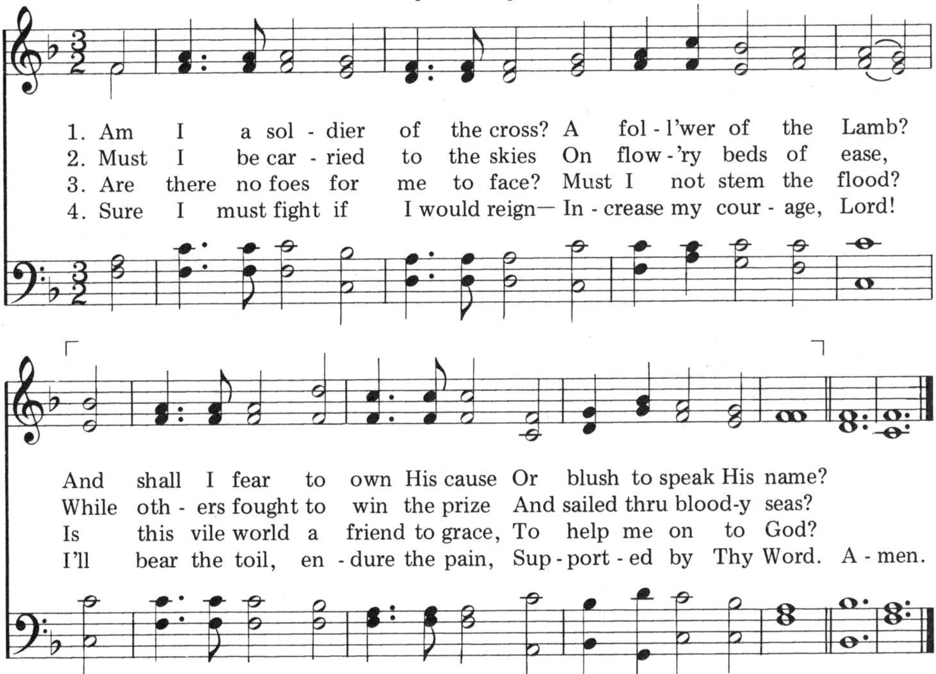

1. Am I a sol - dier of the cross? A fol - l'wer of the Lamb?
And shall I fear to own His cause Or blush to speak His name?

2. Must I be car - ried to the skies On flow - 'ry beds of ease,
While oth - ers fought to win the prize And sailed thru blood-y seas?

3. Are there no foes for me to face? Must I not stem the flood?
Is this vile world a friend to grace, To help me on to God?

4. Sure I must fight if I would reign— In - crease my cour - age, Lord!
I'll bear the toil, en - dure the pain, Sup - port - ed by Thy Word. A - men.

TEXT: Isaac Watts
MUSIC: Thomas A. Arne

ARLINGTON
C.M.

483 Lead On, O King Eternal

You guided Your people to make for Yourself a glorious name. Isa. 63:14

1. Lead on, O King E - ter - nal, The day of march has come;
2. Lead on, O King E - ter - nal, Till sin's fierce war shall cease,
3. Lead on, O King E - ter - nal, We fol - low, not with fears;
Hence-forth in fields of con - quest Your tents shall be our home.
And ho - li - ness shall whis - per The sweet A - men of peace;
For glad - ness breaks like morn - ing Wher - e'er Your face ap - pears;
Through days of prep - a - ra - tion Your grace has made us strong,
For not with swords loud clash - ing, Nor roll of stir - ring drums,
Your cross is lift - ed o'er us; We jour - ney in its light:
And now, O King E - ter - nal, We lift our bat - tle song.
With deeds of love and mer - cy The heav'n-ly king - dom comes.
The crown a - waits the con - quest; Lead on, O God of might. A - men.

TEXT: Ernest W. Shurtleff
MUSIC: Henry T. Smart; Last stanza harmonization by Bruce Greer
A higher setting may be found at No. 226

LANCASHIRE
7.6.7.6.D.

Optional last stanza harmonization
Unison - Broader
comes. 3. Lead on, O King E - ter - nal, We
fol - low, not with fears; For glad - ness breaks like morn - ing Where-
e'er Your face ap - pears; Your cross is lift - ed o'er us; We
jour - ney in its light: The crown a - waits the con - quest; Lead
8va 8va
Optional choral ending - sing parts
cresc. rit. ff
on, O God of might. Lead on, O King, Lead on!
8va

484 Who Is on the Lord's Side?

Put on the full armor of God, so that . . . you may be able to stand your ground. Eph. 6:13

1. Who is on the Lord's side? Who will serve the King? Who will
2. Not for weight of glo - ry, Not for crown and palm, En - ter
3. Je - sus, Thou hast bought us, Not with gold or gem, But with
4. Fierce may be the con - flict, Strong may be the foe, But the
be His help - ers, Oth - er lives to bring? Who will leave the
we the ar - my, Raise the war - rior psalm; But for love that
Thine own life - blood, For Thy di - a - dem. With Thy bless - ing
King's own ar - my None can o - ver - throw. Round His stand - ard
world's side? Who will face the foe? Who is on the
claim - eth Lives for whom He died; He whom Je - sus
fill - ing Each who comes to Thee, Thou hast made us
rang - ing; Vic - t'ry is se - cure; For His truth un -
Lord's side? Who for Him will go? By Thy call of mer - cy,
nam - eth Must be on His side. By Thy love con - strain - ing,
will - ing, Thou hast made us free. By Thy grand re - demp - tion,
chang - ing Makes the tri - umph sure. Joy - ful - ly en - list - ing

TEXT: Frances Ridley Havergal
MUSIC: C. Luise Reichardt; arranged by John Goss

ARMAGEDDON
6.5.6.5.D. with Refrain

By Thy grace di - vine, We are on the Lord's side, Sav-ior, we are Thine.
By Thy grace di - vine, We are on the Lord's side, Sav-ior, we are Thine.
By Thy grace di - vine, We are on the Lord's side, Sav-ior, we are Thine.
By Thy grace di - vine, We are on the Lord's side, Sav-ior, we are Thine.

The Battle Belongs to the Lord 485

The battle is not yours, but God's. 2 Chr. 20:15

Unison

1. In heav-en-ly ar-mor we'll en - ter the land, the battle belongs to the Lord! No wea-pon that's fashioned against us will stand, the bat-tle be-longs to the Lord!
2. When the pow-er of dark-ness comes in like a flood, the battle belongs to the Lord! He's raised up a stan - dard, the pow'r of His blood, the bat-tle be-longs to the Lord!

Refrain

We sing glo - ry, hon - or, pow-er and strength to the Lord. We sing glo - ry, hon - or, power and strength to the Lord!

TEXT and MUSIC: Jamie Owens-Collins; arranged by Robert F. Douglas

THE BATTLE
11.8.11.8. with Refrain

486 Faith Is the Victory

This is the victory that has overcome the world, even our faith. 1 John 5:4

1. En - camped a - long the hills of light, Ye Chris - tian sol - diers, rise,
2. His ban - ner o - ver us is love, Our sword the Word of God;
3. On ev - ery hand the foe we find Drawn up in dread ar - ray;
4. To him that o - ver - comes the foe, White rai - ment shall be giv'n;
And press the bat - tle ere the night Shall veil the glow - ing skies.
We tread the road the saints a - bove With shouts of tri - umph trod.
Let tents of ease be left be - hind, And on - ward to the fray;
Be - fore the an - gels he shall know His name con-fessed in heav'n.
A - gainst the foe in vales be - low Let all our strength be hurled;
By faith they, like a whirl-wind's breath, Swept on o'er ev - 'ry field;
Sal - va - tion's hel - met on each head, With truth all girt a - bout,
Then on - ward from the hills of light, Our hearts with love a - flame,
Faith is the vic - to - ry, we know, That o - ver-comes the world.
The faith by which they con-quered death Is still our shin - ing shield.
The earth shall trem-ble 'neath our tread, And ech - o with our shout.
We'll van - quish all the hosts of night, In Je - sus' con - quering name.

TEXT: John H. Yates
MUSIC: Ira D. Sankey

SANKEY
C.M.D. with Refrain

Refrain
Faith is the vic - to - ry! Faith is the vic - to - ry!
O, glo - ri - ous vic - to - ry, That o - ver-comes the world.

INNER PEACE AND JOY

Peace, Perfect Peace 487

My peace I give you . . . not . . . as the world gives. John 14:27

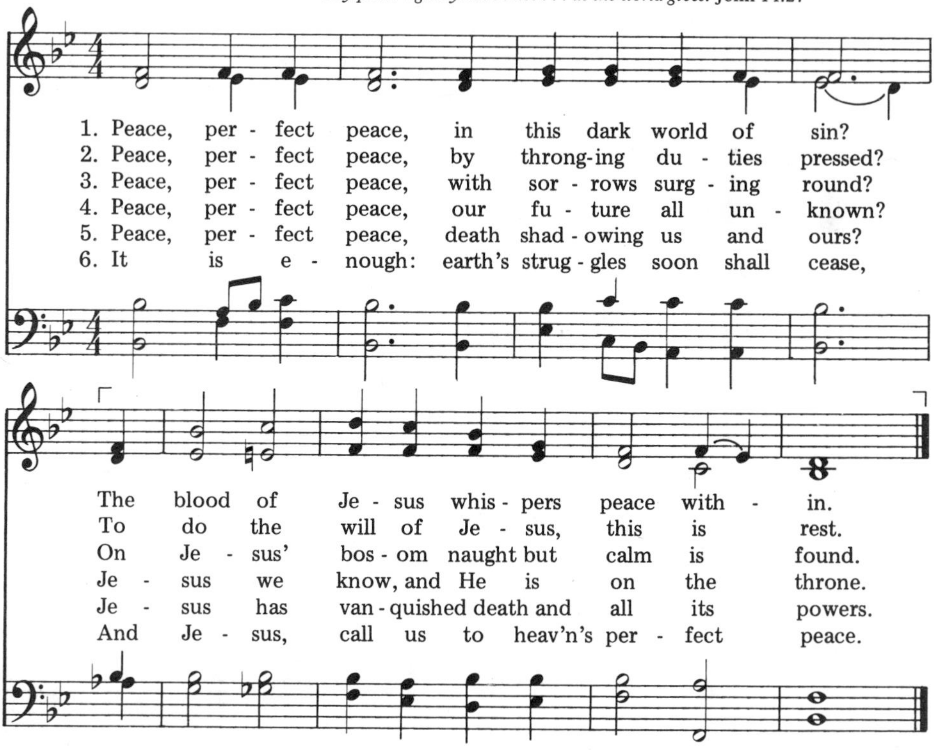

1. Peace, perfect peace, in this dark world of sin?
The blood of Jesus whispers peace within.

2. Peace, perfect peace, by thronging duties pressed?
To do the will of Jesus, this is rest.

3. Peace, perfect peace, with sorrows surging round?
On Jesus' bosom naught but calm is found.

4. Peace, perfect peace, our future all unknown?
Jesus we know, and He is on the throne.

5. Peace, perfect peace, death shadowing us and ours?
Jesus has vanquished death and all its powers.

6. It is enough: earth's struggles soon shall cease,
And Jesus, call us to heav'n's perfect peace.

TEXT: Edward H. Bickersteth
MUSIC: George T. Caldbeck; arranged by Charles J. Vincent

PAX TECUM
Irregular meter

488 He Keeps Me Singing

Sing to the Lord, for He has done glorious things. Isa. 12:5

1. There's with-in my heart a mel - o - dy— Je - sus whis-pers sweet and low,
2. All my life was wrecked by sin and strife, Dis-cord filled my heart with pain;
3. Feast-ing on the rich - es of His grace, Rest-ing 'neath His shel-t'ring wing,
4. Tho sometimes He leads thru wa - ters deep, Tri - als fall a - cross the way,
5. Soon He's com-ing back to wel-come me Far be - yond the star - ry sky;

"Fear not, I am with thee— peace, be still," In all of life's ebb and flow.
Je - sus swept a - cross the bro - ken strings, Stirr'd the slumb'ring chords a-gain.
Al - ways look-ing on His smil - ing face— That is why I shout and sing.
Tho sometimes the path seems rough and steep, See His foot-prints all the way.
I shall wing my flight to worlds un-known, I shall reign with Him on high.

Optional descant
Je - sus, Je - sus— Sweet - est name I know,
Refrain
Je - sus, Je - sus, Je - sus— Sweet -est name I know,

TEXT and MUSIC: Luther B. Bridgers
Descant by Eugene Thomas

SWEETEST NAME
9.7.9.7. with Refrain

Fills my long - ing, Keeps me sing-ing as I go.
Fills my ev - 'ry long - ing, Keeps me sing-ing as I go.

Rejoice in the Lord Always 489

4 Part Canon (optional)

Rejoice in the Lord! Phil. 3:1

I

Re - joice in the Lord al - ways, a - gain I say, re - joice!

II

Re - joice in the Lord al - ways, a - gain I say, re - joice!

III

Re - joice, re-joice, a - gain I say, re - joice!

IV

Re - joice, re-joice, a - gain I say, re - joice!

TEXT: Philippians 4:4
MUSIC: Traditional

REJOICE
Irregular meter

490 I Am His, and He Is Mine

Your life is now hidden with Christ in God. Col. 3:3

1. Loved with ev - er - last - ing love, Led by grace that love to know;
2. Heav'n a - bove is soft - er blue, Earth a - round is sweet-er green!
3. Things that once were wild a - larms Can - not now dis - turb my rest;
4. His for - ev - er, on - ly His; Who the Lord and me shall part?
Gra - cious Spir - it from a - bove, Thou hast taught me it is so!
Some-thing lives in ev - ery hue Christ - less eyes have nev - er seen:
Closed in ev - er - last - ing arms, Pil - lowed on the lov - ing breast.
Ah, with what a rest of bliss Christ can fill the lov - ing heart!
O, this full and per - fect peace! O, this trans - port all di - vine!
Birds with glad - der songs o'er - flow, Flow'rs with deep - er beau - ties shine,
O, to lie for - ev - er here, Doubt and care and self re - sign,
Heav'n and earth may fade and flee, First - born light in gloom de - cline;
1
2
In a love which can - not cease, I am His, and He is mine. mine.
Since I know, as now I know, I am His, and He is mine. mine.
While He whis - pers in my ear, I am His, and He is mine. mine.
But while God and I shall be, I am His, and He is mine. mine.

TEXT: George W. Robinson
MUSIC: James Mountain

EVERLASTING LOVE
7.7.7.7.D.

PERFECT PEACE

A Brief Service in Recognition of His Provision

Suggested Hymn Stanzas

To facilitate an uninterrupted flow from stanza to stanza, the suggested stanzas have been marked with an arrow: ►
Thou Wilt Keep Him in Perfect Peace, complete
It Is Well with My Soul, stanzas 1, 3
Like a River Glorious, complete

WORSHIP LEADER: "These things I have spoken to you, that in Me you may have peace. In the world you have tribulation, but take courage; I have overcome the world."

PEOPLE: Therefore having been justified by faith, we have peace with God through our Lord Jesus Christ.

WORSHIP LEADER: And He came and preached peace to you who were far away, and peace to those who were near.

PEOPLE: Be anxious for nothing, but in everything by prayer and supplication with thanksgiving let your requests be made known to God. And the peace of God, which surpasses all comprehension, shall guard your hearts and your minds in Christ Jesus.

WORSHIP LEADER: Finally, brethren, whatever is true, whatever is honorable, whatever is right, whatever is pure, whatever is lovely, whatever is of good repute, if there is any excellence and if anything worthy of praise, let your mind dwell on these things. The things you have learned and received and heard and seen in me, practice these things; and the God of peace shall be with you.

PEOPLE: For it was the Father's good pleasure for all the fulness to dwell in Him, and through Him to reconcile all things to Himself, having made peace through the blood of His cross; through Him, I say, whether things on earth or things in heaven.

WORSHIP LEADER: And let the peace of Christ rule in your hearts, to which indeed you were called in one body; and be thankful.

John 16:33; Rom. 5:1; Eph. 2:17;
Phil. 4:6-9; Col. 1:19-20; 3:15. (NASB)

"PERFECT PEACE—A Brief Service in Recognition of His Provision"

492 Thou Wilt Keep Him in Perfect Peace

You will keep in perfect peace him whose mind is steadfast. Isa. 26:3

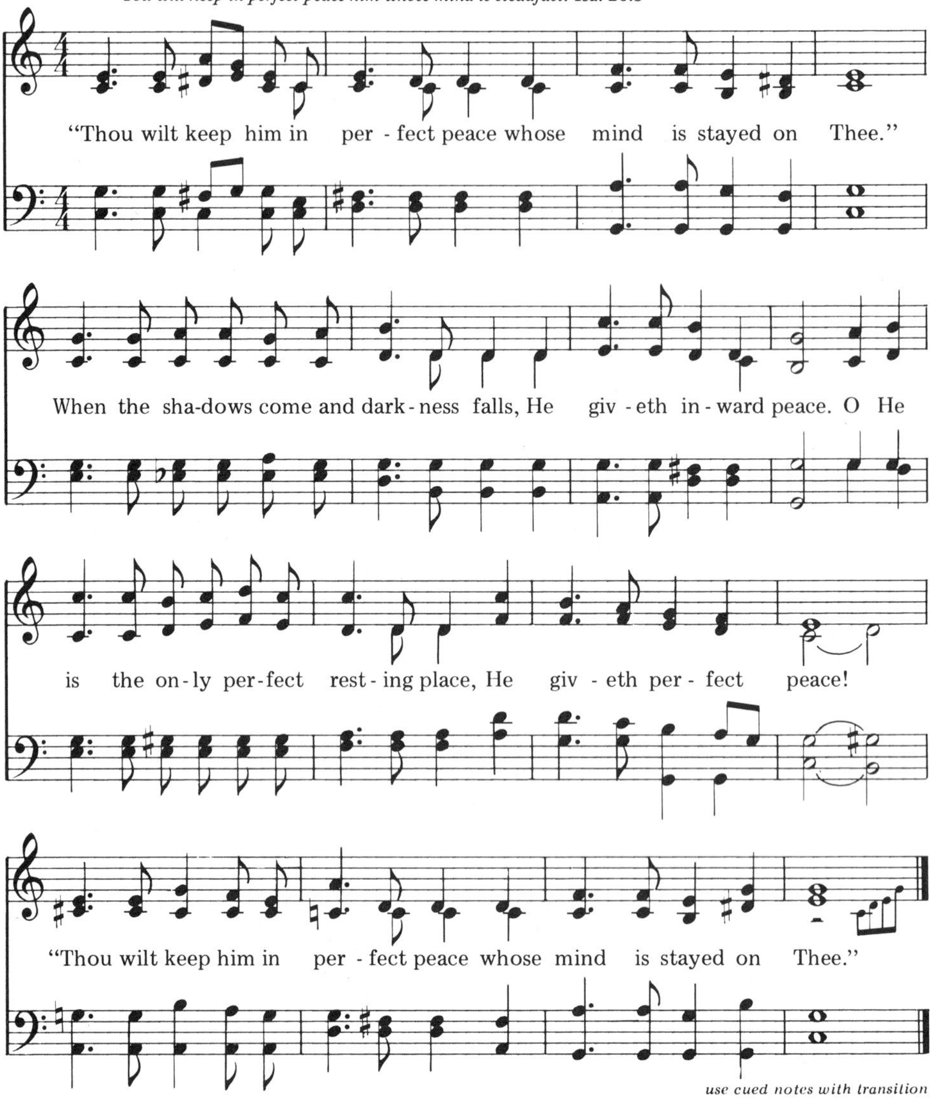
"Thou wilt keep him in per - fect peace whose mind is stayed on Thee."
When the sha-dows come and dark - ness falls, He giv - eth in - ward peace. O He
is the on - ly per - fect rest - ing place, He giv - eth per - fect peace!
"Thou wilt keep him in per - fect peace whose mind is stayed on Thee."

use cued notes with transition to "It Is Well with My Soul"

TEXT and MUSIC: Vivian Kretz; based on Isaiah 26:3

PERFECT PEACE
Irregular meter

Optional transition to "It Is Well with My Soul"

cresc.
decresc.

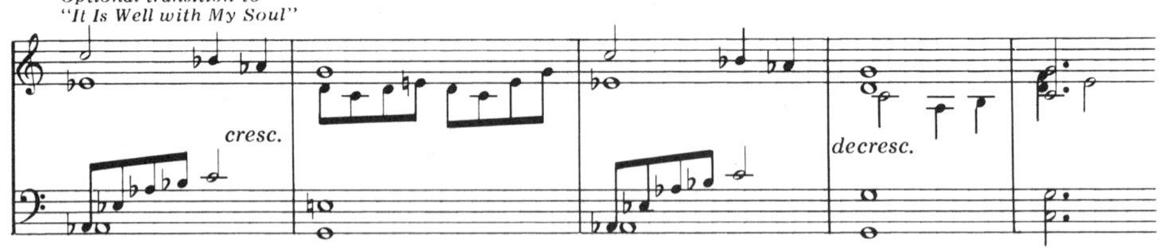

It Is Well with My Soul 493

Praise the Lord, O my soul, and forget not all His benefits. Ps. 103:2

1. When peace like a river attendeth my way,
When sorrows like sea billows roll;
Whatever my lot, Thou hast taught me to say,
"It is well, it is well with my soul."

2. Though Satan should buffet, tho' trials should come,
Let this blest assurance control,
That Christ has regarded my helpless estate,
And hath shed His own blood for my soul.

3. My sin— O, the bliss of this glorious thought,
My sin— not in part but the whole,
Is nailed to the cross and I bear it no more,
Praise the Lord, praise the Lord, O my soul!

4. And, Lord, haste the day when the faith shall be sight,
The clouds be rolled back as a scroll,
The trump shall resound and the Lord shall descend,
"Even so"— it is well with my soul.

Refrain

It is well with my soul, (It is well with my soul,)
It is well, it is well with my soul.

TEXT: Horatio G. Spafford
MUSIC: Philip P. Bliss

VILLE DU HAVRE
11.8.11.9. with Refrain

Optional transition to
"Like a River Glorious"
faster tempo

494 Like a River Glorious

. . . your peace would have been like a river. Isa. 48:18

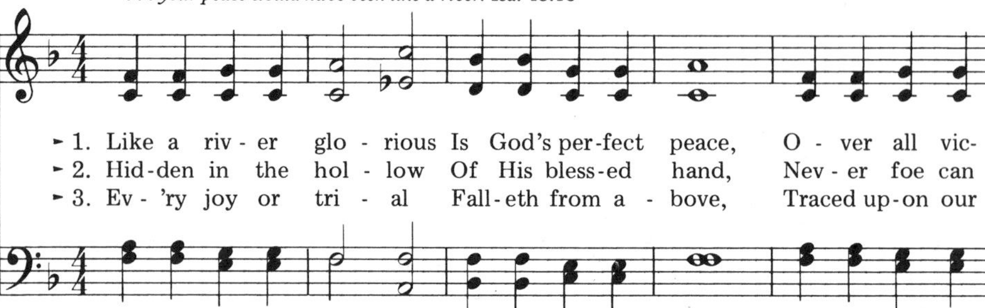
1. Like a riv - er glo - rious Is God's per-fect peace, O - ver all vic-
2. Hid-den in the hol - low Of His bless-ed hand, Nev - er foe can
3. Ev - 'ry joy or tri - al Fall-eth from a - bove, Traced up-on our

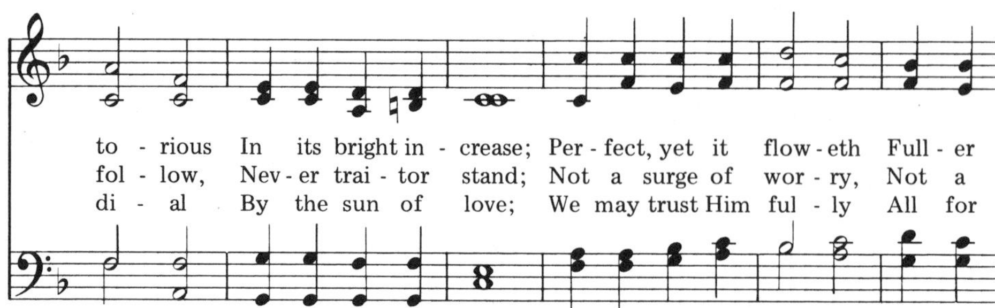
to - rious In its bright in - crease; Per - fect, yet it flow-eth Full - er
fol - low, Nev-er trai - tor stand; Not a surge of wor - ry, Not a
di - al By the sun of love; We may trust Him ful - ly All for

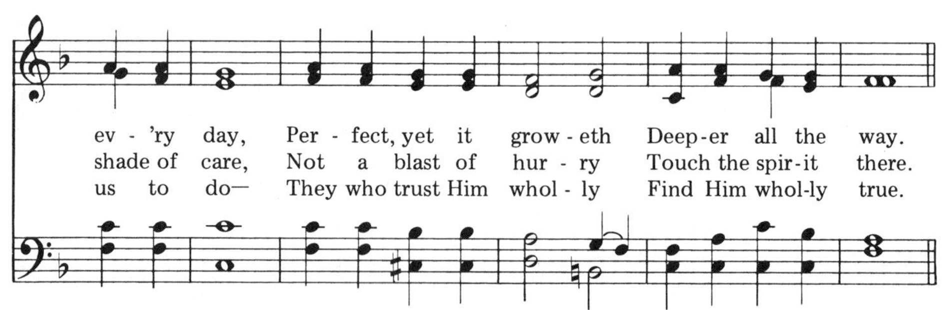
ev - 'ry day, Per - fect, yet it grow-eth Deep-er all the way.
shade of care, Not a blast of hur - ry Touch the spir-it there.
us to do— They who trust Him whol - ly Find Him whol-ly true.

TEXT: Frances Ridley Havergal
MUSIC: James Mountain; Descant and choral ending by James C. Gibson

WYE VALLEY
6.5.6.5.D. with Refrain

Descant
Stayed up - on Je - ho - vah, Hearts are ful - ly blest—
Refrain
Stayed up - on Je - ho - vah, Hearts are ful - ly blest—

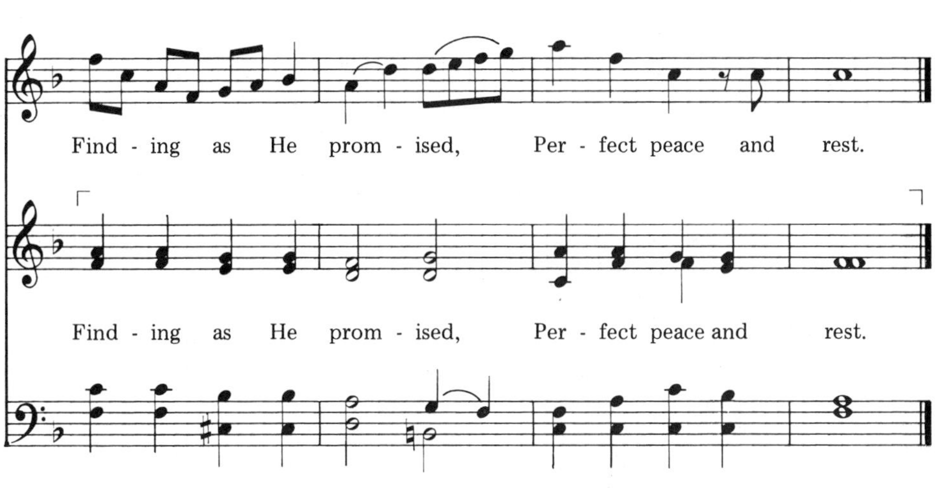
Find - ing as He prom - ised, Per - fect peace and rest.
Find - ing as He prom - ised, Per - fect peace and rest.

Optional choral ending
mf
rit. e dim.
Find-ing, as He prom-ised, Per - fect peace and rest.

The End of "PERFECT PEACE—A Brief Service in Recognition of His Provision"

495 Heaven Came Down

What counts is a new creation. Gal. 6:15

1. O what a won - der - ful, won - der - ful day— Day I will
2. Born of the Spir - it with life from a - bove In - to God's
3. Now I've a hope that will sure - ly en - dure Aft - er the
nev - er for - get; Aft - er I'd wan-dered in dark-ness a - way,
fam - ily di - vine, Jus - ti -fied ful - ly thro' Cal - va - ry's love,
pass - ing of time; I have a fu - ture in heav - en for sure,
Je - sus my Sav - ior I met. O what a ten - der, com-pas-sion-ate friend—
O what a stand-ing is mine! And the trans-ac-tion so quick - ly was made
There in those man-sions sub-lime. And it's be-cause of that won - der-ful day
He met the need of my heart; Shad - ows dis - pel - ling, With
When as a sin - ner I came, Took of the of - fer Of
When at the cross I be - lieved; Rich - es e - ter - nal And

TEXT and MUSIC: John W. Peterson

HEAVEN CAME DOWN
Irregular meter

joy I am tell - ing, He made all the dark-ness de - part!
grace He did prof - fer— He saved me, O praise His dear name!
bless-ings su - per - nal From His pre-cious hand I re - ceived.
Refrain
Heav - en came down and glo - ry filled my soul, (filled my soul,)
When at the cross the Sav-ior made me whole; (made me whole;) My
sins were washed a - way And my night was turned to day—
Heav - en came down and glo - ry filled my soul! (filled my soul!)

496 He Hideth My Soul

He will hide me . . . and set me high upon a rock. Ps. 27:5

1. A won - der-ful Sav - ior is Je - sus my Lord, A won - der-ful
2. A won - der-ful Sav - ior is Je - sus my Lord— He tak - eth my
3. With num-ber-less bless-ings each mo-ment He crowns, And, filled with His
4. When clothed in His brightness trans-port - ed I rise, To meet Him in
Sav - ior to me; He hid - eth my soul in the cleft of the
bur - den a - way; He hold - eth me up and I shall not be
full - ness di - vine, I sing in my rap - ture, "O glo - ry to
clouds of the sky, His per - fect sal - va - tion, His won - der-ful
rock, Where riv - ers of pleas-ure I see.
moved, He giv - eth me strength as my day.
God For such a Re - deem - er as mine!"
love, I'll shout with the mil - lions on high.
Refrain
He hid - eth my soul
in the cleft of the rock That shad-ows a dry, thirst-y land;
He hid - eth my life in the depths of His love, And cov - ers me

TEXT: Fanny J. Crosby
MUSIC: William J. Kirkpatrick

KIRKPATRICK
11.8.11.8. with Refrain

there with His hand, And cov - ers me there with His hand.

Near to the Heart of God 497

It is good to be near God. Ps. 73:28

1. There is a place of qui - et rest Near to the heart of God,
2. There is a place of com-fort sweet Near to the heart of God,
3. There is a place of full re - lease Near to the heart of God,

A place where sin can - not mo-lest, Near to the heart of God.
A place where we our Sav - ior meet, Near to the heart of God.
A place where all is joy and peace, Near to the heart of God.

Refrain

O Je - sus, blest Re - deem - er, Sent from the heart of God,

Hold us who wait be - fore Thee Near to the heart of God.

TEXT and MUSIC: Cleland B. McAfee

McAFEE
C.M. with Refrain

498 Peace Like a River

The peace of God . . . will guard your hearts and your minds in Christ Jesus. Phil. 4:7

TEXT and MUSIC: Traditional

PEACE LIKE A RIVER
7.7.10.D.

Sunshine in My Soul 499

God . . . made His light shine in our hearts. 2 Cor. 4:6

1. There is sun - shine in my soul to - day, More glo - ri - ous and bright
2. There is mu - sic in my soul to - day, A car - ol to my King,
3. There is spring-time in my soul to - day, For when the Lord is near
4. There is glad - ness in my soul to - day, And hope and love and praise,
Than glows in an - y earth - ly sky, For Je - sus is my light.
And Je - sus, lis - ten - ing can hear The songs I can - not sing.
The dove of peace sings in my heart, The flow'rs of grace ap - pear.
For bless - ings which He gives me now, For joys in fu - ture days.
Refrain
3
O there's sun - shine, bless - ed sun-shine, When the peace - ful, hap - py mo-ments
roll; When Je - sus shows His smil - ing face, There is sun-shine in my soul.

TEXT: Eliza E. Hewitt
MUSIC: John R. Sweney

SUNSHINE
9.6.8.6. with Refrain

500 Wonderful Peace

May the Lord of peace Himself give you peace at all times. 2 Thess. 3:16

1. Far a - way in the depths of my spir - it to - night Rolls a
2. What a treas - ure I have in this won - der - ful peace, Bur - ied
3. I am rest - ing to - night in this won - der - ful peace, Rest - ing
4. And I think when I rise to that Cit - y of peace, Where the
5. O my soul, are you here with - out com - fort or rest, March-ing
mel - o - dy sweet - er than psalm; In ce - les - tial - like strains it un -
deep in the heart of my soul; So se - cure that no pow - er can
sweet - ly in Je - sus' con - trol; For I'm kept from all dan - ger by
Au - thor of peace I shall see, That one strain of the song which the
down the rough path-way of time? Make the Sav- ior your friend when the
Refrain
ceas - ing - ly falls O'er my soul like an in - fi - nite calm.
mine it a - way, While the years of e - ter - ni - ty roll.
night and by day, And His glo - ry is flood-ing my soul. Peace! peace!
ran-somed will sing, In that heav - en - ly king-dom shall be:
shad-ows grow dark; Oh, ac - cept this sweet peace so sub - lime.
won-der-ful peace, Com-ing down from the Fa-ther a - bove; Sweep o - ver my

TEXT: W. D. Cornell, altered
MUSIC: W. G. Cooper

WONDERFUL PEACE
12.9.12.9. with Refrain

spir - it for - ev - er, I pray, In fath-om -less bil - lows of love.

Jesus, Thou Joy of Loving Hearts 501

I have told you this so that My joy may be in you. John 15:11

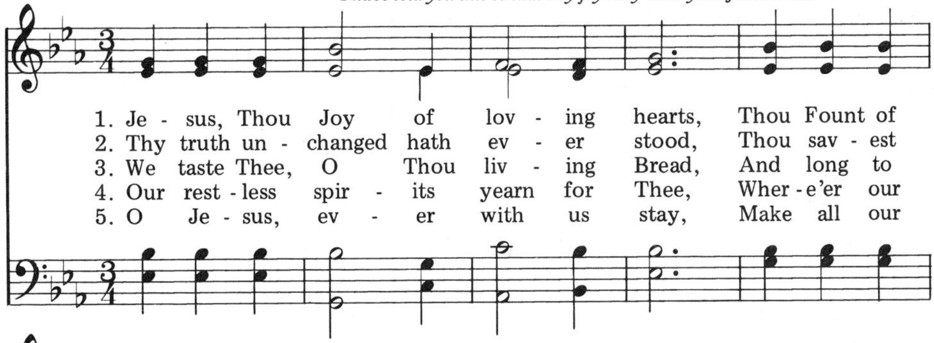

1. Je - sus, Thou Joy of lov - ing hearts, Thou Fount of
2. Thy truth un - changed hath ev - er stood, Thou sav - est
3. We taste Thee, O Thou liv - ing Bread, And long to
4. Our rest - less spir - its yearn for Thee, Wher - e'er our
5. O Je - sus, ev - er with us stay, Make all our

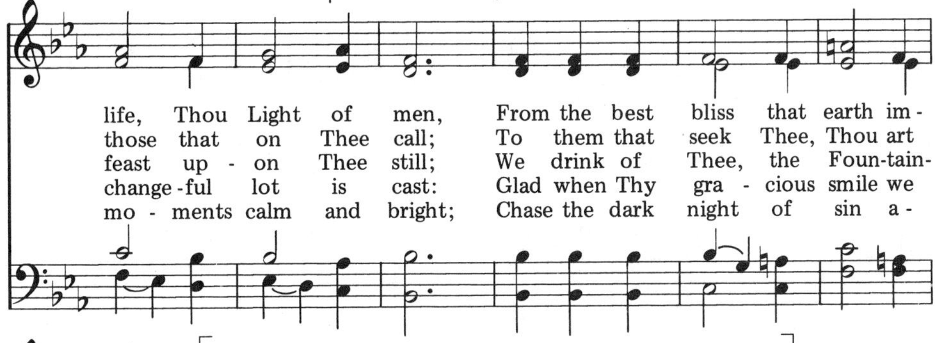

life, Thou Light of men, From the best bliss that earth im -
those that on Thee call; To them that seek Thee, Thou art
feast up - on Thee still; We drink of Thee, the Foun-tain-
change - ful lot is cast: Glad when Thy gra - cious smile we
mo - ments calm and bright; Chase the dark night of sin a -

parts, We turn un - filled to Thee a - gain.
good, To them that find Thee, all in all.
head, And thirst our souls from Thee to fill.
see, Blest when our faith can hold Thee fast.
way, Shed o'er the world Thy ho - ly light. A - men.

TEXT: Attributed to Bernard of Clairvaux; translated by Ray Palmer
MUSIC: Henry Baker

QUEBEC
L.M.

502 In Heavenly Love Abiding

If you obey My commands, you will remain in My love. John 15:10

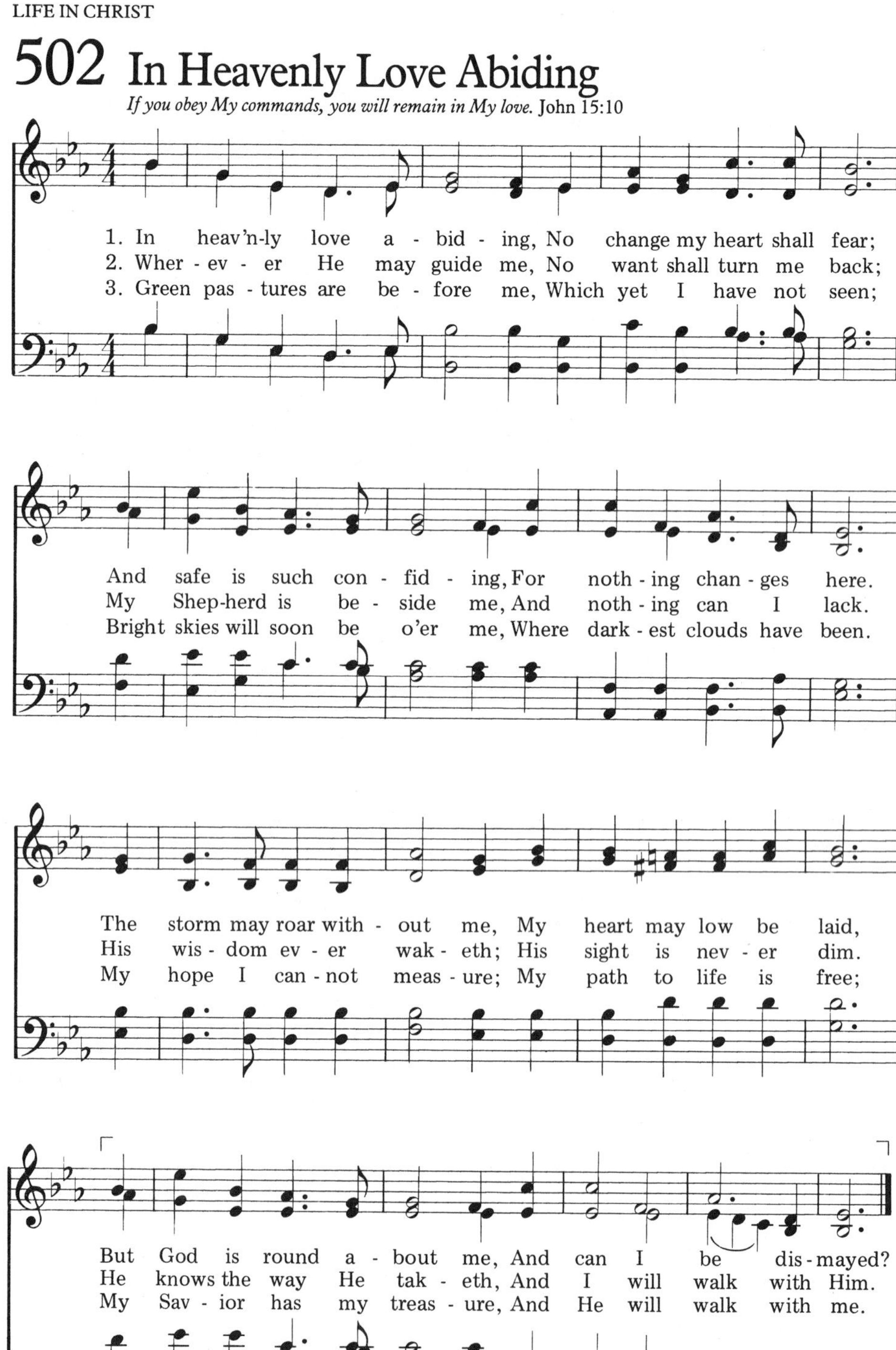
1. In heav'n-ly love a - bid - ing, No change my heart shall fear;
2. Wher - ev - er He may guide me, No want shall turn me back;
3. Green pas - tures are be - fore me, Which yet I have not seen;
And safe is such con - fid - ing, For noth - ing chan - ges here.
My Shep-herd is be - side me, And noth - ing can I lack.
Bright skies will soon be o'er me, Where dark - est clouds have been.
The storm may roar with - out me, My heart may low be laid,
His wis - dom ev - er wak - eth; His sight is nev - er dim.
My hope I can - not meas - ure; My path to life is free;
But God is round a - bout me, And can I be dis - mayed?
He knows the way He tak - eth, And I will walk with Him.
My Sav - ior has my treas - ure, And He will walk with me.

TEXT: Anna L. Waring
MUSIC: Felix Mendelssohn

SEASONS
7.6.7.6.D.

Jesus, I Am Resting, Resting 503

There remains, then, a Sabbath-rest for the people of God. Heb. 4:9

1. Je - sus, I am rest - ing, rest - ing In the joy of what Thou art;
2. O, how great Thy lov - ing kind - ness, Vast - er, broad-er than the sea!
3. Sim - ply trust - ing Thee, Lord Je - sus, I be-hold Thee as Thou art,
4. Ev - er lift Thy face up - on me As I work and wait for Thee;
(Ref.) Je - sus, I am rest - ing, rest - ing In the joy of what Thou art;
I am find - ing out the great - ness Of Thy lov - ing heart.
O, how mar - vel - ous Thy good - ness, Lav - ished all on me!
And Thy love, so pure, so change-less, Sat - is - fies my heart;
Rest - ing 'neath Thy smile, Lord Je - sus, Earth's dark shad - ows flee.
I am find - ing out the great - ness Of Thy lov - ing heart.
Fine
Thou hast bid me gaze up - on Thee, And Thy beau-ty fills my soul,
Yes, I rest in Thee, Be - lov - ed, Know what wealth of grace is Thine,
Sat - is - fies its deep-est long-ings, Meets, sup-plies its ev - ery need,
Bright-ness of my Fa - ther's glo - ry, Sun - shine of my Fa - ther's face,
D.C. for Refrain
For by Thy trans - form - ing pow - er, Thou hast made me whole.
Know Thy cer - tain - ty of prom - ise, And have made it mine.
Com - pass-eth me round with bless - ings: Thine is love in - deed!
Keep me ev - er trust - ing, rest - ing, Fill me with Thy grace.

TEXT: Jean S. Pigott
MUSIC: James Mountain

TRANQUILITY
8.7.8.5.D. with Refrain

504 He Touched Me

Jesus . . . touched the man. "I am willing," He said. "Be clean!" Matt. 8:3

1. Shack - led by a heav - y bur - den, 'Neath a load of guilt and shame; Then the hand of Je - sus touched me, And now I am no long - er the same.
2. Since I met this bless - ed Sav - ior, Since He cleansed and made me whole; I will nev - er cease to praise Him, I'll shout it while e - ter - ni - ty rolls.
Refrain
He touched me, O, He touched me, And O, the joy that floods my soul; Some-thing hap-pened, and now I know, He touched me and made me whole.

TEXT and MUSIC: William J. Gaither

HE TOUCHED ME
Irregular meter

Love Lifted Me 505

He loved us and sent His Son as an atoning sacrifice for our sins. 1 John 4:10

1. I was sink-ing deep in sin, Far from the peace-ful shore, Ver - y deep-ly
2. All my heart to Him I give, Ev - er to Him I'll cling, In His bless-ed
3. Souls in dan-ger, look a-bove, Je - sus com-plete - ly saves; He will lift you
stained with-in, Sink-ing to rise no more; But the Mas - ter of the sea
pres - ence live, Ev - er His prais - es sing; Love so might - y and so true
by His love Out of the an - gry waves; He's the Mas - ter of the sea,
Heard my de-spair - ing cry, From the wa-ters lift - ed me, Now safe am I.
Mer - its my soul's best songs; Faith-ful, lov-ing ser-vice, too, To Him be - longs.
Bil - lows His will o - bey; He your Sav-ior wants to be, Be saved to - day.
Refrain
Love lift - ed me! Love lift - ed me! When noth - ing
e - ven me! e - ven me!
else could help, Love lift - ed me. Love lift - ed me.
1
2

TEXT: James Rowe
MUSIC: Howard E. Smith

SAFETY
7.6.7.6.7.6.7.4. with Refrain

506 I Will Sing of My Redeemer

In Him we have redemption through His blood. Eph. 1:7

1. I will sing of my Re-deem-er And His won-drous love to me;
2. I will tell the won-drous sto-ry, How, my lost es-tate to save,
3. I will praise my dear Re-deem-er, His tri-um-phant pow'r I'll tell,
4. I will sing of my Re-deem-er And His heav'n-ly love to me;
On the cru-el cross He suf-fered, From the curse to set me free.
In His bound-less love and mer-cy, He the ran-som free-ly gave.
How the vic-to-ry He giv-eth O-ver sin and death and hell.
He from death to life hath bro't me, Son of God with Him to be.
Refrain
Sing, O sing of my Re-deem-er,
of my Re-deem-er, Sing, O sing of my Re-deem-er,
With His blood He pur-chased me;
He pur-chased me, With His blood, He pur-chased me;

TEXT: Philip P. Bliss
MUSIC: James McGranahan
Alternate tune: HYFRYDOL at No. 89

MY REDEEMER
8.7.8.7. with Refrain

On the cross He sealed my par - don,
He sealed my par-don, On the cross He sealed my par-don,
Paid the debt and made me free.
and made me free, and made me free.

Through It All 507

Trials . . . have come so that your faith . . . may be proved genuine. 1 Pet. 1:6-7

Through it all, Through it all, I've learned to trust in Je - sus, I've learned to trust in God; Through it all, Through it all, I've learned to de - pend up - on His Word.

TEXT and MUSIC: Andraé Crouch

THROUGH IT ALL
Irregular meter

508 I Will Sing the Wondrous Story

They . . . sang the song . . . of the Lamb: "Great and marvelous are Your deeds." Rev. 15:2-3

1. I will sing the won-drous sto - ry Of the Christ who died for me—
2. I was lost but Je - sus found me—Found the sheep that went a - stray,
3. Days of dark - ness still come o'er me, Sor - row's paths I of - ten tread;
4. He will keep me till the riv - er Rolls its wa - ters at my feet;
How He left His home in glo - ry For the cross of Cal - va - ry.
Threw His lov - ing arms a - round me, Drew me back in - to His way.
But the Sav - ior still is with me—By His hand I'm safe - ly led.
Then He'll bear me safe - ly o - ver, Where the loved ones I shall meet.
Refrain
Yes, I'll sing the won-drous sto - ry Of the Christ who died for me,
Sing it with the saints in glo - ry, Gath-ered by the crys-tal sea.

TEXT: Francis H. Rowley
MUSIC: Peter P. Bilhorn
Alternate tune: HYFRYDOL at No. 89

WONDROUS STORY
8.7.8.7. with Refrain

MY LIFE, MY JOY, MY ALL

A Brief Service of Testimony and Praise

Suggested Hymn Stanzas

To facilitate an uninterrupted flow from stanza to stanza,
the suggested stanzas have been marked with an arrow: ►
Jesus Is All the World to Me, stanza 1
Now I Belong to Jesus, stanzas 1, 3
My Savior's Love, stanzas 1, 4
O, How He Loves You and Me, complete

WORSHIP LEADER:
I will proclaim the name of the Lord. Oh, praise the greatness of our God!

PEOPLE:
He is the Rock, His works are perfect, and all His ways are just. A faithful God who does no wrong, upright and just is He.

WORSHIP LEADER:
The Lord lives! Praise be to my Rock! Exalted be God, the Rock, my Savior! I will praise you, O Lord. Although you were angry with me, your anger has turned away and you have comforted me.

PEOPLE:
Surely God is my salvation; I will trust and not be afraid. The Lord, the Lord, is my strength and my song; He has become my salvation. With joy you will draw water from the wells of salvation.

WORSHIP LEADER:
Praise be to the God and Father of our Lord Jesus Christ! In His great mercy He has given us new birth into a living hope through the resurrection of Jesus Christ from the dead, and into an inheritance that can never perish, spoil or fade—kept in heaven for you, who through faith are shielded by God's power until the coming of the salvation that is ready to be revealed in the last time.

Deut. 32:3-4; 2 Sam. 22:47;
Isa. 12:1-3; 1 Pet. 1:3-5. (NIV)

"MY LIFE, MY JOY, MY ALL—A Brief Service of Testimony and Praise"

510 Jesus Is All the World to Me

To me, to live is Christ. Phil. 1:21

1. Je - sus is all the world to me, My life, my joy, my all;
2. Je - sus is all the world to me, My Friend in tri - als sore;
3. Je - sus is all the world to me, And true to Him I'll be;
4. Je - sus is all the world to me, I want no bet - ter friend;
He is my strength from day to day, With - out Him I would fall.
I go to Him for bless-ings, and He gives them o'er and o'er.
O, how could I this Friend de - ny, When He's so true to me?
I trust Him now, I'll trust Him when Life's fleet - ing days shall end.
When I am sad to Him I go, No oth - er one can cheer me so;
He sends the sun - shine and the rain, He sends the har - vest's gold - en grain;
Fol - low - ing Him I know I'm right, He watch - es o'er me day and night;
Beau - ti - ful life with such a Friend; Beau - ti - ful life that has no end;
When I am sad He makes me glad, He's my Friend.
Sun - shine and rain, har - vest of grain, He's my Friend.
Fol - low - ing Him by day and night, He's my Friend.
E - ter - nal life, e - ter - nal joy, He's my Friend.
Opt. segue to "Now I Belong to Jesus"

TEXT and MUSIC: Will L. Thompson

ELIZABETH
Irregular meter

Now I Belong to Jesus 511

Whether we live or die, we belong to the Lord. Rom. 14:8

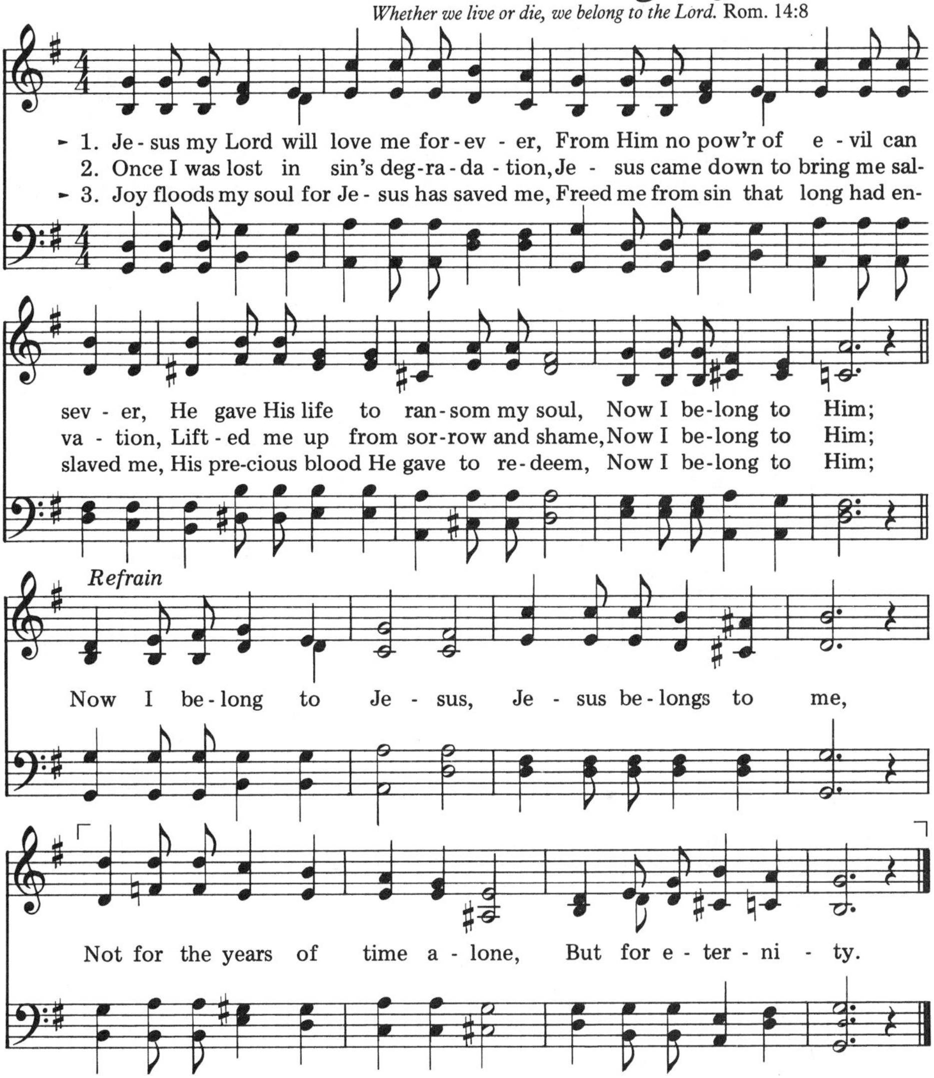

1. Jesus my Lord will love me forever, From Him no pow'r of evil can sever, He gave His life to ransom my soul, Now I belong to Him;
2. Once I was lost in sin's degradation, Jesus came down to bring me salvation, Lifted me up from sorrow and shame, Now I belong to Him;
3. Joy floods my soul for Jesus has saved me, Freed me from sin that long had enslaved me, His precious blood He gave to redeem, Now I belong to Him;

Refrain

Now I belong to Jesus, Jesus belongs to me,
Not for the years of time alone, But for eternity.

TEXT and MUSIC: Norman J. Clayton

ELLSWORTH
10.10.9.6. with Refrain

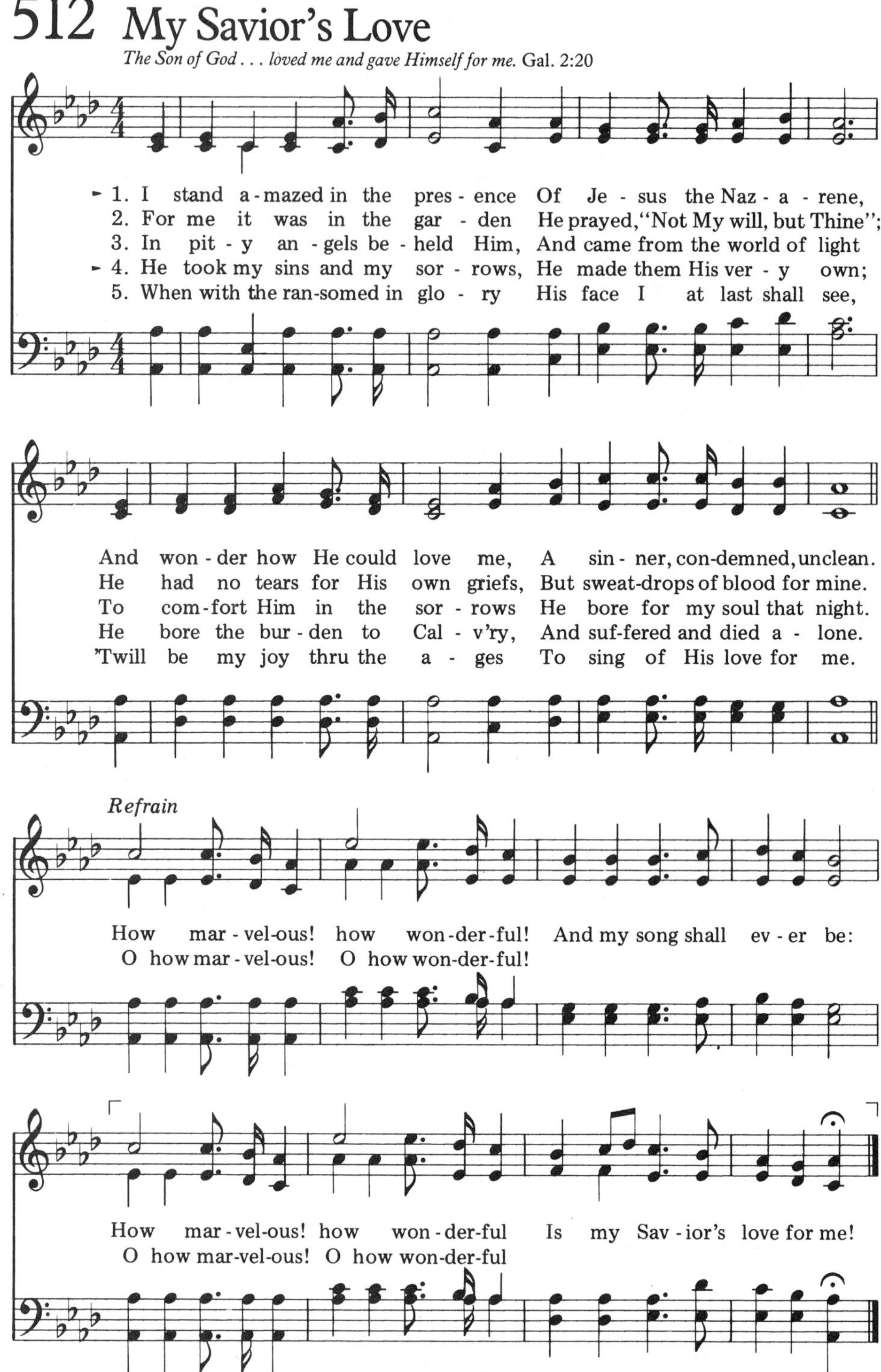
512 My Savior's Love
The Son of God . . . loved me and gave Himself for me. Gal. 2:20
1. I stand a-mazed in the pres-ence Of Je-sus the Naz-a-rene,
2. For me it was in the gar-den He prayed, "Not My will, but Thine";
3. In pit-y an-gels be-held Him, And came from the world of light
4. He took my sins and my sor-rows, He made them His ver-y own;
5. When with the ran-somed in glo-ry His face I at last shall see,
And won-der how He could love me, A sin-ner, con-demned, unclean.
He had no tears for His own griefs, But sweat-drops of blood for mine.
To com-fort Him in the sor-rows He bore for my soul that night.
He bore the bur-den to Cal-v'ry, And suf-fered and died a-lone.
'Twill be my joy thru the a-ges To sing of His love for me.
Refrain
How mar-vel-ous! how won-der-ful! And my song shall ev-er be:
O how mar-vel-ous! O how won-der-ful!
How mar-vel-ous! how won-der-ful Is my Sav-ior's love for me!
O how mar-vel-ous! O how won-der-ful

TEXT and MUSIC: Charles H. Gabriel

MY SAVIOR'S LOVE
8.7.8.7. with Refrain

O, How He Loves You and Me 513

As the Father has loved Me, so have I loved you. John 15:9

Optional transition to
"O, How He Loves You and Me"
mp
1. O, how He loves you and me. O, how He loves you and me; He gave His life, what more could He give? O, how He loves you; O, how He loves me; O, how He loves you and me!
2. Je-sus to Cal-v'ry did go, His love for man-kind to show; What He did there brought hope from de-spair: O, how He loves you; O, how He loves me; O, how He loves you and me!
Optional choral ending - a cappella preferred
very rubato
1. O, how He loves you;
2. O, how He loves me;
O, how He loves you and me, you and me.
me.
me.

TEXT and MUSIC: Kurt Kaiser

PATRICIA
Irregular meter

The end of "MY LIFE, MY JOY, MY ALL—A Brief Service of Testimony and Praise"

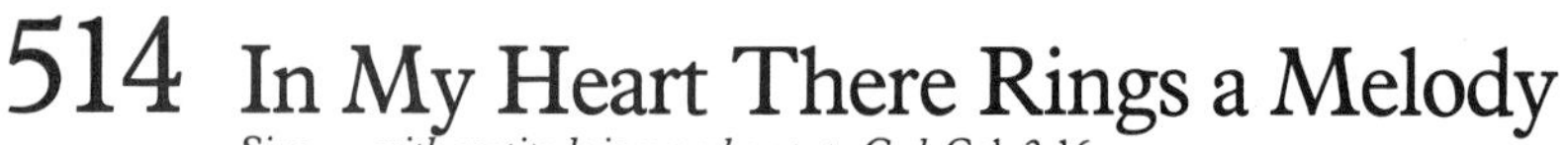

514 In My Heart There Rings a Melody

Sing . . . with gratitude in your hearts to God. Col. 3:16

1. I have a song that Jesus gave me,
It was sent from heav'n above;
There never was a sweeter melody,
'Tis a melody of love.

2. I love the Christ who died on Cal-v'ry,
For He washed my sins away;
He put within my heart a melody,
And I know it's there to stay.

3. 'Twill be my endless theme in glory,
With the angels I will sing;
'Twill be a song with glorious harmony,
When the courts of heaven ring.

Refrain

In my heart there rings a melody,
There rings a melody with heaven's harmony;
In my heart there rings a melody,
There rings a melody of love.

TEXT and MUSIC: Elton M. Roth

HEART MELODY
Irregular meter

Since Jesus Came into My Heart 515

If anyone is in Christ, he is a new creation. 2 Cor. 5:17

1. What a won-der-ful change in my life has been wrought Since Je-sus came in-to my heart! I have light in my soul for which long I have sought, Since Je-sus came in-to my heart!
2. I have ceased from my wan-d'ring and go - ing a-stray, Since Je-sus came in-to my heart! And my sins, which were man-y, are all washed a-way,
3. I shall go there to dwell in that Cit - y, I know, Since Je-sus came in-to my heart! And I'm hap-py, so hap-py, as on-ward I go,
Refrain
Since Je-sus came in-to my heart, Since Je-sus came in-to my heart, Floods of joy o'er my soul like the sea bil-lows roll, Since Je-sus came in-to my heart.

TEXT: Rufus H. McDaniel
MUSIC: Charles H. Gabriel

McDANIEL
12.8.12.8. with Refrain

516 He's Everything to Me

When I consider Your heavens, . . . what is man that You are mindful of him? Ps. 8:3-4

In the stars His hand-i - work I see, On the wind He speaks with
maj - es - ty, Tho He rul - eth o - ver land and sea, What is
that to me? I will cel - e - brate Na - tiv - i - ty, for it
has a place in his - to - ry; Sure, He came to set His peo - ple free—
What is that to me? Till by faith I met Him face to face

TEXT and MUSIC: Ralph Carmichael

WOODLAND HILLS
Irregular meter

And I felt the won-der of His grace— Then I knew that
He was more than just a God who did-n't care, That lived a - way out
there And now He walks be - side me day by day, Ev - er
watch-ing o'er me lest I stray, Help-ing me to find that nar - row way—
1
He's ev - 'ry-thing to me.
2
He's ev - 'ry - thing to me.

517 I'd Rather Have Jesus

I consider everything a loss compared to the surpassing greatness of knowing Christ. Phil. 3:8

1. I'd rath - er have Je - sus than sil - ver or gold; I'd rath - er be His than have rich - es un - told; I'd rath - er have Je - sus than hous - es or lands. I'd rath - er be led by His nail-pierced hand
2. I'd rath - er have Je - sus than men's ap - plause; I'd rath - er be faith - ful to His dear cause; I'd rath - er have Je - sus than world-wide fame. I'd rath - er be true to His ho - ly name
3. He's fair - er than lil - ies of rar - est bloom; He's sweet-er than hon - ey from out the comb; He's all that my hun - ger - ing spir - it needs. I'd rath - er have Je - sus and let Him lead
(small notes, last stanza)
Refrain
Than to be the king of a vast do - main Or be held in sin's dread sway.
I'd rath - er have Je - sus than an - y - thing This world af - fords to - day.

TEXT: Rhea F. Miller
MUSIC: George Beverly Shea

I'D RATHER HAVE JESUS
Irregular meter

The Longer I Serve Him 518

God . . . I serve with my whole heart in preaching the gospel of His Son. Rom. 1:9

1. Since I start-ed for the King-dom, Since my life He con-trols,
Since I gave my heart to Je-sus, The long-er I serve Him, the sweet-er He grows.

2. Ev-ery need He is sup-ply-ing, Plen-teous grace He be-stows;
Ev-ery day my way gets bright-er, The long-er I serve Him, the sweet-er He grows.

Refrain

The long-er I serve Him the sweet-er He grows,
The more that I love Him, more love He be-stows;
Each day is like heav-en, my heart o-ver-flows,
The long-er I serve Him the sweet-er He grows.

TEXT and MUSIC: William J. Gaither

THE SWEETER HE GROWS
8.6.8.11. with Refrain

519 Something Beautiful

This son of mine was dead and is alive again; he was lost and is found. Luke 15:24

Some-thing beau-ti-ful, some-thing good; All my con - fu - sion He un-der - stood; All I had to of - fer Him was bro-ken - ness and strife, But He made some - thing beau-ti - ful of my life.

TEXT: Gloria Gaither
MUSIC: William J. Gaither

SOMETHING BEAUTIFUL
Irregular meter

520 Redeemed

You were redeemed . . . with the precious blood of Christ, a lamb. 1 Pet. 1:18-19

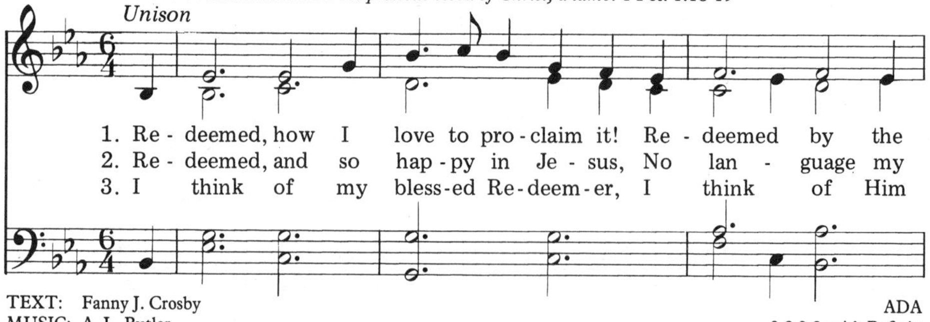
Unison
1. Re - deemed, how I love to pro - claim it! Re - deemed by the
2. Re - deemed, and so hap - py in Je - sus, No lan - guage my
3. I think of my bless-ed Re-deem-er, I think of Him

TEXT: Fanny J. Crosby
MUSIC: A. L. Butler
This tune and *Redeemed* by Kirkpatrick, No. 521, may be sung as a medley

ADA
9.8.9.8. with Refrain

blood of the Lamb; Re - deemed thro' His in - fi - nite mer - cy, His
rap - ture can tell; I know that the light of His pres-ence With
all the day long; I sing, for I can - not be si - lent; His
Refrain— Sing Parts
child, and for - ev - er, I am.
me doth con - tin - ual - ly dwell. Re - deemed, re -
love is the theme of my song.
Unison
deemed, Re - deemed by the blood of the Lamb; Re -
deemed, thro' His in - fi - nite mer - cy, His child and for - ev - er, I
Optional transition to last verse of "Redeemed"—
by Kirkpatrick found on next page
am. am.
slight accel.

521 Redeemed

You were redeemed . . . with the precious blood of Christ, a lamb. 1 Pet. 1:18-19

1. Re-deemed, how I love to pro-claim it! Re-deemed by the blood of the Lamb;
2. Re-deemed and so hap-py in Je - sus, No lan-guage my rap-ture can tell;
3. I think of my bless-ed Re-deem - er, I think of Him all the day long;
4. I know I shall see in His beau - ty The King in whose law I de - light;
Re-deemed through His in-fi-nite mer - cy, His child, and for-ev - er I am.
I know that the light of His pres-ence With me doth con-tin-ual-ly dwell.
I sing, for I can-not be si - lent; His love is the theme of my song.
Who lov - ing - ly guard-eth my foot-steps, And giv-eth me songs in the night.
Refrain
Re - deemed, re - deemed, Re - deemed by the blood of the Lamb;
re-deemed, re-deemed,
Re - deemed, re - deemed, His child, and for-ev - er, I am.
re-deemed, re-deemed,

TEXT: Fanny J. Crosby
MUSIC: William J. Kirkpatrick

REDEEMED
9.8.9.8. with Refrain

He Lifted Me 522

He lifted me out of the slimy pit . . . He set my feet on a rock. Ps. 40:2

1. In lov - ing kind - ness Je - sus came My soul in mer - cy to re-claim,
2. He called me long be - fore I heard, Be - fore my sin - ful heart was stirred,
3. His brow was pierced with man-y a thorn, His hands by cru - el nails were torn,
4. Now on a high - er plane I dwell, And with my soul I know 'tis well;

And from the depths of sin and shame Thro' grace He lift - ed me.
But when I took Him at His word, For - giv'n He lift - ed me.
When from my guilt and grief, for-lorn, In love He lift - ed me.
Yet how or why, I can - not tell, He should have lift - ed me.
(He lift-ed me.)

Refrain

From sink - ing sand He lift - ed me, With ten - der hand He lift - ed me,

From shades of night to plains of light, O praise His name, He lift - ed me!

TEXT and MUSIC: Charles H. Gabriel

HE LIFTED ME
8.8.8.6. with Refrain

523 Yesterday, Today and Tomorrow

Christ died for our sins . . . He was raised . . . according to the Scriptures. 1 Cor. 15:3-4

Unison or 2-part
Introduction
p
Yes-ter-day He died for me, yes-ter-day,
yes-ter-day, Yes-ter-day He died for me, yes-ter-day, Yes-ter-day He
died for me, died for me— This is his-to - ry.
mp
To-day He lives for me,
to-day, to-day, To-day He lives for me, to-day, To-day He
lives for me, lives for me— This is vic-to - ry.
mf
3
To-mor-row He

TEXT: Jack Wyrtzen
MUSIC: Don Wyrtzen

YESTERDAY, TODAY AND TOMORROW
Irregular meter

comes for me,
He comes,
He comes,
To-mor-row He comes for me,
He comes, Tomorrow He comes for me, comes for me—This is mys-ter - y.
f
O friend, do you know Him?
know Him?
know Him?
O friend, do
you know Him? know Him?
O friend, do you know Him? do you know Him? Je-sus
Christ the Lord,
Je-sus Christ the Lord,
Je - sus Christ the Lord!

524 It Took a Miracle

The grace of God that brings salvation has appeared to all. Titus 2:11

1. My Fa - ther is om - ni - po - tent, And that you can't de - ny;
2. Tho here His glo - ry has been shown, We still can't ful - ly see
3. The Bi - ble tells us of His pow'r And wis - dom all way thru,
A God of might and mir - a - cles— 'Tis writ - ten in the sky.
The won - ders of His might, His throne— 'Twill take e - ter - ni - ty.
And ev - 'ry lit - tle bird and flow'r Are tes - ti - mo - nies too.
Refrain
It took a mir - a - cle to put the stars in place, It took a
mir - a - cle to hang the world in space; But when He saved my soul,
Cleansed and made me whole, It took a mir - a - cle of love and grace.

TEXT and MUSIC: John W. Peterson

MONTROSE
C.M. with Refrain

I Will Praise Him 525

To Him who . . . has freed us from our sins by His blood. Rev. 1:5

1. When I saw the cleans-ing foun-tain, O-pen wide for all my sin,
2. Tho' the way seems straight and nar-row, All I claimed was swept a-way;
3. Bless-ed be the name of Je-sus! I'm so glad He took me in;
4. Glo-ry, glo-ry to the Fa-ther! Glo-ry, glo-ry to the Son!
I o-beyed the Spir-it's woo-ing When He said, "Wilt thou be clean?"
My am-bi-tions, plans and wish-es At my feet in ash-es lay.
He's for-giv-en my trans-gres-sions, He has cleansed my heart from sin.
Glo-ry, glo-ry to the Spir-it! Glo-ry to the Three in One!
Refrain
I will praise Him! I will praise Him! Praise the Lamb for sin-ners slain;
Give Him glo-ry, all ye peo-ple, For His blood can wash a-way each stain.

TEXT and MUSIC: Margaret J. Harris

I WILL PRAISE HIM
8.7.8.7. with Refrain

526 All That Thrills My Soul

Christ is all, and is in all. Col. 3:11

1. Who can cheer the heart like Je - sus, By His pres-ence all di - vine?
2. Love of Christ so free - ly giv - en, Grace of God be - yond de - gree,
3. What a won - der - ful re - demp-tion! Nev - er can a mor - tal know
4. Ev - 'ry need His hand sup - ply - ing, Ev - 'ry good in Him I see;
5. By the crys - tal flow - ing riv - er With the ran-somed I will sing,
True and ten - der, pure and pre - cious, O how blest to call Him mine!
Mer - cy high - er than the heav - en, Deep - er than the deep-est sea!
How my sin, tho red like crim - son, Can be whit - er than the snow.
On His strength di - vine re - ly - ing, He is all in all to me.
And for - ev - er and for - ev - er Praise and glo - ri - fy the King.
Refrain
All that thrills my soul is Je - sus, He is more than life to me;
to me;
And the fair - est of ten thou - sand In my bless-ed Lord I see.

TEXT and MUSIC: Thoro Harris

HARRIS
8.7.8.7.D.

Glory to His Name 527

Without the shedding of blood there is no forgiveness. Heb. 9:22

1. Down at the cross where my Sav - ior died, Down where for cleans-ing from sin I cried, There to my heart was the blood ap-plied; Glo-ry to His name!
2. I am so won - drous-ly saved from sin, Je - sus so sweet - ly a - bides with-in, There at the cross where He took me in; Glo-ry to His name!
3. O pre-cious foun-tain that saves from sin, I am so glad I have en - tered in; There Je - sus saves me and keeps me clean; Glo-ry to His name!
4. Come to this foun - tain so rich and sweet; Cast your poor soul at the Sav-ior's feet; Plunge in to - day and be made com-plete; Glo-ry to His name!

Refrain

Glo - ry to His name, Glo - ry to His name; There to my heart was the blood ap - plied; Glo - ry to His name!

TEXT: Elisha A. Hoffman
MUSIC: John H. Stockton

GLORY TO HIS NAME
9.9.9.5. with Refrain

528 No One Ever Cared for Me Like Jesus

What is man that You care for him . . . ? Ps. 144:3

1. I would love to tell you what I think of Je - sus
2. All my life was full of sin when Je - sus found me,
3. Ev - 'ry day He comes to me with new as - sur - ance,
Since I found in Him a friend so strong and true; I would
All my heart was full of mis - er - y and woe; Je - sus
More and more I un - der - stand His words of love; But I'll
tell you how He chang'd my life com - plete - ly— He did some-thing
placed His strong and lov - ing arms a - round me, And He led me
nev - er know just why He came to save me, Till some day I
that no oth - er friend could do.
in the way I ought to go.
see His bless-ed face a - bove.
Refrain
No one ev - er cared for me like
Je - sus, There's no oth-er friend so kind as He; No one else could

TEXT and MUSIC: Charles F. Weigle

WEIGLE
12.11.12.11. with Refrain

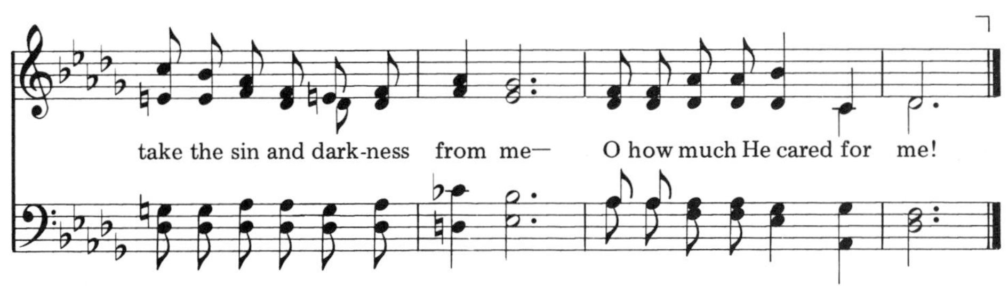
take the sin and dark-ness from me— O how much He cared for me!

O, How I Love Jesus 529

Though you have not seen Him, you love Him. 1 Pet. 1:8

1. There is a name I love to hear, I love to sing its worth;
It sounds like mu - sic in my ear, The sweet - est name on earth.

2. It tells me of a Sav - ior's love, who died to set me free;
It tells me of His pre - cious blood, The sin - ner's per - fect plea.

3. It tells me what my Fa - ther hath In store for ev - 'ry day,
And, tho I tread a dark-some path, Yields sun - shine all the way.

4. It tells of One whose lov - ing heart Can feel my deep - est woe,
Who in each sor - row bears a part That none can bear be - low.

Refrain

O, how I love Je - sus, O, how I love Je - sus,
O, how I love Je - sus— Be - cause He first loved me!

TEXT: Frederick Whitfield
MUSIC: Traditional American melody

O, HOW I LOVE JESUS
C.M. with Refrain

530 Saved, Saved!

He saved us . . . because of His mercy. Titus 3:5

Unison
1. I've found a Friend who is all to me, His love is ev - er true; I love to tell how He lifted me, And what His grace can do for you.
2. He saves me from ev-ery sin and harm, Secures my soul each day; I'm lean-ing strong on His might-y arm; I know He'll guide me all the way.
3. When poor and need-y and all a-lone, In love He said to me, "Come un-to Me and I'll lead you home, To live with Me e-ter-nal-ly."
Refrain (parts optional)
Saved by His pow'r di-vine, Saved to new life sub-lime!
Saved by His pow'r, Saved to new life,

TEXT and MUSIC: Jack P. Scholfield

SCHOLFIELD
8.6.8.8. with Refrain

Life now is sweet and my joy is com-plete, For I'm saved, saved, saved!
Satisfied 531
He satisfies the thirsty and fills the hungry with good things. Ps. 107:9
1. All my life long I had pant - ed For a drink, from some clear spring,
2. Feed-ing on the husks a - round me, Till my strength was al - most gone,
3. Well of wa - ter ev - er spring-ing, Bread of life so rich and free,
That I hoped would quench the burn-ing Of the thirst I felt with - in.
Longed my soul for some-thing bet - ter, On-ly still to hun-ger on.
Un - told wealth that nev - er fail - eth, My Re - deem - er is to me.
Refrain
Hal-le - lu - jah! I have found Him Whom my soul so long has craved!
Je - sus sat - is-fies my long - ings— Thru His blood I now am saved.

TEXT: Clara T. Williams
MUSIC: Ralph E. Hudson

SATISFIED
8.7.8.7. with Refrain

532 O Happy Day!

Let us rejoice and be glad in His salvation. Isa. 25:9

1. O hap-py day that fixed my choice On Thee, my Sav - ior and my God!
2. O hap-py bond that seals my vows To Him who mer - its all my love!
3. 'Tis done, the great trans - ac - tion's done— I am my Lord's and He is mine;
4. Now rest, my long - di - vid - ed heart, Fixed on this bliss - ful cen-ter, rest,
Well may this glow - ing heart re - joice And tell its rap- tures all a - broad.
Let cheer-ful an - thems fill His house, While to that sa - cred shrine I move.
He drew me, and I fol-lowed on, Charmed to con-fess the voice di - vine.
Nor ev - er from my Lord de - part, With Him of ev - 'ry good pos-sessed.
Refrain
Hap - py day, hap - py day, When Je - sus washed my sins a - way!
He taught me how to watch and pray And live re - joic - ing ev-ery day;
Hap - py day, hap - py day, When Je - sus washed my sins a - way!

TEXT: Philip Doddridge
MUSIC: Edward F. Rimbault

HAPPY DAY
L.M. with Refrain

O Perfect Love 533

Husbands, love your wives. Col. 3:19 *Women . . . love their husbands.* Titus 2:4

1. O per - fect love, all hu - man thought tran - scend - ing,
2. O per - fect Life, be Thou their full as - sur - ance
3. Grant them the joy which bright-ens earth - ly sor - row;
4. Hear us, O Fa - ther, gra - cious and for - giv - ing,
Low - ly we kneel in prayer be - fore Thy throne,
Of ten - der char - i - ty and stead - fast faith,
Grant them the peace which calms all earth - ly strife,
Through Je - sus Christ, Thy co - e - ter - nal Word,
That theirs may be the love which knows no end - ing,
Of pa - tient hope, and qui - et, brave en - dur - ance,
And to life's day the glo - rious, un - known mor - row
Who, with the Ho - ly Ghost, by all things liv - ing
Whom Thou for - ev - er - more dost join in one.
With child - like trust that fears not pain nor death.
That dawns up - on e - ter - nal love and life.
Now and to end - less a - ges art a - dored. A - men.

TEXT: Dorothy F. Gurney, stanzas 1, 2, 3; John Ellerton, stanza 4
MUSIC: Joseph Barnby

SANDRINGHAM
11.10.11.10.

534 She Will Be Called Blessed

Her children . . . call her blessed; her husband . . . praises her. Prov. 31:28

Stanza 1, Spoken

Worship Leader: Her strength and her dignity clothe her with beauty;
In works of her hands she excells.
A heart of compassion she turns to the needy;
In service to others, she gives of herself.

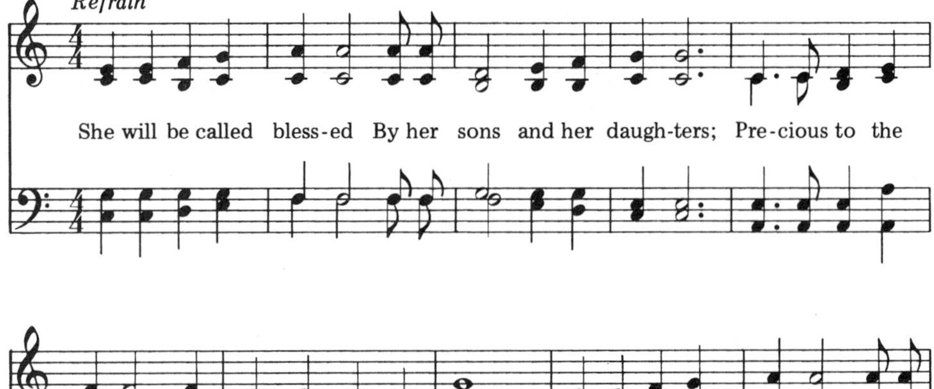
Refrain
She will be called bless-ed By her sons and her daugh-ters; Pre-cious to the

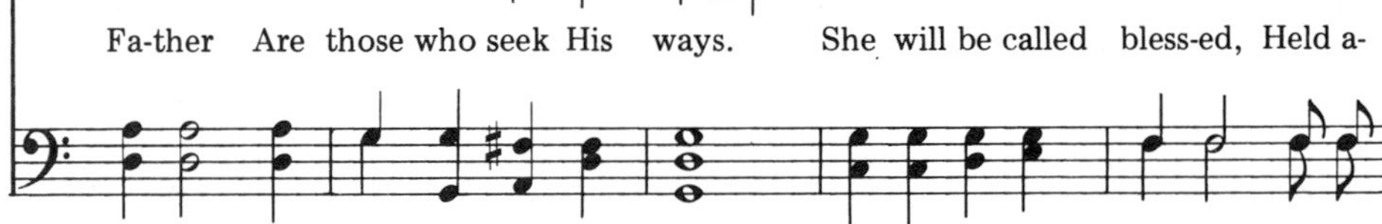
Fa-ther Are those who seek His ways. She will be called bless-ed, Held a-

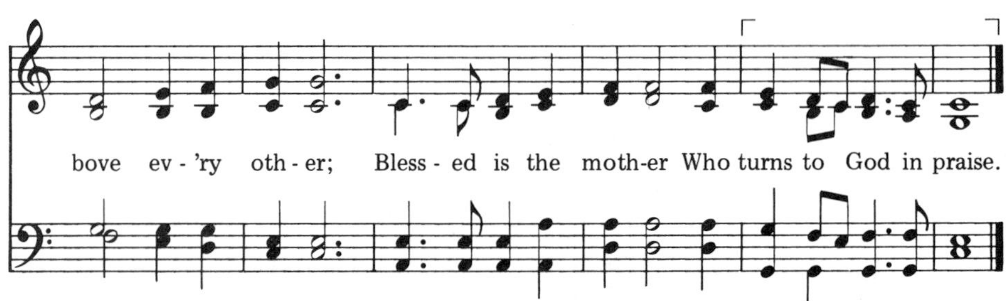
bove ev - 'ry oth - er; Bless - ed is the moth-er Who turns to God in praise.

Optional: instruments may play the final 8 bars of the Refrain while worship leader recites stanza 2.

Stanza 2, Spoken

Worship Leader: She rises each morning to see her household;
She looks toward the future with joy.
She teaches her children true lessons of kindness;
And shares with them wisdom the world can't destroy.

Repeat the Refrain

TEXT: Elizabeth de Gravelles; based on Proverbs 31:10-31
MUSIC: Joseph Barlowe

IRENE
13.12.13.12.

A Christian Home 535

From infancy you have known the holy Scriptures. 2 Tim. 3:15
1. O give us homes built firm up-on the Sav-ior, Where Christ is Head and Coun-sel-lor and Guide; Where ev-ery child is taught His love and fa-vor And gives His heart to Christ, the cru-ci-fied: How sweet to know that though his foot-steps wa-ver His faith-ful Lord is walk-ing by his side!
2. O give us homes with god-ly fa-thers, moth-ers, Who al-ways place their hope and trust in Him; Whose ten-der pa-tience tur-moil nev-er both-ers, Whose calm and cour-age trou-ble can-not dim; A home where each finds joy in serv-ing oth-ers, And love still shines, tho days be dark and grim.
3. O Lord, our God, our homes are Thine for-ev-er! We trust to Thee their prob-lems, toil, and care; Their bonds of love no en-e-my can sev-er If Thou art al-ways Lord and Mas-ter there: Be Thou the cen-ter of our least en-deav-or— Be Thou our Guest, our hearts and homes to share.
A-men.

TEXT: Barbara B. Hart
MUSIC: Jean Sibelius
A higher setting may be found at No. 347

FINLANDIA (altered)
11.10.11.10.11.10.

536 Happy the Home When God Is There

As for me and my household, we will serve the Lord. Josh. 24:15

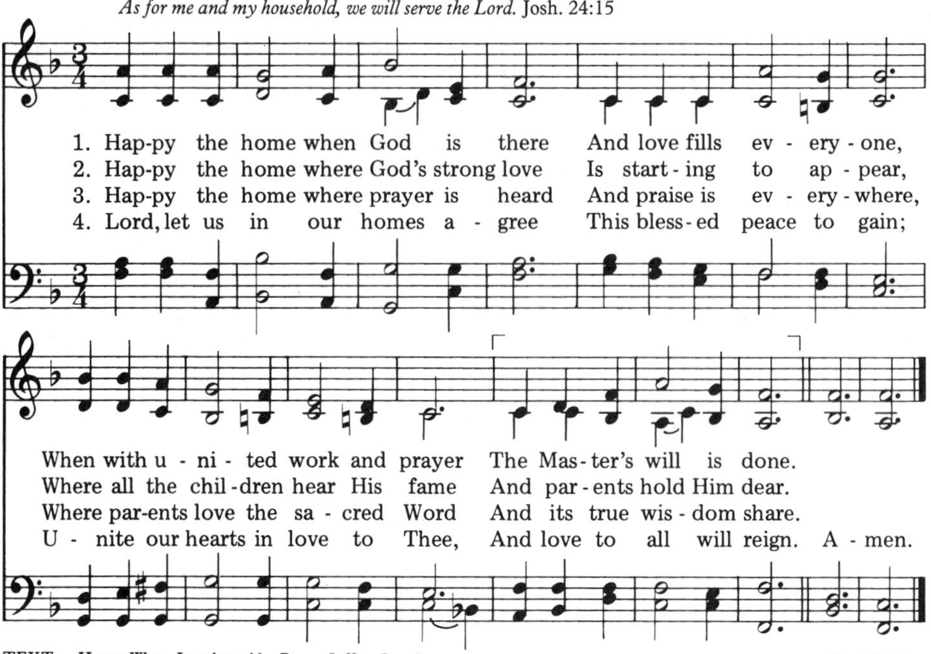
1. Hap-py the home when God is there And love fills ev - ery - one,
2. Hap-py the home where God's strong love Is start - ing to ap - pear,
3. Hap-py the home where prayer is heard And praise is ev - ery - where,
4. Lord, let us in our homes a - gree This bless - ed peace to gain;
When with u - ni - ted work and prayer The Mas - ter's will is done.
Where all the chil - dren hear His fame And par - ents hold Him dear.
Where par-ents love the sa - cred Word And its true wis - dom share.
U - nite our hearts in love to Thee, And love to all will reign. A - men.

TEXT: Henry Ware, Jr.; altered by Bryan Jeffery Leech
MUSIC: John B. Dykes
A higher setting may be found at No. 79

ST. AGNES
C.M.

537 As for Me and My House

Unless the Lord builds the house, its builders labor in vain. Ps. 127:1

As for me and my house, we will serve the Lord; As for me and my
house, we will praise His name. For un - less He builds the house we have

TEXT: Elizabeth de Gravelles; based on Joshua 24:15
MUSIC: Kurt Kaiser

WE WILL SERVE
Irregular meter

worked in vain; As for me and my house we will serve the Lord.

When I Can Read My Title Clear 538

I am going . . . to prepare a place for you. John 14:2

1. When I can read my ti - tle clear To man- sions in the skies,
2. Should earth a - gainst my soul en - gage And fier - y darts be hurled,
3. Let cares like a wild del - uge come And storms of sor - row fall!

Fine

D.S. I'll bid fare - well to ev - ery fear And wipe my weep - ing eyes.
D.S. Then I can smile at Sa - tan's rage And face a frown - ing world.
D.S. May I but safe - ly reach my home, My God, my heaven, my all.

D.S.
And wipe my weep - ing eyes, And wipe my weep - ing eyes,
And face a frown - ing world, And face a frown - ing world,
My God, my heaven, my all, My God, my heaven, my all,

TEXT: Isaac Watts
MUSIC: Traditional American melody; from *Kentucky Harmony,* 1816

PISGAH
8.6.8.6.6.6.8.6.

539 O That Will Be Glory

Our present sufferings are not worth comparing with the glory. Rom. 8:18

1. When all my la - bors and tri - als are o'er, And I am safe on that beau - ti - ful shore, Just to be near the dear Lord I a - dore Will through the a - ges be glo - ry for me.
2. When by the gift of His in - fi - nite grace, I am ac - cord - ed in heav - en a place, Just to be there and to look on His face
3. Friends will be there I have loved long a - go; Joy like a riv - er a - round me will flow; Yet, just a smile from my Sav - ior, I know,

Refrain

O that will be glo-ry for me, Glo-ry for me, glo-ry for me;
O that will be glo-ry for me, Glo-ry for me, glo-ry for me;
When by His grace I shall look on His face, That will be glo - ry, be glo - ry for me.

rit.

TEXT and MUSIC: Charles H. Gabriel

GLORY SONG
10.10.10.10. with Refrain

AN UPWARD LOOK

A Brief Service of Joyful Anticipation

Suggested Hymn Stanzas

To facilitate an uninterrupted flow from stanza to stanza, the suggested stanzas have been marked with an arrow: ►

He the Pearly Gates Will Open, stanzas 1, 3
When We All Get to Heaven, stanzas 1, 3, 4
When the Roll Is Called Up Yonder, stanzas 1, 3

WORSHIP LEADER:

Then I saw a new heaven and a new earth, for the first heaven and the first earth had passed away, and there was no longer any sea. I saw the Holy City, the New Jerusalem, coming down out of heaven from God, prepared as a bride beautifully dressed for her husband. And I heard a loud voice from the throne saying, "Now the dwelling of God is with men, and He will live with them. They will be His people, and God Himself will be with them and be their God. He will wipe every tear from their eyes. There will be no more death or mourning or crying or pain, for the old order of things has passed away."

I did not see a temple in the city, because the Lord God Almighty and the Lamb are its temple. The city does not need the sun or the moon to shine on it, for the glory of God gives it light, and the Lamb is its lamp. On no day will its gates ever be shut, for there will be no night there. Nothing impure will ever enter it, nor will anyone who does what is shameful or deceitful, but only those whose names are written in the Lamb's book of life.

Revelation 21:1-4, 22-23, 25, 27. (NIV)

Optional introduction to "He the Pearly Gates Will Open"

"AN UPWARD LOOK—A Brief Service of Joyful Anticipation"

541 He the Pearly Gates Will Open

Those who wash their robes . . . may go through the gates into the city. Rev. 22:14

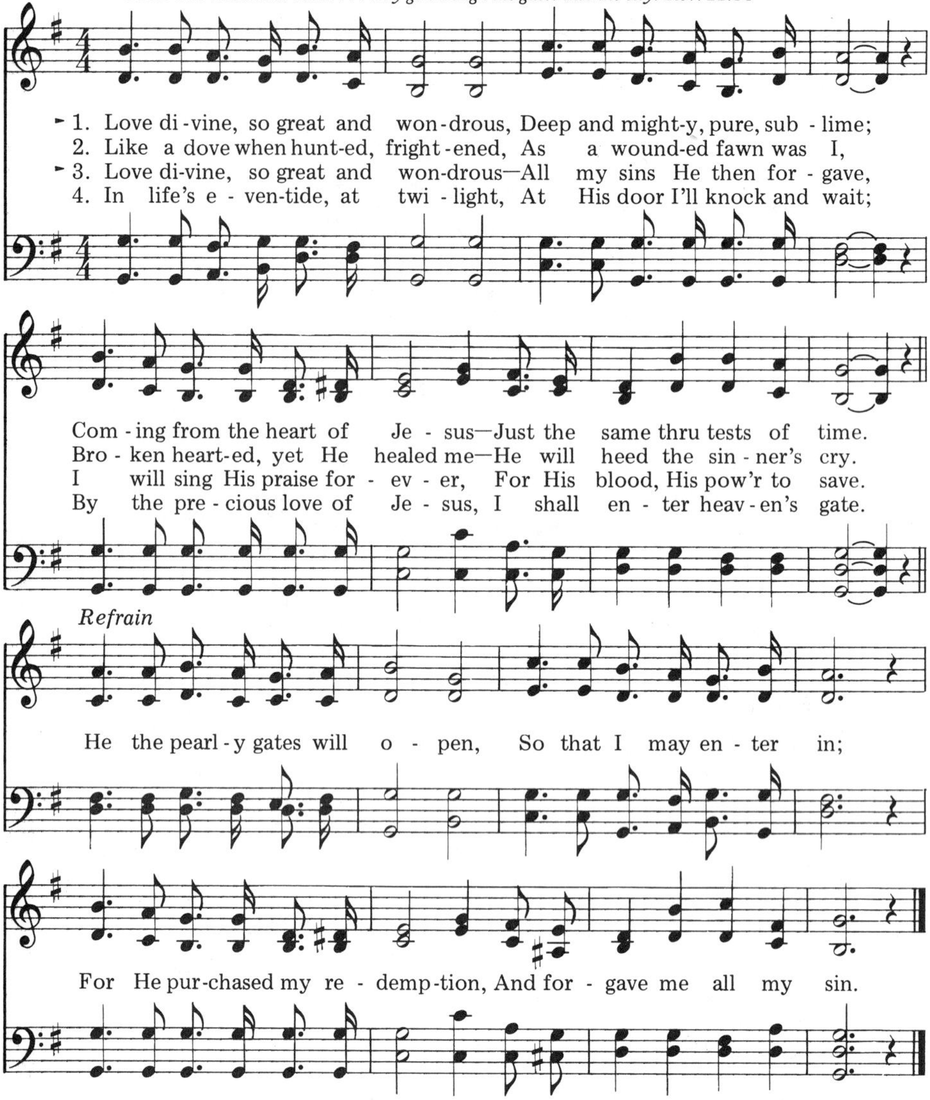

1. Love di-vine, so great and won-drous, Deep and might-y, pure, sub - lime; Com - ing from the heart of Je - sus—Just the same thru tests of time.
2. Like a dove when hunt-ed, fright - ened, As a wound-ed fawn was I, Bro - ken heart-ed, yet He healed me—He will heed the sin - ner's cry.
3. Love di-vine, so great and won-drous—All my sins He then for - gave, I will sing His praise for - ev - er, For His blood, His pow'r to save.
4. In life's e - ven-tide, at twi - light, At His door I'll knock and wait; By the pre - cious love of Je - sus, I shall en - ter heav - en's gate.

Refrain

He the pearl - y gates will o - pen, So that I may en - ter in;
For He pur-chased my re - demp-tion, And for - gave me all my sin.

TEXT: Frederick A. Blom; translated by Nathaniel Carlson
MUSIC: Elsie Ahlwén

PEARLY GATES
8.7.8.7. with Refrain

When We All Get to Heaven 542

We . . . will be caught up . . . to . . . be with the Lord forever. 1 Thess. 4:17

1. Sing the won-drous love of Je - sus, Sing His mer - cy and His grace;
2. While we walk the pil - grim path - way Clouds will o - ver - spread the sky;
3. Let us then be true and faith - ful, Trust - ing, serv - ing ev - ery day;
4. On - ward to the prize be - fore us! Soon His beau - ty we'll be - hold;
In the man - sions bright and bless - ed He'll pre - pare for us a place.
But when trav - 'ling days are o - ver, Not a shad - ow, not a sigh.
Just one glimpse of Him in glo - ry Will the toils of life re - pay.
Soon the pearl - y gates will o - pen, We shall tread the streets of gold.
Refrain
When we all get to heav - en, What a day of re-
When we all
What a
joic - ing that will be! When we all see
day of re - joic - ing that will be! When we all
Je - sus, We'll sing and shout the vic - to - ry.
and shout the vic - to - ry.

TEXT: Eliza E. Hewitt
MUSIC: Emily D. Wilson

HEAVEN
8.7.8.7. with Refrain

Optional transition to "When the Roll Is Called Up Yonder"

f

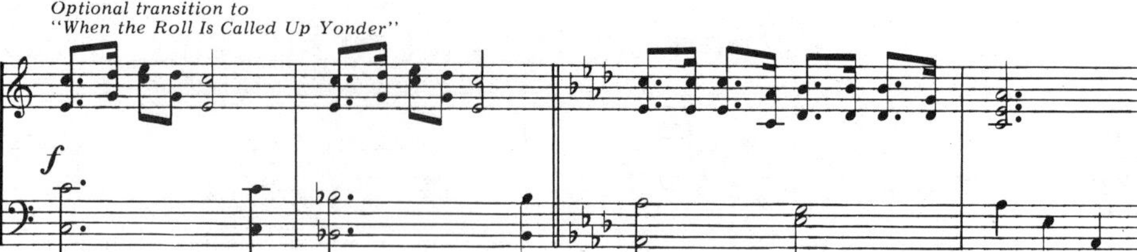

543 When the Roll Is Called Up Yonder

The Lord Himself will come down . . . with the trumpet call of God. 1 Thess. 4:16

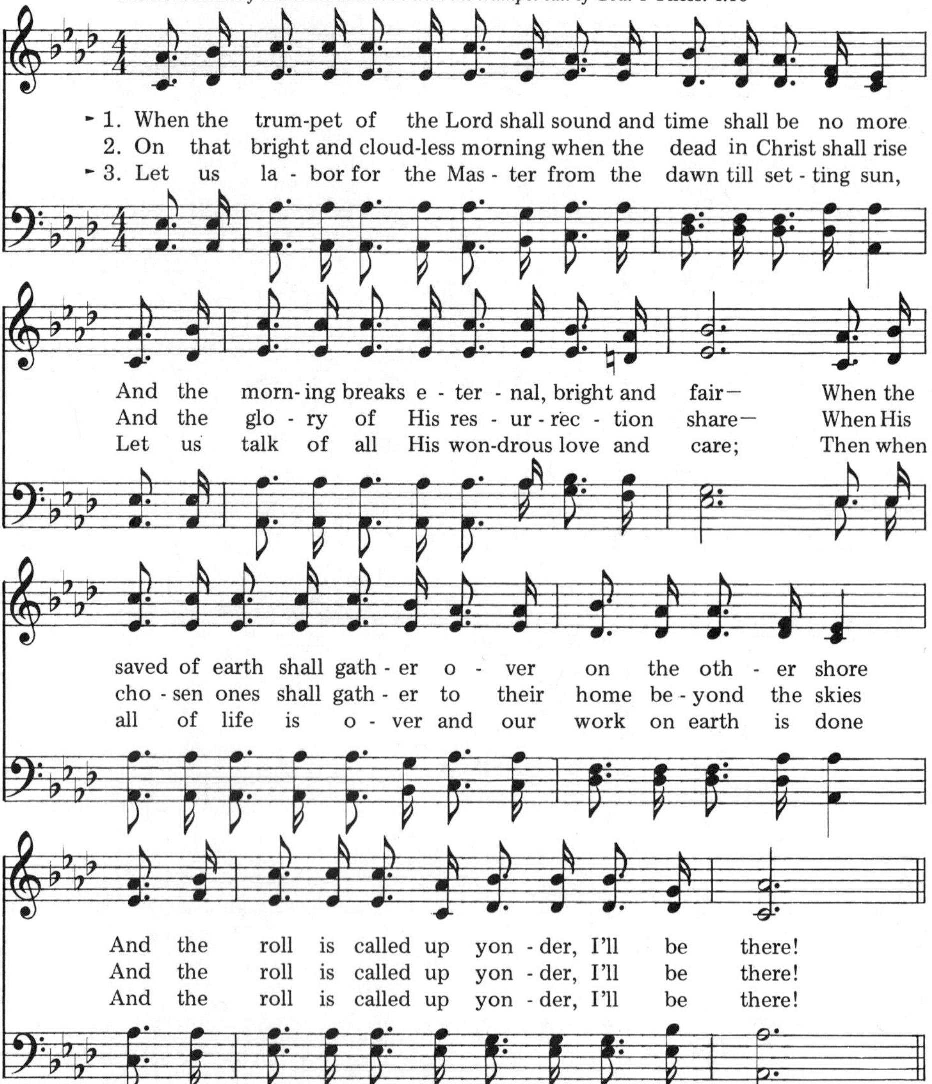
1. When the trum-pet of the Lord shall sound and time shall be no more
2. On that bright and cloud-less morning when the dead in Christ shall rise
3. Let us la - bor for the Mas - ter from the dawn till set - ting sun,
And the morn-ing breaks e - ter - nal, bright and fair— When the
And the glo - ry of His res - ur - rec - tion share— When His
Let us talk of all His won-drous love and care; Then when
saved of earth shall gath - er o - ver on the oth - er shore
cho - sen ones shall gath - er to their home be - yond the skies
all of life is o - ver and our work on earth is done
And the roll is called up yon - der, I'll be there!
And the roll is called up yon - der, I'll be there!
And the roll is called up yon - der, I'll be there!

TEXT and MUSIC: James M. Black

ROLL CALL
Irregular meter

Refrain
When the roll is called up yonder, When the
When the roll
roll is called up yonder, When the roll
When the roll
when the roll
is called up yon-der—When the roll is called up yon-der I'll be there!
Optional choral ending
When we all see
f
We all see
When we all see Je - sus, We'll sing and
ff
shout the vic - to - ry, the vic - to - ry.
8va
8va

The end of "AN UPWARD LOOK—A Brief Service of Joyful Anticipation"

544 We'll Understand It Better By and By

Faith is the substance of things hoped for, the evidence of things not seen. Heb. 11:1

1. Tri - als dark on ev - 'ry hand, And we can - not un - der - stand
2. Oft our cher-ished plans have failed, Dis - ap - point-ments have pre - vailed,
3. Temp - ta - tions, hid - den snares Of - ten take us un - a - wares,
All the ways that God would lead us to that bless-ed Prom-ised Land;
And we've wan - dered in the dark-ness, heav-y - heart-ed and a - lone;
And our hearts are made to bleed for some tho't-less word or deed,
But He'll guide us with His eye, And we'll fol - low till we die; We will
But we're trust - ing in the Lord, And, ac - cord-ing to His Word, We will
And we won - der why the test When we try to do our best, But we'll
un - der-stand it bet - ter by and by.
Refrain
By and by, when the morn-ing comes, When the saints of God are gath-ered home, We will tell the sto - ry

TEXT and MUSIC: Charles A. Tindley; arranged by B. B. McKinney

BY AND BY
Irregular meter

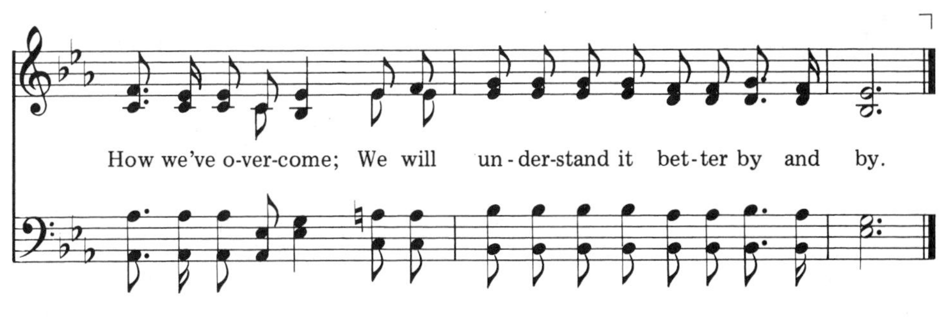
How we've o-ver-come; We will un-der-stand it bet-ter by and by.

We Shall See His Lovely Face 545

They will see His face. Rev. 22:4

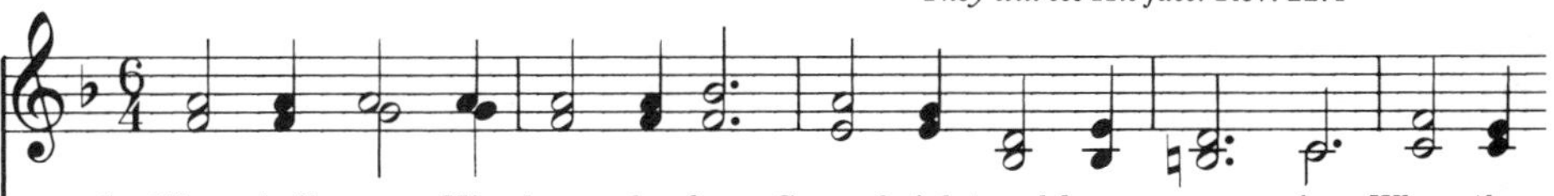

1. We shall see His love-ly face Some bright, gold-en morn-ing, When the
2. God shall wipe a-way all tears Some bright, gold-en morn-ing, When the
3. We shall meet to part no more, Some bright, gold-en morn-ing, At the

clouds have rift-ed, And the shades have flown; Sor-row will be turned to joy,
jour-ney's end-ed, And the course is run; No more cry-ing, pain or death
gates of glo-ry Where our loved ones stand; Songs of vic-t'ry fill the skies

Heart-aches gone for-ev-er; No more night, on-ly light, When we see His face.
In that hour of glad-ness, Tri-als cease, all is peace, When we see His face.
In that hour of greet-ing, End-less days, end-less praise, When we see His face.

TEXT and MUSIC: Norman J. Clayton

CLAYTON
6.6.6.5.D.

546 For All the Saints

They will rest from their labor, for their deeds will follow them. Rev. 14:13

Unison
1. For all the saints who from their la - bors rest, Who
2. Thou wast their rock, their for - tress, and their might,
3. O may Thy sol - diers, faith - ful, true, and bold,
4. O blest com - mu - nion, fel - low - ship di - vine!
5. But lo! there breaks a yet more glo - rious day: The
6. From earth's wide bounds, from o - cean's far - thest coast, Thru
Thee by faith be - fore the world con - fessed, Thy
Thou, Lord, their cap - tain in the well - fought fight;
Fight as the saints who no - bly fought of old, And
We fee - bly strug - gle, they in glo - ry shine; Yet
saints tri - um - phant rise in bright ar - ray; The
gates of pearl streams in the count - less host,
name, O Je - sus, be for - ev - er blest:
Thou, in the dark - ness drear, their one true Light:
win with them the vic - tor's crown of gold:
all are one in Thee, for all are Thine:
King of glo - ry pass - es on His way:
Sing - ing to Fa - ther, Son, and Ho - ly Ghost:

TEXT: William W. How
MUSIC: Ralph Vaughan Williams

SINE NOMINE
10.10.10. with Alleluias

Al - le - lu - ia! Al - le - lu - ia!

The Kingdom of God 547

I saw a new heaven and a new earth. Rev. 21:1

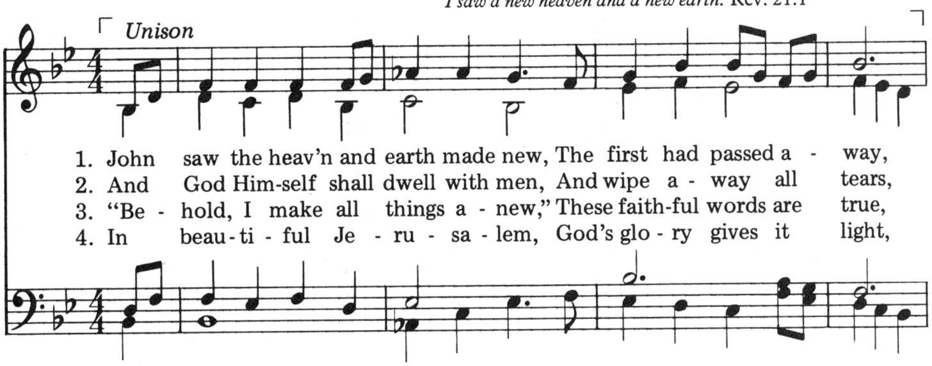

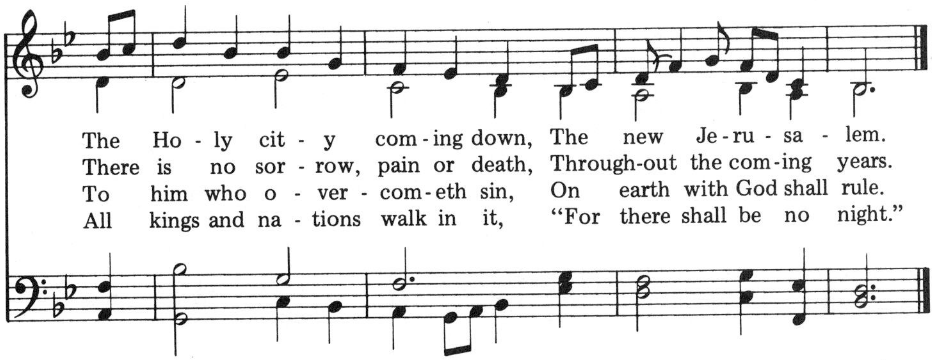

Unison

1. John saw the heav'n and earth made new, The first had passed a - way, The Ho - ly cit - y com - ing down, The new Je - ru - sa - lem.
2. And God Him-self shall dwell with men, And wipe a - way all tears, There is no sor - row, pain or death, Through-out the com-ing years.
3. "Be - hold, I make all things a - new," These faith-ful words are true, To him who o - ver - com-eth sin, On earth with God shall rule.
4. In beau - ti - ful Je - ru - sa - lem, God's glo - ry gives it light, All kings and na - tions walk in it, "For there shall be no night."

TEXT: Louise Lapp; based on Revelation 21
MUSIC: Traditional Spiritual melody; arranged by H.T. Burleigh

McKEE
C.M.

548 Beyond the Sunset

There will be no more death or mourning or crying or pain. Rev. 21:4

1. Be - yond the sun - set, O bliss - ful morn - ing, When with our Sav - ior heaven is be - gun; Earth's toil-ing end - ed, O glo - rious dawn - ing, Be - yond the sun - set, when day is done.
2. Be - yond the sun - set no clouds will gath - er, No storms will threat-en, no fears an - noy; O day of glad - ness, O day un - end - ing, Be - yond the sun - set, e - ter - nal joy!
3. Be - yond the sun - set, O glad re - un - ion, With our dear loved ones who've gone be - fore; In that fair home - land we'll know no part - ing, Be - yond the sun - set, for - ev - er - more!

TEXT: Virgil P. Brock
MUSIC: Blanche Kerr Brock

SUNSET
10.9.10.9.

549 Face to Face

Now we see . . . as in a mirror; then we shall see face to face. 1 Cor. 13:12

1. Face to face with Christ my Sav - ior, Face to face—what will it be—
2. On - ly faint-ly now I see Him, With the dark-ling veil be - tween;
3. What re - joic - ing in His pres - ence When are ban-ished grief and pain;
4. Face to face! O bliss - ful mo - ment! Face to face—to see and know;

TEXT: Carrie E. Breck; based on 1 Corinthians 13:12
MUSIC: Grant C. Tullar

FACE TO FACE
8.7.8.7. with Refrain

This tune and *Saved by Grace,* No. 550, may be sung as a medley.

When with rap-ture I be-hold Him, Je-sus Christ who died for me?
But a bless-ed day is com-ing When His glo-ry shall be seen.
When the crook-ed ways are straight-ened And the dark things shall be plain.
Face to face with my Re-deem-er, Je-sus Christ who loves me so.
Refrain
Face to face I shall be-hold Him, Far be-yond the star-ry sky; Face to face in all His glo-ry, I shall see Him by and by. by.
Optional transition to "Saved by Grace"
Saved by Grace 550
For it is by grace you have been saved, through faith. Eph. 2:8
And I shall see Him face to face, shall see to face, And tell the sto-ry—Saved by grace; And I shall see Him face to face, shall see to face, And tell the sto-ry—Saved by grace.

TEXT: Fanny J. Crosby
MUSIC: George C. Stebbins; arranged by Robert F. Douglas
This tune and *Face to Face,* No. 549, may be sung as a medley.

SAVED BY GRACE
L.M.

551 Soon and Very Soon

"Yes, I am coming soon." Amen. Come, Lord Jesus. Rev. 22:20

1., 4. Soon and ver - y soon, We are going to see the King;
2. No more cry-ing there, We are going to see the King;
3. No more dy-ing there, We are going to see the King;

Soon and ver - y soon, We are going to see the King;
No more cry - ing there, We are going to see the King;
No more dy - ing there, We are going to see the King;

Soon and ver - y soon, We are going to see the King;
No more cry -ing there, We are going to see the King; Hal-le-
No more dy - ing there, We are going to see the King;

lu - jah! Hal-le - lu - jah! We're going to see the King.

1,3 | 2,4

going to see the King. Hal - le - lu - jah! Hal - le - lu - jah!

TEXT and MUSIC: Andraé Crouch

SOON AND VERY SOON
Irregular meter

On Jordan's Stormy Banks 552

Let us, therefore, make every effort to enter that rest. Heb. 4:11

1. On Jor-dan's storm-y banks I stand, And cast a wish-ful eye
2. All o'er those wide ex - tend-ed plains Shines one e - ter - nal day;
3. No chill-ing winds nor poi-s'nous breath Can reach that health-ful shore;
4. When shall I reach that hap - py place, And be for - ev - er blest?
To Ca - naan's fair and hap - py land, Where my pos - ses - sions lie.
There God the Son for - ev - er reigns And scat-ters night a - way.
Sick - ness and sor - row, pain and death Are felt and feared no more.
When shall I see my Fa-ther's face, And in His bos - om rest?
Refrain
I am bound for the prom-ised land, I am bound for the prom-ised land;
O who will come and go with me? I am bound for the prom-ised land.

TEXT: Samuel Stennett
MUSIC: Traditional American melody; arranged by Rigdon M. McIntosh

PROMISED LAND
C.M. with Refrain

553 Sweet By and By

We do not have an enduring city, but we are looking for the city that is to come. Heb. 13:14

1. There's a land that is fair - er than day, And by faith we can see it a - far, For the Fa - ther waits o - ver the way To pre- pare us a dwell - ing place there.
2. We shall sing on that beau - ti - ful shore The me - lo - di - ous songs of the blest; And our spir - its shall sor - row no more— Not a sigh for the bless - ing of rest.
3. To our boun - ti - ful Fa - ther a - bove We will of - fer our trib - ute of praise, For the glo - ri - ous gift of His love And the bless - ings that hal - low our days.
Refrain
In the sweet by and by, We shall meet on that beau - ti - ful shore; In the sweet by and by, We shall meet on that beau-ti-ful shore.
In the sweet by and by, by and by, In the sweet by and by,

TEXT: Sanford F. Bennett
MUSIC: Joseph P. Webster

SWEET BY AND BY
9.9.9.9. with Refrain

I'll Fly Away 554

We . . . would prefer to be away from the body and at home with the Lord. 2 Cor. 5:8

1. Some glad morn-ing when this life is o'er, I'll fly a - way; To a home on God's ce - les - tial shore, I'll fly a - way.
2. When the shad-ows of this life have gone, fly a-way, fly a-way; Like a bird from pris - on bars has flown, fly a-way, fly a-way.
3. Just a few more wea - ry days and then, To a land where joys shall nev - er end,
Refrain
I'll fly a - way, O glo-ry, I'll fly a - way; in the morn-ing; When I die, hal - le - lu - jah, by and by, I'll fly a - way. fly a-way, fly a-way.
Optional choral ending
ff
I'll fly a - way.

TEXT and MUSIC: Albert E. Brumley

I'LL FLY AWAY
9.4.9.4. with Refrain

555 We're Marching to Zion

You have come to Mount Zion . . . the city of the living God. Heb. 12:22

1. Come, we that love the Lord, And let our joys be known,
2. Let those re - fuse to sing Who nev - er knew our God,
3. The hill of Zi - on yields A thou - sand sa - cred sweets
4. Then let our songs a - bound And ev - ery tear be dry;
Join in a song with sweet ac-cord, Join in a song with sweet ac-cord
But chil-dren of the heav'n-ly King, But chil-dren of the heav'n-ly King
Be - fore we reach the heav'n-ly fields, Be - fore we reach the heav'n-ly fields
We're march-ing thro' Im-manuel's ground, We're march-ing thro' Im-man-uel's ground
And thus sur - round the throne, And thus sur-round the throne.
May speak their joys a - broad, May speak their joys a - broad.
Or walk the gold - en streets, Or walk the gold - en streets.
To fair - er worlds on high, To fair - er worlds on high.
Refrain
We're march-ing to *Zi - on, Beau-ti-ful, beau-ti-ful Zi - on;
We're march-ing up-ward to Zi - on, The beau-ti-ful cit - y of God.

TEXT: Isaac Watts; Robert Lowry, Refrain
MUSIC: Robert Lowry

MARCHING TO ZION
6.6.8.8.6.6. with Refrain

*Psalm 2:6. By extension this refers to the New Jerusalem.

Now Thank We All Our God 556

Give thanks to the Lord . . . make known . . . what He has done. Isa. 12:4

1. Now thank we all our God With heart and hands and voic - es,
2. O may this boun - teous God Thro' all our life be near us,
3. All praise and thanks to God The Fa - ther now be giv - en,
Who won - drous things hath done, In whom His world re - joic - es;
With ev - er joy - ful hearts And bless - ed peace to cheer us;
The Son, and Him who reigns With them in high - est heav - en,
Who, from our moth - er's arms, Hath blest us on our way
And keep us in His grace, And guide us when per - plexed,
The one e - ter - nal God, Whom earth and heav'n a - dore;
With count - less gifts of love, And still is ours to - day.
And free us from all ills In this world and the next.
For thus it was, is now, And shall be ev - er - more. A - men.

TEXT: Martin Rinkart; translated by Catherine Winkworth
MUSIC: Johann Crüger; harmonized by Felix Mendelssohn

NUN DANKET
6.7.6.7.6.6.6.6.

557 In Thanksgiving Let Us Praise Him

With praise and thanksgiving they sang to the Lord. Ezra 3:11

1. From the first bright light of morn-ing, To the last warm glow of dusk;
2. In the sea - son of our plen - ty, In the sea - son of our need;
3. Safe with-in His hand that guides us, Hid-den in His heal-ing wings;
Ev - 'ry breath we take is sa - cred, For it is God's gift to us.
We will find His grace suf - fi - cient, We will find His love com-plete.
Day by day His love pro-vides us Ev - 'ry good and per - fect thing.
In thanks-giv - ing, let us praise Him; In thanks-giv - ing, let us sing
Songs of praise and ad - o - ra - tion To our gra - cious Lord, and King. A-men.

TEXT: Claire Cloninger
MUSIC: Franz Joseph Haydn
A higher setting may be found at No. 278; Alternate tune: BEECHER at No. 92

AUSTRIAN HYMN
8.7.8.7.D.

WITH A SONG OF THANKSGIVING 558

A Brief Service of Praise to God, the Creator

Suggested Hymn Stanzas

To facilitate an uninterrupted flow from stanza to stanza, the suggested stanzas have been marked with an arrow: ►

Come, Ye Thankful People, Come, stanza 1
For the Beauty of the Earth, stanzas 1, 3, 5
We Gather Together, complete

WORSHIP LEADER:
God saw all that He had made, and it was very good.

PEOPLE:
You care for the land and water it; You enrich it abundantly. The streams of God are filled with water to provide the people with grain, for so You have ordained it.

WORSHIP LEADER:
You crown the year with Your bounty, and Your carts overflow with abundance. The grasslands of the desert overflow; the hills are clothed with gladness.

PEOPLE:
The meadows are covered with flocks and the valleys are mantled with grain; they shout for You and sing.

WORSHIP LEADER:
He makes grass grow for the cattle, and plants for man to cultivate—bringing forth food from the earth. How many are Your works, O Lord! In wisdom You made them all; the earth is full of Your creatures.

PEOPLE:
Let them give thanks to the Lord for His unfailing love and His wonderful deeds for men, for He satisfies the thirsty and fills the hungry with good things.

ALL:
But I, with a song of thanksgiving, will sacrifice to You. What I have vowed I will make good. Salvation comes from the Lord.

Gen. 1:31; Ps. 65:9, 11-13; 104:14, 24;
107:8-9; Jonah 2:9. (NIV)

Optional introduction to "Come, Ye Thankful People, Come"

"WITH A SONG OF THANKSGIVING—A Brief Service of Praise to God, the Creator"

559 Come, Ye Thankful People, Come

You crown the year with Your bounty. Ps. 65:11

1. Come, ye thank - ful peo - ple, come— Raise the song of har - vest-home:
2. All the world is God's own field, Fruit un - to His praise to yield;
3. For the Lord our God shall come And shall take His har - vest home;
4. E - ven so, Lord, quick - ly come To Thy fi - nal har - vest-home;
All is safe - ly gath - ered in Ere the win - ter storms be - gin.
Wheat and tares to - geth - er sown, Un - to joy or sor - row grown.
From His field shall in that day All of - fens - es purge a - way;
Gath - er Thou Thy peo - ple in, Free from sor - row, free from sin;
God, our Mak - er, doth pro - vide For our wants to be sup - plied:
First the blade and then the ear, Then the full corn shall ap - pear:
Give His an - gels charge at last In the fire the tares to cast,
There, for - ev - er pu - ri - fied, In Thy pres - ence to a - bide:
Come to God's own tem - ple, come—Raise the song of har - vest-home.
Lord of har - vest, grant that we Wholesome grain and pure may be.
But the fruit - ful ears to store In His gar - ner ev - er - more.
Come, with all Thine an-gels, come— Raise the glo-rious har-vest-home. A - men.

TEXT: Henry Alford
MUSIC: George J. Elvey

ST. GEORGE'S, WINDSOR
7.7.7.7.D.

Optional transition to
"For the Beauty of the Earth"

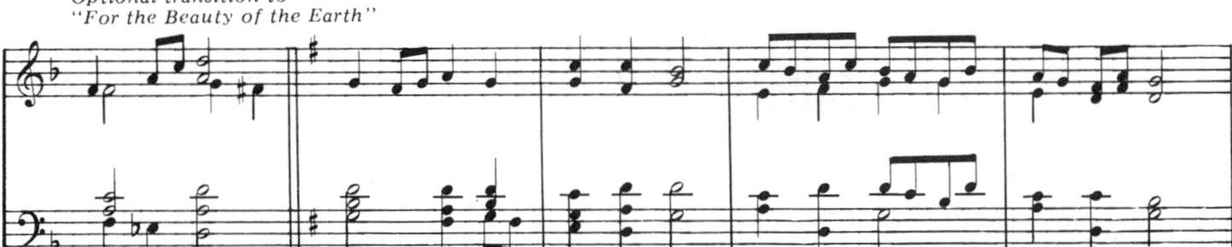

For the Beauty of the Earth 560

Give thanks to the Lord for His unfailing love and His wonderful deeds. Ps. 107:8

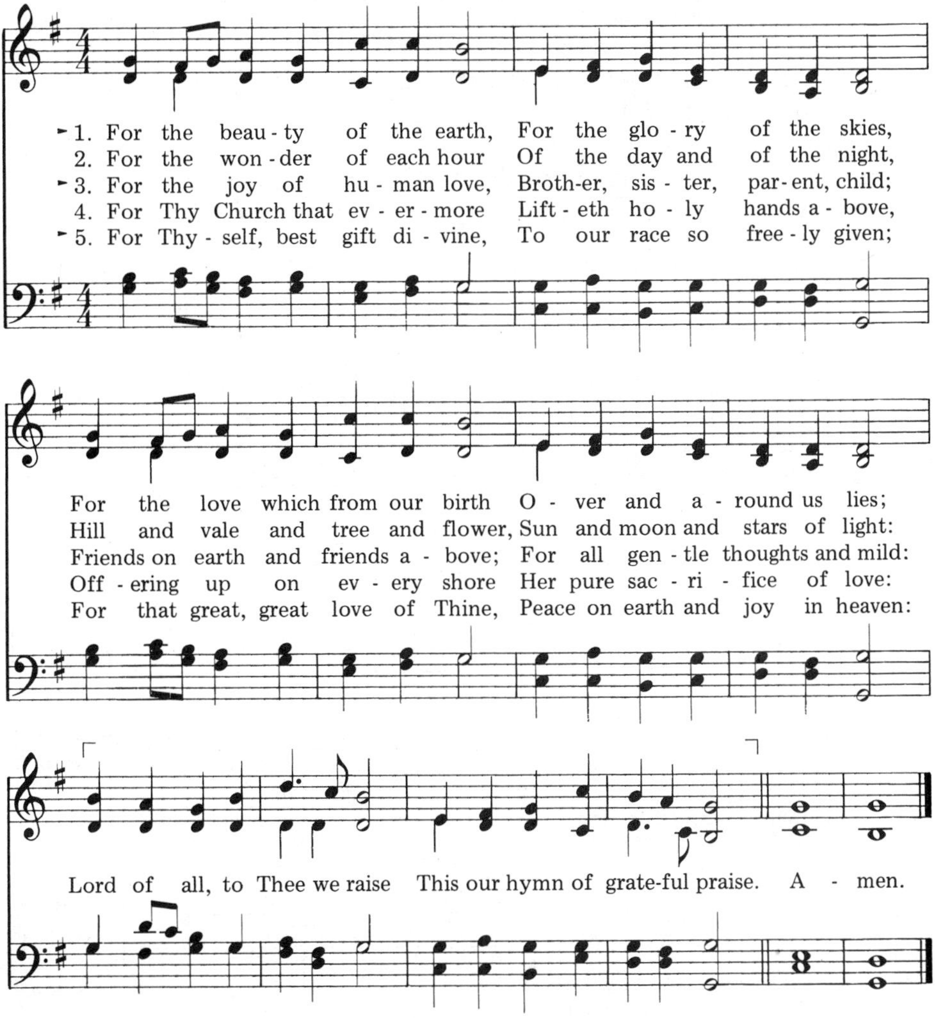
1. For the beau - ty of the earth, For the glo - ry of the skies,
2. For the won - der of each hour Of the day and of the night,
3. For the joy of hu - man love, Broth-er, sis - ter, par - ent, child;
4. For Thy Church that ev - er - more Lift - eth ho - ly hands a - bove,
5. For Thy - self, best gift di - vine, To our race so free - ly given;
For the love which from our birth O - ver and a - round us lies;
Hill and vale and tree and flower, Sun and moon and stars of light:
Friends on earth and friends a - bove; For all gen - tle thoughts and mild:
Off - ering up on ev - ery shore Her pure sac - ri - fice of love:
For that great, great love of Thine, Peace on earth and joy in heaven:
Lord of all, to Thee we raise This our hymn of grate-ful praise. A - men.

TEXT: Folliott S. Pierpoint, altered
MUSIC: Conrad Kocher; arranged by William H. Monk

DIX
7.7.7.7.7.7.

561 We Gather Together

May God be gracious to us and bless us. Ps. 67:1

Optional transition to "We Gather Together"
mf
f
1. We gath - er to - geth - er to ask the Lord's bless - ing;
2. Be - side us to guide us, our God with us join - ing,
3. We all do ex - tol Thee, Thou Lead - er tri - um - phant,
He chas - tens and has - tens His will to make known;
Or - dain - ing, main - tain - ing His king - dom di - vine;
And pray that Thou still our De - fend - er wilt be.
The wick - ed op - press - ing now cease from dis - tress - ing,
So from the be - gin - ning the fight we were win - ning:
Let Thy con-gre - ga - tion es - cape trib - u - la - tion:
Sing prais - es to His name: He for - gets not His own.
Thou, Lord, wast at our side, all glo - ry be Thine!
Thy name be ev - er praised! O Lord, make us free! A - men.

TEXT: Netherlands Folk hymn; translated by Theodore Baker
MUSIC: Netherlands Folk song; arranged by Edward Kremser
Last stanza harmonization by Dick Bolks

KREMSER
12.11.12.11.

Optional last stanza harmonization
Broader
Unison
Thine! 3. We all do ex - tol Thee, Thou
Lead - er tri - um - phant, And pray that Thou still our De -
fend - er wilt be. Let Thy con - gre - ga - tion es -
cape trib - u - la - tion: Thy name be ev - er praised! O
Play cued notes if choral ending is sung
Optional choral ending
rit.
Lord make us free! Lord, make us free!

The end of "WITH A SONG OF THANKSGIVING—A Brief Service of Praise to God, the Creator"

562 Rejoice, Ye Pure in Heart

Rejoice in the Lord and be glad, you righteous; sing. Ps. 32:11

1. Re - joice, ye pure in heart, Re - joice, give thanks, and sing.
2. With all the an - gel choirs, With all the saints on earth,
3. Yes, on through life's long path, Still chant - ing as we go;
4. Still lift your stan - dard high, Still march in firm ar - ray;

Your fes - tal ban - ner wave on high, The cross of Christ your King.
Pour out the strains of joy and bliss, True rap - ture, no - blest mirth!
From youth to age, by night and day, In glad - ness and in woe.
As war - riors through the dark - ness toil Till dawns the gold - en day.

Refrain

Re - joice, re - joice, Re - joice, give thanks, and sing! A - men.
Re - joice, re - joice,

TEXT: Edward H. Plumptre
MUSIC: Arthur H. Messiter

MARION
S.M. with Refrain

563 Count Your Blessings

Many, O Lord my God, are the wonders You have done. Ps. 40:5

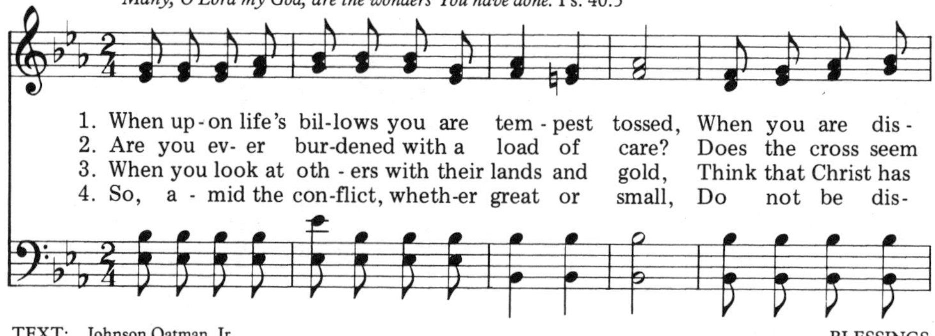
1. When up - on life's bil - lows you are tem - pest tossed, When you are dis -
2. Are you ev - er bur - dened with a load of care? Does the cross seem
3. When you look at oth - ers with their lands and gold, Think that Christ has
4. So, a - mid the con - flict, wheth - er great or small, Do not be dis -

TEXT: Johnson Oatman, Jr.
MUSIC: Edwin O. Excell

BLESSINGS
11.11.11.11. with Refrain

cour - aged, think-ing all is lost, Count your man-y bless - ings, name them
heav - y you are called to bear? Count your man-y bless - ings, ev - 'ry
prom - ised you His wealth un - told; Count your man-y bless - ings, mon - ey
cour - aged, God is o - ver all; Count your man-y bless - ings, an - gels
one by one, And it will sur - prise you what the Lord hath done.
doubt will fly, And you will be sing - ing as the days go by.
can - not buy Your re - ward in heav - en, nor your home on high.
will at - tend, Help and com-fort give you to your jour - ney's end.
Refrain
Count your bless-ings, name them one by one; Count your
Count your man-y bless-ings, name them one by one; Count your man-y
bless-ings, see what God hath done; Count your bless-ings,
bless-ings, see what God hath done; Count your man-y bless-ings,
name them one by one; Count your man-y bless-ings, see what God hath done.

564 We Are So Blessed

God . . . has blessed us . . . with every spiritual blessing in Christ. Eph. 1:3

We are so blessed by the gifts from Your hand, I just can't un - der - stand Why You've loved us so much. We are
so blessed, we just can't find a way or the words that can say, Thank You
Lord, for Your touch. When we're emp - ty You fill us 'Til we o - ver - flow, When we're hun - gry You feed us and cause us to know;
We are so blessed, Take what we have to

TEXT and MUSIC: William J. Gaither, Gloria Gaither, Greg Nelson; arranged by Keith Phillips

SO BLESSED
Irregular meter

3
3
3
bring; Take it all, ev - 'ry - thing, Lord, we love You so much.
3
3
3

We Thank You, Lord 565

We give thanks to You, O God, we give thanks, for Your Name is near. Ps. 75:1

4 Part Canon
I
II
1. We thank You for Your love, We thank You for Your care,
2. We thank You for Your Son, We thank You for Your Word,

III
IV
We thank You for Your faith - ful - ness, We thank You, Lord.
We thank You for e - ter - nal life, We thank You, Lord.

TEXT and MUSIC: Gerald S. Henderson

COLIN
6.6.8.4.

For Health and Strength 566

God . . .richly provides us with everything for our enjoyment. 1 Tim. 6:17

4 Part Canon
I
II
III
IV
For health and strength, and dai-ly food, We praise Thy Name, O Lord.

TEXT and MUSIC: Traditional Dutch Folk song

GRACE
Irregular meter

567 Another Year Is Dawning

Teach us to number our days aright, that we may gain a heart of wisdom. Ps. 90:12

1. An - oth - er year is dawn - ing: Dear Fa - ther, let it be,
2. An - oth - er year of mer - cies, Of faith - ful - ness and grace;
3. An - oth - er year of serv - ice, Of wit - ness for Thy love;
In work - ing or in wait - ing, An - oth - er year with Thee;
An - oth - er year of glad - ness In the shin - ing of Thy face;
An - oth - er year of train - ing For ho - lier work a - bove.
An - oth - er year of prog - ress, An - oth - er year of praise,
An - oth - er year of lean - ing Up - on Thy lov - ing breast;
An - oth - er year is dawn - ing: Dear Fa - ther, let it be,
An - oth - er year of prov - ing Thy pres - ence all the days.
An - oth - er year of trust - ing, Of qui - et, hap - py rest.
On earth or else in heav - en, An - oth - er year for Thee. A - men.

TEXT: Frances Ridley Havergal
MUSIC: Samuel S. Wesley
A higher setting may be found at No. 277

AURELIA
7.6.7.6.D.

God of the Ages 568

From everlasting to everlasting You are God. Ps. 90:2

Unison
1. God of the a - ges, His - to - ry's Mak - er,
2. God of this morn - ing, Glad-ly Your chil - dren
3. God of to - mor - row, Strong O-ver - com - er,
4. Lord of past a - ges, Lord of this morn - ing,
Plan-ning our path - way, Hold - ing us fast,
Wor-ship be - fore You, Trust - ing - ly bow:
Princ - es of dark - ness Own Your com-mand:
Lord of the fu - ture, Help us, we pray:
Shap - ing in mer - cy All that con - cerns us:
Teach us to know You Al - ways a - mong us,
What then can harm us? We are Your peo - ple,
Teach us to trust You, Love and o - bey You,
Fa - ther, we praise You, Lord of the past.
Qui - et - ly sov - 'reign— Lord of our now.
Now and for - ev - er Kept by Your hand.
Crown You each mo - ment Lord of to - day.

TEXT: Margaret Clarkson
MUSIC: Traditional Gaelic melody; arranged by Tom Fettke

BUNESSAN
5.5.5.4.D.

569 Battle Hymn of the Republic

We are more than conquerors through Him who loved us. Rom. 8:37

1. Mine eyes have seen the glo - ry of the com - ing of the Lord,
2. I have seen Him in the watch-fires of a hun-dred cir-cling camps,
3. He has sound - ed forth the trum - pet that shall nev - er sound re - treat,
4. In the beau - ty of the lil - ies Christ was born a - cross the sea,
He is tramp-ling out the vin - tage where the grapes of wrath are stored;
They have build - ed Him an al - tar in the eve - ning dews and damps;
He is sift - ing out the hearts of men be - fore His judg-ment seat;
With a glo - ry in His bos - om that trans - fig - ures you and me;
He hath loosed the fate - ful light - ning of His ter - ri - ble swift sword—
I can read His right - eous sen - tence by the dim and flar - ing lamps—
O be swift, my soul, to an - swer Him! be ju - bi - lant, my feet!
As He died to make men ho - ly, let us live to make men free,
His truth is march-ing on.
His day is march-ing on.
Our God is march-ing on.
While God is march-ing on.
Refrain
Glo - ry! glo-ry, hal - le - lu - jah! Glo - ry!

TEXT: Julia Ward Howe
MUSIC: Traditional American melody;
Descant and arrangement of last Refrain by Eugene Thomas

BATTLE HYMN
15.15.15.6. with Refrain

glo-ry, hal-le - lu - jah! Glo - ry! glo-ry, hal - le - lu - jah! His truth is march-ing on.
Descant
Glo - ry!
Optional repeat of last Refrain
on. ritard
Glo - ry! glo - ry, hal - le-
glo-ry, hal-le-lu - jah! Glo - ry! glo-ry, hal-le-lu - jah! Glo - ry!
lu - jah! Glo-ry! glo-ry, hal-le - lu - jah! Glo - ry! glo-ry, hal-le-
rall.
glo-ry, hal-le-lu-jah! His truth is march-ing on. A - men, a - men.
Optional choral ending
rall.
lu - jah! His truth is march-ing on. A - men, a - men.

570

ONE NATION, UNDER GOD
A Medley

Suggested Hymn Stanzas

To facilitate an uninterrupted flow from stanza to stanza,
the suggested stanzas have been marked with an arrow: ►
My Country, 'Tis of Thee, stanzas 1, 4
America, the Beautiful, stanza 1
God of Our Fathers, stanzas 1, 2, 4

WORSHIP LEADER: **Righteousness exalts a nation, but sin is a disgrace to any people.**
PEOPLE: **Blessed is the nation whose God is the Lord.**

Prov. 14:34; Ps. 33:12. (NIV)

571 My Country, 'Tis of Thee

Righteousness exalts a nation, but sin is a disgrace to any people. Prov. 14:34

► 1. My coun - try, 'tis of thee, Sweet land of lib - er - ty, Of thee I sing: Land where my fa - thers died, Land of the pil - grim's pride, From ev - 'ry moun - tain side Let free - dom ring!
2. My na - tive coun - try, thee, Land of the no - ble free, Thy name I love: I love thy rocks and rills, Thy woods and tem - pled hills; My heart with rap - ture thrills Like that a - bove.
3. Let mu - sic swell the breeze, And ring from all the trees Sweet free-dom's song: Let mor - tal tongues a - wake, Let all that breathe par - take; Let rocks their si - lence break, The sound pro - long.
► 4. Our fa - thers' God, to Thee, Au - thor of lib - er - ty, To Thee we sing: Long may our land be bright With free-dom's ho - ly light; Pro - tect us by Thy might, Great God, our King!

Opt. segue to "America, the Beautiful"

TEXT: Samuel F. Smith
MUSIC: *Thesaurus Musicus,* c. 1745

AMERICA
6.6.4.6.6.6.4.

America, the Beautiful 572

Show proper respect to everyone . . . fear God. 1 Pet. 2:17

1. O beau - ti - ful for spa - cious skies, For am - ber waves of grain,
2. O beau - ti - ful for pil - grim feet, Whose stern im - pas - sioned stress
3. O beau - ti - ful for he - roes proved In lib - er - at - ing strife,
4. O beau - ti - ful for pa - triot dream That sees be - yond the years
For pur - ple moun - tain maj - es - ties A - bove the fruit - ed plain!
A thor - ough-fare for free - dom beat A - cross the wil - der - ness!
Who more than self their coun - try loved, And mer - cy more than life!
Thine al - a - bas - ter cit - ies gleam, Un-dimmed by hu - man tears!
A - mer - i - ca! A - mer - i - ca! God shed His grace on thee,
A - mer - i - ca! A - mer - i - ca! God mend thine ev - ery flaw,
A - mer - i - ca! A - mer - i - ca! May God thy gold re - fine,
A - mer - i - ca! A - mer - i - ca! God shed His grace on thee,
And crown thy good with broth - er - hood From sea to shin - ing sea! *sea!
Con - firm thy soul in self - con - trol, Thy lib - er - ty in law!
Till all suc - cess be no - ble - ness, And ev - ery gain di - vine!
And crown thy good with broth - er - hood From sea to shin - ing sea!

*Opt. segue to "God of Our Fathers"

TEXT: Katharine Lee Bates
MUSIC: Samuel A. Ward

MATERNA
C.M.D.

573 God of Our Fathers

In You our fathers . . . trusted and You delivered them. Ps. 22:4

Trumpets
before each stanza
1. God of our fathers, whose almighty hand Leads forth in beauty all the starry band Of shining worlds in splendor thru the skies, Our grateful songs before Thy throne arise.
2. Thy love divine hath led us in the past, In this free land by Thee our lot is cast; Be Thou our Ruler, Guardian, Guide, and Stay, Thy Word our law, Thy paths our chosen way.
3. From war's alarms, from deadly pestilence, Be Thy strong arm our ever-sure defense; Thy true religion in our hearts increase, Thy bounteous goodness nourish us in peace.
4. Refresh Thy people on their toilsome way, Lead us from night to never-ending day; Fill all our lives with love and grace divine, And glory, laud, and praise be ever Thine! Amen.

TEXT: Daniel C. Roberts
MUSIC: George W. Warren
Last stanza harmonization by Kurt Kaiser

NATIONAL HYMN
10.10.10.10.

Optional last stanza harmonization
Unison
4. Re - fresh Thy peo - ple on their toil-some way,
Lead us from night to nev - er - end - ing day;
Fill all our lives with love and grace di - vine,
And glo - ry, laud, and praise be ev - er Thine!
A - men, A - men.

The end of "ONE NATION, UNDER GOD—A Medley"

574 If My People's Hearts Are Humbled

If My people . . . will humble themselves . . . then will I . . . heal their land. 2 Chr. 7:14

1. If My peo-ple's hearts are hum-bled, If they pray and seek My face;
2. Then My eyes will see their sor - row, Then My ears will hear their plea.
If they turn a - way from e - vil, I will not with - hold My grace.
If My peo - ple's hearts are hum-bled I will set their na - tion free.
I will hear their prayers from heav - en; I will par - don ev - 'ry sin.
If My peo-ple's hearts are hum-bled, If they pray and seek My face;
If My peo-ple's hearts are hum-bled, I will sure - ly heal their land.
If they turn a - way from e - vil, I will not with - hold My grace.

TEXT: Claire Cloninger; based on 2 Chronicles 7:14
MUSIC: John Zundel
A higher setting may be found at No. 268; Alternate tune: AUSTRIAN HYMN at No. 278

BEECHER
8.7.8.7.D.

Eternal Father, Strong to Save 575

He guided them to their desired haven. Let them give thanks to the Lord. Ps. 107:30-31

1. E - ter - nal Fa - ther, strong to save, Whose arm hath bound the
2. O Christ, the Lord of hill and plain O'er which our traf - fic
3. O Spir - it, whom the Fa - ther sent To spread a - broad the
4. O Trin - i - ty of love and power, Our breth-ren shield in
rest - less wave, Who bids the might - y o - cean deep Its
runs a - main By moun - tain pass or val - ley low: Wher-
fir - ma - ment: O Wind of heav - en, by Thy might Save
dan - ger's hour; From rock and tem - pest, fire and foe, Pro -
own ap - point - ed lim - its keep: O hear us when we
ev - er, Lord, our breth - ren go, Pro - tect them by Thy
all who dare the ea - gle's flight, And keep them by Thy
tect them where - so - e'er they go; Thus ev - er - more shall
cry to Thee For those in per - il on the sea.
guard - ing hand From ev - ery per - il on the land.
watch - ful care From ev - ery per - il in the air.
rise to Thee Glad praise from air and land and sea. A - men.

TEXT: William Whiting, stanzas 1, 4; Robert Nelson Spencer, stanzas 2, 3
MUSIC: John Bacchus Dykes

MELITA
8.8.8.8.8.8.

576 The Star-Spangled Banner

Live as free men . . . live as servants of God. 1 Pet. 2:16

1. O say, can you see, by the dawn's ear-ly light, What so proud-ly we hailed at the twi-light's last gleam-ing, Whose broad stripes and bright stars, thro' the per-il-ous fight, O'er the ram-parts we watched, were so gal-lant-ly stream-ing? And the rock-ets' red glare, the bombs burst-ing in air, Gave proof thro' the night that our flag was still

2. O thus be it ev-er, when free men shall stand Be-tween their loved homes and the war's des-o-la-tion! Blest with vic-t'ry and peace, may the heav'n-res-cued land Praise the Pow'r that hath made and pre-served us a na-tion! Then con-quer we must, when our cause it is just; And this be our mot-to: "In God is our

TEXT: Francis Scott Key
MUSIC: Attributed to John Stafford Smith

NATIONAL ANTHEM
Irregular meter

there. O say, does that star span-gled ban-ner yet wave
trust!" And the star-span-gled ban - ner in tri-umph shall wave
O'er the land of the free and the home of the brave?
O'er the land of the free and the home of the brave!

Blessed the Nation 577

Blessed are the people whose God is the Lord. Ps. 144:15

1. Bless - ed the na - tion whose God is the Lord; Bless - ed the land where He reigns. Bless - ed the peo - ple who trust in His Word, And wor - ship His glo - ri - ous name.
2. He is a lov - ing and mer - ci - ful God; We are but chil - dren of dust. He is our Re - fuge, our Strength and our Shield; And He is the Lord that we trust.
3. Bless - ed the na - tion whose God is the Lord; Bless - ed the land where He reigns. Bless - ed the peo - ple who trust in His Word, And wor - ship His glo - ri - ous name.

TEXT: Elizabeth de Gravelles; based on Psalm 144:15
MUSIC: Joseph Barlowe

CARMEL
10.7.10.8.

578 All Things Bright and Beautiful

God saw all that He had made, and it was very good. Gen. 1:31

Unison
Refrain: All things bright and beau-ti-ful, All crea-tures great and small, And all things wise and won-der-ful; The Lord God made them all.
rit. last time
Fine
1. Each lit-tle flow'r that o-pens up, Each lit-tle bird that sings, He made their glow-ing col-ors and He made their ti-ny wings. The pur-ple head-ed moun-tain, The riv-er run-ning by, The
2. The cold wind in the win-ter-time, The pleas-ant sum-mer sun, The ripe fruits in the gar-den now, He made them ev-'ry-one; He gave us eyes to see them all, And lips that we might tell How

TEXT: Cecil F. Alexander, altered
MUSIC: Sonny Salsbury; arranged by Lee Herrington

SALSBURY
Irregular meter

D.C. for Refrain
sun - set and the morn-ing light That bright-ens up the sky.
great is the Al - might-y God Who has made all things well.
Jesus Loves Me 579
Christ loved us and gave Himself up for us. Eph. 5:2
1. Je - sus loves me! this I know, For the Bi - ble tells me so; Lit - tle
2. Je - sus loves me! He who died Heav-en's gate to o - pen wide; He will
3. Je - sus loves me! He will stay Close be-side me all the way; He's pre-
ones to Him be-long, They are weak but He is strong.
wash a - way my sin, Let His lit - tle child come in.
pared a home for me, And some day His face I'll see.
Refrain
Yes, Je-sus loves me!
Yes, Je - sus loves me! Yes, Je - sus loves me! The Bi - ble tells me so.

TEXT: Anna B. Warner, altered
MUSIC: William B. Bradbury

JESUS LOVES ME
7.7.7.7. with Refrain

580 Jesus Loves the Little Children

Let the little children come to Me, and do not hinder them. Matt. 19:14

Je - sus loves the lit - tle chil - dren, All the chil - dren of the world. Red and yel - low, black and white, They are pre - cious in His sight— Je - sus loves the lit - tle chil - dren of the world.

TEXT: Reverend C. H. Woolston
MUSIC: George F. Root

CHILDREN
8.7.7.7.11.

581 Commit Thy Way

Commit your way to the Lord; trust in Him and He will do this. Ps. 37:5

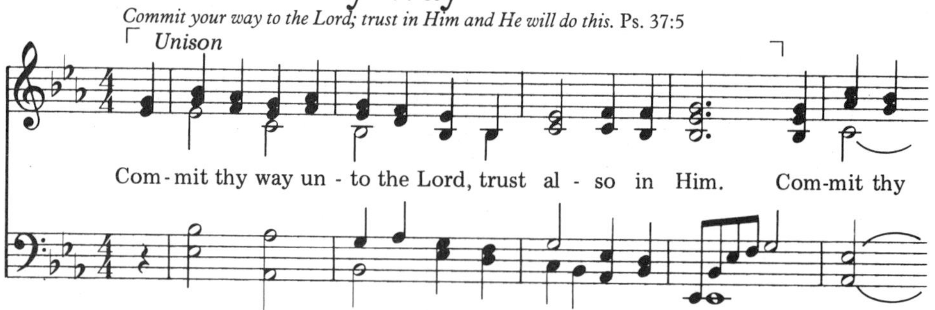
Unison
Com - mit thy way un - to the Lord, trust al - so in Him. Com - mit thy

TEXT: Psalm 37:5
MUSIC: Kurt Kaiser

COMMIT THY WAY
Irregular meter

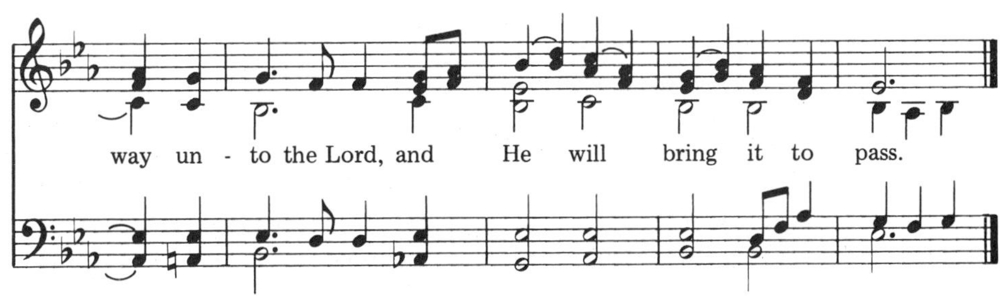
way un - to the Lord, and He will bring it to pass.

Reach Your Hand 582

Love one another deeply, from the heart. 1 Pet. 1:22

Unison

1. Reach your hand as far as it goes, and I'll reach mine. Do you sup - pose that we can make the world so small that there will be no walls at all? 2. Let's

(2.) stretch our arms so ver - y much that if we try, our fin - gers touch; and when they do, we'll know it's true that you love me, and I love you. 3. Oh,

(3.) Fa - ther dear, we give to You our hands, our feet, our hearts, to do just as You will, for we would be a wit - ness for the world to see.

1,2 | 3

TEXT: Gerald DiPego, stanzas 1, 2; Kurt Kaiser, stanza 3
MUSIC: Kurt Kaiser

REACH YOUR HAND
L.M.

583 The Wise May Bring Their Learning

God . . . will not forget your work and the love you have shown Him. Heb. 6:10

1. The wise may bring their learn - ing, The rich may bring their wealth,
2. We'll bring Him hearts that love Him; We'll bring Him thank-ful praise,
3. We'll bring the lit - tle du - ties We have to do each day;

And some may bring their great - ness, And some bring strength and health;
And young souls meek - ly striv - ing To walk in ho - ly ways:
We'll try our best to please Him, At home, at school, at play:

We, too, would bring our treas - ures To of - fer to the King;
And these shall be the treas - ures We of - fer to the King,
And bet - ter are these treas - ures To of - fer to our King,

We have no wealth or learn - ing: What shall we chil - dren bring?
And these are gifts that e - ven The poor - est child may bring.
Than rich - est gifts with - out them; Yet these a child may bring.

TEXT: Anonymous; from *The Book of Praise for Children,* 1881
MUSIC: Joe E. Parks

ELDER MOUNTAIN
7.6.7.6.D.

It Is Good to Sing Thy Praises 584

It is good to praise the Lord. Ps. 92:1

1. It is good to sing Thy prais-es And to thank Thee, O Most High,
2. Thou has filled my heart with glad-ness Thro the works Thy hands have wrought;
3. But the good shall live be-fore Thee, Plant-ed in Thy dwell-ing place,
Show-ing forth Thy lov-ing-kind-ness When the morn-ing lights the sky.
Thou hast made my life vic-to-rious, Great Thy works and deep Thy thought.
Fruit-ful trees and ev-er ver-dant, Nour-ished by Thy bound-less grace.
It is good when night is fall-ing Of Thy faith-ful-ness to tell,
Thou, O Lord, on high ex-alt-ed, Reign-est ev-er-more in might;
In His good-ness to the right-eous God His right-eous-ness dis-plays;
While with sweet, me-lo-dious prais-es Songs of ad-o-ra-tion swell.
All Thy en-e-mies shall per-ish, Sin be ban-ished from Thy sight.
God my Rock, my Strength, my Ref-uge, Just and true are all His ways. A-men.

TEXT: *The Psalter;* based on Psalm 92
MUSIC: Leavitt's *The Christian Lyre,* 1831; attributed to Wolfgang A. Mozart; arranged by Hubert P. Main
A lower setting may be found at No. 377

ELLESDIE
8.7.8.7.D.

585 Brethren, We Have Met to Worship

Worship the Lord in the splendor of His holiness. 1 Chr. 16:29

1. Breth-ren, we have met to wor - ship And a - dore the Lord our God;
2. Let us love our God su - preme-ly, Let us love each oth - er too;

Will you pray with all your pow - er, While we try to preach the Word?
Let us love and pray for sin - ners Till our God makes all things new.

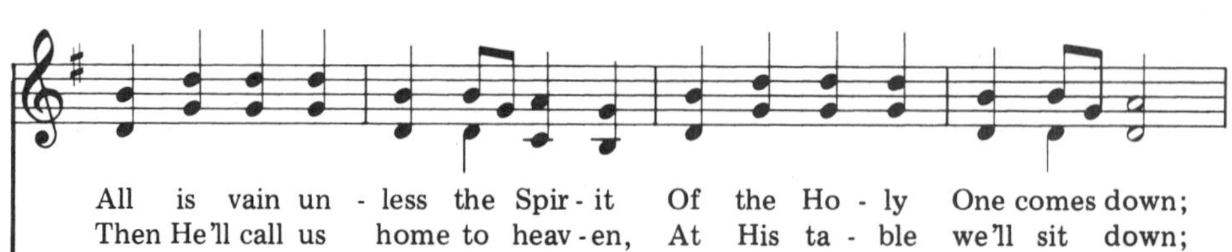

All is vain un - less the Spir - it Of the Ho - ly One comes down;
Then He'll call us home to heav - en, At His ta - ble we'll sit down;

Breth-ren, pray, and ho - ly man - na Will be show-ered all a - round.
Christ will gird Him - self and serve us With sweet man-na all a - round.

TEXT: George Atkins
MUSIC: William Moore

HOLY MANNA
8.7.8.7.D.

Jesus, Stand Among Us 586

Jesus . . . stood among them and said, "Peace be with you!" John 20:19

1. Je - sus, stand a - mong us In Thy ris - en power;
2. Breathe the Ho - ly Spir - it In - to ev - ery heart;
Let this time of wor - ship Be a hal-lowed hour.
Bid the fears and sor - rows From each soul de - part. A - men.

TEXT: William Pennefather
MUSIC: Friedrich Filitz

BEMERTON
6.5.6.5.

All Praise to Our Redeeming Lord 587

The whole body, joined . . . together . . . grows and builds itself up in love. Eph. 4:16

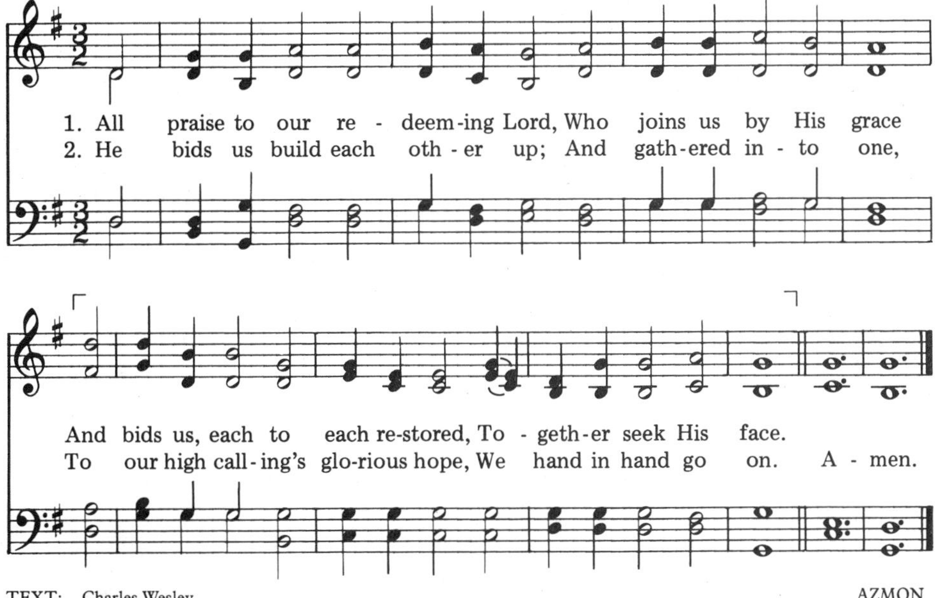
1. All praise to our re - deem-ing Lord, Who joins us by His grace
2. He bids us build each oth - er up; And gath-ered in - to one,
And bids us, each to each re-stored, To - geth-er seek His face.
To our high call-ing's glo-rious hope, We hand in hand go on. A - men.

TEXT: Charles Wesley
MUSIC: Carl G. Gläser; arranged by Lowell Mason
A higher setting may be found at No. 76

AZMON
C.M.

588 We Have Come into His House

They came to Him, clasped His feet and worshiped Him. Matt. 28:9

TEXT and MUSIC: Bruce Ballinger

WORSHIP HIM
Irregular meter

Come into His Presence 589

Come before Him with joyful songs. Ps. 100:2

4 Part Canon

1. Come in - to His pres-ence sing-ing Al - le-lu - ia, al - le-lu - ia, al - le-lu - ia.
2. Come in - to His pres-ence sing-ing Je - sus is Lord, Je - sus is Lord, Je - sus is Lord.
3. Praise the Lord together singing Worthy the Lamb, worthy the Lamb, worthy the Lamb.
4. Praise the Lord to-geth-er sing-ing Glo - ry to God, glo - ry to God, glo - ry to God.

TEXT and MUSIC: Source unknown

HIS PRESENCE
8.4.4.4.

This Is the Day 590

This is the day the Lord has made; let us rejoice and be glad in it. Ps. 118:24

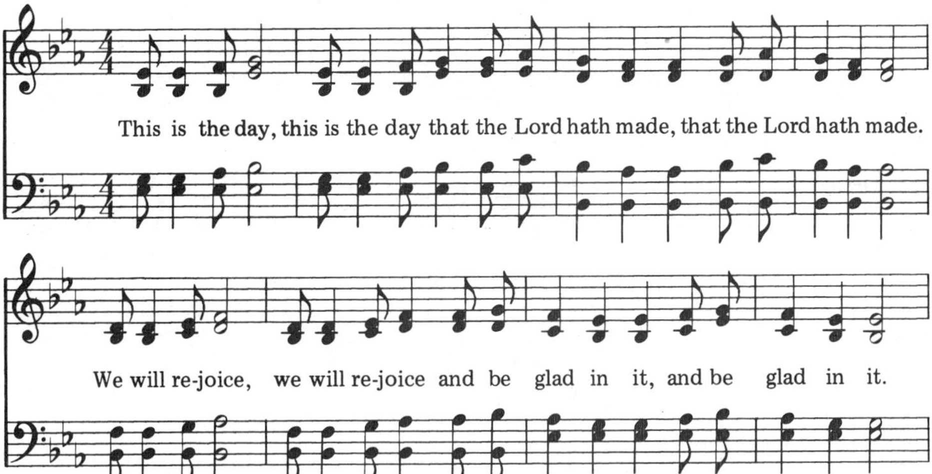

This is the day, this is the day that the Lord hath made, that the Lord hath made.

We will re-joice, we will re-joice and be glad in it, and be glad in it.

This is the day that the Lord hath made; We will re-joice and be glad in it.

This is the day, this is the day that the Lord hath made.

TEXT and MUSIC: Les Garrett; adapted from Psalm 118:24

THIS IS THE DAY
Irregular meter

591 Come Let Us Reason

Though your sins are like scarlet, they shall be as white as snow. Isa. 1:18

"Come, let us rea - son to - geth - er," that's what
God says. "Come, let us rea - son to -
geth - er," says the Lord. Lord. "Tho' your sins be as
scar - let, they shall be as white as snow;
Tho' they be red as crim - son, they shall be as wool."
1, 3
fine
2
D.C. al Fine
3

TEXT and MUSIC: Ken Medema; arranged by David Allen

COME LET US REASON
Irregular meter

In This Quiet Moment 592

In quietness and trust is your strength. Isa. 30:15

Unison
In this qui - et mo - ment, Je - sus, speak to me.
Fill my heart with Thy love di - vine, Your pow - er let me see.

TEXT and MUSIC: Larry Mayfield

QUIET MOMENT
Irregular meter

O Worship the Lord 593

Worship the Lord in the splendor of His holiness. Ps. 96:9

O wor - ship the Lord in the beau - ty of ho - li - ness;
Serve Him with glad - ness, all the earth. A - men.

TEXT: Psalm 96:9
MUSIC: Robert G. McCutchan

McCUTCHAN
Irregular meter

594 The Lord Is in His Holy Temple

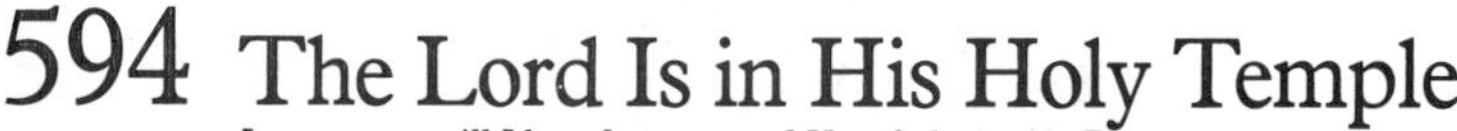

In reverence will I bow down toward Your holy temple. Ps. 5:7

The Lord is in His ho - ly tem - ple, The Lord is in His ho - ly tem - ple; Let all the earth keep si-lence, Let all the earth keep si - lence be - fore Him, Keep si-lence, keep si-lence be - fore Him. A - men.

TEXT: Habakkuk 2:20
MUSIC: George F. Root

QUAM DILECTA
Irregular meter

595 Now to the King of Heaven

To the only wise God be glory forever through Jesus Christ! Rom. 16:27

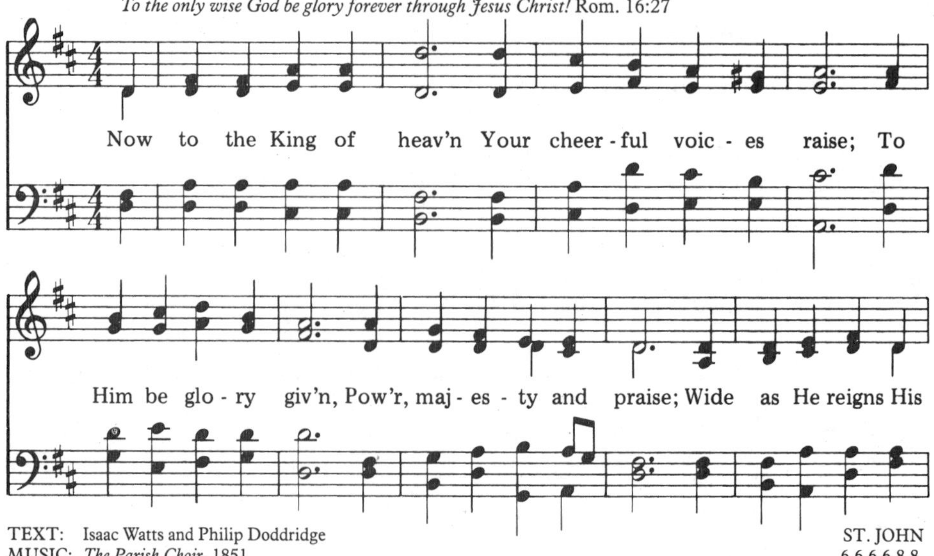
Now to the King of heav'n Your cheer - ful voic - es raise; To
Him be glo - ry giv'n, Pow'r, maj - es - ty and praise; Wide as He reigns His

TEXT: Isaac Watts and Philip Doddridge
MUSIC: *The Parish Choir,* 1851

ST. JOHN
6.6.6.6.8.8.

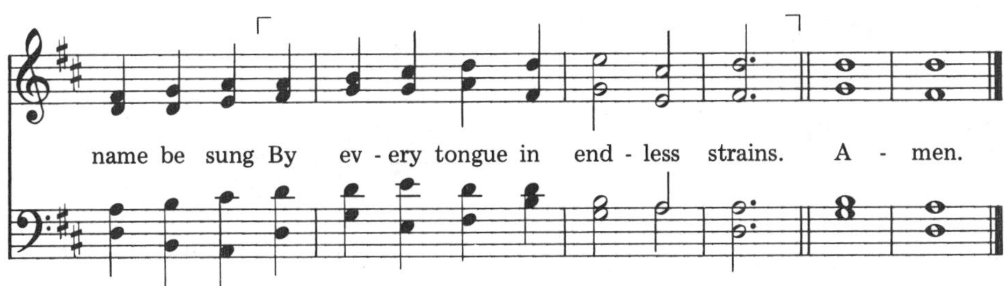
name be sung By ev - ery tongue in end - less strains. A - men.

Praise Ye the Name of the Lord 596

Sing the glory of His name; make His praise glorious! Ps. 66:2

Choir Unison

Praise ye the name of the Lord of Hosts. Praise Him, praise Him, all ye peo - ple. Let all the na - tions praise the Lord.

keyboard play cued notes only

8va 8va

ff *Sing Parts*

Praise ye the Lord!

rit. e rall. *fff*

Let all the na - tions praise the Lord!

TEXT and MUSIC: Gordon Young

PRAISE YE
Irregular meter

597 Christ, We Do All Adore Thee

Worthy is the Lamb . . . to receive . . . honor and glory and praise! Rev. 5:12

p
Christ, we do all a - dore Thee, and we do praise Thee for - ev - er;
mp
cresc.
Christ, we do all a - dore Thee, and we do praise Thee for - ev - er,
mf
decresc.
For on the ho - ly cross hast Thou the world from sin re - deem - ed.
p
decresc.
Christ, we do all a - dore Thee, and we do praise Thee for - ev - er.
pp
pp
*Instruments
Christ, we do all a - dore Thee!
*These 2 measures may be omitted.

TEXT: *Adoramus Te,* English version by Theodore Baker
MUSIC: Theodore Dubois; from *The Seven Last Words of Christ*

ADORE THEE
Irregular meter

Cast Thy Burden upon the Lord 598

Cast your cares on the Lord and He will sustain you. Ps. 55:22

Cast thy bur - den up - on the Lord, and He shall sus -
tain thee; He nev - er will suf - fer the
right - eous to fall: He is at thy right hand.
Optional ending
Thy mer - cy, Lord, is great and far a - bove the heav'ns: Let
none be made a - sham - ed that wait up - on Thee. A - men.

TEXT: Based on Psalm 55:22
MUSIC: Felix Mendelssohn; from *Elijah*

CAST THY BURDEN
Irregular meter

599 Spoken Calls to Worship

1 The earth is the Lord's, and everything in it, the world, and all who live in it. Lift up your heads, O you gates; lift them up, you ancient doors, that the King of glory may come in. Who is He, this King of glory? The Lord Almighty—He is the King of glory. Ps. 24:1, 9-10

2 Come, let us sing for joy to the Lord; let us shout aloud to the Rock of our salvation. Let us come before Him with thanksgiving and extol Him with music and song. Ps. 95:1-2

3 Come, let us bow down in worship, let us kneel before the Lord our Maker; for He is our God and we are the people of His pasture, the flock under His care. Ps. 95:6-7

4 Shout for joy to the Lord, all the earth. Worship the Lord with gladness; come before Him with joyful songs. Know that the Lord is God. It is He who made us, and we are His; we are His people, the sheep of His pasture. Ps. 100:1-3

5 Enter His gates with thanksgiving and His courts with praise; give thanks to Him and praise His name. For the Lord is good and His love endures forever; His faithfulness continues through all generations. Ps. 100:4-5

6 Praise the Lord. Praise God in His sanctuary; praise Him in His mighty heavens. Praise Him for His acts of power; praise Him for His surpassing greatness. Let everything that has breath praise the Lord. Praise the Lord. Ps. 150:1-2, 6

7 Come to Me, all you who are weary and burdened, and I will give you rest. Take My yoke upon you and learn from Me, for I am gentle and humble in heart, and you will find rest for your souls. For My yoke is easy and My burden is light. Matt. 11:28-30

8 Worthy is the Lamb, who was slain, to receive power and wealth and wisdom and strength and honor and glory and praise! To Him who sits on the throne and to the Lamb be praise and honor and glory and power, for ever and ever! Rev. 5:12-13

9 I will sing of the Lord's great love forever; with my mouth I will make Your faithfulness known through all generations. I will declare that Your love stands firm forever, that You established Your faithfulness in heaven itself. Ps. 89:1-2

10 Be still, and know that I am God; I will be exalted among the nations, I will be exalted in the earth. Ps. 46:10

11 Ascribe to the Lord the glory due His name; worship the Lord in the splendor of His holiness. Ps. 29:2

12 It is good to praise the Lord and make music to Your name, O Most High, to proclaim Your love in the morning and Your faithfulness at night. Ps. 92:1-2

13 You are my God, and I will give You thanks; You are my God, and I will exalt You. Give thanks to the Lord, for He is good; His love endures forever. Ps. 118:28-29

14 Yet a time is coming and has now come when the true worshipers will worship the Father in spirit and truth, for they are the kind of worshipers the Father seeks. God is spirit, and His worshipers must worship in spirit and in truth. John 4:23-24

All Spoken Calls to Worship are from the NIV.

If You Will Only Let God Guide You 600

We wait in hope for the Lord; He is our Help and our Shield. Ps. 33:20

1. If you will on - ly let God guide you, And hope in
2. On - ly be still, and wait His lei - sure In cheer - ful
3. Sing, pray, and swerve not from His ways, But do your
Him thru all your ways, What-ev - er comes, He'll stand be - side you,
hope, with heart con - tent To take what - e'er the Fa - ther's plea-sure
part in con-science true; Trust His rich prom - is - es of grace,
To bear you thru the e - vil days; Who trusts in God's un-
And all dis - cern - ing love have sent; Nor doubt our in - most
So shall they be ful - filled in you; God hears the call of
chang - ing love Builds on the rock that can - not move.
wants are known To Him who chose us for His own.
those in need, The souls that trust in Him in - deed.

TEXT: Georg Neumark; translated by Catherine Winkworth, altered
MUSIC: Georg Neumark

NEUMARK
9.8.9.8.8.8.

601 Lord, Dismiss Us with Thy Blessing

May Your blessing be on Your people. Ps. 3:8

1. Lord, dis - miss us with Thy bless-ing, Fill our hearts with joy and peace;
2. Thanks we give and ad - o - ra - tion For Thy gos - pel's joy - ful sound;

Let us each, Thy love pos-sess - ing, Tri - umph in re - deem - ing grace.
May the fruits of Thy sal - va - tion In our hearts and lives a - bound.

O re - fresh us, O re - fresh us, Trav-eling through this wil-der-ness.
Ev - er faith - ful, ev - er faith - ful To the truth may we be found. A - men.

TEXT: John Fawcett, altered
MUSIC: Tattersall's *Psalmody,* 1794

SICILIAN MARINERS
8.7.8.7.8.7.

602 God Be with You

The grace of our Lord Jesus Christ be with you. 1 Thess. 5:28

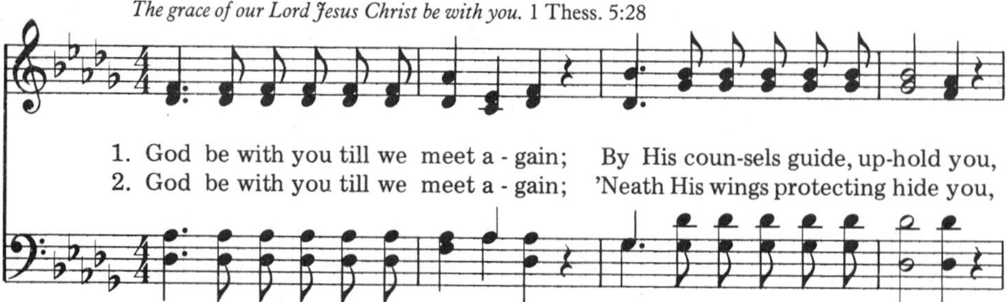
1. God be with you till we meet a - gain; By His coun-sels guide, up-hold you,
2. God be with you till we meet a - gain; 'Neath His wings protecting hide you,

TEXT: Jeremiah E. Rankin
MUSIC: William G. Tomer

GOD BE WITH YOU
Irregular meter

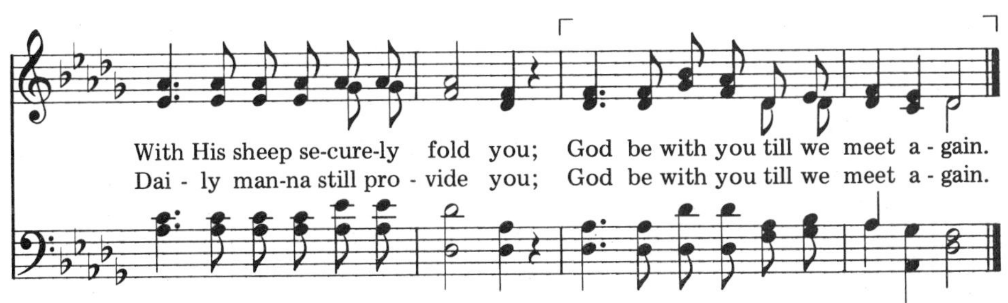
With His sheep se-cure-ly fold you; God be with you till we meet a - gain.
Dai - ly man-na still pro - vide you; God be with you till we meet a - gain.

The Lord Whom We Love 603

. . . to prepare God's people for works of service. Eph. 4:12

The Lord whom we love, whom we wor-ship and a - dore, We will serve through-

out this com-ing week. He it is who binds us to - geth-er,

And He it is who sends us a - part, To be God's

peo-ple, be God's peo-ple, A - men, a - men.

TEXT and MUSIC: Kurt Kaiser

BROOKS
Irregular meter

604 Savior, Again to Thy Dear Name

The Lord blesses His people with peace. Ps. 29:11

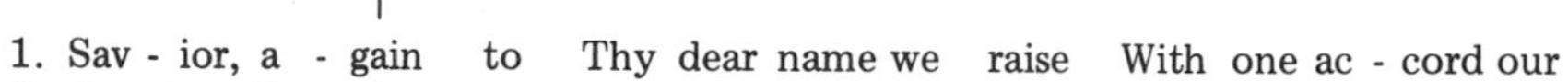

1. Sav - ior, a - gain to Thy dear name we raise With one ac - cord our
2. Grant us Thy peace up - on our home-ward way; With Thee be - gan, with

part - ing hymn of praise; Once more we bless Thee ere our wor-ship cease;
Thee shall end the day; Guard Thou the lips from sin, the hearts from shame,

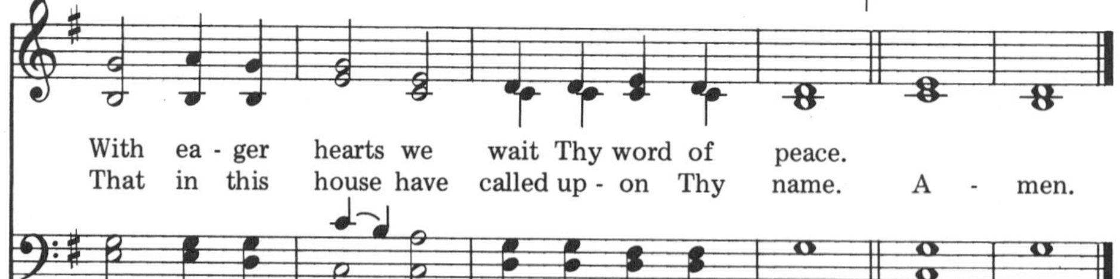
With ea - ger hearts we wait Thy word of peace.
That in this house have called up - on Thy name. A - men.

TEXT: John Ellerton
MUSIC: Edward J. Hopkins; arranged by Joseph Barlowe

ELLERS
10.10.10.10.

605 When This Song of Praise Shall Cease

Mercy, peace and love be yours in abundance. Jude 2

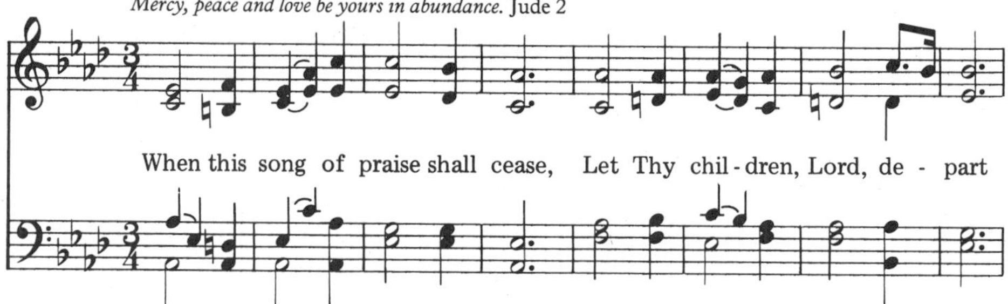
When this song of praise shall cease, Let Thy chil - dren, Lord, de - part

TEXT: William Bradbury, altered
MUSIC: Louis M. Gottschalk

MERCY
7.7.7.7.

With the bless - ing of Thy peace, And Thy love in ev - 'ry heart. A - men.

Grace, Love and Fellowship 606

May . . . grace . . . love . . . and . . . fellowship . . . be with you all. 2 Cor. 13:14

Unison

May the grace of Christ, our Sav - ior, and the love of God, our

Fa - ther, and the fel - low - ship of the Spir - it be with us.

1

2

May the us for - ev - er, and

rit.

ev - er, for - ev - er - more, A - men.

TEXT and MUSIC: Tom Fettke; based on 2 Cor. 13:14

CANE PEAK
Irregular meter

607 The Lord Bless You and Keep You

The Lord bless you and keep you . . . and give you peace. Num. 6:24, 26

p
The Lord bless you and keep you; The Lord lift His coun - te-nance up -
on you, and give you peace, and give you peace;
and give you peace, and give you peace;
cresc.
The Lord make His face to shine up - on you,
decresc.
The Lord make His face to shine up - on you,
The Lord
and be gra - cious un - to you, be gra - cious,
and be gra - cious, and be gra - cious,
p
dim. e rit.
Optional ending
1
The Lord be gra-cious, gra - cious un - to you. A - men.

TEXT: Numbers 6:24-26
MUSIC: Peter C. Lutkin

BENEDICTION
Irregular meter

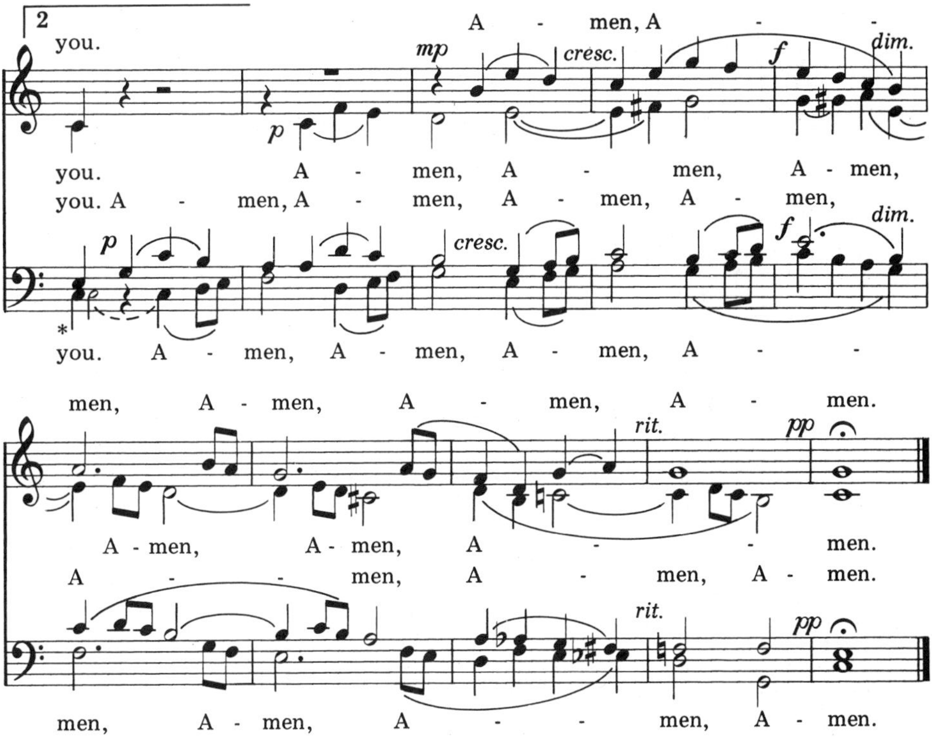
2
you.
A - men, A - -
mp cresc. f dim.
p
you. A - men, A - men, A - men,
you. A - men, A - men, A - men, A - men,
p cresc. f dim.
*
you. A - men, A - men, A - men, A - -
men, A - men, A - men, A - men.
rit. pp
A - men, A - men, A - men.
A - - men, A - men, A - men.
rit. pp
men, A - men, A - - men, A - men.

*The "Amens" may be used separately. Bass begins with first "Amen" on the downbeat of the measure (cued half-note).

May the Grace of Christ, Our Savior 608

The grace of the Lord Jesus be with God's people. Rev. 22:21

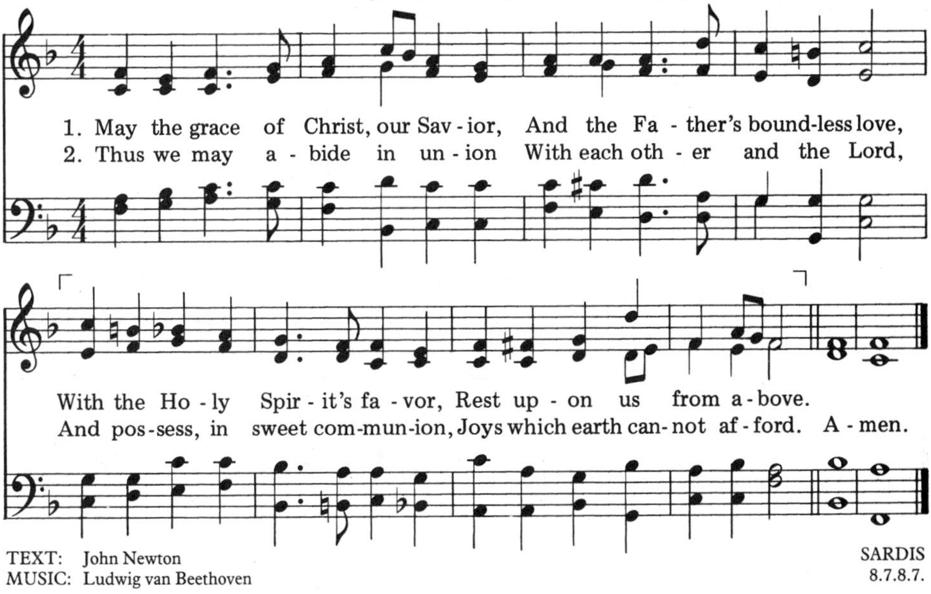
1. May the grace of Christ, our Sav - ior, And the Fa - ther's bound-less love,
2. Thus we may a - bide in un - ion With each oth - er and the Lord,
With the Ho - ly Spir - it's fa - vor, Rest up - on us from a - bove.
And pos-sess, in sweet com-mun-ion, Joys which earth can- not af - ford. A - men.

TEXT: John Newton
MUSIC: Ludwig van Beethoven

SARDIS
8.7.8.7.

609 Lord, Let Us Now Depart in Peace

Peace to you. 3 John 14

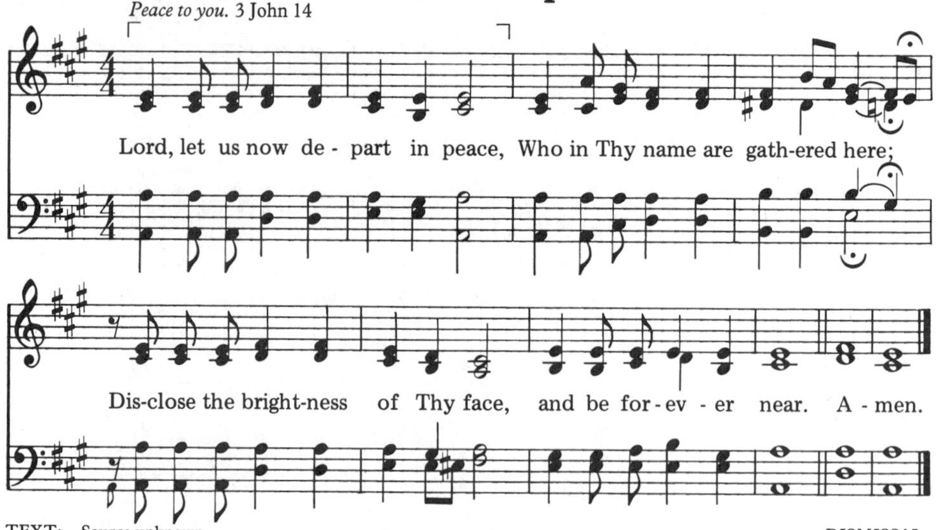
Lord, let us now de - part in peace, Who in Thy name are gath-ered here;
Dis-close the bright-ness of Thy face, and be for - ev - er near. A - men.

TEXT: Source unknown
MUSIC: George Whelpton

DISMISSAL
Irregular meter

610 Go Now and Live for the Savior

Live a life worthy of the Lord. Col. 1:10

Go now, and live for the Sav - ior; Go, may this
joy be your joy too. Go, may this pres - ence ev - er
guide you; Go, live this life the whole day through.

TEXT and MUSIC: Kurt Kaiser

GO NOW
8.8.9.8.

Now unto the King 611

Now to the King eternal, immortal, invisible, the only God, be honor. 1 Tim. 1:17

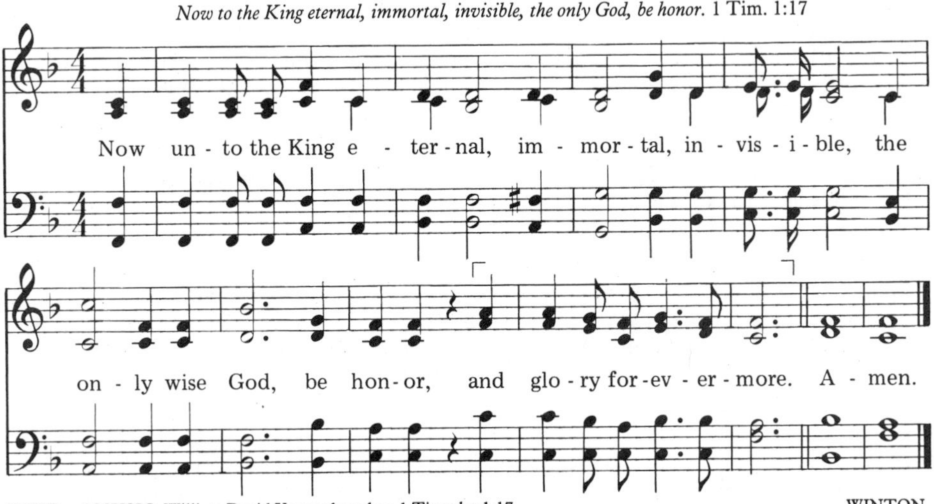
Now un - to the King e - ter - nal, im - mor - tal, in - vis - i - ble, the
on - ly wise God, be hon - or, and glo - ry for - ev - er - more. A - men.

TEXT and MUSIC: William David Young; based on 1 Timothy 1:17

WINTON
Irregular meter

Benediction 612

May the grace of the Lord Jesus Christ . . . be with you all. 2 Cor. 13:14

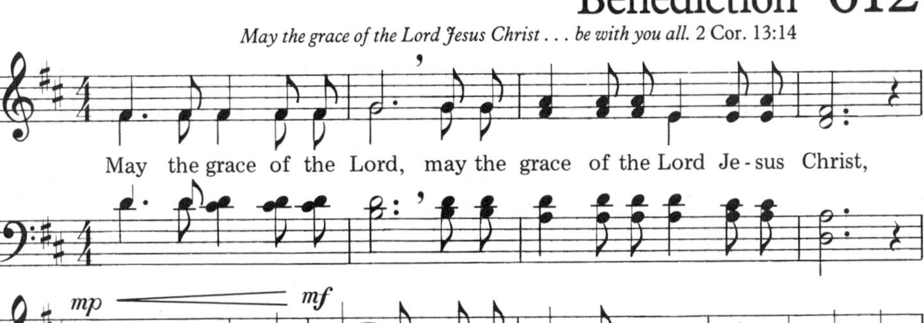
May the grace of the Lord, may the grace of the Lord Je - sus Christ,
mp
mf
and the love of God, and the fel - low-ship of the Ho - ly
the

sub. p
ten.
Spir - it, be with you all. A - men.
ten.

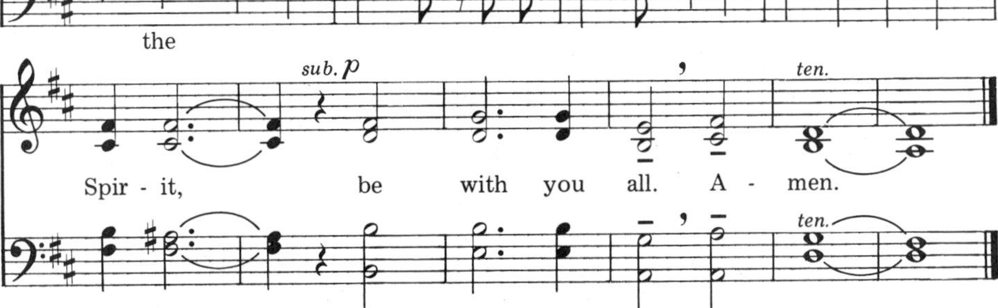

TEXT: 2 Corinthians 13:14
MUSIC: Ken Barker

PAUL
Irregular meter

613 Spoken Benedictions

1 The Lord bless you and keep you; the Lord make His face shine upon you and be gracious to you; the Lord turn His face toward you and give you peace. Num. 6:24-26

2 May the grace of the Lord Jesus Christ, and the love of God, and the fellowship of the Holy Spirit be with you all. 2 Cor. 13:14

3 May the God of peace, who through the blood of the eternal covenant brought back from the dead our Lord Jesus, that great Shepherd of the sheep, equip you with everything good for doing His will, and may He work in us what is pleasing to Him, through Jesus Christ, to whom be glory for ever and ever. Amen. Heb. 13:20-21

4 To Him who is able to keep you from falling and to present you before His glorious presence without fault and with great joy—to the only God our Savior be glory, majesty, power and authority, through Jesus Christ our Lord, before all ages, now and forevermore! Amen. Jude 24-25

5 May our Lord Jesus Christ Himself and God our Father, who loved us and by His grace gave us eternal encouragement and good hope, encourage your hearts and strengthen you in every good deed and word. 2 Thess. 2:16-17

6 And the God of all grace, who called you to His eternal glory in Christ, after you have suffered a little while, will Himself restore you and make you strong, firm and steadfast. To Him be the power for ever and ever. Amen. 1 Pet. 5:10-11

7 Now to Him who is able to do immeasurably more than all we ask or imagine, according to His power that is at work within us, to Him be glory in the church and in Christ Jesus throughout all generations, for ever and ever! Amen. Eph. 3:20-21

8 The grace of our Lord Jesus Christ be with you. 1 Thess. 5:28

9 Now to the King eternal, immortal, invisible, the only God, be honor and glory for ever and ever. Amen. 1 Tim. 1:17

10 The grace of the Lord Jesus be with God's people. Amen. Rev. 22:21

All Spoken Benedictions are from the NIV.

Hear Our Prayer, O Lord 614

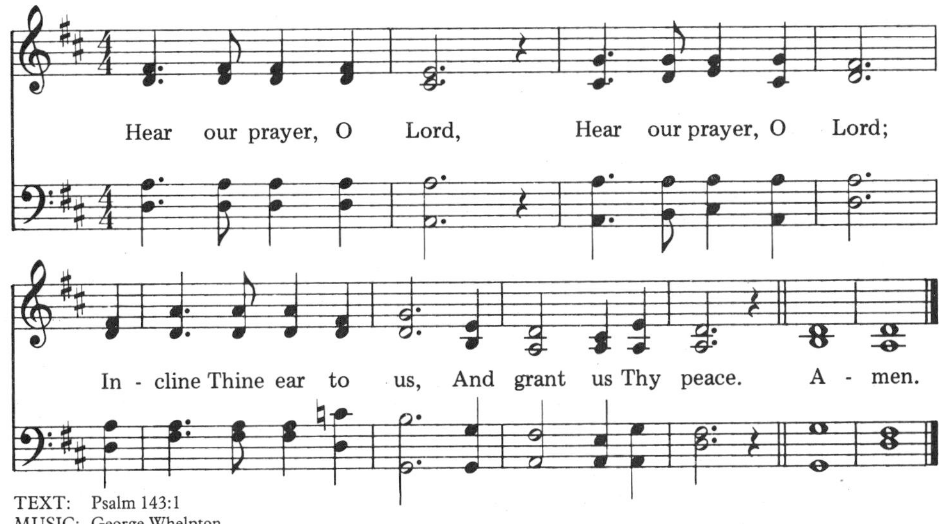
Hear our prayer, O Lord, Hear our prayer, O Lord;
In - cline Thine ear to us, And grant us Thy peace. A - men.

TEXT: Psalm 143:1
MUSIC: George Whelpton

Spirit Divine, Hear Our Prayer 615

Spir - it Di - vine, hear our prayer, And make our
hearts Your home; De - scend with all Your gra - cious
pow'r, Come, Ho - ly Spir - it, come. A - men.

TEXT: Andrew Reed
MUSIC: Bill Wolaver

616 Hear Our Prayer, O Heavenly Father

Hear our prayer, O heav'n-ly Fa-ther, for the dear Re-deem-er's sake. A - men.

TEXT: Traditional
MUSIC: Attributed to Frederic Chopin

617 Thou Wilt Keep Him in Perfect Peace

Thou wilt keep him in per-fect peace Whose mind is stayed on Thee. A-men.

TEXT: Isaiah 26:3
MUSIC: *Scottish Psalter,* 1615

DUKE'S TUNE
Irregular meter

618 Let the Words of My Mouth

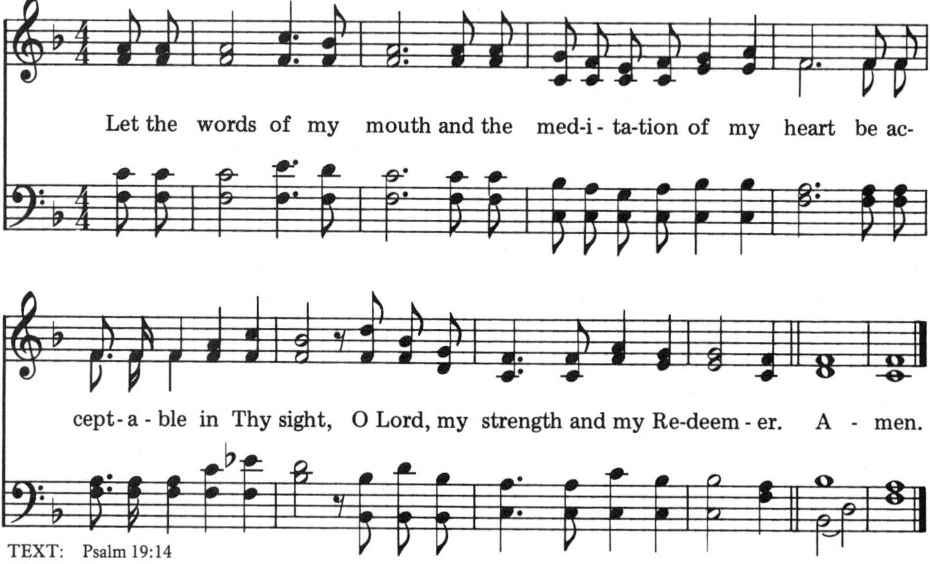
Let the words of my mouth and the med-i-ta-tion of my heart be ac-
cept-a-ble in Thy sight, O Lord, my strength and my Re-deem-er. A - men.

TEXT: Psalm 19:14
MUSIC: Adolph Baumbach

We Give You Thanks 619

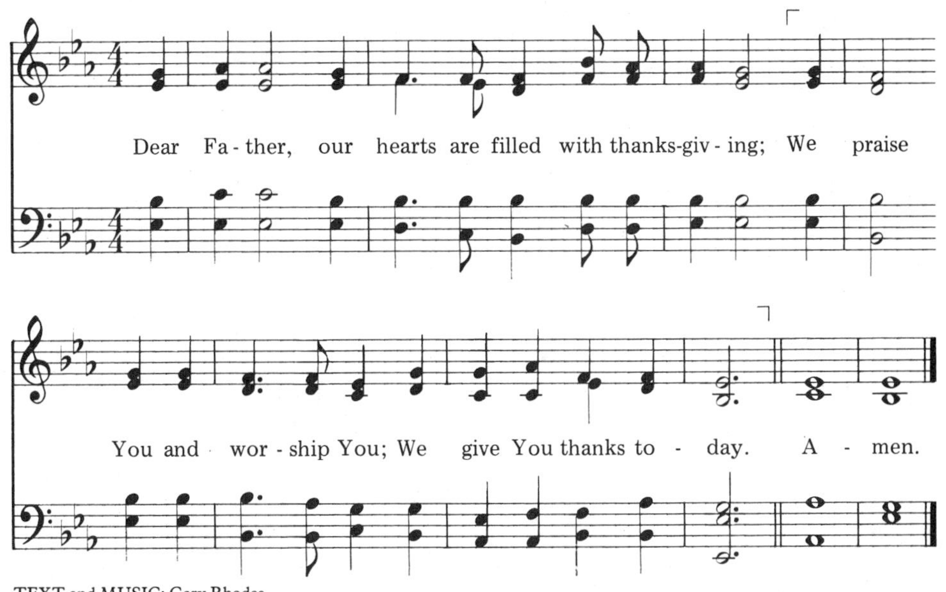
Dear Fa - ther, our hearts are filled with thanks-giv - ing; We praise
You and wor - ship You; We give You thanks to - day. A - men.

TEXT and MUSIC: Gary Rhodes

We Give Thee But Thine Own 620

We have given You only what comes from Your hand. 1 Chr. 29:14

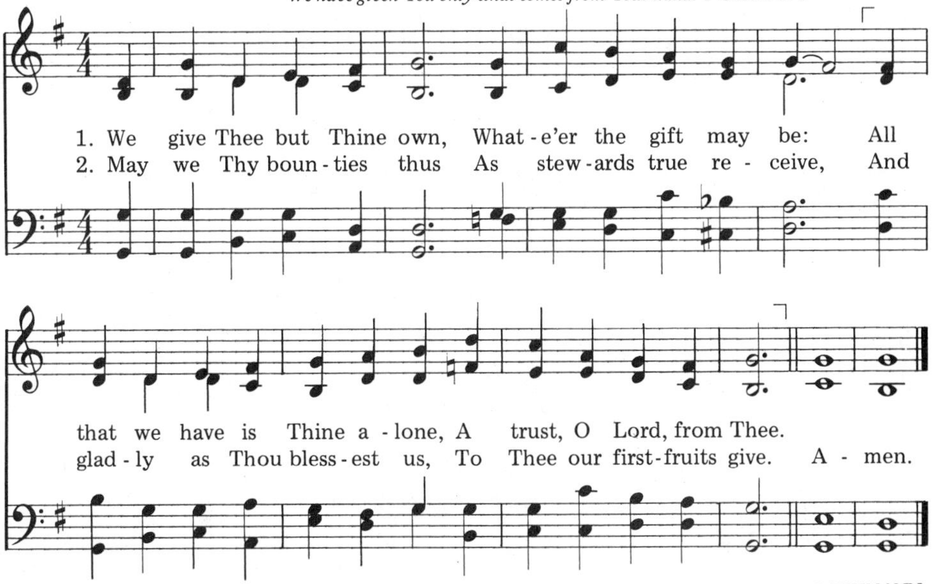

1. We give Thee but Thine own, What - e'er the gift may be: All that we have is Thine a - lone, A trust, O Lord, from Thee.

2. May we Thy boun - ties thus As stew - ards true re - ceive, And glad - ly as Thou bless - est us, To Thee our first-fruits give. A - men.

TEXT: William W. How
MUSIC: Mason and Webb's *Cantica Laudis,* 1850

SCHUMANN
S.M.

621 God's Ways Are Wonderful

Whoever sows generously will also reap generously. 2 Cor. 9:6

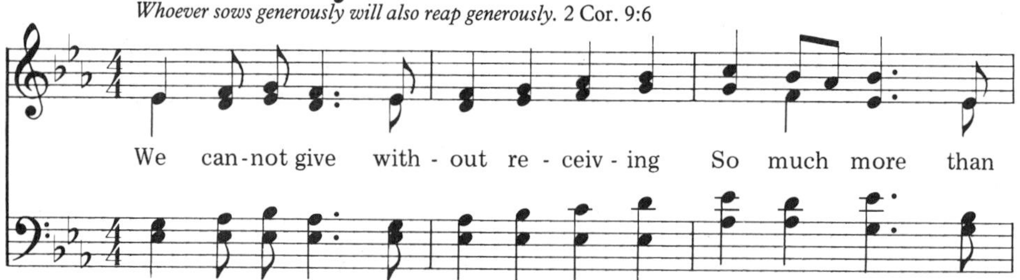
We can-not give with - out re - ceiv - ing So much more than

we have giv - en. God's ways are won-der-ful, God's ways are won-der - ful.

TEXT and MUSIC: Kurt Kaiser

GOD'S WAYS
Irregular meter

622 Gloria Patri

Ascribe to the Lord the glory due His name. Ps. 96:8

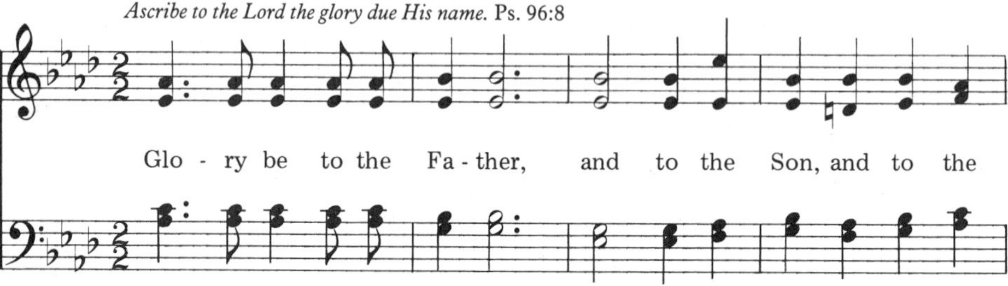
Glo - ry be to the Fa - ther, and to the Son, and to the

Ho - ly Ghost: as it was in the be - gin - ning, is

TEXT: *Gloria Patri;* Traditional, 2nd century
MUSIC: Christoph Meineke

MEINEKE
Irregular meter

now and ev - er shall be, world with-out end. A - men, A - men.

Gloria Patri 623

Ascribe to the Lord the glory due His name. Ps. 96:8

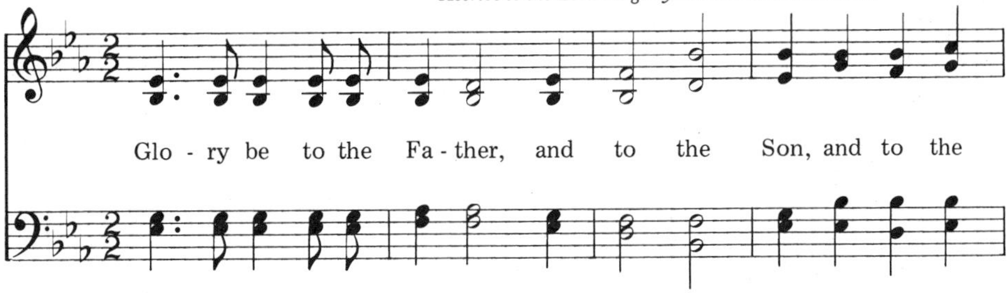

Glo - ry be to the Fa - ther, and to the Son, and to the

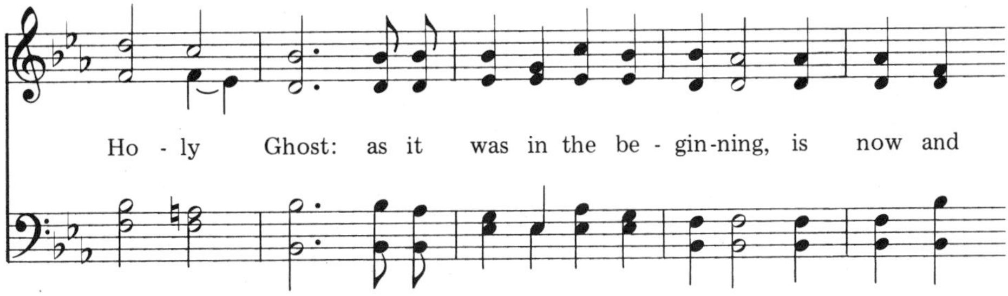

Ho - ly Ghost: as it was in the be - gin-ning, is now and

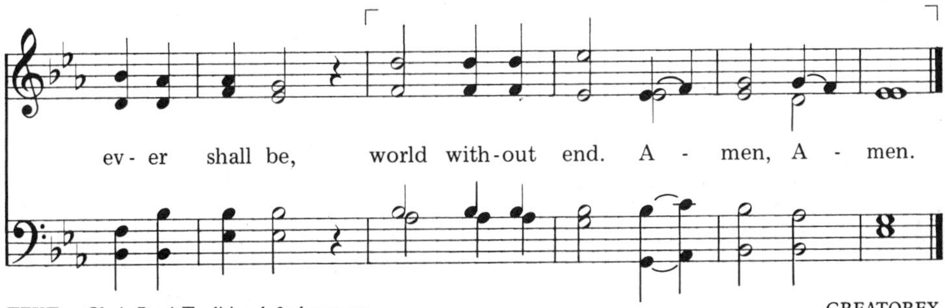

ev - er shall be, world with-out end. A - men, A - men.

TEXT: *Gloria Patri;* Traditional, 2nd century
MUSIC: Henry W. Greatorex

GREATOREX
Irregular meter

624 Doxology

Praise be to the God and Father of our Lord Jesus Christ, who has blessed us. Eph. 1:3

Praise God from whom all bless-ings flow; Praise Him, all crea-tures here be - low;
Praise Him a-bove, ye heav'n-ly host; Praise Fa-ther, Son and Ho-ly Ghost. A - men.
Praise God from whom all bless-ings flow; Praise Him, all crea - tures here be - low;
Praise Him a-bove, ye heav'n-ly host; Praise Fa-ther, Son and Ho-ly Ghost. A - men.

TEXT: Thomas Ken
MUSIC: *Genevan Psalter,* 1551; attributed to Louis Bourgeois

OLD HUNDREDTH
L.M.

625 Doxology

Praise be to the God and Father of our Lord Jesus Christ, who has blessed us. Eph. 1:3

TEXT: Thomas Ken
MUSIC: *Genevan Psalter,* 1551; attributed to Louis Bourgeois

OLD HUNDREDTH
L.M.

Doxology 626

Praise be to the God and Father of our Lord Jesus Christ, who has blessed us. Eph. 1:3

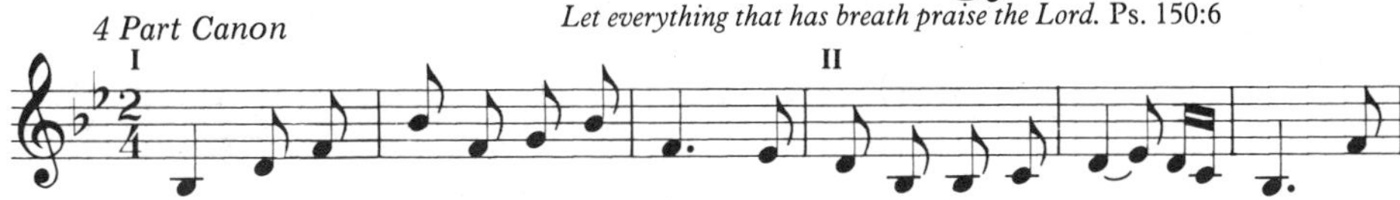

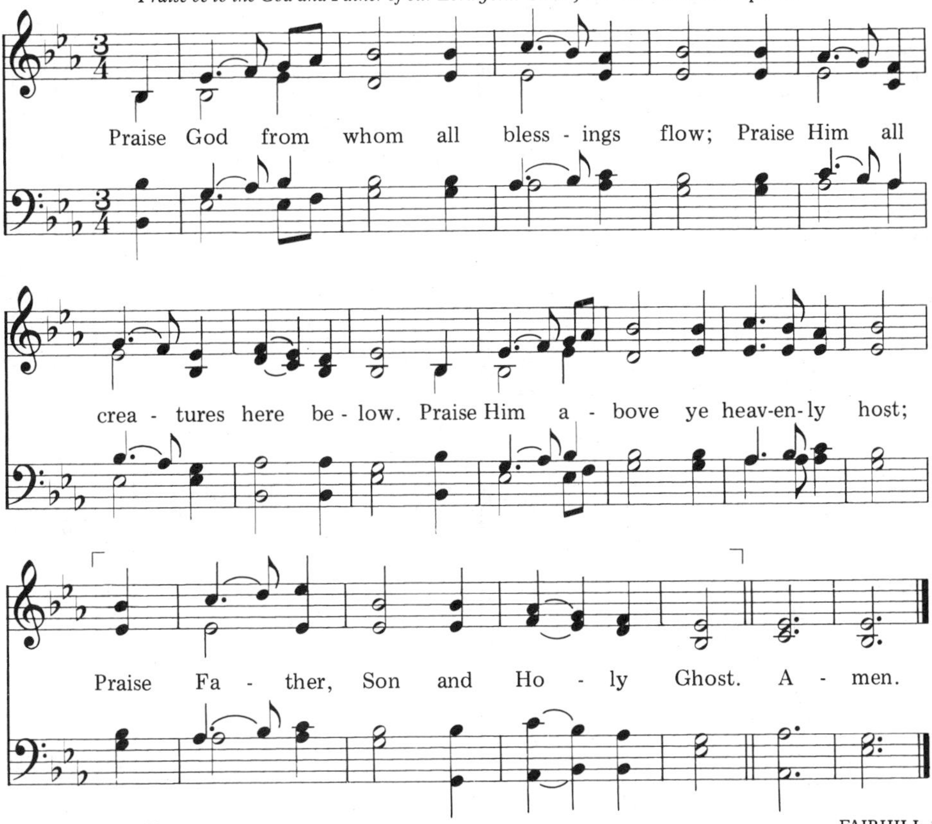
Praise God from whom all bless - ings flow; Praise Him all
crea - tures here be - low. Praise Him a - bove ye heav-en-ly host;
Praise Fa - ther, Son and Ho - ly Ghost. A - men.

TEXT: Thomas Ken
MUSIC: Jimmy Owens

FAIRHILL
L.M.

A Doxology Canon 627

Let everything that has breath praise the Lord. Ps. 150:6

4 Part Canon
I
II
Praise God from whom all bless-ings flow; Praise Him, all crea-tures here be - low; Praise
III
IV
Him a-bove, ye heav - n'ly host; Praise Fa-ther, Son and Ho - ly Ghost.

TEXT: Thomas Ken
MUSIC: Gerald S. Henderson

PRAISE GOD
L.M.

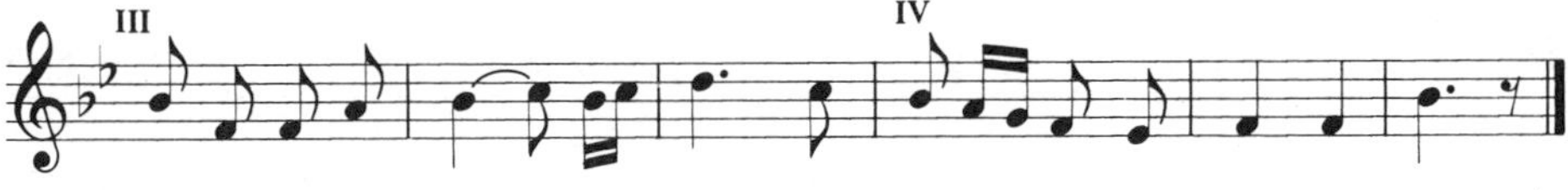

628 Amens

I. GENEVA — Louis Bourgeois

A - - men.

II. TWOFOLD — Dresden

A - men, A - men.

III. TWOFOLD — Greek

A - men, A - men.

IV. THREEFOLD — Denmark

A-men, A-men, A - men.

V. THREEFOLD — Traditional

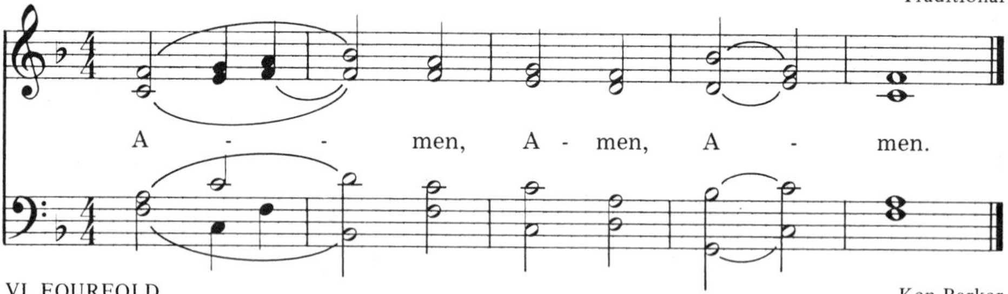

A - - men, A - men, A - men.

VI. FOURFOLD — Ken Barker

A - men, A - men, A - - men, A - men.

VII. FOURFOLD
John Stainer
A - men, A - men, A - men, A - men.

VIII. FIVEFOLD

Kurt Kaiser

A - men, A - men, A -
A - men, A - men, A -
A - men, A - men, A -
A - - men, A - men, A -
- men, A - men, A - - men.
men, A - - men, A - - men.
men, A - - men, A - - men.
- - men, A - men, A - - men.

IX. SEVENFOLD

John Stainer

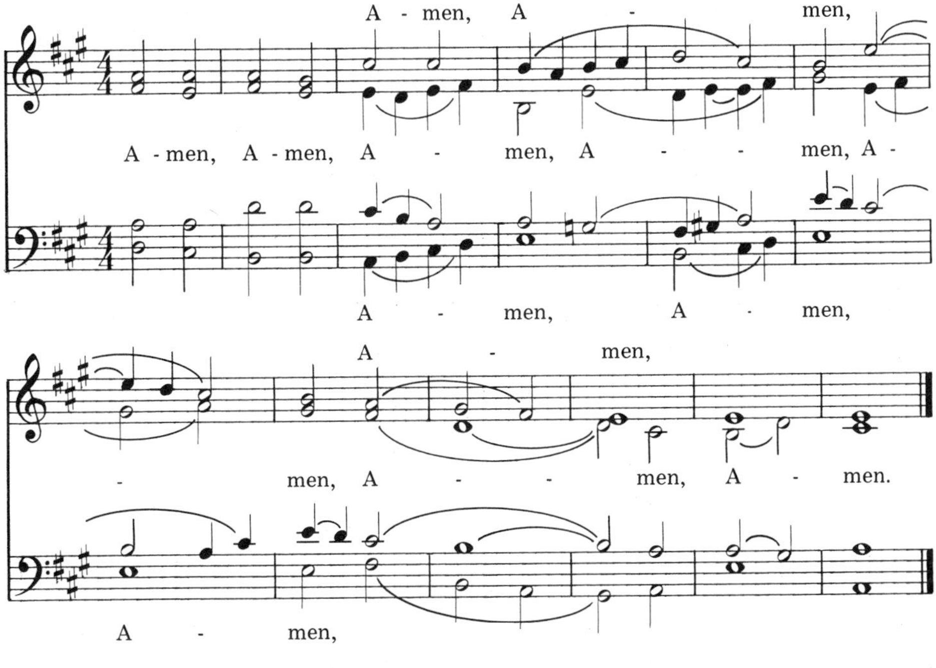

A - men, A - men,

A - men, A - men, A - men, A - - men, A -

A - men, A - men,

A - men,

- men, A - - men, A - men.

A - men,

SCRIPTURE RESOURCES

for Worship and Celebration
including
Scriptures for Individual, Unison, Responsive or Antiphonal Reading
and
Psalms for Unison Reading or Personal Meditation

O God, whose Word
is quick and powerful, and sharper
than any two-edged sword, grant us grace
to receive Thy truth in
faith and love.

PREFACE

From time immemorial Scripture has been read to the congregation of God's people. Examples abound in the Bible; here are two:

1. "[Ezra] read [the Law] aloud from daybreak till noon . . . And all the people listened attentively to the Book of the Law." Neh. 8:3 (NIV)

2. "Blessed is the one who reads the words of this prophecy, and blessed are those who hear it and take to heart what is written in it." Rev. 1:3 (NIV)

1 Timothy 4:13 is particularly relevant for the Church. Here Paul instructed Timothy: "Devote yourself to the public reading of Scripture, to preaching and to teaching." The combining of the public reading of Scripture with preaching and teaching in this verse would seem to indicate that the latter are to be based on the text of Scripture itself. In any case, it is clear that Scripture reading is to be a vital part of the Church's worship services.

We have provided a number of Scripture resources that are appropriate for a wide variety of applications. There are sections with:

1. Scripture readings for individual, unison, responsive or antiphonal reading.
2. Psalms for unison reading or personal meditation.

In addition, the body of the hymnal contains:

3. Scripture readings introducing the *Brief Services.*
4. Spoken calls to worship.
5. Spoken benedictions.
6. Scripture verses appearing with hymn titles. (These verses could furnish guidance in the selection of appropriate hymns for certain Biblical texts.)

Now we "commit you to God and to the word of His grace, which can build you up and give you an inheritance among all those who are sanctified". Acts 20:32 (NIV)

Dr. Kenneth L. Barker
Scripture Editor and Theological Consultant

SCRIPTURES FOR INDIVIDUAL, UNISON, RESPONSIVE OR ANTIPHONAL READING

Indexes to Scripture Readings may be found on pages 665 to 673

629 THE TEN COMMANDMENTS

And God spoke all these words: I am the Lord your God, who brought you out of Egypt, out of the land of slavery.

You shall have no other gods before Me.

You shall not make for yourself an idol in the form of anything in heaven above or on the earth beneath or in the waters below. You shall not bow down to them or worship them.

For I, the Lord your God, am a jealous God, punishing the children for the sin of the fathers to the third and fourth generations of those who hate Me, but showing love to a thousand generations of those who love Me and keep My commandments.

You shall not misuse the name of the Lord your God, for the Lord will not hold anyone guiltless who misuses His name.

Remember the Sabbath day by keeping it holy.

Six days you shall labor and do all your work, but the seventh day is a Sabbath to the Lord your God.

On it you shall not do any work, neither you, nor your son or daughter, nor your manservant or maidservant, nor your animals, nor the alien within your gates.

For in six days the Lord made the heavens and the earth, the sea, and all that is in them, but He rested on the seventh day.

Therefore the Lord blessed the Sabbath day and made it holy.

Honor your father and your mother, so that you may live long in the land the Lord your God is giving you.

You shall not murder.

You shall not commit adultery.

You shall not steal.

You shall not give false testimony against your neighbor.

You shall not covet your neighbor's house. You shall not covet your neighbor's wife, or his manservant or maidservant, his ox or donkey, or anything that belongs to your neighbor.

Ex. 20:1-17 (NIV)

630 TEACHING CHILDREN

Take heed to yourself, and diligently keep yourself, lest you forget the things your eyes have seen, and lest they depart from your heart all the days of your life. And teach them to your children and your grandchildren.

Now this is the commandment, and these are the statutes and judgments which the Lord your God has commanded to teach you, that you may observe them in the land which you are crossing over to possess;

That you may fear the Lord your God, to keep all His statutes and His commandments which I command you, you and your son and your grandson, all the days of your life, and that your days may be prolonged.

Therefore hear, O Israel, and be careful

to observe it, that it may be well with you, and that you may multiply greatly as the Lord God of your fathers has promised you—a land flowing with milk and honey.

Hear, O Israel: The Lord our God, the Lord is one!

You shall love the Lord your God with all your heart, with all your soul, and with all your might.

And these words which I command you today shall be in your heart;

You shall teach them diligently to your children, and shall talk of them when you sit in your house, when you walk by the way, when you lie down, and when you rise up.

You shall bind them as a sign on your hand, and they shall be as frontlets between your eyes.

You shall write them on the doorposts of your house and on your gates.

Train up a child in the way he should go, and when he is old he will not depart from it.

And you, fathers, do not provoke your children to wrath, but bring them up in the training and admonition of the Lord.

Deut. 4:9; 6:1-9; Prov. 22:6; Eph. 6:4 (NKJV)

631 OBEDIENCE

You shall therefore love the Lord your God, and always keep His charge, His statutes, His ordinances, and His commandments.

For this commandment which I command you today is not too difficult for you, nor is it out of reach.

It is not in heaven, that you should say, Who will go up to heaven for us to get it for us and make us hear it, that we may observe it?

Nor is it beyond the sea, that you should say, Who will cross the sea for us to get it for us and make us hear it, that we may observe it?

But the word is very near you, in your mouth and in your heart, that you may observe it.

This book of the law shall not depart from your mouth, but you shall meditate on it day and night, so that you may be careful to do according to all that is written in it; for then you will make your way prosperous, and then you will have success.

Has the Lord as much delight in burnt offerings and sacrifices as in obeying the voice of the Lord? Behold, to obey is better than sacrifice, and to heed than the fat of rams.

He who has My commandments and keeps them, he it is who loves Me; and he who loves Me shall be loved by My Father, and I will love him, and will disclose Myself to him.

Jesus answered and said to him, If anyone loves Me, he will keep My word; and My Father will love him, and We will come to him, and make Our abode with him.

Although He was a Son, He learned obedience from the things which He suffered.

By faith Abraham, when he was called, obeyed by going out to a place which he was to receive for an inheritance; and he went out, not knowing where he was going.

And by this we know that we have come to know Him, if we keep His commandments.

Deut. 11:1; 30:11-14; Josh. 1:8; 1 Sam. 15:22; John 14:21,23; Heb. 5:8; 11:8; 1 John 2:3 (NASB)

632 FORGIVENESS

Come now, and let us reason together, says the Lord, Though your sins are like scarlet, they shall be as white as snow; though they are red like crimson, they shall be as wool.

No more shall every man teach his neighbor, and every man his brother, saying, Know the Lord, for they all shall know Me, from the least of them to the greatest of them, says the Lord. For I will forgive their iniquity, and their sin I will remember no more.

Who is a God like You, pardoning iniquity and passing over the transgression of the remnant of His heritage?

He does not retain His anger forever, because He delights in mercy.

If you forgive men their trespasses, your heavenly Father will also forgive you.

But if you do not forgive men their trespasses, neither will your Father forgive your trespasses.

Peter came to Him and said, Lord, how often shall my brother sin against me, and I forgive him? Up to seven times?

Jesus said to him, I do not say to you, up to seven times, but up to seventy times seven.

Be kind to one another, tenderhearted, forgiving one another, just as God in Christ also forgave you.

If we say that we have no sin, we deceive ourselves, and the truth is not in us.

If we confess our sins, He is faithful and just to forgive us our sins and to cleanse us from all unrighteousness.

If we say that we have not sinned, we make Him a liar, and His word is not in us.

My little children, these things I write to you, that you may not sin. And if anyone sins, we have an Advocate with the Father, Jesus Christ the righteous.

And He Himself is the propitiation for our sins, and not for ours only but also for the whole world.

Isa. 1:18; Jer. 31:34; Mic. 7:18; Matt. 6:14-15; 18:21-22; Eph. 4:32; 1 John 1:8-2:2 (NKJV)

633 SCRIPTURE

The grass withers and the flowers fall, but the word of our God stands forever. Continue in what you have learned and have become convinced of, because you know those from whom you learned it;

And how from infancy you have known the holy Scriptures, which are able to make you wise for salvation through faith in Christ Jesus.

All Scripture is God-breathed and is useful for teaching, rebuking, correcting and training in righteousness;

So that the man of God may be thoroughly equipped for every good work.

For the word of God is living and active. Sharper than any double-edged sword, it penetrates even to dividing soul and spirit, joints and marrow; it judges the thoughts and attitudes of the heart.

Nothing in all creation is hidden from God's sight. Everything is uncovered and laid bare before the eyes of Him to whom we must give account.

We did not follow cleverly invented stories when we told you about the power and coming of our Lord Jesus Christ, but we were eyewitnesses of His majesty.

For He received honor and glory from God the Father when the voice came to Him from the Majestic Glory, saying, This is My Son, whom I love; with Him I am well pleased.

We ourselves heard this voice that came from heaven when we were with Him on the sacred mountain.

And we have the word of the prophets made more certain, and you will do well to pay attention to it, as to a light shining in a dark place, until the day dawns and the morning star rises in your hearts.

Above all, you must understand that no prophecy of Scripture came about by the prophet's own interpretation.

For prophecy never had its origin in the will of man, but men spoke from God as they were carried along by the Holy Spirit.

Isa. 40:8; 2 Tim. 3:14-17; Heb. 4:12-13; 2 Pet. 1:16-21 (NIV)

634 THE MESSIANIC KING

There will be no more gloom for those who were in distress. In the past He humbled the land of Naphtali, but in the future He will honor Galilee of the Gentiles, by the way of the sea, along the Jordan—

The people walking in darkness have seen a great Light; on those living in the land of the shadow of death a Light has dawned.

You have enlarged the nation and increased their joy; they rejoice before You as people rejoice at the harvest, as men rejoice when dividing the plunder.

For as in the day of Midian's defeat, You have shattered the yoke that burdens them, the bar across their shoulders, the rod of their oppressor.

Every warrior's boot used in battle and every garment rolled in blood will be destined for burning, will be fuel for the fire.

For to us a Child is born, to us a Son is given, and the government will be on His shoulders. And He will be called Wonderful Counselor, Mighty God, Everlasting Father, Prince of Peace.

Of the increase of His government and peace there will be no end. He will reign on David's throne and over his kingdom, establishing and upholding it with justice and righteousness from that time on and forever.

The zeal of the Lord Almighty will accomplish this.

Isa. 9:1-7 (NIV)

635 CHRIST'S INCARNATION

In the beginning was the Word, and the Word was with God, and the Word was God.

He was in the beginning with God;

All things were made through Him, and without Him was not anything made that was made.

In Him was Life, and the Life was the Light of men.

The Light shines in the darkness, and the darkness has not overcome it.

There was a man sent from God, whose name was John.

He came for testimony, to bear witness to the Light, that all might believe through Him.

He was not the Light, but came to bear witness to the Light.

The true Light that enlightens every man was coming into the world.

He was in the world, and the world was made through Him, yet the world knew Him not.

He came to His own home, and His own people received Him not.

But to all who received Him, who believed in His name, He gave power to become children of God;

Who were born, not of blood nor of the will of the flesh nor of the will of man, but of God.

And the Word became flesh and dwelt among us, full of grace and truth; we have beheld His glory, glory as of the only Son from the Father.

John 1:1-14 (RSV)

636 THE MAGI'S VISIT

Now when Jesus was born in Bethlehem of Judea in the days of Herod the king, behold, wise men from the East came to Jerusalem, saying,

Where is He who has been born king of the Jews? For we have seen His star in the East, and have come to worship Him.

When Herod the king heard this, he was troubled, and all Jerusalem with him;

And assembling all the chief priests and scribes of the people, he inquired of them where the Christ was to be born.

They told him, In Bethlehem of Judea; for so it is written by the prophet:

And you, O Bethlehem, in the land of Judah, are by no means least among the rulers of Judah; for from you shall come a ruler who will govern my people Israel.

Then Herod summoned the wise men secretly and ascertained from them what time the star appeared;

And he sent them to Bethlehem, saying, Go and search diligently for the Child, and when you have found Him bring me word, that I too may come and worship Him.

When they had heard the king they went their way; and lo, the star which they had seen in the East went before them, till it came to rest over the place where the Child was.

When they saw the star, they rejoiced exceedingly with great joy;

And going into the house they saw the Child with Mary His mother, and they fell down and worshiped Him. Then, opening their treasures, they offered Him gifts, gold and frankincense and myrrh.

And being warned in a dream not to return to Herod, they departed to their own country by another way.

Matt. 2:1-12 (RSV)

637 CHRIST'S BAPTISM

In those days John the Baptist came preaching in the wilderness of Judea, and saying, Repent, for the kingdom of heaven is at hand!

For this is he who was spoken of by the prophet Isaiah, saying: The voice of one crying in the wilderness: Prepare the way of the Lord, Make His paths straight.

When he saw many of the Pharisees and Sadducees coming to his baptism, he said to them, Brood of vipers! Who has warned you to flee from the wrath to come?

Therefore bear fruits worthy of repentance.

I indeed baptize you with water unto repentance, but He who is coming after me is mightier than I, whose sandals I am not worthy to carry.

He will baptize you with the Holy Spirit and fire.

His winnowing fan is in His hand, and He will thoroughly purge His threshing floor, and gather His wheat into the barn; but He will burn up the chaff with unquenchable fire.

Then Jesus came from Galilee to John at the Jordan to be baptized by him.

And John tried to prevent Him, saying, I have need to be baptized by You, and are You coming to Me?

But Jesus answered and said to him, Permit it to be so now, for thus it is fitting for us to fulfill all righteousness. Then he allowed Him.

Then Jesus, when He had been baptized, came up immediately from the water; and behold, the heavens were opened to Him, and He saw the Spirit of God descending like a dove and alighting upon Him.

And suddenly a voice came from heaven, saying, This is My beloved Son, in whom I am well pleased.

Matt. 3:1-3, 7-8, 11-17 (NKJV)

638 CHRIST'S TRIUMPHAL ENTRY

As they approached Jerusalem and came to Bethphage on the Mount of Olives, Jesus sent two disciples, saying to them,

Go to the village ahead of you, and at once you will find a donkey tied there, with her colt by her. Untie them and bring them to Me.

If anyone says anything to you, tell him that the Lord needs them, and he will send them right away.

This took place to fulfill what was spoken through the prophet:

Say to the Daughter of Zion, See, your King comes to you, gentle and riding on a donkey, on a colt, the foal of a donkey.

The disciples went and did as Jesus had instructed them.

They brought the donkey and the colt, placed their cloaks on them, and Jesus sat on them.

A very large crowd spread their cloaks on the road, while others cut branches from the trees and spread them on the road.

The crowds that went ahead of Him and those that followed shouted,

Hosanna to the Son of David! Blessed is He who comes in the name of the Lord! Hosanna in the highest!

When Jesus entered Jerusalem, the whole city was stirred and asked, Who is this?

The crowds answered, This is Jesus, the prophet from Nazareth in Galilee.

Matt. 21:1-11 (NIV)

639 CHRIST'S SUFFERINGS

Who has believed our message and to whom has the arm of the Lord been revealed?

He grew up before Him like a tender shoot, and like a root out of dry ground.

He had no beauty or majesty to attract us to Him, nothing in His appearance that we should desire Him.

He was despised and rejected by men, a man of sorrows, and familiar with suffering.

Like one from whom men hide their faces He was despised, and we esteemed Him not.

Surely He took up our infirmities and carried our sorrows, yet we considered Him stricken by God, smitten by Him, and afflicted.

But He was pierced for our transgressions, He was crushed for our iniquities; the punishment that brought us peace was upon Him, and by His wounds we are healed.

We all, like sheep, have gone astray, each of us has turned to his own way; and the Lord has laid on Him the iniquity of us all.

He was oppressed and afflicted, yet He did not open His mouth; He was led like a lamb to the slaughter, and as a sheep before her shearers is silent, so He did not open His mouth.

By oppression and judgment, He was taken away.

And who can speak of His descendants? For He was cut off from the land of the living; for the transgression of my people He was stricken.

He was assigned a grave with the wicked, and with the rich in His death, though He had done no violence, nor was any deceit in His mouth.

Isa. 53:1-9 (NIV)

640 CHRIST'S DEATH

Then Pilate took Jesus and scourged Him.

And the soldiers plaited a crown of thorns, and put it on His head, and arrayed Him in a purple robe;

They came up to Him, saying, Hail, King of the Jews! and struck Him with their hands.

Pilate went out again, and said to them, See, I am bringing Him out to you, that you may know that I find no crime in Him.

So Jesus came out, wearing the crown of thorns and the purple robe. Pilate said to them, Behold the Man!

When the chief priests and the officers saw Him, they cried out, Crucify Him, crucify Him! Pilate said to them, Take Him yourselves and crucify Him, for I find no crime in Him.

Then he handed Him over to them to be crucified.

So they took Jesus, and He went out, bearing His own cross, to the place called the place of a skull, which is called in Hebrew Golgotha.

There they crucified Him, and with Him two others, one on either side, and Jesus between them.

Pilate also wrote a title and put it on the cross; it read, Jesus of Nazareth, the King of the Jews.

John 19:1-6, 16-19 (RSV)

641 CHRIST'S ASCENSION

The former account I made, O Theophilus, of all that Jesus began both to do and teach, until the day in which He was taken up, after He through the Holy Spirit had given commandments to the apostles whom He had chosen;

To whom He also presented Himself alive after His suffering by many infallible proofs, being seen by them during forty days and speaking of the things pertaining to the kingdom of God.

And being assembled together with them, He commanded them not to depart from Jerusalem, but to wait for the Promise of the Father, which, He said, you have heard from Me;

For John truly baptized with water, but you shall be baptized with the Holy Spirit not many days from now.

Therefore, when they had come together, they asked Him, saying, Lord, will You at this time restore the kingdom to Israel?

And He said to them, It is not for you to know times or seasons which the Father has put in His own authority.

But you shall receive power when the Holy Spirit has come upon you; and you shall be witnesses to Me in Jerusalem, and in all Judea and Samaria, and to the end of the earth.

Now when He had spoken these things, while they watched, He was taken up, and a cloud received Him out of their sight.

And while they looked steadfastly toward heaven as He went up, behold, two men stood by them in white apparel;

Who also said, Men of Galilee, why do you stand gazing up into heaven? This same Jesus, who was taken up from you into heaven, will so come in like manner as you saw Him go into heaven.

Acts 1:1-11 (NKJV)

642 CHRIST'S EXALTATION

If therefore there is any encouragement in Christ, if there is any consolation of love;

If there is any fellowship of the Spirit, if any affection and compassion;

Make my joy complete by being of the same mind, maintaining the same love, united in spirit, intent on one purpose.

Do nothing from selfishness or empty conceit, but with humility of mind let each of you regard one another as more important than himself;

Do not merely look out for your own personal interests, but also for the interests of others.

Have this attitude in yourselves which was also in Christ Jesus;

Who, although He existed in the form of God, did not regard equality with God a thing to be grasped;

But emptied Himself, taking the form of a bond-servant, and being made in the likeness of men.

And being found in appearance as a man, He humbled Himself by becoming obedient to the point of death, even death on a cross.

Therefore also God highly exalted Him, and bestowed on Him the name which is above every name;

That at the name of Jesus every knee should bow, of those who are in heaven, and on earth, and under the earth;

And that every tongue should confess that Jesus Christ is Lord, to the glory of God the Father.

Phil. 2:1-11 (NASB)

643 CHRIST'S RETURN

Brothers, we do not want you to be ignorant about those who fall asleep, or to grieve like the rest of men, who have no hope.

We believe that Jesus died and rose again and so we believe that God will bring with Jesus those who have fallen asleep in Him.

According to the Lord's own word, we tell you that we who are still alive, who are left till the coming of the Lord, will certainly not precede those who have fallen asleep.

For the Lord Himself will come down from heaven, with a loud command, with the voice of the archangel and with the trumpet call of God, and the dead in Christ will rise first.

After that, we who are still alive and are left will be caught up with them in the clouds to meet the Lord in the air. And so we will be with the Lord forever.

Therefore encourage each other with these words.

1 Thess. 4:13-18 (NIV)

644 THE HOLY SPIRIT

I will pray the Father, and He will give you another Helper, that He may abide with you forever;

Even the Spirit of truth, whom the world cannot receive, because it neither sees Him nor knows Him; but you know Him, for He dwells with you and will be in you.

I will not leave you orphans; I will come to you.

Now I go away to Him who sent Me, and none of you asks Me, Where are You going?

But because I have said these things to you, sorrow has filled your heart.

Nevertheless I tell you the truth. It is to your advantage that I go away; for if I do not go away, the Helper will not come to you; but if I depart, I will send Him to you.

And when He has come, He will convict the world of sin, and of righteousness, and of judgment:

Of sin, because they do not believe in Me;

Of righteousness, because I go to My Father and you see Me no more;

Of judgment, because the ruler of this world is judged.

I still have many things to say to you, but you cannot bear them now.

However, when He, the Spirit of truth, has come, He will guide you into all truth; for He will not speak on His own authority, but whatever He hears He will speak; and He will tell you things to come.

He will glorify Me, for He will take of what is Mine and declare it to you.

All things that the Father has are Mine. Therefore I said that He will take of Mine and declare it to you.

John 14:16-18; 16:5-15 (NKJV)

645 MISSIONS

The eleven disciples proceeded to Galilee, to the mountain which Jesus had designated.

And when they saw Him, they worshiped Him; but some were doubtful.

And Jesus came up and spoke to them, saying, All authority has been given to Me in heaven and on earth. Go therefore and make disciples of all the nations, baptizing them in the name of the Father and the Son and the Holy Spirit, teaching them to observe all that I commanded you; and lo, I am with you always, even to the end of the age.

Do you not say, There are yet four months, and then comes the harvest? Behold, I say to you, lift up your eyes, and look on the fields, that they are white for harvest.

The word is near you, in your mouth and in your heart—that is, the word of faith which we are preaching;

That if you confess with your mouth Jesus as Lord, and believe in your

heart that God raised Him from the dead, you shall be saved;

For with the heart man believes, resulting in righteousness, and with the mouth he confesses, resulting in salvation.

For the Scripture says, Whoever believes in Him will not be disappointed.

For there is no distinction between Jew and Greek; for the same Lord is Lord of all, abounding in riches for all who call upon Him;

For whoever will call upon the name of the Lord will be saved.

How then shall they call upon Him in whom they have not believed? And how shall they believe in Him whom they have not heard? And how shall they hear without a preacher?

And how shall they preach unless they are sent? Just as it is written, How beautiful are the feet of those who bring glad tidings of good things!

Matt. 28:16-20; John 4:35; Rom. 10:8-15 (NASB)

646 THE CHURCH

He said to them, But who do you say that I am?

And Simon Peter answered and said, You are the Christ, the Son of the living God.

Jesus answered and said to him, Blessed are you, Simon Bar-Jonah, for flesh and blood has not revealed this to you, but My Father who is in heaven.

And I also say to you that you are Peter, and on this rock I will build My church, and the gates of Hades shall not prevail against it.

And I will give you the keys of the kingdom of heaven, and whatever you bind on earth will be bound in heaven, and whatever you loose on earth will be loosed in heaven.

As the body is one and has many members, but all the members of that one body, being many, are one body, so also is Christ.

For by one Spirit we were all baptized into one body—whether Jews or Greeks, whether slaves or free—and have all been made to drink into one Spirit.

He put all things under His feet, and gave Him to be head over all things to the church, which is His body, the fullness of Him who fills all in all.

You are no longer strangers and foreigners, but fellow citizens with the saints and members of the household of God;

Having been built on the foundation of the apostles and prophets, Jesus Christ Himself being the chief cornerstone;

In whom the whole building being joined together, grows into a holy temple in the Lord;

In whom you also are being built together for a habitation of God in the Spirit.

Husbands, love your wives, just as Christ also loved the church and gave Himself for it, that He might sanctify and cleanse it with the washing of water by the word;

That He might present it to Himself a glorious church, not having spot or wrinkle or any such thing, but that it should be holy and without blemish.

Matt. 16:15-19; 1 Cor. 12:12-13; Eph. 1:22-23; 2:19-22; 5:25-27 (NKJV)

647 THE LORD'S SUPPER

I received from the Lord what I also

delivered to you, that the Lord Jesus on the night when He was betrayed took bread;

And when He had given thanks, He broke it, and said, This is My body which is for you. Do this in remembrance of Me.

In the same way also the cup, after supper, saying, This cup is the new covenant in My blood. Do this, as often as you drink it, in remembrance of Me.

For as often as you eat this bread and drink the cup, you proclaim the Lord's death until He comes.

Whoever, therefore, eats the bread or drinks the cup of the Lord in an unworthy manner will be guilty of profaning the body and blood of the Lord.

Let a man examine himself, and so eat of the bread and drink of the cup.

For any one who eats and drinks without discerning the body eats and drinks judgment upon himself.

That is why many of you are weak and ill, and some have died.

But if we judged ourselves truly, we should not be judged.

But when we are judged by the Lord, we are chastened so that we may not be condemned along with the world.

1 Cor. 11:23-32 (RSV)

648 THE BEATITUDES

Now when He saw the crowds, He went up on a mountainside and sat down.

His disciples came to Him and He began to teach them, saying:

Blessed are the poor in spirit, for theirs is the kingdom of heaven.

Blessed are those who mourn, for they will be comforted.

Blessed are the meek, for they will inherit the earth.

Blessed are those who hunger and thirst for righteousness, for they will be filled.

Blessed are the merciful, for they will be shown mercy.

Blessed are the pure in heart, for they will see God.

Blessed are the peacemakers, for they will be called sons of God.

Blessed are those who are persecuted because of righteousness, for theirs is the kingdom of heaven.

Blessed are you when people insult you, persecute you and falsely say all kinds of evil against you because of Me.

Rejoice and be glad, because great is your reward in heaven, for in the same way they persecuted the prophets who were before you.

Matt. 5:1-12 (NIV)

649 THE VINE AND THE BRANCHES

I am the true vine, and My Father is the vinedresser.

Every branch in Me that does not bear fruit, He takes away; and every branch that bears fruit, He prunes it, that it may bear more fruit.

You are already clean because of the word which I have spoken to you.

Abide in Me, and I in you. As the branch cannot bear fruit of itself, unless it abides in the vine, so neither can you, unless you abide in Me.

I am the vine, you are the branches; he who abides in Me, and I in him, he bears much fruit; for apart from Me you can do nothing.

If anyone does not abide in Me, he is thrown away as a branch, and dries up; and they gather them, and cast them into the fire, and they are burned.

If you abide in Me, and My words abide in you, ask whatever you wish, and it shall be done for you.

By this is My Father glorified, that you bear much fruit, and so prove to be My disciples.

Just as the Father has loved Me, I have also loved you; abide in My love.

If you keep My commandments, you will abide in My love; just as I have kept My Father's commandments, and abide in His love.

These things I have spoken to you, that My joy may be in you, and that your joy may be made full.

This is My commandment, that you love one another, just as I have loved you.

Greater love has no one than this, that one lay down his life for his friends.

You are My friends, if you do what I command you.

No longer do I call you slaves, for the slave does not know what his master is doing.

But I have called you friends, for all things that I have heard from My Father I have made known to you.

You did not choose Me, but I chose you, and appointed you, that you should go and bear fruit, and that your fruit should remain, that whatever you ask of the Father in My name, He may give to you.

This I command you, that you love one another.

John 15:1-17 (NASB)

650 THE LORD'S PRAYER

When you pray, you shall not be like the hypocrites. For they love to pray standing in the synagogues and on the corners of the streets, that they may be seen by men. Assuredly, I say to you, they have their reward.

But you, when you pray, go into your room, and when you have shut your door, pray to your Father who is in the secret place; and your Father who sees in secret will reward you openly.

But when you pray, do not use vain repetitions as the heathen do. For they think that they will be heard for their many words.

Therefore do not be like them. For your Father knows the things you have need of before you ask Him.

In this manner, therefore, pray: Our Father in heaven, Hallowed be Your name.

Your kingdom come. Your will be done on earth as it is in heaven.

Give us this day our daily bread.

And forgive us our debts, as we forgive our debtors.

And do not lead us into temptation, but deliver us from the evil one.

For Yours is the kingdom and the power and the glory forever. Amen.

For if you forgive men their trespasses, your heavenly Father will also forgive you.

But if you do not forgive men their trespasses, neither will your Father forgive your trespasses.

Matt. 6:5-15 (NKJV)

651 DISCIPLESHIP

A student is not above his teacher, nor a servant above his master.

It is enough for the student to be like his teacher, and the servant like his master.

If anyone comes to Me and does not hate his father and mother, his wife and children, his brothers and sisters—yes, even his own life—he cannot be My disciple.

And anyone who does not carry his cross and follow Me cannot be My disciple.

When Jesus spoke again to the people, He said, I am the Light of the world. Whoever follows Me will never walk in darkness, but will have the Light of Life.

To the Jews who had believed Him, Jesus said, If you hold to My teaching, you are really My disciples.

Then you will know the truth, and the truth will set you free.

A new command I give you: Love one another. As I have loved you, so you must love one another.

By this all men will know that you are My disciples, if you love one another.

This is to My Father's glory, that you bear much fruit, showing yourselves to be My disciples.

Matt. 10:24-25; Luke 14:26-27; John 8:12, 31-32; 13:34-35; 15:8 (NIV)

652 COMFORT

Let not your hearts be troubled; believe in God, believe also in Me.

In My Father's house are many rooms; if it were not so, would I have told you that I go to prepare a place for you?

And when I go and prepare a place for you, I will come again and will take you to Myself, that where I am you may be also.

If you love Me, you will keep My commandments.

And I will pray the Father, and He will give you another Counselor, to be with you for ever.

Peace I leave with you; My peace I give to you; not as the world gives do I give to you. Let not your hearts be troubled, neither let them be afraid.

Blessed be the God and Father of our Lord Jesus Christ, the Father of mercies and God of all comfort, who comforts us in all our affliction, so that we may be able to comfort those who are in any affliction, with the comfort with which we ourselves are comforted by God.

For as we share abundantly in Christ's sufferings, so through Christ we share abundantly in comfort too.

If we are afflicted, it is for your comfort and salvation; and if we are comforted, it is for your comfort, which you experience when you patiently endure the same sufferings that we suffer.

Our hope for you is unshaken; for we know that as you share in our sufferings, you will also share in our comfort.

John 14:1-3, 15-16,27; 2 Cor. 1:3-7 (RSV)

653 GOD'S LOVE

For God so loved the world that He gave His only begotten Son, that whoever believes in Him should not perish but have everlasting life.

God demonstrates His own love toward us, in that while we were still sinners, Christ died for us.

Behold what manner of love the Father has bestowed on us, that we should be called children of God! Therefore the world does not know us, because it did not know Him.

He who does not love does not know God, for God is love.

In this the love of God was manifested toward us, that God has sent His only begotten Son into the world, that we might live through Him.

In this is love, not that we loved God, but that He loved us and sent His Son to be the propitiation for our sins.

Beloved, if God so loved us, we also ought to love one another.

No one has seen God at any time. If we love one another, God abides in us, and His love has been perfected in us.

There is no fear in love; but perfect love casts out fear, because fear involves torment. But he who fears has not been made perfect in love.

We love Him because He first loved us.

John 3:16; Rom. 5:8; 1 John 3:1; 4:8-12, 18-19 (NKJV)

654 THE NEW BIRTH

Now there was a man of the Pharisees named Nicodemus, a member of the Jewish ruling council.

He came to Jesus at night and said, Rabbi, we know You are a teacher who has come from God. For no one could perform the miraculous signs You are doing if God were not with him.

In reply Jesus declared, I tell you the truth, no one can see the kingdom of God unless he is born again.

How can a man be born when he is old? Nicodemus asked. Surely he cannot enter a second time into his mother's womb to be born!

Jesus answered, I tell you the truth, no one can enter the kingdom of God unless he is born of water and the Spirit.

Flesh gives birth to flesh, but the Spirit gives birth to spirit.

You should not be surprised at My saying, You must be born again.

The wind blows wherever it pleases. You hear its sound, but you cannot tell where it comes from or where it is going. So it is with everyone born of the Spirit.

Just as Moses lifted up the snake in the desert, so the Son of Man must be lifted up, that everyone who believes in Him may have eternal life.

For God so loved the world that He gave His one and only Son, that whoever believes in Him shall not perish but have eternal life.

For God did not send His Son into the world to condemn the world, but to save the world through Him.

Therefore, if anyone is in Christ, he is a new creation; the old has gone, the new has come!

John 3:1-8, 14-17; 2 Cor. 5:17 (NIV)

655 PRAYER

Ask, and it will be given you; seek, and you will find; knock, and it will be opened to you.

For every one who asks receives, and he who seeks finds, and to him who knocks it will be opened.

Or what man of you, if his son asks him for bread, will give him a stone?

Or if he asks for a fish, will give him a serpent? If you then, who are evil, know how to give good gifts to your children, how much more will your Father who is in heaven give good things to those who ask Him!

Therefore I tell you, whatever you ask in prayer, believe that you have received it, and it will be yours.

And whenever you stand praying, forgive, if you have anything against any one; so that your Father also who is in heaven may forgive you your trespasses.

Whatever you ask in My name, I will do it, that the Father may be glorified in the Son; if you ask anything in My name, I will do it.

Likewise the Spirit helps us in our weakness; for we do not know how to pray as we ought, but the Spirit Himself intercedes for us with sighs too deep for words.

And He who searches the hearts of men knows what is the mind of the Spirit, because the Spirit intercedes for the saints according to the will of God.

Pray at all times in the Spirit, with all prayer and supplication. To that end keep alert with all perseverance, making supplication for all the saints.

Since then we have a great High Priest who has passed through the heavens, Jesus, the Son of God, let us hold fast our confession.

For we have not a High Priest who is unable to sympathize with our weaknesses, but One who in every respect has been tempted as we are, yet without sin.

Let us then with confidence draw near to the throne of grace, that we may receive mercy and find grace to help in time of need.

This is the confidence which we have in Him, that if we ask anything according to His will He hears us.

And if we know that He hears us in whatever we ask, we know that we have obtained the requests made of Him.

Matt. 7:7-11; Mark 11:24-25; John 14:13-14; Rom 8:26-27; Eph. 6:18; Heb. 4:14-16; 1 John 5:14-15 (RSV)

656 GIVING

Give, and it will be given to you. A good measure, pressed down, shaken together and running over, will be poured into your lap. For with the measure you use, it will be measured to you.

In everything I did, I showed you that by this kind of hard work we must help the weak, remembering the words the Lord Jesus Himself said: It is more blessed to give than to receive.

On the first day of every week, each one of you should set aside a sum of money in keeping with his income, saving it up, so that when I come no collections will have to be made.

Just as you excel in everything—in faith, in speech, in knowledge, in complete earnestness and in your love for us—see that you also excel in this grace of giving.

For you know the grace of our Lord Jesus Christ, that though He was rich, yet for your sakes He became poor, so that you through His poverty might become rich.

If the willingness is there, the gift is acceptable according to what one has, not according to what he does not have.

Remember this: Whoever sows sparingly will also reap sparingly, and whoever sows generously will also reap generously. Each man should give what he has decided in his heart to give, not reluctantly or under compulsion, for God loves a cheerful giver.

Thanks be to God for His indescribable Gift!

Luke 6:38; Acts 20:35; 1 Cor. 16:2; 2 Cor. 8:7,9,12; 9:6-7,15 (NIV)

657 FAITHFULNESS

Who then is the faithful and sensible slave whom his master put in charge of his household to give them their food at the proper time?

Blessed is that slave whom his master finds so doing when he comes.

Truly I say to you, that he will put him in charge of all his possessions.

His master said to him, Well done, good and faithful slave; you were faithful with a few things, I will put you in charge of many things, enter into the joy of your master.

He who is faithful in a very little thing is faithful also in much; and he who is unrighteous in a very little thing is unrighteous also in much.

If therefore you have not been faithful in the use of unrighteous mammon, who will entrust the true riches to you?

And if you have not been faithful in the use of that which is another's, who will give you that which is your own?

No servant can serve two masters; for either he will hate the one, and love the other, or else he will hold to one, and despise the other. You cannot serve God and mammon.

It is required of stewards that one be found trustworthy.

The things which you have heard from Me in the presence of many witnesses, these entrust to faithful men, who will be able to teach others also.

Do not fear what you are about to suffer.

Be faithful until death; and I will give you the crown of life.

Matt. 24:45-47; 25:21; Luke 16:10-13; 1 Cor. 4:2; 2 Tim. 2:2; Rev. 2:10 (NASB)

658 ETERNAL LIFE

As Moses lifted up the serpent in the wilderness, so must the Son of Man be lifted up, that whoever believes in Him may have eternal life.

For God so loved the world that He gave His only Son, that whoever believes in Him should not perish but have eternal life.

He who believes in the Son has eternal life; he who does not obey the Son shall not see life, but the wrath of God rests upon him.

Truly, truly, I say to you, he who hears My word and believes Him who sent Me, has eternal life; he does not come into judgment, but has passed from death to life.

My sheep hear My voice, and I know them, and they follow Me; and I give them eternal life, and they shall never perish, and no one shall snatch them out of My hand.

My Father, who has given them to Me, is greater than all, and no one is able to snatch them out of the Father's hand.

This is the testimony, that God gave us eternal life, and this life is in His Son.

He who has the Son has life; he who has not the Son of God has not life.

I write this to you who believe in the name of the Son of God, that you may know that you have eternal life.

We know that the Son of God has come and has given us understanding, to know Him who is true; and we are in Him who is true, in His Son Jesus Christ. This is the true God and eternal life.

John 3:14-16,36; 5:24; 10:27-29; 1 John 5:11-13,20 (RSV)

659 SALVATION BY GRACE

From His fulness have we all received, grace upon grace. For the law was given through Moses; grace and truth came through Jesus Christ.

Law came in, to increase the trespass; but where sin increased, grace abounded all the more, so that, as sin reigned in death, grace also might reign through righteousness to eternal life through Jesus Christ our Lord.

But God, who is rich in mercy, out of the great love with which He loved us, even when we were dead through our trespasses, made us alive together with Christ (by grace you have been saved);

And raised us up with Him and made us sit with Him in the heavenly places in Christ Jesus, that in the coming ages He might show the immeasurable riches of His grace in kindness toward us in Christ Jesus.

For by grace you have been saved through faith; and this is not your own doing, it is the gift of God—not because of works, lest any man should boast.

The grace of God has appeared for the salvation of all men, training us to renounce irreligion and worldly passions, and to live sober, upright, and godly lives in this world.

When the goodness and loving kindness of God our Savior appeared, He saved us, not because of deeds done by us in righteousness, but in virtue of His own mercy, by the washing of regeneration and renewal in the Holy Spirit;

Which He poured out upon us richly through Jesus Christ our Savior, so that we might be justified by His grace and become heirs in hope of eternal life.

John 1:16-17; Rom. 5:20-21; Eph. 2:4-9; Titus 2:11-12; 3:4-7 (RSV)

660 REDEMPTION

For even the Son of Man did not come to be served, but to serve, and to give His life as a ransom for many.

But now a righteousness from God, apart from law, has been made known, to which the Law and the Prophets testify.

This righteousness from God comes through faith in Jesus Christ to all who believe. There is no difference;

For all have sinned and fall short of the glory of God, and are justified freely by His grace through the redemption that came by Christ Jesus.

God presented Him as a sacrifice of atonement, through faith in His blood. He did this to demonstrate His justice, because in His forbearance He had left the sins committed beforehand unpunished—

He did it to demonstrate His justice at the present time, so as to be just and the one who justifies the man who has faith in Jesus.

In Him we have redemption through His blood, the forgiveness of sins, in accordance with the riches of God's grace that He lavished on us with all wisdom and understanding.

For this reason Christ is the mediator of a new covenant, that those who are called may receive the promised eternal inheritance—now that He has died as a ransom to set them free from the sins committed under the first covenant.

For you know that it was not with perishable things such as silver or gold that you were redeemed from the empty way of life handed down to you from your forefathers;

But with the precious blood of Christ, a lamb without blemish or defect.

Mark 10:45; Rom. 3:21-26; Eph. 1:7-8; Heb. 9:15; 1 Pet. 1:18-19 (NIV)

661 CHRISTIAN LOVE

If I speak in the tongues of men and of angels, but have not love, I am only a resounding gong or a clanging cymbal.

If I have the gift of prophecy and can fathom all mysteries and all knowledge, and if I have a faith that can move mountains, but have not love, I am nothing.

If I give all I possess to the poor and surrender my body to the flames, but have not love, I gain nothing.

Love is patient, love is kind. It does not envy, it does not boast, it is not proud.

It is not rude, it is not self-seeking, it is not easily angered, it keeps no record of wrongs.

Love does not delight in evil but rejoices with the truth.

It always protects, always trusts, always hopes, always perseveres.

Love never fails. But where there are prophecies, they will cease; where there are tongues, they will be stilled; where there is knowledge, it will pass away.

For we know in part and we prophesy in part, but when perfection comes, the imperfect disappears.

When I was a child, I talked like a child, I thought like a child, I reasoned like a child. When I became a man, I put childish ways behind me.

Now we see but a poor reflection, as in a mirror; then we shall see face to face. Now I know in part; then I shall know fully, even as I am fully known.

And now these three remain: faith, hope and love. But the greatest of these is love.

1 Cor. 13 (NIV)

662 FAITH

Now faith is the assurance of things hoped for, the conviction of things not seen.

For by it the men of old gained approval.

By faith we understand that the worlds were prepared by the word of God, so that what is seen was not made out of things which are visible.

And without faith it is impossible to please Him, for he who comes to God must believe that He is, and that He is a rewarder of those who seek Him.

By faith Abraham, when he was called, obeyed by going out to a place which he was to receive for an inheritance; and he went out, not knowing where he was going.

By faith he lived as an alien in the land of promise, as in a foreign land, dwelling in tents with Isaac and Jacob, fellow heirs of the same promise.

For he was looking for the city which has foundations, whose architect and builder is God.

By faith even Sarah herself received ability to conceive, even beyond the proper time of life, since she considered Him faithful who had promised.

Therefore, also, there was born of one man, and him as good as dead at that, as many descendants as the stars of heaven in number, and innumerable as the sand which is by the seashore.

By faith Abraham, when he was tested, offered up Isaac; and he who had received the promises was offering up his only begotten son.

It was he to whom it was said, In Isaac your descendants shall be called.

He considered that God is able to raise men even from the dead; from which he also received him back as a type.

Heb. 11:1-3,6,8-12,17-19 (NASB)

663 FAMILY

Wives, submit to your own husbands, as to the Lord.

For the husband is head of the wife, as also Christ is head of the church; and He is the Savior of the body.

Therefore, just as the church is subject to Christ, so let the wives be to their own husbands in everything.

Husbands, love your wives, just as Christ also loved the church and gave Himself for it, that He might sanctify and cleanse it with the washing of water by the word, that He might present it to Himself a glorious church, not having spot or wrinkle or any such thing, but that it should be holy and without blemish.

So husbands ought to love their own wives as their own bodies; he who loves his wife loves himself.

For no one ever hated his own flesh, but nourishes and cherishes it, just as the Lord does the church.

For we are members of His body, of His flesh and of His bones.

For this reason a man shall leave his father and mother and be joined to his wife, and the two shall become one flesh.

This is a great mystery, but I speak concerning Christ and the church.

Nevertheless let each one of you in particular so love his own wife as himself, and let the wife see that she respects her husband.

Children, obey your parents in the Lord, for this is right.

Honor your father and mother, which is the first commandment with promise:

That it may be well with you and you may live long on the earth.

And you, fathers, do not provoke your children to wrath, but bring them up in the training and admonition of the Lord.

Eph. 5:22-6:4 (NKJV)

664 UNITY

As a prisoner for the Lord, then, I urge you to live a life worthy of the calling you have received.

Be completely humble and gentle; be patient, bearing with one another in love.

Make every effort to keep the unity of the Spirit through the bond of peace.

There is one body and one Spirit—just as you were called to one hope when you were called—

One Lord, one faith, one baptism;

One God and Father of all, who is over all and through all and in all.

If you have any encouragement from being united with Christ, if any comfort from His love, if any fellowship with the Spirit, if any tenderness and compassion;

Then make my joy complete by being likeminded, having the same love, being one in spirit and purpose.

Do nothing out of selfish ambition or vain conceit, but in humility consider others better than yourselves.

Each of you should look not only to your own interests, but also to the interests of others.

Eph. 4:1-6; Phil. 2:1-4 (NIV)

665 GOVERNMENT

Let every soul be subject to the governing authorities. For there is no authority except from God, and the authorities that exist are appointed by God.

Therefore whoever resists the authority resists the ordinance of God, and those who resist will bring judgment on themselves.

For rulers are not a terror to good works, but to evil. Do you want to be unafraid of the authority? Do what is good, and you will have praise from the same.

For he is God's minister to you for good. But if you do evil, be afraid; for he does not bear the sword in vain; for he is God's minister, an avenger to execute wrath on him who practices evil.

Therefore you must be subject, not only because of wrath but also for conscience' sake.

For because of this you also pay taxes, for they are God's ministers attending continually to this very thing.

Render therefore to all their due: taxes to whom taxes are due, customs to whom customs, fear to whom fear, honor to whom honor.

Therefore submit yourselves to every ordinance of man for the Lord's sake, whether to the king as supreme, or to governors, as to those who are sent by him for the punishment of evildoers and for the praise of those who do good.

For this is the will of God, that by doing good you may put to silence the ignorance of foolish men—as free, yet not using your liberty as a cloak for vice, but as servants of God.

Honor all people. Love the brotherhood. Fear God. Honor the king.

Rom. 13:1-7; 1 Pet. 2:13-17 (NKJV)

666 WORK

Now we command you, brethren, in the name of our Lord Jesus Christ, that you keep away from any brother who is living in idleness and not in accord with the tradition that you received from us.

For you yourselves know how you ought to imitate us; we were not idle when we were with you, we did not eat any one's bread without paying;

But with toil and labor we worked night and day, that we might not burden any of you.

It was not because we have not that right, but to give you in our conduct an example to imitate.

For even when we were with you, we gave you this command: If any one will not work, let him not eat.

For we hear that some of you are living in idleness, mere busybodies, not doing any work.

Now such persons we command and exhort in the Lord Jesus Christ to do their work in quietness and to earn their own living.

Brethren, do not be weary in well-doing.

2 Thess. 3:6-13 (RSV)

667 THE CHRISTIAN'S RESURRECTION

If for this life only we have hoped in Christ, we are of all men most to be pitied.

But in fact Christ has been raised from the dead, the first fruits of those who have fallen asleep.

For as by a man came death, by a Man has come also the resurrection of the dead.

For as in Adam all die, so also in Christ shall all be made alive.

Some one will ask, How are the dead raised? With what kind of body do they come?

You foolish man! What you sow does not come to life unless it dies.

And what you sow is not the body which is to be, but a bare kernel, perhaps of wheat or of some other grain.

But God gives it a body as He has chosen, and to each kind of seed its own body.

So is it with the resurrection of the dead. What is sown is perishable, what is raised is imperishable.

It is sown in dishonor, it is raised in glory. It is sown in weakness, it is raised in power.

It is sown a physical body, it is raised a spiritual body. If there is a physical body, there is also a spiritual body.

For this perishable nature must put on the imperishable, and this mortal nature must put on immortality.

When the perishable puts on the imperishable, and the mortal puts on immortality, then shall come to pass the saying that is written:

Death is swallowed up in victory. O death, where is thy victory? O death, where is thy sting?

The sting of death is sin, and the power of sin is the law. But thanks be to God, who gives us the victory through our Lord Jesus Christ.

Therefore, my beloved brethren, be steadfast, immovable, always abounding in the work of the Lord, knowing that in the Lord your labor is not in vain.

1 Cor. 15:19-22, 35-38, 42-44, 53-58 (RSV)

668 JUSTIFICATION THROUGH FAITH

Therefore having been justified by faith, we have peace with God through our Lord Jesus Christ;

Through whom also we have obtained our introduction by faith into this grace in which we stand; and we exult in hope of the glory of God.

And not only this, but we also exult in our tribulations, knowing that tribulation brings about perseverance;

And perseverance, proven character; and proven character, hope;

And hope does not disappoint, because the love of God has been poured out within our hearts through the Holy Spirit who was given to us.

For while we were still helpless, at the right time Christ died for the ungodly.

For one will hardly die for a righteous man; though perhaps for the good man someone would dare even to die.

But God demonstrates His own love toward us, in that while we were yet sinners, Christ died for us.

Much more then, having now been justified by His blood, we shall be saved from the wrath of God through Him.

For if while we were enemies, we were reconciled to God through the death of His Son, much more, having been reconciled, we shall be saved by His life.

And not only this, but we also exult in God through our Lord Jesus Christ, through whom we have now received the reconciliation.

So then as through one transgression there resulted condemnation to all men, even so through one act of righteousness there resulted justification of life to all men.

Rom. 5:1-11,18 (NASB)

669 MATURITY

He gave some as apostles, and some as prophets, and some as evangelists, and some as pastors and teachers, for the equipping of the saints for the work of service, to the building up of the body of Christ;

Until we all attain to the unity of the faith, and of the knowledge of the Son of God, to a mature man, to the measure of the stature which belongs to the fulness of Christ.

As a result, we are no longer to be children, tossed here and there by waves, and carried about by every wind of doctrine, by the trickery of men, by craftiness in deceitful scheming;

But speaking the truth in love, we are to grow up in all aspects into Him, who is the head, even Christ, from whom the whole body, being fitted and held together by that which every joint supplies, according to the proper working of each individual part, causes the growth of the body for the building up of itself in love.

Though by this time you ought to be teachers, you have need again for someone to teach you the elementary principles of the oracles of God, and you have come to need milk and not solid food.

For everyone who partakes only of milk is not accustomed to the word of righteousness, for he is a babe.

But solid food is for the mature, who because of practice have their senses trained to discern good and evil.

Therefore leaving the elementary teaching about the Christ, let us press on to maturity.

Eph. 4:11-16; Heb. 5:12-6:1 (NASB)

670 CHRIST'S PRIESTHOOD

Holy brethren, who share in a heavenly call, consider Jesus, the Apostle and High Priest of our confession.

For we have not a High Priest who is unable to sympathize with our weaknesses, but One who in every respect has been tempted as we are, yet without sin.

Let us then with confidence draw near to the throne of grace, that we may receive mercy and find grace to help in time of need.

He holds His priesthood permanently, because He continues for ever.

Consequently He is able for all time to save those who draw near to God through Him, since He always lives to make intercession for them.

For it was fitting that we should have such a High Priest, holy, blameless,

unstained, separated from sinners, exalted above the heavens.

He has no need, like those high priests, to offer sacrifices daily, first for His own sins and then for those of the people; He did this once for all when He offered up Himself.

And every priest stands daily at his service, offering repeatedly the same sacrifices, which can never take away sins.

But when Christ had offered for all time a single sacrifice for sins, He sat down at the right hand of God, then to wait until His enemies should be made a stool for His feet.

For by a single offering He has perfected for all time those who are sanctified.

Therefore, brethren, since we have confidence to enter the sanctuary by the blood of Jesus, by the new and living way which He opened for us through the curtain, that is, through His flesh, and since we have a great priest over the house of God;

Let us draw near with a true heart in full assurance of faith, with our hearts sprinkled clean from an evil conscience and our bodies washed with pure water.

Heb. 3:1; 4:15-16; 7:24-27; 10:11-14, 19-22 (RSV)

671 CHRIST'S TEMPTATION

Then Jesus was led by the Spirit into the desert to be tempted by the devil.

After fasting forty days and forty nights, He was hungry.

The tempter came to Him and said, If you are the Son of God, tell these stones to become bread.

Jesus answered, It is written: Man does not live on bread alone, but on every word that comes from the mouth of God.

Then the devil took Him to the holy city and had Him stand on the highest point of the temple.

If you are the Son of God, he said, throw Yourself down.

For it is written: He will command His angels concerning You, and they will lift You up in their hands, so that You will not strike Your foot against a stone.

Jesus answered him, It is also written: Do not put the Lord your God to the test.

Again, the devil took Him to a very high mountain and showed Him all the kingdoms of the world and their splendor.

All this I will give you, he said, if You will bow down and worship me.

Jesus said to him, Away from Me, Satan! For it is written: Worship the Lord your God, and serve Him only.

Then the devil left Him, and angels came and attended Him.

Matt. 4:1-11 (NIV)

672 ASSURANCE

We know that God causes all things to work together for good to those who love God, to those who are called according to His purpose.

For whom He foreknew, He also predestined to become conformed to the image of His Son, that He might be the firstborn among many brethren;

And whom He predestined, these He also called; and whom He called, these

He also justified; and whom He justified, these He also glorified.

What then shall we say to these things? If God is for us, who is against us?

He who did not spare His own Son, but delivered Him up for us all, how will He not also with Him freely give us all things?

Who will bring a charge against God's elect? God is the one who justifies.

Who is the one who condemns? Christ Jesus is He who died, yes, rather who was raised, who is at the right hand of God, who also intercedes for us.

Who shall separate us from the love of Christ? Shall tribulation, or distress, or persecution, or famine, or nakedness, or peril, or sword?

Just as it is written, For Thy sake we are being put to death all day long; we were considered as sheep to be slaughtered.

But in all these things we overwhelmingly conquer through Him who loved us.

For I am convinced that neither death, nor life, nor angels, nor principalities, nor things present, nor things to come, nor powers,

Nor height, nor depth, nor any other created thing, shall be able to separate us from the love of God, which is in Christ Jesus our Lord.

Rom. 8:28-39 (NASB)

673 SANCTIFICATION

Count yourselves dead to sin but alive to God in Christ Jesus.

Therefore do not let sin reign in your mortal body so that you obey its evil desires.

Do not offer the parts of your body to sin, as instruments of wickedness, but rather offer yourselves to God, as those who have been brought from death to life; and offer the parts of your body to Him as instruments of righteousness.

For sin shall not be your master, because you are not under law, but under grace.

Just as you used to offer the parts of your body in slavery to impurity and to ever-increasing wickedness, so now offer them in slavery to righteousness leading to holiness.

When you were slaves to sin, you were free from the control of righteousness.

What benefit did you reap at that time from the things you are now ashamed of? Those things result in death!

But now that you have been set free from sin and have become slaves to God, the benefit you reap leads to holiness, and the result is eternal life.

Live by the Spirit, and you will not gratify the desires of the sinful nature.

For the sinful nature desires what is contrary to the Spirit, and the Spirit what is contrary to the sinful nature. They are in conflict with each other, so that you do not do what you want.

But if you are led by the Spirit, you are not under law.

The acts of the sinful nature are obvious: sexual immorality, impurity and debauchery;

Idolatry and witchcraft; hatred, discord, jealousy, fits of rage, selfish ambition, dissensions, factions and envy; drunkenness, orgies, and the like.

I warn you, as I did before, that those

who live like this will not inherit the kingdom of God.

But the fruit of the Spirit is love, joy, peace, patience, kindness, goodness, faithfulness,

Gentleness and self-control. Against such things there is no law.

Those who belong to Christ Jesus have crucified the sinful nature with its passions and desires.

Since we live by the Spirit, let us keep in step with the Spirit.

Rom. 6:11-14, 19-22; Gal. 5:16-25 (NIV)

674 DEDICATED SERVICE

I appeal to you therefore, brethren, by the mercies of God, to present your bodies as a living sacrifice, holy and acceptable to God, which is your spiritual worship.

Do not be conformed to this world but be transformed by the renewal of your mind, that you may prove what is the will of God, what is good and acceptable and perfect.

For by the grace given to me I bid every one among you not to think of himself more highly than he ought to think, but to think with sober judgment, each according to the measure of faith which God has assigned him.

For as in one body we have many members, and all the members do not have the same function, so we, though many, are one body in Christ, and individually members one of another.

Let love be genuine; hate what is evil, hold fast to what is good;

Love one another with brotherly affection; outdo one another in showing honor.

Never flag in zeal, be aglow with the Spirit, serve the Lord.

Rejoice in your hope, be patient in tribulation, be constant in prayer.

Contribute to the needs of the saints, practice hospitality.

Bless those who persecute you; bless and do not curse them.

Rejoice with those who rejoice, weep with those who weep.

Live in harmony with one another; do not be haughty, but associate with the lowly; never be conceited.

Repay no one evil for evil, but take thought for what is noble in the sight of all. If possible, so far as it depends upon you, live peaceably with all.

Do not be overcome by evil, but overcome evil with good.

Rom. 12:1-5, 9-18, 21 (RSV)

675 PERSEVERANCE

Do you not know that those who run in a race all run, but only one receives the prize? Run in such a way that you may win.

And everyone who competes in the games exercises self-control in all things. They then do it to receive a perishable wreath, but we an imperishable.

Therefore I run in such a way, as not without aim; I box in such a way, as not beating the air;

But I buffet my body and make it my slave, lest possibly, after I have preached to others, I myself should be disqualified.

Work out your salvation with fear and trembling;

For it is God who is at work in you, both to will and to work for His good pleasure.

I press on in order that I may lay hold of that for which also I was laid hold of by Christ Jesus.

Brethren, I do not regard myself as having laid hold of it yet; but one thing I do: forgetting what lies behind and reaching forward to what lies ahead,

I press on toward the goal for the prize of the upward call of God in Christ Jesus.

We have become partakers of Christ, if we hold fast the beginning of our assurance firm until the end.

Since we have so great a cloud of witnesses surrounding us, let us also lay aside every encumbrance, and the sin which so easily entangles us, and let us run with endurance the race that is set before us,

Fixing our eyes on Jesus, the author and perfecter of faith, who for the joy set before Him endured the cross, despising the shame, and has sat down at the right hand of the throne of God.

For consider Him who has endured such hostility by sinners against Himself, so that you may not grow weary and lose heart.

As an example, brethren, of suffering and patience, take the prophets who spoke in the name of the Lord.

Behold, we count those blessed who endured. You have heard of the endurance of Job and have seen the outcome of the Lord's dealings, that the Lord is full of compassion and is merciful.

Be all the more diligent to make certain about His calling and choosing you; for as long as you practice these things, you will never stumble;

For in this way the entrance into the eternal kingdom of our Lord and Savior Jesus Christ will be abundantly supplied to you.

Building yourselves up on your most holy faith; praying in the Holy Spirit;

Keep yourselves in the love of God, waiting anxiously for the mercy of our Lord Jesus Christ to eternal life.

Now to Him who is able to keep you from stumbling, and to make you stand in the presence of His glory blameless with great joy, be glory, majesty, dominion and authority, before all time and now and forever. Amen.

1 Cor. 9:24-27; Phil. 2:12-13; 3:12-14; Heb. 3:14; 12:1-3; James 5:10-11; 2 Pet. 1:10-11; Jude 20-21, 24, 25 (NASB)

676 RIGHTEOUSNESS

And he believed the Lord; and he reckoned it to him as righteousness.

Righteousness exalts a nation, but sin is a reproach to any people.

For I am not ashamed of the gospel: it is the power of God for salvation to every one who has faith, to the Jew first and also to the Greek.

For in it the righteousness of God is revealed through faith for faith; as it is written, He who through faith is righteous shall live.

Now we know that whatever the law says it speaks to those who are under the law, so that every mouth may be stopped, and the whole world may be held accountable to God.

For no human being will be justified in His sight by works of the law, since through the law comes knowledge of sin.

But now the righteousness of God has been manifested apart from law, although the law and the prophets bear witness to it, the righteousness of God through faith in Jesus Christ for all who believe.

For there is no distinction; since all have sinned and fall short of the glory of God, they are justified by His grace as a gift, through the redemption which is in Christ Jesus, whom God put forward as an expiation by His blood, to be received by faith.

This was to show God's righteousness, because in His divine forbearance He had passed over former sins;

It was to prove at the present time that He Himself is righteous and that He justifies him who has faith in Jesus.

The promise to Abraham and his descendants, that they should inherit the world, did not come through the law but through the righteousness of faith.

Then as one man's trespass led to condemnation for all men, so one man's act of righteousness leads to acquittal and life for all men.

For as by one man's disobedience many were made sinners, so by one man's obedience many will be made righteous.

Law came in, to increase the trespass; but where sin increased, grace abounded all the more, so that, as sin reigned in death, grace also might reign through righteousness to eternal life through Jesus Christ our Lord.

Brethren, my heart's desire and prayer to God for them is that they may be saved.

I bear them witness that they have a zeal for God, but it is not enlightened.

For, being ignorant of the righteousness that comes from God, and seeking to establish their own, they did not submit to God's righteousness.

For Christ is the end of the law, that every one who has faith may be justified.

Gen. 15:6; Prov. 14:34; Rom. 1:16-17; 3:19-26; 4:13; 5:18-21; 10:1-4 (RSV)

677 GLORIFICATION

The sufferings of this present time are not worthy to be compared with the glory that is to be revealed to us.

For the anxious longing of the creation waits eagerly for the revealing of the sons of God.

For the creation was subjected to futility, not of its own will, but because of Him who subjected it, in hope that the creation itself also will be set free from its slavery to corruption into the freedom of the glory of the children of God.

For we know that the whole creation groans and suffers the pains of childbirth together until now.

And not only this, but also we ourselves, having the first fruits of the Spirit, even we ourselves groan within ourselves, waiting eagerly for our adoption as sons, the redemption of our body.

For in hope we have been saved, but hope that is seen is not hope; for why does one also hope for what he sees?

But if we hope for what we do not see, with perseverance we wait eagerly for it.

And in the same way the Spirit also helps our weakness; for we do not know how to pray as we should, but the Spirit Himself intercedes for us with groanings too deep for words;

And He who searches the hearts knows what the mind of the Spirit is, because He intercedes for the saints according to the will of God.

And we know that God causes all things to work together for good to those who love God, to those who are called according to His purpose.

For whom He foreknew, He also predestined to become conformed to the image of His Son, that He might be the firstborn among many brethren;

And whom He predestined, these He also called; and whom He called, these He also justified; and whom He justified, these He also glorified.

Rom. 8:18-30 (NASB)

678 GOD'S GOODNESS

O give thanks to the Lord, for He is good; for His steadfast love endures for ever!

Deliver us, O God of our salvation, and gather and save us from among the nations, that we may give thanks to Thy holy name, and glory in Thy praise.

Blessed be the Lord, the God of Israel, from everlasting to everlasting! Then all the people said Amen! and praised the Lord.

The Lord is good, a stronghold in the day of trouble; He knows those who take refuge in Him.

You have heard that it was said, You shall love your neighbor and hate your enemy.

But I say to you, Love your enemies and pray for those who persecute you, so that you may be sons of your Father who is in heaven;

For He makes His sun rise on the evil and on the good, and sends rain on the just and on the unjust.

For if you love those who love you, what reward have you? Do not even the tax collectors do the same?

And if you salute only your brethren, what more are you doing than others? Do not even the Gentiles do the same?

You, therefore, must be perfect, as your heavenly Father is perfect.

What man of you, if his son asks him for bread, will give him a stone?

Or if he asks for a fish, will give him a serpent?

If you then, who are evil, know how to give good gifts to your children, how much more will your Father who is in heaven give good things to those who ask Him!

So whatever you wish that men would do to you, do so to them; for this is the law and the prophets.

We know that in everything God works for good with those who love Him, who are called according to His purpose.

For those whom He foreknew He also predestined to be conformed to the image of His Son, in order that He might be the firstborn among many brethren.

And those whom He predestined He also called; and those whom He called He also justified; and those whom He justified He also glorified.

Everything created by God is good, and nothing is to be rejected if it is received with thanksgiving.

Every good endowment and every perfect gift is from above, coming down from the Father of lights with whom there is no variation or shadow due to change.

You have tasted the kindness of the Lord.

1 Chr. 16:34-36; Nah. 1:7; Matt. 5:43-48; 7:9-12; Rom. 8:28-30; 1 Tim. 4:4; James 1:17; 1 Pet. 2:3 (RSV)

679 WISDOM

The proverbs of Solomon the son of David, king of Israel: To know wisdom and instruction, To perceive the words of understanding,

To receive the instruction of wisdom, justice, judgment, and equity;

To give prudence to the simple, To the young man knowledge and discretion—

A wise man will hear and increase learning, And a man of understanding will attain wise counsel,

To understand a proverb and an enigma, The words of the wise and their riddles.

The fear of the Lord is the beginning of knowledge, But fools despise wisdom and instruction.

Happy is the man who finds wisdom, And the man who gains understanding;

For her proceeds are better than the profits of silver, And her gain than fine gold.

The fear of the Lord is the beginning of wisdom, And the knowledge of the Holy One is understanding.

If any of you lacks wisdom, let him ask of God, who gives to all liberally and without reproach, and it will be given to him.

Who is wise and understanding among you? Let him show by good conduct that his works are done in the meekness of wisdom.

But if you have bitter envy and self-seeking in your hearts, do not boast and lie against the truth.

This wisdom does not descend from above, but is earthly, sensual, demonic.

For where envy and self-seeking exist, confusion and every evil thing will be there.

But the wisdom that is from above is first pure, then peaceable, gentle, willing to yield, full of mercy and good fruits, without partiality and without hypocrisy.

Now the fruit of righteousness is sown in peace by those who make peace.

Prov. 1:1-7; 3:13-14; 9:10; James 1:5; 3:13-18 (NKJV)

680 JOY

Though the fig tree should not blossom, and there be no fruit on the vines, though the yield of the olive should fail, and the fields produce no food, though the flock should be cut off from the fold, and there be no cattle in the stalls,

Yet I will exult in the Lord, I will rejoice in the God of my salvation.

I thank my God in all my remembrance of you,

Always offering prayer with joy in my every prayer for you all,

In view of your participation in the gospel from the first day until now.

For I am confident of this very thing, that He who began a good work in you will perfect it until the day of Christ Jesus.

Some, to be sure, are preaching Christ even from envy and strife, but some also from good will;

The latter do it out of love, knowing that I am appointed for the defense of the gospel;

The former proclaim Christ out of selfish ambition, rather than from pure motives, thinking to cause me distress in my imprisonment.

What then? Only that in every way, whether in pretense or in truth, Christ is proclaimed; and in this I rejoice, yes, and I will rejoice.

Therefore, my beloved brethren whom I long to see, my joy and crown, so stand firm in the Lord, my beloved.

Rejoice in the Lord always; again I will say, rejoice!

Hab. 3:17-18; Phil. 1:3-6, 15-18; 4:1,4 (NASB)

681 RECONCILIATION

If when we were enemies we were reconciled to God through the death of His Son, much more, having been reconciled, we shall be saved by His life.

And not only that, but we also rejoice in God through our Lord Jesus Christ, through whom we have now received the reconciliation.

Now all things are of God, who has reconciled us to Himself through Jesus Christ, and has given us the ministry of reconciliation,

That is, that God was in Christ reconciling the world to Himself, not imputing their trespasses to them, and has committed to us the word of reconciliation.

Therefore we are ambassadors for Christ, as though God were pleading through us: we implore you on Christ's behalf, be reconciled to God.

Now in Christ Jesus you who once were far off have been made near by the blood of Christ.

For He Himself is our peace, who has made both one, and has broken down the middle wall of division between us, having abolished in His flesh the enmity, that is, the law of commandments contained in ordinances, so as to create in Himself one new man from the two, thus making peace,

And that He might reconcile them both to God in one body through the cross, thereby putting to death the enmity.

And He came and preached peace to you who were afar off and to those who were near.

For through Him we both have access by one Spirit to the Father.

Rom. 5:10-11; 2 Cor. 5:18-20; Eph. 2:13-18 (NKJV)

682 VICTORY OVER SIN

What shall we say then? Shall we continue in sin that grace may abound?

Certainly not! How shall we who died to sin live any longer in it?

Or do you not know that as many of us as were baptized into Christ Jesus were baptized into His death?

Therefore we were buried with Him through baptism into death, that just as Christ was raised from the dead by the glory of the Father, even so we also should walk in newness of life.

For if we have been united together in the likeness of His death, certainly we also shall be in the likeness of His resurrection,

Knowing this, that our old man was crucified with Him, that the body of sin might be done away with, that we should no longer be slaves of sin.

For he who has died has been freed from sin.

Now if we died with Christ, we believe that we shall also live with Him, knowing that Christ, having been raised from the dead, dies no more. Death no longer has dominion over Him.

For the death that He died, He died to sin once for all; but the life that He lives, He lives to God.

Likewise you also, reckon yourselves to be dead indeed to sin, but alive to God in Christ Jesus our Lord.

Therefore do not let sin reign in your mortal body, that you should obey it in its lusts.

And do not present your members as instruments of unrighteousness to sin, but present yourselves to God as being alive from the dead, and your members as instruments of righteousness to God.

Rom. 6:1-13 (NKJV)

683 CHRIST, BREAD OF LIFE

Jesus said to them, I am the bread of life; he who comes to Me shall not hunger, and he who believes in Me shall never thirst.

But I said to you, that you have seen Me, and yet do not believe.

All that the Father gives Me shall come to Me, and the one who comes to Me I will certainly not cast out.

For I have come down from heaven, not to do My own will, but the will of Him who sent Me.

And this is the will of Him who sent Me, that of all that He has given Me I lose nothing, but raise it up on the last day.

For this is the will of My Father, that everyone who beholds the Son and believes in Him, may have eternal life; and I Myself will raise him up on the last day.

The Jews therefore were grumbling about Him, because He said, I am the bread that came down out of heaven.

And they were saying, Is not this Jesus, the Son of Joseph, whose father and mother we know? How does He now say, I have come down out of heaven?

Jesus answered and said to them, Do not grumble among yourselves.

No one can come to Me, unless the Father who sent Me draws him; and I will raise him up on the last day.

It is written in the prophets, And they shall all be taught of God. Everyone who has heard and learned from the Father, comes to Me.

Not that any man has seen the Father, except the One who is from God; He has seen the Father.

Truly, truly, I say to you, he who believes has eternal life.

I am the bread of life.

John 6:35-48 (NASB)

684 SPIRITUAL GIFTS

Now concerning spiritual gifts, brethren, I do not want you to be unaware.

To each one is given the manifestation of the Spirit for the common good.

For to one is given the word of wisdom through the Spirit, and to another the word of knowledge according to the same Spirit;

To another faith by the same Spirit, and to another gifts of healing by the one Spirit,

And to another the effecting of miracles, and to another prophecy, and to another the distinguishing of spirits, to another various kinds of tongues, and to another the interpretation of tongues.

But one and the same Spirit works all these things, distributing to each one individually just as He wills.

Now you are Christ's body, and individually members of it.

And God has appointed in the church, first apostles, second prophets, third teachers, then miracles, then gifts of healings, helps, administrations, various kinds of tongues.

All are not apostles, are they? All are not prophets, are they?

All are not teachers, are they? All are not workers of miracles, are they?

All do not have gifts of healings, do they? All do not speak with tongues, do they? All do not interpret, do they?

But earnestly desire the greater gifts. And I show you a still more excellent way.

Pursue love, yet desire earnestly spiritual gifts, but especially that you may prophesy.

For one who speaks in a tongue does not speak to men, but to God; for no one understands, but in his spirit he speaks mysteries.

But one who prophesies speaks to men for edification and exhortation and consolation.

Let all things be done properly and in an orderly manner.

1 Cor. 12:1, 7-11, 27-31; 14:1-3, 40 (NASB)

685 CHRISTIAN CONDUCT

If then you have been raised with Christ, seek the things that are above, where Christ is, seated at the right hand of God.

Set your minds on things that are above, not on things that are on earth.

For you have died, and your life is hid with Christ in God.

When Christ who is our life appears, then you also will appear with Him in glory.

Put to death therefore what is earthly in you: fornication, impurity, passion, evil desire, and covetousness, which is idolatry.

On account of these the wrath of God is coming.

In these you once walked, when you lived in them.

But now put them all away: anger, wrath, malice, slander, and foul talk from your mouth.

Do not lie to one another, seeing that you have put off the old nature with its practices and have put on the new nature, which is being renewed in knowledge after the image of its creator.

Here there cannot be Greek and Jew, circumcised, barbarian, Scythian, slave, free man, but Christ is all, and in all.

Col. 3:1-11 (RSV)

686 THE GOOD SAMARITAN

A certain lawyer stood up and tested Him, saying, Teacher, what shall I do to inherit eternal life?

He said to him, What is written in the Law? What is your reading of it?

So he answered and said, You shall love the Lord your God with all your heart, with all your soul, with all your strength, and with all your mind, and your neighbor as yourself.

And He said to him, You have answered rightly; do this and you will live.

But he, wanting to justify himself, said to Jesus, And who is my neighbor?

Then Jesus answered and said: A certain man went down from Jerusalem to Jericho, and fell among thieves, who stripped him of his clothing, wounded him, and departed, leaving him half dead.

Now by chance a certain priest came down that road. And when he saw him, he passed by on the other side.

Likewise a Levite, when he arrived at the place, came and looked, and passed by on the other side.

But a certain Samaritan, as he journeyed, came where he was. And when he saw him, he had compassion on him, and went to him and bandaged his wounds, pouring on oil and wine; and he set him on his own animal, brought him to an inn, and took care of him.

On the next day, when he departed, he took out two denarii, gave them to the innkeeper, and said to him, Take care of him; and whatever more you spend, when I come again, I will repay you.

So which of these three do you think was neighbor to him who fell among the thieves?

And he said, He who showed mercy on him. Then Jesus said to him, Go and do likewise.

Luke 10:25-37 (NKJV)

687 PASSOVER AND THE LAST SUPPER

Then came the Day of Unleavened Bread, when the Passover must be killed.

And He sent Peter and John, saying, Go and prepare the Passover for us, that we may eat.

So they said to Him, Where do You want us to prepare?

And He said to them, Behold, when you have entered the city, a man will meet you carrying a pitcher of water; follow him into the house which he enters.

Then you shall say to the master of the house, The Teacher says to you, Where is the guest room in which I may eat the Passover with My disciples?

Then he will show you a large, furnished upper room; there make ready.

So they went and found it as He had said to them, and they prepared the Passover.

And when the hour had come, He sat down, and the twelve apostles with Him.

Then He said to them, With fervent desire I have desired to eat this Passover with you before I suffer;

For I say to you, I will no longer eat of it until it is fulfilled in the kingdom of God.

Then He took the cup, and gave thanks, and said, Take this and divide it among yourselves;

For I say to you, I will not drink of the fruit of the vine until the kingdom of God comes.

And He took bread, gave thanks and broke it, and gave it to them, saying, This is My body which is given for you; do this in remembrance of Me.

Likewise He also took the cup after supper, saying, This cup is the new covenant in My blood, which is shed for you.

Luke 22:7-20 (NKJV)

688 THE CHRISTIAN'S BAPTISM

Go and make disciples of all nations, baptizing them in the name of the

Father and of the Son and of the Holy Spirit.

Repent and be baptized, every one of you, in the name of Jesus Christ for the forgiveness of your sins. And you will receive the gift of the Holy Spirit.

The jailer called for lights, rushed in and fell trembling before Paul and Silas.

He then brought them out and asked, Sirs, what must I do to be saved?

They replied, Believe in the Lord Jesus, and you will be saved—you and your household.

Then they spoke the word of the Lord to him and to all the others in his house.

At that hour of the night the jailer took them and washed their wounds; then immediately he and all his family were baptized.

The jailer brought them into his house and set a meal before them; he was filled with joy because he had come to believe in God—he and his whole family.

Don't you know that all of us who were baptized into Christ Jesus were baptized into His death?

We were therefore buried with Him through baptism into death in order that, just as Christ was raised from the dead through the glory of the Father, we too may live a new life.

In Him you were also circumcised, in the putting off of the sinful nature, not with a circumcision done by the hands of men but with the circumcision done by Christ,

Having been buried with Him in baptism and raised with Him through your faith in the power of God, who raised Him from the dead.

Matt. 28:19; Acts 2:38; 16:29-34; Rom. 6:3-4; Col. 2:11-12 (NIV)

689 FELLOWSHIP

That which was from the beginning, which we have heard, which we have seen with our eyes, which we have looked upon and touched with our hands, concerning the word of life—

The life was made manifest, and we saw it, and testify to it, and proclaim to you the eternal life which was with the Father and was made manifest to us—

That which we have seen and heard we proclaim also to you, so that you may have fellowship with us; and our fellowship is with the Father and with His Son Jesus Christ.

And we are writing this that our joy may be complete.

This is the message we have heard from Him and proclaim to you, that God is light and in Him is no darkness at all.

If we say we have fellowship with Him while we walk in darkness, we lie and do not live according to the truth;

But if we walk in the light, as He is in the light, we have fellowship with one another, and the blood of Jesus His Son cleanses us from all sin.

If we say we have no sin, we deceive ourselves, and the truth is not in us.

If we confess our sins, He is faithful and just, and will forgive our sins and cleanse us from all unrighteousness.

If we say we have not sinned, we make Him a liar, and His word is not in us.

1 John 1 (RSV)

PSALMS FOR UNISON READING OR PERSONAL MEDITATION

690 PSALM 1

Blessed is the man
who does not walk in the counsel
of the wicked
or stand in the way of sinners
or sit in the seat of mockers.
But his delight is in the law
of the Lord,
and on His law he meditates
day and night.
He is like a tree planted by
streams of water,
which yields its fruit in season
and whose leaf does not wither.
Whatever he does prospers.

Not so the wicked!
They are like chaff
that the wind blows away.
Therefore the wicked will not
stand in the judgment,
nor sinners in the assembly
of the righteous.

For the Lord watches over the
way of the righteous,
but the way of the wicked
will perish.

691 PSALM 2

Why do the nations conspire
and the peoples plot in vain?
The kings of the earth take
their stand
and the rulers gather together
against the Lord
and against His Anointed One.
Let us break their chains,
they say,
and throw off their fetters.
The One enthroned in heaven laughs;
the Lord scoffs at them.
Then He rebukes them in His anger
and terrifies them in His
wrath, saying,

I have installed My King
on Zion, My holy hill.
I will proclaim the decree
of the Lord:

He said to Me, You are my Son;
today I have become Your Father.
Ask of Me,
and I will make the nations
Your inheritance,
the ends of the earth
Your possession.
You will rule them with an
iron scepter;
You will dash them to pieces
like pottery.

Therefore, you kings, be wise;
be warned, you rulers of the earth.
Serve the Lord with fear
and rejoice with trembling.
Kiss the Son, lest He be angry
and you be destroyed in your way,
for His wrath can flare up in
a moment.
Blessed are all who take
refuge in Him.

692 PSALM 16

Keep me safe, O God,
for in You I take refuge.

I said to the Lord, You are my Lord;
apart from You I have no good
thing.
As for the saints who are in
the land,
they are the glorious ones in
whom is all my delight.
The sorrows of those will increase
who run after other gods.
I will not pour out their libations
of blood
or take up their names on my lips.

Psalm readings from The Holy Bible, New International Version

Lord, You have assigned me my
portion and my cup;
You have made my lot secure.
The boundary lines have fallen for
me in pleasant places;
surely I have a delightful
inheritance.

I will praise the Lord, who
counsels me;
even at night my heart instructs me.
I have set the Lord always before me.
Because He is at my right hand,
I will not be shaken.

Therefore my heart is glad
and my tongue rejoices;
my body also will rest secure,
because You will not abandon me
to the grave,
nor will You let Your Holy
One see decay.
You have made known to me the
path of life;
You will fill me with joy in
Your presence,
with eternal pleasures at
Your right hand.

693 PSALM 19

The heavens declare the
glory of God;
the skies proclaim the work
of His hands.
Day after day they pour forth speech;
night after night they
display knowledge.
There is no speech or language
where their voice is not heard.
Their voice goes out into all
the earth,
their words to the ends of
the world.

The law of the Lord is perfect,
reviving the soul.
The statutes of the Lord are
trustworthy,
making wise the simple.
The precepts of the Lord are right,
giving joy to the heart.
The commands of the Lord are radiant,
giving light to the eyes.
The fear of the Lord is pure,
enduring forever.

The ordinances of the Lord are sure
and altogether righteous.
They are more precious than gold,
than much pure gold;
they are sweeter than honey,
than honey from the comb.
By them is Your servant warned;
in keeping them there is
great reward.

Who can discern his errors?
Forgive my hidden faults.
Keep Your servant also from
willful sins;
may they not rule over me.
Then will I be blameless,
innocent of great transgression.

May the words of my mouth and the
meditation of my heart
be pleasing in Your sight,
O Lord, my Rock and my Redeemer.

694 PSALM 22

My God, my God, why have
You forsaken me?
Why are You so far from saving me,
so far from the words of
my groaning?
O my God, I cry out by day, but
You do not answer,
by night, and am not silent.

Yet You are enthroned as
the Holy One;
You are the praise of Israel.
In You our fathers put their trust;
they trusted and You delivered them.
They cried to You and were saved;
in You they trusted and were
not disappointed.

Dogs have surrounded me;
a band of evil men has encircled me,
they have pierced my hands

and my feet.
I can count all my bones;
people stare and gloat over me.
They divide my garments among them
and cast lots for my clothing.

But You, O Lord, be not far off;
O my Strength, come quickly
to help me.

Deliver my life from the sword,
my precious life from the power
of the dogs.
Rescue me from the mouth
of the lions;
save me from the horns
of the wild oxen.

I will declare Your name to
my brothers;
in the congregation I will
praise You.

From You comes my praise in
the great assembly;
before those who fear You will I
fulfill my vows.
The poor will eat and be satisfied;
they who seek the Lord
will praise Him—
may your hearts live forever!
All the ends of the earth
will remember and turn to the Lord,
and all the families of the nations
will bow down before Him,
for dominion belongs to the Lord
and He rules over the nations.

695 PSALM 23

The Lord is my shepherd,
I shall not be in want.
He makes me lie down in
green pastures,
He leads me beside quiet waters,
He restores my soul.
He guides me in paths of
righteousness
for His name's sake.
Even though I walk
through the valley of the
shadow of death,
I will fear no evil,
for You are with me;
Your rod and Your staff,
they comfort me.

You prepare a table before me
in the presence of my enemies.
You anoint my head with oil;
my cup overflows.
Surely, goodness and love
will follow me
all the days of my life,
and I will dwell in the house
of the Lord
forever.

696 PSALM 24

The earth is the Lord's, and
everything in it,
the world, and all who live in it;
for He founded it upon the seas
and established it upon the waters.

Who may ascend the hill of the Lord?
Who may stand in His holy place?
He who has clean hands and
a pure heart,
who does not lift up his soul
to an idol
or swear by what is false.
He will receive blessing from
the Lord
and vindication from God his
Savior.
Such is the generation of those
who seek Him,
who seek Your face, O God of Jacob.

Lift up your heads, O you gates;
be lifted up, you ancient doors,
that the King of glory may come in.
Who is this King of glory?
The Lord strong and mighty,
the Lord mighty in battle.
Lift up your heads, O you gates;
lift them up, you ancient doors,
that the King of glory may come in.
Who is He, this King of glory?
The Lord Almighty—
He is the King of glory.

697 PSALM 27

The Lord is my light and
my salvation—
whom shall I fear?
The Lord is the stronghold
of my life—
of whom shall I be afraid?
When evil men advance against me
to devour my flesh,
when my enemies and my
foes attack me,
they will stumble and fall.
Though an army besiege me,
my heart will not fear;
though war break out against me,
even then will I be confident.

One thing I ask of the Lord,
this is what I seek:
that I may dwell in the house
of the Lord
all the days of my life,
to gaze upon the beauty of
the Lord
and to seek Him in His temple.

Hear my voice when I call, O Lord;
be merciful to me and answer me.
My heart says of you, Seek His face!
Your face, Lord, I will seek.
Do not hide Your face from me,
do not turn Your servant
away in anger;
You have been my helper.
Do not reject me or forsake me,
O God my Savior.
Though my father and mother
forsake me,
the Lord will receive me.
Teach me Your way, O Lord;
lead me in a straight path
because of my oppressors.

I am still confident of this:
I will see the goodness of the Lord
in the land of the living.
Wait for the Lord;
be strong and take heart
and wait for the Lord.

698 PSALM 32

Blessed is he
whose transgressions are forgiven,
whose sins are covered.
Blessed is the man
whose sin the Lord does not
count against him
and in whose spirit is no deceit.

When I kept silent,
my bones wasted away
through my groaning all day long.
For day and night
Your hand was heavy upon me;
my strength was sapped
as in the heat of summer.

Then I acknowledged my sin to You
and did not cover up my iniquity.
I said, I will confess
my transgressions to the Lord—
and You forgave
the guilt of my sin.

Therefore let everyone who is godly
pray to You
while You may be found;
surely when the mighty waters rise,
they will not reach him.
You are my hiding place;
You will protect me from trouble
and surround me with
songs of deliverance.

I will instruct you and teach you
in the way you should go;
I will counsel you and
watch over you.
Do not be like the horse or the mule,
which have no understanding
but must be controlled by bit
and bridle
or they will not come to you.
Many are the woes of the wicked,
but the Lord's unfailing love
surrounds the man who trusts
in Him.

Rejoice in the Lord and be
glad, you righteous;
sing, all you who are
upright in heart!

699 PSALM 33

Sing joyfully to the Lord,
you righteous;
it is fitting for the upright
to praise Him.
Sing to Him a new song;
play skillfully, and shout for joy.

For the word of the Lord is
right and true;
He is faithful in all He does.
The Lord loves righteousness
and justice;
the earth is full of His
unfailing love.

By the word of the Lord were
the heavens made,
their starry host by the
breath of His mouth.
Let all the earth fear the Lord;
let all the people of the
world revere Him.
For He spoke, and it came to be;
He commanded, and it stood firm.
The Lord foils the plans of
the nations;
He thwarts the purposes of
the peoples.
But the plans of the Lord
stand firm forever,
the purposes of His heart
through all generations.

We wait in hope for the Lord;
He is our help and our shield.
In Him our hearts rejoice,
for we trust in His holy name.
May Your unfailing love rest upon
us, O Lord,
even as we put our hope in You.

700 PSALM 40

I waited patiently for the Lord;
He turned to me and heard my cry.
He lifted me out of the slimy pit,
out of the mud and mire;
He set my feet on a rock
and gave me a firm place to stand.
He put a new song in my mouth,
a hymn of praise to our God.
Many will see and fear
and put their trust in the Lord.

Blessed is the man
who makes the Lord his trust,
who does not look to the proud,
to those who turn aside to
false gods.
Many, O Lord my God,
are the wonders You have done.
The things You planned for us
no one can recount to You;
were I to speak and tell of them,
they would be too many to declare.

Sacrifice and offering You
did not desire,
but my ears You have pierced;
burnt offerings and sin offerings
You did not require.
Then I said, Here I am, I
have come—
it is written about me in the scroll.
I desire to do Your will, O my God;
Your law is within my heart.
I proclaim righteousness in
the great assembly;
I do not seal my lips,
as you know, O Lord.
I do not hide Your righteousness
in my heart;
I speak of Your faithfulness
and salvation.
I do not conceal Your love
and Your truth
from the great assembly.

701 PSALM 42

As the deer pants for
streams of water,
so my soul pants for You, O God.
My soul thirsts for God, for
the living God.
When can I go and meet with God?
My tears have been my food
day and night,
while men say to me all day long,
Where is your God?
These things I remember

as I pour out my soul:
how I used to go with the
multitude,
leading the procession to
the house of God,
with shouts of joy and thanksgiving
among the festive throng.

Why are you downcast, O my soul?
Why so disturbed within me?
Put your hope in God,
for I will yet praise Him,
my Savior and my God.

My soul is downcast within me;
therefore I will remember You
from the land of the Jordan,
the heights of Hermon—
from Mount Mizar.
Deep calls to deep
in the roar of Your waterfalls;
all Your waves and breakers
have swept over me.

By day the Lord directs His love,
at night His song is with me—
a prayer to the God of my life.
I say to God my Rock,
Why have You forgotten me?
Why must I go about mourning,
oppressed by the enemy?
My bones suffer mortal agony
as my foes taunt me,
saying to me all day long,
Where is your God?

Why are you downcast, O my soul?
Why so disturbed within me?
Put your hope in God,
for I will yet praise Him,
my Savior and my God.

702 **PSALM 46**

God is our refuge and strength,
an ever present help in trouble.
Therefore we will not fear, though
the earth give way
and the mountains fall into the
heart of the sea,
though its waters roar and foam
and the mountains quake
with their surging.

There is a river whose streams
make glad the city of God,
the holy place where the
Most High dwells.
God is within her, she will not fall;
God will help her at break of day.
Nations are in uproar, kingdoms fall;
He lifts His voice, the earth melts.

The Lord Almighty is with us;
the God of Jacob is our fortress.

Come and see the works of the Lord,
the desolations He has brought
on the earth.
He makes wars cease to the ends
of the earth;
He breaks the bow and
shatters the spear,
He burns the shields with fire.
Be still, and know that I am God;
I will be exalted among the nations,
I will be exalted in the earth.

The Lord Almighty is with us;
the God of Jacob is our fortress.

703 **PSALM 51**

Have mercy on me, O God,
according to Your unfailing love;
according to Your great compassion
blot out my transgressions.
Wash away all my iniquity
and cleanse me from my sin.

For I know my transgressions,
and my sin is always before me.
Against You, You only, have
I sinned
and done what is evil in Your sight,
so that You are proved right
when You speak
and justified when You judge.
Surely I was sinful at birth,
sinful from the time my mother
conceived me.
Surely You desire truth in
the inner parts;

You teach me wisdom in
the inmost place.

Cleanse me with hyssop, and I
will be clean;
wash me, and I will be
whiter than snow.
Let me hear joy and gladness;
let the bones You have
crushed rejoice.
Hide Your face from my sins
and blot out all my iniquity.

Create in me a pure heart, O God,
and renew a steadfast spirit
within me.
Do not cast me from Your presence
or take Your Holy Spirit from me.
Restore to me the joy of
Your salvation
and grant me a willing spirit,
to sustain me.

Then I will teach transgressors
Your ways,
and sinners will turn back to You.
You do not delight in sacrifice,
or I would bring it;
You do not take pleasure in
burnt offerings.
The sacrifices of God are a
broken spirit;
a broken and contrite heart,
O God, You will not despise.

704 PSALM 65

Praise awaits You, O God, in Zion;
to You our vows will be fulfilled.
O You who hear prayer,
to You all men will come.
When we were overwhelmed by sins,
You forgave our transgressions.
Blessed is the man You choose
and bring near to live in
Your courts!
We are filled with the good things
of Your house,
of Your holy temple.

You answer us with awesome deeds
of righteousness,
O God our Savior,
the hope of all the ends
of the earth
and of the farthest seas.
Those living far away fear
Your wonders;
where morning dawns and
evening fades
You call forth songs of joy.
You care for the land and water it;
You enrich it abundantly.
The streams of God are filled
with water
to provide the people with grain,
for so You have ordained it.
You crown the year with
Your bounty,
and Your carts overflow
with abundance.
The grasslands of the desert overflow;
the hills are clothed with gladness.

The meadows are covered with flocks
and the valleys are mantled
with grain;
they shout for joy and sing.

705 PSALM 84

How lovely is Your dwelling place,
O Lord Almighty!
My soul yearns, even faints,
for the courts of the Lord;
my heart and my flesh cry out
for the living God.

Even the sparrow has found a home,
and the swallow a nest for herself,
where she may have her young—
a place near Your altar,
O Lord Almighty, my King
and my God.
Blessed are those who dwell
in Your house;
they are ever praising You.

Blessed are those whose strength
is in You,
who have set their hearts
on pilgrimage.
As they pass through the
Valley of Baca,

they make it a place of springs;
the autumn rains also cover
it with pools.
They go from strength to strength
till each appears before God in Zion.

Hear my prayer, O Lord God
Almighty;
listen to me, O God of Jacob.

Better is one day in Your courts
than a thousand elsewhere;
I would rather be a doorkeeper in
the house of my God
than dwell in the tents
of the wicked.

For the Lord God is a sun and shield;
the Lord bestows favor and honor;
no good thing does He withhold
from those whose walk is blameless.

O Lord Almighty,
blessed is the man who
trusts in You.

706 PSALM 90

Lord, You have been our
dwelling place
throughout all generations.
Before the mountains were born
or You brought forth the earth
and the world,
from everlasting to everlasting
You are God.

You turn men back to dust,
saying, Return to dust, O
sons of men.
For a thousand years in Your sight
are like a day that has just gone by,
or like a watch in the night.

You have set our iniquities
before You,
our secret sins in the light of
Your presence.
All our days pass away
under Your wrath;
we finish our years with a moan.
The length of our days is
seventy years—
or eighty, if we have the strength;
yet their span is but trouble
and sorrow,
for they quickly pass, and
we fly away.

Satisfy us in the morning with
Your unfailing love,
that we may sing for joy and be
glad all our days.
Make us glad for as many days as
You have afflicted us,
for as many years as we
have seen trouble.

May Your deeds be shown to
Your servants,
Your splendor to their children.

May the favor of the Lord our God
rest upon us;
establish the work of our
hands for us—
yes, establish the work of
our hands.

707 PSALM 91

He who dwells in the shelter of
the Most High
will rest in the shadow of
the Almighty.
I will say of the Lord, He is my
refuge and my fortress,
my God, in whom I trust.

Surely He will save you from
the fowler's snare
and from the deadly pestilence.
He will cover you with His feathers,
and under His wings you will
find refuge;
His faithfulness will be your
shield and rampart.
You will not fear the terror
of night,
nor the arrow that flies by day,
nor the pestilence that stalks
in the darkness,
nor the plague that destroys
at midday.

A thousand may fall at your side,
ten thousand at your right hand,
but it will not come near you.
You will only observe with your eyes
and see the punishment of
the wicked.

If you make the Most High
your dwelling—
even the Lord, who is my refuge—
then no harm will befall you,
no disaster will come near your tent.
For He will command His angels
concerning you
to guard you in all your ways;
they will lift you up in their hands,
so that you will not strike your
foot against a stone.

Because he loves Me, says the Lord,
I will rescue him;
I will protect him, for he
acknowledges My name.
He will call upon Me, and I
will answer him;
I will be with him in trouble,
I will deliver him and honor him.
With long life will I satisfy him
and show him My salvation.

708 PSALM 95

Come, let us sing for joy to the Lord;
let us shout aloud to the Rock
of our salvation.
Let us come before Him with
thanksgiving
and extol Him with music and song.

For the Lord is the great God,
the great King above all gods.
In His hand are the depths
of the earth,
and the mountain peaks belong
to Him.
The sea is His, for He made it,
and His hands formed the dry land.

Come, let us bow down in worship,
let us kneel before the
Lord our Maker;
for He is our God
and we are the people of
His pasture,
the flock under His care.

Today, if you hear His voice,
do not harden your hearts as
you did at Meribah,
as you did that day at Massah
in the desert,
where your fathers tested
and tried Me,
though they had seen what I did.
For forty years I was angry with
that generation;
I said, They are a people whose
hearts go astray,
and they have not known My ways.
So I declared on oath in My anger,
They shall never enter My rest.

709 PSALM 100

Shout for joy to the Lord,
all the earth.
Worship the Lord with gladness;
come before Him with joyful songs.
Know that the Lord is God.
It is He who made us, and
we are His;
we are His people, the sheep
of His pasture.

Enter His gates with thanksgiving
and His courts with praise;
give thanks to Him and
praise His name.
For the Lord is good and His
love endures forever;
His faithfulness continues
through all generations.

710 PSALM 103

Praise the Lord, O my soul;
all my inmost being, praise
His holy name.
Praise the Lord, O my soul,
and forget not all His benefits—
who forgives all your sins
and heals all your diseases,
who redeems your life from the pit

and crowns you with love
and compassion,
who satisfies your desires with
good things
so that your youth is renewed
like the eagle's.
The Lord is compassionate
and gracious,
slow to anger, abounding in love.
He will not always accuse,
nor will He harbor His anger
forever;
He does not treat us as our
sins deserve
or repay us according to
our iniquities.
For as high as the heavens are
above the earth,
so great is His love for those
who fear Him;
as far as the east is from the west,
so far has He removed our
transgressions from us.
As a father has compassion
on his children,
so the Lord has compassion on
those who fear Him;
for He knows how we are formed,
He remembers that we are dust.
As for man, his days are like grass,
he flourishes like a flower
of the field;
the wind blows over it and it is gone,
and its place remembers it no more.
But from everlasting to everlasting
the Lord's love is with those
who fear Him,
and His righteousness with their
children's children—
with those who keep His covenant
and remember to obey His precepts.

The Lord has established His
throne in heaven,
and His kingdom rules over all.
Praise the Lord, O my soul.

711 **PSALM 110**

The Lord says to my Lord:
Sit at My right hand
until I make Your enemies
a footstool for Your feet.

The Lord will extend Your mighty
scepter from Zion;
You will rule in the midst
of Your enemies.

Your troops will be willing
on Your day of battle.
Arrayed in holy majesty,
from the womb of the dawn
You will receive the dew of
Your youth.

The Lord has sworn
and will not change His mind:
You are a priest forever,
in the order of Melchizedek.

The Lord is at Your right hand;
He will crush kings on the day
of His wrath.
He will judge the nations,
heaping up the dead
and crushing the rulers of
the whole earth.
He will drink from a brook
beside the way;
therefore He will lift up His head.

712 **PSALM 118**

Give thanks to the Lord, for
He is good;
His love endures forever.

In my anguish I cried to the Lord,
and He answered by setting me free.
The Lord is with me; I will
not be afraid.
What can man do to me?
The Lord is with me; He is my helper.
I will look in triumph on
my enemies.

It is better to take refuge in
the Lord
than to trust in man.
It is better to take refuge in
the Lord
than to trust in princes.

I was pushed back and about to fall,
but the Lord helped me.
The Lord is my strength and my song;
He has become my salvation.

Shouts of joy and victory
resound in the tents of the
righteous:
The Lord's right hand has done
mighty things!
The Lord's right hand is
lifted high;
the Lord's right hand has done
mighty things!

I will not die but live,
and will proclaim what the
Lord has done.
The Lord has chastened me severely,
but He has not given me
over to death.

Open for me the gates of
righteousness;
I will enter and give thanks
to the Lord.
This is the gate of the Lord
through which the righteous
may enter.
I will give You thanks, for
You answered me;
You have become my salvation.

The stone the builders rejected
has become the capstone;
the Lord has done this, and it is
marvelous in our eyes.
This is the day the Lord has made;
let us rejoice and be glad in it.

713 PSALM 121

I lift up my eyes to the hills—
where does my help come from?
My help comes from the Lord,
the Maker of heaven and earth.

He will not let your foot slip—
He who watches over you
will not slumber;
indeed, He who watches over Israel
will neither slumber nor sleep.

The Lord watches over you—
the Lord is your shade at
your right hand;
the sun will not harm you by day,
nor the moon by night.

The Lord will keep you
from all harm—
He will watch over your life;
the Lord will watch over your
coming and going
both now and forevermore.

714 PSALM 139

O Lord, You have searched me
and You know me.
You know when I sit and
when I rise;
You perceive my thoughts from afar.
You discern my going out and
my lying down;
You are familiar with all my ways.
Before a word is on my tongue
You know it completely, O Lord.

Where can I go from Your Spirit?
Where can I flee from Your
presence?
If I go up to the heavens,
You are there;
if I make my bed in the depths,
You are there.
If I rise on the wings of the dawn,
if I settle on the far side
of the sea,
even there Your hand will guide me,
Your right hand will hold me fast.

For You created my inmost being;
You knit me together in my
mother's womb.
I praise You because I am fearfully
and wonderfully made;
Your works are wonderful,
I know that full well.
My frame was not hidden from You
when I was made in the secret place.
When I was woven together in the
depths of the earth,
Your eyes saw my unformed body.
All the days ordained for me

were written in Your book
before one of them came to be.

How precious to me are Your
thoughts, O God!
How vast is the sum of them!

Were I to count them,
they would outnumber the
grains of sand.
When I awake,
I am still with You.

Search me, O God, and know my
heart;
test me and know my
anxious thoughts.
See if there is any offensive
way in me,
and lead me in the way everlasting.

715 PSALM 145

I will exalt You, my God the King;
I will praise Your name for
ever and ever.

Great is the Lord and most
worthy of praise;
His greatness no one can fathom.
One generation will commend Your
works to another;
they will tell of Your mighty acts.
They will tell of the glory of
Your kingdom
and speak of Your might,
so that all men may know of
Your mighty acts
and the glorious splendor
of Your kingdom.
Your kingdom is an
everlasting kingdom,
and Your dominion endures through
all generations.

The Lord is faithful to all
His promises
and loving toward all He has made.
The Lord upholds all those who fall
and lifts up all who are bowed
down.
The eyes of all look to You,
and You give them their food at
the proper time.
You open Your hand
and satisfy the desires of
every living thing.

The Lord is righteous in all His ways
and loving toward all He has made.
The Lord is near to all who
call on Him,
to all who call on Him in truth.

He fulfills the desires of those
who fear Him;
He hears their cry and saves them.
The Lord watches over all
who love Him,
but all the wicked He will destroy.

My mouth will speak in praise
of the Lord.
Let every creature praise
His holy name
for ever and ever.

AFFIRMATIONS OF FAITH AND TE DEUM

716 THE APOSTLES' CREED

I believe in God the Father Almighty, maker of heaven and earth:

And in Jesus Christ His only Son, our Lord; who was conceived by the Holy Spirit, born of the Virgin Mary, suffered under Pontius Pilate, was crucified, dead, and buried; He descended into hades; the third day He rose again from the dead; He ascended into heaven, and sitteth on the right hand of God, the Father Almighty; from thence He shall come to judge the quick and the dead.

I believe in the Holy Spirit, the holy Christian church, the communion of saints, the forgiveness of sins, the resurrection of the body, and the life everlasting. Amen.

717 THE NICENE CREED

I believe in one God the Father Almighty, Maker of heaven and earth, and of all things visible and invisible:

And in one Lord Jesus Christ, the only-begotten Son of God, begotten of His Father before all worlds, God of God, Light of Light, very God of very God, begotten, not made, being of one substance with the Father, by whom all things were made;

Who for us men and for our salvation came down from heaven,
and was incarnate by the Holy Spirit of the Virgin Mary,
and was made man, and crucified also for us under Pontius Pilate;
He suffered and was buried, and the third day He rose again
according to the Scriptures, and ascended into heaven,
and sitteth on the right hand of the Father;
And He shall come again with glory to judge both the quick
and the dead;
Whose kingdom shall have no end.

And I believe in the Holy Spirit, the Lord and Giver of life, who proceedeth from the Father and the Son, who with the Father and the Son together is worshiped and glorified; who spoke by the prophets. And I believe in one catholic and apostolic church; I acknowledge one baptism for the remission of sins, and I look for the resurrection of the dead, and the life of the world to come. Amen.

718 A CONTEMPORARY AFFIRMATION OF FAITH

We believe in Jesus Christ the Lord,
Who was promised to the people of Israel,
Who came in the flesh to dwell among us,
Who announced the coming of the rule of God,
Who gathered disciples and taught them,
Who died on the cross to free us from sin,
Who rose from the dead to give us life and hope,
Who reigns in heaven at the right hand of God,
Who comes to judge and bring justice to victory.

We believe in God His Father,
Who raised Him from the dead,
Who created and sustains the universe,
Who acts to deliver His people in times of need,
Who desires all men everywhere to be saved,
Who rules over the destinies of men and nations,
Who continues to love men even when they reject Him.

We believe in the Holy Spirit,
Who is the form of God present in the church,
Who moves men to faith and obedience,
Who is the guarantee of our deliverance,
Who leads us to find God's will in the Word,
Who assists those whom He renews in prayer,
Who guides us in discernment,
Who impels us to act together.

We believe God has made us His people,
To invite others to follow Christ,
To encourage one another to deeper commitment,
To proclaim forgiveness of sins and hope,
To reconcile men to God through word and deed,
To bear witness to the power of love over hate,
To proclaim Jesus the Lord over all,
To meet the daily tasks of life with purpose,
To suffer joyfully for the cause of right,
To the ends of the earth,
To the end of the age,
To the praise of His glory. Amen.

719 TE DEUM

We praise Thee, O God:
We acknowledge Thee to be the Lord.
All the earth doth worship Thee, the Father everlasting.
To Thee all angels cry aloud;
The heavens and all the powers therein.
To Thee cherubim and seraphim continually do cry:
Holy, Holy, Holy, Lord God of Sabaoth.
Heaven and earth are full of the majesty of Thy glory.
The glorious company of the apostles praise Thee.
The goodly fellowship of the prophets praise Thee.
The noble army of martyrs praise Thee.
The holy Church, throughout all the world, doth acknowledge Thee.
The Father of an infinite majesty;
Thine adorable, true, and only Son,
Also the Holy Spirit, the comforter.
Thou art the King of glory, O Christ.
Thou art the everlasting Son of the Father.
When Thou tookest upon Thee to deliver man,
Thou didst humble Thyself to be born of a virgin.
When Thou hadst overcome the sharpness of death,
Thou didst open the kingdom of heaven to all believers.
Thou sittest at the right hand of God, in the glory of the Father.
We believe that Thou shalt come to be our Judge.
We therefore pray Thee, help Thy servants,
Whom Thou hast redeemed with Thy precious blood.
Make them to be numbered with Thy saints in glory everlasting.
O Lord, save Thy people, and bless Thy heritage.
Govern them, and lift them up forever.
Day by day we magnify Thee;
And we worship Thy name ever, world without end.
Vouchsafe, O Lord, to keep us this day without sin.
O Lord, have mercy upon us, have mercy upon us.
O Lord, let Thy mercy be upon us, as our trust is in Thee.
O Lord, in Thee have I trusted;
Let me never be confounded.

INDEXES FOR SCRIPTURAL RESOURCES

CONTENTS

ALPHABETICAL INDEX OF SCRIPTURE AND OTHER READINGS

A Contemporary Affirmation of Faith, 718
A Living Hope, 403
Advent of Our Lord, The, 122
An Upward Look, 540
Apostles' Creed, The, 716
Assurance, 672
Beatitudes, The, 648
Benedictions (Spoken), 613
Calls to Worship (Spoken), 599
Christ, Bread of Life, 683
Christ's Ascension, 641
Christ's Baptism, 637
Christ's Death, 640
Christ's Exaltation, 642
Christ's Incarnation, 635
Christ's Priesthood, 670
Christ's Return, 643
Christ's Sufferings, 639
Christ's Temptation, 671
Christ's Triumphal Entry, 638
Christian Conduct, 685
Christian Love, 661
Christian's Baptism, The, 688
Christian's Resurrection, The, 667
Church, The, 646
Comfort, 652
Dedicated Service, 674
Discipleship, 651
Eternal Life, 658
Faith, 662
Faithfulness, 657
Family, 663
Fellowship, 689
For Unto Us a Child Is Born, 142
Forgiveness, 632
Give Him Glory, 86
Giving, 656
Gloria in Excelsis Deo, 130
Glorification, 677
Glory in the Cross, 182
God's Amazing Grace, 200
God's Goodness, 678
God's Love, 653
Good Samaritan, The, 686
Government, 665
He Is Risen! Alleluia!, 214
Holy Spirit, The, 644
How Majestic Is Your Name, 28
I Know a Fount, 194
In His Image, 386
Joy, 680
Justification through Faith, 668
Lead Us, O God, 48
Living Church, The, 290
Lord Is My Shepherd, The, 459
Lord's Prayer, The, 650
Lord's Supper, The, 647
Magi's Visit, The, 636
Maturity, 669
Messianic King, The, 634
Missions, 645
My God, I Love Thee, 361
My Life, My Joy, My All, 509
Name of Jesus, The, 99
New Birth, The, 654
Nicene Creed, The, 717
Obedience, 631
One Nation, Under God, 570
Passover and the Last Supper, 687
Perfect Peace, 491
Perseverance, 675
Praise God in His Sanctuary, 7
Prayer, 655
Psalm 1, 690
Psalm 2, 691
Psalm 16, 692
Psalm 19, 693
Psalm 22, 694
Psalm 23, 695
Psalm 24, 696
Psalm 27, 697
Psalm 32, 698
Psalm 33, 699
Psalm 40, 700
Psalm 42, 701
Psalm 46, 702
Psalm 51, 703
Psalm 65, 704
Psalm 84, 705
Psalm 90, 706
Psalm 91, 707
Psalm 95, 708
Psalm 100, 709
Psalm 103, 710
Psalm 110, 711
Psalm 118, 712
Psalm 121, 713
Psalm 139, 714
Psalm 145, 715
Reconciliation, 681
Redemption, 660
Righteousness, 676
Salvation by Grace, 659
Sanctification, 673
Scripture, 633
Soldiers of Christ, Arise, 476
Spiritual Gifts, 684
Te Deum, 719
Teaching Children, 630
Ten Commandments, The, 629
Unity, 664
Victory over Sin, 682
Vine and the Branches, The, 649
Wisdom, 679
With a Song of Thanksgiving, 558
Work, 666

TOPICAL INDEX OF SCRIPTURE AND OTHER READINGS

The subject headings for this index are coordinated with the subject headings in the Topical Index of Hymns

GOD OUR FATHER

His Adoration and Praise
Praise God in His Sanctuary, 7
My Life, My Joy, My All, 509
The Lord's Prayer, 650
God's Love, 653
Te Deum, 719

His Majesty and Power
How Majestic Is Your Name, 28
The Ten Commandments, 629
Obedience, 631
The Lord's Prayer, 650
Prayer, 655
Eternal Life, 658
Government, 665

His Guidance and Care
The Ten Commandments, 629
Obedience, 631
Forgiveness, 632
Scripture, 633
Christ's Exaltation, 642
Christ's Return, 643
The Holy Spirit, 644
The Beatitudes, 648
The Vine and the Branches, 649
The Lord's Prayer, 650
Discipleship, 651
Comfort, 652
God's Love, 653
The New Birth, 654
Prayer, 655
Salvation by Grace, 659
Redemption, 660
The Christian's Resurrection, 667
Justification Through Faith, 668
Maturity, 669
Christ's Priesthood, 670
Christ's Temptation, 671
God's Goodness, 678

His Works in Creation
How Majestic Is Your Name, 28
With a Song of Thanksgiving, 558
The Ten Commandments, 629
Christ's Incarnation, 635
Faith, 662

His Love and Mercy
God's Amazing Grace, 200
The Ten Commandments, 629
Forgiveness, 632
Comfort, 652
God's Love, 653
The New Birth, 654
Prayer, 655
Eternal Life, 658
Salvation by Grace, 659
Redemption, 660
Justification Through Faith, 668
God's Goodness, 678

JESUS OUR SAVIOR

His Adoration and Praise
Give Him Glory, 86
The Name of Jesus, 99
Christ's Triumphal Entry, 638
Christ's Exaltation, 642
The Lord's Supper, 647
Te Deum, 719

His Advent and Birth
The Advent of Our Lord, 122
Gloria in Excelsis Deo, 130
For Unto Us a Child Is Born, 142
The Messianic King, 634
Christ's Incarnation, 635
The Magi's Visit, 636

His Life, Ministry, and Teaching
Christ's Baptism, 637
Christ's Triumphal Entry, 638
The Holy Spirit, 644
Missions, 645
The Church, 646
The Beatitudes, 648
The Vine and the Branches, 649
The Lord's Prayer, 650
Discipleship, 651
Comfort, 652
The New Birth, 654
Prayer, 655
Faithfulness, 657
Eternal Life, 658
Christ's Temptation, 671
Christ, Bread of Life, 683
The Good Samaritan, 684

His Triumphal Entry
Christ's Triumphal Entry, 638

His Suffering and Death
Christ's Sufferings, 639
Christ's Death, 640
The Lord's Supper, 647
God's Love, 653
Salvation by Grace, 659
Redemption, 660
Justification Through Faith, 668
Christ's Priesthood, 670

His Redemption
Christ's Death, 640
The Lord's Supper, 647
God's Love, 653
The New Birth, 654
Eternal Life, 658
Salvation by Grace, 659
Redemption, 660
Justification Through Faith, 668
Christ's Priesthood, 670

His Cross
Glory in the Cross, 182
Christ's Death, 640
Christ's Exaltation, 642

His Cleansing Blood
I Know a Fount, 194
Forgiveness, 632
The Lord's Supper, 647
Redemption, 660
Justification Through Faith, 668
Christ's Priesthood, 670

His Grace, Love, and Mercy
God's Amazing Grace, 200
The Lord Is My Shepherd, 459
Forgiveness, 632
The Messianic King, 634
Christ's Incarnation, 635
Christ's Exaltation, 642
The Church, 646
The Vine and the Branches, 649
Comfort, 652
Prayer, 655
Giving, 656
Salvation by Grace, 659
Redemption, 660
Justification Through Faith, 668
Christ's Priesthood, 670

His Resurrection
He Is Risen! Alleluia!, 214
Christ's Ascension, 641
Christ's Return, 643
The Christian's Resurrection, 667

His Ascension and Reign
Give Him Glory, 86
The Name of Jesus, 99
The Messianic King, 634
Christ's Ascension, 641
Christ's Exaltation, 642
Prayer, 655
Christ's Priesthood, 670

His Second Coming
Christ's Return, 643
Comfort, 652

THE HOLY SPIRIT

Scripture, 633
Christ's Baptism, 637
Christ's Ascension, 641
The Holy Spirit, 644
The Church, 646
Comfort, 652
The New Birth, 654
Prayer, 655
Unity, 664

THE HOLY TRINITY

Scripture, 633
Christ's Baptism, 637
Christ's Ascension, 641
Christ's Exaltation, 642
The Holy Spirit, 644
Missions, 645
The Church, 646
Comfort, 652
The New Birth, 654
Prayer, 655
Salvation by Grace, 659
Unity, 664
Justification Through Faith, 668
Christ's Temptation, 671

THE WORD OF GOD

The Ten Commandments, 629
Teaching Children, 630
Obedience, 631
Scripture, 633
Missions, 645
The Vine and the Branches, 649
Maturity, 669
Christ's Temptation, 671

THE CHURCH

Its Nature and Foundation
Forgiveness, 632
Scripture, 633
The Holy Spirit, 644
The Church, 646
The New Birth, 654
Prayer, 655
Giving, 656
Faithfulness, 657
Justification Through Faith, 668

Fellowship of Believers
Christ's Exaltation, 642
The Vine and the Branches, 649
Christian Love, 661
Unity, 664
Maturity, 669
Spiritual Gifts, 684
Fellowship, 689

Renewal and Revival
The Living Church, 290
Soldiers of Christ, Arise, 476
Obedience, 631
Discipleship, 651
Faithfulness, 657
Unity, 664
Maturity, 669

Missions and Evangelism
The Living Church, 290
Missions, 645
God's Love, 653
The New Birth, 654
Faithfulness, 657

Dedication of Children
The Ten Commandments, 629
Teaching Children, 630
Family, 663

Baptism
Missions, 645
The Church, 646
Unity, 664
The Christian's Baptism, 688

The Lord's Supper
Christ's Death, 640
The Lord's Supper, 647
Redemption, 660
Passover and the Last Supper, 687

LIFE IN CHRIST

Salvation
Forgiveness, 632
The Holy Spirit, 644
God's Love, 653
The New Birth, 654
Eternal Life, 658

Salvation by Grace, 659
Redemption, 660
Justification Through Faith, 668
Righteousness, 676
Reconciliation, 681

Assurance and Trust
Lead Us, O God, 48
A Living Hope, 403
The Lord Is My Shepherd, 459
My Life, My Joy, My All, 509
Comfort, 652
God's Love, 653
Prayer, 655
Eternal Life, 658
Faith, 662
Christ's Priesthood, 670
Assurance, 672
Christ, Bread of Life, 683

Commitment and Consecration
The Living Church, 290
Obedience, 631
The Beatitudes, 648
The Vine and the Branches, 649
Discipleship, 651
Faithfulness, 657
Unity, 664
Maturity, 669
Dedicated Service, 674

Aspiration
My God, I Love Thee, 361
In His Image, 386
Obedience, 631
Christ's Exaltation, 642
The Beatitudes, 648
The Vine and the Branches, 649
Discipleship, 651
Prayer, 655
Faithfulness, 657
Christian Love, 661
Unity, 664
Maturity, 669
Perseverance, 675
Wisdom, 679
Victory Over Sin, 682

Faith and Hope
A Living Hope, 403
My Life, My Joy, My All, 509
An Upward Look, 540
Christ's Return, 643
Comfort, 652
God's Love, 653
Prayer, 655
Eternal Life, 658
Faith, 662
Unity, 664
The Christian's Resurrection, 667
Justification Through Faith, 668
Maturity, 669
Glorification, 677
The Apostles' Creed, 716
The Nicene Creed, 717

Comfort and Encouragement
A Living Hope, 403
The Lord Is My Shepherd, 459
Perfect Peace, 491
Christ's Exaltation, 642
Christ's Return, 643
The Holy Spirit, 644
The Vine and the Branches, 649
The Lord's Prayer, 650
Comfort, 652
God's Love, 653
Prayer, 655
Eternal Life, 658
Faith, 662
The Christian's Resurrection, 667
Christ's Priesthood, 670
Christ's Temptation, 671
Assurance, 672

Prayer and Intercession
Lead Us, O God, 48
The Living Church, 290
The Vine and the Branches, 649
The Lord's Prayer, 650
Prayer, 655
Christ's Priesthood, 670

Holiness and Purity
In His Image, 386
The Ten Commandments, 629
Obedience, 631
The Church, 646
The Lord's Supper, 647
The Beatitudes, 648
The Vine and the Branches, 649
Maturity, 669
Christ's Priesthood, 670
Christ's Temptation, 671
Sanctification, 673
Victory Over Sin, 682
Christian Conduct, 685
Fellowship, 689

Stewardship and Service
Christ's Exaltation, 642
Missions, 645
The Vine and the Branches, 649
Discipleship, 651
Prayer, 655
Giving, 656
Faithfulness, 657
Unity, 664
Work, 666
Dedicated Service, 674
Spiritual Gifts, 684
The Good Samaritan, 686

Provision and Leading
Lead Us, O God, 48
The Lord Is My Shepherd, 459
The Holy Spirit, 644
The Lord's Prayer, 650
Comfort, 652
God's Love, 653
Prayer, 655
Giving, 656
Eternal Life, 658
Faith, 662
Work, 666
Christ's Priesthood, 670
Wisdom, 679
Christ, Bread of Life, 683

Spiritual Warfare
Soldiers of Christ, Arise, 476
The Church, 646
The Lord's Prayer, 650

Discipleship, 651
Prayer, 655
Faithfulness, 657
Christ's Temptation, 671
Perseverance, 675
Victory Over Sin, 682

Inner Peace and Joy
A Living Hope, 403
The Lord Is My Shepherd, 459
Perfect Peace, 491
Forgiveness, 632
Christ's Return, 643
The Holy Spirit, 644
The Beatitudes, 648
The Vine and the Branches, 649
The Lord's Prayer, 650
Comfort, 652
God's Love, 653
Prayer, 655
Eternal Life, 658
The Christian's Resurrection, 667
Justification Through Faith, 668
Christ's Priesthood, 670
Joy, 680
Reconciliation, 681
Fellowship, 689

Testimony and Praise
My Life, My Joy, My All, 509
With a Song of Thanksgiving, 558
Missions, 645
The Lord's Supper, 647
The Beatitudes, 648
The Vine and the Branches, 649
Discipleship, 651
God's Love, 653
The New Birth, 654
Faithfulness, 657
Eternal Life, 658
Salvation by Grace, 659
Redemption, 660
Faith, 662
Unity, 664
Maturity, 669

Family and Home
The Ten Commandments, 629
Teaching Children, 630
Obedience, 631
Forgiveness, 632
Scripture, 633
The Church, 646
The Beatitudes, 648
Discipleship, 651
Prayer, 655
Christian Love, 661
Faith, 662
Family, 663
Unity, 664
Government, 665
Work, 666
Maturity, 669
Christ's Temptation, 671

LIFE EVERLASTING

An Upward Look, 540
Christ's Return, 643
The Lord's Prayer, 650
Comfort, 652
Faithfulness, 657
Eternal Life, 658
The Christian's Resurrection, 667
Glorification, 677

SPECIAL TIMES AND SEASONS

Thanksgiving and Harvest
With a Song of Thanksgiving, 558
Christ's Return, 643
Missions, 645
The Church, 646
The Vine and the Branches, 649
The Lord's Prayer, 650
Prayer, 655
Giving, 656
Family, 663
Unity, 664
Work, 666
The Christian's Resurrection, 667

New Year
Obedience, 631
Christ's Exaltation, 642
Missions, 645
The Beatitudes, 648
The Vine and the Branches, 649
Discipleship, 651
The New Birth, 654
Prayer, 655
Giving, 656
Faithfulness, 657
Christian Love, 661
Family, 663
Unity, 664
Maturity, 669
Christ's Priesthood, 670

Patriotic
One Nation, Under God, 571
The Ten Commandments, 629
Missions, 645
The Church, 646
The Lord's Prayer, 650
Discipleship, 651
Government, 665
Work, 666
Righteousness, 676
Wisdom, 679
The Good Samaritan, 686

Anniversaries
The Vine and the Branches, 649
The Lord's Prayer, 650
Comfort, 652
God's Love, 653
Prayer, 655
Faithfulness, 657
Christian Love, 661
Faith, 662
Family, 663
Unity, 664
Maturity, 669

SCRIPTURAL INDEX OF SCRIPTURE READINGS

Genesis
1:31 558
15:6 676

Exodus
20:1-17 629

Numbers
6:24-26 613

Deuteronomy
4:9 630
6:1-9 630
11:1 631
30:11-14 631
32:3-4 509

Joshua
1:8 631

1 Samuel
15:22 631

2 Samuel
22:47 509

1 Chronicles
16:34-36 678

Psalms
1 690
2 691
8 28
16 692
19 693
22 694
23 695
23:1 459
24 696
24:1, 9-10 599
27 697
29:2 599
31:1-3 48
32 698
33 699
33:12 570
40 700
42 701
46 702
46:10 599
48:14 459
51 703
65 704
65:9, 11-13 558
84 705
89:1-2 599
90 706
91 707
92:1-2 599
95 708
95:1-2, 6-7 599
100 709
100:1-3, 4-5 599
103 710
104:14, 24 558
107:8-9 558
110 711
118 712
118:28-29 599
121 713
139 714
145 715
150 7
150:1-2, 6 599

Proverbs
1:1-7 679
3:13-14 679
9:10 679
14:34 570, 676
22:6 630

Isaiah
1:18 632
9:1-7 634
12:1-3 509
40:8 633
40:11 459
53:1-9 639

Jeremiah
31:34 632

Ezekiel
34:15-16 459

Jonah
2:9 558

Micah
7:18 632

Nahum
1:7 678

Habakkuk
3:17-18 680

Matthew
1:18-23 142
2:1-12 636
3:1-3, 7-8, 11-17 637
4:1-11 671
5:1-12 648
5:43-48 678
6:5-15 650
6:14-15 632
7:7-11 655
7:9-12 678
10:24-25 651
11:28-30 599
16:15-19 646
18:21-22 632
21:1-11 638
24:45-47 657
25:21 657
28:1-6 214
28:16-20 645
28:19 688

Mark
10:45 660
11:24-25 655

Luke
2:8-14 130
6:38 656
10:25-37 686
14:26-27 651
16:10-13 657
22:7-20 687

John
1:1-14 635
1:16-17 200, 659
3:1-8, 14-17 654
3:14-16, 36 658
3:16 653
4:23-24 599
4:35 645
5:24 658
6:35-38 683
8:12, 31-32 651
10:11 459
10:27-29 658
12:23, 28-33 182
13:1 200
13:34-35 651
14:1-3, 15-16, 27 652
14:13-14 655
14:16-18 644
14:21, 23 631
15:1-17 649
15:8 651
16:5-15 644
16:33 491
19:1-6, 16-19 640

Acts
1:1-11 641
2:38 688
16:29-34 688
20:35 656

Romans
1:16-17 676
3:19-26 676
3:21-26 660
4:13 676
5:1 491
5:1-2, 5-6, 9-10 403
5:1-11, 18 668
5:8 200, 653
5:10-11 681
5:18-21 676
5:20-21 659
6:1-13 682

6:3-4 688
6:11-14, 19-22 673
8:18-30 677
8:26-27 655
8:28-30 678
8:28-39 672
8:29 386
10:1-4 676
10:8-15 645
12:1-5, 9-18, 21 674
13:1-7 665

1 Corinthians
2:2 386
4:2 657
9:24-27 675
11:23-32 647
12:1, 7-11, 27-31 684
12:12-13 646
13 661
14:1-3, 40 684
15:19-22, 35-38, 42-44, 53-58 667
16:2 656

2 Corinthians
1:3-7 652
3:18 386
5:17 654
5:18-20 681
8:7, 9, 12 656
8:9 200
9:6-7, 15 656
13:14 613

Galatians
4:19 386
5:16-25 673
6:14 182

Ephesians
1:7-8 660
1:22-23 646
2:4-5 200
2:4-9 659
2:13-18 681
2:17 491
2:19-22 646
3:20-21 613
4:1-6 664
4:11-16 669
4:32 632
5:22-6:4 663
5:25-27 646
6:4 630
6:10-17 476
6:18 655

Philippians
1:3-6, 15-18 680
2:1-4 664
2:1-11 642
2:5 386
2:8-9 182
2:9-11 99
2:12-13 675
3:8-10 386
3:12-14 675
4:1, 4 680
4:6-9 491

Colossians
1:15-20 86
1:19-20 491
2:11-12 688
3:1-11 685
3:15 491

1 Thessalonians
4:13-18 643
5:28 613

2 Thessalonians
2:16-17 613
3:6-13 666

1 Timothy
1:17 613
4:4 678

2 Timothy
2:2 657
3:14-17 633

Titus
2:11-12 659
3:4-7 659

Hebrews
3:1 670
3:14 675
4:12-13 633
4:14-16 655
4:15-16 670
5:8 631
5:12-6:1 669
6:17-20 403
7:24-27 670
9:15 660
10:11-14, 19-22 670
11:1-3, 6, 8-12, 17-19 662
11:8 631
12:1-3 675
12:2 86, 182
13:20-21 459, 613

James
1:5 679
1:17 678
3:13-18 679
5:10-11 675

1 Peter
1:3-5 509
1:18-19 660
1:18-19, 21 194
2:3 678
2:13-17 665
2:21 386
5:4 459
5:10-11 613

2 Peter
1:10-11 675
1:16-21 633

1 John
1 689
1:8-2:2 632
2:3 631
2:6 386
3:1 653
4:8-12, 18-19 653
4:9-10 200
5:11-13, 20 658
5:14-15 655

Jude
20-21, 24, 25 675
24, 25 613

Revelation
2:10 657
5:12-13 86, 599
7:17 459
21:1-4, 22-23, 25, 27 540
22:21 613

INDEX OF SPOKEN CALLS TO WORSHIP AND BENEDICTIONS

CALLS TO WORSHIP, 599
Psalm 24:1, 9-10
Psalm 29:2
Psalm 46:10
Psalm 89:1-2
Psalm 92:1-2
Psalm 95:1-2
Psalm 95:6-7
Psalm 100:1-3
Psalm 100:4-5
Psalm 118:28-29
Psalm 150:1-2, 6
Matthew 11:28-30
John 4:23-24
Revelation 5:12-13

BENEDICTIONS, 613
Numbers 6:24-26
2 Corinthians 13:14
Ephesians 3:20-21
1 Thessalonians 5:28
2 Thessalonians 2:16-17
1 Timothy 1:17
Hebrews 13:20-21
1 Peter 5:10-11
Jude 24-25
Revelation 22:21

INDEX OF NON-SCRIPTURAL READINGS

WHO SHALL COME by Mary E. Caldwell, 122
Theme: JESUS OUR SAVIOR - His Advent
GOD OF THE LIVING CHURCH by Alfred H. Ackley, 290
Theme: THE CHURCH - Revival and Renewal
MY ETERNAL KING by Francis Xavier; translated by Edward Caswall, 361
Theme: COMMITMENT AND CONSECRATION
OUR LOVE FOR GOD AND HIS SON
AFFIRMATIONS OF FAITH
The Apostles' Creed, 716
The Nicene Creed, 717
A Contemporary Affirmation of Faith, 718
TE DEUM, 719

INDEXES FOR THE HYMNS

CONTENTS

INDEX OF SCRIPTURE APPEARING WITH HYMN TITLES

Scripture	Hymn
Genesis	
1:31	578
17:1	36
Exodus	
15:13	461
15:26	343
20:11	59
Leviticus	
11:44	379
19:2	437
Numbers	
6:24, 26	607
14:21	32
Deuteronomy	
11:1	55
21:23	177
31:6	419
32:3	6
33:27	354
Joshua	
1:9	292
24:15	536
1 Samuel	
17:47	472
1 Kings	
18:21	475
1 Chronicles	
16:25	16
16:29	585
16:34	41
21:13	68
29:13	85
29:14	620
2 Chronicles	
7:14	574
20:15	485
29:30	19
Ezra	
3:11	557
Nehemiah	
8:10	411
9:5	21
Job	
12:10	344
Psalms	
3:8	601
5:7	594
5:8	49
8:1	30
8:3-4	516
8:9	35
18:1	362
18:2	93
18:3	38
18:30, 32	333
19:1	62
22:4	573
23:1	53
23:3	50
23:6	45
26:8	280
27:5	496
27:8	325
27:11	395
29:11	604
31:23	80
32:11	562
33:20	600
35:28	76
37:5	581
40:2	522
40:5	563
40:17	303
42:11	401
46:7	26
46:10	347
47:1	24
48:1	4
48:14	460
50:12	58
51:7	436
51:10	440
55:22	57, 598
57:8-9	60
57:10-11	5
61:2	348
62:7	353
63:3	69
65:11	559
66:2	596
67:1	561
68:32	263
71:24	70
72:8	231
73:28	497
75:1	565
84:11	412
85:6	295
86:1	428
87:3	278
89:1	457
90:1	52
90:2	568
90:12	567
91:4	356
92:1	584
95:3	267
95:6	14
96:8	622, 623
96:9	165, 593
98:4	23
100:1	20
100:2	589
103:1	3
103:2	493
103:11	61
103:22	13
104:1	10
107:8	560
107:9	531
107:30-31	575
115:1	11
116:1	364
118:24	590
119:18	381
119:105	272
119:130	269
119:151	393
126:3	66
127:1	537
134:2	107
136:1	63
138:2	264
139:14	1
139:23	434, 438, 439
144:3	528
144:15	577
145:1	12
145:3	31
146:2	113
147:5	39
148:1, 7	9
148:13	64
149:1	18
150:6	627
Proverbs	
10:22	2
11:11	452
14:34	571
31:28	534
Ecclesiastes	
3:11	465
Song of Solomon	
2:11-12	396
Isaiah	
1:18	591
6:3	22
7:4	421
7:14	123
9:6	146
9:7	155
11:1	160
12:4	556
12:5	488
25:4	466
25:9	532
26:3	492
28:16	277
30:15	592
33:17	88
40:9	298
40:11	458
41:13	463
42:11-12	138
43:2	46
48:18	494
52:7	229
53:3	175
53:6	340
55:9	54
55:12	244
58:11	51
61:1	124, 336
63:14	483
64:8	371
Jeremiah	
1:7	444
8:22	423
20:9	294
23:5	162
31:3	67
Lamentations	
3:22-23	43
Ezekiel	
34:26	289
36:26	40
Daniel	
4:37	8
Micah	
5:2	141
5:5	152
Nahum	
1:7	47
Habakkuk	
3:2	291
Zechariah	
2:10	120
4:6	248
9:9	153
9:10	33
13:1	196
Matthew	
1:21	126
1:23	134
2:1	166
2:2	82
2:6	131
2:10-11	163
3:15	319
4:19	375
5:8	383
6:9	268, 426
6:24	359
6:33	42
7:24	402, 404
8:3	504
9:36	315
9:38	288
10:8	447
10:32	235
10:39	378
11:28	326
11:29	414
16:24	367
18:20	256
19:14	580
21:9	174
24:30	241
28:6	221
28:9	226, 588
28:18	301
28:19	296
28:20	308
Mark	
6:41	274
8:34	449
8:36	443
9:23	420
10:16	318
11:22	408
15:17	178
15:25	181
16:6-7	222
Luke	
1:31-33	84
1:35	148
1:46	150
1:47	151
1:49	27
2:7	157, 158
2:8	136
2:9	128
2:10	144
2:11	135
2:13	132
2:14	133
2:15	145
2:16	147
2:17	137
2:18	139
2:20	161
2:32	129
4:22	109
5:11	470
9:23	377
11:2, 4	427
14:22	331
15:4	464
15:18	341
15:24	519
19:6	125
21:28	245
22:19	322
23:33	338
24:52	223
John	
1:11	127
1:14	110
1:16	121
1:29	197
3:15	205
3:16	207
4:14	398
4:23	265
4:35	305
4:42	81

6:37 342
6:63 270
6:68 117
9:25 202
10:3 462
10:14-15 468
10:27 373
11:25 218
12:13 173
12:26 376
12:28 29
12:32 304
12:46 159
13:1 351
13:35 284
14:1 350
14:2 538
14:3 239
14:6 114
14:13 90
14:15 391
14:16 257
14:19 213
14:27 487
15:5 332
15:9 513
15:10 502
15:11 501
15:13 453
15:15 422
16:15 254
18:37 230
19:25 183
19:37 185
20:19 586
20:20 425
20:21 310, 311
20:22 251, 259
20:28 225

Acts
1:3 215
2:24 216
2:36 360
2:42 323
3:1 433
4:12 102
5:42 100
8:4 297
8:35 172
10:34-35 285
10:36 156
14:23 346
16:9 316
16:31 330

Romans
1:9 518
1:16 300
3:24 187
3:25 193
4:20 34
5:6 170
5:8 209
5:11 119
5:20 201
6:4 320
6:13 366
8:2 250
8:15 15
8:17 352
8:18 539
8:29 388
8:32 302
8:37 569
8:39 374
9:5 87
10:9 105
12:1 368
12:11 455
13:14 469
14:8 511
16:26 349
16:27 595

1 Corinthians
1:2 94
1:18 188,208
1:30 206
2:2 176
2:4 258
3:11 276
3:16 260
4:2 448
6:19-20 210
8:6 149
9:19 313
10:4 204
11:1 384
11:24 321
11:25 324
11:26 140
12:3 101
13:12 549
15:3-4 523
15:20 224
15:54 227
15:55 217
15:57 473
16:13 477, 481

2 Corinthians
1:3 83
2:14 479
3:17 253
3:18 335
4:4 307
4:6 499
5:8 554
5:15 372
5:17 515
6:2 328
8:5 154
8:9 198
9:6 621
9:15 98
12:9 56
13:14 606, 612

Galatians
2:20 512
3:13 339
3:28 286
4:19 387
5:16 247
5:22 252
5:25 249
6:14 385
6:15 495

Ephesians
1:3 564, 624, 625, 626
1:7 506
1:12 75
1:21 111
2:7 203
2:8 550
3:12 410
3:15 282
3:17-18 211, 212
4:3 287
4:8 232
4:12 603
4:16 587
5:2 579
5:18 261
5:19-20 108
5:25 357
6:4 317
6:10-11 478
6:13 484
6:14 474

Philippians
1:9 363
1:10 456
1:20 394
1:21 510
2:5 390
2:8 186
2:9-11 96, 97
2:15-16 312
3:1 489
3:7 382
3:8 517
3:14 399
4:4 228
4:6 435
4:7 498
4:13 380

Colossians
1:10 610
1:27 406
2:5 355
2:13 189
3:3 490
3:11 526
3:16 514
3:17 116
3:24 446

1 Thessalonians
1:6 400
4:14 219
4:16 543
4:17 542
5:28 602

2 Thessalonians
1:12 112
3:16 500

1 Timothy
1:15 306
1:17 25, 611
2:3-4 431
2:5 471
3:16 167
6:15 77
6:15-16 104
6:17 566

2 Timothy
1:12 409
2:2 450
2:3 482
2:4 480
2:15 445
2:19 275
3:15 535
3:16 273

Titus
2:4 533
2:11 524
2:12 370
2:13-14 89
3:5 530

Hebrews
1:4 103
2:6 65
2:9 74
2:18 430
3:15 329
4:3 405
4:7 327
4:9 503
4:11 552
4:15 417
4:16 416
6:10 583
6:11 369
7:19 392
7:25 199
9:22 527
9:28 236
10:13 243
10:19 432
10:20 169
10:22 358
11:1 544
12:2 184
12:3 79
12:14 441, 442
12:22 555
13:5 467
13:8 95
13:14 553
13:15 171
13:16 454
13:20 192

James
4:6 415
4:8 365, 397
5:13 345
5:16 407

1 Peter
1:3 115
1:6-7 507
1:8 529
1:18-19 520, 521
1:22 582
2:7 413
2:9 283
2:16 576
2:17 572
5:7 418

2 Peter
1:4 271
3:9 337
3:18 389

1 John
1:7 195
2:6 451
3:1 44, 71
3:2 237
3:14 281
3:18 314
4:4 255
4:9 92
4:10 505
4:11 309
4:19 424
5:4 486
5:14 429

3 John
14 609

Jude
2 605
3 279
14 238
23 299

Revelation
1:5 525
1:7 246
1:18 220
3:2 293
3:4 240
4:8 262
4:11 73
5:9 106
5:12 180, 597
5:13 72, 78
7:9 233
7:10 17
7:14 190
12:5 164
12:11 191
13:8 179
14:13 546
15:2-3 508
15:4 266
17:14 168
19:1 91
19:6 37
19:12 234
19:16 143
21:1 547
21:4 548
22:4 545
22:12 242
22:13 118
22:14 541
22:17 334
22:20 551
22:21 608

INDEX OF SCRIPTURE TEXTS AND ADAPTATIONS IN HYMNS

Genesis
28:10-22 393

Exodus
15:26 343

Numbers
6:24-26 607

Joshua
24:15 537

2 Samuel
22:47 38

Nehemiah
8:10 411

Psalms
4:8 49
5:8 49
8 35
18:1 93
18:3 38
19 62
19:14 618
23 45, 53
37:5 581
42 401
46:10 343
47:1 24
55:22 598
57:9-11 5
63:3, 4 69
89:1 457
90 52
92 584
95:6-7 14
96:9 593
98:4 23
100 20
103 3, 13
118:24 590
119:105 272
136 63
139:23 438
143:1 614
144:15 577
148 9

Proverbs
31:10-31 534

Isaiah
6:3 22, 32
9:6, 7 146
26:3 492, 617
33:20, 21 278
55:12 244

Ezekiel
34:26 289

Habakkuk
2:20 594

Matthew
6:9-13 426
6:33 42
7:7 42
10:8 447
14:19 274
21:15, 16 174
28:6, 7 221
28:18 447
28:18-20 301

Luke
1:46-55 27

John
1:14-17 121
3:16 205
3:16, 17 207
13:35 284
20:21 310, 311
20:22 251

1 Corinthians
13:12 549

2 Corinthians
3:17 253
13:14 606, 612

Philippians
2:5-11 235
4:4 228, 489

1 Thessalonians
4:16, 17 246

1 Timothy
1:17 25

2 Timothy
1:12b 409

James
4:8 397

1 John
3:1 71
3:2 246
4:4 255

Revelation
1:7 246
3:4 240
4:11 73
5:9 73
5:12 180
5:12, 13 78
7:9 240
21 547

INDEX OF BRIEF SERVICES AND MEDLEYS

Brief Services

7 **PRAISE GOD IN HIS SANCTUARY - A Brief Service of Worship and Exaltation**
Theme: God Our Father - His Adoration and Praise
Selections included: *Praise to the Lord, the Almighty; Praise the Lord! Ye Heavens, Adore Him; O Worship the King*

28 **HOW MAJESTIC IS YOUR NAME - A Brief Service in Recognition of God's Majesty and Power**
Theme: God Our Father - His Majesty and Power
Selections included: *Glorify Thy Name; How Majestic Is Your Name; Great Is the Lord*

48 **LEAD US, O GOD - A Brief Service of Prayer and Petition**
Theme: God Our Father - His Guidance and Care
Selections included: *Lead Me, Lord; The Lord's My Shepherd, I'll Not Want; Guide Me, O Thou Great Jehovah; O God, Our Help in Ages Past*

86 **GIVE HIM GLORY - A Brief Service Exalting Our Lord, Jesus Christ**
Theme: Jesus Our Savior - His Adoration and Praise
Selections included: *May Jesus Christ Be Praised; Fairest Lord Jesus; Our Great Savior*

99 **THE NAME OF JESUS - A Brief Service of Worship and Praise**
Theme: Jesus Our Savior - His Adoration and Praise
Selections included: *There Is No Name So Sweet on Earth; His Name Is Wonderful; There's Something About That Name; Blessed Be the Name*

122 **THE ADVENT OF OUR LORD - A Brief Service of Joyful Expectation**
Theme: Jesus Our Savior - His Advent
Selections included: *O Come, O Come, Emmanuel; Come, Thou Long-Expected Jesus; Joy to the World!*

130 **GLORIA IN EXCELSIS DEO - A Brief Service of Proclamation and Praise**
Theme: Jesus Our Savior - His Birth
Selections included: *Angels from the Realms of Glory; Angels We Have Heard on High; Hark! the Herald Angels Sing*

142 **FOR UNTO US A CHILD IS BORN - A Brief Service in Celebration of Our Lord's Birth**
Theme: Jesus Our Savior - His Birth
Selections included: *Infant Holy, Infant Lowly; How Great Our Joy!; O Come, All Ye Faithful; For Unto Us a Child Is Born*

182 **GLORY IN THE CROSS - A Brief Service of Reflection and Praise**
Theme: Jesus Our Savior - His Cross
Selections included: *Beneath the Cross of Jesus; In the Cross of Christ I Glory; When I Survey the Wondrous Cross*

194 **I KNOW A FOUNT - A Medley**
Theme: Jesus Our Savior - His Blood
Selections included: *I Know a Fount; Nothing But the Blood*

200 **GOD'S AMAZING GRACE - A Brief Service in Recognition of His Love and Provision**
Theme: Jesus Our Savior - His Grace, Love and Mercy
Selections included: *Grace Greater Than Our Sin; Amazing Grace; And Can It Be?*

214 **HE IS RISEN! ALLELUIA! - A Brief Service in Celebration of Our Lord's Resurrection**
Theme: Jesus Our Savior - His Resurrection
Selections included: *Alleluia! Alleluia!; Christ Arose; Christ the Lord Is Risen Today*

290 **THE LIVING CHURCH - A Brief Service of Prayer and Challenge**
Theme: The Church - Renewal and Revival
Selections included: *O Breath of Life; God of Grace and God of Glory; Rise Up, O Church of God*

361 **MY GOD, I LOVE THEE - A Brief Service of Adoration and Commitment**
Theme: Life in Christ - Commitment and Consecration
Selections included: *I Love Thee; More Love to Thee; My Jesus, I Love Thee*

386 IN HIS IMAGE - A Brief Service of Aspiration and Hope
Theme: Life in Christ - Aspiration
Selections included: *O to Be Like Thee!; I Would Be Like Jesus; More About Jesus*

403 A LIVING HOPE - A Brief Service of Affirmation and Renewal
Theme: Life in Christ - Faith and Hope
Selections included: *The Solid Rock; My Faith Has Found a Resting Place; My Hope Is in the Lord*

459 THE LORD IS MY SHEPHERD - A Brief Service in Recognition of His Leadership
Theme: Life in Christ - Provision and Leading
Selections included: *All the Way My Savior Leads Me; He Leadeth Me; Savior, Like a Shepherd Lead Us*

476 SOLDIERS OF CHRIST, ARISE - A Brief Service of Challenge and Victory
Theme: Life in Christ - Spiritual Warfare
Selections included: *Stand Up, Stand Up for Jesus; Soldiers of Christ, Arise; Onward, Christian Soldiers*

491 PERFECT PEACE - A Brief Service in Recognition of His Provision
Theme: Life in Christ - Inner Peace and Joy
Selections included: *Thou Wilt Keep Him in Perfect Peace; It Is Well with My Soul; Like a River Glorious*

509 MY LIFE, MY JOY, MY ALL - A Brief Service of Testimony and Praise
Theme: Life in Christ - Testimony and Praise
Selections included: *Jesus Is All the World to Me; Now I Belong to Jesus; My Savior's Love; O, How He Loves You and Me*

540 AN UPWARD LOOK - A Brief Service of Joyful Anticipation
Theme: Life Everlasting
Selections included: *He the Pearly Gates Will Open; When We All Get to Heaven; When the Roll Is Called Up Yonder*

558 WITH A SONG OF THANKSGIVING - A Brief Service of Praise to God, the Creator
Theme: Thanksgiving
Selections included: *Come, Ye Thankful People, Come; For the Beauty of the Earth; We Gather Together*

570 ONE NATION, UNDER GOD - A Medley
Theme: Patriotic
Selections included: *My Country, 'Tis of Thee; America, the Beautiful; God of Our Fathers*

Medleys

55-56 Theme: God Our Father - His Guidance and Care
Selections included: *Day by Day - A Prayer*
Day by Day

152-153 Theme: Jesus Our Savior - His Birth
Selections included: *I Heard the Bells on Christmas Day*
Come On, Ring Those Bells

194-195 Theme: Jesus Our Savior - His Blood
Selections included: *I Know a Fount*
Nothing But the Blood

520-521 Theme: Life in Christ - Testimony and Praise
Selections included: *Redeemed (Ada)*
Redeemed (Kirkpatrick)

549-550 Theme: Life Everlasting
Selections included: *Face to Face*
Saved by Grace

570-573 Theme: Patriotic
Selections included: *My Country, 'Tis of Thee*
America, the Beautiful
God of Our Fathers

INDEX OF DESCANTS, LAST STANZA HARMONIZATIONS AND CHORAL ENDINGS

DESCANTS

Battle Hymn of the Republic, 569
Blessed Assurance, 345
Child of Love, 156
Faith of Our Fathers, 279
He Keeps Me Singing, 488
Holy God, We Praise Thy Name, 12
Holy, Holy, Holy, 262
Hosanna, Loud Hosanna, 174
I Will Call upon the Lord, 38
Jesus Shall Reign, 231
Like a River Glorious, 494
My Hope Is in the Lord, 406
O Worship the King, 10
Onward, Christian Soldiers, 479
Our Great Savior, 89
Pure and Holy, 437
Rejoice, the Lord Is King, 228
Rise Up, O Church (Men) of God, 293
Seek Ye First, 42
To God Be the Glory, 66
We Praise Thee, O God, Our Redeemer, 16

LAST STANZA HARMONIZATIONS AND SETTINGS

Alleluia, 91
Battle Hymn of the Republic, 569
Because He Lives, 213
Come, Thou Almighty King, 267
Crown Him with Many Crowns, 234
God of Our Fathers, 573
Hallelujah, What a Savior!, 175
How Great Thou Art, 4
I Sing the Mighty Power of God, 59
In the Name of the Lord, 90
Jesus Shall Reign, 231
Lead On, O King Eternal, 483
O For a Thousand Tongues, 76
O Worship the King, 10
Rise Up, O Church (Men) of God, 293
Take My Life and Let It Be, 379
We Gather Together, 561
We Will Glorify, 72
When I Survey the Wondrous Cross, 185

CHORAL ENDINGS

All Hail the Power of Jesus' Name (Coronation), 97
And Can It Be?, 203
Battle Hymn of the Republic, 569
Blessed Be the Name, 103
Christ the Lord Is Risen Today, 217
Come, Christians, Join to Sing, 108
Come, Thou Almighty King, 267
Crown Him with Many Crowns, 234
Faith of Our Fathers, 279
For Unto Us a Child Is Born, 146
Great Is the Lord, 31
Great Is Thy Faithfulness, 43
Hark! the Herald Angels Sing, 133
Hosanna, Loud Hosanna, 174
How Great Thou Art, 4
I Have Decided to Follow Jesus, 376
I Sing the Mighty Power of God, 59
I'll Fly Away, 554
In Remembrance, 322
Joy to the World!, 125
Lead On, O King Eternal, 483
Like a River Glorious, 494
Love Divine, All Loves Excelling, 92
More About Jesus, 389
My Hope Is in the Lord, 406
My Jesus, I Love Thee, 364
O For a Thousand Tongues, 76
O God, Our Help in Ages Past, 52
O, How He Loves You and Me, 513
Our Great Savior, 89
Rejoice, the Lord Is King, 228
Resurrection Canon, 221
Savior, Like a Shepherd Lead Us, 462
The Savior Is Waiting, 329
To God Be the Glory, 66
We Gather Together, 561
We Praise Thee, O God, Our Redeemer, 16
We Shall Behold Him, 237
When I Survey the Wondrous Cross, 185
When the Roll Is Called Up Yonder, 543

INDEX OF COPYRIGHT OWNERS

The use of the valid copyrights of the following publishers and individuals is gratefully acknowledged. In each case, rearranging, photocopying, or reproduction by any other means, as well as the use of the song in performance for profit, is specifically prohibited by law without the written permission of the copyright owner.

ALBERT E. BRUMLEY AND SONS, *Down In Memory Lane, Powell, MO 65730:* Selections 294, 473, 554

BIRDWING MUSIC/CHERRY LANE MUSIC PUB. CO., INC. *c/o Sparrow Corp., 9255 Deering Ave., Chatsworth, CA 91311:* Selections 15, 206

BROADMAN PRESS *The Sunday School Board, 127 Ninth Ave. North, Nashville, TN 37234:* Selections 85, 251, 302, 322, 360, 367, 408, 455, 520

BUG AND BEAR MUSIC (exclusive admin. by LCS MUSIC GROUP) *P.O. Box 7409, Dallas, TX 75209:* Selections 104, 272

CHANCEL MUSIC (a div. of WORD, INC.) *5221 N. O'Connor Blvd., Suite 1000, Irving, TX 75039:* Selection 456

CHERRY BLOSSOM MUSIC CO. *c/o Sparrow Corp., 9255 Deering Ave., Chatsworth, CA 91311:* Selection 411

CHRISTIAN ARTISTS MUSIC *P.O. Box 1984, Thousand Oaks, CA 91360:* Selection 134

CHRISTIAN PUBLICATIONS *3825 Hartzdale Dr., Camp Hill, PA 17011:* Selection 472

CHURCH HYMNAL CORP., THE *800 2nd Ave. (at 42nd St.) New York, NY 10017:* Selection 575

COVENANT PRESS (Covenant Book Concern) *5101 N. Francisco Ave. North, Chicago, IL 60625:* Selection 254

CRUMP, ELUNED AND DILYS EVANS *Tan-y-Coed, Uxbridge Square, Caernarvon, North Wales LL552:* Selections 211, 475

DUNAMIS MUSIC *8319 Lankershim Blvd., N. Hollywood, CA 91605:* Selection 115

DUNKERLEY, DESMOND *23 Haslemere Road, Southsea, Portsmouth, Hants PO4 8BB England:* Selection 285

EVANGELICAL COVENANT CHURCH, THE *5101 N. Francisco Ave. North, Chicago, IL 60625:* Selection 315

FAIRHILL MUSIC *P.O. Box 933, Newbury Park, CA 91320:* Selection 485

FARJEON, ELEANOR (see Harold Ober Associates, Inc.): Selection 60

FARJEON, GERVASE AND M.S.H. JONES (See Harold Ober Associates, Inc.): Selection 60

FARNSWORTH MUSIC (Division of Music by Hummingbird) *P.O. Box 120753, Nashville, TN 37212:* Selection 437

F.E.L. PUBLICATIONS, LTD. *2545 Chandler Ave., Suite 5, Las Vegas, NV 89120:* Selection 284

FOX PUBLICATIONS *P.O. Box 333, Tarzana, CA 91356:* Selection 300

FRED BOCK MUSIC COMPANY *P.O. Box 333, Tarzana, CA 91356:* Selections 73, 283, 536

G. SCHIRMER, INC. *866 3rd Ave., New York, NY 10022:* Selections 3, 139, 347, 426, 535

GAITHER MUSIC COMPANY (William J. Gaither) *P.O. Box 737, Alexandria, IN 46001:* Selections 90, 98, 102, 107, 114, 213, 238, 250, 282, 359, 446, 458, 504, 518, 519, 564

GOOD LIFE PUBLICATIONS *c/o Columbia Pictures Publications, P.O. Box 4340, Hialeah, FL 33041:* Selection 417

HAROLD OBER ASSOCIATES, INC. *40 East 49th Street, New York, NY 10017:* Selection 60

HILL AND RANGE SONGS, INC. (All rights controlled by Unichappel Music, Inc.—Rightsong Music, Publisher) *c/o Hal Leonard Pub. Corp., 8112 West Bluemound Rd., Milwaukee, WI 53213:* Selection 463

HIS EYE MUSIC *c/o Sparrow Corp., 9255 Deering Ave., Chatsworth, CA 91311:* Selection 411

HOLLIS MUSIC, INC. *c/o The Richman Organization, 10 Columbus Circle, New York, NY 10019:* Selection 150

HOPE PUBLISHING CO. *Carol Stream, IL 60188:* Selections 27, 43, 176, 198, 245, 429, 514, 568

HOUSE OF MERCY (admin. by Maranatha! Music) *P.O. Box 31050, Laguna Hills, CA 92654-1050:* Selection 80

HYMN SOCIETY OF AMERICA (represented by Hope Publishing Co.) *Carol Stream, IL 60188:* Selection 454

HYMNS ANCIENT AND MODERN, LTD. *St. Mary's Works, St. Mary's Plain, Norwich, Norfolk NR3 3BH, England:* Selection 304

INTERVARSITY CHRISTIAN FELLOWSHIP *InterVarsity Press, Box 1400, Downers Grove, IL 60515:* Selection 117

JOHN T. BENSON PUBLISHING CO. (The Benson Co., Inc.) *365 Great Circle Dr., Nashville, TN 37228:* Selections 179, 237

JOHN W. PETERSON MUSIC COMPANY *13610 N. Scottsdale Rd., #10-221, Scottsdale, AZ 85254:* Selections 239, 464, 495, 524

JOY OF THE LORD PUBLISHING *c/o Sparrow Corp., 9255 Deering Ave., Chatsworth, CA 91311:* Selection 411

LANNY WOLFE MUSIC *c/o Pathway Press, P.O. Box 2250, Cleveland, TN 37320:* Selection 255

LATTER RAIN MUSIC *c/o Sparrow Corp., 9255 Deering Ave., Chatsworth, CA 91311:* Selections 93, 222

LeFEVRE-SING PUBLISHING CO. *P.O. Box 460, Smyrna, GA 30081:* Selection 332

LEXICON MUSIC, INC. (Assigned to MacKenzie and Associates, Inc.), *23 Music Sq. E., Suite 101, Nashville, TN 37203:* Selections 11, 13, 23, 24, 40, 53, 256, 266, 309, 447, 516, 551, 626

LILLENAS PUBLISHING CO. *P.O. Box 527, Kansas City, MO 64141:* Selections 83, 165, 244, 281, 400, 415, 583

LIVING WAY MINISTRIES *14300 Sherman Way, Van Nuys, CA 91405-2499:* Selections 225, 407

LUTHERAN CHURCH IN AMERICA, Board of Publications *2900 Queen Ln., Philadelphia, PA 19129:* Selection 44

MAKANUME MUSIC (Assigned to MacKenzie and Associates, Inc.) *23 Music Sq. E., Suite 101, Nashville, TN 37203:* Selection 40

MANNA MUSIC, INC. *25510 Ave. Stanford, Suite 101-102, Valencia, CA 91355:* Selections 4, 91, 101, 153, 192, 252, 507

MARANATHA! MUSIC *P.O. Box 31050, Laguna Hills, CA 92654-1050:* Selections 14, 29, 42, 71, 77, 265, 383, 465

MEADOWGREEN MUSIC CO. *54 Music Sq. E., Suite 305, Nashville, TN 37203:* Selections 30, 31, 272, 287

MEECE MUSIC (admin. by WORD MUSIC, a div. of WORD, INC.) *5221 N. O'Connor Blvd., Suite 1000, Irving, TX 75039:* Selection 209

MOODY PRESS (Moody Bible Institute of Chicago) *820 N. LaSalle Dr., Chicago, IL 60610-3283:* Selection 247

NAZARENE PUBLISHING HOUSE *P.O. Box 527, Kansas City, MO 64141:* Selections 67, 169, 526

NORMAN CLAYTON PUB. CO. (a div. of WORD, INC.) *5221 N. O'Connor Blvd., Suite 1000, Irving, TX 75039:* Selections 35, 59, 66, 105, 406, 511, 545, 561

OOH'S AND AH'S MUSIC (Assigned to MacKenzie and Associates, Inc.) *23 Music Sq. E., Suite 101, Nashville, TN 37203:* Selection 40

ORTLUND, ANNE *32 Whitewater Drive, Corona Del Mar, CA 92625:* Selection 316

OXFORD UNIVERSITY PRESS *Ely House, 37 Dover St., London W1X 4AH, England:* Selections 27, 64, 108, 167, 546

PARAGON MUSIC CORP. (The Benson Company, Inc.) *365 Great Circle Dr., Nashville, TN 37228:* Selection 113

PEARCE, ALMEDA J. (Mrs. Rowan) *502 Elizabeth Drive, Lancaster, PA 17601:* Selection 240

PRESBYTERIAN OUTLOOK, THE *512 East Main Street, Richmond, VA 23219:* Selection 293

PRISM TREE MUSIC *P.O. Box 3194, Redding, CA 96049:* Selection 394

RIVER OAKS MUSIC CO. (admin. Meadowgreen Music Group) *54 Music Sq. E., Suite 305, Nashville, TN 37203:* Selections 90, 197, 303, 564

ROCKSMITH MUSIC *c/o Trust Music Management, 6255 Sunset Blvd., Suite 705, Hollywood, CA 90028:* Selection 74

RODEHEAVER CO., THE (a div. of WORD, INC.) *5221 N. O'Connor Blvd., Suite 1000, Irving, TX 75039:* Selections 65, 186, 189, 219, 220, 258, 372, 388, 420, 421, 425, 452, 515, 517, 548

SACRED SONGS (a div. of WORD, INC.) *5221 N. O'Connor Blvd., Suite 1000, Irving, TX 75039:* Selections 329, 398, 596, 610

SALVATIONIST PUBLISHING AND SUPPLIES LIMITED *117-121 Judd Street, King's Cross, London, WC1H 9NN, England:* Selection 418

SANDI'S SONGS MUSIC *c/o John Helvering Agency, P.O. Box 2940, Anderson, IN 46001:* Selection 90

SCRIPTURE IN SONG (admin. by Maranatha! Music) *P.O. Box 31050, Laguna Hills, CA 92654-1050:* Selections 5, 112, 590

SHEPHERD'S FOLD MUSIC (a div. of Jubilee Communications, Inc.) *c/o Gaither Music Co., P.O. Box 737, Alexandria, IN 46001:* Selections 197, 303

SHERLOCK, HUGH *2 Nicks Avenue, Box 426, Kingston B. Jamaica, The Carribean:* Selection 305

SINGSPIRATION MUSIC (a div. of the Zondervan Corp.) *365 Great Circle Dr., Nashville, TN 37228:* Selections 45, 69, 72, 180, 310, 311, 331, 335, 378, 505, 523, 528, 535

SMITH, LEONARD E., JR./NEW JERUSALEM MUSIC *P.O. Box 225 Pine Mill Rd., Clarksboro, NJ 08020:* Selection 229

SOME-O-DAT MUSIC (admin. by DAYSPRING MUSIC, a div. of WORD, INC.) *5221 N. O'Connor Blvd., Suite 1000, Irving, TX 75039:* Selection 114

SOUND III, INC. *c/o Tempo Music Publications, 3773 W. 95th St., Leawood, KS 66206:* Selections 38, 588

STEVE ADAMS MUSIC (all rights controlled by Franklin House Publishing, Inc.) *P.O. Box 989, Franklin, TN 37065:* Selection 253

STRAIGHTWAY MUSIC (a div. of Jubilee Communications, Inc.) *c/o Gaither Music Co., P.O. Box 737, Alexandria, IN 46001:* Selections 288, 324, 437

UNITED CHURCH PRESS, THE *United Church Board for Homeland Ministries, 132 W. 31st Street, New York, NY 10001:* Selection 119

WHOLE ARMOR PUB. CO. *2821 Bransford Ave., Nashville, TN 37204:* Selection 36

WORD MUSIC (a div. of WORD, INC.) *5221 N. O'Connor Blvd., Suite 1000, Irving, TX 75039:* Selections 10, 12, 16, 32, 35, 39, 54, 55, 57, 60, 61, 63, 76, 78, 84, 89, 92, 97, 104, 105, 108, 121, 123, 125, 126, 129, 138, 140, 143, 146, 149, 154, 156, 159, 162, 164, 171, 174, 185, 187, 203, 205, 212, 218, 221, 223, 228, 230, 231, 234, 235, 242, 243, 246, 260, 262, 263, 267, 279, 287, 293, 305, 308, 311, 312, 314, 318, 323, 343, 344, 345, 376, 379, 382, 391, 396, 397, 401, 434, 437, 438, 439, 442, 457, 467, 469, 474, 479, 480, 483, 488, 494, 513, 534, 537, 550, 557, 565, 568, 569, 573, 574, 577, 578, 581, 582, 591, 592, 603, 606, 611, 612, 615, 619, 621, 627

WORK, MRS. JOHN W. III *1030 17th Ave. North, Nashville, TN 37208:* Selection 138

WORLD STUDENT CHRISTIAN FEDERATION *27 Ch. des Crets de Pregny, 1218 Grand-Saconnex, Geneva, Switzerland:* Selection 227

Any omission or inaccuracy of copyright notices on individual hymns will be corrected in subsequent printings wherever valid information is offered by the claimants.

ALPHABETICAL INDEX OF TUNES

A PERFECT HEART (Irreg.), 40
ABBA FATHER (Irreg.), 15
ABERYSTWYTH (7.7.7.7.D.), 466
ACCLAIM (8.8.8.5.), 75
ACKLEY (Irreg.), 220
ADA (9.8.9.8. w/Ref.), 520
ADAMS (Irreg.), 253
ADELAIDE (5.4.5.4.D.), 371
ADESTE FIDELES (Irreg.), 145
ADESTE FIDELES (Ref. only), (7.7.10.), 82
ADORE THEE (Irreg.), 597
AFFIRMATIVE (L.M.), 480
ALETTA (7.7.7.7.), 273
ALL SAINTS, NEW (C.M.D.), 316
ALL THE WAY (8.7.8.7.D.), 460
ALL TO CHRIST (6.6.7.7. w/Ref.), 210
ALL YOUR ANXIETY (Irreg.), 418
ALLELUIA (L.M.), 91
AMAZING GRACE (C.M.), 202
AMERICA (6.6.4.6.6.6.4.), 571
AMY (C.M.), 318
ANGEL'S STORY (7.6.7.6.D.), 369
ANNAMARIE (7.7.7.5.D. w/Ref.), 407
ANTIOCH (C.M.), 125
ANY ROOM (8.7.8.7. w/Ref.), 328
APPALACHIA (8.8.9.8.), 401
ARIEL (8.8.6.8.8.6.6.), 110
ARISE (8.7.8.7. w/Ref.), 334
ARLINGTON (C.M.), 482
ARMAGEDDON (6.5.6.5.D. w/Ref.), 484
ASHLYNE (6.5.6.5.D.), 235
ASPIRATION CANON (8.6.8.6.8.6.), 391
ASSAM (Irreg.), 376
ASSURANCE (9.10.9.9. w/Ref.), 345
AURELIA (7.6.7.6.D.), 277, 567
AUSTRIAN HYMN (8.7.8.7.D.), 9, 278, 557
AWAY IN A MANGER (11.11.11.11.), 157
AZMON (C.M.), 76, 440, 587

BALM IN GILEAD (Irreg.), 423
BATTLE HYMN (15.15.15.6. w/Ref.), 569
BE CALM MY SOUL (L.M.), 421
BE EXALTED (Irreg.), 5
BE GLORIFIED (Irreg.), 394
BE JOYFUL (Irreg.), 223
BE STILL AND KNOW (8.8.8.), 343
BEACH SPRING (8.7.8.7.D.), 455
BEECHER (8.7.8.7.D.), 92, 268, 574
BEHOLD THE LAMB (Irreg.), 179
BEMERTON (6.5.6.5.), 586
BENEDICTION (Irreg.), 607
BENTON HARBOR (8.7.8.7. w/Ref.), 81
BETHANY (6.4.6.4.6.6.6.4.), 393
BINGHAMTON (10.11.11.11. w/Ref.), 352
BLESS HIS HOLY NAME (Irreg.), 13
BLESSED BE THE NAME (C.M. w/Ref.), 103
BLESSINGS (11.11.11.11. w/Ref.), 563
BLOTT EN DAG (Irreg.), 56
BOND OF LOVE (Irreg.), 281
BOYLSTON (S.M.), 448
BRADBURY (8.7.8.7.D.), 462
BREAD OF LIFE (6.4.6.4.D.), 274
BROOKS (Irreg.), 603
BULLINGER (8.5.8.3.), 346
BUNESSAN (5.5.5.4.D.), 60, 212, 568
BY AND BY (Irreg.), 544
BY GRACE MADE STRONG (11.10.11.10. w/Coda), 311

CALLING TODAY (10.8.10.7. w/Ref.), 327
CALVARY (9.9.9.4. w/Ref.), 338
CALVARY COVERS IT (Irreg.), 189
CAMACHA (6.4.6.4.6.6.6.4.), 395
CANE PEAK (Irreg.), 606
CANONBURY (L.M.), 450
CANTIQUE DE NOËL (11.10.11.10.11.10.11.10.10.), 148
CARMEL (10.7.10.8.), 577
CARMICHAEL (11.7.11.7. w/Ref), 329
CAROL (C.M.D.), 128
CAST THY BURDEN (Irreg.), 598
CASTLE (9.11.11.10.), 154
CATHERINE (Irreg.), 63
CELEBRATE JESUS (Irreg.), 324
CHAUTAUQUA (Ref. only) (Irreg.), 22
CHILD OF LOVE (Irreg.), 156
CHILDREN (8.7.7.7.11.), 580
CHILDREN PRAYING (Irreg.), 429
CHRIST AROSE (6.5.6.4. w/Ref.), 216
CHRISTMAS (C.M. w/Repeats), 135
CLAP YOUR HANDS (Irreg.), 24
CLAYTON (6.6.6.5.D.), 545
CLEANSING FOUNTAIN (C.M.D.), 196
CLOSE TO THEE (8.7.8.7.6.6.8.7.), 365
CLOSER WALK (Irreg.), 380
COLIN (6.6.8.4.), 565
COME LET US REASON (Irreg.), 591
COME, HOLY SPIRIT (8.7.8.7.D.), 250
COMFORTER (12.12.12.6. w/Ref.), 257
COMING AGAIN (7.7.7.7. w/Ref.), 239
COMING HOME (8.5.8.5. w/Ref.), 341
COMMIT THY WAY (Irreg.), 581
CONSOLATOR (11.10.11.10.), 416
CONSTANCY (8.7.8.7. w/Ref.), 368
CONVERSE (8.7.8.7.D.), 435
CORONATION (C.M. w/Repeats), 97
COVER ME (Irreg.), 469
CRADLE SONG (11.11.11.11.), 158
CREATION (L.M.D.), 62
CRIMOND (C.M.), 50
CROFT (11.11.7.7.11.), 397
CROWNING DAY (Irreg.), 236
CRUCIFER (10.10.10.10.), 304
CRUCIFIX (7.6.7.6.D.), 340
CRUSADERS' HYMN (5.6.8.5.5.8.), 88
CULL CANYON (7.7.7.7.), 171
CWM RHONDDA (8.7.8.7.8.7.7.), 51, 292

DARWALL (6.6.6.6.8.8.), 111, 117, 228
DAVID (10.11.10.10.), 434
DENNIS (S.M.), 286
DET AR ETT FAST ORD (9.8.9.8.), 291
DIADEM (C.M. w/Ref.), 96
DIADEMATA (S.M.D.), 234, 478
DIAPASON (Irreg.), 246
DISMISSAL (Irreg.), 609
DIVINUM MYSTERIUM (8.7.8.7.8.7.7.), 118
DIX (7.7.7.7.7.7.), 163, 560
DOMINUS REGIT ME (8.7.8.7.), 468
DONA NOBIS PACEM (Irreg.), 32
DUKE STREET (L.M.), 231
DUKE'S TUNE (Irreg.), 617
DUNBAR (8.8.8.6. w/Ref.), 370
DUNCANNON (C.M. w/Ref.), 176

EASTER HYMN (7.7.7.7. w/Alleluias), 217
EASTER SONG (Irreg.), 222
EBENEZER (8.7.8.7.D.), 211, 475
EIN' FESTE BURG (8.7.8.7.6.6.6.7.), 26
EL NATHAN (C.M. w/Ref.), 409
EL SHADDAI (Irreg.), 36
ELATA (C.M.), 126
ELDER MOUNTAIN (7.6.7.6.D.), 583
ELIZABETH (Irreg.), 510
ELLACOMBE (7.6.7.6.D.), 59, 174
ELLERS (10.10.10.10.), 439, 604
ELLESDIE (8.7.8.7.D.), 377, 584
ELLSWORTH (10.10.9.6. w/Ref.), 511
EMMANUEL (Irreg.), 134
ENGLAND (Irreg.), 39
ERMUNTRE DICH (8.7.8.7.8.8.7.7.), 129

ES IST EIN' ROS' (7.6.7.6.6.7.6.), 160
EVANGEL (7.6.7.6.D. w/Ref.), 424
EVENTIDE (10.10.10.10.), 419
EVERLASTING LOVE (7.7.7.7.D.), 490
EXCELLENCE (Irreg.), 456

FACE TO FACE (8.7.8.7. w/Ref.), 549
FAIRHILL (L.M.), 626
FAITHFUL MEN (6.6.11.6.6.9.), 288
FAITHFULNESS (11.10.11.10. w/Ref.), 43
FALLS CREEK (8.6.8.7. w/Ref.), 367
FAMILY OF GOD (Irreg.), 282
FAYE (Irreg.), 55
FEDERAL STREET (L.M.), 317
FILL ME NOW (8.7.8.7. w/Ref.), 261
FILL MY CUP (Irreg.), 398
FILLMORE (Irreg.), 457
FINLANDIA (10.10.10.10.10.10.), 347
FINLANDIA (altered) (11.10.11.10.11.10.), 535
FISCHER (11.11.11.11. w/Ref.), 436
FLEMMING (11.11.11.6.), 264
FOOTSTEPS (9.4.9.4. w/Ref.), 470
FOR UNTO US (Irreg.), 146
FOUNDATION (11.11.11.11.), 275
FREELY, FREELY (9.9.9.9. w/Ref.), 447

GALILEE (8.7.8.7.), 375
GARDEN (Irreg.), 425
GEIBEL (7.6.7.6.D. w/Ref.), 481
GENTLE SHEPHERD (Irreg.), 458
GERMAN FOLK (10.12.10.), 78
GERMANY (L.M.), 193
GIFT OF LIFE (6.7.8.6.), 205
GIVE ME JESUS (8.7.8.7. w/Ref.), 443
GLADNESS (10.10.10.10. w/Ref.), 357
GLORIA (7.7.7.7. w/Ref.), 132
GLORIFY THY NAME (Irreg.), 29
GLORIOUS NAME (8.7.8.7. w/Ref.), 85
GLORY SONG (10.10.10.10. w/Ref.), 539
GLORY TO HIS NAME (9.9.9.5. w/Ref.), 527
GO (Irreg.), 308
GO NOW (8.8.9.8.), 610
GO TELL IT (Irreg.), 138
GO YE (8.8.12.8.), 301
GOD BE WITH YOU (Irreg.), 602
GOD CARES (C.M. w/Ref.), 47
GOD IS SO GOOD (Irreg.), 41
GOD LEADS US (11.8.11.8. w/Ref.), 46
GOD'S PEOPLE (10.11.11.8. w/Ref.), 312
GOD'S WAYS (Irreg.), 621
GOLDEN CHAIN (Ref. only) (8.7.8.7.), 100
GORDON (11.11.11.11.), 364
GRACE (Irreg.), 566
GREAT IS THE LORD (Irreg.), 31
GREATER IS HE (8.8.8.7.), 255
GREATOREX (Irreg.), 623
GREEN (Irreg.), 206
GREENRIDGE (11.11.11.11.), 140
GREENSLEEVES (8.7.8.7. w/Ref.), 137
GROSSER GOTT (7.8.7.8.7.7.), 12

HALLELUJAH CHORUS (Irreg.), 37
HALLOWED BE THE NAME (Irreg.), 84
HAMBURG (L.M.), 185
HANKEY (7.6.7.6.D. w/Ref.), 297
HANNAH (Ref. only) (9.8.9.8.), 218
HANOVER (10.10.11.11.), 17
HAPPY DAY (L.M. w/Ref.), 532
HARRIS (8.7.8.7.D.), 526
HARTFORD (Irreg.), 473
HE CARETH FOR YOU (Irreg.), 57
HE GIVETH MORE GRACE (Irreg.), 415
HE IS HERE (Irreg.), 256
HE IS LORD (11.10.12.10. w/Ref.), 105
HE LEADETH ME (L.M. w/Ref.), 461
HE LIFTED ME (8.8.8.6. w/Ref.), 522
HE ROSE TRIUMPHANTLY (6.6.6.6. w/Ref.), 219
HE TOUCHED ME (Irreg.), 504
HEARN (7.8.8.8.), 112
HEART MELODY (Irreg.), 514
HEAVEN (8.7.8.7. w/Ref.), 542
HEAVEN CAME DOWN (Irreg.), 495
HENDON (7.7.7.7. w/Repeat), 379
HICKS (Irreg.), 93
HIDING IN THEE (11.11.11.11. w/Ref.), 348
HIGHER GROUND (L.M. w/Ref.), 399
HIMLADUVA (8.7.8.7.), 254
HINGHAM (11.10.11.10. w/Ref.), 356
HIS NAME IS LIFE (Irreg.), 114
HIS PRESENCE (8.4.4.4.), 589
HOLINESS (6.5.6.5.D.), 441
HOLY MANNA (8.7.8.7.D.), 454, 585
HOLY, HOLY (Irreg.), 266
HOW GREAT THOU ART (11.10.11.10. w/Ref.), 4
HOW MAJESTIC (Irreg.), 30
HUDSON (C.M. w/Ref.), 188
HURSLEY (L.M.), 412
HYFRYDOL (8.7.8.7.D.), 61, 89, 124, 233
HYMN TO JOY (8.7.8.7.D.), 1, 215

I AM THINE (10.7.10.7. w/Ref.), 358
I CAN SAFELY GO (11.11.11.11. w/Ref.), 467
I KNOW A FOUNT (10.10.10.15.), 194
I LOVE THEE (11.11.11.11.), 362
I LOVE YOU, LORD (Irreg.), 80
I WILL PRAISE HIM (8.7.8.7. w/Ref.), 525
I WONDER AS I WANDER (Irreg.), 139
I'D RATHER HAVE JESUS (Irreg.), 517
I'LL FLY AWAY (9.4.9.4. w/Ref.), 554
I'LL GO (9.7.9.7.9.8. w/Ref.), 444
IN DULCI JUBILO (Irreg.), 151
IN HIS TIME (Irreg.), 465
IRA (C.M.), 313
IRBY (8.7.8.7.7.7.), 155
IRENE (13.12.13.12.), 534
ITALIAN HYMN (6.6.4.6.6.6.4.), 267
IVERSON (Irreg.), 247
IVES (8.7.8.7.8.8.8.7.), 400

JANICE (12.10.13.10.), 165
JESU, MEINE FREUDE (6.6.5.6.6.5.7.8.6.), 413
JESUS IS KING (Irreg.), 230
JESUS LOVES ME (7.7.7.7. w/Ref.), 579
JESUS SAVES (7.6.7.6.7.7.7.6.), 306
JESUS, I COME (Irreg.), 336
JOYFUL NOISE (12.8.12.8.10.8.10.8.), 23
JOYFUL SONG (Irreg.), 106
JÜNGST (Irreg.), 144

KENOSIS (6.6.6.6.8.8.), 453
KING IS COMING (Irreg.), 238
KING OF HEAVEN (Irreg.), 104
KING OF KINGS (Irreg.), 77
KINGS OF ORIENT (8.8.4.4.6. w/Ref.), 166
KINGSFOLD (C.M.D.), 167
KINGSTON (8.7.8.7.D.), 305
KIRKPATRICK (11.8.11.8. w/Ref.), 496
KREMSER (12.11.12.11.), 16, 561

LAFFERTY (Irreg.), 42
LAMB OF GLORY (7.8.7.8. w/Ref.), 197
LANCASHIRE (7.6.7.6.D.), 226, 483
LANDAS (C.M. w/Ref.), 405
LASST UNS ERFREUEN (L.M. w/Alleluias), 64
LAUDA ANIMA (Andrews) (8.7.8.7.8.7.), 3
LAUDES DOMINI (6.6.6.6.6.6.), 87
LEAD ME, LORD (Irreg.), 49
LEMMEL (Ref. only) (Irreg.), 335
LENOX (6.6.6.6.8.8. w/Repeat), 199
LEONI (6.6.8.4.D.), 34, 472
LET US BREAK BREAD (Irreg.), 323
LET'S JUST PRAISE THE LORD (Irreg.), 107
LIVING (10.10.10.10. w/Ref.), 372
LLANFAIR (7.7.7.7. w/Alleluias), 232
LOBE DEN HERREN (14.14.4.7.8.), 8
LORD OF ALL (Irreg.), 359
LORD, WE PRAISE YOU (4.4.4.4.), 83
LORDSHIP OF CHIRST (10.7.10.6. w/Ref.), 360
LOVE OF GOD (Irreg.), 67

LOWLINESS (7.7.7.7. w/Ref.), 168
LYONS (10.10.11.11.), 10

MACCABEUS (10.11.11.11. w/Ref.), 227
MADRID (6.6.6.6.D.), 108
MAITLAND (C.M.), 449
MAJESTY (Irreg.), 74
MALOTTE (Irreg.), 426
MAN OF SORROWS (7.7.7.8.), 175
MANNA (Irreg.), 252
MANNER OF LOVE (Irreg.), 71
MANOAH (C.M.), 70, 321
MAORI (10.10.10.10.), 438
MARANATHA (Irreg.), 265
MARCHING TO ZION (6.6.8.8.6.6. w/Ref.), 555
MARGARET (Irreg.), 127
MARION (S.M. w/Ref.), 562
MARTYRDOM (C.M.), 208
MARYTON (L.M.), 320, 451
MATERNA (C.M.D.), 572
MEECE (Irreg.), 209
MEINECKE (Irreg.), 622
MELITA (8.8.8.8.8.8.), 402, 575
MENDELSSOHN (7.7.7.7.D. w/Ref.), 133
MERCY (7.7.7.7.), 248, 605
MESSAGE (10.8.8.7.7. w/Ref.), 296
MIEIR (Irreg.), 101
MINERVA (C.M. w/Ref.), 330
MIT FREUDEN ZART (8.7.8.7.8.8.7.), 6
MONTROSE (C.M. w/Ref.), 524
MOODY (9.9.9.9. w/Ref.), 201
MORE LOVE TO THEE (6.4.6.4.6.6.4.), 363
MORECAMBE (10.10.10.10.), 249
MORRIS (9.10.9.10.), 392
MUNICH (7.6.7.6.D.), 269
MUSKOGEE (11.10.11.8. w/Ref.), 408
MY REDEEMER (8.7.8.7. w/Ref.), 506
MY SAVIOR'S LOVE (8.7.8.7. w/Ref.), 512
MY TRIBUTE (Irreg.), 11
McAFEE (C.M. w/Ref.), 497
McCABE (11.6.11.6. w/Ref.), 307
McCUTCHAN (Irreg.), 593
McDANIEL (12.8.12.8. w/Ref.), 515
McKEE (C.M.), 547

NAME OF THE LORD (Irreg.), 90
NATIONAL ANTHEM (Irreg.), 576
NATIONAL HYMN (10.10.10.10.), 573
NATIVITY CANON (4.6.6.4.), 149
NEAR THE CROSS (7.6.7.6. w/Ref.), 385
NEED (6.4.6.4. w/Ref.), 428
NEIDLINGER (10.6.10.7. w/Ref.), 162
NETTLETON (8.7.8.7.D.), 2
NEUMARK (9.8.9.8.8.8.), 600
NICAEA (11.12.12.10.), 262
NO NOT ONE (10.6.10.6. w/Ref.), 422
NO ONE UNDERSTANDS (8.7.8.7. w/Ref.), 417
NORRIS (8.8.8.9. w/Ref.), 373
NU GLÄDJENS TIMME (C.M. w/Ref.), 161
NUN DANKET (6.7.6.7.6.6.6.6.), 556
NUSBAUM (Irreg.), 333

O HEARKEN YE (8.8.6.6.D.), 150
O SANCTISSIMA (4.5.7.6.6.7.), 119
O'SHIELDS (Irreg.), 38
O, HOW I LOVE JESUS (C.M. w/Ref.), 529
OLD HUNDREDTH (L.M.), 20, 624, 625
OLD RUGGED CROSS (Irreg.), 186
OLIVET (6.6.4.6.6.6.4.), 410
ONE DAY (11.10.11.10. w/Ref.), 170
ONE SMALL CHILD (Irreg.), 164
ONLY BELIEVE (8.10.8.10.), 420
ONLY ONE LIFE (7.6.7.6.7.6.12.6.), 378
OPEN OUR EYES (11.12.11.11.), 383
ORTONVILLE (C.M. w/Repeats), 109
ORWIGSBURG (10.9.10.9. w/Ref.), 430
OTHELLO (C.M. w/Ref.), 339
OUR GOD REIGNS (Irreg.), 229

PASS IT ON (Irreg.), 309
PASS ME NOT (8.5.8.5. w/Ref.), 337
PASSION CHORALE (7.6.7.6.D.), 178
PATRICIA (Irreg.), 513
PAUL (Irreg.), 612
PAX TECUM (Irreg.), 487
PEACE LIKE A RIVER (7.7.10.D.), 498
PEARCE (11.10.11.10.), 240
PEARLY GATES (8.7.8.7. w/Ref.), 541
PENITENTIA (10.10.10.10.), 325
PEOPLE NEED THE LORD (Irreg.), 303
PERFECT PEACE (Irreg.), 492
PISGAH (8.6.8.6.6.6.8.6.), 538
PLAINFIELD (7.8.7.8. w/Ref.), 195
POWER IN THE BLOOD (10.9.10.8. w/Ref.), 191
PRAISE GOD (L.M.), 627
PRAISE YE (Irreg.), 596
PRAYING FOR YOU (9.9.11.11. w/Ref.), 431
PRECIOUS LORD (6.6.9.6.6.9.), 463
PRECIOUS NAME (8.7.8.7. w/Ref.), 116
PROMISED LAND (C.M. w/Ref.), 552
PROMISES (11.11.11.9. w/Ref.), 271
PURE AND HOLY (7.7.7.7. w/Ref.), 437

QUAM DILECTA (Irreg.), 594
QUEBEC (L.M.), 501
QUIET MOMENT (Irreg.), 592

RATHBUN (8.7.8.7.), 184
REACH OUT (Irreg.), 314
REACH YOUR HAND (L.M.), 582
RED (Irreg.), 322
REDEEMED (9.8.9.8. w/Ref.), 521
REGENT SQUARE (8.7.8.7.8.7.), 131, 225, 241, 276
REJOICE (Irreg.), 489
RESCUE (11.10.11.10. w/Ref.), 299
REST (8.6.8.8.6.), 427
RESURRECTION (Irreg.), 213
RESURRECTION CANON (11.11.11.), 221
RETREAT (L.M.), 319, 432
REVIVE US AGAIN (11.11. w/Ref.), 295
RING THOSE BELLS (Irreg.), 153
ROLL CALL (Irreg.), 543
ROMERO (7.7.9.7.), 113
RONDINELLA (10.9.10.9. w/Ref.), 387
ROOM AT THE CROSS (Irreg.), 331
RUSSIAN HYMN (11.10.11.9.), 33

SAFETY (7.6.7.6.7.6.7.4. w/Ref.), 505
SAGINA (8.8.8.8.8.8. w/Ref.), 203
ST. AGNES (C.M.), 79, 536
ST. ANNE (C.M.), 52
ST. BRENDAN'S (Irreg.), 284
ST. CATHERINE (8.8.8.8.8.8.), 279
ST. CHRISTOPHER (7.6.8.6.8.6.8.6.), 183
ST. DENIO (11.11.11.11.), 25
ST. GEORGE'S, WINDSOR (7.7.7.7.D.), 559
ST. GERTRUDE (6.5.6.5.D. w/Ref.), 479
ST. JOHN (6.6.6.6.8.8.), 595
ST. LEONARDS (8.7.8.5.), 390
ST. LOUIS (8.6.8.6.7.6.8.6.), 141
ST. MARGARET (8.8.8.8.6.), 374
ST. PETER (C.M.), 94, 285
ST. THEODULPH (7.6.7.6.D.), 173
ST. THOMAS (S.M.), 18, 21, 120, 280, 293
SALSBURY (Irreg.), 578
SANDRINGHAM (11.10.11.10.), 533
SANKEY (C.M.D. w/Ref.), 486
SARDIS (8.7.8.7.), 608
SATISFIED (8.7.8.7. w/Ref.), 531
SAVED BY GRACE (L.M.), 550
SCALES (11.11.11.11. w/Ref.), 294
SCHOLFIELD (8.6.8.8. w/Ref.), 530
SCHULER (10.7.10.7. w/Ref.), 452
SCHUMANN (S.M.), 620
SCOTT (Irreg.), 381
SEASONS (7.6.7.6.D.), 502
SECOND COMING (Irreg.), 245
SERVING (Irreg.), 446

SHELTER (L.M. w/Ref.), 353
SHEPHERD OF LOVE (Irreg.), 464
SHOWALTER (10.9.10.9. w/Ref.), 354
SHOWERS OF BLESSING (8.7.8.7. w/Ref.), 289
SICILIAN MARINERS (8.7.8.7.8.7.), 601
SINE NOMINE (10.10.10. w/Alleluias), 546
SING PRAISE (Irreg.), 263
SLANE (10.10.10.10.), 382
SLANE (Altered) (6.5.6.5.D.), 442
SO BLESSED (Irreg.), 564
SOLI DEO GLORIA (Irreg.), 35
SOLID ROCK (L.M. w/Ref.), 404
SOMETHING BEAUTIFUL (Irreg.), 519
SOMETHING FOR JESUS (6.4.6.4.6.6.6.4.), 445
SOMETIMES ALLELUIA (Irreg.), 115
SOON AND VERY SOON (Irreg.), 551
SPRING HILL (C.M. w/Ref.), 388
SPRINGTIME (Irreg.), 396
STAINER (Irreg.), 207
STILLE NACHT (Irreg.), 147
STORY OF JESUS (8.7.8.7.D. w/Ref.), 172
SULLIVAN (Irreg.), 302
SUNSET (10.9.10.9.), 548
SUNSHINE (9.6.8.6. w/Ref.), 499
SURELY GOODNESS AND MERCY (Irreg.), 45
SURRENDER (8.7.8.7. w/Ref.), 366
SWEET BY AND BY (9.9.9.9. w/Ref.), 553
SWEET HOUR (L.M.D.), 433
SWEETEST NAME (9.7.9.7. w/Ref.), 95, 488
SWENEY (L.M. w/Ref.), 389
SYMPHONY (11.11.13.8.9.), 283

TABERNACLE (8.7.8.7. w/Ref.), 258
TALLIS' CANON (L.M.), 54
TERRA BEATA (S.M.D.), 58
THANK YOU (8.8.8.7.), 98
THAT NAME (Irreg.), 102
THE BATTLE (11.8.11.8. w/Ref.), 485
THE BLOOD (Irreg.), 192
THE FIRST NOEL (Irreg.), 136
THE JOY OF THE LORD (8.8.7.7.8.), 411
THE NEW 23RD (Irreg.), 53
THE SWEETER HE GROWS (8.6.8.11. w/Ref.), 518
THE TREES OF THE FIELD (Irreg.), 244
THE UNVEILED CHRIST (8.7.8.7. w/Ref.), 169
THIS IS THE DAY (Irreg.), 590
THOMPSON (11.7.11.7. w/Ref.), 326
THOUSAND CANDLES (8.7.8.6.), 159
THROUGH IT ALL (Irreg.), 507
THY LOVING KINDNESS (10.10.10.10.), 69
THY WORD (Irreg.), 272
TIDINGS (11.10.11.10. w/Ref.), 298
TO BE LIKE JESUS (10.7.10.7.), 384
TO GOD BE THE GLORY (11.11.11.11. w/Ref.), 66
TOPLADY (7.7.7.7.7.7.), 204
TORONTO (11.10.11.10. w/Coda), 310
TRANQUILITY (8.7.8.5.D. w/Ref.), 503
TRENTHAM (S.M.), 259
TRUETT (7.6.8.6. w/Ref.), 251
TRUST AND OBEY (6.6.9.D. w/Ref.), 349
TRUST IN JESUS (8.7.8.7. w/Ref.), 350
TRUSTING JESUS (7.7.7.7. w/Ref.), 355
TRYGGARE KAN INGEN VARA (L.M.), 44
TUCKER (Irreg.), 300

VENI EMMANUEL (L.M. w/Ref.), 123, 243
VICKI (Irreg.), 121
VILLE DU HAVRE (11.8.11.9. w/Ref.), 493
VOX DILECTI (C.M.D.), 414

W ZLOBIE LEZY (8.7.8.7.8.8.7.7.), 143
WAITING (S.M.), 242
WAKEFIELD (6.6.12. w/Ref.), 406
WALKER (8.7.8.7.), 187
WALTHAM (L.M.), 152
WASHED IN THE BLOOD (11.9.11.9. w/Ref.), 190
WAY OF THE CROSS (Irreg.), 471
WE SHALL BEHOLD HIM (Irreg.), 237
WE WILL GLORIFY (9.7.9.6.), 72
WE WILL SERVE (Irreg.), 537
WE WILL STAND (Irreg.), 474
WEBB (7.6.7.6.D.), 477
WEBER (S.M.), 287
WEIGLE (12.11.12.11. w/Ref.), 528
WELCOME (8.7.8.7.), 260
WELLESLEY (8.7.8.7.), 68
WERE YOU THERE? (Irreg.), 181
WHITTLE (10.10.10.10. w/Ref.), 351
WHOLE WORLD (Irreg.), 344
WINTON (Irreg.), 611
WITHOUT HIM (8.7.8.7. w/Ref.), 332
WONDER OF IT ALL (Irreg.), 65
WONDERFUL GRACE (Irreg.), 198
WONDERFUL PEACE (12.9.12.9. w/Ref.), 500
WONDROUS LOVE (12.9.6.6.12.9.), 177
WONDROUS STORY (8.7.8.7. w/Ref.), 508
WOODLAND HILLS (Irreg.), 516
WOODLANDS (10.10.10.10.), 27
WOODWORTH (L.M.), 342
WORDS OF LIFE (8.6.8.6.6.6. w/Ref.), 270
WORSHIP AND ADORE (7.6.6.6.8.6.), 19
WORSHIP AND BOW DOWN (Irreg.), 14
WORSHIP HIM (Irreg.), 588
WORTHY (Irreg.), 73
WORTHY IS THE LAMB (Irreg.), 180
WYE VALLEY (6.5.6.5.D. w/Ref.), 494
WYE VALLEY (abridged) (6.5.6.5.D.), 315

YESTERDAY, TODAY AND TOMORROW (Irreg.), 523

ZUVERSICHT (7.8.7.8.7.7.), 224

METRICAL INDEX OF TUNES

Common Meter
C.M. (8.6.8.6.)
AMAZING GRACE, 202
AMY, 318
ANTIOCH, 125
ARLINGTON, 482
AZMON, 76, 440, 587
CRIMOND, 50
ELATA, 126
IRA, 313
MAITLAND, 449
MANOAH, 70, 321
MARTYRDOM, 208
McKEE, 547
ST. AGNES, 79, 536
ST. ANNE, 52
ST. PETER, 94, 285

C.M. with Refrain
BLESSED BE THE NAME, 103
DIADEM, 96
DUNCANNON, 176
EL NATHAN, 409
GOD CARES, 47
HUDSON, 188
LANDAS, 405
MINERVA, 330
MONTROSE, 524
McAFEE, 497
NU GLÄDJENS TIMME, 161
O, HOW I LOVE JESUS, 529
OTHELLO, 339
PROMISED LAND, 552
SPRING HILL, 388

C.M. with Repeats
CHRISTMAS, 135
CORONATION, 97
ORTONVILLE, 109

Common Meter Double
C.M.D. (8.6.8.6.8.6.8.6.)
ALL SAINTS, NEW, 316
CAROL, 128
CLEANSING FOUNTAIN, 196
ELLACOMBE, 59
KINGSFOLD, 167
MATERNA, 572
VOX DILECTI, 414

C.M.D. with Refrain
SANKEY, 486

Long Meter
L.M. (8.8.8.8.)
ALLELUIA, 91
CANONBURY, 450
DUKE STREET, 231
FAIRHILL, 626
FEDERAL STREET, 317
GERMANY, 193
HAMBURG, 185
HURSLEY, 412
MARYTON, 320, 451
OLD HUNDREDTH, 20, 624, 625
PRAISE GOD, 627
QUEBEC, 501
REACH YOUR HAND, 582
RETREAT, 319, 432
SAVED BY GRACE, 550
TALLIS' CANON, 54
WALTHAM, 152
WOODWORTH, 342

L.M. with Alleluias
LASST UNS ERFREUEN, 64

L.M. with Refrain
HAPPY DAY, 532
HE LEADETH ME, 461
HIGHER GROUND, 399
SHELTER, 353
SOLID ROCK, 404
SWENEY, 389
VENI EMMANUEL, 123, 243

Long Meter Double
L.M.D. (8.8.8.8.8.8.8.8.)
CREATION, 62
SWEET HOUR, 433

Short Meter
S.M. (6.6.8.6.)
BOYLSTON, 448
DENNIS, 286
ST. THOMAS, 18, 21, 120, 280, 293
SCHUMANN, 620
TRENTHAM, 259
WAITING, 242
WEBER, 287

S.M. with Refrain
MARION, 562

Short Meter Double
S.M.D. (6.6.8.6.6.6.8.6.)
DIADEMATA, 234, 478
TERRA BEATA, 58

4.4.4.4.
LORD, WE PRAISE YOU, 83

4.5.7.6.6.7.
O SANCTISSIMA, 119

4.6.6.4.
NATIVITY CANON, 149

5.4.5.4.D.
ADELAIDE, 371

5.5.5.4.D.
BUNESSAN, 60, 212, 568

5.6.8.5.5.8.
CRUSADERS' HYMN, 88

6.4.6.4.D
BREAD OF LIFE, 274

6.4.6.4. with Refrain
NEED, 428

6.4.6.4.6.6.4.
MORE LOVE TO THEE, 363

6.4.6.4.6.6.6.4.
BETHANY, 393
CAMACHA, 395
SOMETHING FOR JESUS, 445

6.5.6.4. with Refrain
CHRIST AROSE, 216

6.5.6.5.
BEMERTON, 586

6.5.6.5.D.
ASHLYNE, 235
HOLINESS, 441
SLANE (Altered), 442
WYE VALLEY (abridged), 315

6.5.6.5.D. with Refrain
ARMAGEDDON, 484
ST. GERTRUDE, 479
WYE VALLEY, 494

6.6.4.6.6.6.4.
AMERICA, 571
ITALIAN HYMN, 267
OLIVET, 410

6.6.5.6.6.5.7.8.6.
JESU, MEINE FREUDE, 413

6.6.6.5.D.
CLAYTON, 545

6.6.6.6. with Refrain
HE ROSE TRIUMPHANTLY, 219

6.6.6.6.6.6.
LAUDES DOMINI, 87

6.6.6.6.D.
MADRID, 108

6.6.6.6.8.8.
DARWALL, 111, 117, 228
KENOSIS, 453
ST. JOHN, 595

6.6.6.6.8.8. with Repeat
LENOX, 199

6.6.7.7. with Refrain
ALL TO CHRIST, 210

6.6.8.4.
COLIN, 565

6.6.8.4.D.
LEONI, 34, 472

6.6.8.8.6.6. with Refrain
MARCHING TO ZION, 555

6.6.9.6.6.9.
PRECIOUS LORD, 463

6.6.9.D. with Refrain
TRUST AND OBEY, 349

6.6.11.6.6.9.
FAITHFUL MEN, 288

6.6.12. with Refrain
WAKEFIELD, 406

6.7.6.7.6.6.6.6.
NUN DANKET, 556

6.7.8.6.
GIFT OF LIFE, 205

7.6.6.6.8.6.
WORSHIP AND ADORE, 19

7.6.7.6. with Refrain
NEAR THE CROSS, 385

7.6.7.6.D.
ANGEL'S STORY, 369
AURELIA, 277, 567
CRUCIFIX, 340
ELDER MOUNTAIN, 583
ELLACOMBE, 174
LANCASHIRE, 226, 483
MUNICH, 269
PASSION CHORALE, 178
ST. THEODULPH, 173
SEASONS, 502
WEBB, 477

7.6.7.6.D. with Refrain
EVANGEL, 424
GEIBEL, 481
HANKEY, 297

7.6.7.6.6.7.6.
ES IST EIN' ROS', 160

7.6.7.6.7.6.7.4. w/Refrain
SAFETY, 505

7.6.7.6.7.6.12.6.
ONLY ONE LIFE, 378

7.6.7.6.7.7.7.6.
JESUS SAVES, 306

7.6.8.6. with Refrain
TRUETT, 251

7.6.8.6.8.6.8.6.
ST. CHRISTOPHER, 183

7.7.7.5.D. with Refrain
ANNAMARIE, 407

7.7.7.7.
ALETTA, 273
CULL CANYON, 171
MERCY, 248, 605

7.7.7.7. with Alleluias
EASTER HYMN, 217
LLANFAIR, 232

7.7.7.7. with Refrain
COMING AGAIN, 239
GLORIA, 132
JESUS LOVES ME, 579
LOWLINESS, 168
PURE AND HOLY, 437
TRUSTING JESUS, 355

7.7.7.7. with Repeat
HENDON, 379

7.7.7.7.D.
ABERSYSTWYTH, 466
EVERLASTING LOVE, 490
ST. GEORGE'S, WINDSOR, 559

7.7.7.7.D. with Refrain
MENDELSSOHN, 133

7.7.7.7.7.7.
DIX, 163, 560
TOPLADY, 204

7.7.7.8.
MAN OF SORROWS, 175

7.7.9.7.
ROMERO, 113

7.7.10.
ADESTE FIDELES (Refrain only), 82

7.7.10.D.
PEACE LIKE A RIVER, 498

7.8.7.8. with Refrain
LAMB OF GLORY, 197
PLAINFIELD, 195

7.8.7.8.7.7.
GROSSER GOTT, 12
ZUVERSICHT, 224

7.8.8.8.
HEARN, 112

8.4.4.4.
HIS PRESENCE, 589

8.5.8.3.
BULLINGER, 346

8.5.8.5. with Refrain
COMING HOME, 341
PASS ME NOT, 337

8.6.8.6.6.6. with Refrain
WORDS OF LIFE, 270

8.6.8.6.6.6.8.6.
PISGAH, 538

8.6.8.6.7.6.8.6.
ST. LOUIS, 141

8.6.8.6.8.6.
ASPIRATION CANON, 391

8.6.8.7. with Refrain
FALLS CREEK, 367

8.6.8.8. with Refrain
SCHOLFIELD, 530

8.6.8.8.6.
REST, 427

8.6.8.11. with Refrain
THE SWEETER HE GROWS, 518

8.7.7.7.11.
CHILDREN, 580

8.7.8.5.
ST. LEONARDS, 390

8.7.8.5.D. with Refrain
TRANQUILITY, 503

8.7.8.6.
THOUSAND CANDLES, 159

8.7.8.7.
DOMINUS REGIT ME, 468
GALILEE, 375
GOLDEN CHAIN (Refrain only), 100
HIMLADUVA, 254
RATHBUN, 184
SARDIS, 608

WALKER, 187
WELCOME, 260
WELLESLEY, 68

8.7.8.7. with Refrain

ANY ROOM, 328
ARISE, 334
BENTON HARBOR, 81
CONSTANCY, 368
FACE TO FACE, 549
FILL ME NOW, 261
GIVE ME JESUS, 443
GLORIOUS NAME, 85
GREENSLEEVES, 137
HEAVEN, 542
I WILL PRAISE HIM, 525
MY REDEEMER, 506
MY SAVIOR'S LOVE, 512
NO ONE UNDERSTANDS, 417
PEARLY GATES, 541
PRECIOUS NAME, 116
SATISFIED, 531
SHOWERS OF BLESSING, 289
SURRENDER, 366
TABERNACLE, 258
THE UNVEILED CHRIST, 169
TRUST IN JESUS, 350
WITHOUT HIM, 332
WONDROUS STORY, 508

8.7.8.7.D.

ALL THE WAY, 460
AUSTRIAN HYMN, 9, 278, 557
BEACH SPRING, 455
BEECHER, 92, 268, 574
BRADBURY, 462
COME, HOLY SPIRIT, 250
CONVERSE, 435
EBENEZER, 211, 475
ELLESDIE, 377, 584
HARRIS, 526
HOLY MANNA, 454, 585
HYFRYDOL, 61, 89, 124, 233
HYMN TO JOY, 1, 215
KINGSTON, 305
NETTLETON, 2

8.7.8.7.D. with Refrain

STORY OF JESUS, 172

8.7.8.7.6.6.6.7.

EIN' FESTE BURG, 26

8.7.8.7.6.6.8.7.

CLOSE TO THEE, 365

8.7.8.7.7.7.

IRBY, 155

8.7.8.7.8.7.

LAUDA ANIMA (Andrews), 3
REGENT SQUARE, 131, 225, 241, 276

SICILIAN MARINERS, 601

8.7.8.7.8.7.7.

CWM RHONDDA, 51, 292
DIVINUM MYSTERIUM, 118

8.7.8.7.8.8.7.

MIT FREUDEN ZART, 6

8.7.8.7.8.8.7.7.

ERMUNTRE DICH, 129
W ZLOBIE LEZY, 143

8.7.8.7.8.8.8.7.

IVES, 400

8.8.4.4.6. with Refrain

KINGS OF ORIENT, 166

8.8.6.6.D.

O HEARKEN YE, 150

8.8.6.8.8.6.6.

ARIEL, 110

8.8.7.7.8.

THE JOY OF THE LORD, 411

8.8.8.

BE STILL AND KNOW, 343

8.8.8.5.

ACCLAIM, 75

8.8.8.6. with Refrain

DUNBAR, 370
HE LIFTED ME, 522

8.8.8.7.

GREATER IS HE, 255
THANK YOU, 98

8.8.8.8.

AFFIRMATIVE, 480
BE CALM MY SOUL, 421
TRYGGARE KAN INGEN VARA, 44

8.8.8.8.6.

ST. MARGARET, 374

8.8.8.8.8.8.

MELITA, 402, 575
ST. CATHERINE, 279

8.8.8.8.8.8. with Refrain

SAGINA, 203

8.8.8.9. with Refrain

NORRIS, 373

8.8.9.8.

APPALACHIA, 401
GO NOW, 610

8.8.12.8.

GO YE, 301

8.10.8.10.

ONLY BELIEVE, 420

9.4.9.4. with Refrain

FOOTSTEPS, 470
I'LL FLY AWAY, 554

9.6.8.6. with Refrain

SUNSHINE, 499

9.7.9.6.

WE WILL GLORIFY, 72

9.7.9.7. with Refrain

SWEETEST NAME, 488

9.7.9.7.9.8. with Refrain

I'LL GO, 444

9.8.9.8.

DET AR ETT FAST ORD, 291
HANNAH (Refrain only), 218

9.8.9.8. with Refrain

ADA, 520
REDEEMED, 521

9.8.9.8.8.8.

NEUMARK, 600

9.9.9.4. with Refrain

CALVARY, 338

9.9.9.5. with Refrain

GLORY TO HIS NAME, 527

9.9.9.9. with Refrain

FREELY, FREELY, 447
MOODY, 201
SWEET BY AND BY, 553

9.9.11.11. with Refrain

PRAYING FOR YOU, 431

9.10.9.9. with Refrain

ASSURANCE, 345

9.10.9.10.

MORRIS, 392

9.10.10.10.

SWEETEST NAME, 95

9.11.11.10.

CASTLE, 154

10.6.10.6. with Refrain

NO NOT ONE, 422

10.6.10.7. with Refrain

NEIDLINGER, 162

10.7.10.6. with Refrain
LORDSHIP OF CHRIST, 360

10.7.10.7.
TO BE LIKE JESUS, 384

10.7.10.7. with Refrain
I AM THINE, 358
SCHULER, 452

10.7.10.8.
CARMEL, 577

10.8.8.7.7. with Refrain
MESSAGE, 296

10.8.10.7. with Refrain
CALLING TODAY, 327

10.9.10.8. with Refrain
POWER IN THE BLOOD, 191

10.9.10.9.
SUNSET, 548

10.9.10.9. with Refrain
ORWIGSBURG, 430
RONDINELLA, 387
SHOWALTER, 354

10.10.9.6. with Refrain
ELLSWORTH, 511

10.10.10. with Alleluias
SINE NOMINE, 546

10.10.10.10.
CRUCIFER, 304
ELLERS, 439, 604
EVENTIDE, 419
MAORI, 438
MORECAMBE, 249
NATIONAL HYMN, 573
PENITENTIA, 325
SLANE, 382
THY LOVING KINDNESS, 69
WOODLANDS, 27

10.10.10.10. with Refrain
GLADNESS, 357
GLORY SONG, 539
LIVING, 372
WHITTLE, 351

10.10.10.10.10.10.
FINLANDIA, 347

10.10.10.15.
I KNOW A FOUNT, 194

10.10.11.11.
HANOVER, 17
LYONS, 10

10.11.10.10.
DAVID, 434

10.11.11.8. with Refrain
GOD'S PEOPLE, 312

10.11.11.11. with Refrain
BINGHAMTON, 352
MACCABEUS, 227

10.12.10.
GERMAN FOLK, 78

11.6.11.6. with Refrain
McCABE, 307

11.7.11.7. with Refrain
CARMICHAEL, 329
THOMPSON, 326

11.8.11.8. with Refrain
GOD LEADS US, 46
KIRKPATRICK, 496
THE BATTLE, 485

11.8.11.9. with Refrain
VILLE DU HAVRE, 493

11.9.11.9. with Refrain
WASHED IN THE BLOOD, 190

11.10.11.8. with Refrain
MUSKOGEE, 408

11.10.11.9.
RUSSIAN HYMN, 33

11.10.11.10.
CONSOLATOR, 416
PEARCE, 240
SANDRINGHAM, 533

11.10.11.10. with Coda
BY GRACE MADE STRONG, 311
TORONTO, 310

11.10.11.10. with Refrain
FAITHFULNESS, 43
HINGHAM, 356
HOW GREAT THOU ART, 4
ONE DAY, 170
RESCUE, 299
TIDINGS, 298

11.10.11.10.11.10.
FINLANDIA (altered), 535

11.10.11.10.11.10.11.10.10.
CANTIQUE DE NOËL, 148

11.10.12.10. with Refrain
HE IS LORD, 105

11.11. with Refrain
REVIVE US AGAIN, 295

11.11.7.7.11.
CROFT, 397

11.11.11.
RESURRECTION CANON, 221

11.11.11.6.
FLEMMING, 264

11.11.11.9. with Refrain
PROMISES, 271

11.11.11.11.
AWAY IN A MANGER, 157
CRADLE SONG, 158
FOUNDATION, 275
GORDON, 364
GREENRIDGE, 140
I LOVE THEE, 362
ST. DENIO, 25

11.11.11.11. with Refrain
BLESSINGS, 563
FISCHER, 436
HIDING IN THEE, 348
I CAN SAFELY GO, 467
SCALES, 294
TO GOD BE THE GLORY, 66

11.11.13.8.9.
SYMPHONY, 283

11.12.11.11.
OPEN OUR EYES, 383

11.12.12.10.
NICAEA, 262

12.8.12.8. with Refrain
McDANIEL, 515

12.8.12.8.10.8.10.8.
JOYFUL NOISE, 23

12.9.6.6.12.9.
WONDROUS LOVE, 177

12.9.12.9. with Refrain
WONDERFUL PEACE, 500

12.10.13.10.
JANICE, 165

12.11.12.11.
KREMSER, 16, 561

12.11.12.11. with Refrain
WEIGLE, 528

12.12.12.6. with Refrain
COMFORTER, 257

13.12.13.12.
IRENE, 534

14.14.4.7.8.
LOBE DEN HERREN, 8

15.15.15.6. with Refrain
BATTLE HYMN, 569

Irregular meter
A PERFECT HEART, 40
ABBA FATHER, 15
ACKLEY, 220
ADAMS, 253
ADESTE FIDELES, 145
ADORE THEE, 597
ALL YOUR ANXIETY, 418
ASSAM, 376
BALM IN GILEAD, 423
BE EXALTED, 5
BE GLORIFIED, 394
BE JOYFUL, 223
BEHOLD THE LAMB, 179
BENEDICTION, 607
BLESS HIS HOLY NAME, 13
BLOTT EN DAG, 56
BOND OF LOVE, 281
BROOKS, 603
BY AND BY, 544
CALVARY COVERS IT, 189
CANE PEAK, 606
CAST THY BURDEN, 598
CATHERINE, 63
CELEBRATE JESUS, 324
CHAUTAUQUA (Refrain only), 22
CHILD OF LOVE, 156
CHILDREN PRAYING, 429
CLAP YOUR HANDS, 24
CLOSER WALK, 380
COME LET US REASON, 591
COMMIT THY WAY, 581
COVER ME, 469
CROWNING DAY, 236
DIAPASON, 246
DISMISSAL, 609
DONA NOBIS PACEM, 32
DUKE'S TUNE, 617
EASTER SONG, 222
EL SHADDAI, 36
ELIZABETH, 510
EMMANUEL, 134
ENGLAND, 39
EXCELLENCE, 456
FAMILY OF GOD, 282
FAYE, 55
FILL MY CUP, 398
FILLMORE, 457
FOR UNTO US, 146
GARDEN, 425
GENTLE SHEPHERD, 458
GLORIFY THY NAME, 29
GO, 308
GO TELL IT, 138
GOD BE WITH YOU, 602
GOD IS SO GOOD, 41
GOD'S WAYS, 621
GRACE, 566
GREAT IS THE LORD, 31
GREATOREX, 623
GREEN, 206
HALLELUJAH CHORUS, 37
HALLOWED BE THE NAME, 84
HARTFORD, 473
HE CARETH FOR YOU, 57
HE GIVETH MORE GRACE, 415
HE IS HERE, 256
HE TOUCHED ME, 504
HEART MELODY, 514
HEAVEN CAME DOWN, 495
HICKS, 93
HIS NAME IS LIFE, 114
HOLY, HOLY, 266
HOW MAJESTIC, 30
I LOVE YOU, LORD, 80
I WONDER AS I WANDER, 139
I'D RATHER HAVE JESUS, 517
IN DULCI JUBILO, 151
IN HIS TIME, 465
IVERSON, 247
JESUS IS KING, 230
JESUS, I COME, 336
JOYFUL SONG, 106
JÜNGST, 144
KING IS COMING, 238
KING OF HEAVEN, 104
KING OF KINGS, 77
LAFFERTY, 42
LEAD ME, LORD, 49
LEMMEL (Refrain only), 335
LET US BREAK BREAD, 323
LET'S JUST PRAISE THE LORD, 107
LORD OF ALL, 359
LOVE OF GOD, 67
MAJESTY, 74
MALOTTE, 426
MANNA, 252
MANNER OF LOVE, 71
MARANATHA, 265
MARGARET, 127
MEECE, 209
MEINECKE, 622
MIEIR, 101
MY TRIBUTE, 11
McCUTCHAN, 593
NAME OF THE LORD, 90
NATIONAL ANTHEM, 576
NUSBAUM, 333
O'SHIELDS, 38
OLD RUGGED CROSS, 186
ONE SMALL CHILD, 164
OUR GOD REIGNS, 229
PASS IT ON, 309
PATRICIA, 513
PAUL, 612
PAX TECUM, 487
PEOPLE NEED THE LORD, 303
PERFECT PEACE, 492
PRAISE YE, 596
QUAM DILECTA, 594
QUIET MOMENT, 592
REACH OUT, 314
RED, 322
REJOICE, 489
RESURRECTION, 213
RING THOSE BELLS, 153
ROLL CALL, 543
ROOM AT THE CROSS, 331
ST. BRENDAN'S, 284
SALSBURY, 578
SCOTT, 381
SECOND COMING, 245
SERVING, 446
SHEPHERD OF LOVE, 464
SING PRAISE, 263
SO BLESSED, 564
SOLI DEO GLORIA, 35
SOMETHING BEAUTIFUL, 519
SOMETIMES ALLELUIA, 115
SOON AND VERY SOON, 551
SPRINGTIME, 396
STAINER, 207
STILLE NACHT, 147
SULLIVAN, 302
SURELY GOODNESS AND MERCY, 45
THAT NAME, 102
THE BLOOD, 192
THE FIRST NOEL, 136
THE NEW 23RD, 53
THE TREES OF THE FIELD, 244
THIS IS THE DAY, 590
THROUGH IT ALL, 507
THY WORD, 272
TUCKER, 300
VICKI, 121
WAY OF THE CROSS, 471
WE SHALL BEHOLD HIM, 237
WE WILL SERVE, 537
WE WILL STAND, 474
WERE YOU THERE?, 181
WHOLE WORLD, 344
WINTON, 611
WONDER OF IT ALL, 65
WONDERFUL GRACE, 198
WOODLAND HILLS, 516
WORSHIP AND BOW DOWN, 14
WORSHIP HIM, 588
WORTHY, 73
WORTHY IS THE LAMB, 180
YESTERDAY, TODAY AND TOMORROW, 523

INDEX OF KEYS

MAJOR KEYS

Key of A

Face to Face, 549
Lo, He Comes with Clouds Descending, 241
Lord, Let Us Now Depart in Peace, 609
The King Is Coming, 238

Key of A flat

All Hail the Power of Jesus' Name (Diadem), 96
Are You Washed in the Blood?, 190
Arise, My Soul, Arise, 199
Because He Lives, 213
Blessed Be the Name, 103
Come and Praise the Lord Our King, 171
Come, Christians, Join to Sing, 108
Gloria Patri (Meinecke), 622
Glory to His Name, 527
He Rose Triumphantly, 219
Heavenly Spirit, Gentle Spirit, 254
Holy Ghost, with Light Divine, 248
Hosanna, Loud Hosanna, 174
How Firm a Foundation, 275
I Am Trusting Thee, Lord Jesus, 346
I Will Sing of My Redeemer, 506
If My People's Hearts Are Humbled, 574
I'll Fly Away, 554
Immortal, Invisible, 25
In Remembrance, 322
In the Garden, 425
It Is Good to Sing Thy Praises, 584
Jesus Calls Us, 375
Jesus Loves the Little Children, 580
Jesus, Thy Blood and Righteousness, 193
Leaning on the Everlasting Arms, 354
Love Divine, All Loves Excelling, 92
Majestic Sweetness Sits Enthroned, 109
More Love to Thee, 363
Must Jesus Bear the Cross Alone?, 449
My Savior's Love, 512
O Breath of Life, 291
O for a Thousand Tongues, 76
O, How He Loves You and Me, 513
O That Will Be Glory, 539
O Worship the King, 10
Open My Eyes, That I May See, 381
Praise Ye the Triune God, 264
Precious Lord, Take My Hand, 463
Psalm 136, 63
Redeemed (Kirkpatrick), 521
Saved, Saved!, 530
Since Jesus Came into My Heart, 515
Take the Name of Jesus with You, 116
The Blood Will Never Lose Its Power, 192
The Longer I Serve Him, 518
The Spacious Firmament, 62
The Star-Spangled Banner, 576
Thou Art Worthy, 73
To God Be the Glory, 66
We Bless the Name of Christ, the Lord, 319
When the Roll Is Called Up Yonder, 543
When This Song of Praise Shall Cease, 605
Whiter Than Snow, 436
Who Is He in Yonder Stall?, 168

Key of B flat

A Doxology Canon, 627
All Glory, Laud and Honor, 173
All That Thrills My Soul, 526
America, the Beautiful, 572
Angels from the Realms of Glory, 131
At the Name of Jesus, 235
Battle Hymn of the Republic, 569
Be Exalted, O God, 5
Christ Is Made the Sure Foundation, 276
Fill My Cup, Lord, 398
From Every Stormy Wind That Blows, 432
Glorify Thy Name, 29
Go, 308
God, Our Father, We Adore Thee, 268
God Will Take Care of You, 47
Hallelujah, What a Savior!, 175
Have You Any Room for Jesus?, 328
He Lives, 220
He's Everything to Me, 516
How Great Thou Art, 4
I Gave My Life for Thee, 453
I Know that My Redeemer Liveth, 218
I Sing the Mighty Power of God, 59
In the Cross of Christ I Glory, 184
It Came upon the Midnight Clear, 128
Jesus Is Calling, 327
Jesus Is Coming Again, 239
Just a Closer Walk with Thee, 380
Love Lifted Me, 505
Macedonia, 316
Majesty, 74
My Tribute, 11
O Zion, Haste, 298
Old Time Power, 258
Our Day of Joy Is Here Again, 161
Our God Reigns, 229
Peace, Perfect Peace, 487
Rescue the Perishing, 299
Rock of Ages, 204
Silent Night! Holy Night!, 147
Stand Up, Stand Up for Jesus (Webb), 477
Standing on the Promises, 271
Tell Me the Old, Old Story, 424
The Bond of Love, 281
The Comforter Has Come, 257
The Kingdom of God, 547
The Lord's Prayer, 426
The Old Rugged Cross, 186
The Wise May Bring Their Learning, 583
The Wonder of It All, 65
There Is a Fountain, 196
There Is Power in the Blood, 191
There Shall Be Showers of Blessing, 289
There's a Wideness in God's Mercy, 68
We Are Gathered for Thy Blessing, 258
What Can I Give Him?, 154
Who Is on the Lord's Side?, 484
Worship Christ the Risen King, 225
Worthy Is the Lamb, 180

Key of C

A Charge to Keep I Have, 448
A Mighty Fortress Is Our God, 26
A Nativity Prayer, 126
As for Me and My House, 537
At Calvary, 338
Be Joyful, 223
Be Still and Know, 343
Christ Arose, 216
Christ the Lord Is Risen Today, 217
Christ, We Do All Adore Thee, 597
Clap Your Hands, 24
Come Celebrate Jesus, 324
Come into His Presence, 589
Come, Ye Disconsolate, 416
Dear Lord and Father of Mankind, 427
Emmanuel, 134
Eternal Father, Strong to Save, 575
God of the Ages, 568
Good Shepherd, Take This Little Child, 318
Great Is the Lord, 31
Have Faith in God, 408
He Leadeth Me, 461
Hear Now the Name, 407
Holy, Holy, 266
How Great Our Joy!, 144
How Majestic Is Your Name, 30
I Have Decided to Follow Jesus, 376
Is It the Crowning Day?, 236
It Is Well with My Soul, 493
Jesus Is the Sweetest Name I Know, 95
Jesus Lives, and So Shall I, 224
Jesus Loves Me, 579
Lift High the Cross, 304
Lord, We Praise You, 83
Make Me a Blessing, 452
May Jesus Christ Be Praised, 87
Morning Has Broken, 60
O God, Our Help in Ages Past, 52
O Holy Night!, 148
O Sacred Head, Now Wounded, 178
O the Deep, Deep Love of Jesus (Bunessan), 212
One Day!, 170
People Need the Lord, 303
Praise the Name of Jesus, 93
Rejoice, the Lord Is King, 228
She Will Be Called Blessed, 534

Sometimes "Alleluia", 115
Spirit of God, Descend upon My Heart, 249
Sweet Hour of Prayer, 433
The Lord Bless You and Keep You, 607
The Majesty and Glory of Your Name, 35
The New 23rd, 53
The Solid Rock (Melita), 402
Thou Wilt Keep Him in Perfect Peace (Perfect Peace), 492
Under His Wings, 356
We Come, O Christ, to You, 117
We Shall Behold Him, 237
What If It Were Today?, 245
When He Shall Come, 240
When We All Get to Heaven, 542
While Shepherds Watched Their Flocks, 135
Wonderful Grace of Jesus, 198
Yesterday, Today and Tomorrow, 523

Key of D

A Communion Hymn for Christmas, 140
Adoration, 165
Another Year Is Dawning, 567
Anywhere with Jesus, 467
Benediction, 612
Beyond the Sunset, 548
Blessed Assurance, 345
Break Thou the Bread of Life, 274
Children of the Heavenly Father, 44
Come Holy Spirit, Dove Divine, 320
Come Let Us Reason, 591
Come Let Us Worship and Bow Down, 14
Come, Thou Fount of Every Blessing, 2
Cover Me, 469
God Leads Us Along, 46
God So Loved the World, 207
God the Omnipotent, 33
Grace, Love and Fellowship, 606
Great Is Thy Faithfulness, 43
Hallelujah Chorus, 37
He Careth for You, 57
Hear Our Prayer, O Lord, 614
His Name Is Life, 114
Holy, Holy, Holy, 262
How Sweet the Name of Jesus Sounds, 94
I Am His, and He Is Mine, 490
I Know a Fount, 194
I Know Whom I Have Believed, 409
I Lay My Sins on Jesus, 340
I Surrender All, 366
I Will Call upon the Lord, 38
I Will Praise Him!, 525
I'll Tell the World That I'm a Christian, 300
In His Time, 465
In My Life Lord, Be Glorified, 394
Jesus Shall Reign, 231
Jesus, We Just Want to Thank You, 98
Joy to the World!, 125
Lord, Dismiss Us with Thy Blessing, 601
Make a Joyful Noise, 23
My Faith Looks Up to Thee, 410
Now to the King of Heaven, 595
O to Be Like Thee!, 387
Only One Life, 378
Open Our Eyes, Lord, 383
Pass It On, 309
Praise, My Soul, the King of Heaven, 3
Praise Ye the Name of the Lord, 596
Resurrection Canon, 221
Saved by Grace, 550
Shepherd of Love, 464
Tell Me the Story of Jesus, 172
Tell Out, My Soul, 27
The Day of Resurrection, 226
The First Noel, 136
The Joy of the Lord, 411
The Lord Is in His Holy Temple, 594
The Love of God, 67
There Is a Redeemer, 206
Thou Didst Leave Thy Throne, 127
We Praise Thee, O God, Our Redeemer, 16
We Will Glorify, 72
Welcome, Welcome, 260
What a Wonderful Savior!, 81

Key of D flat

Beneath the Cross of Jesus, 183
God Be with You, 602
He Hideth My Soul, 496
I Just Came to Praise the Lord, 113
I Must Tell Jesus, 430
I Want to Be Like Jesus, 400
I Will Sing of the Mercies, 457
I'd Rather Have Jesus, 517
Jesus Is Lord of All (McClard), 360
Jesus Paid It All, 210
Join All the Glorious Names, 111
Just As I Am, 342
Lead On, O King Eternal, 483
Near to the Heart of God, 497
Nearer, Still Nearer, 392
No One Ever Cared for Me Like Jesus, 528
No One Understands Like Jesus, 417
O Could I Speak the Matchless Worth, 110
Only Believe, 420
Savior, Like a Shepherd Lead Us, 462
The Unveiled Christ, 169
We Gather Together, 561

Key of E flat

A Child of the King, 352
A Christian Home, 535
Abba Father, Abba Father, 15
Abide with Me, 419
All Creatures of Our God and King, 64
All for Jesus, 368
All Things Bright and Beautiful, 578
All Your Anxiety, 418
At the Cross, 188
Be Thou My Vision, 382
Behold the Lamb, 179
Behold, What Manner of Love, 71
Bless His Holy Name, 13
Break Forth, O Beauteous Heavenly Light, 129
Breathe on Me, 251
Bring Back the Springtime, 396
Cast Thy Burden upon the Lord, 598
Come on, Ring Those Bells, 153
Commit Thy Way, 581
Count Your Blessings, 563
Crown Him with Many Crowns, 234
Day by Day, 56
Day by Day - A Prayer, 55
Doxology (Owens), 626
Easter Song, 222
El Shaddai, 36
Fairest Lord Jesus, 88
Faith Is the Victory, 486
Footprints of Jesus, 470
Footsteps of Jesus, 470
Freely, Freely, 447
Gloria Patri (Greatorex), 623
Go Now and Live for the Savior, 610
God Is So Good, 41
God of Our Fathers, 573
God's Ways Are Wonderful, 621
Hallowed Be the Name, 84
Have Thine Own Way, Lord, 371
He Giveth More Grace, 415
Here, O My Lord, I See Thee Face to Face, 325
Hiding in Thee, 348
I Heard the Bells on Christmas Day, 152
I Love Thee, 362
I Love You, Lord, 80
I Will Serve Thee, 446
I Will Sing the Wondrous Story, 508
I'll Go Where You Want Me to Go, 444
In Christ There Is No East or West, 285
In Heavenly Love Abiding, 502
In This Quiet Moment, 592
Jesus, Name Above All Names, 112
Jesus, Thou Joy of Loving Hearts, 501
Lead Me, Lord, 49
Lead Me to Calvary, 176
Let Us Break Bread Together, 323
Lord, Lay Some Soul upon My Heart, 313
Lord, Listen to Your Children Praying, 429
May the Mind of Christ, My Savior, 390
O Master, Let Me Walk with Thee, 451
O Perfect Love, 533
O Thou Joyful, O Thou Wonderful, 119
O Word of God Incarnate, 269
Of the Father's Love Begotten, 118
On Jordan's Stormy Banks, 552
Onward, Christian Soldiers, 479
Praise the Lord! Ye Heavens, Adore Him, 9
Pure and Holy, 437
Reach Your Hand, 582
Redeemed (Ada), 520
Satisfied, 531
Seek Ye First, 42

Sing Praise to God Who Reigns Above, 6
Soldiers of Christ, Arise, 478
Something Beautiful, 519
Surely Goodness and Mercy, 45
Take Time to Be Holy (Slane), 442
Teach Me Thy Way, O Lord, 395
The Church's One Foundation, 277
There's Something About That Name, 102
Thine Is the Glory, 227
This Is My Father's World, 58
This Is the Day, 590
Through It All, 507
Thy Loving Kindness, 69
Thy Word, 272
To Be God's People, 312
To Be Like Jesus, 384
We Are So Blessed, 564
We Give You Thanks, 619
We Have Come into His House, 588
We'll Understand It Better By and By, 544
Were You There?, 181
We've a Story to Tell to the Nations, 296
Where the Spirit of the Lord Is, 253

Key of F

A Perfect Heart, 40
A Shelter in the Time of Storm, 353
A Thousand Candles, 159
According to Thy Gracious Word, 321
Am I a Soldier of the Cross?, 482
Angels We Have Heard on High, 132
Aspiration Canon, 391
Away in a Manger (Away in a Manger), 157
Away in a Manger (Cradle Song), 158
Be Still, My Soul, 347
Blessed the Nation, 577
Blessing and Honor, 78
Blest Be the Tie That Binds, 286
Breathe on Me, Breath of God, 259
Child of Love, 156
Cleanse Me (Maori), 438
Come, Holy Spirit, 250
Come, Thou Almighty King, 267
Come, We That Love the Lord, 18
Come, Ye Thankful People, Come, 559
Draw Nigh to God, 397
Faithful Men, 288
Father, I Adore You, 265
Fill Me Now, 261
For God So Loved, 205
For Health and Strength, 566
Gentle Shepherd, 458
Give Me Jesus, 443
Glorious Is Thy Name, 85
Glorious Things of Thee Are Spoken, 278
Go, Tell It on the Mountain, 138
Good Christian Men, Rejoice, 151
Great Are You, O Lord, 39
Greater Is He That Is in Me, 255
Hail the Day That Sees Him Rise, 232
Happy the Home When God Is There, 536
Hark! the Herald Angels Sing, 133
He Is Coming, 246
He Touched Me, 504
Heaven Came Down, 495
He's Got the Whole World in His Hands, 344
His Name Is Wonderful, 101
Holy Bible, Book Divine, 273
Holy God, We Praise Thy Name, 12
Holy Lord, 32
I Am a Soldier of the Cross!, 480
I Am Praying for You, 431
I Love Thy Kingdom, Lord, 280
I'll Live for Him, 370
In Thanksgiving, Let Us Praise Him, 557
Jesus Is Born, 149
Jesus Is Lord of All (Gaither), 359
Jesus, Stand Among Us, 586
Lavish Love, Abundant Beauty, 61
Let the Words of My Mouth, 618
Let Your Heart Be Broken, 315
Let's Just Praise the Lord, 107
Like a River Glorious, 494
Living for Jesus, 372
Lo! How a Rose E'er Blooming, 160
May the Grace of Christ, Our Savior, 608
Moment by Moment, 351
My Country, 'Tis of Thee, 571
My Jesus, I Love Thee, 364
Near the Cross, 385
Nearer, My God, to Thee, 393
No, Not One!, 422
Now Thank We All Our God, 556
Now Unto the King, 611
O Happy Day!, 532
O Jesus, I Have Promised, 369
O Little Town of Bethlehem, 141
Once in Royal David's City, 155
Only Trust Him, 330
Our Great Savior, 89
Peace Like a River, 498
Psalm 42, 401
Reach Out and Touch, 314
Rejoice in the Lord Always, 489
Revive Us Again, 295
Rise Up, O Church (Men) of God, 293
Set My Soul Afire, 294
So Send I You, 310
So Send I You - by Grace Made Strong, 311
Soon and Very Soon, 551
Spirit Divine, Hear Our Prayer, 615
Spirit of the Living God, 247
Sun of My Soul, 412
Take My Life and Let It Be, 379
Take Time to Be Holy (Holiness), 441
The Advent of Our God, 120
The Family of God, 282
The Lord Whom We Love, 603
The Lord's My Shepherd, I'll Not Want, 50
The Savior Is Waiting, 329
The Solid Rock (Solid Rock), 404
There Is a Balm in Gilead, 423
There Is No Name So Sweet on Earth, 100
This Child We Dedicate to Thee, 317
Thou Wilt Keep Him in Perfect Peace (Duke's Tune), 617
Trust and Obey, 349
Trusting Jesus, 355
Turn Your Eyes upon Jesus, 335
We Are God's People, 283
We Shall See His Lovely Face, 545
We Thank You, Lord, 565
We Will Stand, 474
What a Friend We Have in Jesus, 435
When I Survey the Wondrous Cross, 185
Where He Leads Me, 373
Wherever He Leads I'll Go, 367
While We Are Waiting, Come, 242
Without Him, 332
Wonderful Words of Life, 270

Key of G

Alas! and Did My Savior Bleed?, 208
All Hail the Power of Jesus' Name (Coronation), 97
All People That on Earth Do Dwell, 20
All the Way My Savior Leads Me, 460
Alleluia, 91
Alleluia! Alleluia!, 215
Alleluia! Sing to Jesus, 233
Amazing Grace, 202
And Can It Be?, 203
As with Gladness Men of Old, 163
Be Calm My Soul, 421
Begin, My Tongue, Some Heavenly Theme, 70
Brethren, We Have Met to Worship, 585
Calvary Covers It All, 189
Cleanse Me (Ellers), 439
Close to Thee, 365
Come, All Christians, Be Committed, 455
Come, Thou Long-Expected Jesus, 124
Doxology, 624
Doxology (Alternate Rhythm), 625
Faith of Our Fathers, 279
For All the Saints, 546
For the Beauty of the Earth, 560
For Unto Us a Child Is Born, 146
Glorious Is Thy Name, Most Holy, 454
Go Ye into All the World, 301
God of Grace and God of Glory, 292
Grace Greater Than Our Sin, 201
Guide Me, O Thou Great Jehovah, 51
He Is Lord, 105
He Keeps Me Singing, 488
He Lifted Me, 522
He the Pearly Gates Will Open, 541
Hear Our Prayer, O Heavenly Father, 616
Higher Ground, 399
His Way, 54
His Way with Thee, 333
I Am Thine, O Lord, 358
I Love to Tell the Story, 297
I Need Thee Every Hour, 428

I Would Be Like Jesus, 388
In My Heart There Rings a Melody, 514
In the Name of the Lord, 90
Infant Holy, Infant Lowly, 143
Isaiah 6:3, 22
It Took a Miracle, 524
Jesus, I Am Resting, Resting, 503
Jesus, I Come, 336
Jesus, I My Cross Have Taken, 377
Jesus Is All the World to Me, 510
Jesus Loves Even Me, 357
Jesus Saves!, 306
Jesus, the Very Thought of Thee, 79
Joyful, Joyful, We Adore Thee, 1
King of Heaven, Lord Most High, 104
Lamb of Glory, 197
Lord, I'm Coming Home, 341
Lord, Speak to Me, 450
Lord, Thy Church on Earth Is Seeking, 305
More About Jesus, 389
My Faith Has Found a Resting Place, 405
My Hope Is in the Lord, 406
Nothing But the Blood, 195
Now I Belong to Jesus, 511
O Come, All Ye Faithful, 145
O Come, Let Us Adore Him, 82
O for a Heart to Praise My God, 440
O Hearken Ye, 150
O, How I Love Jesus, 529
O Love That Will Not Let Me Go, 374
O Worship the Lord, 593
Our God Has Made Us One, 287
Pass Me Not, 337
Praise Him! Praise Him!, 106
Praise the Savior, 75
Praise to the Lord, the Almighty, 8
Reaching for Excellence, 456
Rejoice, Ye Pure in Heart, 562
Room at the Cross for You, 331
Savior, Again to Thy Dear Name, 604
Send the Light, 307
Share His Love, 302
Since I Have Been Redeemed, 339
Softly and Tenderly, 326
Something for Thee, 445
Stand Up and Bless the Lord, 21
Stand Up, Stand Up for Jesus (Geibel), 481
Sunshine in My Soul, 499
Sweet By and By, 553
Sweet, Sweet Spirit, 252
The Birthday of a King, 162
The King of Love My Shepherd Is, 468
The Way of the Cross Leads Home, 471
The Word Made Flesh, 121
'Tis So Sweet to Trust in Jesus, 350
Victory in Jesus, 473
We Are the Reason, 209
We Give Thee but Thine Own, 620
We Worship and Adore You, 19
We're Marching to Zion, 555
When I Can Read My Title Clear, 538
Wonderful Peace, 500
Ye Servants of God, 17

MINOR KEYS

Key of A minor

Jesus Is King, 230

Key of C minor

In His Cross I Glory, 187
Jesus, Priceless Treasure, 413
They'll Know We Are Christians by Our Love, 284

Key of D minor

He Is Here, He Is Here, 256
Sing Praise, 263
What Wondrous Love Is This, 177

Key of E minor

Jesus, Lover of My Soul, 466
King of Kings, 77
O Come, Messiah, Come Again, 243
O Come, O Come, Emmanuel, 123
O Sing a Song of Bethlehem, 167
O the Deep, Deep Love of Jesus (Ebenezer), 211
One Small Child, 164
Search Me, 434
The Battle Belongs to the Lord, 485
The Battle Is the Lord's, 472
The Trees of the Field, 244
We Three Kings, 166
What Child Is This?, 137

Key of F minor

Come, Ye Sinners, Poor and Needy, 334
Once to Every Man and Nation, 475
The God of Abraham Praise, 34

Key of G minor

All Praise to Our Redeeming Lord, 587
I Heard the Voice of Jesus Say, 414
I Wonder as I Wander, 139
If You Will Only Let God Guide You, 600

Worship & Celebrate

INDEX OF AUTHORS, COMPOSERS, SOURCES, TRANSLATORS AND ARRANGERS

Ackley, Alfred Henry (1887-1960): 220
Ackley, Bentley DeForest (1872-1958): 219, 388
Adam, Adolphe (1803-1856): 148
Adams, Sarah Flower (1805-1848): 393
Adams, Stephen R. (1943-): 253
Addison, Joseph (1672-1719): 62
Adkins, Donna (1940-): 29
Adoramus Te: 597
Ahlwén, Elsie (1905-): 541
Ahnfelt, Oscar (1813-1882): 56
Akers, Doris Mae (1922-): 252
Alexander, Cecil Frances Humphreys (1818-1895): 155, 375, 578
Alexander, James Waddell (1804-1859): 178
Alford, Henry (1810-1871): 559
Allen, Chester G. (1838-1878): 106
Allen, David Jonathan (1941-): 15, 303, 324, 379, 382, 383, 437, 442, 479, 591
Allen, George Nelson (1812-1877): 449, 463
American Folk hymn: 177
American melody, Traditional: 2, 196, 202, 275, 334, 455, 529, 538, 552, 569
Andrews, Mark (1875-1939): 3
Anonymous: 343, 583
Appalachian carol: 139
Appalachian Folk melody: 401
Appalachian melody, Traditional: 230
Arne, Thomas Augustus (1710-1778): 482
Atkins, George, (18th century): 585
Atkinson, Frederick Cook (1841-1897): 249

Babcock, Maltbie Davenport (1858-1901): 58
Bach, Johann Sebastian (1685-1750): 178
Baker, Henry (1835-1910): 501
Baker, Henry Williams (1821-1877): 118, 468
Baker, Theodore (1851-1934): 160, 561, 597
Ball, Diane (1941-): 465
Ballinger, Bruce (1945-): 588
Barham-Gould, Arthur Cyril (1891-1953): 390
Baring-Gould, Sabine (1834-1924): 479
Barker, Brenda Faye (1959-): 63
Barker, Kenneth Paul (1955-): 12, 55, 63, 231, 279, 318, 434, 612, 628
Barlowe, Joseph (1941-): 121, 129, 143, 439, 534, 577, 604
Barnby, Joseph (1838-1896): 87, 533
Bartlett, Eugene Monroe, Jr. (1918-): 294
Bartlett, Eugene Monroe, Sr. (1895-1941): 473
Bateman, Christian Henry (1813-1889): 108
Bates, Katherine Lee (1859-1929): 572
Batya, Naomi (1961-): 77
Baumbach, Adolph (1830-1880): 618
Baxter, Lydia (1809-1874): 116
Beethoven, Ludwig van (1770-1827): 1, 215, 608
Bennard, George (1873-1958): 186
Bennett, Sanford Fillmore (1836-1898): 553
Benson, Louis F. (1855-1930): 167
Berg, Carolina Sandell (1832-1903): 44, 56
Bernard of Clairvaux (1091-1153): 79, 501
Bethune, George W. (1805-1862): 100
Bickersteth, Edward Henry (1825-1906): 487
Bilhorn, Peter Philip (1865-1936): 508
Billings, William (1746-1800): 480
Black, James Milton (1856-1938): 543
Blanchard, Richard Eugene (1925-): 398
Blandy, E.W. (19th century): 373
Bliss, Philip Paul (1838-1876): 175, 270, 357, 453, 493, 506
Blom, Frederick Arvid (1867-1927): 541
Blomquist, Joel (1840-1930): 254, 291
Bock, Fred (1939-): 283
Bode, John Ernest (1816-1874): 369
Bohemian Brethren's *Kirchengesänge* (1566), Berlin: 6
Bolks, Richard (1934-): 59, 561
Bonar, Horatius (1808-1889): 325, 340, 414
Borop, Niles (1956-): 104, 287
Borthwick, Jane Laurie (1813-1897): 347
Bottome, Frank (1823-1894): 257
Bourgeois, Louis (1510- 1561): 20, 624, 625
Bowring, John (1792-1872): 184,
Bradbury, William Batchelder (1816-1868): 100, 273, 342, 404, 433, 461, 462, 579, 605
Brahms, Johannes (1833-1897): 283
Breck, Carrie E. (1855-1934): 549
Bridgers, Luther Burgess (1884-1948): 488
Bridges, Matthew (1800-1894): 234
Broadwood, Lucy (19th century): 167
Brock, Blanche Kerr (1888-1958): 548
Brock, Virgil P. (1887-1978): 548
Brooks, Phillips (1835-1893): 126, 141
Brown, Charles F. (1942-): 312, 314
Brown, Mary (19th century): 444
Brumley, Albert E. (1905-): 554
Budry, Edmond Louis (1854-1932): 227
Buell, Harriet Eugenia (1834-1910): 352
Bullinger, Ethelbert William (1837-1913): 346
Burleigh, Harry T. (1866-1949): 547
Burt, Alfred S. (1920-1954): 150
Burton, John, Sr. (1773-1822): 273
Butler, Aubrey Lee (1933-): 520
Byrne, Mary Elizabeth (1880-1931): 382

Caldbeck, George Thomas (1852-1918): 487
Caldwell, Mary E. (1909-): 122
Calkin, Jean Baptiste (1827-1905): 152
Campbell, Thomas (1777-1844): 203
Canaidau y Cyssegr (1839), John Roberts': 25
Cantica Laudis (1850), Mason and Webb's: 620
Cantus Diversi (1751), Wade's: 82
Card, Michael (1957-): 36
Carlson, Nathaniel (1879-1957): 541
Carman, (1956-): 114
Carmichael, Ralph Richard (1927-): 53, 329, 516
Carter, Russell Kelso (1849-1926): 271
Cason, Don (1954-): 154, 242
Caswall, Edward (1814-1878): 79, 87
Cennick, John (1718-1755): 241
Chambers, Brent (1948-): 5
Chandler, John (1806-1876): 120
Chapman, J. Wilbur (1859-1918): 89, 170
Charles, Elizabeth Rundle (1828-1896): 264
Charlesworth, Vernon J. (1839-1915): 353
Chisholm, Thomas Obediah (1866-1960): 43, 372, 387, 400
Chopin, Frederic (1810-1849): 616
Chorley, Henry F. (1808-1872): 33

Christiansen, Avis Marguerite Burgeson (1895-): 378
Christian Harmony (1805), Ingalls': 362
Christmas Carols (1833), W. Sandys': 136
Clark, William H. (19th century): 103
Clarkson, Edith Margaret (1915-): 2, 117, 140, 310, 311, 472, 568
Clayton, Norman John (1903-): 406, 511, 545
Clephane, Elizabeth Cecelia (1830-1869): 183
Cloninger, Claire (1942-): 105, 242, 318, 324, 557, 574
Cluff, Samuel O'Malley (1837-1910): 431
Coelho, Terrye (1952-): 265
Coffin, Charles (1676-1749): 120
Coffin, Henry Sloane (1877-1954): 123
Coffman, Samuel Frederick (1872-1954): 319
Collection of Church Music (1851), Henry W. Greatorex's: 70, 321
Columbian Harmony (1825), William Moore's: 454
Colvin, Herbert (1923-): 10
Conkey, Ithamar (1815-1867): 184
Conty, Sophie (1961-): 77
Converse, Charles Crozat (1832-1918): 435
Cooke, Oliver (1873-1945): 194
Cooper, W. G. (19th century): 500
Cornell, W. D. (19th century): 500
Cory, Julia Cady (1882-1963): 16
Courtney, Ragan (1941-): 322
Cowper, William (1731-1800): 54, 196
Cox, Frances Elizabeth (1812-1897): 6
Croft, Colbert (1941-): 397
Croft, Joyce (1944-): 397
Croft, William (1678-1727): 17, 52
Croly, George (1780-1860): 249
Crosby, Fanny Jane (1820-1915): 66, 106, 172, 299, 327, 337, 345, 358, 365, 385, 443, 460, 496, 520, 521, 550
Crouch, Andraé (1945-): 11, 13, 192, 507, 551
Crüger, Johann (1598-1662): 224, 413, 556
Cull, Robert (1949-): 383
Culverwell, Andrew (1944-): 153, 469
Cummings, William Hayman (1831-1915): 133
Cushing, William Orcutt (1823-1902): 348, 356
Cutler, Henry Stephen (1824-1902): 316

Damascus, John of (c. 696-754): 226
Darwall, John (1731-1789): 111, 117, 228
Dauermann, Stuart (1944-): 244
de Giardini, Felice (1716-1796): 267
de Gravelles, Elizabeth (1942-): 534, 537, 577
Dearle, Edward (1806-1891): 325
Di Pego, Gerald (20th century): 582
Dix, William Chatterton (1837-1898): 137, 163, 233
Dixon, Helen Cadbury Alexander (1877-1969): 467
Doane, William Howard (1832-1915): 66, 116, 299, 337, 358, 363, 385, 424
Doddridge, Phillip (1702-1751): 532, 595
Doherty, Dave (1951-): 14
Dorsey, Thomas A. (1899-): 463
Douglas, Charles Winfred (1867-1944): 118
Douglas, Robert Franklin (1941-): 76, 84, 90, 162, 185, 322, 397, 438, 485, 550
Doxology, Jewish: 34
Draper, William Henry (1855-1933): 64
Dubois, Theodore (1837-1924): 597
Dudley-Smith, Timothy (1926-): 27
Duffield, George, Jr. (1818-1888): 477, 481
Dunbar, C.R. (19th century): 370
Dunlop, Merrill Everett (1905-): 378
Dutch Folk song, Traditional: 566
Dwight, John Sullivan (1813-1893): 148
Dwight, Timothy (1752-1817): 280
Dykes, John Bacchus (1823-1876): 79, 262, 402, 414, 468, 536, 575

Edmunds, Lidie H. (19th century): 405
Edson, Lewis (1748-1820): 199
Elijah (1846), Felix Mendelssohn's: 598
Ellerton, John (1826-1893): 33, 533, 604
Elliot, Emily Elizabeth Steele (1836-1897): 127
Elliott, Charlotte (1789-1871): 342
Elliott, Ruth (1887-): 454
Ellis, Peter (1950-): 61
Ellor, James (1819-1899): 96
Elvey, George Job (1816-1893): 234, 478, 559
English, Tina (1952-): 156
English carol, Traditional: 136, 137
English Folk song: 205
English melody, Traditional: 39
Evans, David (1874-1948): 108
Everett, Asa B. (1828-1875): 470
Excell, Edwin Othello (1851-1921): 202, 339, 563

Faber, Frederick William (1814-1863): 68, 279
Falk, Johannes D. (1768-1826): 119
Farjeon, Eleanor (1881-1965): 60
Farnsworth, Bob (1952-): 437
Fawcett, John (1740-1817): 286, 601
Featherston, William Ralph (1846-1873): 364
Fettke, Thomas Eugene (1941-): 35, 60, 89, 97, 105, 123, 140, 146, 165, 212, 237, 243, 568, 606
Filitz, Friedrich (1804-1876): 586
Fillmore, James Henry (1849-1936): 218, 457
Fischer, William Gustavus (1835-1912): 297, 436
Flemming, Friedrich Ferdinand (1778-1813): 264
Flint, Annie Johnson (1862-1932): 415
Folk song, Traditional: 380
Fosdick, Harry Emerson (1878-1969): 292
Foundling Hospital Collection (1796): 9
Fox, Baynard L. (1932-1982): 300
Francis, Samuel Trevor (1834-1925): 211, 212
Franck, Johann (1618-1677): 413
Franz, Ignace (1719-1790): 12
Frazer, George West (1830-1896): 268
French carol, Traditional: 132
French melody, Traditional: 132, 156
Fry, Steve (1954-): 15

Gabriel, Charles Hutchinson (1856-1932): 307, 399, 471, 512, 515, 522, 539
Gaelic melody, Traditional: 60, 212, 568
Gaither, Gloria (1942-): 90, 98, 102, 107, 114, 213, 238, 250, 282, 359, 446, 458, 519, 564
Gaither, William J. (1936-): 98, 102, 107, 114, 213, 238, 250, 282, 359, 446, 458, 504, 518, 519, 564
Gardiner, William (1770-1853): 10
Garrett, Les (1944-): 590
Gauntlett, Henry John (1805-1876): 155
Geibel, Adam (1855-1933): 481
Geistliche Kirchengesäng (1599), Cologne: 64
Geistliche Kirchengesäng (1623), Cologne: 160
Gellert, Christian Furchtegott (1715-1769): 224
Genevan Psalter (1551): 20, 624, 625
Gerhardt, Paul (1607-1676): 178
German carol, Traditional: 144
German carol (16th century): 160
German Folk song: 78, 221
German hymn, Anonymous: 88
German melody (14th century): 151
German melody, Traditional: 75, 144, 413
Gesangbuch der Herzogl (1784), Württemburg: 59, 174

Gibson, James C. (1944-): 345, 494
Gilman, Samuel (1791-1858): 317
Gilmore, Joseph Henry (1834-1918): 461
Girard, Chuck (1943-): 115
Gladden, Washington (1836-1918): 451
Gläser, Carl Gotthelf (1784-1829): 76, 440, 587
Gloria Patri (2nd century), Traditional: 622, 623
Gordon, Adoniram Judson (1836-1895): 364
Goss, John (1800-1880): 484
Gottschalk, Louis Moreau (1829-1869): 248, 605
Grant, Amy (1960-): 272
Grant, David (1833-1893): 50
Grant, Robert (1779-1838): 10
Grape, John Thomas (1835-1915): 210
Greatorex, Henry Wellington (1813-1858): 623
Greatorex, Walter (1877-1949): 27
Greek melody, Traditional: 340
Green, Lilly (1951-): 84
Green, Melody (20th century): 206
Greer, Bruce (1961-): 174, 391, 483
Gregorian Chant: 185
Grétry, André (1741-1831): 405
Groves, Alexander (1842-1909): 274
Grüber, Franz Xaver (1787-1863): 147
Gurney, Dorothy Frances Blomfield (1858-1932): 533

Hall Elvina Mabel (1820-1889): 210
Hall, O.D. (1936-): 267
Hanby, Benjamin Russell (1833-1867): 168
Handel, George Frederick (1685-1759): 37, 125, 135, 146, 218, 227
Hankey, Arabella Catherine (1834-1911): 297, 424
Harkin, Danna (20th century): 401
Harkness, Robert (1880-1961): 61, 89, 124, 233
Harris, Margaret Jenkins (1903-): 525
Harris, Thoro (1874-1955): 526
Hart, Barbara B. (1916-): 535
Hart, Joseph (1712-1768): 334
Hassler, Hans Leo (1564-1612): 178
Hastings, Thomas (1784-1872): 109, 204, 319, 416, 432
Hatch, Edwin (1835-1889): 251, 259
Hatton, John (c. 1710-1793): 231
Havergal, Frances Ridley (1836-1879): 346, 379, 450, 453, 484, 494, 567
Hawks, Annie Sherwood (1835-1918): 428
Haydn, Franz Joseph (1732-1809): 9, 62, 278, 557
Haydn, Johann Michael (1737-1806): 10
Hayes, Mark (1953-): 234
Hayford, Jack Williams (1934-): 74, 225, 407
Head, Bessie Porter (1850-1936): 291
Hearn, Naida (1944-): 112
Heber, Reginald (1783-1826): 262
Hebrew Folk song, Ancient: 77
Hebrew melody, Traditional: 34, 472
Hedge, Frederick H. (1805-1890): 26
Helmore, Thomas (1811-1890): 123, 243
Helvering, Sandi Patti (1956-): 90
Hemy, Henri Frederick (1818-1888): 279
Henderson, Gerald Samuel (1941-): 32, 39, 54, 78, 149, 205, 221, 230, 246, 263, 480, 565, 627
Herrell, N.B. (1877-1954): 169
Herring, Anne (1945-): 222
Herrington, Leland Howard (1941-): 71, 179, 256, 343, 457, 578
Hewitt, Eliza Edmunds (1851-1920): 389, 499, 542
Hicks, Roy, Jr. (20th century): 93
Hine, Stuart Wesley Keene (1899-): 4
Hodges, Edward (1796-1867): 1, 215
Hoffman, Elisha Albright (1839-1929): 81, 190, 354, 430, 527
Holck, Douglas Allen (1943-): 66
Holcomb, Steve (1952-): 16
Holden, Oliver (1765-1844): 97
Hollihan, James (1955-): 474
Hopkins, Edward J. (1818-1901): 439, 604
Hopkins, John Henry, Jr. (1820-1891): 166
How, William Walsham (1823-1897): 269, 546, 620
Howe, Julia Ward (1819-1910): 569
Hoyle, Richard Birch (1875-1939): 227
Hudson, Mike (1950-): 437
Hudson, Ralph E. (1843-1901): 103, 188, 370, 531
Huff, Ronn (1938-): 235, 442
Hugg, George C. (1848-1907): 422
Hughes, John (1873-1932): 51, 292
Hull, Eleanor Henrietta (1860-1935): 382
Husband, John Jenkins (1760-1825): 295
Hussey, Jennie Evelyn (1874-1958): 176
Hustad, Donald Paul (1918-): 139, 426
Hutson, Wihla (1901-): 150
Hymns for the Young (1836), Dorothy A Thrupp's: 462

Indian Folk melody: 376
Ingalls, Jeremiah (1764-1828): 362
Irish Folk melody: 382, 442
Irish hymn: Ancient: 382
Irvine, Jessie Seymour (1836-1887): 50
Israeli Fok song: 263
Iverson, Daniel (1890-): 247
Ives, David Livingstone (1921-): 400

Jackson, Robert (1842-1914): 259
James, Mary D. (1810-1883): 368
James, Michael (1941-): 329, 401, 406
Johnson, Linda Lee (1947-): 35, 105
Johnston, Julia Harriette (1849-1919): 201
Jones, Lewis Edgar (1865-1936): 191
Joy, Edward Henry (1871-1949): 418
Judas, Maccabbaeus (1746), George Frederick Handel's: 227
Jude, William Herbert (1851-1922): 375
Judson, Adoniram (1788-1850): 320
Jüngst, Hugo (1853-1923): 144

Kaiser, Kurt Frederic (1934-): 57, 223, 260, 309, 311, 396, 456, 467, 513, 537, 573, 581, 582, 603, 610, 621, 628
Karlsson, Evie (1956-): 159
Katholisches Gesangbuch (1774), Vienna: 12, 412
Katholisches Gesangbuch (1828), Würzburg: 87
Katterjohn, Henry (1869-1931): 119
Keble, John (1792-1866): 412
Kelly, Thomas (1769-1855): 75
Ken, Thomas (1637-1710): 624, 625, 626, 627
Kentucky Harmony (1816): 538
Kethe, William (? -1593): 20
Key, Francis Scott (1779-1843): 576
Kilpatrick, Bob (1952-): 394
Kirchengesänge (1566), Bohemian Brethren's, Berlin: 6
Kirkland, Camp (1846-): 228
Kirkpatrick, William James (1838-1921): 103, 158, 176, 257, 306, 341, 350, 387, 405, 496, 521
Kitchin, George W. (1827-1912): 304
Klein, Laurie (1950-): 80
Knapp, Phoebe Palmer (1839-1908): 345
Kocher, Conrad (1786-1872): 163, 560
Kohler, Emmy (1858-1925): 159
Kremser, Edward (1838-1914): 16, 561
Kretz, Vivian (20th century): 492

Ladd, Debi Parker (1961-): 63
Lafferty, Karen (1948-): 42
Lapp, Louise (19th century): 547

Lathbury, Mary Artemisia (1841-1913): 22, 274
Latin carol (14th century): 151
Latin hymn: 123, 145, 276
Latin poem, Medieval: 178
Leavitt, Joshua (1794-1873): 584
Leech, Bryan Jeffery (1931-): 283, 315, 456, 536
LeFevre, Mylon R. (1944-): 332
Lehman, Frederick M. (1868-1953): 67
Lemmel, Helen Howarth (1864-1961): 335
Liles, Dwight (1957-): 104
Lillenas, Haldor (1885-1959): 198
Linn, Joseph (1945-): 203
Lloyd, Eva B. (1912-): 455
Loizeaux, Alfred Samuel (1877-1962): 268
Long, Lela (19th century): 95
Longfellow, Henry Wadsworth (1807-1882): 152
Longstaff, William Dunn (1822-1894): 441, 442
Lowden, Carl Harold (1883-1963): 372
Lowell, James Russel (1819-1891): 475
Lowry, Robert (1826-1899): 195, 216, 428, 445, 460, 555
Luther, Martin (1483-1546): 26
Lutkin, Peter Christian (1858-1931): 607
Lvov, Alexis F. (1799-1870): 33
Lyon, Meyer (1751-1799): 34, 472
Lyra Davidica (1708), London: 217
Lyte, Henry Francis (1793-1847): 3, 377, 419

Mackay, William Paton (1839-1885): 295
Madan, Martin (1725-1790): 241
Main, Hubert Platt (1839-1925): 377
Maker, Frederick Charles (1844-1927): 183, 427
Malan, Henri Abraham César (1787-1864): 379
Malotte, Albert Hay (1895-1964): 426
Mann, Arthur Henry (1850-1929): 369
Maori melody: 438
Marsh, Charles Howard (1886-1956): 170, 236
Martin, Civilla Durfee (1869-1948): 47
Martin, Walter Stillman (1862-1935): 47
Mason, Lowell (1792-1872): 76, 110, 125, 185, 196, 286, 393, 410, 440, 448, 587
Matheson, George (1842-1906): 374
Matthews, Timothy Richard (1826-1910): 127
Mayfield, Larry (1944-): 592
McAfee, Cleland Boyd (1866-1944): 497
McClard, LeRoy (1926-): 360
McCutchan, Robert Guy (1877-1958): 593
McDaniel, Rufus Henry (1850-1940): 515
McFarland, John Thomas (1851-1913): 157, 158
McGee, Bob (1949-): 134
McGranahan, James (1840-1907): 289, 301, 409, 506
McGuire, Dony (1951-): 40
McHugh, Phill (1951-): 90, 197, 303
McIntosh, Rigdon McCoy (1836-1899): 552
McKinney, Baylus Benjamin (1886-1952): 85, 251, 367, 408, 544
Medema, Ken (1943-): 429, 591
Medley, Samuel (1738-1799): 110
Meece, David (1952-): 164, 209
Meineke, Christoph (1782-1850): 622
Melodia Sacra (1815), Weyman's: 135
Mendelssohn, Felix (1809-1847): 133, 269, 502, 556, 598
Merrill, William Pierson (1867-1954): 293
Messiter, Arthur Henry (1834-1916): 562
Mieir, Audrey (1916-): 101
Miles, C. Austin (1868-1946): 425
Miller, Rhea F. (1894-1966): 517
Millhuff, Charles (1938-): 238
Mills, Pauline M. (1898-): 73
Mitchell, Hubert (1907-): 415
Mitchell, Hugh (1914-): 69
Mohr, Joseph (1792-1848): 147
Monk, William Henry (1823-1889): 419, 560
Monsell, John Samuel Bewley (1811-1875): 165
Montgomery, James (1771-1854): 21, 131, 321
Moody, May Whittle (1870-1963): 351
Moore, Thomas (1779-1852): 416
Moore, William (19th century): 454, 585
Morris, Lelia Naylor (1862-1929): 245, 260, 392
Mote, Edward (1797-1874): 402, 404
Mountain, James (1844-1933): 315, 490, 494, 503
Mozart, Wolfgang Amadeus (1756-1791): 377, 584
Münster Gesangbuch (1677): 88
Murray, James Ramsey (1841-1905): 157

Naegeli, Johann Georg (1773-1836): 286
Neale, John Mason (1818-1866): 118, 123, 151, 173, 226, 276
Neander, Joachim (1650-1680): 8
Neidlinger, William Harold (1900-): 162
Nelson, Greg (1948-): 197, 303, 564
Netherlands Folk song: 16, 561
Netherlands Folk hymn: 561
Neumark, Georg (1621-1681): 600
Neuvermehrtes Gesangbuch (1693), Meiningen: 269
Newbolt, Michael R. (1874-1956): 304
Newell, William Reed (1868-1956): 338
Newton, John (1725-1807): 94, 202, 278, 608
Nichol, Henry Ernest (1862-1928): 296
Nicholson, James L. (1828-1876): 436
Nicholson, Sydney Hugo (1875-1947): 304
Niles, John Jacob (1892-1980): 139
Ninth Symphony (1839), Ludwig van Beethoven's: 1, 215
Noel, Caroline Maria (1817-1877): 235
Norris, John Samuel (1844-1907): 373
Nusbaum, Cyrus S. (1861-1937): 333

Oakeley, Frederick (1802-1880): 145
Oatman, Johnson, Jr. (1856-1922): 399, 422, 563
Oliver, Henry Kemble (1800-1885): 317
Olivers, Thomas (1725-1799): 34
Olson, Ernst William (1870-1958): 44
Orr, James Edwin (1912-): 438, 439
Ortlund, Anne (1923-): 316
O'Shields, Michael (1948-): 38
Osler, Edward (1798-1863): 9
Owens, Carol (1931-): 447
Owens, Jimmy (1930-): 23, 24, 256, 266, 626
Owens, Priscilla Jane (1829-1907): 306
Owens-Collins, Jamie (1955-): 485
Oxenham, John (1852-1941): 285

Palmer, Ray (1808-1887): 410, 501
Palmgren, Gerhard W. (1880-1959): 254
Paris, Twila (1958-): 72, 288
Parker, Debi J. (1961-): 63
Parker, Edwin Pond (1836-1925): 248
Parks, Joe Eldridge (1927-): 583
Parry, Joseph (1841-1903): 466
Patillo, Leon (1947-): 308
Peace, Albert Lister (1844-1912): 374
Pearce, Almeda J. (1893-): 240
Pennefather, William (1816-1873): 586
Perronet, Edward (1726-1792): 96, 97
Peterson, John Willard (1921-): 45, 239, 310, 417, 464, 495, 524
Phelps, Sylvanus Dryden (1816-1895): 445
Phillips, Keith (1941-): 206, 218, 272, 323, 564
Pierpoint, Folliott Sanford (1835-1917): 560
Pigott, Jean Sophia (1845-1882): 503

Plainsong melody: 112, 123, 243
Plainsong melody (13th century): 118
Plumptre, Edward Hayes (1821-1891): 562
Polish carol, Traditional: 143
Pollard, Adelaide Addison (1862-1934): 371
Pounds, Jessie Brown (1861-1921): 218, 467, 471
Praetorius, Michael (1571-1621): 160
Prentiss, Elizabeth Payson (1818-1878): 363
Prichard, Rowland Hugh (1811-1887): 61, 89, 124, 233
Prior, Charles Edwin (1856-1927): 444
Prudentius, Aurelius Clemens (348-413): 118
Psalmody (1794), Tattersall's: 119, 601
Psalteriolum Cantionum Catholicarum (1710): 123
Purifoy, John (1952-): 121

Rader, Paul (1879-1938): 258, 420
Rambo, Dottie (1934-): 179, 237
Rambo, Reba (1951-): 40
Ramsey, Benjamin Mansell (1849-1923): 395
Rankin, Jeremiah Eames (1828-1904): 602
Read, Daniel (1757-1836): 260
Red, Buryl (1936-): 322
Redner, Lewis Henry (1831-1908): 141
Reed, Andrew (1787-1862): 248, 615
Rees, John P. (1828-1900): 202
Reichardt, C. Luise (1780-1826): 484
Reinagle, Alexander Robert (1799-1877): 94, 285
Repository of Sacred Music (1813), John Wyeth's: 2
Reynolds, William J. (1920-): 302
Rhodes, Gary (1955-): 262, 619
Rimbault, Edward Francis (1816-1876): 532
Rinkart, Martin (1586-1649): 556
Rippon, John (1751-1836): 96, 97, 275
Rist, Johann (1607-1667): 129
Roberts, Daniel Crane (1841-1907): 573
Roberts, John (1822-1877): 232
Robinson, George Wade (1838-1877): 490
Robinson, Robert (1735-1790): 2
Roe, Gloria (1938-): 421
Romero, Wayne (1950-): 113
Root, George Frederick (1820-1895): 580, 594
Rosasco, John (1948-): 324
Rossetti, Christina (1830-1894): 154
Roth, Elton Menno (1891-1951): 514
Rounsefell, Carrie Esther (1861-1930): 444
Rowe, James (1865-1933): 388, 505
Rowley, Francis Harold (1854-1952): 508
Rubin, Steffi Geiser (1950-): 244
Runyan, William Marion (1870-1957): 43

Sacred Melodies (1815), William Gardiner's: 10, 193
Salsbury, Sonny (1938-): 578
Sammis, John H. (1846-1919): 349
Sandys, William (1792-1874): 136
Sankey, Ira David (1840-1908): 313, 348, 353, 355, 356, 431, 486
Schaff, Philip (1819-1893): 224
Schlegel, Katharina Amalia von (1697- ?): 347
Schlesische Volkslieder (1842): 88
Scholfield, Jack P. (1882-1972): 530
Scholtes, Peter (1938-): 284
Schop, Johann (1590-1664): 129
Schuler, George Stark (1882-1973): 452
Schumann, Robert Alexander (1810-1856): 450
Schütz, Johann Jakob (1640-1690): 6
Scott, Clara H. (1841-1897): 381
Scottish Psalter (1565): 20
Scottish Psalter (1615): 617
Scottish Psalter (1650): 50
Scriven, Joseph Medlicott (1820-1886): 435
Sears, Edmund Hamilton (1810-1876): 128
Seiss, Joseph Augustus (1823-1904): 88
Selection of Hymns (1787), Rippon's: 275
Shea, George Beverly (1909-): 65, 517
Shepherd, Thomas (1665-1739): 449
Sheppard, Franklin Lawrence (1852-1930): 58
Sherlock, Hugh (1905-): 305
Sherwin, William Fiske (1826-1888): 22, 274
Showalter, Anthony Johnson (1858-1924): 354
Shurtleff, Ernest Warburton (1862-1917): 483
Sibelius, Jean (1865-1957): 347, 535
Sinclair, Jerry (1943-): 91
Skillings, Otis (1935-): 83, 281
Skoog, Andrew L. (1856-1934): 56, 161
Slade, Mary B. C. (1826-1882): 470
Sleeper, William True (1819-1904): 336
Smart, Henry Thomas (1813-1879): 131, 225, 226, 241, 276, 483
Smith, Alfred Barney (1916-): 45
Smith, Deborah Davis (1958-): 31
Smith, Henry Percy (1825-1898): 320, 451
Smith, Howard E. (1863-1918): 505
Smith, John Stafford (1750-1836): 576
Smith, Michael Whitaker (1957-): 30, 31, 272
Smith, Oswald Jeffray (1889-): 219
Smith, Samuel Francis (1808-1895): 571
Smith, Walter Chalmers (1824-1908): 25
Smith, Leonard E., Jr. (1942-): 229
Southern Harmony (1835), William Walker's: 177, 334
Spaeth, Harriet Krauth (1845-1925): 160
Spafford, Horatio Gates (1828-1888): 493
Spanish melody, Traditional: 108
Spencer, Robert Nelson (1877-1961): 575
Spiritual, Traditional: 138, 181, 323, 344, 423, 547
St. Francis of Assisi, (1182-1226): 64
St. Richard of Chichester, (1197-1253): 55
Stainer, John (1840-1901): 136, 151, 207, 628
Stanphill, Ira Forest (1914-): 331
Stead, Louisa M.R. (1850-1917): 350
Stebbins, George Coles (1846-1945): 327, 336, 371, 441, 550
Steele, David Horatio (1950-): 165
Stennett, Samuel (1727-1795): 109, 552
Stites, Edgar Page (1836-1921): 355
Stockton, John Hart (1813-1877): 330, 527
Stokes, Elwood Haines (1815-1895): 261
Stone, Samuel John (1839-1900): 277
Stowell, Hugh (1799-1865): 432
Stralsund Gesangbuch (1665): 8
Sullivan, Arthur Seymour (1842-1900): 479
Sumner, John B. (1838-1918): 352
Swedish carol: 159
Swedish Folk melody: 44
Sweney, John R. (1837-1899): 172, 261, 389, 443, 499

Taff, Russ (1953-): 474
Taff, Tori (1956-): 474
Tallis, Thomas (1505-1585): 54
Tate, Nahum (1652-1715): 135
Taylor, Mrs. Walter G. (1932-): 189
Te Deum (4th century): 12
Teschner, Melchior (1584-1635): 173
Messiah (1741), George Frederick Handel's: 37, 146
The Book of Praise for Children (1881): 583
The Christian Lyre (1831), Leavitt's: 377, 584
The Diapason (1860): 246
The Parish Choir (1851): 595
The Psalter: 584
The Sacred Harp (1844): 455

The Seven Last Words of Christ (1899), Theodore Dubois': 597
Theodulph of Orleans (c. 760-821): 173
Thesaurus Musicus (c. 1745): 571
Thomas, Eugene (1941-): 74, 80, 108, 114, 159, 197, 229, 293, 308, 344, 376, 488, 569
Thompson, John (1950-): 36
Thompson, Will Lamartine (1847-1909): 326, 510
Thomson, Mary Ann (1834-1923): 298
Threlfall, Jennette (1821-1880): 174
Thring, Godfrey (1823-1903): 234
Thrupp, Dorothy Ann (1779-1847): 462
Tindley, Charles A. (1851-1933): 544
Tomer, William Gould (1833-1896): 602
Toplady, Augustus Montague (1740-1778): 204
Tourjee, Lizzie Shove (1858-1913): 68
Towner, Daniel Brink (1850-1919): 201, 338, 349
Traditional (others have been categorized under specific source, e.g., American, German, etc.): 19, 41, 82, 105, 171, 384, 489, 498, 616
Trapp, Vann Owen (1934-): 243
Troutbeck, Dr. John (1832-1899): 129
Tucker, Dr. Leon (19th century): 313
Tullar, Grant Colfax (1869-1950): 549

Union Harmony (1837), Caldwell's: 275

Vail, Silas Jones (1818-1884): 365
Vale, Allene G. (20th century): 411
Van De Venter, Judson W. (1855-1939): 366
van Dyke, Henry (1852-1933): 1
Van Tine, Patricia (1949-): 71
Vaughan Williams, Ralph (1872-1958): 167, 546
Vincent, Charles J. (1852-1934): 487
Virginia Harmony (1831), Carrell and Clayton's: 202

Wade, John Francis (1711-1786): 145
Walch, James (1837-1901): 298
Walford, William W. (1772-1850): 433
Walker, Tricia (1953-): 187
Walton, James George (1821-1905): 279
Walworth, Clarence Augustus (1820-1900): 12
Ward, Samuel Augustus (1847-1903): 572
Ware, Henry, Jr. (1794-1843): 536
Waring, Anna Laetitia (1823-1910): 502
Warner, Anna Bartlett (1820-1915): 579
Warren, George William (1828-1902): 573
Watts, Isaac (1674-1748): 18, 52, 59, 70, 111, 125, 185, 188, 208, 231, 480, 482, 538, 555, 595
Webb, George James (1803-1887): 477
Webbe, Samuel (1740-1816): 416
Weber, Jim (1958-): 287
Webster, Joseph Philbrick (1819-1875): 553
Weeden, Winfield Scott (1847-1908): 366
Weigle, Charles F. (1871-1966): 528
Welsh Hymn melody: 232
Welsh Hymn melody, Traditional: 25
Wesley, Charles (1707-1788): 17, 76, 92, 124, 133, 199, 203, 217, 228, 232, 241, 440, 448, 466, 478, 587
Wesley, John (1703-1791): 193
Wesley, Samuel Sebastian (1810-1876): 49, 277, 567
Whelpton, George (1847-1930): 609, 614
Whitcomb, George Walker (? -1941): 236
Whitfield, Frederick (1829-1904): 529
Whiting, William (1825-1878): 575
Whittier, John Greenleaf (1807-1892): 427
Whittingham, William (1524-1579): 50
Whittle, Daniel Webster (1840-1901): 289, 328, 351, 409
Wilkinson, Kate Barclay (1859-1928): 390
Williams, Aaron (1731-1776): 18, 21, 120, 280, 293
Williams, C.C. (? -1882): 328
Williams, Clara Tear (1858-1937): 531
Williams, Peter (1722-1796): 51
Williams, Thomas John (1869-1944): 211, 475
Williams, William (1717-1791): 51
Willis, Richard Storrs (1819-1900): 88, 128
Wilson, Emily Divine (1865-1942): 542
Wilson, Hugh (1764-1824): 208
Wilson, Ira Bishop (1880-1950): 452
Winkworth, Catherine (1827-1878): 8, 413, 556, 600
Wolaver, Bill (1958-): 138, 615
Wolfe, Lanny (1942-): 255
Wood, James H. (1921-): 455
Woolston, Reverend C. H. (19th century): 580
Wordsworth, Christopher (1807-1885): 215
Work, John W., Jr. (1871-1925): 138
Wyeth, John (1770-1858): 2
Wyrtzen, Don (1942-): 180, 523
Wyrtzen, Jack (1913-): 523

Yates, John Henry (1837-1900): 486
Young, G. A. (1903-): 46
Young, Gordon (1919-): 596
Young, John Freeman (1820-1885): 147
Young, William David (1941-): 126, 171, 305, 611

Zinzendorf, Nicolaus Ludwig von (1700-1760): 193
Zundel, John (1815-1882): 92, 268, 574

Worship & Celebrate

TOPICAL INDEX OF HYMNS

ADORATION AND PRAISE
God Our Father
A Mighty Fortress Is Our God, 26
Abba Father, 15
All Creatures of Our God and King, 64
All People That on Earth Do Dwell, 20
Be Exalted, O God, 5
Bless His Holy Name, 13
Children of the Heavenly Father, 44
Clap Your Hands, 24
Come Let Us Worship and Bow Down, 14
Come, Thou Almighty King, 267
Come, Thou Fount of Every Blessing, 2
Come, We That Love the Lord, 18
Doxology, 624
Doxology (Alternate Rhythm), 625
Doxology (Owens), 626
El Shaddai, 36
Father, I Adore You, 265
For the Beauty of the Earth, 560
Gloria Patri (Greatorex), 623
Gloria Patri (Meinecke), 622
Glorify Thy Name, 29
God Is So Good, 41
God, Our Father, We Adore Thee, 268
Great Are You, O Lord, 39
Great Is Thy Faithfulness, 43
Hallelujah Chorus, 37
Holy God, We Praise Thy Name, 12
Holy, Holy, 266
How Great Thou Art, 4
Isaiah 6:3, 22
It Is Good to Sing Thy Praises, 584
Joyful, Joyful, We Adore Thee, 1
Make a Joyful Noise, 23
My Tribute, 11
O God, Our Help in Ages Past, 52
O Worship the King, 10
Praise, My Soul, the King of Heaven, 3
Praise the Lord! Ye Heavens, Adore Him, 9
Praise to the Lord, the Almighty, 8
Praise Ye the Triune God, 264
Sing Praise to God Who Reigns Above, 6
Stand Up and Bless the Lord, 21
The God of Abraham Praise, 34
The Majesty and Glory of Your Name, 35
The Wonder of It All, 65
To God Be the Glory, 66
We Praise Thee, O God, Our Redeemer, 16
We Worship and Adore You, 19
Ye Servants of God, 17

ADORATION AND PRAISE
Jesus Our Savior
All for Jesus, 368
All Glory, Laud and Honor, 173
All Hail the Power of Jesus' Name (Coronation), 97
All Hail the Power of Jesus' Name (Diadem), 96
All That Thrills My Soul, 526
Alleluia, 91
Alleluia! Alleluia!, 215
Amazing Grace, 202
Blessed Assurance, 345
Blessed Be the Name, 103
Blessing and Honor, 78
Christ Is Made the Sure Foundation, 276
Christ, We Do All Adore Thee, 597
Come and Praise the Lord Our King, 171
Come, Christians, Join to Sing, 108
Fairest Lord Jesus, 88
Glorious Is Thy Name, 85
Glory to His Name, 527
Grace Greater Than Our Sin, 201
Hallowed Be the Name, 84
He Is Here, He Is Here, 256
He Is Lord, 105
He Touched Me, 504
His Name Is Life, 114
His Name Is Wonderful, 101
How Great Our Joy!, 144
How Sweet the Name of Jesus Sounds, 94
I Am His, and He Is Mine, 490
I Just Came to Praise the Lord, 113
I Love Thee, 362
I Love You, Lord, 80
I Will Sing of My Redeemer, 506
I'd Rather Have Jesus, 517
In the Name of the Lord, 90
Jesus, I Am Resting, Resting, 503
Jesus Is the Sweetest Name I Know, 95
Jesus, Name Above All Names, 112
Jesus, the Very Thought of Thee, 79
Jesus, Thou Joy of Loving Hearts, 501
Jesus, We Just Want to Thank You, 98
Join All the Glorious Names, 111
King of Heaven, Lord Most High, 104
King of Kings, 77
Let's Just Praise the Lord, 107
Lord, We Praise You, 83
Love Divine, All Loves Excelling, 92
Majestic Sweetness Sits Enthroned, 109
Majesty, 74
May Jesus Christ Be Praised, 87
My Jesus, I Love Thee, 364
O Come, Let Us Adore Him, 82
O Could I Speak the Matchless Worth, 110
O for a Thousand Tongues, 76
O the Deep, Deep Love of Jesus (Bunessan), 212
O the Deep, Deep Love of Jesus (Ebenezer), 211
Our Great Savior, 89
Praise Him! Praise Him!, 106
Praise the Name of Jesus, 93
Praise the Savior, 75
Sometimes "Alleluia", 115
Take the Name of Jesus with You, 116
There Is No Name So Sweet on Earth, 100
There's Something About That Name, 102
Thou Art Worthy, 73
We Come, O Christ, to You, 117
We Will Glorify, 72
What a Wonderful Savior!, 81

ADVENT
(see CHRIST - Advent)

AMENS
628

ASCENSION
(see CHRIST - Ascension and Reign)

ASPIRATION
A Charge to Keep I Have, 448
Aspiration Canon, 391
Be Thou My Vision, 382
Breathe on Me, 251
Breathe on Me, Breath of God, 259
Bring Back the Springtime, 396
Come, Thou Fount of Every Blessing, 2
Day by Day - A Prayer, 55
Dear Lord and Father of Mankind, 427
Draw Nigh to God, 397
Fill Me Now, 261
Fill My Cup, Lord, 398
Footsteps of Jesus, 470
Higher Ground, 399
I Am Thine, O Lord, 358
I Want to Be Like Jesus, 400
I Would Be Like Jesus, 388
In My Life Lord, Be Glorified, 394
Just a Closer Walk with Thee, 380
Lead Me to Calvary, 176
Make Me a Blessing, 452
May the Mind of Christ, My Savior, 390
More About Jesus, 389
More Love to Thee, 363
My Faith Looks Up to Thee, 410
Near the Cross, 385
Nearer, My God, to Thee, 393
Nearer, Still Nearer, 392
O for a Heart to Praise My God, 440
O to Be Like Thee!, 387
Open My Eyes, That I May See, 381
Open Our Eyes, Lord, 383
Psalm 42, 401
Search Me, 434
Set My Soul Afire, 294
Spirit of God, Descend upon My Heart, 249
Teach Me Thy Way, O Lord, 395
To Be Like Jesus, 384

ASSURANCE

A Child of the King, 352
A Mighty Fortress Is Our God, 26
A Shelter in the Time of Storm, 353
All the Way My Savior Leads Me, 460
Amazing Grace, 202
Be Calm My Soul, 421
Be Still and Know, 343
Be Still, My Soul, 347
Blessed Assurance, 345
Children of the Heavenly Father, 44
Christ Is Made the Sure Foundation, 276
Day by Day, 56
God Will Take Care of You, 47
Grace Greater Than Our Sin, 201
He Leadeth Me, 461
He Lives, 220
He's Got the Whole World in His Hands, 344
Hiding in Thee, 348
How Firm a Foundation, 275
I Am His, and He Is Mine, 490
I Am Trusting Thee, Lord Jesus, 346
I Know Whom I Have Believed, 409
Is It the Crowning Day?, 236
Jesus, I Am Resting, Resting, 503
Jesus Lives, and So Shall I, 224
Jesus Loves Even Me, 357
Leaning on the Everlasting Arms, 354
Moment by Moment, 351
My Faith Has Found a Resting Place, 405
My Hope Is in the Lord, 406
No, Not One!, 422
O God, Our Help in Ages Past, 52
Praise the Savior, 75
Standing on the Promises, 271
Surely Goodness and Mercy, 45
The Solid Rock (Melita), 402
The Solid Rock (Solid Rock), 404
This Is My Father's World, 58
'Tis So Sweet to Trust in Jesus, 350
Trust and Obey, 349
Trusting Jesus, 355
Under His Wings, 356
We Shall Behold Him, 237
We'll Understand It Better By and By, 544
Yesterday, Today and Tomorrow, 523

ATONEMENT
(see CHRIST - Atonement)

BABY DEDICATION
(see DEDICATION OF CHILDREN AND PARENTS)

BAPTISM

All the Way My Savior Leads Me, 460
Come Holy Spirit, Dove Divine, 320
I'll Live for Him, 370
Jesus, I My Cross Have Taken, 377
Just As I Am, 342
O Happy Day!, 532
O Master, Let Me Walk with Thee, 451
Take My Life and Let It Be, 379
Trust and Obey, 349
We Bless the Name of Christ, the Lord, 319
Where He Leads Me, 373
Wherever He Leads I'll Go, 367

BENEDICTIONS

Benediction, 612
Go Now and Live for the Savior, 610
Lord, Let Us Now Depart in Peace, 609
May the Grace of Christ, Our Savior, 608
Now unto the King, 611
The Lord Bless You and Keep You, 607

BIBLE
(see WORD OF GOD)

BLOOD OF CHRIST
(See CHRIST - Cleansing Blood)

BROTHERHOOD
(see SOCIAL CONCERN)

CALLS TO WORSHIP
(Choral)

Cast Thy Burden upon the Lord, 598
Christ, We Do All Adore Thee, 597
Now to the King of Heaven, 595
O Worship the Lord, 593
Praise Ye the Name of the Lord, 596
The Lord Is in His Holy Temple, 594

CALLS TO WORSHIP
(Spoken)

599

CANONS AND ROUNDS

A Doxology Canon, 627
Aspiration Canon, 391
Be Joyful, 223
Behold, What Manner of Love, 71
Blessing and Honor, 78
Clap Your Hands, 24
Father, I Adore You, 265
For God So Loved, 205
For Health and Strength, 566
Great Are You, O Lord, 39
He Is Coming, 246
His Way, 54
Holy Lord, 32
I Am a Soldier of the Cross!, 480
In His Cross I Glory, 187
Jesus Is Born, 149
Jesus Is King, 230
King of Kings, 77
Make a Joyful Noise, 23
Rejoice in the Lord Always, 489
Resurrection Canon, 221
Search Me, 434
Sing Praise, 263
We Thank You, Lord, 565

CHILDREN'S HYMNS

All Things Bright and Beautiful, 578
Children of the Heavenly Father, 44
Commit Thy Way, 581
Fairest Lord Jesus, 88
Gentle Shepherd, 458
God Leads Us Along, 46
Jesus Loves Even Me, 357
Jesus Loves Me, 579
Jesus Loves the Little Children, 580
Reach Your Hand, 582
Savior, Like a Shepherd Lead Us, 462
The Wise May Bring Their Learning, 583
This Is My Father's World, 58
Yesterday, Today and Tomorrow, 523

CHORUSES
(Scripture and Praise)

A Nativity Prayer, 126
A Perfect Heart, 40
Abba Father, Abba Father, 15
As for Me and My House, 537
Be Exalted, O God, 5
Bless His Holy Name, 13
Child of Love, 156
Come Celebrate Jesus, 324
Come Let Us Reason, 591
Come Let Us Worship and Bow Down, 14
Come on, Ring Those Bells, 153
Commit Thy Way, 581
Cover Me, 469
Day by Day - A Prayer, 55
Draw Nigh to God, 397
El Shaddai, 36
Emmanuel, 134
Gentle Shepherd, 458
Glorify Thy Name, 29
Go Ye into All the World, 301
God Is So Good, 41
Great Is the Lord, 31
Greater Is He That Is in Me, 255
He Careth for You, 57
He Is Lord, 105
He's Everything to Me, 516
His Name Is Life, 114
His Name Is Wonderful, 101
How Majestic Is Your Name, 30
I Know a Fount, 194
I Know That My Redeemer Liveth, 218
I Love You, Lord, 80
I Will Call upon the Lord, 38
I Will Serve Thee, 446
I Will Sing of the Mercies, 457
In My Life Lord, Be Glorified, 394
In the Name of the Lord, 90
In This Quiet Moment, 592
Isaiah 6:3, 22
Jesus Is the Sweetest Name I Know, 95
Jesus Loves the Little Children, 580
Jesus, Name Above All Names, 112
Lead Me, Lord, 49
Let's Just Praise the Lord, 107

Lord, Lay Some Soul upon My Heart, 313
Lord, Listen to Your Children Praying, 429
Majesty, 74
O, How He Loves You and Me, 513
Only Believe, 420
Open Our Eyes, Lord, 383
People Need the Lord, 303
Praise the Name of Jesus, 93
Saved by Grace, 550
Seek Ye First, 42
Something Beautiful, 519
Sometimes "Alleluia", 115
Spirit of the Living God, 247
Sweet, Sweet Spirit, 252
The Bond of Love, 281
The Family of God, 282
The King Is Coming, 238
The New 23rd, 53
The Trees of the Field, 244
There Is No Name So Sweet on Earth, 100
There's Something About That Name, 102
This Is the Day, 590
Thou Art Worthy, 73
Thou Wilt Keep Him in Perfect Peace, 492
Through It All, 507
Thy Loving Kindness, 69
Thy Word, 272
To Be Like Jesus, 384
Turn Your Eyes upon Jesus, 335
We Are the Reason, 209
We Will Stand, 474
We Worship and Adore You, 19
Welcome, Welcome, 260
What Can I Give Him?, 154
Where the Spirit of the Lord Is, 253
Worthy Is the Lamb, 180
Yesterday, Today and Tomorrow, 523

CHRIST - Adoration and Praise

(see ADORATION AND PRAISE - Jesus Our Savior)

CHRIST - Advent

(see also CHRIST - Birth)

Come, Thou Long-Expected Jesus, 124
Joy to the World!, 125
O Come, Let Us Adore Him, 82
O Come, O Come, Emmanuel, 123
O Thou Joyful, O Thou Wonderful 119
Of the Father's Love Begotten, 118
The Advent of Our God, 120
The Word Made Flesh, 121

CHRIST - Ascension and Reign

Alleluia! Sing to Jesus, 233
At the Name of Jesus, 235
Christ Arose, 216
Crown Him with Many Crowns, 234
Hail the Day That Sees Him Rise, 232
He Rose Triumphantly, 219
Jesus Is King, 230
Jesus Shall Reign, 231
Our God Reigns, 229
Rejoice, the Lord Is King, 228

CHRIST - Atonement, Crucifixion, Suffering and Death

A Perfect Heart, 40
Alas! and Did My Savior Bleed?, 208
Alleluia! Alleluia!, 215
Amazing Grace, 202
And Can It Be?, 203
Are You Washed in the Blood?, 190
At Calvary, 338
At the Cross, 188
Behold the Lamb, 179
Beneath the Cross of Jesus, 183
Calvary Covers It All, 189
For God So Loved, 205
Glory to His Name, 527
God So Loved the World, 207
Grace Greater Than Our Sin, 201
Hallelujah, What a Savior!, 175
He Is Lord, 105
He Rose Triumphantly, 219
He the Pearly Gates Will Open, 541
His Way with Thee, 333
I Am Thine, O Lord, 358
I Know a Fount, 194
I Lay My Sins on Jesus, 340
I Will Sing of My Redeemer, 506
I'll Live for Him, 370
In His Cross I Glory, 187
In the Cross of Christ I Glory, 184
Jesus Paid It All, 210
Jesus Saves!, 306
Jesus, Thy Blood and Righteousness, 193
Lead Me to Calvary, 176
Lift High the Cross, 304
Living for Jesus, 372
Near the Cross, 385
Nothing But the Blood, 195
O Sacred Head, Now Wounded, 178
One Day!, 170
Praise Him! Praise Him!, 106
Redeemed (Ada), 520
Redeemed (Kirkpatrick), 521
Rock of Ages, 204
Room at the Cross for You, 331
The Blood Will Never Lose Its Power, 192
The Old Rugged Cross, 186
The Unveiled Christ, 169
There Is a Fountain, 196
There Is a Redeemer, 206
There Is Power in the Blood, 191
'Tis So Sweet to Trust in Jesus, 350
We Are the Reason, 209
We Come, O Christ, to You, 117
Were You There?, 181
What a Wonderful Savior!, 81
What Wondrous Love Is This, 177
When I Survey the Wondrous Cross, 185
Worthy Is the Lamb, 180

CHRIST - Birth

(see also CHRIST - Advent, CHRIST - Epiphany)

A Communion Hymn for Christmas, 140
A Nativity Prayer, 126
A Thousand Candles, 159
Angels from the Realms of Glory, 131
Angels We Have Heard on High, 132
Away in a Manger (Away in a Manger), 157
Away in a Manger (Cradle Song), 158
Break Forth, O Beauteous Heavenly Light, 129
Child of Love, 156
Come on, Ring Those Bells, 153
Emmanuel, 134
For Unto Us a Child Is Born, 146
Go, Tell It on the Mountain, 138
Good Christian Men, Rejoice, 151
Hark! the Herald Angels Sing, 133
How Great Our Joy!, 144
I Heard the Bells on Christmas Day, 152
I Wonder as I Wander, 139
Infant Holy, Infant Lowly, 143
It Came upon the Midnight Clear, 128
Jesus Is Born, 149
Joy to the World!, 125
Lo! How a Rose E'er Blooming, 160
O Come, All Ye Faithful, 145
O Hearken Ye, 150
O Holy Night!, 148
O Little Town of Bethlehem, 141
Once in Royal David's City, 155
Our Day of Joy Is Here Again, 161
Silent Night! Holy Night!, 147
The Birthday of a King, 162
The First Noel, 136
Thou Didst Leave Thy Throne, 127
What Can I Give Him?, 154
What Child Is This?, 137
While Shepherds Watched Their Flocks, 135

CHRIST - Cleansing Blood

(see CHRIST - Atonement)

CHRIST - Cross

(see CHRIST - Atonement)

CHRIST - Death

(see CHRIST - Atonement)

CHRIST - Epiphany

Adoration, 165
As with Gladness Men of Old, 163
Break Forth, O Beauteous Heavenly Light, 129
Fairest Lord Jesus, 88
Go, Tell It on the Mountain, 138
O Sing a Song of Bethlehem, 167
One Small Child, 164
We Three Kings, 166

CHRIST - Example
Be Thou My Vision, 382
Footsteps of Jesus, 470
I Want to Be Like Jesus, 400
I Would Be Like Jesus, 388
Lord, Speak to Me, 450
May the Mind of Christ, My Savior, 390
More About Jesus, 389
O Master, Let Me Walk with Thee, 451
O to Be Like Thee!, 387
Take Time to Be Holy (Holiness), 441
Take Time to Be Holy (Slane), 442
Teach Me Thy Way, O Lord, 395
Where He Leads Me, 373
Wherever He Leads I'll Go, 367

CHRIST - Friend
Alleluia! Sing to Jesus, 233
Close to Thee, 365
Come, Christians, Join to Sing, 108
He Lives, 220
In the Garden, 425
Jesus Is All the World to Me, 510
Leaning on the Everlasting Arms, 354
Moment by Moment, 351
No, Not One!, 422
No One Ever Cared for Me Like Jesus, 528
No One Understands Like Jesus, 417
O Could I Speak the Matchless Worth, 110
O Jesus, I Have Promised, 369
Our Great Savior, 89
Room at the Cross for You, 331
Saved, Saved!, 530
'Tis So Sweet to Trust in Jesus, 350
What a Friend We Have in Jesus, 435

CHRIST - Grace, Love and Mercy
Alas! and Did My Savior Bleed?, 208
Amazing Grace, 202
And Can It Be?, 203
Arise, My Soul, Arise, 199
At Calvary, 338
Come, Thou Fount of Every Blessing, 2
For God So Loved, 205
Give Me Jesus, 443
God So Loved the World, 207
Grace Greater Than Our Sin, 201
He Giveth More Grace, 415
He the Pearly Gates Will Open, 541
I Will Sing of the Mercies, 457
It Took a Miracle, 524
Jesus, Lover of My Soul, 466
Jesus Loves Even Me, 357
Jesus Loves Me, 579
Jesus Paid It All, 210
Lamb of Glory, 197
Love Divine, All Loves Excelling, 92
Love Lifted Me, 505
May the Grace of Christ, Our Savior, 608
My Savior's Love, 512
O, How He Loves You and Me, 513
O, How I Love Jesus, 529
O Perfect Love, 533
O the Deep, Deep Love of Jesus (Bunessan), 212
O the Deep, Deep Love of Jesus (Ebenezer), 211
Rock of Ages, 204
Tell Me the Old, Old Story, 424
The Word Made Flesh, 121
There Is a Redeemer, 206
We Are the Reason, 209
What Wondrous Love Is This, 177
Wonderful Grace of Jesus, 198

CHRIST - His Name
All Hail the Power of Jesus' Name (Coronation), 97
All Hail the Power of Jesus' Name (Diadem), 96
At the Name of Jesus, 235
Blessed Be the Name, 103
Emmanuel, 134
Freely, Freely, 447
He Keeps Me Singing, 488
Hear Now the Name, 407
His Name Is Life, 114
His Name Is Wonderful, 101
How Sweet the Name of Jesus Sounds, 94
In the Name of the Lord, 90
Jesus Is the Sweetest Name I Know, 95
Jesus, Name Above All Names, 112
Join All the Glorious Names, 111
Praise Him! Praise Him!, 106
Praise the Name of Jesus, 93
Take the Name of Jesus with You, 116
There Is No Name So Sweet on Earth, 100
We Bless the Name of Christ, the Lord, 319

CHRIST - Life and Ministry
Come and Praise the Lord Our King, 171
Come, Thou Long-Expected Jesus, 124
O Sing a Song of Bethlehem, 167
One Day!, 170
Tell Me the Story of Jesus, 172
The Unveiled Christ, 169
Thou Didst Leave Thy Throne, 127
Who Is He in Yonder Stall?, 168
Yesterday, Today and Tomorrow, 523

CHRIST - Lordship
A Child of the King, 352
Adoration, 165
All Glory, Laud and Honor, 173
Crown Him with Many Crowns, 234
He Is Lord, 105
His Name Is Wonderful, 101
I Am Trusting Thee, Lord Jesus, 346
I Love You, Lord, 80
Jesus Is King, 230
Jesus Is Lord of All (Gaither), 359
Jesus Is Lord of All (McClard), 360
Joy to the World!, 125
King of Heaven, Lord Most High, 104
King of Kings, 77
Let's Just Praise the Lord, 107
Lord, We Praise You, 83
Majesty, 74
Praise Him! Praise Him!, 106
Rejoice, the Lord Is King, 228
The Birthday of a King, 162
Thou Didst Leave Thy Throne, 127
What Child Is This?, 137
Who Is He in Yonder Stall?, 168

CHRIST - Our Love for
Close to Thee, 365
I Just Came to Praise the Lord, 113
I Love Thee, 362
I Love You, Lord, 80
Lord, We Praise You, 83
More Love to Thee, 363
My Jesus, I Love Thee, 364
O, How I Love Jesus, 529

CHRIST - Resurrection
Alleluia! Alleluia!, 215
Be Joyful, 223
Because He Lives, 213
Christ Arose, 216
Christ the Lord Is Risen Today, 217
Crown Him with Many Crowns, 234
Easter Song, 222
He Is Lord, 105
He Lives, 220
He Rose Triumphantly, 219
I Know That My Redeemer Liveth, 218
Jesus Lives, and So Shall I, 224
One Day!, 170
Our God Reigns, 229
Resurrection Canon, 221
The Day of Resurrection, 226
Thine Is the Glory, 227
Were You There?, 181
Worship Christ the Risen King, 225

CHRIST - Savior
(see CHRIST - Atonement, CHRIST - Salvation)

CHRIST - Second Coming
Hallelujah, What a Savior!, 175
He Is Coming, 246
Is It the Crowning Day?, 236
Jesus Is Coming Again, 239
Lo, He Comes with Clouds Descending, 241
O Come, Messiah, Come Again, 243
One Day!, 170
The King Is Coming, 238
The Trees of the Field, 244
We Shall Behold Him, 237
What If It Were Today?, 245
When He Shall Come, 240
While We Are Waiting, Come, 242

CHRIST - Triumphal Entry
All Glory, Laud and Honor, 173
Hosanna, Loud Hosanna, 174

CHRISTIAN EXPERIENCE
(see TESTIMONY AND PRAISE)

CHRISTMAS
(see CHRIST - Birth)

CHURCH - Fellowship of Believers (Unity)
Blest Be the Tie That Binds, 286
Brethren, We Have Met to Worship, 585
Come, Christians, Join to Sing, 108
Good Christian Men, Rejoice, 151
In Christ There Is No East or West, 285
Joyful, Joyful, We Adore Thee, 1
Let Us Break Bread Together, 323
Let's Just Praise the Lord, 107
Our God Has Made Us One, 287
Sometimes "Alleluia", 115
Sweet, Sweet Spirit, 252
The Bond of Love, 281
The Church's One Foundation, 277
The Family of God, 282
They'll Know We Are Christians by Our Love, 284
We Are God's People, 283
We Will Stand, 474
Where the Spirit of the Lord Is, 253

CHURCH - Nature and Foundation
Christ Is Made the Sure Foundation, 276
Faith of Our Fathers, 279
Glorious Things of Thee Are Spoken, 278
How Firm a Foundation, 275
I Love Thy Kingdom, Lord, 280
The Church's One Foundation, 277

CLOSING OF SERVICE - Benedictions
(see BENEDICTIONS)

CLOSING OF SERVICE - Benedictions - Spoken
613

CLOSING OF SERVICE - Hymns and Songs
Blest Be the Tie That Binds, 286
God Be with You, 602
Grace, Love and Fellowship, 606
If You Will Only Let God Guide You, 600
Lord, Dismiss Us with Thy Blessing, 601
Savior, Again to Thy Dear Name, 604
Seek Ye First, 42
Sweet, Sweet Spirit, 252
Take the Name of Jesus with You, 116
The Bond of Love, 281
The Lord Bless You and Keep You, 607
The Lord Whom We Love, 603
When This Song of Praise Shall Cease, 605

COMFORT AND ENCOURAGEMENT
A Mighty Fortress Is Our God, 26
Abide with Me, 419
All Your Anxiety, 418
Be Calm My Soul, 421
Cast Thy Burden upon the Lord, 598
Children of the Heavenly Father, 44
Come, Holy Spirit, 250
Come, Ye Disconsolate, 416
Day by Day, 56
God Will Take Care of You, 47
Guide Me, O Thou Great Jehovah, 51
He Careth for You, 57
He Giveth More Grace, 415
Heavenly Spirit, Gentle Spirit, 254
His Way, 54
I Heard the Voice of Jesus Say, 414
I Must Tell Jesus, 430
Jesus, Lover of My Soul, 466
Jesus, Priceless Treasure, 413
My Faith Looks Up to Thee, 410
My Savior's Love, 512
Near to the Heart of God, 497
Nearer, Still Nearer, 392
No, Not One!, 422
No One Understands Like Jesus, 417
O God, Our Help in Ages Past, 52
O Love That Will Not Let Me Go, 374
Only Believe, 420
Sun of My Soul, 412
Tell Me the Old, Old Story, 424
The Comforter Has Come, 257
The Joy of the Lord, 411
The King of Love My Shepherd Is, 468
The Lord's My Shepherd, I'll Not Want, 50
The New 23rd, 53
There Is a Balm in Gilead, 423
This Is My Father's World, 58
Through It All, 507
What a Friend We Have in Jesus, 435
Where the Spirit of the Lord Is, 253
Wonderful Peace, 500

COMMITMENT AND CONSECRATION
A Charge to Keep I Have, 448
All for Jesus, 368
Breathe on Me, 251
Breathe on Me, Breath of God, 259
Cleanse Me (Ellers), 439
Cleanse Me (Maori), 438
Close to Thee, 365
Come, All Christians, Be Committed, 455
Come, Thou Fount of Every Blessing, 2
Commit Thy Way, 581
Fill Me Now, 261
Give Me Jesus, 443
Have Thine Own Way, Lord, 371
His Way with Thee, 333
I Am Thine, O Lord, 358
I Have Decided to Follow Jesus, 376
I Love Thee, 362
I Surrender All, 366
I'll Live for Him, 370
Jesus Calls Us, 375
Jesus, I My Cross Have Taken, 377
Jesus Is Lord of All (Gaither), 359
Jesus Is Lord of All (McClard), 360
Living for Jesus, 372
More Love to Thee, 363
Must Jesus Bear the Cross Alone?, 449
My Jesus, I Love Thee, 364
O Jesus, I Have Promised, 369
O Love That Will Not Let Me Go, 374
O Master, Let Me Walk with Thee, 451
Only One Life, 378
Reaching for Excellence, 456
Revive Us Again, 295
Seek Ye First, 42
Set My Soul Afire, 294
Something for Thee, 445
Spirit of God, Descend upon My Heart, 249
Take My Life and Let It Be, 379
Take Time to Be Holy (Holiness), 441
Take Time to Be Holy (Slane), 442
Where He Leads Me, 373
Wherever He Leads I'll Go, 367
Whiter Than Snow, 436

COMMUNION
(see LORD'S SUPPER)

CONCERN FOR OTHERS
(see MISSIONS AND EVANGELISM)

CONFESSION
(see REPENTANCE AND FORGIVENESS)

CONSECRATION
(see COMMITMENT AND CONSECRATION)

CREATION
(see GOD - Creation)

DEDICATION OF BUILDING
(see CHURCH - Nature and Foundation)

DEDICATION OF CHILDREN AND PARENTS
Because He Lives, 213
Children of the Heavenly Father, 44
God Leads Us Along, 46
Good Shepherd, Take This Little Child, 318
This Child We Dedicate to Thee, 317

DEDICATION OF CHRISTIAN WORKERS
(see COMMITMENT AND CONSECRATION, DISCIPLESHIP, STEWARDSHIP AND SERVICE)

DEDICATION OF LIFE
(see COMMITMENT AND CONSECRATION, DISCIPLESHIP, STEWARDSHIP AND SERVICE)

DISCIPLESHIP
A Charge to Keep I Have, 448
Beneath the Cross of Jesus, 183
Come, All Christians, Be Committed, 455
Dear Lord and Father of Mankind, 427
Footsteps of Jesus, 470
I Gave My Life for Thee, 453
I Have Decided to Follow Jesus, 376
I'll Go Where You Want Me to Go, 444
I'll Live for Him, 370
Jesus Calls Us, 375
Jesus, I My Cross Have Taken, 377
Living for Jesus, 372
Lord, Lay Some Soul upon My Heart, 313
Lord, Speak to Me, 450
Must Jesus Bear the Cross Alone?, 449
O Jesus, I Have Promised, 369
O Master, Let Me Walk with Thee, 451
Once to Every Man and Nation, 475
Onward, Christian Soldiers, 479
Pass It On, 309
Reach Out and Touch, 314
Rise Up, O Church (Men) of God, 293
Take My Life and Let It Be, 379
Take Time to Be Holy (Holiness), 441
Take Time to Be Holy (Slane), 442
Trust and Obey, 349
Where He Leads Me, 373
Wherever He Leads I'll Go, 367
Who Is on the Lord's Side?, 484

DOXOLOGIES
A Doxology Canon, 627
Doxology, 624
Doxology (Alternate Rhythm), 625
Doxology (Owens), 626

EASTER
(see CHRIST - Resurrection)

EDUCATION, CHRISTIAN
Be Thou My Vision, 382
Holy Bible, Book Divine, 273
Lead On, O King Eternal, 483
Lord, Speak to Me, 450
May the Mind of Christ, My Savior, 390
More About Jesus, 389
O Master, Let Me Walk with Thee, 451
O Word of God Incarnate, 269
Open My Eyes, That I May See, 381
Spirit of God, Descend upon My Heart, 249
Teach Me Thy Way, O Lord, 395
Tell Me the Story of Jesus, 172

ENCOURAGEMENT
(see COMFORT AND ENCOURAGEMENT)

ETERNAL LIFE
(see LIFE EVERLASTING, CHRIST - Second Coming)

EVANGELISM
(see MISSIONS AND EVANGELISM)

EVENING HYMNS
Abide with Me, 419
God Be with You, 602
Savior, Again to Thy Dear Name, 604
Share His Love, 302
Sun of My Soul, 412

FAITH AND HOPE
A Shelter in the Time of Storm, 353
Alleluia! Sing to Jesus, 233
Be Still, My Soul, 347
Because He Lives, 213
Faith Is the Victory, 486
For All the Saints, 546
Have Faith in God, 408
Hear Now the Name, 407
I Am Trusting Thee, Lord Jesus, 346
I Know Whom I Have Believed, 409
Is It the Crowning Day?, 236
Jesus, Lover of My Soul, 466
Like a River Glorious, 494
My Faith Has Found a Resting Place, 405
My Faith Looks Up to Thee, 410
My Hope Is in the Lord, 406
Only Believe, 420
Only Trust Him, 330
Take the Name of Jesus with You, 116
The Joy of the Lord, 411
The Solid Rock (Melita), 402
The Solid Rock (Solid Rock), 404
'Tis So Sweet to Trust in Jesus, 350
Trust and Obey, 349

FAMILY AND HOME
A Christian Home, 535
As for Me and My House, 537
Happy the Home When God Is There, 536
I Would Be Like Jesus, 388
O Perfect Love, 533
She Will Be Called Blessed, 534

FATHER'S DAY
A Christian Home, 535
As for Me and My House, 537
Faith of Our Fathers, 279
Faithful Men, 288
For the Beauty of the Earth, 560
God of Our Fathers, 573
Happy the Home When God Is There, 536
Now Thank We All Our God, 556
O Perfect Love, 533

FELLOWSHIP OF BELIEVERS
(see CHURCH - Fellowship of Believers)

FELLOWSHIP WITH CHRIST
Day by Day - A Prayer, 55
Face to Face, 549
He Keeps Me Singing, 488
He Lives, 220
Here, O My Lord, I See Thee Face to Face, 325
In the Garden, 425
Jesus Is All the World to Me, 510
Jesus, the Very Thought of Thee, 79
Just a Closer Walk with Thee, 380
No, Not One!, 422
O Master, Let Me Walk with Thee, 451
Saved, Saved!, 530
Trust and Obey, 349
What a Friend We Have in Jesus, 435

FELLOWSHIP WITH GOD
Abide with Me, 419
Breathe on Me, Breath of God, 259
Close to Thee, 365
Day by Day, 56
He's Everything to Me, 516
How Firm a Foundation, 275
I Am His, and He Is Mine, 490
I Am Thine, O Lord, 358
In the Garden, 425
Leaning on the Everlasting Arms, 354
Near to the Heart of God, 497
Nearer, My God, to Thee, 393
The Bond of Love, 281

FORGIVENESS
(see REPENTANCE AND FORGIVENESS, CHRIST - Grace, Love and Mercy, GOD - Love and Mercy)

FUNERAL HYMNS
(see also COMFORT AND ENCOURAGEMENT)
A Mighty Fortress Is Our God, 26
Abide with Me, 419
All Your Anxiety, 418
Be Still, My Soul, 347
Come, Ye Disconsolate, 416
He Giveth More Grace, 415
He Leadeth Me, 461
He the Pearly Gates Will Open, 541
I Know That My Redeemer Liveth, 218
I Must Tell Jesus, 430
In the Garden, 425
Jesus Lives, and So Shall I, 224
Jesus, Lover of My Soul, 466
My Faith Looks Up to Thee, 410
My Jesus, I Love Thee, 364
Near to the Heart of God, 497
Nearer, My God, to Thee, 393
No, Not One!, 422

No One Understands Like Jesus, 417
O God, Our Help in Ages Past, 52
O Love That Will Not Let Me Go, 374
Precious Lord, Take My Hand, 463
Take the Name of Jesus with You, 116
The King of Love My Shepherd Is, 468
The Lord's My Shepherd, I'll Not Want, 50
We Shall See His Lovely Face, 545
What a Friend We Have in Jesus, 435
What Wondrous Love Is This, 177
Where the Spirit of the Lord Is, 253

GLORIAS

Gloria Patri (Greatorex), 623
Gloria Patri (Meinecke), 622

GOD - Attributes

All People That on Earth Do Dwell, 20
El Shaddai, 36
God Is So Good, 41
God of Grace and God of Glory, 292
God the Omnipotent, 33
Hallelujah Chorus, 37
Holy, Holy, 266
Holy, Holy, Holy, 262
Holy Lord, 32
Immortal, Invisible, 25
Isaiah 6:3, 22
King of Heaven, Lord Most High, 104
O Worship the King, 10
Praise, My Soul, the King of Heaven, 3
Sing Praise to God Who Reigns Above, 6
We Praise Thee, O God, Our Redeemer, 16

GOD - Creation
(Nature)

All Creatures of Our God and King, 64
All Things Bright and Beautiful, 578
Fairest Lord Jesus, 88
Great Is Thy Faithfulness, 43
He's Everything to Me, 516
He's Got the Whole World in His Hands, 344
How Great Thou Art, 4
I Sing the Mighty Power of God, 59
Joyful, Joyful, We Adore Thee, 1
Lavish Love, Abundant Beauty, 61
Morning Has Broken, 60
Psalm 136, 63
The Spacious Firmament, 62
The Trees of the Field, 244
This Is My Father's World, 58
Thou Art Worthy, 73

GOD - Father

Be Thou My Vision, 382
Children of the Heavenly Father, 44
Day by Day, 56
Dear Lord and Father of Mankind, 427
Eternal Father, Strong to Save, 575
Father, I Adore You, 265
For God So Loved, 205
God Be with You, 602
God, Our Father, We Adore Thee, 268
God Will Take Care of You, 47
Great Is Thy Faithfulness, 43
Holy God, We Praise Thy Name, 12
Holy, Holy, Holy, 262
How Great Thou Art, 4
If You Will Only Let God Guide You, 600
Immortal, Invisible, 25
Joyful, Joyful, We Adore Thee, 1
Now Thank We All Our God, 556
O God, Our Help in Ages Past, 52
O Love That Will Not Let Me Go, 374
Praise, My Soul, the King of Heaven, 3
Tell Out, My Soul, 27
The God of Abraham Praise, 34
This Is My Father's World, 58
To God Be the Glory, 66

GOD - Guidance and Care

A Mighty Fortress Is Our God, 26
Children of the Heavenly Father, 44
Come, Thou Fount of Every Blessing, 2
Come, Ye Thankful People, Come, 559
Day by Day, 56
Day by Day - A Prayer, 55
Eternal Father, Strong to Save, 575
For the Beauty of the Earth, 560
God Is So Good, 41
God Leads Us Along, 46
God Will Take Care of You, 47
Great Is Thy Faithfulness, 43
Guide Me, O Thou Great Jehovah, 51
He Careth for You, 57
Hiding in Thee, 348
His Way, 54
Lavish Love, Abundant Beauty, 61
Lead Me, Lord, 49
Lead On, O King Eternal, 483
Now Thank We All Our God, 556
O God, Our Help in Ages Past, 52
Praise to the Lord, the Almighty, 8
Seek Ye First, 42
Sing Praise to God Who Reigns Above, 6
Surely Goodness and Mercy, 45
The Lord's My Shepherd, I'll Not Want, 50
The New 23rd, 53
We Are So Blessed, 564

GOD - Holy Spirit
(see HOLY SPIRIT)

GOD - Love and Mercy

Begin, My Tongue, Some Heavenly Theme, 70
Behold, What Manner of Love, 71
Great Is Thy Faithfulness, 43
O Love That Will Not Let Me Go, 374
Psalm 136, 63
Share His Love, 302
Surely Goodness and Mercy, 45
The Love of God, 67
The Wonder of It All, 65
There's a Wideness in God's Mercy, 68
Thy Loving Kindness, 69
To God Be the Glory, 66

GOD - Majesty and Power

A Mighty Fortress Is Our God, 26
A Perfect Heart, 40
El Shaddai, 36
Glorify Thy Name, 29
God the Omnipotent, 33
Great Are You, O Lord, 39
Great Is the Lord, 31
Hallelujah Chorus, 37
Holy, Holy, Holy, 262
Holy Lord, 32
How Majestic Is Your Name, 30
I Sing the Mighty Power of God, 59
I Will Call upon the Lord, 38
Immortal, Invisible, 25
O Worship the King, 10
Tell Out, My Soul, 27
The God of Abraham Praise, 34
The Majesty and Glory of Your Name, 35
Ye Servants of God, 17

GOD - Trinity
(see TRINITY)

GRACE
(see GOD - Love and Mercy, CHRIST - Grace, Love and Mercy)

HEALING

Be Still and Know, 343
He Touched Me, 504
Hear Now the Name, 407
How Sweet the Name of Jesus Sounds, 94
I Lay My Sins on Jesus, 340
Jesus, I Come, 336
Jesus Is Lord of All (Gaither), 359
Jesus Is Lord of All (McClard), 360
Jesus, We Just Want to Thank You, 98
Moment by Moment, 351
My Faith Has Found a Resting Place, 405
No, Not One!, 422
Praise, My Soul, the King of Heaven, 3
Praise to the Lord, the Almighty, 8
There Is a Balm in Gilead, 423
There's a Wideness in God's Mercy, 68

HEAVEN
(see LIFE EVERLASTING)

HOLINESS AND PURITY

Cleanse Me (Ellers), 439
Cleanse Me (Maori), 438
Give Me Jesus, 443
O for a Heart to Praise My God, 440
Pure and Holy, 437
Search Me, 434
Take Time to Be Holy (Holiness), 441
Take Time to Be Holy (Slane), 442
Whiter Than Snow, 436

HOLY SPIRIT

Breathe on Me, 251
Breathe on Me, Breath of God, 259
Cleanse Me (Ellers), 439
Cleanse Me (Maori), 438
Come, Holy Spirit, 250
Come Holy Spirit, Dove Divine, 320
Fill Me Now, 261
Greater Is He That Is In Me, 255
He Is Here, He Is Here, 256
Heavenly Spirit, Gentle Spirit, 254
Holy Ghost, with Light Divine, 248
Jesus, Stand Among Us, 586
O Breath of Life, 291
Spirit of God, Descend upon My Heart, 249
Spirit of the Living God, 247
Sweet, Sweet Spirit, 252
The Comforter Has Come, 257
We Are Gathered for Thy Blessing, 258
Welcome, Welcome, 260
Where the Spirit of the Lord Is, 253

HOLY TRINITY
(see TRINITY)

HOME
(see FAMILY AND HOME)

HOPE
(see FAITH AND HOPE)

INVITATION AND ACCEPTANCE
(see also REPENTANCE AND FORGIVENESS)

All Your Anxiety, 418
Are You Washed in the Blood?, 190
Come, Ye Sinners, Poor and Needy, 334
Have You Any Room for Jesus?, 328
I Am Praying for You, 431
I Have Decided to Follow Jesus, 376
I Surrender All, 366
Jesus Calls Us, 375
Jesus, I Come, 336
Jesus Is Calling, 327
Just As I Am, 342
Lord, I'm Coming Home, 341
Only Trust Him, 330
Room at the Cross for You, 331
Softly and Tenderly, 326
The Savior Is Waiting, 329
Thou Didst Leave Thy Throne, 127
Turn Your Eyes upon Jesus, 335

JOY

Be Joyful, 223
Good Christian Men, Rejoice, 151
How Great Our Joy!, 144
Jesus, Thou Joy of Loving Hearts, 501
Joyful, Joyful, We Adore Thee, 1
Rejoice, the Lord Is King, 228
The Day of Resurrection, 226

JUDGMENT

Jesus, Thy Blood and Righteousness, 193
Lo, He Comes with Clouds Descending, 241

LEADING
(see PROVISION AND LEADING, GOD - Guidance and Care)

LIFE EVERLASTING

Beyond the Sunset, 548
Face to Face, 549
For All the Saints, 546
He Keeps Me Singing, 488
He the Pearly Gates Will Open, 541
I Am His, and He Is Mine, 490
I'll Fly Away, 554
Jesus Lives, and So Shall I, 224
Must Jesus Bear the Cross Alone?, 449
My Faith Looks Up to Thee, 410
O Could I Speak the Matchless Worth, 110
O That Will Be Glory, 539
On Jordan's Stormy Banks, 552
Saved by Grace, 550
Soon and Very Soon, 551
Sweet By and By, 553
The King of Love My Shepherd Is, 468
The Kingdom of God, 547
The New 23rd, 53
The Way of the Cross Leads Home, 471
We Shall See His Lovely Face, 545
We'll Understand It Better By and By, 544
We're Marching to Zion, 555
When I Can Read My Title Clear, 538
When the Roll Is Called Up Yonder, 543
When We All Get to Heaven, 542

LORD'S DAY
(see OPENING OF SERVICE)

LORD'S SUPPER
(see also CHRIST - Atonement)

A Communion Hymn for Christmas, 140
According to Thy Gracious Word, 321
Break Thou the Bread of Life, 274
Come Celebrate Jesus, 324
Here, O My Lord, I See Thee Face to Face, 325
In Remembrance, 322
Let Us Break Bread Together, 323

LOVE - God's Love
(see also GOD - Love and Mercy)

Children of the Heavenly Father, 44
For God So Loved, 205
God So Loved the World, 207
I Am His, and He Is Mine, 490
I Will Sing of My Redeemer, 506
In Heavenly Love Abiding, 502
Jesus, Lover of My Soul, 466
Jesus Loves Even Me, 357
Jesus Loves Me, 579
Joyful, Joyful, We Adore Thee, 1
Lavish Love, Abundant Beauty, 61
Love Divine, All Loves Excelling, 92
Love Lifted Me, 505
No One Ever Cared for Me Like Jesus, 528
O, How He Loves You and Me, 513
O Love That Will Not Let Me Go, 374
O the Deep, Deep Love of Jesus (Bunessan), 212
O the Deep, Deep Love of Jesus (Ebenezer), 211
Of the Father's Love Begotten, 118
Share His Love, 302
The Love of God, 67
Thy Loving Kindness, 69
When I Survey the Wondrous Cross, 185

LOVE - Our Love for God

Joyful, Joyful, We Adore Thee, 1
More Love to Thee, 363
My Jesus, I Love Thee, 364
O, How I Love Jesus, 529

LOVE - Our Love for Others

Blest Be the Tie That Binds, 286
Joyful, Joyful, We Adore Thee, 1
People Need the Lord, 303
The Bond of Love, 281
They'll Know We Are Christians by Our Love, 284

LOYALTY AND COURAGE
(see also SPIRITUAL WARFARE)

A Charge to Keep I Have, 448
Faith Is the Victory, 486
Greater Is He That Is In Me, 255
I Must Tell Jesus, 430
I Need Thee Every Hour, 428
Near the Cross, 385
O Jesus, I Have Promised, 369
Take the Name of Jesus with You, 116
Who Is on the Lord's Side?, 484

MARRIAGE
(see FAMILY AND HOME)

MEMORIAL DAY

America, the Beautiful, 572
Battle Hymn of the Republic, 569
God of Our Fathers, 573
Once to Every Man and Nation, 475
We Gather Together, 561

MEMORIAL OCCASIONS

Faith of Our Fathers, 279
For All the Saints, 546
God of Our Fathers, 573
O God, Our Help in Ages Past, 52
We Gather Together, 561

MERCY

(see GOD - Love and Mercy, CHRIST - Grace, Love and Mercy)

MISSIONS AND EVANGELISM

All Hail the Power of Jesus' Name (Coronation), 97
All Hail the Power of Jesus' Name (Diadem), 96
Anywhere with Jesus, 467
Faith of Our Fathers, 279
Faithful Men, 288
Freely, Freely, 447
Go, 308
Go, Tell It on the Mountain, 138
Go Ye into All the World, 301
I Love to Tell the Story, 297
I'll Go Where You Want Me to Go, 444
I'll Tell the World That I'm a Christian, 300
In Christ There Is No East or West, 285
Jesus Loves the Little Children, 580
Jesus Saves!, 306
Jesus Shall Reign, 231
Let Your Heart Be Broken, 315
Lift High the Cross, 304
Lord, Lay Some Soul upon My Heart, 313
Lord, Speak to Me, 450
Lord, Thy Church on Earth Is Seeking, 305
Macedonia, 316
Make Me a Blessing, 452
O for a Thousand Tongues, 76
O Zion, Haste, 298
Only One Life, 378
Open My Eyes, That I May See, 381
Our God Reigns, 229
Pass It On, 309
People Need the Lord, 303
Reach Out and Touch, 314
Rescue the Perishing, 299
Send the Light, 307
Set My Soul Afire, 294
Share His Love, 302
So Send I You, 310
So Send I You - by Grace Made Strong, 311
Take My Life and Let It Be, 379
Take the Name of Jesus with You, 116
Tell Me the Story of Jesus, 172
The Church's One Foundation, 277
To Be God's People, 312
We've a Story to Tell to the Nations, 296
When He Shall Come, 240
Wherever He Leads I'll Go, 367
Ye Servants of God, 17

MORNING

Holy, Holy, Holy, 262
May Jesus Christ Be Praised, 87
Morning Has Broken, 60
Sun of My Soul, 412
This Is the Day, 590

MOTHER'S DAY

A Christian Home, 535
For the Beauty of the Earth, 560
Happy the Home When God Is There, 536
Now Thank We All Our God, 556
O Perfect Love, 533
She Will Be Called Blessed, 534

NATION

(see PATRIOTIC)

NATURE

(see GOD - Creation)

NEW YEAR

(see also COMMITMENT AND CONSECRATION)

Another Year Is Dawning, 567
God of the Ages, 568
Guide Me, O Thou Great Jehovah, 51
If You Will Only Let God Guide You, 600
Lead On, O King Eternal, 483
Now Thank We All Our God, 556
O God, Our Help in Ages Past, 52
Savior, Like a Shepherd Lead Us, 462

OBEDIENCE (see also COMMITMENT AND CONSECRATION, ASPIRATION, STEWARDSHIP AND SERVICE, SPIRITUAL WARFARE)

Seek Ye First, 42
Trust and Obey, 349

OFFERTORIES (see RESPONSES - Offertories)

OPENING OF SERVICE - Calls to Worship

Cast Thy Burden upon the Lord, 598
Christ, We Do All Adore Thee, 597
Now to the King of Heaven, 595
O Worship the Lord, 593
Praise Ye the Name of the Lord, 596
The Lord Is in His Holy Temple, 594

OPENING OF SERVICE - Calls to Worship - Spoken

599

OPENING OF SERVICE - Hymns and Songs

(see also ADORATION AND PRAISE)

All People That on Earth Do Dwell, 20
All Praise to Our Redeeming Lord, 587
Brethren, We Have Met to Worship, 585
Come Celebrate Jesus, 324
Come, Christians, Join to Sing, 108
Come into His Presence, 589
Come Let Us Reason, 591
Come, Thou Almighty King, 267
Come, We That Love the Lord, 18
Holy, Holy, 266
In This Quiet Moment, 592
It Is Good to Sing Thy Praises, 584
Jesus, Stand Among Us, 586
Let Us Break Bread Together, 323
Open My Eyes, That I May See, 381
Open Our Eyes, Lord, 383
Stand Up and Bless the Lord, 21
This Is the Day, 590
We Are Gathered for Thy Blessing, 258
We Have Come into His House, 588
Welcome, Welcome, 260

PALM SUNDAY

(see CHRIST - Triumphal Entry)

PATRIOTIC

America, the Beautiful, 572
Battle Hymn of the Republic, 569
Blessed the Nation, 577
Eternal Father, Strong to Save, 575
God of Our Fathers, 573
If My People's Hearts Are Humbled, 574
My Country, 'Tis of Thee, 571
The Star-Spangled Banner, 576

PEACE

He Hideth My Soul, 496
He Keeps Me Singing, 488
Heaven Came Down, 495
I Am His, and He Is Mine, 490
I Know Whom I Have Believed, 409
In Heavenly Love Abiding, 502
In My Heart There Rings a Melody, 514
It Is Well with My Soul, 493
Jesus, I Am Resting, Resting, 503
Jesus, Thou Joy of Loving Hearts, 501
Like a River Glorious, 494
My Faith Has Found a Resting Place, 405
Near to the Heart of God, 497
Now I Belong to Jesus, 511
O Happy Day!, 532
Peace Like a River, 498
Peace, Perfect Peace, 487
Rejoice in the Lord Always, 489
Rejoice, Ye Pure in Heart, 562
Saved, Saved!, 530
Since Jesus Came into My Heart, 515
Sunshine in My Soul, 499
The Joy of the Lord, 411
Thou Wilt Keep Him in Perfect Peace, 492
Wonderful Peace, 500

PENTECOST
(see HOLY SPIRIT)

PRAISE
(see ADORATION AND PRAISE)

PRAYER AND INTERCESSION
A Nativity Prayer, 126
Dear Lord and Father of Mankind, 427
From Every Stormy Wind That Blows, 432
I Am Praying for You, 431
I Must Tell Jesus, 430
I Need Thee Every Hour, 428
In the Garden, 425
Lord, Listen to Your Children Praying, 429
Search Me, 434
Sweet Hour of Prayer, 433
The Lord's Prayer, 426
What a Friend We Have in Jesus, 435

PRAYER RESPONSES (see RESPONSES - Prayer)

PROMISES
Draw Nigh to God, 397
God Will Take Care of You, 47
I Heard the Voice of Jesus Say, 414
Seek Ye First, 42
The Joy of the Lord, 411

PROVISION AND LEADING
(see also GOD - Guidance and Care)
All the Way My Savior Leads Me, 460
Anywhere with Jesus, 467
Cover Me, 469
Footsteps of Jesus, 470
Gentle Shepherd, 458
He Leadeth Me, 461
I Will Sing of the Mercies, 457
In His Time, 465
Jesus, Lover of My Soul, 466
Precious Lord, Take My Hand, 463
Savior, Like a Shepherd Lead Us, 462
Shepherd of Love, 464
The King of Love My Shepherd Is, 468
The Way of the Cross Leads Home, 471

PURITY
(see HOLINESS AND PURITY)

REDEMPTION (see REPENTANCE AND FORGIVENESS, ATONEMENT, CHRIST - Grace, Love and Mercy)

REFUGE
(see GUIDANCE AND CARE, FAITH AND HOPE)

RENEWAL AND REVIVAL
Faithful Men, 288
God of Grace and God of Glory, 292
Lord, Thy Church on Earth Is Seeking, 305
O Breath of Life, 291
Revive Us Again, 295
Rise Up, O Church (Men) of God, 293
Set My Soul Afire, 294
There Shall Be Showers of Blessing, 289

REPENTANCE AND FORGIVENESS
At Calvary, 338
Cleanse Me (Ellers), 439
Cleanse Me (Maori), 438
Come, Ye Sinners, Poor and Needy, 334
I Lay My Sins on Jesus, 340
If My People's Hearts Are Humbled, 574
Jesus, I Come, 336
Just As I Am, 342
Lord, I'm Coming Home, 341
Pass Me Not, 337
Since I Have Been Redeemed, 339
Turn Your Eyes upon Jesus, 335
Whiter Than Snow, 436

RESPONSES - Benedictions
(see BENEDICTIONS)

RESPONSES - Offertories
Glorify Thy Name, 29
God Is So Good, 41
God's Ways Are Wonderful, 621
We Give Thee but Thine Own, 620

RESPONSES - Prayer
Day by Day - A Prayer, 55
Hear Our Prayer, O Heavenly Father, 616
Hear Our Prayer, O Lord, 614
Lead Me, Lord, 49
Let the Words of My Mouth, 618
Spirit Divine, Hear Our Prayer, 615
Thou Wilt Keep Him in Perfect Peace (Duke's Tune), 617
We Give You Thanks, 619

RESURRECTION
(see CHRIST - Resurrection)

REVIVAL
(see RENEWAL AND REVIVAL)

SALVATION
(see also INVITATION AND ACCEPTANCE, REPENTANCE AND FORGIVENESS)
All for Jesus, 368
And Can It Be?, 203
At Calvary, 338
At the Cross, 188
Calvary Covers It All, 189
Come, Ye Sinners, Poor and Needy, 334
For God So Loved, 205
Freely, Freely, 447
Glory to His Name, 527
God So Loved the World, 207
Have You Any Room for Jesus?, 328
He Touched Me, 504
Heaven Came Down, 495
His Way with Thee, 333
I Know a Fount, 194
I Know Whom I Have Believed, 409
I Surrender All, 366
It Took a Miracle, 524
Jesus Is Calling, 327
Jesus Paid It All, 210
Jesus Saves!, 306
Jesus, Thy Blood and Righteousness, 193
Lord, I'm Coming Home, 341
Love Divine, All Loves Excelling, 92
Love Lifted Me, 505
My Faith Has Found a Resting Place, 405
My Hope Is in the Lord, 406
My Tribute, 11
Nothing But the Blood, 195
Now I Belong to Jesus, 511
O Happy Day!, 532
One Day!, 170
Only Trust Him, 330
Our Great Savior, 89
Praise Him! Praise Him!, 106
Praise to the Lord, the Almighty, 8
Praise Ye the Triune God, 264
Rock of Ages, 204
Room at the Cross for You, 331
Satisfied, 531
Saved, Saved!, 530
Since I Have Been Redeemed, 339
Sing Praise to God Who Reigns Above, 6
Softly and Tenderly, 326
Tell Me the Old, Old Story, 424
The Blood Will Never Lose Its Power, 192
The Church's One Foundation, 277
The Love of God, 67
The Savior Is Waiting, 329
The Way of the Cross Leads Home, 471
There Is a Fountain, 196
There Is Power in the Blood, 191
Thou Didst Leave Thy Throne, 127
To God Be the Glory, 66
Turn Your Eyes upon Jesus, 335
Victory in Jesus, 473
Without Him, 332
Yesterday, Today and Tomorrow, 523

SANCTIFICATION (see HOLINESS AND PURITY, ASPIRATION, CHRIST - Cleansing Blood, HOLY SPIRIT, COMMITMENT AND CONSECRATION)

SECOND COMING
(see CHRIST - Second Coming)

SERVICE
(see STEWARDSHIP AND SERVICE)

SERVICE MUSIC - Amens
628

SERVICE MUSIC - Benedictions
(see BENEDICTIONS)

SERVICE MUSIC - Calls to Worship
(see CALLS TO WORSHIP)

SERVICE MUSIC - Doxologies
(see DOXOLOGIES)

SERVICE MUSIC - Glorias
(see GLORIAS)

SERVICE MUSIC - Offertories
(see RESPONSES - Offertories)

SERVICE MUSIC - Prayer Responses
(see RESPONSES - Prayer)

SOCIAL CONCERN
(see also LOVE - Our Love For Others)
Footsteps of Jesus, 470
Joyful, Joyful, We Adore Thee, 1
Let Your Heart Be Broken, 315
Macedonia, 316

SPIRITUAL WARFARE
A Mighty Fortress Is Our God, 26
Am I a Soldier of the Cross?, 482
Faith Is the Victory, 486
For All the Saints, 546
God of Grace and God of Glory, 292
He Keeps Me Singing, 488
I Am a Soldier of the Cross!, 480
It Is Well with My Soul, 493
Lead On, O King Eternal, 483
Lift High the Cross, 304
O God, Our Help in Ages Past, 52
O Jesus, I Have Promised, 369
Once to Every Man and Nation, 475
Onward, Christian Soldiers, 479
Rise Up, O Church (Men) of God, 293
Soldiers of Christ, Arise, 478
Stand Up, Stand Up for Jesus (Geibel), 481
Stand Up, Stand Up for Jesus (Webb), 477
The Battle Belongs to the Lord, 485
The Battle Is the Lord's, 472
Victory in Jesus, 473
We Will Stand, 474
When I Can Read My Title Clear, 538
Who Is on the Lord's Side?, 484

STEWARDSHIP AND SERVICE
A Charge to Keep I Have, 448
Come, All Christians, Be Committed, 455
Freely, Freely, 447
Give Me Jesus, 443
Glorious Is Thy Name, Most Holy, 454
God's Ways Are Wonderful, 621
I Gave My Life for Thee, 453
I Will Serve Thee, 446
I'll Go Where You Want Me to Go, 444
Jesus Is Lord of All (Gaither), 359
Jesus Is Lord of All (McClard), 360
Let Your Heart Be Broken, 315
Lord, Speak to Me, 450
Make Me a Blessing, 452
Must Jesus Bear the Cross Alone?, 449
O Master, Let Me Walk with Thee, 451
O to Be Like Thee!, 387
Reaching for Excellence, 456
Something for Thee, 445
Take My Life and Let It Be, 379
The Wise May Bring Their Learning, 583
We Give Thee but Thine Own, 620

SUBMISSION
(see COMMITMENT AND CONSECRATION, STEWARDSHIP AND SERVICE)

SURRENDER
(see COMMITMENT AND CONSECRATION, REPENTANCE AND FORGIVENESS)

TEMPTATION
A Charge to Keep I Have, 448
At the Name of Jesus, 235
Faith Is the Victory, 486
Greater Is He That Is In Me, 255
I Must Tell Jesus, 430
I Need Thee Every Hour, 428
Lead Me to Calvary, 176
Near the Cross, 385
O Jesus, I Have Promised, 369
O Sacred Head, Now Wounded, 178
Spirit of God, Descend upon My Heart, 249
Take the Name of Jesus with You, 116

TESTIMONY AND PRAISE
Alas! and Did My Savior Bleed?, 208
All That Thrills My Soul, 526
All the Way My Savior Leads Me, 460
Amazing Grace, 202
At Calvary, 338
At the Cross, 188
Because He Lives, 213
Beneath the Cross of Jesus, 183
Blessed Assurance, 345
Fill My Cup, Lord, 398
Freely, Freely, 447
Give Me Jesus, 443
Glory to His Name, 527
Go, Tell It on the Mountain, 138
He Keeps Me Singing, 488
He Leadeth Me, 461
He Lifted Me, 522
He Lives, 220
He Touched Me, 504
Heaven Came Down, 495
He's Everything to Me, 516
I Am His, and He Is Mine, 490
I Have Decided to Follow Jesus, 376
I Heard the Voice of Jesus Say, 414
I Just Came to Praise the Lord, 113
I Know That My Redeemer Liveth, 218
I Know Whom I Have Believed, 409
I Lay My Sins on Jesus, 340
I Love to Tell the Story, 297
I Will Praise Him!, 525
I Will Sing of My Redeemer, 506
I Will Sing of the Mercies, 457
I Will Sing the Wondrous Story, 508
I'd Rather Have Jesus, 517
I'll Tell the World That I'm a Christian, 300
In His Cross I Glory, 187
In My Heart There Rings a Melody, 514
It Is Well with My Soul, 493
It Took a Miracle, 524
Jesus Is All the World to Me, 510
Jesus Is King, 230
Jesus Lives, and So Shall I, 224
Jesus Loves Even Me, 357
Jesus Paid It All, 210
Living for Jesus, 372
Love Lifted Me, 505
Moment by Moment, 351
My Savior's Love, 512
My Tribute, 11
No One Ever Cared for Me Like Jesus, 528
Nothing But the Blood, 195
Now I Belong to Jesus, 511
O Could I Speak the Matchless Worth, 110
O for a Thousand Tongues, 76
O Happy Day!, 532
O, How He Loves You and Me, 513
O, How I Love Jesus, 529
O the Deep, Deep Love of Jesus (Bunessan), 212
O the Deep, Deep Love of Jesus (Ebenezer), 211
Peace Like a River, 498
Praise Him! Praise Him!, 106
Redeemed (Ada), 520
Redeemed (Kirkpatrick), 521
Satisfied, 531
Saved, Saved!, 530
Since I Have Been Redeemed, 339
Since Jesus Came into My Heart, 515
Something Beautiful, 519
Standing on the Promises, 271
Sunshine in My Soul, 499
Tell Out, My Soul, 27
The Blood Will Never Lose Its Power, 192
The Joy of the Lord, 411

The King of Love My Shepherd Is, 468
The Longer I Serve Him, 518
The Old Rugged Cross, 186
The Solid Rock (Melita), 402
The Solid Rock (Solid Rock), 404
The Way of the Cross Leads Home, 471
Through It All, 507
'Tis So Sweet to Trust in Jesus, 350
Under His Wings, 356
Without Him, 332
Yesterday, Today and Tomorrow, 523

THANKSGIVING
(Thankfulness)
Come, Ye Thankful People, Come, 559
Count Your Blessings, 563
For Health and Strength, 566
For the Beauty of the Earth, 560
I Just Came to Praise the Lord, 113
In Thanksgiving, Let Us Praise Him, 557
Jesus, We Just Want to Thank You, 98
Lord, We Praise You, 83
Now Thank We All Our God, 556
Psalm 136, 63
Rejoice, Ye Pure in Heart, 562
This Is My Father's World, 58
We Are So Blessed, 564
We Gather Together, 561
We Give You Thanks, 619
We Thank You, Lord, 565

TRINITY
Come, Thou Almighty King, 267
Father, I Adore You, 265
God, Our Father, We Adore Thee, 268
Holy, Holy, 266
Holy, Holy, Holy, 262
Praise Ye the Triune God, 264
Sing Praise, 263

TRIUMPHAL ENTRY
(see CHRIST - Triumphal Entry)

TRUST
(see also ASSURANCE)
A Child of the King, 352
A Shelter in the Time of Storm, 353
Be Still and Know, 343
Be Still, My Soul, 347
Because He Lives, 213
Blessed Assurance, 345
He Careth for You, 57
He's Got the Whole World in His Hands, 344
Hiding in Thee, 348
I Am Trusting Thee, Lord Jesus, 346
Jesus Loves Even Me, 357
Leaning on the Everlasting Arms, 354
Moment by Moment, 351
Praise the Savior, 75
'Tis So Sweet to Trust in Jesus, 350
Trust and Obey, 349
Trusting Jesus, 355
Under His Wings, 356

UNITY
(see CHURCH - Fellowship of Believers)

VICTORY
(see also SPIRITUAL WARFARE)
Arise, My Soul, Arise, 199
Because He Lives, 213
Greater Is He That Is In Me, 255
Jesus Is Lord of All (Gaither), 359
Jesus Is Lord of All (McClard), 360
Jesus Lives, and So Shall I, 224
Joyful, Joyful, We Adore Thee, 1
Like a River Glorious, 494
O God, Our Help in Ages Past, 52
O Jesus, I Have Promised, 369
So Send I You - by Grace Made Strong, 311
The Blood Will Never Lose Its Power, 192
The Solid Rock (Melita), 402
The Solid Rock (Solid Rock), 404
There Is Power in the Blood, 191
Victory in Jesus, 473

WARFARE
(see SPIRITUAL WARFARE)

WEDDING
Day by Day, 56
Great Is Thy Faithfulness, 43
Happy the Home When God Is There, 536
Joyful, Joyful, We Adore Thee, 1
Love Divine, All Loves Excelling, 92
Now Thank We All Our God, 556
O God, Our Help in Ages Past, 52
O Perfect Love, 533
Rejoice, Ye Pure in Heart, 562
Savior, Like a Shepherd Lead Us, 462
The Bond of Love, 281
The King of Love My Shepherd Is, 468
The Lord's Prayer, 426

WITNESSING
(see MISSIONS AND EVANGELISM)

WORD OF GOD
According to Thy Gracious Word, 321
Break Thou the Bread of Life, 274
Holy Bible, Book Divine, 273
How Firm a Foundation, 275
Jesus Loves Even Me, 357
Jesus Loves Me, 579
O Word of God Incarnate, 269
Standing on the Promises, 271
Thy Word, 272
Wonderful Words of Life, 270

WORSHIP
(see also ADORATION AND PRAISE)
Be Thou My Vision, 382
In This Quiet Moment, 592
Jesus, Priceless Treasure, 413
Let Us Break Bread Together, 323
O Worship the Lord, 593
Spirit of God, Descend upon My Heart, 249
Sun of My Soul, 412
Sweet, Sweet Spirit, 252
We Are So Blessed, 564
We Have Come into His House, 588

YOUTH SONGS AND HYMNS
Come Celebrate Jesus, 324
Come Let Us Reason, 591
Cover Me, 469
Day by Day - A Prayer, 55
Easter Song, 222
Father, I Adore You, 265
Freely, Freely, 447
Go, 308
Greater Is He That Is In Me, 255
Hallowed Be the Name, 84
He's Everything to Me, 516
He's Got the Whole World in His Hands, 344
Holy, Holy, 266
I Have Decided to Follow Jesus, 376
I Will Serve Thee, 446
In His Time, 465
In My Life Lord, Be Glorified, 394
In the Name of the Lord, 90
King of Kings, 77
Lord, Listen to Your Children Praying, 429
Majesty, 74
Morning Has Broken, 60
Open Our Eyes, Lord, 383
Pass It On, 309
Peace Like a River, 498
People Need the Lord, 303
Praise the Name of Jesus, 93
Rejoice in the Lord Always, 489
Shepherd of Love, 464
Sometimes "Alleluia", 115
Soon and Very Soon, 551
Sweet, Sweet Spirit, 252
The Battle Belongs to the Lord, 485
The Bond of Love, 281
The New 23rd, 53
The Trees of the Field, 244
There Is a Redeemer, 206
They'll Know We Are Christians by Our Love, 284
This Is the Day, 590
Thy Word, 272
Turn Your Eyes upon Jesus, 335
We Are the Reason, 209
We Come, O Christ, to You, 117
We Shall Behold Him, 237
We Will Glorify, 72
We Will Stand, 474
Worthy Is the Lamb, 180

ZEAL
(see also SPIRITUAL WARFARE, VICTORY, LOYALTY AND COURAGE)
O for a Thousand Tongues, 76
When We All Get to Heaven, 542

ALPHABETICAL INDEX OF HYMNS

Titles are in **bold face** type; First lines are in regular type.

A Charge to Keep I Have, 448
A Child of the King, 352
A Christian Home, 535
A Communion Hymn for Christmas, 140
A Doxology Canon, 627
A Mighty Fortress Is Our God, 26
A Nativity Prayer, 126
A Perfect Heart, 40
A pilgrim was I, and a wand'ring, **45**
A Shelter in the Time of Storm, 353
A Thousand Candles, 159
A wonderful Savior is Jesus my Lord, **496**
Abba Father, 15
Abide with Me, 419
According to Thy Gracious Word, 321
Adoration, 165
Alas! and Did My Savior Bleed?, 208
Alas! and did my Savior bleed? (At the Cross), **188**
All Creatures of Our God and King, 64
All for Jesus, 368
All Glory, Laud and Honor, 173
All Hail the Power of Jesus' Name (CORONATION), 97
All Hail the Power of Jesus' Name (DIADEM), 96
All my life long I had panted, **531**
All my tomorrows, **359**
All People That on Earth Do Dwell, 20
"All power is given unto Me," **301**
All praise to Him who reigns above, **103**
All Praise to Our Redeeming Lord, 587
All That Thrills My Soul, 526
All the Way My Savior Leads Me, 460
All Things Bright and Beautiful, 578
All to Jesus I surrender, **366**
All Your Anxiety, 418
Alleluia, 91
Alleluia! Alleluia!, 215
Alleluia, Alleluia! The majesty, **35**
Alleluia! Born is the King of kings, **149**
Alleluia! Christ is risen from the dead, **221**
Alleluia! Sing to Jesus, 233
Almighty Father give us a vision, **312**
Am I a Soldier of the Cross?, 482
Amazing Grace, 202
Amens, 628
America, the Beautiful, 572
And Can It Be?, 203
And I shall see Him face to face, **550**
Angels from the Realms of Glory, 131
Angels We Have Heard on High, 132
Another Year Is Dawning, 567
Anywhere with Jesus, 467
Are You Washed in the Blood?, 190
Arise, My Soul, Arise, 199
As for Me and My House, 537
As the hart longs, **401**
As with Gladness Men of Old, 163
Aspiration Canon, 391
At Calvary, 338
At the Cross, 188
At the Name of Jesus, 235
Away in a Manger (AWAY IN A MANGER), 157
Away in a Manger (CRADLE SONG), 158

Battle Hymn of the Republic, 569
Be Calm My Soul, 421
Be Exalted, O God, 5
Be Joyful, 223
Be not dismayed whate'er betide, **47**
Be Still and Know, 343
Be Still, My Soul, 347
Be Thou My Vision, 382
Because He Lives, 213
Because the Lord is my Shepherd, **53**
Begin, My Tongue, Some Heavenly Theme, 70
Behold the Lamb, 179
Behold, What Manner of Love, 71
Beneath the Cross of Jesus, 183
Benediction, 612
Beyond the Sunset, 548
Bless His Holy Name, 13
Bless the Lord, O my soul, **13**
Bless the Lord who reigns in beauty, **40**
Blessed Assurance, 345
Blessed Be the Name, 103
Blessed Savior, we adore Thee, **85**
Blessed the Nation, 577
Blessing and Honor, 78
Blest Be the Tie That Binds, 286
Break Forth, O Beauteous Heavenly Light, 129
Break Thou the Bread of Life, 274
Breathe on Me, 251
Breathe on Me, Breath of God, 259
Brethren, We Have Met to Worship, 585
Bring Back the Springtime, 396

Calvary Covers It All, 189
Cast Thy Burden upon the Lord, 598
Child of Love, 156
Children of the Heavenly Father, 44
Christ Arose, 216
Christ has for sin atonement made, **81**
Christ Is Made the Sure Foundation, 276
Christ the Lord Is Risen Today, 217
Christ, We Do All Adore Thee, 597
Clap Your Hands, 24
Cleanse Me (ELLERS), 439
Cleanse Me (MAORI), 438
Close to Thee, 365

Come, All Christians, Be Committed, 455
Come and join the reapers, **288**
Come and Praise the Lord Our King, 171
Come as a wisdom to children, **250**
Come Celebrate Jesus, 324
Come, Christians, Join to Sing, 108
Come, every soul by sin oppressed, **330**
Come, Holy Spirit, 250
Come, Holy Spirit, Dove Divine, 320
Come into His Presence, 589
Come Let Us Reason, 591
Come Let Us Worship and Bow Down, 14
Come on, Ring Those Bells, 153
Come, Thou Almighty King, 267
Come, Thou Fount of Every Blessing, 2
Come, Thou Long-Expected Jesus, 124
Come, We That Love the Lord, 18
Come, we that love the Lord (We're Marching to Zion), **555**
Come, Ye Disconsolate, 416
Come, Ye Sinners, Poor and Needy, 334
Come, Ye Thankful People, Come, 559
Commit Thy Way, 581
Count Your Blessings, 563
Cover Me, 469
Crown Him with Many Crowns, 234

Day by Day, 56
Day by Day - A Prayer, 55
Dear Father, our hearts are filled, **619**
Dear Lord and Father of Mankind, 427
Down at the cross where my Savior died, **527**
Doxology, 624
Doxology (ALTERNATE RHYTHM), 625
Doxology (OWENS), 626
Draw Nigh to God, 397
Dying with Jesus, by death reckoned mine, **351**

Earthly pleasures vainly call me, **388**
Easter Song, 222
El Shaddai, 36
Emmanuel, 134
Emptied of His glory, **105**
Encamped along the hills of light, **486**
Eternal Father, Strong to Save, 575

Face to Face, 549
Fairest Lord Jesus, 88
Faith Is the Victory, 486
Faith of Our Fathers, 279
Faithful Men, 288
Far away in the depths of my spirit, **500**
Far dearer than all, **189**
Father, I Adore You, 265
Father, we love you, **29**
Fill Me Now, 261
Fill My Cup, Lord, 398
Footsteps of Jesus, 470
For All the Saints, 546
For God So Loved, 205
For Health and Strength, 566
For the Beauty of the Earth, 560
For Unto Us a Child Is Born, 146
Freely, Freely, 447
From Every Stormy Wind That Blows, 432
From the first bright light, **557**

Gathered round Your table, **140**
Gentle Shepherd, 458
Give Me Jesus, 443
Give thanks to the Lord, **63**
Gloria Patri (GREATOREX), 623
Gloria Patri (MEINECKE), 622
Glorify Thy Name, 29
Glorious Is Thy Name, 85
Glorious Is Thy Name, Most Holy, 454
Glorious Things of Thee Are Spoken, 278
Glory be to the Father (GREATOREX), **623**
Glory be to the Father (MEINECKE), **622**
Glory to His Name, 527
Go, 308
Go Now and Live for the Savior, 610
Go, Tell It on the Mountain, 138
Go Ye into All the World, 301
God Be with You, 602
God forgave my sin in Jesus' name, **447**
God Is So Good, 41
God Leads Us Along, 46
God moves in a mysterious way, **54**
God of Grace and God of Glory, 292
God of Our Fathers, 573
God of the Ages, 568
God, Our Father, We Adore Thee, 268
God, our Father, we adore You, **39**
God sent His Son, they called Him Jesus, **213**
God So Loved the World, 207
God the Omnipotent, 33
God Will Take Care of You, 47
God's Ways Are Wonderful, 621
Good Christian Men, Rejoice, 151
Good Shepherd, Take This Little Child, 318
Grace Greater Than Our Sin, 201
Grace, Love and Fellowship, 606
Great Are You, O Lord, 39
Great Is the Lord, 31
Great Is Thy Faithfulness, 43
Greater Is He That Is in Me, 255
Guide Me, O Thou Great Jehovah, 51

Hail the Day That Sees Him Rise, 232
Hallelujah Chorus, 37
Hallelujah! Hallelujah!, **37**
Hallelujah, What a Savior!, 175
Hallowed Be the Name, 84
Happy the Home When God Is There, 536
Hark! the Herald Angels Sing, 133
Have Faith in God, 408
Have Thine Own Way, Lord, 371
Have You Any Room for Jesus? 328
Have you been to Jesus for the cleansing, **190**
He Careth for You, 57
He Giveth More Grace, 415
He Hideth My Soul, 496
He Is Coming, 246

He Is Here, He Is Here, 256
He Is Lord, 105
He Keeps Me Singing, 488
He Leadeth Me, 461
He Lifted Me, 522
He Lives, 220
He Rose Triumphantly, 219
He the Pearly Gates Will Open, 541
He Touched Me, 504
Hear Now the Name, 407
Hear Our Prayer, O Heavenly Father, 616
Hear Our Prayer, O Lord, 614
Hear the bells ringing, **222**
Hear the story from God's Word, **197**
Heaven Came Down, 495
Heavenly Spirit, Gentle Spirit, 254
Here, O My Lord, I See Thee Face to Face, 325
He's Everything to Me, 516
He's Got the Whole World in His Hands, 344
Hiding in Thee, 348
Higher Ground, 399
His Name Is Life, 114
His name is Master, **114**
His Name Is Wonderful, 101
His Way, 54
His Way with Thee, 333
Holy Bible, Book Divine, 273
Holy Ghost, with Light Divine, 248
Holy God, We Praise Thy Name, 12
Holy, Holy, 266
Holy, Holy, Holy, 262
Holy, holy, holy, Lord God of hosts, **22**
Holy, holy, Lord, God almighty, **32**
Holy Lord, 32
Holy Spirit, breathe on me, **251**
Hosanna, Loud Hosanna, 174
Hover o'er me, Holy Spirit, **261**
How can I say thanks, **11**
How Firm a Foundation, 275
How Great Our Joy!, 144
How Great Thou Art, 4
How lovely on the mountains, **229**
How Majestic Is Your Name, 30
How Sweet the Name of Jesus Sounds, 94

I Am a Soldier of the Cross!, 480
I Am His, and He Is Mine, 490
I Am Praying for You, 431
I am so glad that our Father in heav'n, **357**
I Am Thine, O Lord, 358
I Am Trusting Thee, Lord Jesus, 346
I am weak but Thou art strong, **380**
I can hear my Savior calling, **373**
I come to the garden alone, **425**
I Gave My Life for Thee, 453
I have a Savior, **431**
I have a song I love to sing, **339**
I have a song that Jesus gave me, **514**
I Have Decided to Follow Jesus, 376
I have one deep, supreme desire, **400**
I hear the Savior say, **210**
I heard an old, old story, **473**
I Heard the Bells on Christmas Day, 152
I Heard the Voice of Jesus Say, 414
I Just Came to Praise the Lord, 113
I Know a Fount, 194
I know, I know that Jesus liveth, **218**
I know not why God's wondrous grace, **409**
I Know That My Redeemer Liveth, 218
I Know Whom I Have Believed, 409
I Lay My Sins on Jesus, 340
I Love Thee, 362
I Love Thy Kingdom, Lord, 280
I Love to Tell the Story, 297
I Love You, Lord, 80
I must needs go home, **471**
I Must Tell Jesus, 430
I Need Thee Every Hour, 428
I serve a risen Savior, **220**
I Sing the Mighty Power of God, 59
I stand amazed in the presence, **512**
I Surrender All, 366
I Want to Be Like Jesus, 400
I want to be like Jesus Christ, **391**
I was sinking deep in sin, **505**
I Will Call upon the Lord, 38
I will give thanks to Thee, **5**
I Will Praise Him!, 525
I Will Serve Thee, 446
I Will Sing of My Redeemer, 506
I Will Sing of the Mercies, 457
I Will Sing the Wondrous Story, 508
I Wonder as I Wander, 139
I Would Be Like Jesus, 388
I would love to tell you, **528**
I'd Rather Have Jesus, 517
If My People's Hearts Are Humbled, 574
If You Will Only Let God Guide You, 600
I'll Fly Away, 554
I'll Go Where You Want Me to Go, 444
I'll Live for Him, 370
I'll Tell the World That I'm a Christian, 300
I'm pressing on the upward way, **399**
I'm so glad I'm a part, **282**
Immortal, Invisible, 25
Immortal, invisible King of heaven, **104**
In Christ There Is No East or West, 285
In heavenly armor, **485**
In Heavenly Love Abiding, 502
In His Cross I Glory, 187
In His Time, 465
In loving kindness Jesus came, **522**
In My Heart There Rings a Melody, 514
In My Life, Lord, Be Glorified, 394
In Remembrance, 322
In shady, green pastures, **46**
In Thanksgiving, Let Us Praise Him, 557
In the Cross of Christ I Glory, 184
In the cross of Christ I glory (CANON), **187**
In the Garden, 425
In the little village of Bethlehem, **162**
In the Name of the Lord, 90
In the stars His handiwork I see, **516**

In This Quiet Moment, 592
Infant Holy, Infant Lowly, 143
Is It the Crowning Day?, 236
Is there a heart o'erbound by sorrow, **418**
Isaiah 6:3, 22
It Came upon the Midnight Clear, 128
It Is Good to Sing Thy Praises, 584
It Is Well with My Soul, 493
It may not be on the mountain's height, **444**
It only takes a spark, **309**
It Took a Miracle, 524
I've found a friend, **530**
I've got peace like a river, **498**
I've wandered far away, **341**

Jesus Calls Us, 375
Jesus, I Am Resting, Resting, 503
Jesus, I Come, 336
Jesus, I My Cross Have Taken, 377
Jesus Is All the World to Me, 510
Jesus Is Born, 149
Jesus Is Calling, 327
Jesus Is Coming Again, 239
Jesus is coming to earth again, **245**
Jesus Is King, 230
Jesus Is Lord of All (GAITHER), 359
Jesus Is Lord of All (McCLARD), 360
Jesus is Savior and Lord of my life, **360**
Jesus is tenderly calling you home, **327**
Jesus Is the Sweetest Name I Know, 95
Jesus, Jesus, blessed Lord Thou art, **156**
Jesus, Jesus, Jesus, **102**
Jesus, keep me near the cross, **385**
Jesus Lives, and So Shall I, 224
Jesus, Lover of My Soul, 466
Jesus Loves Even Me, 357
Jesus Loves Me, 579
Jesus Loves the Little Children, 580
Jesus may come today, **236**
Jesus my Lord will love me forever, **511**
Jesus, Name Above All Names, 112
Jesus Paid It All, 210
Jesus, Priceless Treasure, 413
Jesus Saves!, 306
Jesus Shall Reign, 231
Jesus, Stand Among Us, 586
Jesus, the Very Thought of Thee, 79
Jesus, Thou Joy of Loving Hearts, 501
Jesus, Thy Blood and Righteousness, 193
Jesus, We Just Want to Thank You, 98
Jesus! what a Friend for sinners, **89**
John saw the heaven and earth, **547**
Join All the Glorious Names, 111
Joy to the World!, 125
Joyful, Joyful, We Adore Thee, 1
Just a Closer Walk with Thee, 380
Just As I Am, 342

King of Heaven, Lord Most High, 104
King of Kings, 77
King of my life, I crown Thee now, **176**

Lamb of Glory, 197
Lavish Love, Abundant Beauty, 61
Lead Me, Lord, 49
Lead Me to Calvary, 176
Lead On, O King Eternal, 483
Leaning on the Everlasting Arms, 354
Let the Words of My Mouth, 618
Let us Break Bread Together 323
Let Your Heart Be Broken, 315
Let's Just Praise the Lord, 107
Lift High the Cross, 304
Like a River Glorious, 494
Like the woman at the well, **398**
Living for Jesus, 372
Lo, He Comes with Clouds Descending, 241
Lo! How a Rose E'er Blooming, 160
Lord, Dismiss Us with Thy Blessing, 601
Lord, I'm Coming Home, 341
Lord Jesus, I long to be perfectly whole, **436**
Lord, Lay Some Soul upon My Heart, 313
Lord, Let Us Now Depart in Peace, 609
Lord, Listen to Your Children Praying, 429
Lord, Speak to Me, 450
Lord, Thy Church on Earth Is Seeking, 305
Lord, We Praise You, 83
Love Divine, All Loves Excelling, 92
Love divine, so great and wondrous, **541**
Love Lifted Me, 505
Loved with everlasting love, **490**
Low in the grave He lay, **216**

Macedonia, 316
Majestic Sweetness Sits Enthroned, 109
Majesty, 74
Make a Joyful Noise, 23
Make Me a Blessing, 452
"Man of Sorrows!," **175**
Marvelous grace of our loving Lord, **201**
Marvelous message we bring, **239**
May Jesus Christ Be Praised, 87
May the Grace of Christ, Our Savior, 608
May the grace of Christ, our Savior (Grace, Love and Fellowship), **606**
May the grace of the Lord, **612**
May the Mind of Christ, My Savior, 390
Mine eyes have seen the glory, **569**
Moment by Moment, 351
More About Jesus, 389
More Love to Thee, 363
Morning Has Broken, 60
Must Jesus Bear the Cross Alone?, 449
My Country, 'Tis of Thee, 571
My Faith Has Found a Resting Place, 405
My Faith Looks Up to Thee, 410
My Father is omnipotent, **524**
My Father is rich in houses and lands, **352**
My hope is built on nothing less (MELITA), **402**
My hope is built on nothing less (SOLID ROCK), **404**
My Hope Is in the Lord, 406
My Jesus, I Love Thee, 364
My life, my love I give to Thee, **370**

My Savior's Love, 512
My Tribute, 11

Near the Cross, 385
Near to the Heart of God, 497
Nearer, My God, to Thee, 393
Nearer, Still Nearer, 392
No, Not One!, 422
No One Ever Cared for Me Like Jesus, 528
No One Understands Like Jesus, 417
Nothing But the Blood, 195
Now I Belong to Jesus, 511
Now Thank We All Our God, 556
Now to the King of Heaven, 595
Now Unto the King, 611

O beautiful for spacious skies, **572**
O Breath of Life, 291
O Come, All Ye Faithful, 145
O Come, Let Us Adore Him, 82
O Come, Messiah, Come Again, 243
O Come, O Come, Emmanuel, 123
O Could I Speak the Matchless Worth, 110
O for a Heart to Praise My God, 440
O for a Thousand Tongues, 76
O give us homes built firm, **535**
O God, Our Help in Ages Past, 52
O Happy Day!, 532
O Hearken Ye, 150
O holy Child of Bethlehem, **126**
O Holy Night!, 148
O, How He Loves You and Me, 513
O, How I Love Jesus, 529
O Jesus, I Have Promised, 369
O Little Town of Bethlehem, 141
O Lord, my God, **4**
O Lord, our Lord, **30**
O Love That Will Not Let Me Go, 374
O Master, Let Me Walk with Thee, 451
O Perfect Love, 533
O Sacred Head, Now Wounded, 178
O say, can you see, **576**
O Sing a Song of Bethlehem, 167
O spread the tidings 'round, **257**
O That Will Be Glory, 539
O the Deep, Deep Love of Jesus (BUNESSAN), 212
O the Deep, Deep Love of Jesus (EBENEZER), 211
O Thou Joyful, O Thou Wonderful, 119
O to Be Like Thee!, 387
O Word of God Incarnate, 269
O Worship the King, 10
O Worship the Lord, 593
O Zion, Haste, 298
Of the Father's Love Begotten, 118
Oh, Jesus my Savior, **246**
Oh safe to the Rock that is higher than I, **348**
Oh, the King is coming, **238**
Old-Time Power, 258
On a hill far away, **186**
On Jordan's Stormy Banks, 552
Once in Royal David's City, 155
Once our blessed Christ of beauty, **169**
Once to Every Man and Nation, 475
One Day!, 170
One Small Child, 164
Only Believe, 420
Only One Life, 378
Only Trust Him, 330
Onward, Christian Soldiers, 479
Open My Eyes, That I May See, 381
Open Our Eyes, Lord, 383
Our blessed Lord was slain, **219**
Our Day of Joy Is Here Again, 161
Our Father, which art in heaven, **426**
Our God Has Made Us One, 287
Our God Reigns, 229
Our Great Savior, 89
Out in the highways and byways of life, **452**
Out of my bondage, sorrow and night, **336**

Pass It On, 309
Pass Me Not, 337
Peace Like a River, 498
Peace, Perfect Peace, 487
People Need the Lord, 303
Praise God from whom all blessings flow, **624**
Praise God from whom all blessings flow (A Doxology Canon), **627**
Praise God from whom all blessings flow (Alternate Rhythm), **625**
Praise God from whom all blessings flow (OWENS), **626**
Praise Him! Praise Him!, 106
Praise, My Soul, the King of Heaven, 3
Praise the Lord! Ye Heavens, Adore Him, 9
Praise the Name of Jesus, 93
Praise the Savior, 75
Praise to the Lord, the Almighty, 8
Praise ye the Father, **264**
Praise Ye the Name of the Lord, 596
Praise Ye the Triune God, 264
Precious Lord, Take My Hand, 463
Psalm 42, 401
Psalm 136, 63
Pure and Holy, 437

Reach for the glorious prize, **456**
Reach Out and Touch, 314
Reach Your Hand, 582
Reaching for Excellence, 456
Redeemed (ADA), 520
Redeemed (KIRKPATRICK), 521
Rejoice in the Lord Always, 489
Rejoice, the Lord Is King, 228
Rejoice, Ye Pure in Heart, 562
Rescue the Perishing, 299
Resurrection Canon, 221
Revive Us Again, 295
Rise, O Church, **225**
Rise Up, O Church (Men) of God, 293
Rock of Ages, 204
Room at the Cross for You, 331

Satisfied, 531
Saved by Grace, 550
Saved, Saved!, 530
Savior, Again to Thy Dear Name, 604
Savior, Like a Shepherd Lead Us, 462
Savior, Thy dying love, **445**
Search Me, 434
Search me, O God (Cleanse Me - ELLERS), **439**
Search me, O God (Cleanse Me - MAORI), **438**
Search me, O God (SEARCH ME), **434**
Seek Ye First, 42
Send the Light, 307
Set My Soul Afire, 294
Shackled by a heavy burden, **504**
Share His Love, 302
She Will Be Called Blessed, 534
Shepherd of Love, 464
Silent Night! Holy Night!, 147
Simply trusting every day, **355**
Since I Have Been Redeemed, 339
Since I started for the Kingdom, **518**
Since Jesus Came into My Heart, 515
Sing Praise, 263
Sing Praise to God Who Reigns Above, 6
Sing the wondrous love of Jesus, **542**
Sing them over again to me, **270**
So Send I You, 310
So Send I You - by Grace Made Strong, 311
Softly and Tenderly, 326
Soldiers of Christ, Arise, 478
Some glad morning when, **554**
Something Beautiful, 519
Something for Thee, 445
Sometimes "Alleluia," 115
Soon and Very Soon, 551
Spirit Divine, Hear our Prayer, 615
Spirit of God, Descend upon My Heart, 249
Spirit of the Living God, 247
Stand Up and Bless the Lord, 21
Stand Up, Stand Up for Jesus (GEIBEL), 481
Stand Up, Stand Up for Jesus (WEBB), 477
Standing on the Promises, 271
Sun of My Soul, 412
Sunshine in My Soul, 499
Surely Goodness and Mercy, 45
Sweet By and By, 553
Sweet Hour of Prayer, 433
Sweet, Sweet Spirit, 252
Sweetly, Lord, have we heard, **470**

Take My Life and Let It Be, 379
Take the Name of Jesus with You, 116
Take the world, but give me Jesus, **443**
Take Time to Be Holy (HOLINESS), 441
Take Time to Be Holy (SLANE), 442
"Take up thy cross and follow Me," **367**
Teach Me Thy Way, O Lord, 395
Tell Me the Old, Old Story, 424
Tell Me the Story of Jesus, 172
Tell Out, My Soul, 27
The Advent of Our God, 120
The Battle Belongs to the Lord, 485
The Battle Is the Lord's, 472
The Birthday of a King, 162
The blood that Jesus shed for me, **192**
The Blood Will Never Lose Its Power, 192
The Bond of Love, 281
The Church's One Foundation, 277
The Comforter Has Come, 257
The cross upon which Jesus died, **331**
The Day of Resurrection, 226
The Family of God, 282
The First Noel, 136
The God of Abraham Praise, 34
The Joy of the Lord, 411
The King Is Coming, 238
The King of Love My Shepherd Is, 468
The Kingdom of God, 547
The Longer I Serve Him, 518
The Lord Bless You and Keep You, 607
The Lord Is in His Holy Temple, 594
The Lord Whom We Love, 603
The Lord's My Shepherd, I'll Not Want, 50
The Lord's our Rock, in Him we hide, **353**
The Lord's Prayer, 426
The Love of God, 67
The love of God is broader, **302**
The Majesty and Glory of Your Name, 35
The New 23rd, 53
The Old Rugged Cross, 186
The Savior Is Waiting, 329
The sky shall unfold, **237**
The Solid Rock (MELITA), 402
The Solid Rock (SOLID ROCK), 404
The Spacious Firmament, 62
The Star-Spangled Banner, 576
The Trees of the Field, 244
The Unveiled Christ, 169
The vision of a dying world, **316**
The Way of the Cross Leads Home, 471
The Wise May Bring Their Learning, 583
The Wonder of It All, 65
The Word Made Flesh, 121
There Is a Balm in Gilead, 423
There Is a Fountain, 196
There is a name I love to hear, **529**
There is a place of quiet rest, **497**
There Is a Redeemer, 206
There Is No Name So Sweet on Earth, 100
There Is Power in the Blood, 191
There is strength in the name, **90**
There is sunshine in my soul today, **499**
There Shall Be Showers of Blessing, 289
There's a call comes ringing, **307**
There's a land that is fairer, **553**
There's a sweet, sweet spirit in this place, **252**
There's a Wideness in God's Mercy, 68
There's not a friend like the lowly Jesus, **422**
There's Something About That Name, 102
There's the wonder of sunset, **65**
There's within my heart a melody, **488**
They'll Know We Are Christians by Our Love, 284
Thine Is the Glory, 227

This Child We Dedicate to Thee, 317
This Is My Father's World, 58
This Is the Day, 590
Thou Art Worthy, 73
Thou Didst Leave Thy Throne, 127
Thou my everlasting portion, **365**
Thou Wilt Keep Him in Perfect Peace (DUKE'S TUNE), 617
Thou Wilt Keep Him in Perfect Peace (PERFECT PEACE), 492
Through It All, 507
Thy Loving Kindness, 69
Thy Word, 272
'Tis So Sweet to Trust in Jesus, 350
To Be God's People, 312
To Be Like Jesus, 384
To God Be the Glory, 66
Trials dark on every hand, **544**
Trust and Obey, 349
Trusting Jesus, 355
Turn Your Eyes upon Jesus, 335

Under His Wings, 356

Victory in Jesus, 473

We Are Gathered for Thy Blessing, 258
We Are God's People, 283
We are one in the bond of love, **281**
We are one in the Spirit, **284**
We Are So Blessed, 564
We Are the Reason, 209
We Bless the Name of Christ, the Lord, 319
We cannot give without receiving, **621**
We Come, O Christ, to You, 117
We Gather Together, 561
We Give Thee but Thine Own, 620
We Give You Thanks, 619
We Have Come into His House, 588
We have heard the joyful sound, **306**
We light a thousand candles, **159**
We love to sing of Christ our King, **100**
We praise Thee, O God!, **295**
We Praise Thee, O God, Our Redeemer, 16
We Shall Behold Him, 237
We Shall See His Lovely Face, 545
We thank you for Your love, **565**
We Thank You, Lord, 565
We Three Kings, 166
We Will Glorify, 72
We Will Stand, 474
We Worship and Adore You, 19
Welcome, Welcome, 260
We'll Understand It Better By and By, 544
We're Marching to Zion, 555
Were You There?, 181
We've a Story to Tell to the Nations, 296
What a fellowship, what a joy divine, **354**
What a Friend We Have in Jesus, 435
What a wonderful change in my life, **515**
What a Wonderful Savior!, 81
What Can I Give Him?, 154
What can wash away my sin?, **195**
What Child Is This?, 137
What If It Were Today?, 245
What Wondrous Love Is This, 177
When all my labors and trials are o'er, **539**
When He Shall Come, 240
When I Can Read My Title Clear, 538
When I saw the cleansing fountain, **525**
When I Survey the Wondrous Cross, 185
When in the spring the flowers, **396**
When morning gilds the skies, **87**
When peace like a river attendeth my way, **493**
When the Roll Is Called Up Yonder, 543
When the trumpet of the Lord, **543**
When This Song of Praise Shall Cease, 605
When upon life's billows, **563**
When We All Get to Heaven, 542
When we walk with the Lord, **349**
Where He Leads Me, 373
Where the Spirit of the Lord Is, 253
Wherever He Leads I'll Go, 367
While by the sheep we watched, **144**
While Shepherds Watched Their Flocks, 135
While We Are Waiting, Come, 242
Whiter Than Snow, 436
Who can cheer the heart like Jesus?, **526**
Who Is He in Yonder Stall?, 168
Who Is on the Lord's Side?, 484
Without Him, 332
Wonderful Grace of Jesus, 198
Wonderful Peace, 500
Wonderful Words of Life, 270
Worship Christ the Risen King, 225
Worship the Lord in the beauty, **165**
Worthy Is the Lamb, 180
Would you be free from the burden of sin?, **191**
Would you live for Jesus, **333**

Ye Servants of God, 17
Years I spent in vanity and pride, **338**
Yesterday He died for me, **523**
Yesterday, Today and Tomorrow, 523
You shall go out with joy, **244**
You're my brother, you're my sister, **474**